JOHN BAPTIST SCALABRINI

Apostle to Emigrants

JOHN BAPTIST SCALABRINI

Apostle to Emigrants

MARCO CALIARO and MARIO FRANCESCONI

New York
CENTER FOR MIGRATION STUDIES
1977

This translation of *L'Apostolo degli Emigranti: Giovanni Battista Scalabrini, Vescovo di Piacenza* (Editrice Ancora Milano: N.A. 2029, giugno 1968) was done by Alba I. Zizzamia.

JOHN BAPTIST SCALABRINI

Apostle to Emigrants

First Edition

Center for Migration Studies
209 Flagg Place
Staten Island, New York 10304

ISBN 0-913256-24-2
Library of Congress Catalog Card Number: 76-44922
Printed in the United States of America

Preface

The purpose of this biography, which replaces the out of print volume of F. Gregori, *La vita e l'opera di un grande Vescovo, Mons. Giov. Battista Scalabrini* (Turin 1934), is to provide a substantially complete documentation of the thought, the work and, above all, the spirituality of John Baptist Scalabrini.

We did not intend to repeat all those passing events which are more pertinent to newspaper accounts than to history; nor did we intend to exhaust all pastoral aspects of the activities of Bishop Scalabrini. This would require us to write the history of the diocese of Piacenza from 1876 to 1905. Even less did we intend to say the last word on the main problems of that period. In this regard we limited ourselves to a general framework, used as a premise in order to avoid repetitions, and to brief explanations which we gradually considered necessary, referring to the relative bibliography considerably enriched in the last years.

Our main goal was to present the essential traits of Scalabrini's personality, the parameters of his work, and the teachings of his message, valid not only for his but also for our time.

We thank all those who generously helped us, particularly the Very Reverend G. Tessarolo, C.S., Superior General of the Scalabrinian Congregation, B. Gallo, G. Danesi, F. Prevedello, A. Perotti, G. Martina, F. Molinari, A. Fappani, C. Bello, F. Bianconi.

M.G. and M.F.

CONTENTS

John Baptist Scalabrini
1837-1905

Historical Background

"To make every sacrifice to extend the kingdom of Jesus Christ in men's souls; to risk one's life if necessary for the spiritual well-being of one's beloved flock; to get down on one's knees before the world, so to speak, in order to beg from it, as a favor, the permission to do it some good — this is the spirit, the character, the only ambition of the Bishop...And indeed what truly good and beneficent work does not earn the protection and encouragement of the Bishop. He may perhaps be repaid with ingratitude. It does not matter. His charity never fails: *numquam excidit*...God is love, and the more closely a soul is united with God, so much the more does it bear a fullness of charity. That is why the Bishop loves not only God, not only his brothers, but also everything that is worthy of love. Everything, I repeat, without exception. He loves every true thing, every beautiful thing, every great thing, every good thing, every holy thing: matter and spirit, reason and faith, nature and grace, civilization and religion, Church and State, family and fatherland. He loves all the harmonies of human nature, and he loves them because in his heart, which in the fullness of the Holy Spirit is united to God, who is truth, beauty, goodness, life, and the essence of love, there cannot be anything but fullness of love."

"He who loves the Pope loves Italy...Transcending all political parties and apart from all that is unrelated to Religion, with nothing but words of love for everyone, we help the public authorities to reshape the moral order through the efficacy of our ministry...Faithful to the precept to render to God what is of God, we do not fail to render to Caesar that which is Caesar's. Love of Religion and love of country harmonize and fuse in our hearts; and in our teaching as in our actions they will by the Grace of God always be united."[1]

This was Scalabrini's concept of the episcopate: the apostolate is the supreme preoccupation of the Bishop; it is not his only concern but the one which draws together and unifies all his interests. He is assigned by the Holy Spirit to share the life of man and of the people of God; he fully accepts all pastoral responsibilities and therefore all dangers which he cannot escape without failing in the sum total of his duties. The desire to work for souls without being distracted by strictly worldly matters did not isolate the Bishop of Piacenza from the world. In fact it led him to take on not only all the religious problems, but also the social, political and cultural questions which were of concern to the life of the Church in his time.

Pius IX dubbed him the Apostle of the Catechism, Pius XII called him Apostle of the Emigrants — two titles indicating the place which the problems of the Church and of humanity occupied in his life and his activities. He was inescapably and deeply bound to his own time. He did not avoid its struggles, nor did he take refuge — as some Italian Catholics of his century were easily tempted to do — in a historical period different from his own.

To understand the characteristics of his apostolic activity, to explain the position he took, and to take the true measure of his stature, we must consider the history of the Church in Italy in the period covered by his life span (1839-1905). It is the period that coincides with the conflict between the Holy See and the Italian State, from its very beginnings to the time when the tension began to subside.

Scalabrini was nine years old in 1848 when Pius IX pronounced his "Bless Italy, O Lord", and priests and seminarians in Milan took part in the *Cinque Gironate*. He was twenty and about to complete his studies in philosophy at the seminary of San Abbondio in Como when Garibaldi took the city — prelude to the annexation of Lombardy — and the seminarians, divided between "liberals" and "intransigents", threw themselves into the polemics of the period.

The Catholics of Lombardy, after a long period of Austrian domination, were particularly susceptible to the appeal of patriotism and national unity, and as a consequence to the need for the Holy See and Italy to be reconciled. They were used besides to a concordatory regime, and the Piedmont government, though it declared it was not bound by the Concordat between the Holy See and Austria, had, nevertheless, permitted legislation regarding religious matters, as stipulated in the Concordat, to remain in force in Lombardy. The enthusiasm generated by the first two wars of independence subsided somewhat. However, anticlerical policies took form in the new government and the rights of the Pope and the Church were usurped with the defeat of the Papal States at Porta Pia. As a result, the Lombard Catholic reservations with respect to the new State became increasingly serious. At the same time, the Liberals reacted with increasing hostility toward the Catholics, whom they termed enemies of the State.

In 1873, Scalabrini denounced the "constant, Satanic efforts to bring about social apostasy, education withdrawn from the watchful eye of the Church...pagan Caesarism, the deification of the State, the insolent violation of the rights of the Church with respect to marriage, to the education of the young, the possession of temporal property and the religious Orders; the unnatural theories of the atheistic state, of the separation of Church and State and all those principles of the new law which are proclaimed as conquests of the great revolution of 1789." At the same time he deprecated "that hybrid Catholicism which is called liberal."[2]

Numerous Lombard priests had supported Father Passaglia, who in 1862 initiated a "Petition of 9000 Italian priests to His Holiness Pius IX and the Catholic Bishops united with him". It begged the Pope to renounce his temporal power, to be content with "moral power", to restore peace between the Church and Italy and to yield Rome as the capital of the new kingdom. There were also many "Rosminiani", or followers of Father Antonio Rosmini, who applied his ideas of reform to the present political situation. Rosmini had singled out "the slavery of ecclesiastical property" as one of the "five wounds of the Church".

At the same time a "Catholic opposition" was developing under the banner of intransigent fidelity to the Pope, defense of his rights, and criticism of the liberalist concept of the Italian State. Milan was the headquarters of the most belligerent and radical defender of intransigentism, the *Osservatore Cattolico*, which made its appearance in 1864. It was published by a group of priests, under the leadership of Monsignor Giuseppe Marinoni, Superior of the Institute for Foreign Missions (Istituto per le Missioni Estere) who a few months before had received young Father Scalabrini's application for admission.

The following incident may help to illustrate the volatile climate of the period. When Scalabrini was rector of the seminary of San Abbondio, it was discovered that some of the students were secretly circulating a poem eulogizing the martyrs of the struggle for independence. It was an ingenuous little contribution to the fiftieth anniversary of the first uprisings of the Risorgimento, which was to be celebrated in 1871. Members of the faculty were not only surprised but scandalized when it turned out that the author of this "liberal" verse was none other than the rector's seventeen year old brother, Angelo. The Bishop "acquitted" the rector of all responsibility, but to avoid any possible pretext for a disturbance thought it best to transfer him to the parish of San Bartolomeo.

Six years later ex-rector Scalabrini became Bishop of Piacenza, and it is interesting to note that his name was submitted to the Holy See by an "intransigent", the Bishop of Pavia, Lucido Maria Parocchi, later Cardinal, at the suggestion of the editors of the *Osservatore Cattolico*. It was also submitted by a saint, who was often attacked by the same publication, Don Bosco. The beginning of Scalabrini's episcopate coincided with the rise to power of the Left, when secularism often degenerated into sectarianism. His "political" activity — if we can call it that — paralleled Leo XIII's policy of reconciliation.

The year 1887 saw the rise and rapid ebb of the great wave of conciliationism, and consequently marked a turning point for Italian Catholics. Some turned to social action as a practical means of "preparation" for future political activity while abstaining from participating in current politics or the present government. Others became "reconciled" to the political fact (preparation in abstention). Bishop Scalabrini was already dedicated to "practical conciliation", in his apostolate for the emigrants. In fact, the 1886 decree of the Holy Office, *non expedit prohibitionem importat,* had led him to withdraw from the controversies which were dividing the Catholic "activists".

Finally, Bishop Scalabrini's death occurred ten days before the publication of the encyclical *Il fermo proposito* with which Pius X began to ratify the ideas for which, as Bishop of Piacenza, he had fought and suffered. It is opportune, therefore, for an understanding of the man and his life, to review briefly this critical period of travail for the Church. It marked the decline of certain of the Church's external structures that were no longer suited to its spiritual and universal stature and the end of the old social order as the new society rushed to "declericalize" the civil institutions. He lived and suffered through this period, refusing to hedge or shirk the responsibilities and consequent risks a pastor of souls has to face in a period of heady transition.

Italian Catholics and Liberalism

The forces which produced the Risorgimento never adequately represented the Italian people, the large majority of whom displayed only a vague aspiration for national unity, and in any event, hoped it could be achieved without prejudice to religious matters. For the greater part of those Italians who called themselves "Liberals", liberalism meant only the desire for the liberty and unity of Italy.

At first there was an attempt to reconcile the Papacy and liberalism. Like La Mennais, the father of Catholic liberalism, Italian "Catholic liberals" accepted the "modern liberties" brought about by the French Revolution, as tools for the Church to use in the new historical situation. In general, however, they did not accept the utilitarian concept of religion which La

Mennais and De Maistre viewed mainly as a great civilizing force. In fact, they pushed in the opposite direction, demanding reform of the Church from within (Capponi, Lambruschini), or through the liberal State itself (Ricasoli). Without going to either extreme, others (Balbo, Cantù, D'Azeglio, Tommaseo, Manzoni, Gioberti) saw in the "modern liberties" values that derived from an inner, religious principle.

Vincenzo Gioberti in particular gave these ideas a political content in relation to the problem of the Risorgimento. He re-evoked the Guelph tradition of the moral supremacy of Italy as the seat of the Papacy and concluded that the bond between the Papacy and Italy could not be broken. Therefore independence and unity were to be achieved through a federation of Italian states headed by the Pope (*Primato morale e civile degli Italiani*, Brussels, 1842-1843).

The neo-Guelph movement contributed to the emergence of the "patriotic" or "national" clergy who supported the Risorgimento. This seemed to ease the conscience of those who wondered whether it was possible to be a good Catholic and "liberal" at the same time. The new Pope, Pius IX, (1846-1878) seemed to bestow the chrism of religion on the Italian revolution; but he quickly dispelled the ambiguity in the new-Guelph position by protesting that, as the Father of all Catholics, he could not declare war on Austria and that, as Pontiff of the Universal Church, he could not preside over a federation of Italian states (Allocution of April 29, 1848).

From that moment on, the Papacy and Liberalism drew further apart. Crisis overtook the Catholic-Liberal movement, which was rocked also by the reaction to the Passaglia petition, Pius IX's condemnation of Liberalism in the encyclical *Quanta cura* and the *Syllabus* (1864), and by the first Vatican Council (1870). Finally it was written off by official Liberalism as well, convinced by now of the impossibility of attempting to "reform" the Church from within.

From then on the label Catholic-Liberals was no longer applied to those who were seeking a theoretical reconciliation between Catholicism and liberalism and were considered unorthodox, but to those who were trying to form a kind of conservative party — for want of a better term — that would gather in both the Catholics who desired conciliation and moderate Liberals in order to form an opposition to radical liberalism and incipient socialism. They were commonly called "*transigent*" (transigenti) Catholics, or, with even greater confusion, "conservatives," but in a much broader sense than that usually given the latter term. "In comparison with the Socialist party," Bishop Scalabrini commented, "all the others become conservative." At the same time, however, he deplored the Liberal conservativism which considered socialism a deadly phenomenon or advocated its outright repression through police methods.[3]

Another Catholic current, on the other hand, was clearly opposed to the nascent Italian State because it was a "Liberal" State and also because its government converted Cabour's formula of a "free Church in a free State" into a policy that "destroyed" Church rights in the name of the State's jurisdiction.

In principle, the *intransigent* current seems to be legitimist, for it was born of opposition to the Liberal revolution and hostility to the changes produced by the French Revolution and developed outside the Church. This original legitimism, however, was soon attenuated, due largely to the review *Civiltà Cattolica* which appeared in 1850, and to Father Taparelli D'Azeglio, who recalled that while all authority derives from God various forms of government are the result of historical circumstances. There were always in the ranks of the *intransigents* some legitimists who laid themselves open to the charges of the Liberals. But the main problem was religious, namely, the problem of the Church in modern society and its relation to secular states.

In the "Piedmont" period of the Risorgimento (1848-1861), the Sardinian kingdom's legislation with respect to ecclesiastical matters was hostile to the Church. This, plus numerous sectarian episodes and generally anti-clerical politics — among them the trumped up nullification of the election of many of the 60 Catholics elected to the sub-Alpine parliament in 1857 — provoked a political reaction on the part of conservative Piedmontese Catholics. In 1861, Father Margotti declared, "We will not be elected or electors".

The Institution of the Congresses

As unification of Italy proceeded — with the liquidation of the Papal States and the occupation of Rome (September 20, 1870) — the *intransigents* developed an increasingly passive attitude, awaiting the inevitable failure of the Liberal "revolution" under the weight of its own misdeeds. The period between 1865 and 1871 saw the rise of Catholic organizations to combat this type of fatalism, to separate the Catholic cause from the legitimist reaction, and above all, to unite the Catholics in a program to defend the Church. The most important of these was the Society of Italian Catholic Youth (Società della Gioventù Cattolica Italiana), founded in 1867. It organized the first Italian Catholic Congress (Venice, 1874), and this in turn established the *Opera dei Congressi e dei Comitati Cattolici* (Institution of Catholic Congresses and Committees), around which a great part of religious socio-political activity centered until 1904.

The *Opera's* over-all complexion was intransigent. But among its members and around its periphery were also many lay-persons, priests and bishops who opposed the excessively centralist and integralist direction of its officers, especially during the presidency of Paganuzzi (1899-1902). The rigid intransigence of the Permanent Committee of the *Opera dei Congressi* was a factor in the transition from the purely religious orientation on which it was founded to political opposition to the new State. The conflict of principle between Catholicism and Liberalism was gradually used to attempt to invalidate the authority of the Liberal State, denounced as the usurper of a legitimate State and as a de jure "legal country" unrepresentative of the de facto "real country".

According to the first electoral laws, in fact, Parliament was chosen by only one percent of the citizenry. In practice, a Catholic population was dominated by a slender Liberal minority, which was for the most part sectarian and Masonic. The radical Liberals it is true should not be confused with the moderates but neither can the destructive legislation adopted be forgotten: expulsion of the Jesuits (1848), the Siccardi laws (1850), the Cavour Law on the suppression of religious corporations (1855), the laws governing charitable institutions, on the *exequatur* and the *placet* (1862-1863), the liquidation of Church property (1866) the abolition of the canonicate chaplaincies collegiate churches (1867), and tithes (1877); the Zanardelli code with its articles against the "abuses" of the clergy (1889); the Crispi Law against charitable institutions (1890) not to mention the imprisonment or banishment of some sixty cardinals and bishops and numerous priests (1860-1861), or the way in which the Papal States were occupied, the offense to the corpse of Pius IX (1881) and the unveiling of a monument to Giordano Bruno (1899).

Thus there were many factors creating Catholic opposition to the new State, given the image it presented of itself, the illuminist ideology which invested it and the antithesis, constantly proclaimed, between the secular state and the Church, viewed as the "enemy" of national unity, progress and liberty. All this was over and above the doctrinal conflict between Catholic and Liberal concepts, the rejection of an "ethical" State legislating in ecclesiastical matters, and the condemnation of the continuous attack on the liberty and independence of the Holy See, for which the Guarantee Act (1871) was no guarantee at all.

Catholic Abstentionism Non-Participation

The *intransigents*, however, did not achieve their political aims. In fact, the Liberals were quite happy not to be faced by a Catholic opposition in Parliament, and they could proceed with ease to structure the State according to their own ideology. The opposition of the *intransigents* took a negative form: namely, abstention from participation in public life, which found increasing support from the Holy See as a sign of protest. In 1866 the Sacred Apostolic Penitentiary declared that participation in political elections was licit "provided there was no prejudice to divine and ecclesiastical laws" but in 1871 this participation was declared to be inexpedient (non expedit) and in 1886 the Holy Office pronounced it illicit.

The positive aspects of *intransigentism*, on the other hand, are rather to be sought in the religious field: courageous witness to the faith and fidelity to Catholicism in the midst of hostility to the Church; the struggle against the individualism, exclusivism and absolutism of the Liberal State;

the long term preparation of the laity, especially at the grass roots, for their eventual insertion, both political and Christian, into the life of the country.

Among the negative aspects were the unrealistic return to the past and a *priori* hostility to the positive values of historical progress, the lack of a clear-cut distinction between religious and civil society, and the consequent continuation of misunderstanding between politics and religion.

Aspects considered controversial were the centralized disciplinary authority outside the local hierarchy, which resulted in strained relations between bishops and the clergy who played a prominent part among the leaders of the *Opera dei Congressi* as well as in the parish committees; the *method* used to advance the status of the laity (also outside the purview of the local hierarchy), although the *fact* of that advancement was deserving of merit.

In any event, it is very dangerous to generalize. The "Catholic movement" was a complex phenomenon; it would be more accurate to speak of "Catholic movements." In fact, it is impossible to classify as *intransigents* or *transigents* many of the personalities who best represented the Catholic camp in the second half of the nineteenth century.

Evolution of Leo XIII's "policy"

Leo XIII guided Catholics through the transition from the defensive attitude adopted by Pius IX to the reconquest of lost positions. He used the new tools of modern society to restore to the Church the role of guide she had exercised in the preceding centuries. In addition to broadening the cultural preparation of the clergy and promoting Thomistic studies, he is noted for his most famous social document, *Rerum Novarum* (1891), and also for the encyclicals *Diuturnum* (1881), *Immortale Dei* (1886) and *Libertas* (1888). While these again condemned Liberalism they also laid the theoretical basis for more active participation by Catholics in modern governments.

For example the new Pope's policy of rapprochement with France was designed to reduce the secularist tendencies of the Third Republic and to prepare the way for future political activity on the part of French Catholics; the Concordat with Germany aimed to end the anti-church harassments of the Kulturkampf.

It was inevitable that Leo should take up the Roman Question. In fact, in the first decade of his pontificate there were various attempts at conciliation or at least rapprochement with Italy, culminating in his address of May 23, 1887: "May all Italians achieve certainty and peace of mind, and may the baneful conflict with the Roman Pontiff finally be ended without prejudice to the reasons of justice and the dignity of the Holy See." Matters took a turn for the worse when Francesco Crispi and Leo XIII leaned increasingly toward *intransigentism*. He moved it, however, from negative protest into the field of social action.

The *intransigents* continued to hold the Liberal State responsible for the growing miseries of the people. While unification did not produce these problems it did exacerbate them; this provided a fertile breeding ground for an opposing ideology, namely, socialism. The Italian Workers Party was born in 1882 and in 1892 became the Italian Socialist Party.

The *transigents*, some out of social conservatism and some from religious motives, then invited the Catholics to join with the moderate wing of the Liberal Party to form a united front against socialism. The *intransigents* did not accept the invitation but turned instead to the "real country" for solidarity with the people against the misdeeds of the "legal country". In 1897-1898 they rejected the "open hand" the Liberals themselves held out to them in order to combat the danger of subversion and they were then accused outright of being subversive. The *Opera dei Congressi* and the *intransigent* newspapers went under in the violent repression of the uprisings of May 1898.

A typical exponent of the extreme radical wing of *intransigentism*, Father David Albertario (1846-1902), was condemned to three years in prison. Bishop Scalabrini referred to him as the champion of a "struggle fiercely fought for the liberty of the Church, for the true and genuine independence of its august Head, for unlimited respect for the word of the Pope, for purely Roman doctrine against everything and everybody." But the exuberant editor of the *Osservatore Cattolica*, in attempting to renew Italian society from the bottom up, fell at times into demagoguery and unleashed a violent polemic against the *transigents*. He hit not only at those who compromised with Liberalism but also at those who supported the Pope's efforts at conciliation and desired only to reveal the true face of the Church, the mystery of salvation, stripping off the layers of political compromise and attachment to temporal power. In the heat of controversy and to achieve a good end, he considered licit means that were neither always good nor honest. Too prompt to cry treason, he appointed himself the paladin of an orthodoxy limited to his own personal vision and political thesis. It would not be just, however, to identify Albertario with the *intransigent* current. In fact, he himself continued to declare he was an *intransigent* even when, under the influence of young Philip Meda, he was converted to the ideas of Christian democracy, and, precisely, to the acceptance of the "fait accompli" and the principle of "preparation in abstention" against which he had previously fought a fierce battle.

Evolution of Italian Catholic Social & Political Action

Italian Catholic social action was given a decisive thrust forward by *Rerum Novarum*, and also by the work of Giuseppe Toniolo who, in 1889, founded the Unione Cattolica per gli Studi Sociali in Italia (Catholic Union for Social Studies in Italy). In 1894 the Union drew up the *Program of Milan*, which became the Magna Carta of Italian Catholic sociology. Though they started out by opting for "corporativism" and mixed unions of workers and employers, Italian Catholics, confronted by the Socialist trade unions, found themselves obliged to accept the "single" trade union, that is, one composed only of workers and presented as the "secretariat of the people" (1895).

Toward the end of the century the Christian Democratic movement began to take shape. The younger generation now accepted without discussion the "fact" of Italian unification. They abandoned the temporal bias and negative attitude of the "old People" and, looking ahead, began to prepare for Catholic participation in the political life of the nation.

Father Romolo Murri, the chief inspiration of the young, politically orientated Christian Democratic current (Toniolo tended to restrict the movement to the social field) reacted against both the distress and conservative attitudes of the old *intransigents* in the crisis of 1898 and against the Liberals who were trying to put the brakes on civic and parliamentary freedoms in order to get through the current crisis of the Liberal State. He took his stand squarely in the field of constitutional freedoms, although he remained faithful to the principle of abstention and opposition. Meda's followers, on the other hand, were already planning to take part in parliament. They were coming to accept, in other words, the political principle commonly upheld by the *transigents*.

The leaders of the *Opera dei Congressi*, after trying for some years to maintain its original orientation, were finally forced to give in. Paganuzzi resigned from the presidency in 1902. Those who continued in the work were the ones who had always maintained a moderate and balanced position, like Toniolo, Medolago Albani and Grossoli. The latter was named president of the *Opera* and won the trust of the new Pope, Pius X. He declared that the Catholic movement could not be anything but Christian Democratic and the Roman Question should be buried. But he was repudiated by the *Osservatore Romano* and submitted his resignation. The Vatican Secretariat of State dissolved the *Opera* (1904) with the exception of the second Group, which dealt with Christian socio-economics and was entrusted to Medolago Albani. Meanwhile, Murri's movement, which wanted at all costs a truly autonomous Catholic party, independent of the hierarchy in political matters, was condemned for the ninth time.

Pius X's intentions were obvious. He had always supported *intransigentism*, but he had never gone along with the idea of strict abstention from political life. He now wished to have a free hand to formulate a different policy toward Italy and gradually to permit participation in the elections. On the other hand he did not approve the "autonomy" of the Murri movement, nor could he tolerate the ambiguity inherent, in a sense, in the *Opera dei Congressi*, which declared itself a religious movement but seemed to be much more of a political-social movement and which indirectly involved the Church in matters not within its province.

The internal contradictions resulting from the lack of distinction between the religious and the socio-political spheres of action had been perceived by the more intelligent and best intentioned, and this accounted for the perplexities of Toniolo and many others, both *intransigent* and *transigent*. In the labyrinth of currents and counter-currents, it is possible to discover among the *intransigents* those who considered an extreme position futile and among the *transigents* some who refused to accept any dealings whatever with the Liberals. The two wings were separated by labels more than anything else and also by intemperate journalists who terrorized — as Scalabrini said — the former and accused the latter of heresy and treason.

The *intransigent* label had various meanings, depending on who was using it or on convenience or in the heat of the argument. As a matter of fact, those favoring a policy of conciliation were generally called *transigent* and those against it were *intransigent*. But it would be unjust and historically incorrect to attribute to the former all the baggage that traveled under the *transigent* label, such as clerico-Liberalism. And it would be equally incorrect to impute to many *intransigents* all the rigidity and narrowness the term often implied.

Intransigents like Toniolo, Rezzara, Montini, Medolago Albani, Meda, Crispolti, Mauri are not to be confused with the legitimists or some of the integralist directors of the *Opera dei Congressi*, or "Institution of the Congresses" much less with the journalists of the *Osservatore Cattolico* and the *Riscossa*. But they did constitute a "noteworthy current, neither radically *intransigent* (in the sense of rejecting any encounter with the State of the Risorgimento) nor *transigent* (in the sense of yielding on the fundamental points of Christian life. It was a current that tried to achieve that *loyal* cooperation and *indirect* rapprochement with the Italian State which Toniolo inspired *with concrete social and economic action.*"[4]

It would also be inaccurate to attribute exclusively to the *intransigents* (according to the current definition) the credit for reevaluating Thomistic philosophy, the struggle for freedom of the schools and religious education, the conquest of communal and provincial administrations, the petitions against divorce, the protests against the anticlerical actions of Liberalism and Masonry, the broad program of social reforms, and the fine network of institutions for the poorer classes, such as workers, clubs, mutual aid societies, cooperatives, rural savings banks, Catholic banks, etc., not to mention religious and social assistance to emigrants. Emigration was perhaps the most conspicuous and dramatic phenomenon of the time: 60,000 Italians left the country in 1870; 100,000 in 1876; 170,000 in 1886; 300,000 in 1896; 800,000 in 1906; 900,000 in 1913.

On the other hand, "conciliationists" like Bishops Scalabrini, Bonomelli, Guindani, Calabiana, Regio, Sanfelice, or like Cardinals Franchi, Nina, Capecelatro, Agliardi, Schiaffino, Galimberti, Laurenti, Alimonda, Giuseppe Pecci (and we might add two future Popes, Cardinal Giocchino Pecci and

Giuseppe Sarto); or like the monsignori around Leo XII — Boccali, Angeli, Marzolini, Volpini, Brunelli, Rotelli — cannot be categorized among the "patriotic clergy" or the writers of the *Rassegna Nazionale*. In the passionate patriotism of the latter groups there is a too exclusive preoccupation with political problems, many links with the early Catholic Liberals and compromise with the very principles of Liberalism and the "free Church in a free State" formula.

The over-all tone of the conciliationist movement, headed in the South by a Capecelatro and in the North by prelates like Scalabrini, Bonomelli and others...is now much more spiritual than it was in the years of unification. It is not, that is, a politico-religious position, with the accent on political, but a form of spirituality which gathers in the themes of the Risorgimento and purifies them through Christian moderation and charity. From this spirituality there arose various forms of assistance and apostolate (here the author cites as example the foundation of the Scalabrini missionaries for emigrants)...And it found cultural expression in calm terms and dignified rather than the polemical terms as in the publication of the so-called national clergy...The aforementioned initiatives of Scalabrini, apostle of the emigrants, were to lead a fine group of priests and laymen to a profound study of one of the most serious and painful problems of the Italian Society of the time, and were also to lead the learned and holy bishop of Piacenza to develop certain of the premises in Leo's famous encyclical against slavery...[5]

The Philosophical Question

The Philosophical disputes between the Thomists and Rosmini's followers heightened the controversies among Catholics in the latter half of the past century. Antonio Rosmini (1797-1855) "perhaps the most vigorous personality in all Italian Catholicism in the 19th century" had been a supporter of Italian unity. For this reason it was inevitable that the disputes provoked by his attempt at an integral restoration of philosophy, "which would avoid the errors of illuminism and the revolution but would preserve, in another context, the deepest and most vital aspirations of these movements", should take on a fatal political coloration and go beyond the limits of calm scientific discussion.[6]

The first charges against the orthodoxy of Rosmini's teachings — accused of ontologism, pantheism and Jansenism — had already appeared in the years between 1839-1854. The Pope had intervened three times to impose silence on the disputants: Gregory XVI in 1843, Pius IX in 1851 and 1854. On the latter occasion, the Congregation of the Index, over which Pius IX presided in person, completely absolved Rosmini's works with the formula *dimittenda esse* (that is, absolved of the charges brought against them) and again imposed silence on the contending parties.

Nevertheless the controversy continued to rage. The *intransigents* elected themselves champions of Thomistic philosophy, and lumping together

Rosminiani and clerico-Liberals, attacked both one and the other. They questioned the formula of absolution and interpreted it to mean that Rosmini's works were to be sent back for further examination. The controversy flared again and the Congregation of the Index felt obliged to intervene. It called to order those who had misinterpreted the Roman formula and declared that "it was not licit to inflict on the works of Rosmini religious censure or censure related to faith and sound morality."[7]

Rosmini's antagonists were not disarmed, however, when, in 1878, Pius IX was succeeded by Leo XIII, who desired to restore Thomist philosophy in the schools, the *intransigents* expended every effort to have Rosmini's works banned and exploited every occasion, as for example, the publication of the encyclical *Aeterni Patris* (August 4, 1879) which urged Catholics to turn again to the teachings of St. Thomas. Obviously the encyclical did not mean a condemnation of other philosophical systems, but that is the way Rosmini's adversaries interpreted it, to the great sorrow of the Pope himself. Soderini, who spent many years at Leo XIII's side and enjoyed his confidence, writes: "The Pope condemned the abuses and aberrations of certain schools, nothing more; hence he was greatly grieved — and there are many who can attest to this — that the document was used as an excuse to descend to certain polemics. Incredible bitterness was caused him by the intemperance and excesses of certain Catholics, and even priests, who would have liked Leo XIII to condemn everyone who did not think the way they did...If they did not dare doubt the orthodoxy of the Pope when he did not follow their whims, they came very near it. He particularly regretted the attacks on the memory of men worthy of great respect, among whom he counted Rosmini."[8]

The controversy became the more distressing and dangerous as it threatened to cause an irreparable break between the clergy and the young seminarians. There were, in fact, numerous followers of Rosmini among the most zealous and scholarly priests — 200 in the diocese of Piacenza alone — and numerous rivalries broke out among the students of different seminaries who were just beginning to stammer in philosophical terms.

On December 14, 1887, with the decree *Post obitum*, the Holy Office condemned forty propositions, most of which were taken from the posthumous writings of Rosmini. There was profound consternation among his followers, but their submission to the Roman decree was exemplary. Members of the Institute of Charity had ample occasion to practice fully their Founder's maxim, "adore, keep silent, and obey"; his other spiritual sons also submitted immediately. There remained the single voice of *Il Rosmini* and later of *Il Nuovo Rosmini,* but these ceased publication on being comdemned. Meanwhile, the most belligerent voices of the opposing camps gradually died down and the hottest phase of the Thomist-Rosmini battle, for all practical purposes, came to an end.

Internal Life of the Church

As we noted above, after the French Revolution and the "revolutions" of the Risorgimento, the political position and "external" juridical status of the Church had been radically changed. While it had lost its temporal goods, it was freer to devote itself to spiritual tasks. The loss of many privileges was compensated by undeniable advantages, while the principles of democracy served to establish its rights.

The education, spiritual formation, discipline and social status of the clergy improved. The laity began to align itself more closely with the hierarchy in order to defend, with courage, the rights and religious interests of the Church. The central ecclesiastical authority and importance of the Roman primacy were strengthened. Pius IX, deprived of temporal sovereignty, found his moral authority increased along with the affection and loyalty of the Catholics and the unity and diffusion of the Church throughout the world.

Religious life reflected for a time the influence of Illuminism and Jansenism, but gradually there emerged a more intense spirit of faith, a livelier "sense of the Church." This was manifested in increasingly frequent reception of the Sacraments, growing attendance at popular "missions," the multiplication of confraternities, pilgrimages, and works of charity, an upsurge in missionary activity, the birth of some 400 religious congregations, and increased devotion to the Eucharist, the Sacred Heart, and the Virgin Mary.

Numerous works and writings favored the resurgence of devotion to the Eucharist, which had almost disappeared under the impact of Jansenism. Its principal architects were S. Julian Eymard, Father Herman Cohen, Msgr. de Segur and Father Faber. Leo XIII wished to give "to his achievements a certain perfection, recommending with greater insistence the devotion to the Most Holy Eucharists" (*Mirae Charitatis,* 1902). The practice of Adoration of the Blessed Sacrament came into being and 1879 saw the first of the Eucharistic Congresses.

Devotion to the Sacred Heart, formerly somewhat overshadowed, was promoted by Pius IX, following the example of St. John Eudes. It gradually lost its sentimental character and became a theological devotion.

Marian Devotion was also encouraged by Pius IX, with the proclamation of the dogma of the Immaculate Conception (1854) and by the apparitions to St. Catherine Labourè (1830) at La Salette (1848) and at Lourdes (1858). Leo XIII wrote nine encyclicals and numerous apostolic letters on the Rosary. Both Popes promoted devotion to St. Joseph.

Thus the 19th century was one of devotional piety often predominantly subjective and sentimental, as reflected more or less in the writings and attitudes of the time. But this must be viewed in the context of reaction against Jansenism, the pervading influence of Romanticism and the inadequate education of the clergy, bitterly deplored by Pius IX, especially in Italy.

Nevertheless, there was substance beneath the externals. The liturgical movement, the expansion of missionary activity, ecumenism, the so-called social apostolate, the reevaluation of human values, and especially the Christocentrism and ecclesiality that characterize contemporary spirituality presuppose the solution of the 19th century problem of reconciliation between religion and culture, faith and science, piety and criticism — a solution due especially to Vatican Council I and Leo XIII. But they also have roots in the last century, especially its latter half, for instance in the renewal of ecclesiological theology and the rise of various liturgical and ecclesial currents which were to bear fruit in the 20th century.

To cite only Italy as an example, the depth and substance of this spirituality is demonstrated by the number of saints it produced, all of them notable for their apostolic and charitable activities. Among them are those who, for one reason or another, were associated with Bishop Scalabrini: St. Anthony M. Gianelli, who promoted the spirituality and morality of St. Alphonsus in the diocese of Piacenza; two typical representatives of the Salesian spirit, St. John Bosco and St. Frances Xavier Cabrini; and the "reformer Pope" St. Pius X. To be noted also are Blessed Luigi Guanella, and the Servants of God Giuseppe Toniolo, Cardinal Andrea Ferrari, Don Luigi Orione, and Mother Rose Gattorno. They represent a host of noble and generous souls. It is not so much the external attitude which reflect the style of the times that we note in them but the profound reality of their spirituality. The characteristic defects of 19th century religiosity — individualism, sentimentalism, scant social concern, lack of a sense of the universality of the Church, anachronistic transfer of monastic forms of asceticism to other "states" in life — certainly cannot be attributed to them.

The Diocese of Piacenza

Scalabrini was Bishop of Piacenza from 1876 to 1905. At that time the diocese of Piacenza, directly responsible to the Holy See since 1818, was composed of 365 parishes; of these one third were scattered through the Po valley, one third among the hills, and another third were on the Appenine mountain, partly in the province of Parma. The diocese numbered 700 priests and 200,000 faithful. The province had been annexed to the Kingdom of Italy in 1860, but it had already declared its own annexation in 1848, before any of the other provinces, thus earning the title of "eldest daughter of Italy."

It had previously been part of the Duchy of Parma and Piacenza. Its people were not dissatisfied with the prudent and goodnatured administration of Maria Luisa but the winds of independence had been blowing for some time through the majority of the educated class and part of the clergy, who were divided between liberals and conservatives. The former were considered, rightly or wrongly, the product of the Collegio Alberoni;[9] the latter of the Seminary — the two institutions (in addition to the Seminary of Bedonia) which trained the diocesan clergy. The Collegio Alberoni was directed by the Lazarist Fathers, most of them from Piedmont and therefore more sensitive to the Risorgimento. The Seminary was characterized by a closer attachment of Thomism and the Jesuits.

In 1848 the ecclesiastical authority (Bishop Luigi Sanvitale) had cooperated by encouraging people and clergy to support the pioneers of the Risorgimento. Many priests remained aloof, however, because they were opposed to doctrinaire Liberalism and because of the persecution which the Liberals had unleashed in March of that year against the Jesuits, who were driven from the city, and against the priests who were devoted to them. They also had a kind of nostalgia for the ducal government. Their opposition grew when the military campaign ended in defeat at Novara and the Liberal government opened its campaign of hostility against the Holy See.

Scalabrini's immediate predecessor, Bishop Antonio Ranza, took possession of his diocese at the same time that the eccentric Charles III of Bourbon regained control of the city amid a very cold welcome on the part of the ecclesiastical authorities and the people (May 1849). Ranza's sympathies were with the *intransigents* but he tried to maintain a neutral position before his clergy. Here as elsewhere the two currents were complicated by a variety of attitudes, from the extreme philo-Liberal wing composed of very few priests who bordered on heterodoxy to the other extreme represented by the legitimists. The great majority, however, were to be found among the moderates of both sides. In general it can be said that the Bishop maintained a strict religious loyalty to the Pope in political matters and displayed a certain tolerance with respect to philosophical differences. Personally he was a great admirer and champion of Thomism, but he did not press those priests who professed Rosmini's philosophy.

He showed admirable forebearance toward the "patriotic clergy." He governed by example rather than with drastic measure, which he feared would produce no good. *Pro bono pacis,* he sang the *Te Deum* in the Cathedral for the departure of the Austrians in 1859, and again for the result of the plebiscite which decreed the annexation of the province to Piedmont in 1860. But he made no secret of his reservations toward that kingdom because of its violation of the Papal States. When Victor Emmanuel II, who had been excommunicated for usurping the territories governed by papal legates, visited Piacenza, the Bishop left the city to comply with the Holy See's directive that the sovereign was not to be received in Church. The King was feted by the hundred or so "patriotic" priests who had signed a petition for annexation and who contributed in part to the indictment of the Bishop. He was arrested, banished to Turin, tried in his absence in Piacenza and sentenced to fourteen months in prison for contempt of the King.

At the end of four months, the Bishop was pardoned and returned to Piacenza, hailed as a confessor, and was eulogized publicly by Pius IX. The "patriotic clergy" subsided but did not yield. Sixty-three signed the Passaglia petition (1862). A priest, who had authored a Passaglia pamphlet and refused to retract it at the Bishop's request even on his deathbed, was refused the last rites. Because he supported the pastor who had to give the last Sacraments, Ranza was tried again, in 1866, and sentenced to a year's exile; but he was able to take advantage of the amnesty declared on the occasion of the annexation of the Veneto.

Later there was considerable confusion in Piacenza between the political and the philosophical question. How slight an occasion could give rise to the confusion is illustrated by an incident which took place in 1867. Father Agostino Moglia, the most famous Rosminian in Piacenza, wrote a brilliant and effective criticism of a book in defense of Passaglia authored by an advocate of the philo-Liberal movement. Some time later he was condemned for a speech against the Liberals' proposal on civil marriage. Slight notice was taken, on the other hand, of a refutation of the same book by a "conservative" canon who considered the Church's judgment on the necessity of temporal power to be irreversible.

Apart from some extremists there, the clergy of the diocese, if not united was nevertheless guided by common sense and avoided extremes. This was the situation when Bishop Scalabrini was named to the diocese. Disturbances even during his episcopate were due to a few extremists. These unfortunately found credence outside the diocese and created the impression that the dissension, always more or less latent among priests trained in institutes which differed in method and doctrinal tradition, was much more serious than it really was.

Attention has recently been focused on Ranza's merits after the long period in which he was forgotten, due to many factors, not the least of which was the personality of his successor.[10] His biographer, Msgr. Alfonso Fermi, rightly declares that Ranza was "an outstanding representative of an impressive current of Neo-Thomist thought, and enjoyed at least a national reputation", but "his episcopate was not exceptional. He walked in the footsteps of his predecessors. He might be called the last of the past epoch. His successor, the Servant of God, Giovanni Battista Scalabrini, is the first of a new era, in which the bishops' pastoral ministry has an entirely different character."[11]

Scalabrini recalled his predecessor's "wisdom, modesty, piety, his detachment from earthly things, his devotion to the Head of the Church, his charity, his life of sacrifice and martyrdom...When I entered the diocese I read with deep veneration the brief notes with which he called his successor's attention to several matters...In them I admired a man of great humility, which is the foundation of all holiness, who accused himself for not having known how to do those things which he was prevented from doing only by the adverse situation of the times, and in his later years, by the ravages of ill health. I admired a man patterned after the great model, Jesus Christ, always equal to himself, averse to quarrels, an enemy of conflict; he rejoiced in the good that came to his sons as if it had come to him; he never complained of his troubles; he was tolerant and prompt to forgive the faults and frailties of his brothers. In short, he was a man who could not help loving everyone and everything that was good, who had compassion for all, who was good to everyone without distinction and took everyone to his paternal heart in Christ Jesus. In those notes I admired a man of unshakeable loyalty to principles, who did not change with the times or places or the persons, a man without self-interest and without thought for his own comfort or disappointments, who walked the straight path of duty no matter what happened, but whose firmness was always accompanied by Christian prudence...I admired a man of ardent zeal for the glory of God and the salvation of souls, who with the greatest humility recommended certain measures to his successor...I read those words with profound respect, I would say also with joy, for they dealt with matters of the greatest importance, and with some that were very dear to me, such as the Catechism and the diocesan Synod, and I followed his recommendations as soon as possible. According to some, who are always quick to pass judgment, I did so too soon. I did so I repeat, profiting from the wisdom of my predecessors, with the affection, if I may say so, and the enthusiasm with which one carries out the last wishes of a wise, pious, and venerated person."[12]

CHAPTER I

Early Life

John Baptist Scalabrini was born on July 8, 1839, at Fino Mornasco (Como) and was baptized on the same day. He was a little over a year old when he was confirmed by Bishop Carlo Romanò of Como.

His childhood was greatly influenced by his parents, Luigi and Colomba Trombetta, both of whom were esteemed by their fellow citizens for their integrity and religious devotion.[1] Luigi was a wine merchant of modest means, but a good provider, and he paid particular attention to the Christian education of his eight children. He was rewarded with the joy of seeing his third eldest consecrated a bishop. Colomba died May 4, 1865, and information regarding her is indirect, gathered by Msgr. Giuseppe Cattaneo, the pastor of Fino Mornasco, in 1902.

"I knew her only by reputation...but I could clearly comprehend the type of woman she was — wise, of strong character, truly Christian, a woman who instilled the principle of true wisdom, the holy fear of God. This was a great good fortune for him, (Scalabrini) and he himself had many occasions to bless the Lord for it."[2]

This judgment is confirmed by the affection with which Scalabrini cherished the memory of his mother. He often spoke of her with enthusiasm and it was clear that he had a special veneration for her.[3] On the tenth anniversary of her death he dedicated his "Little Catechism" to the memory of his "gentle and venerated" mother, "a model of Catholic womanhood, most dear to everyone but especially to the poor." Every year he requested two anniversary Masses in Fino for his parents[4] and the list of his Masses reveals that he frequently offered the Holy Sacrifice of the Mass for his mother. In the draft of a letter dated May 4, 1901, we read: "Today my heart is filled with sadness. It is the thirty-sixth anniversary of the death of my sainted mother."[5] At the distance of thirty-six years, then, the memory of the mother who had taught him Christian wisdom was still vivid in the mind of her son.

His four brothers and three sisters were known as upright and respected persons, but two of them must have occasioned no little sorrow to their brother the bishop. The eldest, Professor Peter Scalabrini, emigrated at the age of eighteen to Argentina, where he eventually was appointed vice-Governor of the city of Paranà. He later became director of the Museum of Natural History and held the chair of Natural Sciences at the University of Buenos Aires. He never abandoned his faith but did neglect his religious duties.[6] His brother Angelo, who first held the post of professor of philosophy at the Liceo Volta in Como and later (1893) became Inspector General of the Italian schools abroad, had, as a young university student, absorbed the positivism of his teacher, Ausonio Franchi.

The Bishop grieved over the fact that his two brothers did not practice their religion and he kept reminding them of their duty in every way he could.[7] He often called Angelo *ad reddendam rationem*[8] and, reminding him of the good Christian education he had received in the family, he would say bitterly, "I don't know where you grew up," — "You are a complete blockhead!"[9] The words were blunt but were prompted by love. Angelo understood this very well. He was skillfully courted for a long time by the Masons, who promised him money, offices and honors, all of which he refused in order not to displease his brother.[10] For the same reason he did not stand for election, for when he wrote to his brother "asking approval for his candidacy as a member of Parliament...the Servant of God replied bluntly that this was forbidden by the Pope and if he wished to cause him displeasure he should accept the nomination."[11] He later returned to the faith and the practice of his religion. The seven hundred page volume in which he gathered the recollections and documents, which are still a precious source for the study of the life and times of Bishop Scalabrini, stands as a grateful tribute to his brother.[12]

We do not know how old John Baptist was when he made his First Holy Communion. His contemporaries recalled that there was a radiant innocence about him and that his devoutness was evident even in his play.[13] Before he indicated any inclination toward the priesthood he took great pleasure in study and "often stayed up through the small hours until his father got up and made him stop studying and praying."[14]

He finished elementary school in his native town, and then his parents sent him to high school at the Liceo Volta in Como. He walked the seven miles there every Monday morning and walked back home on Saturday. He was always an honor student. In a letter to him in 1893 Professor Luigi Mazzoletti, principal of the Ginnasio, recalled that he was "the best pupil in the school."[15] In fact, he always won first prize[16] though among his classmates there were several who later became famous, like Paolo Carcano, who was elected to Parliament and later headed various ministries.

At that time, his favorite church was the Santuario del Crocifisso (Shrine of the Crucifix), where he developed a strong love for the Eucharist and a devotion to the Passion of Christ and to the Sorrowful Mother.[17]

His love of Christ inspired kindness toward those less fortunate than himself. Young as he was, he was given to little economies so that he could help his poorer classmates. At home on weekends he enjoyed helping mother when she gave bread to the needy who knocked on her door. His leaning to the apostolate was clear in adolescence. He attracted young students his own age and became their guide in zealous devotion and in the practice of charity; there gathered around him the vanguard of that Christian youth which he was later to educate for a new age.[18]

There is extant a letter of one of his contemporaries in which she asks Bishop Scalabrini for a grant to enable her son to attend the seminary. In it she recalls happy memories of childhood in Fino when "Your Excellency just home from school used to repeat for all of us boys and girls, gathered in my aunt's courtyard, the lessons you had learned."[19]

Vocation to the Priesthood

As a young student Scalabrini developed a keen attachment to the virtue of purity. It was customary to have pupils memorize long excerpts from the classics and encourage them to test their own talents by writing poetry in the classical manner. Scalabrini, in his innocence and no doubt to the astonishment of his classmates, chose as his theme the glories of St. Louis and of chastity. The composition, in about sixty lines of blank verse, displays good enough literary talent for a fifteen year old, but reveals more the nature of his interior life.[20] Meanwhile, the pastor of Fino Mornasco, Father Philip Gatti, noticed that with the years the boy "advanced in wisdom and nobility of spirit"; and he felt that with proper attention this was a personality that could yield good works in abundance.[21] He therefore tactfully fostered the seeds of vocation, guided his devotion and conduct, and supervised his studies through elementary and middle school.[22] The boy's parents helped also, though without exercising any pressure whatever, for they considered it a blessing from heaven to have a priest in the family. Both pastor and parents, then, were happy when, on graduating from high school, young Scalabrini announced that he would like to enter the seminary.

The Scalabrinis, with the burden of educating their many children, would not have been able perhaps to take on the added expense of seminary fees. The pastor, however, solved the difficulty. The income from a bequest to the parish fund was enough to cover this expense, and through Don Gatti's good offices this was assigned to Scalabrini.

From the minor seminary of St. Abbondio, he went on to the theological seminary, and at the same time served as prefect of discipline together with Luigi Guanella, who was his intimate friend and with whom he practiced preaching.[23] He then went on to the Major Seminary, where he was always first in his class, both in his studies and in his attitude and behavior.[24]

"The sense and love of the divine became part of him, and he advanced both in the knowledge of God and the learning of men, gathering ever new treasures of knowledge and Christian experience."[25]

He was not carried away by the revolutionary movements then turning the heads of many seminarians. He knew which enthusiasms best suited his temperament at this time: study, prayer, obedience.[26] He exercised an apostolate among his peers by his example and by his generous help to students less gifted intellectually than he.

"The Holy Spirit, one of them wrote to him on his election as bishop...has bestowed a fullness of gifts on my dear Scalabrini, who did me so much good. I still remember the affectionate advice I had from him in the Seminary, the novenas we made together, the troubles I had with theology, when, seated on the steps of the great staircase...he helped me with his brotherly and affectionate explanations."[27]

On May 30, 1863, Scalabrini was ordained by Bishop P. L. Speranza of

Bergamo.

Early Ministry

Immediately after ordination, Scalabrini divided his time between the parish of his home town and another in Valtellina, where he functioned as assistant pastor. Among other things, he was one of the founders of the "Pious Union of the Sacred Heart of Jesus," established canonically in the parish of Fino on August 27, 1863.[28]

The following incident illustrates the spirit which animated him.[29] For some time he had cherished the idea of becoming a missionary. A friend of his, Father Valentini, had already gone to the missions, and he was eager to follow his example. He immediately wrote offering his services to the head of the Institute for Foreign Missions in Milan, Bishop Marinoni, who was quite happy to accept his application. But Bishop Marzorati of Como had other ideas. One day he met Scalabrini with Bishop Marinoni and told him bluntly: "I need you; your Indies are in Italy!"

The Bishop's wish admitted no reply. Disappointed though he was, the young priest resigned himself to the loss of his dream. Nevertheless the missionary ideal remained dear to him. He kept up his friendship with Bishop Marinoni, and when he became a bishop in his turn, he gave his priests full freedom to choose the missions if they wanted to.

In a letter dated February 23, 1881, Bishop Marinoni wrote:

"Is it possible that with a clergy as flourishing as that in the diocese of Piacenza there cannot be found a single priest for those peoples who *quaesierunt panem.* Ah! my dear Bishop Scalabrini, I want to see one of your good priests at San Calocero; I want to receive him from the Bishop's hands, with the Bishop's blessing and with a spark of the Bishop's zeal."

Bishop Scalabrini replied:

"San Calocero and its Director are always in my heart, and God knows how ready I am to have my priests become missionaries. Come yourself, go to the Collegio Alberoni, preach, inspire vocations; on this point I give you all the liberty you wish."[30]

Father Opilio Negri of the Collegio Alberoni did join Bishop Marinoni, who wrote to Scalabrini:

"I owe you my sincere thanks for having given me that good Father Opilio, who is a treasure...I am tempted to try for another like him so that we might set out together and the good and Venerable Bishop of Piacenza might then imitate Our Lord, who *misit illos binos ante faciem suam.*

Especially because, Your Excellency having slipped through my fingers, I need a hecatomb to make up for it."[31]

On June 10, 1884, Father Negri left for the Missions with four colleagues. Bishop Marinoni invited the Bishop of Piacenza to conduct the departure ceremony. In his homily, Scalabrini recalled his own desire for that vocation.

"In every man's life there are certain memorable moments which he can never forget. One of these, which I cherish in my heart, is when I knelt before my gentle mother and asked her blessing on my desire to come here to your venerable institution. She gave it to me with some tears, and I was deeply moved as I presented myself to this house. The words I then saw carved over this door: *Seminarium exterarum Missionum*, (Seminary for Foreign Missions) seemed to open for me my whole apostolic future. The conversation I had with the venerable gentleman beside me here, who is truly an honor to the Lombard priesthood, and one whom I cannot ever forget, seemed to assure me that this would indeed be my future destiny according to the Divine Will. But unforeseen circumstances arose, whether as punishment for my sins or from some hidden design of God, and the wooden cross of the missionary became this one of gold I am wearing around my neck, which often causes me to complain to the Lord because he gave me this instead of the other. But then, I must add, may the Will of God be done in all things! I shall never, however, stop thinking of myself...as united with you in spirit, if only as a tertiary, and therefore it is with envy that I look upon you beloved sons, who are about to set out for the distant lands of those without the faith."[32]

The homily given twenty years after his dream had ended, reflects how deep had been his desire to be a missionary. Unable to realize the dream, he dedicated himself whole-heartedly to working for souls in the field to which God had called him. He was assigned to the Seminary of St. Abbondio, where in addition to teaching in the classroom and the pulpit, he was at the service of his students in the confessional. He also taught them, through the example of his pastoral activity in his native town and in the neighboring parishes.[33]

Seminary Professor

A few months after his ordination he was named prefect of discipline and instructor in history and Greek at the Minor Seminary. He was one teacher his students remembered for a long time. On the first centenary of the Seminary of St. Abbondio, the following tribute was written of him:

"He had a lofty concept of the school — to illumine the mind with the light of truth, to inspire the will to good, to fire the imagination through

the harmonious development of the spiritual faculties, in short, to educate
the spirit of his students to high and noble things. He himself was full of
life and of lively intellect; he taught with enthusiasm, and all that was
best and certain in human knowledge he made to serve the divine truths.
This was the way he conceived his role as guide to the young seminarians...He knew that the priest, to be truly the messenger of the Lord must
cherish knowledge. Hence he took into account the best improvements in
teaching methods and brought in a breath of new life...He ended the once
popular tradition of dictating for hours on end those laborious lessons
designed to exercise the memory too much and the intelligence too little.
In addition he did not want his students to cling slavishly to the usual
manuals, which practically spoon fed them. That method, he used to say,
seemed to teach, but in fact it untaught the finest and most necessary
thing. It untaught them how to think. His aim was to arouse in his pupils
an increasingly lively desire to study, to learn, to know."[34]

Canon Sterlocchi, who had been his pupil and undertook to write his
biography on the advice of his uncle, Blessed Luigi Guanella, describes his
methods as follows:

"He did not want us to use any text book for history. He required that
we listen attentively to his exposition and then write a summary of it.
Thus he obliged us to pay attention...In his Greek classes too he used a
method all his own, which it would take too long to describe, but which
made learning easy and pleasant. He also was responsible for instituting
the so-called *Academia*, which was held three times a year and was
attended by all the seminarians, the professors, the Bishop...and other
ecclesiastical authorities."[35]

He taught Greek also at the Collegio Castellini in Camerlata. He had so
mastered this language that he was able to produce a fine Italian translation of
St. Cyrillus of Jerusalem. When Leo XIII sent him his photograph inscribed to
him in Latin distichs, his reply translated them into Greek verse.[36]

Besides Greek and Latin, which he wrote and spoke fluently and with some
style, he had enough knowledge of Hebrew to point out the inaccuracies in a
congratulatory poem dedicated to him on his election as bishop,[37] and he als >
had a great facility for modern languages. This was of great use to him in his
travels abroad. He was invited to preach in the cathedral of Clermont-Ferrand
on the occasion of the eight-hundredth anniversary of the First Crusade, May
17, 1895. He delivered his sermon in French, and it was highly praised in the
press, not only for its content, but also for his mastery of the language. *La
Depeche du Puy-de-Dome* wrote: "He spoke French like a son of France!' *Le
Monde* carried a full summary of the sermon and added that it was "noteworthy

not only for his eloquence but also for the superior manner in which the distinguished Prelate handles the French language."

When he met President Theodore Roosevelt, during his trip to the United States (October 10, 1901), he used French during the interview. He related the conversation to the editor of L'Italia Coloniale, who reported:

"At the beginning of their meeting Roosevelt confessed that he understood French perfectly but could not speak it very well. Bishop Scalabrini said the same with respect to his English and so the one spoke English and the other French and they understood each other perfectly without any difficulty in expressing their thoughts."[38]

From Boston he wrote to his secretary: "I get along fine with my small French. I give talks, sprinkling in a few English phrases, and I keep pushing ahead in American style."[39]

From St. Paul, Minnesota, where he was visiting the seminary, he wrote:

"They read me an address in Latin and I answered in Latin. I had given it some thought and so was not taken by surprise as I was in Detroit. There, at the Polish Seminary, an address was read to me in Latin and I answered somewhat off the cuff."[40]

When three years later at the age of 65, he decided to go to Brazil, he also undertook to learn a new language, despite his many activities.

According to Gregori:

"He began the study of Portuguese with enthusiasm and within a few months he was able to speak it fluently in public, without preparing his remarks ahead of time, as we are told by Prof. Motti, who helped with his study, and as subsequent facts confirmed."[41]

On July 25, 1904, he wrote from Sao Paulo, where he was a guest of the Benedictine:

"Today I shall speak, in Portuguese of course, to the 420 young men being educated by the Benedictines."[42] And on the following day: "The welcome (given me by the Salesians) could not have been more splendid or more cordial. I spoke in Portuguese to the students, replying to the various little speeches addressed to me. The Director General of the government schools and the Vice-President of the Senate were present and were surprised and astonished by the ease with which I spoke their language."[43] From Encantado he wrote: "I answered everyone in Portuguese to their great surprise and pleasure. I had also preached to the seminarians, about forty in all."[44]

And again from Encantado: "I made use of my meager linguistic equipment, preaching in Italian to our emigrants, in Portuguese to the natives, in English, and I even contrived to speak in German."[45]

Rector of St. Abbondio

In 1867 the cholera epidemic spread through the province of Como and Father Scalabrini immediately offered his services to help the sick.

"He did not spare himself, but worked energetically first in the city and then in Portichetto (a hamlet in Fino Mornasco), where he substituted for the old pastor, Father Filippo Gatti. The hamlet was the worst hit for only ten out of sixty survived."[46]

His devotion and charity aroused so much admiration that the survivors preserved the vessels he had used to give the last rites to the sick,[47] and the government voted him a medal for civic valor.[48] But he considered his work a grace, as he wrote to the rector of the seminary, Father Bolzani:

"A few words to send you greetings and to congratulate you in Our Lord for the beautiful grace which, as you wrote, you received to help the poor cholera victims...Let us then thank the Giver, and then let us pray that He will keep you well for the Seminary and the Diocese."[49]

Upon the death of Father Bolzani, Scalabrini was appointed rector of the Seminary of St. Abbondio (October 6, 1868). He was especially anxious to improve the teaching and general training given the students.

"Good teacher that he was he loved them and they loved him in turn, but also knew how to administer good discipline...He reorganized the curriculum so that the students received an integrated education. He did away with the remnants of senile conservatism and the institution soon felt the fresh and lively breeze of modern thought and feeling. The lessons in religion, which he gave to the students in the upper classes, were handed down from one class to another for many years...He warned young scholars not to accept as fruits of the tree of knowledge certain ingenious and seductive hypotheses...Instead he welcomed the progress made by true science, and he expanded upon it in harmony with the faith and religious feeling."[50]

Father Alfonso Bianchi, the son of one of Scalabrini's sisters, provides further testimony:

"On the basis of information I received from Msgr. Gianera, who was for sixty years chancellor of the Diocese of Como and Archdeacon of the

Cathedral, and from Msgr. Cattaneo...Canon Sterlocchi and Father Luigi Guanella, I can affirm that as Rector, Scalabrini brought to the Seminary of St. Abbondio a breath of new life in matters of discipline as well as study, and that he won everyone's heart by his fatherly administration."[51]

Canon Sterlocchi states that he also tried "to improve the seminary's finances, which left much to be desired," and that during the two years of his rectorship, "he was entrusted with other very delicate and important duties, among them the position of Acting Vicar-General and that of pro-Synodal Examiner."[52]

His friendship with Bonomelli,[53] then a parish priest in Lovere, who was invited to give the spiritual retreats in Como's two seminaries, dates from the early months of his term as rector. "To see each other, to speak together, and to feel ourselves immediately bound in intimate friendship was one and the same thing", the Bishop of Cremona later wrote.[54] Scalabrini always deeply appreciated the gift of friendship, which for him had to be governed by "freedom to think and act on different points," and by the "heroic necessity," based on understanding and sincerity, to be utterly frank in pointing out what one considered the other's error.[55] He never forgot his colleagues at the seminary: Father Giuseppe Castelli, later Archpriest in Lugano; Father Giacomo Merizzi, the future bishop of Vigevano; Father Costantino Corticelli and Father Serafino Balestra, who devoted his work to the deaf and dumb.[56]

Educational Background

In his years at the seminary, and to a certain degree in the succeeding years also, Scalabrini continued his own education.

"God had given him," Bishop Bonomelli wrote, "a quick, versatile, sharp, clear and great intelligence. In whatever subject he took up, he succeeded without difficulty, and the most difficult questions — whether in theology, philosophy, history or politics — he treated and explained with such confidence and clarity that he never failed to astonish me. One would think he had made a special study of those questions alone."[57]

Among the results of his studies, in addition to his teaching and preaching, are the eleven lectures on Vatican Council I, which he gave in the cathedral of Como in 1872. These were published the following year at the insistent request of the diocesan clergy. In this, Scalabrini's first work, we note logical reasoning, clarity of exposition, knowledge of the Scriptures, Patristic writings, Church history and the Summa of St. Thomas. Although the book does not constitute an original contribution, it is distinguished for its sound arguments, based entirely on quotations from the Scriptures and St. Thomas, and for its knowledge of contemporary theology.

Scalabrini's ecclesiology reflects the new orientation given it by Mohler, Passaglia, Perrone, Franzelin. His critical sense is evident not only in comparison with the new school of Dollinger but also with the more or less conspicuous divergencies of the French authors, who were nevertheless dear to him, such as Bossuet, Fenelon, Dupanloup, Maret, Barboy. His treatment is not scholarly so much as preeminently pastoral, and this is true of all his later writings. Nevertheless he avoids two common defects of his time: excessive rhetoric and sentimentality, and the use of juridical and rational arguments rather than theological data.

The book reveals his preference for the Greek Fathers and shows that he must have studied them with particular devotion. He indicates in fact that he had begun a translation of a homily of St. Chrysostom and some letters of St. Athanasius which he intended to publish as the most convincing reply to Renan's *Life of Jesus*.[58]

His interest in catechetical problems also dates from this period, and he was later to make a basic contribution to their solution.

Pastor of San Bartolomeo

In 1870 he was named pastor of San Bartolomeo, a typical parish on the outskirts of Como, numbering about ten thousand people. Most of them were factory workers or craftsmen in the textile industries. He took over his new duties on the third Sunday of July, the feast of St. Louis.

Msgr. Cattaneo relates the following:

"He soon knew all his people; he loved them as a father, and he aided them both by his work among them and by his example. Since he never had any other desire but to be a minister of God, he succeeded in being himself a lively and splendid image of the Good Shepherd. And that is what he truly was...His affectionate solicitude reached into families, institutions, schools, factories, and every social class — wherever he found the ignorant to instruct, the afflicted to comfort, souls to win. With the most sensitive tact he welcomed those who returned, never hurting or humiliating them; rather he encouraged them with the friendly words that dissipate temptation, that comfort and complete the work of grace...About him there was a breath of new life; his work was a true and great religious revival, the triumph of the kingdom of Christ among the souls in his care."[59]

His favorites were the children, the sick and the workers. After he became Bishop, he wrote to his successor of San Bartolomeo's, Msgr. Piccinelli:

"San Bartolomeo's is perhaps the most important parish in our diocese and it has special needs; but, unless things have changed it loves its pastor and gives him more consolations than disappointments, even though the latter are not and cannot be lacking. The care of children and the sick are two aspects of the ministry which are most deeply appreciated by the people there, and if you can devote yourself to them in a special way, at least during your first year, you will have won eveyone's heart."[60]

He established a kindergarten,[61] which besides being a charming center, was undoubtedly where the littlest ones absorbed their first notions of the faith. He compiled a short catechism, which he tried out on his small pupils over a long period of time, and finally published in 1875 with the title: "Short Catechism for Kindergarten Use." When we come to the development of his catechetical apostolate, we shall see the importance of this booklet, written as it was by a priest who knew how to become small with the little ones. For those times, in fact, it was a revolutionary innovation in the religious instruction of children.

The older children of San Bartolomeo's also found in the catechism their best school of Christian virtues. It was in Como, in fact, that Scalabrini carried out the reform of religious instruction in the parish which he later prescribed for the whole diocese of Piacenza. Bishop Miotti of Parma describes the results:

"Where the pastor is active, zealous, studious, with a true spirit of self-denial and sacrifice, you will find that catechetical instruction leaves little or nothing to be desired. I could list more than one example...I shall mention only the parish of San Bartolomeo in Como, where my old friend and compatriot, Bishop Scalabrini was pastor for several years...he knew how to make the catechetical schools flourish there."[62]

For the boys, the pastor established an oratory dedicated to St. Joseph. Under his guidance the boys themselves carried the stones and wood for its construction. Thus they had a stake in their oratory, which accomplished an immense amount of good among the youth of the parish. The pastor liked to spend time talking to the boys, and was wont to repeat: "Look, son, your soul is your own. I can help you to save it, but you are the one who has to do it."[63] He particularly stressed religious instruction and frequent reception of the sacraments.

Finally, for the young adults he founded various Catholic associations which grew so dynamic they had a beneficent influence on other sections of the city.

He showed a zealous concern for the sick.

"In his populous parish there were always so many; he was able to express all his great goodness of heart — visiting them often, aiding them if they were poor, consoling them, and helping them to accept their suffering with resignation."[64]

He devoted a great part of his ministry to the sick, visiting them, if possible every evening.[65] To assist them more effectively he started an organization that later became the Conference of St. Vincent de Paul.

The factory workers also experienced his kindness, for he knew their needs. He helped them and sought ways, in the name of justice and understanding between classes, to remedy the evils of the new industrial system.

Later, recalling the distant years of this ministry, he wrote in the pamphlet, *Il Socialismo e l'azione del Clero* (1899) the following revealing passage:

"What I am saying is the fruit of personal experience. Before reading it in books, I learned it from seeing so many social wounds, so many miseries, on which it was my sacred duty to pour the balm of faith and the healing aid of charity.

In the early years of my priesthood, during the months when I was not teaching, I served in various towns in my native diocese and I had time to observe the life of the farmers, in its different forms and varying degrees of well-being, the farm contracts and their economic and moral consequences. I used to walk among those rich fields (property of a wealthy gentleman known for his display of civic charity) made fertile by a hard-working people, a number of whom were pellagrous, and I went into their damp, shutterless hovels with a heavy heart. I was also pastor in a suburb of Como for several years. Among my parishioners were thousands of silk workers, weavers, spinners, dyers. At that time I was able to observe at close hand the miserable condition of these workers, miserable in itself and because of the emergencies which dominated it. What an effect every political or financial crisis, however distant, which slowed or halted industrial activity had on their lives! How deeply they felt every small event! A sickness, for example, or an accident that kept them from daily work! And in addition to these brief interruptions, each of which took a loaf from their poor tables, there were from time to time those great industrial crises when there was no work at all. Then it was sheer misery, hunger in the strict sense of the word, barely disguised for a while by credit at the local store or a salary advance from their employer. Then there was a feverish rush on the part of the men to look for jobs, and of the women to plead for help. Oh, the sadness of the days when, as I climbed the rickety stairs to visit sick workers. I failed to hear the dry, rhythmic clack of the loom. They were sad in every way, because disorder and dishonor often came into the family with poverty. As I observed all their sufferings and heard their complaints (knowing as I did the tireless employers wrongly accused of exploiting the poor, and that kind and charitable landowner whose fields were infected with pellagra) I used to think the evil lay not so much in the will of individuals as in the way work was organized, and that it would be a good thing for everyone if more equitable conditions could be created. If labor gives value to capital, why should it not have a greater share in its profits — enough at least to assure sufficient wholesome food for the workers? If labor is a physical law and a moral duty, why should it not become a legal right? If education is a duty, why is the worker not given time for it by fixing the age at which he can be employed and limiting the hours of work? If hygiene is a social obligation, why (without due preventive measures) are certain occupations permitted which poison and shorten life? Why is the worker not ensured against eventual accidents and why is not some dignified provision made for his helpless old age? This is what I thought..."[66]

Amid the unhappy circumstances of the workers, San Bartolomeo's pastor did not confine himself to commiseration. He threw himself into efforts to find a remedy. He founded charitable organizations and created mutual benefit associations among the workers and farm laborers.

For all his parishioners he was an example of priestly devotion.

"They spoke of his devotion", his successor Msgr. Piccinelli recalled. "A sound, enlightened, communicative, exemplary devotion; a devotion that guides souls to the peak of perfection and is expressed in ardent love for the Most Blessed Sacrament...; a tender filial devotion to the beloved Sorrowful Mother, whose image is the object of special veneration in the Church of San Bartolomeo."[67]

He reorganized the parish records and redecorated the church. He later[68] told how on the day he first went to San Bartolomeo's he had thought of enlarging it when he saw the crowd spilling out of the church into the street. He had immediately had plans drawn up and started to collect the necessary funds, but things went slowly and his appointment as bishop postponed the project for a long time. He did not forget it, however, as we shall note shortly.

Toward the Episcopacy

The young pastor's activity, zeal for souls and gift for administration did not escape the notice of his superiors, who saw in him qualities necessary in a bishop. His nomination was not a surprise to those who knew him. Canon Francesco Poggia, who had been his guest for a day on his way through the city (1870), as soon as he heard of his appointment, wrote him recalling how Scalabrini had observed that the then Vicar-General of Como deserved to be named bishop. And he added:

"As I took leave of your reverence — and this is the pure and simple truth — I was edified by your conversation, in which I noted unusual soundness, perspicacity of mind and goodness of heart. I was impressed by your kind and gentle manner. I could not help saying to myself: Oh, what a good bishop the pastor of San Bartolomeo would be! So it was two Bishops we prophesied one morning..."[69]

Scalabrini himself did not expect the nomination, and he later recounted a curious incident that took place at the time.[70] One of his assistants, Father Pietro Caminada, who was told to take the iodine water cures, had gone to Salsomaggiore, a small city in the diocese of Piacenza, torn apart at the time by quarrels between the faithful and their pastor. One day as he knelt before the image of Our Lady of Grace in the old Church of San Vitale, he prayed for an end to the many troubles of that poor parish, and he seemed to hear an inner voice which said: "Your prayer is granted. Your pastor will be the Bishop of Piacenza and he will remedy all these things."

When he got back to San Bartolomeo, he told Scalabrini about this. The latter shook his head and answered good-naturedly, "I fear, dear Father Pietro, that you have come home cured in body, but..."

"Sick in mind," the other finished for him, but then added, "I don't think so. We shall see what happens."

A few months later, in the middle of December 1875, Scalabrini received the letter of appointment. In it, after a few brief mentions of his activity as a professor, seminary rector and pastor, it states that Scalabrini "a man endowed with seriousness, prudence, learning, integrity and business experience, is worthy of being elevated to the See of Piacenza."[71]

It is easy to imagine the sorrow of both the pastor and his parishioners at the separation.

"He had won the hearts of all of them, even of those who disagreed with him on many things; and this is so true that, when the news came that he had been named Bishop of Piacenza and therefore had to leave the parish, people of all ranks were grieved to hear it. On the day of his departure many clung weeping to his cloak begging him not to leave them. In short, there were such demonstrations of affection that he later said this was the most heart-rending moment of his life."[72]

He never forgot the people of San Bartolomeo. The correspondence between him and his successors reveals the depth of his affection for his flock and how much he continued to love them.

"Why can you not come to Piacenza?" he wrote in 1896 to the newly elected pastor, Msgr. Piccinelli. "I should be deeply obliged to you, for I wish to be the friend of my successor in the parish I love so very much."[73]

He took an interest in the work to enlarge the church and often spoke of it with Msgr. Piccinelli, to whom he also donated what was then a handsome sum. The Monsignor relates:

"When I went to Piacenza to pay my respects, he invited me to stay as his guest for several days. San Bartolomeo was his favorite topic of conversation. While he was talking about it he forgot the burdens of his vast Diocese. — And so, my good Pastor, what's new at San Bartolomeo? Do you still have those crowds of people at Mass and at instructions? And what of the new church? What news of the Oratory?' — My answers were reassuring enough...When I took my leave he gave me a passbook for the Bank of San Antonino, which carried a deposit of 4000 lire plus annual interest; it was a large sum for those days. I tried to refuse it, saying 'Excellency, do not trouble yourself; if you insist, bring it with you as a gift for the church when you come to Como.' And he answered in good Como dialect, 'Take it, take it, who knows what might happen.' I accepted it, thanked him and left, happy as a lark, taking back to the parish the handsome gift and the blessing of their old Pastor."[74]

Naturally the Parish Committee elected him honorary President. In accepting, the Bishop wrote:

"All right! What's done is done. I am very grateful for the affectionate remembrance of my former parishioners, whom I loved so much and whom I still love deeply...I shall do what I can and I shall be happy indeed to see the completion of one of my most fervent wishes."[75]

In 1899 he gave the address at the laying of the cornerstone. He could not be present at the consecration in 1902 because he was on a pastoral visit.

His former parishioners long cherished the memory of him whom they used to call "our Pastor Bishop." In fact, when Como decided in 1913 to honor his memory, the parish of San Bartolomeo asked that his statue be erected in their church. In 1930 on the 25th anniversary of his death, the people still flocked to the commemoration.

Msgr. Piccinelli rightly observed:

"When the memory of a Pastor is still alive after sixty years, it is an evident, incontrovertible, infallible sign that that Pastor was a true father, a true pastor of souls. And that describes exactly the Pastor-Prior John Baptist Scalabrini."[76]

Photo used for
his memorial card.

Scalabrini
1882

CHAPTER II

Bishop of Piacenza

Scalabrini was thirty-six years old when he was named Bishop of Piacenza. His devotion to the Holy See (evident in his lectures on Vatican Council I), his care for the victims of the cholera epidemic, his dedication as a priest and his pastoral activity as pastor of San Bartolomeo undoubtedly were factors in Pius IX's decision to appoint him at what was then considered a young age for a bishop. Despite his relative youth, he had had administrative experience as seminary rector, pastor of a large industrialized suburban parish and finally as pro-Vicar-General, all posts which were a preparation for his new responsibilities.

The news of his appointment took him by surprise, as he himself related later in the Turin paper, *La Stampa:*

"One morning while I was in church, a canon whom I did not know (David Celli from the cathedral of Piacenza) came in and approached me with obvious deference. I asked him if he wished to say Mass. He answered that he had already said his Mass, but he had come to pay his respects to his Bishop — namely, to me who had been named Bishop of

Piacenza. I was stunned, and actually could not believe the announcement. I asked him to stop in at my house and take some refreshment and to leave immediately afterwards, for I did not want this astonishing rumor to spread. He did so, but on the same day the letter bearing the official announcement arrived from Rome."[1]

His first pastoral letter describes his first reactions:

"At this unexpected announcement of my elevation I considered the burden it entailed, a formidable one even for the very angels. Conscious as I was of all that I lacked, I prayed weeping to the God of all mercies to exempt me from these holy duties of the episcopate, which are neither few nor light and to which neither my talents nor my youth are equal, poor as I am in virtue and quite conscious of all my deficiencies. Then, I recognized that in the authority of the Holy Vicar of Jesus Christ this must manifestly be the will of God. Trusting in the grace of Him who gives strength to those on whom he confers honors of office (St. Leo M., Sermo I), I accepted the ministry placed upon me with fear and trembling, but with resignation."[2]

The new bishop's dismay is not surprising, when one considers the concept he had of the dignity and the mission of the office. He constantly returned to the meaning of his office on the occasion of episcopal consecrations and anniversaries. Rather than deliver a eulogy, which could seem to be merely the usual complimentary tribute to the honoree, he chose to describe for the faithful the ideal bishop, doing so as an examination of and a reminder for himself.

"When we consider that a Bishop is the man of God; the dispenser of the Mysteries of Christ Jesus; whose lips should speak the words of salvation to everyone; whose presence should teach how God must be served; who must himself be a living law that brings religion to every heart; who must continually die to himself in order to teach others true Christianity; who must be humble and gentle of heart, firm without arrogance and flexible without weakness, poor and little in his own eyes in the midst of the grandeurs of his office; who must be patient, hard-working, calm, diffident in his own regard but prompt to give preference to others when this is fitting; who must beware the flattery that is the poison of high office; who must welcome sincere advice, be careful to recognize true merit and reward it; who must carry the cross of contradiction and devote himself like a martyr to his sacred ministry — when we think of all this there is reason indeed to be discouraged...and to cry out: 'A great misfortune has befallen us!' Nevertheless, there is reason for courage. It is enough not to be a half bishop, but to be wholly a bishop, loving Jesus Christ with a great love."[3]

"In his supervisory function, which is always difficult and often dangerous, the Bishop...always has three things in mind: the dangers to souls, the crime of silence, and the judgment of God...Truth, only truth is his rule and guide, and he must sacrifice everything rather than betray her...To make every sacrifice to extend the kingdom of Jesus Christ in men's souls, to risk his life if necessary for the welfare of his beloved flock; to get down on one's knees before the world, as it were, in order to beg from it, as a favor, the permission to do it some good — this is the spirit, the character, the only ambition of the Bishop."[4]

It has been said that bishops of the last century were concerned more with the exercise of their authority than with their pastoral ministry; with their hierarchical position rather than with their role in the mystery of salvation, for which they are the *iunctura subministrationis* of the Mystical Body of Christ. Scalabrini vigorously defended the hierarchical authority of the bishop, but always within the context of the only reason for the existence of the bishop as well as the Church; the salvation of souls.

"What is the Bishop's mission? He has one only, but it is a wonderful one and embraces all other missions: to prepare the way of the Lord in the souls...The Bishop is a bridge built by Christ to unite the creature with his Creator, the earth to heaven, men to God. That is his mission. That is the reason in the holy books and in the sacred liturgy why the Bishop is so often called Pontifex."[5]

Two basic ideas guided Scalabrini's thought and action throughout his episcopate. First, the bishop is successor to the Apostles and therefore an apostle, a missionary concerned only with evangelization. The Bishop, placed by the Holy Spirit to direct the Church of God, is responsible for his diocese before God and the Pope. In fact, through the will of Christ, he is the only means of union between the faithful and the Vicar of Christ. There can be no union with the Pope, and therefore with Christ, if there is no union with the bishops. Nor does this mean union doctrine alone. Respect for the hierarchical structure is also essential. In practice, this is union through obedience to the hierarchy. To by-pass the hierarchy is to detach oneself from the unity of the Church, to lacerate the Body of Christ.

Second, the Bishop "is an angel appointed by God to guide us on the paths of righteousness...He who is Priest for eternity annointed him with His holy oil; enriched him with the sevenfold gift of His Spirit; and, placing the Gospel in his hands, said to Him: Go; go and teach men my heavenly doctrine; go and sanctify them with the Sacraments; go and govern them with the power which I communicate to you. *Posuit Episcopos regere Ecclesiam Dei* (He placed the bishops in charge of the government of His church). Through an uninterrupted succession, the Bishop is united with those first chosen by Christ, with those Apostles to whom the Savior said: "As my Father has sent me, so do I send you. He who hears you, hears me. He who scorns you scorns me, and he who scorns me scorns Him who sent me." The bishop, then, continues on earth the redemptive work of Jesus Christ; he is the successor of the Apostles; he is the depository, propagator, judge, avenger, defender and guardian of the faith, in close union with the Bishop of the bishops, the Pope."[6]

The bishop draws his strength from prayer, "from that great principle of hierarchical unity which animates and rules the Church and keeps it ever vigorous, ever young, ever invincible. Yes, in the same way, says St. Cyprian, that the tree's branches draw their vital fluid from its roots, as the rays converge in the sun, so do we bishops draw from the Chair of Peter the word of life and the light of truth: In him and for him we are united with the Supreme Pastor of souls, Christ Jesus."[7]

Through the Pope, the Bishop is intimately united to Christ. "Unworthy as I am, I am your Bishop. Who has given me authority over you if not Jesus Christ, through Him who is His Vicar here on earth? Jesus Christ lives in the bishop, I would say, almost as in a living sacrament. The life of the bishop derives all its vigor from this intimate union with Him, the Prince of Pastors, and with His visible representative, the Pope. It is only through this union that the bishop possesses within the confines of his diocese, the authority to teach, command, forgive and punish. It is only through this union that he preaches the Gospel, administers all the sacraments, consecrates the Ministers of God, who is Judge, Teacher, Pontifex, Lawgiver."[8]

The same thoughts recur in Bishop Scalabrini's letters:

"A bishop is not the master of his own honor as a private citizen is."[9]

"Let us bend our efforts with purity of intention to defend, not our poor persons, but the cause of God and of His Church."[10]

"It is the spirit of our rules," he wrote to his missionaries, "to work in absolute dependence on the bishops. With them we shall succeed in everything, without them in nothing. St. Ignatius Martyr goes so far as to say that he who does anything at all without the knowledge of his bishop does not serve Jesus Christ, but *inservit diabolo*."[11]

"Be very careful then never to undertake anything without the permission of him whom the Holy Spirit set as ruler of the diocese in which you find yourselves. With humility and devotion recognize in him your Father, the one who is to invoke on your labors the blessings of God, and as such surround him with the most reverent love and the most affectionate respect. Then inspire this respect and this love in the minds of our fellow-nationals. Let them see you obedient in all things to the teachings of the bishop, observing his prescriptions, always ready to carry out his wishes and desires, and they will be all the more ready to carry out your wishes and desires. This union with the bishop will render closer and stronger the sense of unity you must have with the Pope — the supreme and infallible

Teacher from whom comes your mission of apostolate in those far-off lands."[12]

Consecration

The twenty-nine years and four months that Bishop Scalabrini served his diocese illustrate far better than any quotation the concept he had of the office entrusted to him.

His appointment was announced at the Consistory of January 28, 1876. He was consecrated two days later in the Collegio Urbano of the Congregation of the Propagation of the Faith by Cardinal Alessandro Franchi, assisted by Archbishops Manetti and Lenti of the titular sees of Sida and Sardica, respectively.

Two circumstances seem almost to have given his life as bishop a certain direction. He was consecrated in the church considered the heart of the missionary expansion of Catholicism, and immediately afterward he went for inspiration to the center of ecclesial unity.

"When the solemn rite that consecrated me as your bishop was ended," he recalled twenty years later, "I went to the tomb of the Prince of the Apostles and fervently beseeched him to obtain for me from God the grace to sacrifice myself completely for the good of the flock entrusted to me. I am certain in my conscience that I have not spared myself, that I have done all that my strength permitted."[13]

On the same day he addressed his first pastoral letter to his clergy and people. A few days later, he left Rome for Como. As the train passed the boundary of his diocese, he knelt to ask the blessing of God and of the patron saints of the territory that had now come under his jurisdiction. He took possession by proxy on February 5th and made his solemn entry on February 13th so that he could be present at the commemoration of the sixth centenary anniversary of the death of Blessed Gregory X of Piacenza, which had already been organized by Bishop Ranza.[14]

He received an enthusiastic welcome from the people of Piacenza, who were charmed by his fatherly manner, youthful appearance and vigorous eloquence. Abbott Placido Schiaffino, later Cardinal, described him at the time as "impressive in his youth, virtue, knowledge and his high and manly purpose."[15]

This purpose revealed itself in the new bishop's address to the faithful at his installation. With deep feeling he repeated the direction his episcopate would take, as he had already outlined it in his first pastoral letter.

"As for myself, debtor to you all, I shall embrace you all in my ministry, in service to you all for the Gospel...Sent first of all to the poor and the unfortunate...I shall suffer with them and I shall work, above all, to help and evangelize the poor...With most ardent fatherly affection I embrace all of you, pastors of souls, conscious as I am of the importance and necessity of your ministry...Nourish the most tender and kindly love for the deaf, the blind, and all others suffering misfortune; make sure that they too receive instruction. Carefully teach young boys and girls the principles of our faith, inculcate in them obedience to God and to their parents. Be ready and willing at all times to help those in need...Do everything in harmony of spirit with God, under the guidance of your Bishop, who stands in God's place...Anxious to preserve harmony and peace among the souls under your care, in all things teach the doctrine professed by Holy Mother Church...With all due reverence and devotion, keep closely united to the Apostolic See, which is the center of unity."[16]

From the beginning, then, the main lines of his administration, the concepts which produced his most important achievements are very clear: works of charity for the poor and the disadvantaged, special instructions for the deaf and dumb, catechetics, unity in the diocese, particularly between priests and bishop, and obedient devotion to the Pope.

CHAPTER III

The Father of His Flock

The Poor

The fatherly concern which characterized all Scalabrini's activities was soon felt by the people of his diocese, as they saw him visiting the sick, helping the poor, including in his pastoral visits hospitals, schools, convents and barracks; suggesting topics for meditation to the seminarians, and hearing the confessions of men who had not been to church in years.[1]

Toward the end of his life he commented:

"I remember the promise I made you on the day of my installation here among you...I warned you that you would not find in me all that you had admired in my predecessors, and I added sincerely: 'I assure you, however, dearly beloved, that you will find in me the heart of a father.' Have my actions fulfilled the promise? I do not dare answer for myself, but I can assure you of this: I have always loved you and your joys were always my joys, your sorrows, my sorrows."[2]

The answer is documented in the depositions of witnesses in the process of inquiry for his canonization. In speaking of his heroic virtue, all of them immediately mention his charity as the principal characteristic of his episcopate — just as the people of the diocese had recognized it as such.[3]

While Bishop Scalabrini considered himself indebted to all his flock, he felt this most keenly in relation to the most troubled among them. He was the tireless evangelizer of all his people, but especially of the poor. All called him Father, but the suffering, the unfortunate, the erring did so with special meaning.

"All human miseries touched his great heart."[4] Everything he did was motivated by his desire to evangelize the poor and by his charity toward all those in whom he saw most intimately reflected the image of Christ crucified. "Whatever activity he wished to undertake, the poor always had priority."[5]

This sense of love was second nature to him and characterized all his contacts with others. While he did not avoid encounters with persons prominent in society or public life, nevertheless he was always most at ease among those tried by poverty and grief. He permitted the former to stop him to speak to him; it was he who stopped the poor to talk with them.[6]

"He was never so happy as when he was among the humble people of this world. He said to me one day: 'On these pastoral visits I most enjoy being with certain poor pastors, those dear and humble priests, who truly work for souls and fear only that they will not save their own! It is so good to be with them. Believe me; as I go my rounds I meet poor little old women who are so filled with God that it is true joy listening to them...' His eyes shone with emotion...He did not brandish the dignity of his office, but muted, not to degrade it, but to raise it through humility...He wore the same smile, the same affectionate dignity, whether he was entering the Vatican, the poor home of a widow or a poverty-worn rectory. He had the same affectionate and affable manner whether he was talking to the Pope or the King, or with the lowliest of his priests, or with a poor worker or housewife who had something to tell him, some worry or trouble to explain to him."[7]

Famines and Misfortunes

He completely won his diocese during the famine which occurred in the third year of his episcopate.

The peasants whose harvest had failed swarmed into the city of Piacenza, where there was no industry that could give them work. The winter of 1879-1880 was exceptionally cold and there was hunger everywhere. The distressing sight of the many beggars dragging themselves through streets, weak from prolonged hunger and poorly clothed became commonplace. The bishop turned the first floor of his residence into a soup kitchen, where the Sisters of St. Anne distributed a thousand meals a day at first, but soon were feeding four thousand. The bishop's means were soon exhausted. His cupboards were emptied to provide clothing, but he did not give up. He challenged the rich to a competition in generosity, and he himself gave them an example. He first sold the pair of horses that had been given him. When these were bought back for him by wealthy persons, he resold them to buy food for the poor. When his funds gave out again, he sacrificed his most precious possession, the chalice Pius IX had given him three days before he died.

The usual "guardians of virtue" reproached what they called his excessive generosity. Bishop Scalabrini replied:

"The Bishop must go on foot to the house of the poor. Jesus walked among the poor of Galilee and Judea. When the people are hungry, the Lord prefers a chalice of brass to one of silver and gold..."[8]

Even Piacenza's anticlerical paper *Il Progresso* called him a "true angel of charity," a man of "incomparable heart."[9] The Liberals promoted a public subscription in admiration and gratitude. In Parliament, deputy Medoro Savini, a native of Piacenza, urged the government to come to the aid of the victims.

"We must do something too," he exclaimed. "We cannot allow the Bishop of Piacenza to be more generous than we..., that bishop of Piacenza, who provides a thousand meals a day for the people. Gentlemen, I bow before that priest (I am not very guilty of clericalism, as you know), because I admire his sublime apostolate. And if all the priests were like him, I would become an altar boy."[10]

When the terrible winter was over, Scalabrini gave his support to the "Comitato per le Cucine Economiche" (Committee for Soup Kitchens). He contributed generously to the establishment of the necessary fund for this work which was providential, especially when the crops failed. Every year his contribution toward the expenses involved ensured the distribution of food and fuel stamps to the poor. In 1893 he personally paid for 6,980 such stamps.[11] In 1900 the Committee formally thanked the Bishop "for the efficacious contribution he has made during the past years, without which the Kitchens would have found it difficult to remain open throughout the whole of the grim winter season."[12] "Suffice to say, he gave more every year than the whole city, the province and the government put together."[13]

Over and over again he arranged at his own expense for the pledges left lying in the pawn shops to be restored to their owners.[14] He was generous with assistance to the Ladies of Charity[15] and in fact to all social assistance and charitable works, many of which had been started under his predecessor.

Toward the end of the century a number of catastrophes befell different parts of Italy. Each of them evoked a moving letter from Scalabrini to the members of his diocese, urging them to give evidence of their Christian concern and of their solidarity with their fellow citizens and, as usual, he set the example.

In 1882 he appealed to his diocese to help the victims of the flood waters of the river Adige. Letters from the bishops of Padua, Adria and Chioggia thank their colleague of Piacenza for the gifts of money and clothing.[16] In 1883, he again appealed to the diocese — this time for the victims of the earthquake of Casamicciola — at a requiem Mass in the Cathedral for those who had died. In response, four of his priests organized a lottery to raise funds. He not only encouraged them but donated another gift he had received from Pius IX, a pectoral cross. This and the chalice he had previously sold had a sentimental value for him much greater than the price they brought, but in his view the gifts of the Pope were the property of the poor.[17]

In the same year, he contributed and promoted other contributions for the ransom of the missionaries and the Sisters taken prisoner by the Mahdi in the Sudan, during the revolt that devastated the missions that had been started by the "untiring apostle," Bishop Comboni.[18]

In 1884, he aided the families suffering as a result of the fire in the powder storage at Pontremoli.[19] He alerted the diocese to the dangers of another epidemic of cholera threatening all of Italy, like the one in 1867, when as a young professor in the Como seminary he had spent himself aiding its victims. In his letter to the various parishes, he asked for prayers, recommended a number of methods to guard against infection, and exhorted his priests not to spare themselves in aiding the sick.[20]

A month later, in the pastoral letter in which he communicated to his people Leo XIII's Encyclical urging prayers to Our Lady of the Rosary to end the epidemic, he noted that the diocese had been almost completely spared.[21] He immediately thought of other areas where the disease was still raging and ordered collections to be taken up in every parish. This concrete assistance to the relief efforts initiated by the Pope is attested to in letters of thanks from the Secretariat of State and several bishops of dioceses that had been hardest hit.[22]

The earthquake in Liguria in 1887 and the flash flood in Campidano in 1889 received the same generous attention.[23] Also in 1887 he celebrated a memorial Mass for those who had died at Dogali and organized aid for the bereaved families.[24] In 1895 and in 1904 avalanches brought calamity to the diocese. Once more he urged his people and clergy, who had done so much for their unknown and distant brothers in times past, to come now to the aid of their neighbors.[25]

With justifiable pride, the Bishop considered Piacenza:

"A splendid and constant proof that where faith, root and source of all good works, remains pure and inviolate; where religion, the inspiration of great and magnanimous deeds, is respected; where the Church, true mother of the people, freely exerts her beneficent influence, there true brotherly love reigns and true miracles of generosity are performed."[26]

Most of the credit was due to the Bishop himself:

"He was incapable of anything but love. He wished all good on everyone and always with remarkable generosity and abundance. He did not know what self-interest was; he received only to give away."[27]

Daily Charity

While the more spectacular misfortunes revealed his greatness of heart, it would be more interesting to learn the full story of the day-to-day charity he exhibited. Millions of lire[28] passed through his hands, which "were like a sieve," as he said himself.[29] "Hands full, pockets empty," he used to say.[30] "He gave everything away," according to his sister Luisa.[31]

Father Saletti, the bursar, was seriously worried on occasion.

"One day I met him in the Bishop's ante chamber, with a dazed look about him. He drew me into a corner and said: 'Do you know? Yesterday I brought the Bishop a half-year's income, and today — would you believe? — he does not have any of it left...?' On another occasion Father Saletti dared to say: "If Your Excellency goes on like this you will die on a heap of straw". Scalabrini answered with a cheerful smile: 'Dear Don Antonino, it would not be too bad for a bishop to die on straw if Jesus Christ was willing to be born on it'."[32]

Several times there was no linen left in the house because he had given it to needy families, until the servants took to locking it away in the cupboards.[33] He did not permit unnecessary expenses. If one was suggested he would observe in a tone that admitted no reply: "And what about my poor?" He endured all sorts of privations himself in order to be able to help those whose misery was a constant appeal.[34]

"His poor" in fact were a besieging multitude,[35] according to letters of thanks still extant. Unfortunately his secretary was unable to save the greater part from destruction,[36] for the Bishop preferred to keep his charities hidden. There is, however, a register of about 229 families, to whom he regularly sent a subsidy, usually once a month.

Among them were widows; parents of seminarians whose tuition he was also carrying; a former teacher who needed a small sum; persons who were sick, or old and alone, and who were able to get along only because of the monthly subsidy from the Bishop; pastors in mountain parishes who would otherwise have gone hungry; priests who needed help to repair their church, a destitute man who needed food for a few days and who asked the Bishop to get his suitcase from the station because he did not have enough money for the baggage check. Then there was the Cardinal of Bologna, who thanked him for an urgently needed loan and called him the instrument the Lord had used to restore his "peace of mind and his joy."[37] The bishop of Osimo asked his help for the Capuchin monastery.[38] The bishop of Como thanked him for paying the board of a seminarian from Como at the Collegio Lombardo.[39] Father Achille Ratti, the future Pius XI, in a letter of recommendation for a person in need wrote:

"It will be a real act of charity. And this is exactly why I have taken the liberty of appealing to you — not to mention the lively memory I hold of your great kindness to me during my brief stay in Piacenza at the beginning of 1900."[40]

Priests in trouble found in Bishop Scalabrini a father who never "abandoned the most unfortunate of his children."[41] Nor was his kindness selective. It included even those who had hurt or offended him.[42] Certain Masonic journalists, moved by his charity, promised to tone down the intemperances of a sectarian paper.[43] "His former concierge, Margherita — although she had stolen almost all the household linen and was caught in the act — he always aided, even with money."[44]

Everyone was helped: those who beseeched his aid with tears and those who approached him in anger or those who, in their illness, were stubborn and difficult to satisfy; those who were grateful and called him savior, the best of all fathers, Providence on earth, and those who did not even say thank you; the widow who had never before seen as much money at one time as the sum the bishop sent her, and the administrator of millions who had gone bankrupt; the curate who could never take a vacation unless the bishop paid his way and took care of his mother while he was gone, and the religious communities of both men and women in his diocese and outside it; the Institute of the Good Shepherd in Piacenza, and twelve orphans in Milan, who had no other recourse but Divine Providence and the goodness of Scalabrini.[45]

Numerous letters attest to the fact that his generosity reached beyond the boundaries of his diocese, not to mention his beloved Como, the parish of San Bartolomeo, and his native Fino Mornasco.[46] His sister Luisa wrote him the deep gratitude of a family he had rescued from distress: "when they heard of your generosity they threw themselves to their knees in front of your picture and the Crucifix, and I didn't know which of the two was more invoked, thanked and blessed."[47] His brother Angelo revealed that for more than twenty years the bishop had deposited with a trusted friend in Como a sum, the interest of which was distributed annually in various charities: "Our dear brother, following the usual impulses of his generous heart, told him to spend, besides the interest, about a half of the capital."[48]

There are extant letters of thanks from a widow in Oneglia, from an Archbishop in Rome who wrote about a subsidy for a sick person, a priest in Turin who received a handsome sum for his church, from persons in Parma, Saluzzo, a priest in Ivrea who was helped to reach his ordination only through the generosity of the Bishop of Piacenza, a family in Bergamo reunited with loved ones who were enabled to return from America through the good offices of the bishop and his brother Angelo...[49]

Various organizations also received his assistance, such as the Biblioteca Circolante Cattolica (Catholic Circulating Library), the Associazione Operaia Cooperativa (Workers' Cooperative Association), various hospitals, the Instituto Scrofolosi, and the Congregation of the Sisters Apostles of the Sacred Heart, whom he saved from financial difficulty.[50]

Even in Brazil, when he visited Italian settlements, he always took thought for those in need: "We never saw him without his hand in his pocket..."[51]

Don Orione, as a young seminarian, delivered a sermon in the presence of Msgr. Scalabrini, who kindly recommended that he spare that big voice of his and, at the same time, invited him for a visit whenever he was in Piacenza. Soon afterwards, Orione accompanied a group of young people on pilgrimage to Bobbio. He was on a tight budget and had not counted on the healthy appetites of his young companions. This fact, together with other unforeseen expenses, left him without funds. He thought of the bishop, told his pilgrims to wait where they were, and set off for Piacenza, where he explained the situation to Scalabrini. He was warmly welcomed and was provided with all he needed and more besides.[52]

Scalabrini also showed a singular and delicate concern for those in prison, whom he visited frequently during the year and always during Lent. He arranged for annual retreats for them, went himself to hear their confessions and said the closing Mass. He preached to them with exquisite kindness, gave them Communion and visited them individually in their cells, taking a special interest in those who were ill. He invariably left a sum of money for their use. "This was something entirely new and never done in the past."[53] He was the first to have a chaplain assigned to the prisons.[54] At Easter and Christmas a special meal was prepared at his expense,[55] and he always visited the prisons in the various towns during his pastoral visitation.[56]

When he preached a retreat to a group of Italian priests in New York, he thanked them for their offering with these words:

"There is a jail in Piacenza where many unfortunates are paying the penalty, often for a passionate impulse or as a result of a bad education. I often go to visit them and I am happy to be able to give them some comfort and help. A little while ago, I passed on to them part of the offering given me for my jubilee by the people and clergy of Piacenza, and I shall pass on to them also this offering you are now giving me."[57]

There is an abundance of incidents recounted on the prison in Piacenza. "As he was about to take Communion one of the condemned prisoners grabbed the bishop's arm and, looking at the Blessed Host, exclaimed: 'You who are God, you know I am innocent.' And then he burst into tears. Msgr. Scalabrini calmed and encouraged the inmate, who received communion with a most lively faith that his innocence would be established."[58]

"In 1898 or 1899 there was among the prisoners the famous Socialist Todeschini. The bishop, leaving the ninety-nine other sheep, sought out this one. Todeschini absolutely refused to let the Bishop enter his cell. The prison personnel could do nothing about it. Then the Servant of God, leaving the group of prison officials, approached the entrance of the cell and called to him. The unhappy man was touched and allowed the bishop to enter. After a short conversation the bishop came out and exclaimed: 'How good is the Lord.' And the phrase is all the more significant since, when he came out of prison, Todeschini went to visit Msgr. Scalabrini. On the same occasion several young men from good Lombard families were introduced to the Servant of God. They were victims of the revolution and were indifferent and apathetic, but the persuasive and fatherly words of the bishop moved them to tears...Thanks to the compassionate solicitude of the Servant of God, another prisoner, after eighteen years of imprisonment, was able to establish his innocence."[59]

Special mention should be made of the charitable aid which Scalabrini gave, almost always personally and as secretly as possible, to families of the nobility that had fallen on hard times. He felt great pity for them: "When one is born poor, poverty is not felt so keenly. That is why I feel so sorry for families that have lost everything."[60]

On one occasion he sold the gems in his pectoral cross to save a marquis from going bankrupt, and then he wrote numerous letters for more help until he had put together the necessary sum, thanks especially to Duke Robert of Bourbon, who was a close friend.[61] He also gave continuous and hidden assistance to four or five families, whom he thus saved from desperation.

"He once told me...that on that day he had saved an impoverished aristocrat from despair and suicide, having given him the help he needed and getting him employment."[62]

The sums involved varied from tens of thousands of lire (equivalent to several millions today) to small sums. But the delicacy and joy with which he gave were always the same. Many expressed gratitude more for the courtesy and gentleness with which they were treated than for the aid itself.

The Father of His Priests

Father Giovanni Squeri recounts how young Francesco Sidoli — later the bishop of Rieti and then archbishop of Genoa — came to be accepted in the seminary.

"He went to Msgr. Scalabrini and kneeling before him said: 'Excellency, I have neither father nor mother; I come from Masnini school, which is now closed. I should like to continue my studies for the priesthood, but I have nothing. Please be a father to me and take me in.' Msgr. Scalabrini, who recounted the incident to me and other professors, was moved by his plea and could not say no. Turning to his chancellor he exclaimed: 'How can I say no? You understand. Accept him and take care of him'."[63]

The Servant of God, Msgr. Francesco Torta, who founded various works for deaf mutes and the blind, recalled:

"He had learned that I wanted to become a priest and had no money, and the very first time I met him...he said: 'I'll take care of it'."[64]

He made Msgr. Torta director of the Oratory of San Giovanni, established to encourage vocations. Four hundred young boys from various parishes frequented the Oratory at that time. In a few years, there were twenty-nine vocations.[65] Torta states that in the twelve years he spent as director — assisted by the young seminarian Count G. B. Nasalli-Rocca, the future Cardinal Archbishop of Bologna — the bishop aided or supported fourteen of the sixteen candidates recommended to him.[66]

"He was singularly generous to poor seminarians, for whom, I personally know, he annually gave several thousand lire."[67] Thus there were many priests in the diocese who could have repeated the same testimony as Msgr. L. Mondini:

"His generosity toward the most needy was great. I myself am proof of it. I would not have been able to enter the seminary, if the Servant of God had not generously made it possible."[68]

His concern extended to seminarians of other dioceses who came to Piacenza to serve their military duty. He always recommended his own seminarians to the bishops of the diocese where they went to serve. He offered to accompany his seminarians and those of the neighboring dioceses to the Lombard Seminary in Rome.[69]

This fatherly concern for the aspirants to the priesthood became, as it were, something sacramental once they were ordained. He was the first to ask the blessing of the young priest he had ordained.[70]

"He was a father to everyone, but especially to the clergy, whom he won with a grace and tact that made them do everything he wished."[71] An example is recounted by Father Enrico Preti, a veteran missionary among the emigrants in Brazil. He tells how a certain pastor had insistently asked for a curate to assist him. On one occasion, following the rather bad advice of a colleague, he raised his voice and used disrespectful language. Msgr. Scalabrini did his best to convince him that it was impossible to grant his request. The pastor kept up his complaining. Scalabrini stood up and without another word went to his room and returned to the study wearing his coat and hat and carrying an umbrella. "All right, here's your curate!" he said. "Let's go!" It is easier to imagine the priest's confusion than to describe it.[72]

On another occasion, while reciting the breviary with an elderly pastor, he noticed a note in the margin, *Hic bibitur* — a little wine here. The pastor kept on going but the bishop interrupted him saying, "Before we go on, we must have something to drink." The pastor started to excuse himself in some confusion. Scalabrini with great good humor reassured him: "There is nothing wrong in that, especially at your age. So let us have a little drink; it won't detract anything from the pious recitation of the Divine Office."[73]

He strove to be "firm without arrogance, yielding without weakness." To moderate the necessary firmness with fatherly kindness was not easy for one of his warm, frank nature and tendency to quick temper. It was the priests who did not measure up to their duties that gave him the most trying times, but he sought always to befriend and reconcile. His remarkable tact did a great deal of good, and his fatherly manner won everyone. "When he could not satisfy a request, he coated the pill with a kindness and courtesy that was almost a satisfaction in itself."[74]

Whenever, in the interests of truth and justice, he found disciplinary measures necessary, he tempered even the most severe with his charity and he felt genuine grief when any further yielding seemed to him a betrayal of his pastoral duty. When he did take severe measures, he always proceeded slowly, seeking to extenuate the blame and soften the punishment. He never acted without warning and he was never vindictive.[75]

Mindful of the Gospel, he first gave a kindly warning, and then a stern one, and afterwards he was sometimes obliged to take severe measures.[76] He was heartbroken, however, when he had to remove a pastor from his parish.[77]

The saddest case of all was that of the schismatic Miraglia,[78] with whom he tried everything he could think of to effect a reconciliation. He sent various priests, canons and pastors of the city, individually and together, to invite him to present himself before the bishop, in the hope of changing his mind. When all else failed, he informed the Holy See.[79]

Several letters are extant that lift the veil a bit on the piteous agony that can invade a priestly heart.

"Excellency, deign to think and provide for me. Yours is a great heart, holy as your intelligence, and among the many sons...and souls you have saved, please place my own unfortunate soul...If your Excellency knew how much good you have done me by remembering me among your own, you would say: Here is another priest who has been saved."[80]

"Thank you, Your Excellency, for your fatherly reply...It is for me a precious document. Besides encouraging me to persevere in the service of souls whom it is my destiny to guide, it gives me confidence that Your Excellency will never abandon an unhappy priest."[81]

"When a few days ago I came to you, in fear and utter discouragement, to lay at your feet the misfortune that had struck me and to ask for advice and help, my discouragement was replaced by an unbounded confidence because of the complete welcome, affectionate compassion and fatherly help which you deigned to accord me. Then you were also good enough to relieve the poverty of my brother. I thank you from the very bottom of my heart..."[82]

"You have done too much, and you still do too much for me. I recognize all this and I thank Your Excellency with all my heart. If it had not been for the charity of Your Excellency, my return to the Church would have been impossible."[83]

Known for "overwhelming generosity of heart," it is not surprising to find this statement in one of Scalabrini's public utterances: "If priests are not angels, it is almost better so, for they can be more compassionate toward their guilty and suffering brothers and help them better."[85]

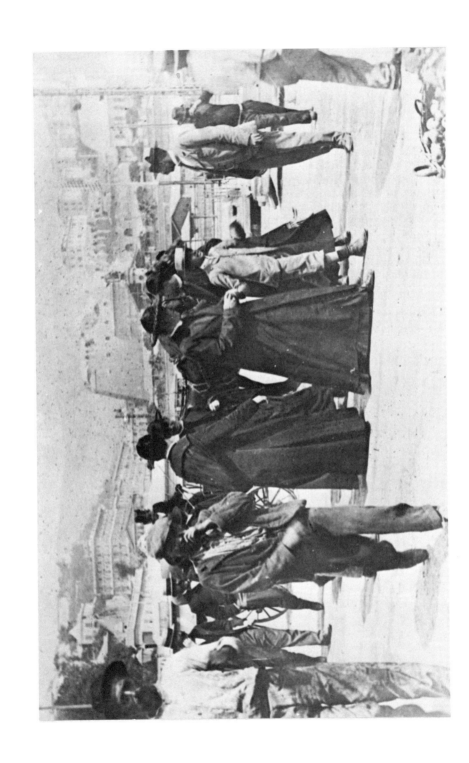

CHAPTER IV

Scalabrini as Teacher

"Bishop Scalabrini was considered an incomparable teacher for both his clergy and his people."[1]

He himself considered a bishop to be God's sentinel, who — seated on his *cathedra* — kept vigilant watch over his flock. "He is charged to give answer to the mysterious question that reaches him every morning from the heights of eternity: Sentinel, what have you discovered in the darkness of the night? *Custos, quid de nocte?* And the darknesses of the night, according to St. Augustine, are the errors, the prejudices, all those obstacles that keep God from entering the souls of men."[2]

If his discourses and pastorals were timely alerts, his most constant and efficacious activity was in the catechetical apostolate.

In an audience for bishops in 1877, Pius IX called him apostle of the catechism, and taking off his pectoral cross he placed it around Bishop Scalabrini's neck.

"Today," Pius IX said, "there is too much concern for the second floor of the house, and not enough attention to the first, which is the foundation. The catechism is the foundation for all preaching and pastoral work. Good catechisms will save society...In witness of the identity of our views we offer our pectoral cross to Bishop Scalabrini and point him out as the Apostle of the Catechism."[3]

For Bishop Scalabrini this was a solemn confirmation of a lifelong commitment, inspired by a passionate desire for the sound instruction of youth.[4] His catechetical activity was unique and incisive, so much so that he was the "great precursor of the Italian movement which is in full flower today," for he "believed in the need for catechetical instruction, was intensely devoted to it, did not gloss over the inadequate methods then in use", but boldly pointed out the way to improve them.[5] The path to renewal of religious education was opened by the hard work of outstanding individuals, "and among these apostles of education," wrote Father Silvio Riva, "Msgr. Scalabrini should be mentioned with special gratitude...I would call him a doctor of catechesis, in the strictly ecclesiastical meaning of the term."[6]

There had been the great catechetical reform to St. Charles Borromeo, imitated in the diocese of Piacenza by Blessed Paolo Burali. St. Peter Canisius had also made basic contributions to the field of catechetical instruction. There had been the Roman Catechism ordered by the Council of Trent and the Christian Doctrine of St. Robert Bellarmine, and later of St. Francis de Sales and St. Alphonsus Liguori. But religious instruction for some time had sadly deteriorated. A great number of catechisms appeared, but not a few of them were condemned by the Church because they were tainted with Jansenism or Illuminism. Pius VII had protested the imposition of the Napoleonic catechism in Italy in contempt of the teaching authority of the bishops. There were excessive differences between diocesan or regional catechetical manuals. The Council of Trent had somewhat remedied the problem by introducing a unified text for pastors. It was hoped that the first Vatican Council would achieve a unified catechism for the people, but the difficulties posed by different languages and divergent national mentalities and methods, the fear of undermining the authority of the bishops, as well as the fact that the Council itself was interrupted, prevented any concrete results in this field. Pius X did achieve the adoption — but only for Italy — of one Catechism in the form of teaching materials based on an intuitive method, and of a cycle of instructions, according to proposal which he himself had put forward while he was Bishop of Mantua and which were developed by Scalabrini at the National Catechetical Congress of Piacenza in 1889. In Northern Italy a certain unity in religious instruction had been achieved on the basis of the catechism of Bishop Casati of Mondovi (1765). This was adopted first in Piedmont, Liguria and Lombardy, and later, in Scalabrini's revised version, in the Emilian Region. In addition to the question of a single catechism, the 19th centruy had witnessed a resurgence of catechetical activity. This was due to the reinstatement of the Jesuits, the appearance of new religious orders of both men and women whose main objective was the education of youth — notably the Salesians of Don Bosco, the Josephites of Murialdo and the Stigmatine Fathers of Bertoni — and the work of outstanding bishops like Cardinal Capecelatro and Bishop Bonomelli. But the people in general had not been reached, as Scalabrini did reach them.[7]

We have already noted, that while he was pastor of San Bartolomeo in Como, Scalabrini had written a *Little Catechism* for kindergarten use.[8]

"Scalabrini's understanding of the child was original," Father Riva observes, "Even though he did not succeed in freeing himself entirely from the pedagogical theories of his time...he had the insight to base his teaching on...a religious psychology of the child: the idea of God develops more rapidly in the ineffable mind of the child and fills it with joy. Over and above various pedagogical concepts, Scalabrini was always the man of God and the man of the Church, concerned about the essential in education...For him religious instruction was *the foundation of the whole educational edifice of man.*"[9]

"But the foundation is not the whole edifice. Therefore, he accompanies catechetical instruction with education in prayer and in religious, moral and social sense. Formation of the personality is viewed in the contest of the moral and natural virtues. Pedagogical elements in children's games are viewed as spontaneous activity and an expression of the inner life..."[10]

When he became Bishop of Piacenza it was immediately clear what his major concern was. His first pastoral care was the improvement of religious instruction. In fact, he never addressed the various Catholic Associations of the diocese, he never conferred with his Collaborators in the Vineyard of the Lord..."without demonstrating his firm desire to establish a catechetical school in every parish."[11]

Two months after his installation as bishop, he issued a pastoral on the teaching of the catechism *(Sull'Insegnamento del Catechismo)* which contains all the elements of his plan. This was to give religious instruction something of a school format very much along the lines advocated by St. Charles Borromeo and Cardinal Frederick Borromeo. He directed that a "School of Christian Doctrine" be established in every parish with at least four classes: for elementary school pupils *(catechismo piccolo)*; a one or two year course to prepare the twelve year olds to receive first Communion *(Catechismo di Prima Comunione)*; a course to complete the instruction, "to develop and strengthen the faith" *(Catechismo grande or di Perseveranza)*; and lastly a course for adults *(Catechismo degli adulti)*, conducted with tests and explanations and designed to prepare parents to teach the catechism to their children.[12] This was to be held before the regular Sunday afternoon catechetical instruction.

At the same time he published a set of rules for the catechetical schools, *Regole per le Scuole della Dottrina Christiana della città e della diocesi.* According to Riva these represented:

"A gigantic effort, inspired by a clear vision of reality and a fervent intention to give religious instruction a dignity, decorum and efficacy which, viewed in the context of the teaching methods then in use, constituted a general reorientation ahead of its time. He was a born educator, a teacher in the best sense of the word. The history of Italian didactics cannot in justice ignore any objective evaluation of his influence; much less can the Church do so in any history of its religious *magisterium.* The parish in Scalabrini's view...is a school, the great school of the faith." But "the school cannot exist except through worthy teachers who possess both virtue and religious learning. And so he founded a training school for religious teachers, which we might envy on many counts and wish we had today, for it represented the finest flower of Scalabrini's educative ministry."[13]

The following year he addressed a pastoral letter to catechism teachers, whose numbers had grown to three thousand. In this pastoral and in his third one,[14] which announced the 1881 reissue of the diocesan catechism,[15] and, above all, in the book[16] in which he treated the broad spectrum of catechetical problems, Scalabrini unfailingly stressed the necessity, the dignity and the efficacy of the catechism.

"It is par excellence the work of the kingdom of heaven and the well-being of souls." — "It is wholly a heavenly science, the science of sciences...the most important and necessary." — "It is the most noble book after Holy Scriptures:" "A universal code," "The great work of Christian regeneration," "The only thing essential for the individual, the family, and society," the "first means of education," because "education without religion is law without legislator, without sanction, without authority, a house with no foundation."

The First Catechetical Congress

In 1876 he founded *Il Catechista Cattolico,* the first catechetical review in Italy and until 1930 the only one. A few years later it had become a national publication, which continued to appear until 1940. He conceived, promoted and was the chairman of the first National Catechetical Congress to be held in Italy or any other country.

The Congress was held in the new church of the seminary from September 24th to 26th in 1889. The honorary president was Cardinal Capecelatro, who brought to it the blessing of the Holy Father whose heart "had been filled with joyous hope" when Msgr. Scalabrini first suggested the project.

Among the four hundred participants were the archbishops of Aquila, Cagliari and Chieti; the bishops of Parma, Cremona, Rimini, Ventimiglia, Bobbio, Foggia, Massa, Carrara, Soana and Pitigliano, the titular bishop of Zama, Msgr. Mascaretti, and the Vicar of Lodi. Ten cardinals, twenty-five archbishops and eight-four bishops sent expressions of support. As chairman, Bishop Scalabrini kept the discussion on strictly religious matters and steered it away from political questions.[17] Largely through his skill and competence, the meeting was not a forum for fine speeches but the point of departure for catechetical renewal in Italy.

"The importance of this Congress," Brother Salvestrini declared recently, "in the history of modern catechetics is such that we may deem it the greatest point of departure for catechetical renewal since the Council of Trent. In many dioceses of Italy, in fact, future catechetical projects drew new vigor from that Congress, the first of its kind in the entire Catholic world, which brought together scattered forces that had not previously had any influence on each other. The Congress consolidated various experiences and acknowledged the need for a psychological and methodological renewal of the traditional catechetical means of instruction."[18]

The Congress reviewed the entire catechetical field. It proposed the adoption of a uniform text. The principal advocate of this was the Bishop of Mantua, Giuseppe Sarto, who, as Pius X, carried out the idea of a uniform catechism for all Italy. The participants also recommended that a chair of catechetics be established in every seminary, that a Confraternity of Christian Doctrine be instituted in every parish, and that religious instruction be formally organized along school lines.[19]

Among the other proposals, mention may be made of those dealing with the publication of a manual for catechists, circulating catechetical libraries, the promotion of Sunday rest, and publication of low-priced edition excerpts from the patristic writings relating to catechesis. Scalabrini immediately made a concrete contribution to this last suggestion by publishing in the *Catechista Cattolico* (1883-1887 and 1890-1892) a translation of the catechesis of St. Cyrillus of Jerusalem. The historical introduction and notes on the text are evidence of his learning, especially in the field of Scriptures, Patristics and history.

In his opening address Cardinal Capecelatro warmly supported an important proposal, which had not been pursued, namely, to base catechetical instruction on Christology. The idea was not lost on Bishop Scalabrini or the Permanent Committee set up to carry out the Congress recommendations and to prepare a second one in five years. Difficulties prevented its being held within the time limit, however. It was not until 1901 that the Committee decided to hold the second Congress in Piacenza in September of 1902. The program was eminently Christological: "The main theme and the ultimate aim of our Congress, is to make Jesus Christ reign in souls," to "bring about the reign of Our Lord in everyone and everything, through the Catechism, or rather through religious instruction." Laymen were to be invited.

"Are not the laity also soldiers of Christ? They must also take up arms for the support and defense of his kingdom...The activity of the clergy has limits beyond which they cannot go, either for lack of means, or limitations of strength, or because situations are unfavorable or actually hostile. The layman can go where the priest cannot. Often an exhortation from him is accepted more readily than from a priest...The laity, too, has its apostolate and, may I say, its apostolic mission."[20]

When several members of the Committee fell ill, the Congress was again postponed,[21] this time until the beginning of 1905. On February 8, Pius X sent the editor of the *Catechista Cattolico*, a Brief of Approval:

"The plan, which you and your co-workers have recently set forth, to hold this year a Second Catechetical Congress, we greatly approve as the one which more than all others leads to the goal We have set for ourselves...In fact the root of all the evils which trouble the present age is a certain ignorance of the fundamentals of our religion, incredible in the midst of so much display of learning and desire for knowledge. We are very pleased to see that you seek the remedy for this disorder with all that is possible and with zealous solicitude. For We have noted this solicitude in the paper attached to your letter which sets forth the matters to be dealt with by the Congress. We deem these matters opportune, no less than does your Bishop who is most versed in this subject. For this reason diligently carry out, under the guidance of your excellent bishop, the work you have begun, confident that your efforts will not fail to receive great help and abundant grace from God."[22]

On May 19, thirteen days before his death, Bishop Scalabrini called a meeting of the Committee.

"With youthful energy and enthusiasm beyond all expectation he set forth and answered three questions: whether the Congress should be held, when and where to hold it. He declared firmly that the Congress must be held, that it must be held that year, and that from every point of view it was best to hold it in Piacenza. Various objections and difficulties of different kinds were put forward in vain. He rebutted them all with a vigorous logic equal to his authority. The next day he named the members of the local committee, which under his direction was about to set briskly to work with the cooperation of willing and competent co-workers, who had already come from all parts of Italy. Plans were being made for the first session, during which a telegram of homage was to be sent to Pius X, when members of His Excellency's household suddenly informed us that he was ill, that he had to undergo surgery, and that he would need absolute rest for some time. We were sorrowed by the grave and unexpected news of the sickness that distressed so dear and venerated a person. A new distress was added because we feared we would not have the comfort of his wise and *youthful* energy in preparing for the Congress. We know that when anyone tried to advise him against taking on the responsibilities of the Congress, he answered playfully in dialect: 'Oh, you are an old man.' — And his would-be adviser was eleven years his junior. But no one feared, not even the closest members of his household, that he might be taken from us...'[23]

At the first Congress, Bishop Giuseppe Alessi proposed the establishment of Higher Schools of Religious Education and was warmly supported by Bishop Scalabrini.[24] The proposal, however, ran into a number of political difficulties. Scalabrini encouraged Alessi to persevere.

"I am increasingly convinced that it is necessary to do good for the sake of good, for the love of God alone, without seeking the approval of men or being disturbed by their disapproval. It is the only way to succeed in what you undertake, do believe me. I have every hope for your work precisely because it is encountering opposition...Your work is blessed by God, and that is enough, whatever anyone says or does, it will win out in the end."[25]

Alessi was encouraged and did persevere and finally saw the fruition of his idea.

As we noted, the first subject dealt with, although it was not on the agenda, was the matter of a uniform text for the catechism.[26] At the end of the discussion, a vote was cast in favor of it on the suggestion of Msgr. Scalabrini, who had accepted with enthusiasm Bishop Giuseppe Sarto's proposal.[27] It was decided to present a petition to Pope Leo XIII over the signature of all the bishops present. Cardinal Capecelatro immediately presented it to the Holy Father, who approved it in principle but reserved the right to study it further. A little later Capecelatro signaled some difficulty: "It seems that there are people in Rome who play politics even with the catechism and those who are concerned with it."[29] On March 23, 1891, he wrote:

"I saw the Holy Father...As for the uniform Catechism he told me he was still very much in favor of it. He added that he had had a catechism, which seemed good to him, printed in Rome: he was going to send it to all the Archbishops of Italy so each could submit their observations on it."[30]

This catechism had certain "merits and defects like all the others", Scalabrini frankly told the Pope. After a while no more was heard about it, and Scalabrini himself let the matter die. He cooperated instead in the adoption of a uniform text for the Emilian region. The one chosen was the text in use in Liguria, revised on the basis of "the extensive and learned work done on it by our Venerable Colleague, the Bishop of Piacenza, who had been given it into his charge."[31]

Scalabrini as Catechist

According to Father Orione, the Congress and the catechetical review opened the way and gave the tone to the catechetical movement that has developed in Italy.[32] In fact, both the Congress and Scalabrini's work in this field had a broad and conspicuous influence on ecclesiastical legislation in the years that followed, and even more recently they were termed "the strongest and most enlightened stimulus to catechetical didactics in the seminaries and every school of religion."[33] Bishop Edward J. Kelly of Boise, Idaho, a few years ago had a part of Scalabrini's *Catechismo Cattolico* translated for his priests and observed that "here the book has been very well received by the priests, who are going to use it for their lay catechists. It was bound to please them since it was written by a genius."[34]

In a certain sense, Scalabrini anticipated modern pedagogical concepts:

"It is a basic principle of Scalabrini's catechetical method that the object and subject of instruction is the whole man, that catechetics is not merely the art of instructing, but is principally the art of educating."[35] Note for example the abundance of intuitive means and active methods he suggests: Love and sympathetic understanding for the student, frequent oral tests, the involvement of the 'whole child' in school and out of school, appealing moral stories, pictures, singing, catechetical contests and parties with prizes, projects for the pupils outside of school hours, cooperation with the parents..., "all with a seriousness and perfection extremely difficult to achieve but without which all the rules, even the wisest, are worth very little."[36]

He urged religious educators to "model themselves on the Divine Teacher." Every month he gathered them together in the city, and either he himself or some one he appointed would talk to them. For the catechists in the rural areas he appointed a Vincentian priest as their spiritual director.

Again ahead of his time, he created a diocesan office for catechetics. The bishop was chairman, assisted by a secretary and, eight general committee members, four of whom were priests and four were laymen. A director for each vicariate had the duty of visiting the various parishes and reporting to the diocesan office. The pastor served as parish director. A chair of catechetics was established in the seminary for the seminarians, who were sent to teach in the parishes, and a training school in religious education was instituted for laymen.

As in his other activities, Scalabrini taught first of all by his example, particularly during his pastoral visits. During one of his visits to the parish of San Bartolomeo he questioned the youngsters as usual. At the end of the function, one eight year old, who had not been asked a question, climbed up the steps to the bishop's chair, catechism in hand. "What are you doing?" the assisting priest asked. "I want the bishop to ask me a question too," the child replied holding out his catechism.[37]

A correspondent for the *Cittadino* of Genoa went to call on the bishop one day and found the rooms of the episcopal palace full of young people, to whom the Bishop himself, the Vicar General and a professor from the seminary were giving religious instruction. His method for explaining the elements of Christian Dictrine to college students was adapted to their level of learning and encouraged them to raise questions and objections, to which he either replied immediately or at an appropriate time in the exposition of his subject. The lesson ended with the recitation of the act of faith and brief prayers.[38]

In the diary he kept during his voyage to the United States, we read under the date of July 28, 1901: "Every day from four until seven I explain the Catechism to several youngsters, and this is a source of great consolation to me."[39]

When he came to Piacenza, Bishop Scalabrini had already inherited a precious catechetical tradition, echoes of which are to be found in previous diocesan synods. It is to be noted also that the city itself was already well known through the reputation of its school system and of pioneers like Giuseppe Taverna, Alfonso Testa, and the Uttini brothers, Ciriaco and Carlo, whose work the bishop utilized in his catechetical reform. "But it is certainly due to Bishop Scalabrini that Piacenza was the first city to promote modern catechesis, as it had been first to join in the crusades and the first to support the unification of Italy."[40] Leo XIII called it the "city of the Catechism."[41]

According to Father Silvio Riva, Bishop Scalabrini's influence in this field reached beyond the confines of his diocese:

"The history of catechetics in Italy and in the Church confirms for him the title of pioneer with respect to the best of today's catechetical practices. His name and his work stand beside those of St. Pius X, for when he codified the catechetical norms he drew on the experience, pastoral norms and conclusions provided by Scalabrini, which served for the entire Catholic Church."[42]

Just as Bishop Scalabrini viewed catechetics as basic to all aspects of Christian life, he also gave it first importance in all his pastoral activity.

"I have said it many times, nor will I tire of repeating it...; we must return to the Catechism, if we wish individuals, families, society to have peace...It is the book that must serve as a norm in all the acts and vicissitudes of life...; not only in private life but in public life as well. In a word, the Catechism must enter into everything, and guide everything, just as the law of God and the Gospel of Christ must guide all things."[43]

In fact, Scalabrini put it first on the agenda of the second Synod. The first chapter is entitled: *"De christianae doctrinae rudimentis* (elements of Christian doctrine), as evidence of the dominant position over all other diocesan activities the bishop attributed to religious instruction. One of the keys to his whole personality was his missionary spirit. For him Christ's missionary injunction lies in the words, "Go, teach..."[44] He therefore equates the vocation to religious teaching with the missionary vocation.

"Many times perhaps you will envy those who, shutting their ears to the voice of flesh and blood, cross the ocean tides for distant lands in order to evangelize peoples in darkness and the shadow of death. But what good do these desires do? Teach the catechism to children and you will be doing something whose merit is as great as the conversion of pagans, and your name will be written in the book of life beside those of the most famous heroes."[45]

Bishop Scalabrini was known as the apostle of the emigrants. Perhaps this is why the title Pius IX gave him of apostle of the catechism is less familiar. But even in his mission for the emigrants, he always stressed the importance of the catechism.

"The troubles in our emigration...can be summed up in this way: Loss of faith through lack of religious instruction...Permit a bishop to mourn such a misfortune! The privation of that spiritual bread which is the word of God..."[46]

The priority he always accorded religious instruction accounts for the fact that he wanted the lay brothers of his Congregation to be called catechists and that he insisted on Italian schools and on Sisters trained to teach and care for children and girls in his missions. He asked that religious instruction be included in any orientation for emigrants. His principal argument for a uniform catechism text was the fact of the new contacts among people as well as increased journeys back and forth "from one part of the world to another".[47]

His favorite devotions, to the Eucharist and the Virgin Mary, were also means of religious instruction.[48]

"He had the intelligence to understand that his mandate to evangelize, received with the fullness of the priesthood, could not be carried out in his time, and still less today, except through catechesis...Bishop Scalabrini understood that souls are enlightened through catechetics: it is the catechism that forms the Christian mentality; other forms of instruction compare with catechesis like a mimeographed copy to the original text... Bishop Scalabrini understood this and was not afraid to place catechesis among the most perfect institutions in the didactic and pedagogical order to want it to be the finest school for men, young and adult, full of the gentle and vigorous spirit of the Divine Teacher, Jesus."[49]

Scalabrini as Preacher

Bishop Scalabrini was also called a tireless apostle of the Word:

"His sermons were unusually frequent and full of content; his splendid Latin allocutions to the synods constitute a lasting record of the great meetings of the diocesan clergy; and the tireless, always careful preaching with which for thirty years he maintained almost daily contact with his people...was anchored, as he was to his style and to his themes, namely the Gospel and the Catechism."[50]

What a tireless preacher he was is evidenced by the fact that during his visit to the United States, which lasted a hundred days filled with traveling and appointments, he gave three hundred and forty talks.[51]

The most difficult judges of all — the priests — attest to the effectiveness of his sermons. During the same American journey he preached a retreat for his missionaries and about thirty other Italian priests. He himself wrote:

"I was always deeply moved when I spoke and those fine priests were even more moved than I. Several of them broke down and wept. It was a new experience: an Italian bishop giving a retreat to Italian priests 3,000 miles from Italy...I was greatly pleased; the priests were enthusiastic."[52]

One of his listeners wrote him from Brooklyn:

"You can never imagine, modest and humble as you are, the immense good that your words — sincere, affectionate and penetrating — of a true man of God have done for all the Italian priests who had the good fortune to hear you. For me it was like listening to the very words of Our Blessed Lord."[53]

He gave retreats in South America also for both priests and Sisters.[54] But above all he was prodigal in his tireless ministry to the people:

"Religious instruction of his people was always one of his most special concerns...One might say he never lost an opportunity to encourage them to do good, preaching sometimes eight or ten times in one day."[55]

This excessive effort was not the least cause of the illnesses that beset him.[56] He always adapted what he said to his audiences,[57] and threw into his sermon the full enthusiasm and energy of his personality.[58] He impressed his hearers with his sincerity and his own obvious conviction.[59]

"Every time I had the good fortune to hear the Servant of God preach, or listen to his exhortations or informal talks I was always impressed by his clear, attractive, moving and persuasive words, but above all by the feeling he created that he was fired and inspired by the most lively faith."[60]

It was a period noted for its rhetoric, but Scalabrini:

"Never used any of the usual oratorical tricks. In fact, his style is often rough, his expressions simple and direct. Whatever he said was so filled with conviction that it was profoundly effective. He did not seem a preacher or lecturer but an apostle."[61] — "He has the easy and persuasive manner of one whose mission it is to reach the heart of his listeners."[62] "His eloquence was scornful of words and filled with substance; it had a warmth which does not inspire some cold and meditated theme but one which grows in the speaker as his talk brings him to the points that most affect him and with the same naturalness communicates itself to his listeners,"[63] "stimulating the emotion characteristic of an audience captivated and excited by true eloquence."[64]

But part of his fascination was undoubtedly due to his personality, "a man of broad vision, tireless work, with a zeal that knew no obstacles or boundaries; and so his words were buttressed by the incontestible efficacy of his deeds."[65]

A curious testimony of the fascination he exercised is given us by Antonio Fogazzaro, to whom Scalabrini described a sermon he had given in Brazil to a crowd of Italians among whom he had noticed a group of Polish immigrants. "They stood around with expressions on their faces so eager that it was touching..."[66]

Thus this good sower of the Word of God cast the good seed from full hands, without stinting, to the end of his life. A few days before his death he spoke in Bobbio "with fatherly sweetness and serenity, and kept his hearers spellbound, avidly drinking in his spontaneous, fluent words, rich in grace and wit."[67]

Also to be noted is the encouragement and stimulus he gave his priests, and especially the pastors, to spread the word of truth with greater generosity and seriousness.

"The priest," he used to say, "is truly the man of God in communicating the truth."[68] "Let us speak the truth, which shines sure and resplendent in the faith; let us speak it in serenity and tranquility, unafraid, patient, and let us place our trust in it, for it has its own invincible strength."[69]

At the third Synod he recommended:

"Do not fail, especially on Sundays and holy days, to explain to the faithful during Holy Mass the Gospel or some other lesson and to explain some mystery of the Holy Sacrifice so that, instructed more in depth, they can participate with greater devotion...At least on Sundays and solemn feast days give the people entrusted to you some religious instruction, according to their needs. Nourish them with wholesome words, teaching them the truths which everyone must know for his own salvation, pointing out simply and briefly the faults that each must avoid and the virtues he must pursue in order to avoid eternal punishment and to attain heavenly glory."[70]

He himself carefully prepared "in prayer and in study,"[71] writing out year after year the homilies he delivered at the pontifical Masses and his principal talks, and preparing copious notes for all other occasions. He required his priests to prepare their sermons carefully. He had equal censure for those who improvised and those who went from pulpit to pulpit declaiming the same stereotyped sermon. He wanted the preparation to be conscientious, careful and adapted to the audience. One day he came upon a member of his staff who was intently reading over a fine written sermon, the cover of which listed the parishes where he had already given it. The bishop took the manuscript from him with a smile and tore it up. "Have this much modesty at least." He also disapproved of those preachers who were engaged twice a year to deliver the same old musty sermon on the souls in Purgatory. Their text, he said was like a "municipal bond" which paid interest every six months.[72]

In the second diocesan Synod, he admonished his clergy thus:

"Let all Preachers and especially pastors and their assistants remember that they are not to speak with the alluring words of human wisdom but with evidence of the spirit and of virtue. They must remember that they are debtors to the learned and the unlearned, and that therefore they must be devoted to simplicity, clarity and brevity. They are not to mount the pulpit unprepared or without having invoked the enlightenment of the Holy Spirit. They are to remember that their words must indeed illumine the minds of their hearers, but even more than that they must move their hearts. While a sermon must never omit some explanation of the noblest truths of the faith, it must also contain some practical application, even when it is a eulogy."[73]

The Pastoral Letters

Msgr. Scalabrini's pastorals are another evidence of his zeal for evangelization and the defense of the truth. There are seventy in all. Some are simple but moving presentations of papal encyclicals or other important papal documents, especially of the monumental teachings of Leo XIII. Others, particularly the Lenten ones, are little dogmatic or moral treatises in which, in a style readily understood by the people but nevertheless rich in substantive teaching and fervor, he sets forth guidelines for a Christian life, defends the Church and his pastors, warns against errors or distortions of the truth, and invariably deals with current subjects.

He knew his own time and his own people. He diagnosed realistically the evils, the sorrows and the confusions of society. He touched its raw wounds without fear and condemned its errors without reticence. At the same time he was a foe of pessimism and, in fact, knew how to discover the positive trends in the spiritual and intellectual ferment that characterized the end of the century:

"We see society agonizing, as it were, to produce a new order of things; but it does not know, in its misery, that it is to prepare itself for the kingdom of the Man-God; it does not know that it is working to prepare the field for the universal victory of the Church and to fulfill the unfailing prophecy of Jesus Christ: *Confidite, ego vici mundum.*"[74]

"Let us open our hearts more than ever; let us hope; but let our hope be calm and patient; let us hope, but without growing weary."[75]

It is with this openness to hope that he directed the educational work for the family and through it for all of society:

"I have always had the idea, Leibniz used to say, that one could reform the human race if one reformed education. Nothing is more true. And since all the reforms that could be introduced are advised or prescribed by the Catholic Religion, we are certain not to err when we affirm that to improve the family, and therefore all of society, it is enough to give a Christian religious education to the growing generation."[76]

This theme of religious education, always uppermost in his mind, is reflected in his pastoral letters, especially those which set forth his solicitude for his flock. All of them constitute a proof that from the day of his consecration he lived and suffered in full the responsibilities of a pastor.

His ideas on instruction and education follow an organic design. In the Pastorals written between 1876 and 1881 he demonstrates that the Catholic religion "is necessary to the well-being of the individual, the family, civil society. It is necessary both for adults and for children, for the learned and the unlearned. It is necessary in private and in public life, in joy and in sorrow, in life and in death."[77] In those written between 1882-1888 he sets forth his concept of Christian life and faith. From 1889 on, while he repeats his ever-present concern for religious education, he deals with more urgent and current topics: the papacy, devotion to the Eucharist, keeping holy the holy days, prayers, social problems. There are some ideas that recur in all the Pastorals. Among them we might note what might be called the outstanding feature of his character as Bishop-Doctor: "the spirit of religion in the family, the spirit of the family in society."[78]

Many of his writings had an influence not only in Italy but abroad as well. This was true for example of his 1887 Pastoral *Cattolici di Nome e Cattolici di fatto* (Catholics in Name and Catholics in Deed), which ran through four editions in two months, the one on *Socialismo e l'Azione de Clero* (Socialism and the Action of the Clergy) and the pamphlet, *L'Emigrazione Italiania in America* (Italian Emigration in America, 1887), which received wide comment in the press.[79]

Priestly Formation

The Bishop of Piacenza was not content to exercise, however generously, his own priestly function. He was deeply concerned with the formation of the most precious instruments of his ministry, so that it could be rightly said, "he made his own clergy."[80] It was a time of "scant pastoral flexibility among the 19th century clergy, who continued to use old methods without creating new tools adapted to new social realities."[81] It was Scalabrini's desire to find a solution to the fundamental problem of priestly training, beginning with the seminary. Nothing touched his concern more deeply than the seminaries, he used to say.

"I love them as the pupil of my eye, because in the growing hopes of the priesthood I see a guarantee of the future well-being of my flock. For this I willingly took on enormous sacrifices, and for this I continue to do all that is possible."[82]

Scalabrini was a worthy successor to Bishop Ranza, who had supported and aided the seminaries. He gave moral and financial aid to the seminary in Bedonia which, established in the mountainous region most rich in vocations, provided almost half the clergy of the diocese. In 1868, he reopened the diocesan seminary, which had been closed because of political events. In the beginning he encountered serious difficulties, but in 1872 when Father Savino Rocca was named rector, the future looked promising although the majority of seminarians were day students.[83]

Scalabrini initiated a campaign for vocations. In every parish he exhorted parents not to hinder but rather to encourage vocations to the priesthood. He constantly urged pastors to be represented in the seminary by at least one student. We have noted the generosity with which he personally subsidized those who could not afford tuition. To help poor seminary students he established in 1892 the Confraternity of Saint Opilio. Each parish, or at lease each vicariate, was to establish a scholarship for a poor student. He himself started off the project by funding one scholarship in the Seminario Urbano and another in the seminary of Bedonia. Sermons on vocations and collections for the Opera S. Opilio were held twice a year in every parish. At the same time he asked pastors to watch for suitable candidates. He warned against the temptation to lose courage or confidence:

"Do not fear that your hopes will be disappointed...Even if among the young levites gathered in the Seminary most will leave and only a few will reach their goal, nevertheless those few will be worth a treasure and will be the joy of both heaven and earth. Among the hundred drops of rain that fall to earth, ninety eight become mud; of the other two, one falls on the forehead of the infant in baptism and gives a son to the Church, the other falls into the priest's chalice, mingles with the Blood of Christ and gives God to men."[84]

Seminary Reform

The new Bishop's aim was to make the seminaries equal to their time. As a first step, he reorganized the courses in literature, philosophy and science.[85] He arranged for students to take the state examinations at the end of high school[86] and sent several of the brighter ones on to the university.

"On the feast of St. Charles, three or four young theology students will leave for Milan to continue their studies and prepare for professorships...It is the only way to keep the seminaries open; a storm is raging around them that I pray with all my heart God will dispel."[87]

He was delighted when in 1880 the philosophical-theological review, *Divus Thomas*, was published by the Collegio Alberoni and became a success. He had warmly supported this enterprise, had found qualified contributing editors for it and generally watched over its fidelity to doctrine. An echo of his concern appears in a letter to Cardinal Giuseppe Pecci:

"You will have received the issues (of the review) by now and I am taking the liberty of asking you, Most Eminent Prince, to give me your worthy opinion. This periodical was founded with the intention of cooperating in the great work of reviving Thomistic philosophy begun by our glorious Holy Father. It meets with general favor, is sought after abroad and has a fine number of associates among scholars, including Your Eminence. I am anxious therefore that this review will prosper for the benefit of the good cause and this is why Your Eminence must do me the favor, which I ask also in the name of the Editors, to tell me clearly Your Eminence's opinion. I am ready to withdraw, explain and amend any expression which is not clearly in accord with the teaching of the Angelic Doctor."[88]

Scalabrini's correspondence with scholars in the field of natural history reveals his desire to get mineral and zoological specimens for the seminary. There is a letter from the geologist Abbot Stoppani which says he is sending minerals and rocks to form the nucleus of a museum of natural history for the school.[89] A few months later, a second letter announces the arrival of fossils and animals.[90] Father Nicolò Zaccarino, who had been Scalabrini's classmate in the seminary in Como, sent the seminary in Piacenza a large collection of minerals[91] and he interested his friend Professor Alessandro Mascarini of Ascoli Piceno in the project, who procured for him several specimens of marine fossils.[92]

A directive addressed to seminary professors and rectors in 1876 sets forth Scalabrini's views on the various courses:

"Philosophy must be above all the basis and foundation of the higher disciplines and it must be derived principally from that of St. Thomas Aquinas. Thomistic philosophy bears the recommendation of centuries and of the Church, not to mention of our reigning Pontiff Pius IX. We choose as the text for this subject in our diocese Father Matteo Liberatore's *Institutiones Philosophiae*. If on certain points it leaves something to be desired for a complete and integral explanation of St. Thomas, we bid the professors to illustrate, with readings and explanations, the thesis of the Angelic Doctor cited therein so that there will remain no question that is not explicated and clarified by the Prince of Christian philosophers. For dogmatic theology we desire that you adopt G. Perrone's *Praelectiones Theologicae*, which also, even if there is some gap in the presentation of one or another question...(a gap which the professors' knowledge and diligence must fill guided by the most important theologians: St. Thomas, Suarez, Billuart and Cardinal Franzelin), nevertheless has advantages over the texts of many other authors... For Moral Theology the text of St. Alphonsus Liguori will be used...If the method is sometimes deficient, the professors will remedy this, stressing the principles of St. Thomas and other outstanding theologians."

Furthermore, he established chairs of Biblical Exegesis, Canon Law, Church History and Liturgy. He ended his decree with an exhortation to love truth and unity, based on a union of spirit and doctrine with the Church and the Apostolic See. Strongly evident is his desire to banish from the seminary and from among his clergy any discord and divisions: "To anyone who might still want to argue: it is not the custom with us, nor in the churches of God (1 *Cor.*, *11:16*)."[93]

Thus Scalabrini not only continued the Thomist tradition, which was revived by Buzzetti, who had founded the chair of philosophy at the beginning of the century, and was continued by Angelo Testa and Bishop Ranza;[94] he also anticipated the directives of Leo XIII. When Leo's directives were promulgated three years later, Scalabrini hastened to reconfirm them solemnly for his diocese, especially in his second synod.[95]

False Accusations

The Vincentian Fathers, who had directed the *Collegio Alberoni* for many years and had given intellectual and spiritual training to half the diocese, had given ample proof of their fidelity to Thomism. Three of them (Barberis, Ramellini, Tornatore, later joined by Msgr. Vinati, professor of the *Seminario Urbano*)[96] were mainly responsible for starting the *Divus Thomas*. Nevertheless, charges of Jansenism were still being made against their teaching.

At the first synod, eighty-two priests wanted to present a memorandum refuting the calumnies. The Bishop answered the charges indirectly in his opening address to the synod, declaring his esteem for the clergy in general and the teachers in the seminary in particular. He then made special mention of the professors of the *Collegio Alberoni*, "the priests of the Congregation of St. Vincent de Paul, who have supported and directed the *Collegio Alberoni* for more than a century, to the general satisfaction of everyone."[97]

In the constitution *De Seminario Clericorum* there is also an indirect reply to the slanders, which came from certain persons who were trying to apply, quite anachronistically, the teachings of St. Thomas to the natural sciences. The *Collegio Alberoni*, in any event, had few competitors in Italy with respect to the quality of its courses and its scientific equipment.

In the encyclical *Aeterni Patris*, Bishop Scalabrini distinguished between directives and suggestions. In "commanding" that the teachings of St. Thomas — "as explained by the most classical scholars as the doctrine which the Church has always venerated" — be taught in the Schools of Theology and Philosophy, he enjoined the directives in the encyclical, which had appeared a month before.

He here quoted the passage in which Leo XIII exhorts the Bishops to spread the wisdom of St. Thomas for the enrichment of all knowledge: "We say the wisdom of St. Thomas: if in fact the Scholastics have reached some interpretation with excessive subtlety, or if something has been taught ill-advisedly, or if there is something which does not accord with the doctrinal findings of a later period, or if it holds little probability, we do not wish that it be presented to our own time in any way."[98]

It may be said that Scalabrini followed in the footsteps of Leo XIII, about whom Count Soderini wrote:

"He particularly regretted the attacks on the memory of men worthy of great respect, among whom he numbered Rosmini. Nor did he intend that on the basis of the encyclical, through excessive zeal and wrongly invoking his name, certain persons only should be considered quasi official interpreters of the Thomistic doctrines and no others, or that these should be expressed in antiquated language, or finally that what remained a matter of opinion should be presented as absolute truth, with no criticism allowed, not even with regard to the contemporary progress of the experimental sciences, which the Angelic Doctor, after all, though of the highest intelligence might have surmised in part, but certainly could not foresee in its entirety...The most enlightened Thomists of the time agreed with this wise attitude, scholars like Cassetta, Segna, Satolli, Cavagnis, Lorenzelli, all of whom later became cardinals, as well as Bishop Talamo, Father Lepidi, and others, among whom the illustrious and courageous Bishop Scalabrini of Piacenza must not be forgotten. With several of these the Pope liked to open his heart, and he deplored the intemperance of those who, he said, 'have forgotten that in order to triumph truth does not need to use constraint or violence'."[99]

To sum up, the witnesses at the Process of Beatification are in agreement that Scalabrini anticipated the dispositions Leo XIII set forth in the encyclical *Aeterni Patris*. We read in the Process that one of his first acts was to introduce the study of St. Thomas in the *Collegio Alberoni*.

"In this connection, I recall that Bishop Scalabrini told me that on the occasion of a private audience, Leo XIII lamented the fact that the *Collegio Alberoni* left something to be desired in the matter of philosophy. He then frankly observed that the Holy Father had been misinformed. When the Pope insisted, Bishop Scalabrini declared bluntly that he was certain of what he claimed, that if more credence was given to others than to the Bishop, there was nothing for the Bishop to do but to lay his mitre at the feet of His Holiness, which he was quite ready to do. The Pope was convinced, told him to come back the next day, and gave him a laudatory brief, which was the best justification for the Servant of God."[100]

In this Brief, Leo XIII congratulated the clergy of Piacenza on the noble account they gave of themselves and the extremely fine expectations they presaged. In addition, he praised and expressed encouragement for the two periodicals of the diocese *Divus Tomas* and *Il Catechista Cattolico* (The Catholic Catechist). In 1878 and in 1883, the Sacred Congregation of the Council had officially bestowed the highest praise on Bishop Scalabrini for the promptness with which he effected the reform in seminary studies along the lines indicated by the Holy See.

Father Giuseppe Cardinali recalled that when he was named rector of the *Seminario Urbano* he found that the Servant of God had already put into effect the reform of the philosophy and theology courses, not only in the *Urbano* but also in the seminary of *Bedonia*. He noted that before *Asterni Patris*, the *Collegio Alberoni* displayed an orientation toward Gioberti and then Rosmini, but that through "the wisdom of the Servant of God" all three institutions followed the "illumined dispositions of Rome."[101] Still another witness recalled a discourse Scalabrini gave the philosophy students at the *Collegio Alberoni* in November of 1877 on the system of St. Thomas, extolling it as capable of solving all metaphysical problems.[102]

Cardinal Nasalli Rocca has recalled the affectionate solicitude Scalabrini had for his seminaries, the direction he gave philosophical and theological studies, and the eminent professors he invited to teach therein, among them, the Thomist Professor Rossignoli, and Monsignors Vinati and Dallepiane. "He insisted that the directives of Leo XIII be faithfully followed."[103]

Thus in the field of ecclesiastical studies Bishop Scalabrini remained faithful to his duty as teacher and pastor as well as executor of the papal directives, notwithstanding the great confusion of the time (his letters speak of the confusion of tongues, the confusion of Babel) and despite the fact that some of his priests were devoted to Rosmini.

"In these delicate matters he was guided by his own vigorous common sense, his love of truth, his zeal for souls. Piacenza, thanks to his efficacious protection, became during his episcopate a worthy center of sacred studies — studies inspired by the immortal motto *nova et vetera* — the old which is rejuvenated in the new, the new which is consecrated in the old."[104]

Continuing Education for Priests

Bishop Scalabrini untiringly urged his priests to continue reading up on the subjects they had pursued in the seminary. In the records of the first diocesan synod we read several stern reflections:

"The Priest must also direct the conscience of the faithful, exhort them with sound teaching and correct those who contradict it. It is obvious that this cannot be done without a profound knowledge of both Dogmatic and Moral Theology...Nor, in order to carry out one's pastoral duties effectively, should knowledge of Mystical Theology be considered of little importance...There are other souls also, wonderfully disposed to all progress toward holiness, but rarely do they find a suitable interpreter and teacher of supernatural ways. For this reason also the words of the prophet are true: *Parvuli petierunt panem, et non erat qui frangeret eis...*" (Little children go begging for bread; no one spares a scrap for them. — Lam., 4:4)[105]

"Whatever time you have free from the Divine Office, from prayer and meditation, from church functions and other necessary activities, do not waste it in idleness, in laziness and in trivial things; but, called as you are to the inheritance of the Lord, meditate day and night on His law...Diligently consult the treatises on both Dogmatic and Moral Theology, the institutions of Canon Law, the books on the Sacred Liturgy and history of the Church, and the works of the Fathers of the Church."[106]

The Bishop attached so much importance to a thorough knowledge of the sacred disciplines that during the second Synod, he devoted a whole address to them:

"Pastors are also Doctors: they must nourish the faithful not only with the Sacraments but also with Doctrine...

This is the knowledge required of the priests of the new law, a knowledge, that is, whereby the number of the elect may be filled, and everyone may be led to the perfection befitting the body of the Church.

Without doubt, if no society can be constituted and endure without knowledge, if it is not possible to fill any office in civil society without the necessary knowledge, how much more will the Church grow and increase with knowledge. With knowledge, ecclesiastical duties will be fulfilled effectively and fruitfully. The Church is founded on faith, but knowledge is necessary to generate and guard the faith; with knowledge, that faith which leads to true blessedness is generated, nourished, defended, fortified...

"Just as it guards the faith, knowledge protects the integrity of morals. What can be expected of the ministry of the priest who does not possess the knowledge he should? What spirit of faith will there be in his performance of the acts of the liturgy; how sure will be the direction he gives in the confessional; what kind of persuasion will there be in his preaching of doctrine; what kind of watch will he keep over the flock entrusted to him? He is the useless servant, and the punishment he merits awaits him: he will be case forth into darkness, bound hand and foot.

"If the Church has at times suffered the defection of her people and the corruption of morals, this must be attributed in large measure to the ignorance of her ministers...

"Although no one denies the need for knowledge, few nevertheless truly dedicate themselves to acquiring it. There are some who before being ordained devote themselves passionately to their studies; but once they have obtained a benefice, they abandon their books, convinced they have learned enough for the uneducated people entrusted to them. It is a vain excuse...Let them study intently, that they may have proper solutions for the new difficulties that will present themselves. Just as soldiers constantly practice their weapons, even when there is no danger of an enemy attack, so priests, if they would not seriously scar their consciences, must never cease to peruse their books, which are their weapons...

"Everyone, therefore, should set aside some time, especially in the morning, to learn or increase his knowledge of something he should know, leaving aside everything else except his duties in justice to his neighbor: the latter in fact must have priority over one's study...Lack of time is no excuse. If one dedicates to study the time lost in useless matters, if one withdraws from the crowd, from idle conversations and dangerous reading, one will have sufficient time for study.

"It is our prayer, Venerable Brothers, that all of you, and especially the young among you, should burn with the desire for knowledge. Love knowledge, which you sought from your youth and held dear as a bride. Take refuge in it when you return home from your ministry, seek in it your rest...

"While we recommend this knowledge to our priests, we do not condemn secular knowledge and cultures. Once ecclesiastical learning is assured, we seek continuously...to acquire secular learning as well."[107]

On other occasions, his feelings seemed to be summed up in the exclamation: "Oh I wish the name cleric meant what it did in the Middle Ages: study, action, sacrifice."[108]

Priestly Holiness

He was even more zealous in the matter of priestly holiness. He could not conceive of the priesthood apart from holiness: in his thinking the two terms were synonymous.

"He who rises above the people in dignity of office," he wrote, "must rise above them in perfection. He who is chosen to represent God must reflect His image in himself in broader outline and with brighter colors. The priest shares to an extraordinary degree an authority that is divine; he shares with Christ the great mission which He received from the Father, and it is only through his fidelity to the God who entrusted the mission to him that he will win the respect of the people and will his ministry bear the most precious fruit."[109]

Following are excerpts from his address to his clergy at the second Synod, in which he stresses the essence and importance of holiness and the means to work toward it. These quotations embody his whole thinking on the subject.

"...Holiness, says St. Thomas, is purity consecrated to God. Not a common purity, not mediocre, but sublime, as St. Chrysostom tells us: holiness is a lofty purity of mind. In any case, the purity of the priest could not be mediocre, for he is like a city on the mountain top which cannot be hidden from view. Holiness, then, is purity consecrated to God: purity dedicated to the honor of God. This holiness, this purity of mind, requires enormous sacrifice. That is holy, in fact, which is entirely consumed on the altar of God. It is obvious, therefore that the life of a priest, free from all unholy habits and wholly spent for the honor of God, constitutes true holiness. I should be unhappy if at this point anyone began to think that such holiness is so far removed from daily life, so difficult to achieve, that it must be reserved to persons who live withdrawn from the world.

"There is no reason for anyone to fear when holiness is mentioned. Holiness, the perfection possible in this life, is not something absolute, free from every imperfection. In fact, even the just man sins seven times a day. Holiness, instead, consists in the constant trust to attain it. This is what St. Bernard taught (Ep. 255 ad Ab. Guar.). I should like to cite here the teaching of St. Augustine on this score: "He is perfect who has no serious sins and tries to avoid venial sins as well: in short, he who runs without tiring along the path of virtue." (De Perfect. Iust. c. 31)...

"The first step or means to holiness is the ardent and generous desire for holiness itself. Since holiness is the goal of the priesthood, all aspirations must be directed to this end. An ordinary desire or resolution is not enough: what is needed is a desire, a will, comparable to hunger and thirst. 'Blessed are they who hunger and thirst for justice, for they shall be filled...'

"Another effective means to achieve holiness lies in the perfect performance of the duties of our vocation...

"The priest must not pursue any other road to holiness except the one pointed out to him by the Lord: to meditate often and perform his duties perfectly...

"The third means to achieve holiness is to keep before one's eyes the model of holiness, to contemplate Him every day and imitate Him. Those who wish to excel in any art do this very thing. We have the absolute example of priestly holiness given us by the Heavenly Father. He has been given to everyone, for to everyone it was said: This is my beloved son in whom I am well pleased; listen to him (Mt., 17:5). But to priests especially it is said: He who would serve me, let him follow me. This is the precept of the Lord which has been set before you too, Venerable Brothers, in your ordination...Keep Christ always in your mind: present to the people His image carved in yourself so that all may rejoice in it and be fired with the desire for holiness. It is written, in fact: Your priests are clothed with justice, and all your saints rejoice. (2 Chron., 6:41)[110]

There is no substitute for the primary source of priestly holiness, the celebration of the Sacrifice of the Mass, center of Christian worship and priestly act *par excellence:*

"The sacrifice is the sum of the worship man owes to his Creator, the Supreme Being, the Master of life and death. And who will offer the sacrifice if not the priest?[111]
The Mass is like the sun of Christianity, the soul, the center of our most holy religion, the most sublime and august mystery of our faith, the most holy action that can be celebrated on earth, the act *par excellence,* but an act that is eminently priestly.[112]

To celebrate the Sacrifice of the Mass with holy and religious devotion, prepare yourselves...with your whole mind concentrated in meditation on so lofty a mystery. To do this more worthily, examine your conscience diligently, carefully and frequently."[113]

Bishop Scalabrini's exhortations to prayer, meditation and the pious practices recommended by the Church were constant:

"...in prayer we approach God, to be filled with the light of interior grace; in prayer lie a thousand shields, all the armor of the strong for priests...Have a set time every day for meditation on heavenly things, and never neglect this. Do not be carried away by the absurd tendency to help others while neglecting yourselves: he who is not good with himself, how can he be good with others? There are often difficulties in the way of this practice, I do not deny: but priests provide ill for themselves if they neglect meditation.[114]
The love of holiness gives rise to frequent and daily meditation on the heavenly law and mysteries. The priest who neglects his daily meditation will not be holy, but will experience desolation. He will be like him who contemplated his face in the mirror and forgot what manner of man he was.
If one has a true love of holiness he will be zealous in seeking to clear his conscience every week, according to the prescription of the synod. He who neglects this duty is far from the path of holiness...
The examination of conscience stems from the same intense desire. This examination is especially necessary for priests, so that they may be conscious of what they are building on the foundation of their faith and vocation, gold or silver, hay or straw."[115]

In an address to the third Synod, we find the following directives:

"Practice all holy prayer diligently. Concentrate, with all the ardor of a chaste mind, in mental prayer a half hour each day. If possible let this be the first thing you do. In fact, mental prayer is the pivot of priestly life; if you are faithful to it, it will benefit you greatly...If you desire to keep or increase the spirit of devotion, never omit, on any day for any reason, the examination of conscience at noon and in the evening, spiritual reading in the afternoon, and the recitation of the Holy Rosary, publicly in church or privately...You who have been established in Holy Orders, approach the sacrament of penance every week, and send us evidence of your weekly confession according to the prescript...Make a Retreat at least every three years, according to the synodal prescription."[116]

In his discourse on priestly studies and knowledge at the second Synod, he also outlined a regular daily schedule:

"...the pastor of souls should arise after six or seven hours of sleep. Not much can be expected of a priest who does not awaken until the sun is high and celebrates Mass in the late morning.

The second point in the schedule is the half-hour of mental prayer. This is the first thing the priest must do, it is the pivot and foundation of pastoral life...

After meditation, the priest must celebrate Mass, and follow it always with an appropriate and devout prayer of thanksgiving. During Mass he is to beseech God to protect him from the love and dangers of the world and to inspire his flock with the spirit of faith and love.

When he has finished the duties of divine worship and the most noble part of his life, the pastor should then put the parish records in order...

Prayer requires that the pastor and priests, toward noon and before sitting down to dinner, make an examination of conscience. No one who truly wishes to keep and intensify the ecclesiastical spirit can neglect the examination of conscience at noon and in the evening...

Interior life is truly intensified if, in the afternoon, each one reads a spiritual book or a Chapter of Scriptures, or venerates the Blessed Virgin... The recitation of the Rosary must never be omitted on any day...

If they observe all these practices, they can carry on their ministry in confidence. I would suggest some general principles for your consideration in this regard. I believe I am speaking to priests who know and practice the law.

The first object of the ministry is the house of the pastor; there must be nothing in it that can offend the people...

The pastor then, as you well know, is debtor to every one, ready always to help everyone. Two extremes are to be avoided, however. We are speaking bluntly, as a father.

Some dedicate themselves so intensely to the salvation of others that they gradually lose their supernatural thrust; they end by losing themselves and not saving others. They must remember that they can be of benefit to others only insofar as they are of benefit to themselves. Therefore they must cultivate piety, for 'pietas ad omnia utilis est', especially in the works of the ministry...

Then there are those who set up shop, as it were, in the parish house. If they are asked, they give help immediately and do not neglect instructing the faithful that come to them. But they are not moved by zeal. They do not give thought to the needs and dangers of their flock. Through rash prudence, pusillanimity, or indolence they neglect the necessary means...That must not be the pastor's life. Remember what the father of the house commanded to his servant: *Exi in viam et saepes et compelle intrare* (Go to the open roads and the hedgerows and force people to come in. — Luke, 14:23). These are the zealous pastors, and they are absolutely necessary our times.

There is another very subtle temptation, which can with little difficulty steal into the souls of those who give direction to others. They see at times that their labor does not yield immediate or abundant fruit. They begin to think the matter is hopeless. They become depressed, they weaken in the ministry...Let them instead be like the ministers of Christ in all patience, remembering the words of the Lord: *Alius est qui seminat et alius est qui metit. Ego misi vos metere quod vos non seminastics. Alii laboraverunt et vos in labores eorum introistis.* (...one sows, another reaps; I sent you to reap a harvest you had not worked for. Others worked for it; and you have come into the rewards of their trouble. — (Jn. 4:37-387) They must sow the word and leave others to gather the fruit. They must remember that in ordination to the priesthood they were given the duty to care for, not necessarily to be successful. They must, however, radiate love, for *caritas omnia credit, omnia sperat, omnia sustinet* (Love...is always ready to excuse, to trust, to hope and to endure whatever comes. — (1 Cor., 13:7).

It is also fundamental to know how to do the works of God. Some undertake the works of God in a human spirit: they gather little or no fruit. You know what the spirit is. *Mitissimus Dei spiritus est et mansuetissimus, qui non turbine glomeratur, non in nubilo lucet, sed merae serenitatis, apertus et simplex* (Tertullian, *Ad Macc.*) Christ worked in this spirit, and his ministers must be inspired with like spirit. Since the Lord is not found in the dissipation of the spiritual life nor in impulsiveness, it is necessary to continue in the sacred ministry with the same spirit of mildness...With any other attitude, pastors and whoever else is dedicated to the care of souls will impede their progress in holiness.

This attitude or spirit of mildness also seems necessary because the works of God are usually prickly with difficulties: these can be met only with generosity and confidence in God. There is no need to wonder, then, if in the ministry one encounters difficulties or persecutions, for all the Saints have experienced these. Instead, we must wonder indeed if everything goes just as we wish.[117]

The following excerpts from Scalabrini's address to the third diocesan Synod would seem to round out the profile of the priest as he envisaged him:

"In your ordination to the priesthood, Venerable Brothers, you have been enrolled through divine mercy in the ecclesiastical order to preserve and propagate the glory of God. Fulfill the ministry of your priestly order; preserve its dignity and honor. In your dress, your walk, your stance, your carriage, conduct yourselves so that you reflect the name and the manner of the Holy Orders you have received. Be satisfied with a frugal meal, and with spare and modest furnishings. In all your life, avoid ostentation, luxury, affectation, and also ambition and vanity...

Do not be greedy for money or for gain. If you are poor, do not desire to become rich lest you fall into many temptations and the snares of the devil. Do not bear your poverty grudgingly. Our heavenly teacher Christ, who at his birth was laid in a manger and who died naked on the cross, loved and taught poverty. They can lack nothing who fear the Lord and call upon his holy name, much less the religious and the priests. On the other hand, those who have fatter incomes should repair the church, adorn it with suitable gifts and provide it with worthy furnishings and vessels. With the tenderness of Christ, distribute the church income from the benefices to the poor, the widows, the sick, to pilgrims, and to all the indigent and the needy. If you deny them the food they need when you can help them, you will be guilty of sin against charity in the sight of God."[118]

The Lombard Seminary

Bishop Scalabrini's solicitude for the education of the clergy is also reflected in the part he played in the reopening of the Lombard Seminary in Rome, in which he had been interested since 1877. On August 9, he wrote to the Bishop of Cremona, telling him that there were plans in Rome to revive the Lombard Seminary, but on a larger scale, as the Seminary of Northern Italy *(Seminario dell'Alta Italia)*. The project, he continued, was looked upon with great favor, among others by Cardinal Borromeo who was already its protector. He went in person to the Holy Father, who gladly approved the plan set before him, and in fact gave it his blessing, expressing a keen desire to have it brought to fruition as soon as possible.

Borromeo, in the name of the Holy Father, asked Scalabrini to write to all the bishops of Northern Italy to ascertain their views.[119] Scalabrini was chosen for this exploratory task because he was the one who originally suggested the plan, as is indicated by a letter from Cardinal Borromeo in which he writes that he had spoken to the Pope "about the ideas of Your Illustrious and Reverend Excellency on starting a national Seminary...like the former Lombard College...The Holy Father agreed entirely with your just desires...Therefore, kindly give me a summary of the regulations on which you intend to establish the new Institution. In addition to the expenses for the building and the four scholarships which Your Excellency guarantees, it is necessary to get agreements with all the bishops of Northern Italy who might wish to share in supporting the students...Finally, I should like to have you think about a good, pious and experienced Ecclesiastic to appoint as rector."[120]

Scalabrini went to work immediately on the project, as is clear from the above-quoted letter of August 9th to Bishop Bonomelli, and from another dated August 13th. In the latter he already proposes some one for the rectorship and suggests sending the students to the Gregorian University. He worked on the Statute of the seminary and actively campaigned for funds for it. He frequently sent large sums for the restoration and remodeling of the building. In October 1878, in a note of thanks for a contribution received from Scalabrini, Cardinal Borromeo wrote:

"The day is approaching when I shall have the consolation of inaugurating the new seminary of Sts. Ambrose and Charles, due mainly to your zeal and work...To all the sacrifices you have made for this institution, I would hope that you will add that of blessing it by staying in it whenever you are in Rome."[121]

The Lombard Seminary, which was then situated next to the church of San Carlo at Corso, was inaugurated on November 4, 1878. In the chapel where St. Charles' heart is preserved, Bishop Scalabrini said Mass for the seminarians, and in the afternoon he gave an address in Latin to an audience of numerous bishops and the canon of St. Peter.

In 1912, in the same church, a statue was erected in honor of Bishop Scalabrini. Cardinal Nasalli-Rocca, then the bishop of Gubbio and a former student at the Lombard Seminary, described Scalabrini at the inaugural ceremonies:

"Beside all the ecclesiastical dignitaries who had given their heart and their contributions to this institution, you would have seen a young bishop, but recently elevated to the honor of the infula, who had consecrated to this fine institution his mind and heart and work."[122]

Of the first students Scalabrini sent to the Lombard Seminary from the diocese of Piacenza, two became bishops: Natale Bruni, Archbishop of Modena, and Ciacomo Randi-Tedeschi, Bishop of Bergamo.

The treatment accorded a third student, a graduate of the *Collegio Alberoni*, prompted Scalabrini to stop sending others to the Lombard Seminary in order "not to create most unhappy divisions among his clergy."[123] This disagreement, however, did not prevent his continuing to take an interest in the institution. A letter from Cardinal Lambrini, written only four months after the above-mentioned incident, thanks the Bishop of Piacenza for a handsome legacy, left to the Lombard Seminary at Scalabrini's suggestion.[124] In 1891, students were again sent from Piacenza, among them Giovanni Battista Nasalli-Rocca, the future Cardinal Archbishop of Bologna.

The Rosminian Question

This summary of Bishop Scalabrini's teaching and the type of training he championed for the clergy would not be complete without a note on his attitude toward the influence of the so-called "philosophical question" in his diocese.

At the end of 1881 or at the beginning of 1882, he wrote as follows to Father Anthony Stoppani, who was a zealous supporter of Rosmini:

"You wish to know from me how much is true of what I said the Holy Father told me personally about the question of Rosmini's philosophy. Here I am to satisfy you. I am guided always and in everything I do, not by what I read in the papers, even Catholic ones, but by him who alone has the authority to regulate in one way rather than another the discipline of the Universal Church. Therefore, also on this matter of freedom in matters of philosophy, I wished to pose the question personally to the Supreme Pontiff. — 'Holy Father,' I said, 'there are many in my diocese who follow Antonio Rosmini's system of philosophy, the most notable among them being the Provost of St. Anne's, Father Moglia, who, having studied it for years, supports that system and defends it vigorously even in his published writings. According to some, who are quick to teach and pass judgment in your name on everyone and everything, supporters of Rosmini and his system should be held no less accountable than others who rebel against your teachings; and I, as bishop, should not only forbid all discussion of the subject but should also have recourse to censures...' 'Oh no!' the Holy Father answered in that grave manner of his so full of kindness, 'No, Bishop! Tell your priests that I have never intended to take away anyone's freedom to discuss arguable teachings. And with regard to Rosmini also, his supporters may very well continue their debates in all peace of conscience provided, of course, that they constantly observe the rules of moderation and charity which We have many times urged, and provided that they remain disposed to submit to whatever decision this Holy See may deem proper to issue in this regard.' This is word for word what I asked and received permission to make public when the occasion arises; this is what I wrote down immediately so that I would not forget, change, augment, tone down or otherwise alter in any way whatever."[125]

Scalabrini used prudently the permission to make the Holy Father's views public. He inserted them in his Pastoral Letter of October 18, 1882, after having stressed the Pope's desire to restore Thomism to first place, but he did so in no arbitrary manner: "But he let it be understood at the same time, very clearly and explicitly, that he desired everyone absolutely to respect the honest freedom of discussion that was and will always be in the Catholic Church in all things in which the Church itself allows freedom."[126]

This letter to Father Stoppani throws light on the Bishop's attitude on the Rosmini question: obedience to the Chair of Peter, shown by the fact that before acting he asked the advice of the Pope; freedom of discussion on debatable questions, but readiness to submit in case of an eventual judgment of the Holy See; above all and always, charity. He held to these principles in his attitude toward the "Rosminians," having at heart only the good souls and particularly the welfare of his diocese.

He personally remained faithful to Thomism, offered to refute Rosminian publications,[127] always deplored the excesses of the champions of both systems, and made a concrete contribution to the rebirth of Thomistic philosophy that earned him the praise of the Holy See. But he was unbudgeable when it came to safeguarding and defending freedom that was allowed both by the nature of purely philosophical questions and the explicit declaration of Leo XIII.

To the "Rosminians" of his diocese he allowed an "honest freedom," while he made every effort to remove all motives for division among his clergy. At the same time he prepared them to submit to the decision of the Pope which, even in 1882, he foresaw would come soon.

"Among my priests there are more than 200 who studied Rosmini. My concern during this time in anticipation of an eventual condemnation, was to win their minds and, while leaving them the liberty granted by the Church, to prepare them for submission whenever the Pope should make his decision. With the help of God I believe I have succeeded. Moglia, who is the leader of the Rosminians, has reassured me many times both for himself and for all the others...Meanwhile I have written to several Rosminians reproving them for the excessive impudence of recent pamphlets and I am ready to write about the censurable propositions you found in the introduction to the Gospel of St. John if you will kindly point them out to me exactly. I have not read the two installments sent to me nor do I have the time now to go over them carefully."[128]

The foreseeable condemnation of Rosmini caused him "immense anxiety," for Scalabrini feared it would be the occasion for apostasy. He offered prayers and penance so that the question might be resolved peacefully.[129] At the same time he did not hesitate to firmly defend those of his clergy who were accused of heresy and rebellion and to expose those who hid under the mantle of the philosophical debate to carry on their disruptive tactics.

Bishop Scalabrini and Father Stoppani

In 1884 an article in *La Civiltà Cattolica* related that Scalabrini abhorred ontological pantheism, Rosmini's theory on the genesis of the soul and particularly the theory of immediate knowledge of the Word in the ideal being.[130] The author of the article was undoubtedly Father Cornoldi, managing editor of *Civiltà Cattolica*, and the most authorative anti-Rosminian of the time. In the preceding summer he had visited the bishops of Piacenza and Cremona and discussed philosophical and political questions with them at length. He had been greatly impressed by them, a fact he conveyed to Leo XIII.[131]

In 1885 Father Stoppani published a book defending those who had signed the Passaglia petition of 1861.[132] This was denounced to the Holy Office. Bishop Bonomelli asked Scalabrini to take soundings in Rome and to do all he could to avoid a condemnation, which he believed would be unjust since the book bore no trace of heterodoxy or disobedience to the Holy See. Its only stigma was its opposition to the intransigent current of thought. Scalabrini used his influence with the Holy Father to turn aside a possible condemnation, and none in fact was pronounced.[133]

Rome understood his interest in Stoppani's book very well. The following year the Holy See charged him with the task of stopping the publication of the periodical *Il Rosmini*, which Stoppani had announced was to take the place of *La Sapienza*.

The Bishop of Cremona had already tried unsuccessfully to dissuade Stoppani from the project, and he had even written to Rome for advice, both for himself and in the name of the Archbishop of Milan.[134] Cardinal Schiaffino reported to the Holy Father the worries of the two prelates and their "praiseworthy solicitude to dissuade Professor Stoppani and the others from carrying out this ill-advised project." He then wrote to Scalabrini:

"The Holy Father's answer was that, since Bishop Bonomelli had not succeeded with Stoppani, I should address myself to you so that you would write to Stoppani or ask him to come to see you, in order to dissuade him (from this project) and convince him to stop others from carrying out the idea; to make Stoppani see that instead of furthering the doctrines with which he is so enamored, he will end up by damaging them."[135]

Scalabrini succeeded only in achieving a certain moderating influence. "I know that they rejected a violent article in refutation of the Pastoral of the Bishop of Concordia."[136] In a later communication, he expressed his pastoral anxiety:

"Did I write you that the Holy Father had charged me to persuade Stoppani to give up the idea of publishing *Il Rosmini*? This mission was a failure! I made a hole in water. I sent to Rome the arguments of Stoppani and Moglia, but since then absolute silence (from Rome). Enough; we shall see what happens. Behind Stoppani there is a seething ferment that gives true cause for worry. If the matter is not handled calmly and prudently, we shall almost have a schism. I seem to be getting along quietly with my Rosminian priests. The moderation with which I have always treated them makes me hope that when there is an authoritative decision they will submit to it. Will that happen with all? May God please that it will?"[137]

His reply to Cardinal Schiaffino's gives further evidence of Scalabrini's moderate and at the same time apostolic attitude:

"*Veni, vidi*...I wish I could add the rest! I asked Professor Stoppani to come to me. I tried to attack him on all fronts and with all possible ammunition, but to no avail. Truly the arguments he set forth were such and so many that I confess I would not know how it could reasonably be possible not to take them into account...As for the Rosminian priests in my diocese, we get along with perfect tranquillity. They know that I do not share their views in philosophical matters, but they also know that I have always left them that freedom of thought permitted by the Church, and that I wish it always to be respected. This is enough for them to bow respectfully to the least of my desires, as for example, what has just happened in the case of the review in question. They have all promised they would not contribute a syllable to it. The only one who offered some observations against this, but always respectfully, was the learned and zealous Provost Moglia, from whom I received two letters which I think it well to send to Your Eminence together with an article by Stoppani, so that you may better know the state of affairs, and, if you think opportune, you may make them known higher up. I would wish, Your Eminence, that you would sound out the Holy Father on how I should conduct myself with Moglia. Is it wise to let him know that notwithstanding his observations it is His (the Holy Father's) wish he not write another single line about Rosmini? What meaning would this have, especially in the doctrinal field? In any case, I shall do whatever you, in the name of the Holy Father, tell me to do. Certainly there can be no wish to risk pushing the Bishops from the wise moderate line that has been and always will be one of the finest qualities of the Church."[138]

Rosmini's forty propositions were finally condemned. From what we know now of Leo XIII, however, it is certain that Scalabrini had interpreted his wishes better than many others, and that he took that drastic decision precisely because of the lack of moderation "on one side and the other."

In June 1889 *Il Rosmini* was also condemned. A few months later *Il Nuovo Rosmini*, which a group of laymen tried to issue in place of the former, also ceased publication. Scalabrini had continued to urge Stoppani to have the publications stopped or at least to detach his responsibilities from the writers who went beyond the limits of obedience to the Pope.[139] From the following letter to Father Cornoldi it would seem he had some success:

"As you know by now, the periodical *Il Rosmini*,[140] of unhappy memory, is now dead, and with it I think one of the principal causes of discord is also dead. The Lord has blessed my efforts in this regard. The one who helped me more than any one else in this affair, I am bound to say, was the lamented Professor Stoppani, who, after all please believe me, was a priest filled with faith and most loyal to the Holy See."[141]

The Decree 'Post Obitum'

Bishop Scalabrini learned of the condemnation of the forty propositions only from the *Osservatore Cattolico*. This strange circumstance prompted some doubt on the authenticity of the report and he therefore wrote immediately to the Pope:

"I am anxious to know if this is truly an authentic action of the Holy See, since I have great reason to doubt this having seen it published only in the *Osservatore* of Milan. I am extremely anxious, I repeat, to know this so that I may do what I can to see that no scandals or conflicts occur. I believe, Most Blessed Father, it will be of no small comfort to you to know that precisely because of this I sent for Father Antonio Stoppani and for the second time I was confirmed in the opinion that I had of him, that he is a priest that few can equal in gifts of the mind and heart, and even less in his gift of faith and his sincere attachment to the Holy See and Your August Person. When he came to me he was naturally most grieved and visibly moved, but he was also resigned despite his immense grief and declared that as soon as he knew with certainty that this was an authentic document of the Holy See, *far from offering the slightest opposition* (These are his exact words) *he would consider it a duty, in fact an honor to submit to you humbly, entirely, unconditionally* and that he was *ready if the occasion demanded it to make a public declaration in this sense.*[142]

Scalabrini's quick action is confirmed by a letter of Father Stoppani to the Bishop of Cremona:

"That good Father Leone writes reproaching me because I went to Piacenza while I did not keep my promise to come there to visit Your Excellency. I went to Piacenza called there by a telegram from Bishop Scalabrini, indicating a grave and urgent matter. This Illustrious Prelate, on the other hand, after three sleepless nights and three days of stomach distress, needed relief, and then he wanted to be reassured that the Rosminians and I personally would conduct ourselves in a manner most befitting good Catholics."[143]

The matter of the stomach ailment and the summons of Stoppani by wire from Milan to have some one to talk to seems to have been an example of Scalabrini's characteristic charity and tact. This is evidenced by the way he announced the decree of condemnation to his priests on March 21, as soon as he received its authentication from Rome.[144] They would certainly not have found it very easy to submit if their Bishop had not wisely been preparing them for it for some time.

Although the condemnation was published in Latin and Italian, he had the letter introducing it printed in Latin and only for his clergy.

Since the impartiality of the judgment of the Holy See, concerned only with the salvation of souls and the purity of doctrine, was evident, he wrote, he was sure that all of them would accept the decree with perfect submission. The Church had spoken, the victory belonged only to Christ and his truth, and especially to obedience. The diocesan priests who had adhered to the teachings of Rosmini in any way had nevertheless always maintained a readiness of spirit to obey as soon as the Church decided to speak; there could be no doubt of their rectitude. It was no longer a time for distinctions or defenses, but for accepting with joy the clarification of the truth: joy for some to see their judgment confirmed, joy for others to be free from the danger of error. Their successors, when they recalled the present quarrels, must be able to praise the priests of Piacenza for their readiness to approve or reprove what was approved or reproved by the Chair of Peter. As for the Institutes of ecclesiastical education, he was happy to confirm the perfect obedience to the directives he had given in 1876 and 1881 for the teaching of Thomistic philosophy in the two seminaries and in the *Collegio Alberoni* and he hoped for increasing progress in the work undertaken. But his principal wish was to see all of them united under one shepherd, one banner, in the name of Christ alone.[145]

All of his priests submitted promptly. The most notable of the Rosminians, Father Agostino Moglia and Father Carlo Uttini, made public declarations.[146] The Pope expressed his satisfaction to Father Cornoldi, who immediately informed Bishop Scalabrini:

"The Pope told me that he had received from Your Excellency, along with the Pastoral, a beautiful letter which mentioned the priests of Piacenza who had submitted. He told me he was very pleased with Your Excellency and wished to demonstrate this. *Deo Gratias.*"[147]

"I Have Fought the Good Fight"

Bishop Scalabrini himself has described what he considered the function of the magisterium:

"The Bishop fulfills all the duties of the good shepherd, guiding his sheep to healthy pastures and clear waters...He speaks, writes and acts. But in speaking, writing and acting he has no other aim but the glory of God and the salvation of souls. No ambiguities, no equivocations, no shamming. On his lips the word is a ray of heavenly light, it is a seed of Christian virtues. His good faith may sometimes be deceived,, but he deceives no one; in fact, it is to keep others from being deceived that he often exposes himself to contradictions and sufferings that are hard to believe. It is not his own comfort, not his own interests that concern him, not the small satisfactions proper to others, but the truth, only the truth is his rule and guide, and he sacrifices everything rather than betray it."[148]

His whole life is proof that he was faithful, with heroic firmness, to this solemn obligation to teach the truth.

"For this truth he was willing to fight strenuously even to the point of suffering and death."[149] — "Having taken up the sword of the spirit, which is the word of God, I shall fight the good fight."[150] — "Guardians and teachers of the truth with orders not to keep it secret, we shall proclaim it without reserve, with apostolic liberty, in every time, in every place, to every one. With the gentle charity of the saints, but not without that noble firmness which commands respect for the solemn rights of the faith, we shall work untiringly..."[151]

Bishop Bonomelli, who knew him more intimately than any one else, declared, "He loved only truth, whomever it might concern."[152] — "To be careful when it is a question of truth?" He used to say. "But to me this would be a betrayal of the Word of God."[153]

His was an absolute love of truth, which did not diminish his absolute dedication to obedience and charity. It is in this sense that we may interpret Fogazzaro's epigram: "immeasurably dedicated and immeasurably free."[154]

A priest of his diocese recalling that in many cities of Italy, including Piacenza, various serious questions of doctrine were being debated, wrote:

"Since the Church, teacher of truth has not yet pronounced the final word on them, everyone believes in good faith that he is sustaining and defending the truth. Likewise it happens that in the passion of debate, they sometimes go beyond the limits of that moderation which is the inseparable companion of truth...We, however, are fortunate, for we have in our Supreme Shepherd a sure and infallible guide...and in our Bishops so many faithful and vigilant sentinels...The writings of those years tell us how much our Bishop contributed to the triumph of truth. He warned us not to seek popular favor and the plaudits of the world. The priest must do his duty without being concerned in any way with praise or blame. He strongly recommended respect for the authority of the Holy Shepherds for the preservation of sound doctrine. In combating error he urged that every respect be shown the person involved, and that on the wounds of our brother we should not pour the vinegar of hatred, which only serves to irritate them the more, but the oil of charity which alleviates and heals them. Discussions should be carried on not out of a mania to confound one's adversary but with the sole purpose of seeking the truth and making sure that it triumphed and was loved. The Bishop professed that he meditated at the feet of Jesus Crucified the counsels he gave his priests. He thus had the consolation of seeing all controversy cease and his wishes fulfilled. And even those who were the most obstinate and the most opposed, embraced one another in the unity of the faith and the bond of charity."[155]

We have stressed this aspect of Scalabrini's character because it seems to us that the love of truth was one of his essential qualities, an indispensable key to the secret of his personality, which was unfortunately not always understood in that troubled time. And it also seems one of the most significant factors in his holiness, for it caused him so much suffering, which he faced and bore courageously: "How little those people have understood me! But God knows the purity of my intentions and that is enough for me."[156]

It was precisely in this sacrifice of self, for the love of truth, that he used to pray to the Divine Teacher: *Fac me cruce inebriari!*[157]

CHAPTER V

The Five Pastoral Visits

"The good Pastor speaks, writes, acts." But in order to act he must first have knowledge on which to act. Bishop Scalabrini took as his model St. Charles Borromeo, not only in his catechetical apostolate but also in what was for both of them the extraordinary commitment to conduct the pastoral visitations in person. In 1876, a few months after his installation in the diocese, he announced his first visit, to begin on December 8th, under the patronage of the Blessed Virgin. The letter announcing the visit he dated, intentionally, November 4, the feast of St. Charles.

He hoped, he wrote, to experience the finest consolation a Bishop could have, "that of getting to know his beloved children and to have them know him."[1]

His aims were to preach Jesus Christ crucified, inspire ever greater faith, promote religious instruction and prod, even quite vigorously, any who were not carrying out their duties, see to the proper ordering of the churches and the liturgy, awaken a sense of Catholicism, and to stimulate the observance of holy days, reception of the sacraments, loyalty to the Holy Father, and "Love, the bond of perfection, and soul of the soul."[2]

Clergy and faithful in each parish were asked to prepare for the visit with prayers to the Holy Spirit and with a spiritual retreat, or at least a series of sermons. Much urging, however, was unnecessary. The announcement was met with enthusiasm and high expectation. In most of the parishes it was three centuries since a bishop had made a pastoral visit. The last to do so had been Paolo Burali (1568-1576), who also modeled himself on St. Charles Borromeo. Yet, according to some historians, not even he had succeeded in reaching some of the tiny parishes lost in the Appenines.[3]

"When Bishop Scalabrini began his first pastoral visit, it is no exaggeration to say that more than 200 parishes could not be reached except by mule or horseback. In the mountains, most of the rectories could not accomodate for the night, however simply, a Bishop and the one or two persons who accompanied him, so that it was not possible for him to go directly from one parish to another as he did later...He had to establish his headquarters, so to speak, in the Vicariate, making one-day trips from there. This meant several hours on horseback, and anyone who knows our mountain and thinks of those goat paths...the ascents where one can keep his seat in the saddle only by clinging to the horse's neck, the steep descents elementary prudence counsels must be traveled on foot...will have to agree that these were far from being pleasure trips."[4]

Bishop Scalabrini was unmoved by the difficulties.

"We know we are greatly inferior to all our illustrious predecessors in the chair of St. Mauro and St. Savino, but we yield to no one in the love we bear you." — "Trusting nothing to our own weak strength but relying entirely on the grace of the Holy Spirit, we beg Him to grant us strength and enlightenment equal to the great desire we have to benefit you, so that your Bishop too may truly say with the Apostle: I have become all things to all men in order to win all to Christ."[5]

How he managed to carry out this generous program is indicated in the following excerpt from a diary kept by one of his co-workers.

"The Bishop arrives towards evening; he goes to the Church and gives a warm and affectionate talk to the crowd waiting for him. The people are devout, joyful, moved to tears. Immediately he begins to hear the men's confessions, which last until late at night.

"The other priests have finished; they are free. It is near midnight, but at the door of the little room where the good Shepherd welcomes them to forgiveness, there is still a long line of penitents...

"He is up very early in the morning, hears confessions again, and at the appointed hour, after a brief homily, he celebrates Mass, during which he distributes communion...

"The Mass is over...one would say the good Bishop had a right to a little rest...What rest!...during these visits rest is unknown...everything conspires to keep him from it. In fact, when the Mass is over and while the people are leaving, the Bishop, to make use of every minute, visits the sacristy, examines the vestments, the altars. Meanwhile, the children to be confirmed are filing into the pews.

"The pews are filled, the doors are closed, and after a short sermon to the children and their sponsors, the Bishop administers the sacrament of confirmation.

"The first round is over, but in some places there are two and three rails full of youngsters. Everybody is tired. The Bishop, still standing, encourages the others, is again at the altar. Now all the children are all confirmed, the church is emptied...

"The Bishop carefully examines the church, the vestments and the liturgical vessels, and has everything noted down so that he can later issue the necessary directives. He then goes to the rectory, and while the others are finally allowed a little rest, the Bishop examines the parish files, the records of baptisms, confirmations, marriages, deaths, the parish statistics. He goes over the church accounts and the bequests.

"It is noon time;...the meal is over...and the bells are joyously calling the people back to church. It is full to overflowing, and we get into the sacristy and choir with difficulty. And here is the Bishop, among the children of the catechism classes. This is where he likes most to be. He listens to them, questions them, gives them a little fatherly sermon, blesses them...

"During the pastoral visit the Bishop is required to perform a special commemoration of the dead. The only way Bishop Scalabrini seems to know how to do this is by leading everyone in procession to the cemetery... He gives one of his characteristic talks to the living; he evokes feeling of great affection...he blesses the dead. The procession returns to the church, and after a closing sermon, the Bishop gives the last blessing to his flock; they are all sad to see him leave.

"Amid a thousand voices of farewell and the sound of the bells, he mounts his horse and leaves...to begin again another day in another parish."[6]

The Bishop of Piacenza spent at least two thousand days in this fashion from that eighth of December in 1876 when he initiated his pastoral visit in the cathedral parish and distributed communion to the faithful for over three hours.

"Not to mention the fact that these periods of pastoral visitation exhausted him," Gregori testified. "Archdeacon Tedeschi, who often accompanied him as a co-visitator, expressed his opinion in these words: — The Bishop works much too hard; if he goes on at this rate, he will surely shorten his life. — This opinion, says Msgr. Piacenza, was confirmed by his pastors, the vicars Forane who followed him in all the suffragan parishes, the priests who preceded him to preach the preparatory mission, by the members of his household and by his own doctor."[7]

But the Bishop felt well recompensed:

"In three weeks I visited twenty mountain parishes, riding several hundred miles on horseback. How fine it is to be with those good people, so filled with faith, far from the noise and pettiness of the world:"[8]

And those good people responded to their Shepherd with equal enthusiasm: "All of us in the mountains and in tiny parishes were extraordinarily moved, for no one could remember having seen a bishop up there, so that some even believed that the Holy Spirit had come down among us."[9]

"He spared himself no work or sacrifice in visiting his diocese many times, riding horseback as much as eight or ten hours and preaching; and the people ran to gather about him with enthusiasm."[10]

"I do not exaggerate. I am recounting what his venerable coworkers told me many times. When our bishop appeared there arose about him a rustle of joy and faith...Even the enemies of our institutions, when they saw him move like Jesus among his people, seeking out his children, soothing with words, that never failed him, their deep sufferings, asking after the sick and the sinners for no other reason...but to help them, sustain them, console them, admitted they were won by so much zeal. If not entirely won over, they were powerless to deny that that wonderful man was something different from all the others."[11]

Newspaper accounts of these visitations are filled with descriptions of enthusiastic crowds, the emotion that swept over them all, especially during the visit to the cemetery and when the bishop was taking his leave. They detail his "prodigious" labors, the people pressing toward him with tears in their eyes to kiss his hand or touch his cloak, the hours and hours he spent hearing confessions, often until midnight, the general communions.[12]

The spiritual results of these journeys were his special reward. He himself says they were abundant, attributing them to the grace and mercy of God, the intercession of Mary Immaculate, the zeal of his priests and co-workers, especially the Vincentian Missionaries:

"The moral impact he had in the diocese through the visitations, conducted in a truly apostolic manner, produced really extraordinary results, especially at the first visit when in addition to the apostolic there was a touch of novelty. People hardened in evil turned to God and scandals were remedied. Marriages were regularized, deep-seated hatreds were ended or at least mitigated, and everywhere there was a reflowering of religious devotion, an awakening of Christian life."[13]

On September 26, 1880, Scalabrini announced that he had completed his first visit to the 365 parishes:

"Now we can say that there is no part of this mystical vineyard, however remote, that we do not know. Taking as our example the prince and model of all pastors, Jesus Christ, we can repeat in all truth: I know my sheep and my sheep know me. We can assert what St. Paul wanted to be able to say to the faithful of Rome: I came to you in joy, by the will of God, and have been comforted with you."[14]

The second series of visits lasted much longer, from April 1882 to the end of 1887, a period of great trials and great achievements. He had to interrupt his activities several times because of illness, but he did not wish the second five year period of his episcopate to end without his having visited all his flock.

Because of uncertain health, he decided in 1888 to entrust the third series of visitations to delegates; but he reserved several parishes for a personal visit and went to each suffragan vicariate to administer confirmation, promulgate decrees and receive all the priests in audience.[15] In October of 1889, immediately after the Catechetical Congress, he came down with an attack of typhoid fever. A month later he still felt the effects of the disease. He found it hard to work, his hands trembled, but he did not lose heart:

"I am neither dead nor dying; but I am somewhat in bad shape, yes. It certainly was not a light attack. It seems it was typhoid, which has shorn my 'brow of all assurance.' Now I am gaining strength but very slowly. I still feel a little weak, especially when I say Mass in the morning. The doctor wants me to go to the Riviera, but I cannot make up my mind. Later perhaps."[17]

Later, feeling a little stronger, he plunged into his work again and started doing the pastoral visits himself. But in the spring of 1890 he wrote to Bonomelli, showing greater concern for his friend's health than for his own:

"I returned from my long journeying exhausted. I keep thinking of you. The idea that your health suffers from this trouble disturbs me greatly."[18]

He was the one who had to give in and take some rest, however, first at Levico and then at Rabbi, but it did not do him very much good. The doctor ordered several months of complete rest, "a most bitter medicine."[19] Two days later, he was already back in his diocese, just in time to encounter bitter trouble.[20] Before two weeks were up, he had to go back to the country again for another period of rest.[21] The Catholic Worker's Union of Piacenza undertook a pilgrimage on September 28th to the shrine of the Madonna of Fontanellato to pray for the bishop's recovery. Toward the end of October he was well enough to return to the city.[22]

The third pastoral visitation was finished by October 1891, and the fourth began in 1893, continuing until 1895. At the end of it the Bishop felt the old weakness returning and took vigorous measures to overcome it, like "ice-cold showers" in winter.[23] He felt he no longer had the strength to undertake these travels every five years:

"It is the fourth visitation, and I think it is my farewell visit; at least it is hardly possible that I shall be able to return to certain places. I hinted at this today at Montecanino and those poor mountain people burst into tears: these are the compensations the Lord prepares to sustain us amid the ingratitudes that accompany the life of a poor bishop."[24]

This was not his farewell, however, for between his two journeys to America — which might also be called pastoral visits — he managed to revisit each one of the parishes, even the most distant and inaccessible. He himself recognized that the work he was doing was "suffocating" although he was "immensely consoled by the sincere faith" of the people.[25] Eight months after his return from the United States he had already visited one hundred and twenty-three parishes:

"This is almost a crazy thing to do, but I want to make up for the time I lost last year. My health, thank God, is excellent. They tell me I am getting younger; yes, it is the youth of the flower that blooms in the morning full of life and is good and wilted by evening. But it does not matter so long as we get where we are going."[26]

A year later he is still tireless, despite his advancing age and the wear and tear his body endured:

"My body is wearing out, and I am moving with long strides toward the last step of all. Meanwhile, I am talking, preaching, writing, journeying on horseback, traveling, sweating, working, so that I may become pleasing at least to the Lord."[27]

Co-workers, members of his household, friends, tried in vain to persuade him to slow down.

"I am unable to slow down nor can I adapt myself to the thought of changing my life, although I shall have to do so. I am getting older, 64; I get tired. Things are becoming increasingly serious. The Socialist tide is swelling. Everything pushes me on to a work that is greater than my weak physical and moral strength, but forward, ever, in the name of the Lord so long as I am able."[28]

He conducted his fifth visit after his journey to Brazil. Ten days before his death, he was visiting one parish and at the same time planning his sixth visitation, which was to begin June 11, 1905:

"Thirty years have passed since this chosen part of Christ's flock was entrusted to my care, and one day, which cannot be far off, I must render to him a most strict accounting...A terrible thought, which is always before my mind, which impels me, spurs me to make amends, in a general visit, for the omissions and failing of my episcopal administration, which has not been a brief one. And so I am announcing, brothers and sons, that I have decided to conduct personally the sixth pastoral visitation in all and every parish of the diocese. If I thought about my age, I should surely be dismayed at the prospect. But so keen in me is the desire to see you again, and to address you one more time as pastor and father, that every difficulty seems nothing, and all labor seems light indeed."

He asked only one recompense of his priests, that he be able personally to distribute the Eucharist to all his flock, from the youngsters making their First Communion to those already on the threshold of eternity.[29]

His desire went unfulfilled, for he died ten days before the visitation was to begin. His accomplishments in this sector of his activity seem somewhat incredible. He can be compared perhaps only to St. Charles Borromeo, and he served in turn as an example for the bishops who knew him. To cite one instance, Bishop Pasquale Morganti of Bobbio, later Archbishop of Revenna, said that what first caught his admiration and he tried hard to imitate was Bishop Scalabrini's zeal for the pastoral visitations and catechetical instruction.[30]

Zeal for Souls

Scalabrini's pastoral visits were perhaps the more conspicuous manifestations of his zeal as bishop, but there is abundant evidence that he never swerved throughout his life from his early determination to spend himself completely and joyously for the good of souls.[31] In fact, the apostolic fervor of his youth constantly increased.[32] He aspired to carry out "every holy work, every good work, every Catholic work."[33]

The aspiration was all the keener because of his awareness of his own time, which fretted him like an open wound. It was a time of "war, not a muted war, veiled in hypocrisies, but open and declared, and a ruthless war against everything most sacred in heaven and on earth, against God and his Christ, against the Church and its visible Head, against Religion and its ministers, against every religious and social order."[34]

To see anyone abandon God caused him a "fever of worry" — a fever to win them back to Christ. He never lost an occasion to be with people, and whether the encounter was accidental or formal, he never missed an opportunity to speak a word of encouragement or exhortation to address a joyful or anxious appeal. His entire public and private life reveal a tactful and courageous awareness of the sacramentality of his office.

"He is the gentlest of souls, his friendliness typically Lombard.He is never chillingly aloof; his deep, sweet glance, his encouraging smile speak the eloquent language of the heart...He does good because he has a heart of gold, not because of any mistaken sense of personal vanity. His words are a soothing balm to the unfortunate. And the poorer and more unfortunate they are, the more he loves and comforts them...We could list a considerable number of cases, where he saved both a life and a soul without anyone knowing about it. This is his most outstanding quality. The beneficent act, hidden, at any cost...Bishop Scalabrini is very aware of his office...Obstacles only serve to increase his efforts a hundredfold."[36]

He was especially happy when, visiting a parish, he found himself surrounded by crowds of children. "This is innocence, come to meet the bishop," he would exclaim. One of his most serious pastoral cares was to devise every possible means to protect their innocence.

He constantly recommended that his priests set up youth centers where young people could gather, where they could be taught Christian doctrine and kept from getting into trouble.

"You must seriously reflect," he warned the second diocesan Synod, "that if you neglect the growing generation, you will have to despair of promoting the faith in your parishes. Therefore try to set up in our city and at least in the principal towns of the diocese a "parish youth center" for children and teen-agers, where they can gather on Sundays and Holy Days for recreation and especially for religious instruction. It is well known, in fact, that in the cities and larger towns children rarely go to church for catechism, and therefore it is difficult for pastors to give them adequate instruction in Christian doctrine without the help of a youth center. Our own experience confirms this and impels us to urge our pastors warmly to institute this wholesome and holy work. You will derive from it innumerable benefits for your parishes, and you will avoid the danger of having other associations, hostile to the faith, set up other recreation centers, which has been done in some places as we know. We know that there will be not a few practical difficulties, we all know that the love of Christ conquers all things and therefore who is inspired by it will accomplish great things. To help prevent these difficulties in so far as it is possible, we shall choose a few priests who are trained in this work. It will be their task, when it is necessary to promote the establishment of these centers, advise on the rules and standards, give counsel, and in short to do all that is necessary so that our desire may be met as promptly as possible."[38]

Again he would say: "Take care of the children and the sick; these are two means to win everything to God. This is what I keep repeating to the pastors of my diocese."[39]

In his pastoral letter on the priesthood, we read: "I especially recommend to your care the children and the working people. Gather the former about you with affection, and with tireless, diligent solicitude, teach them the elements of the faith, instruct them in all the ways of virtue. Gather the workers in fraternal organizations, teach them the merits and nobility of labor, warn them against the arts of the trouble makers and the seductions of the impious."[40]

In the third diocesan Synod, he exhorted his pastors: "Get to know the poor, the widows, the children and all the others who need help from some one else. Assist them with advice, with words of comfort, and with help. If you cannot give them this yourselves, then persuade others to help them."[41]

In Search of Lost Sheep

We have already noted how he sought out those in modest circumstances, the disinherited and tattered members of society, whom he treated as a father does his most beloved children.[42]

With the same love and kindness he sought out those who kept aloof or were hostile to religion, and at that time this scandalized quite a few. In much of the testimony given at diocesan inquiry for his beatification, we detect an echo of wonder or surprise at this apostolic endeavor.

"If he frequented non-religious persons or Masons, he did so to enlighten them and set them on the true path. He used to say that Our Lord had come not to seek the just but the sinners; he used to end every conversation with what he liked to call the little sermon."[43]

"His was an incessant and implacable battle against mortal sin," another witness felt compelled to say. "Bishop Scalabrini showed this in everything he did for himself and for others. If he sought the company of great sinners and Masons, it was the common conviction that he did this to convert them, which often happened. I clearly remember hearing many times...that Bishop Scalabrini used to say: 'I would climb on the shoulders of the devil himself if I were sure he would take me to save a soul'."[44]

When some one reproached him or expressed surprise that he maintained contact with such persons, he would reply: "Let us save souls, and as for the rest let the chips fall where they may."[45] The "rest" included the charge of "Liberal." It seems incredible that his zeal for the spiritual well-being of others should be the basis for an accusation.

In fact, there were numerous returns to the faith as a result of his zeal, so that some said they were afraid to go near him for fear of being converted.

"The journalist Galimberti, editor of the Liberal, Masonic paper *Il Progresso*, used to say that he avoided contact with Bishop Scalabrini because everyone said that he won over to the faith all who drew near him."

The same witness said that Scalabrini had a certain personal charm or attraction, which was something more than a natural gift; it was rather the reflection of his great love:

"That the Servant of God was continually alive with an extraordinary love of the Lord was evident not only in all the external acts of the liturgy, but in all the expressions of his life, so that whoever was near him...was aware that his mind was focused on God and that no discourse of his, whatever the subject, failed to reflect his ardent love of God. This was a source of holy edification and often inspired the negligent to salutary thoughts."[46]

According to Gregori:

"...the Servant of God never avoided encounters or relations with persons of this type (anti-clericals, and perhaps even Masons). But in this also, Bishop Scalabrini was moved by a higher principle, that of winning a soul, in which he succeeded more often than not...I have seen persons enrolled in Masonic orders whom he later converted, as well as threatening documents, of Masonic origin, which indicate that the Servant of God was considered a terrible enemy and quite dangerous to the sect."[47]

Cardinal Nasalli Rocca recalls that at Bishop Scalabrini's death, "an article in an anticlerical paper stated that it had always fought against him because he was dangerous to them, since he attracted so many persons and induced them to noble sentiments."[48] Another witness states that the schismatic Miraglia[49] had come to Piacenza at the instigation of the Masons, in order to offset the Bishop's activity, which was a source of annoyance to the sect especially because of the conversions he effected. Among these conversions is that of a former mayor of Piacenza, who either refused to have a priest as he lay dying or was prevented from calling one.[50] When Bishop Scalabrini, who was out of the city, learned from a friend of the former mayor that he did not expect to live, he immediately returned, though it was already night time, and went to the bedside of the dying man, who requested and received the sacraments from him.[51]

Msgr. Mondini, his Master of Ceremonies, recounts that while the Bishop was beginning his pastoral visit in Castell'Arquato, "some foolish man, observing the people's enthusiasm, began to make fun of them. When the Servant of God reached the door of the church, he knelt and kissed the Crucifix with such ardent devotion, that the unhappy man was deeply moved, burst into tears, and went into the church insisting that he must go to confession. He did so, for the first time in the thirty years that he had lived apart from God, as he himself used to say repeatedly and publicly in the town."[52] Msgr. Mondini also relates the conversion of "a certain sick person who, though on his deathbed, refused to have a priest and in fact, if one was mentioned, replied by taking up the revolver from his night table saying that he would blow out the brains of the first priest who came near him. The Servant of God heard about this and said, 'I'll go'. And he did go; and that poor unfortunate was so impressed by his courage that he was moved to tears and was converted."[53]

The conversion of Enrico de Thierry caused a tremendous stir. He lived on the Appenine where he had started an enterprise to exploit the beechwood forests on Mount Penna. When Bishop Scalabrini went to make his pastoral visit at St. Maria del Taro, de Thierry invited him to dinner, and added rather arrogantly (as he himself said later) that he was a Protestant and convinced that his was the true religion in which he intended to remain until the end of his days.[54] We learn from the ingenuous deposition of one of his servants that "the Servant of God was so tactful that he gradually succeeded in attracting him to the true faith, so that one fine day he baptized him, and we saw the Cavalier come to Mass and receive Communion. And this increased a great deal the esteem and the veneration in which all the people held the Servant of God. I remember, too, that Bishop Scalabrini did a great deal to convert two of the Cavalier's workmen, and he succeeded, and he baptized and confirmed them."[55]

Even his quick journey in Brazil was marked by similar episodes and he himself recounts the conversion of the Busnelli family.[56]

"If he was asked, and it was necessary, he would even go outside his diocese. I happened to meet him in the station at Parma, where he said to me: 'I am going to save a soul'. I learned later that he was going to visit Visconti-Venosta, a cabinet minister. This was not an unusual case. The Servant of God told me that he was often sent for by persons in the public eye who did not wish it known that they were receiving the sacraments."[57]

This work of mercy, visiting the sick who had strayed far from God, was a constant apostolate of the Bishop of Piacenza. In those cases, Msgr. Tammi said, "he did not go, he flew."[58]

Scalabrini himself paid no attention to the charge of "Liberophile." His one motive was to win souls. The obstacle presented at the process of beatification on the basis of this charge by the Promoter of the Faith is refuted by his whole life and by all the evidence, which may be summed up in this typical testimony of D. G. Cardinali:

"The Servant of God was not at all disturbed by this accusation, and he used to say: We must in every way seek to save souls..."[59] Bishop Scalabrini's "Liberalism" was an intense desire for souls. He would have liked to see all ecclesiastical restrictions and penalties on the Liberals removed, without however compromising the essential mission of the Church.

One witness rightly compared his activity to that of Don Bosco:

"This reminds me that he resembled St. John Bosco, whom I had the good fortune to know and to whom I went to confession many times."[60]

Scalabrini was true to the program he had set for his life: "do good, do all the good you can, and do it in the best possible way."[61]

Attitude Toward Evil

Scalabrini's apostolic activity was marked by both zeal and charity:

"We must have deep compassion for the transgression and the transgressors, for apostasy and the apostates, for betrayal and the betrayers, the sin and the sinners (and oh! how willingly we would shed our blood if we could only achieve the conversion of them all!)"[62]

But he was not tolerant toward evil itself. When it was a case of public scandal he rushed to remedy the situation, with a timeliness and firmness that was an example to everyone, including the authorities. The latter, in fact, were often compelled to action because the stand taken by the Bishop, however anxious they were to maintain their anticlerical stance. "He is a fierce one," Bishop Bonomelli once said jokingly when he learned of directives Scalabrini issued in protest to certain public affairs he considered scandalous.[63]

He had been quite grieved some years earlier when a church was opened in Piacenza by an evangelical sect. A pastoral letter and the sermons he gave at Christmas and during the Octave warned the faithful against this new danger. The peace promised in the Gospels, he said, could be guaranteed only by the infallible Church, in which alone there is certainty of the truth and of good.[64]

And freedom? "For me the most just and the most holy of freedoms is to say the truth in the name of Jesus Christ, without hesitation or asperity." For Scalabrini, Protestantism was heresy, hence it was error and sinful. He warned against the dangers of voluntary errors, listing the condemnations of the Popes and ending with a moving tribute to the Catholic Church.[65]

He recognized the good faith and sincerity of Protestants born into their particular faith.[66] But he reproached apostates and renegade Catholics who thought to find an outlet for their pride and a pretext for immorality by changing their religion. He insisted that one of the principal causes of apostasy was ignorance. The true religion "makes only one demand: to be studied." This was an argument dear to this apostle of the catechism. "Divine Revelation does not ask us for blind assent, for a faith without words. God wants our submission to be rational."[67] Religious instruction, Christian doctrine, these were the primary remedies given the faithful as preventives against the dangers of Protestantism and Masonry.[68] But reason is not enough. There must also be heart, a renunciation of sin and a love for our mother, the Church, "the light of all people, our liberty, our salvation, our peace, and our joy..."[69]

The Miraglia Schism

Scalabrini was away in Clermont-Ferrand for the commemoration of the First Crusade when the "Miraglia scandal" exploded in Piacenza.

Father Paolo Miraglia, of the diocese of Patti, had already incurred ecclesiastical censure when, in 1895, he was invited to preach the Marian month by the pastor of Saint Savino, who was unaware of his history.

"He revealed himself after the first ten sermons or so. He inveighed against certain priests who, he said, had written him anonymous letters criticizing his sermons. From the pulpit he began to preach about everything and everybody, reviewing, as the *Corriere della Sera* put it, the foundations of the universe with highly debatable competence, and at times gave out with errors in matters of faith and morals."[70]

The Vicar General warned him, and later took away his faculties. By way of reply Miraglia continued to preach, in secular halls, against the "pharisees," namely, the priests of Piacenza. The latter published a pamphlet defending themselves against his attacks, and he responded by lodging a complaint in the civil court against the thirteen priests who had signed it.

Things were going from bad to worse, but before decreeing any ecclesiastical penalties Bishop Scalabrini tried, with prudence and charity, to reach him in every possible way.

"As soon as I learned of the lawsuit brought by Miraglia against the priests of Piacenza, I tried in every way I could to recall him to wiser counsels. I was most disposed to favor him as much as possible[71] and was grieved at having to take coercive canonical measures against him, and so first of all I sent Father Moglia to him, who urged him to come to me. Miraglia answered: 'There is the same distance from my house to the Bishop's residence as there is from the Bishop's residence to my house. It is he, the Bishop who must come to me...' Notwithstanding this, I sent him another peacemaker, Msgr. Piacenza, of Fiorenzuola. He, too, exhorted him to present himself to me, assuring him that he would be well received. But Miraglia answered: 'I will not go unless I am accompanied by witnesses'. When Piacenza pointed out that if he did not present himself he ran the risk of a canonical admonition from the diocesan Curia, Miraglia added: 'If any one came to give me that, I would throw him down the stairs...' When this attempt also failed, I sent him Father Ricci, who was to try and persuade him to withdraw his lawsuit charges and to assure him, that, in recompense for his submission, I would grant him all that was possible. Ricci, in fact, went to Miraglia's residence and, having asked the concierge if he was home, received this reply: 'Yes sir, he went upstairs a moment ago'. Ricci went up, therefore, and told the maid who answered the door that he wished to see him. She went into the house and then returned to say: 'He isn't here; he has gone to Florence...' I then called together the Diocesan Committee on Ecclesiastical Discipline...and decided to proceed to action. First, however, I wanted to make one more attempt and I had my secretary write to him...begging him to spare me the sorrow of having to publish the canonical precept...a copy of which I was sending him as an act of courtesy and for his information. I enclosed the letter and the canonical precept in an envelope that was both sealed and registered. Miraglia refused to accept it without even opening it, so that I was constrained to make the precept public."[72]

The Bishop then tried his best before pronouncing excommunication and prohibiting the publication of the weekly *Gerolamo Savonarola*, which Miraglia had founded to support his faction. Miraglia appealed to the Pope, rebelled against the canonical warning from Rome, and resisted the renewed and kindly efforts of the Bishop. He opened a schismatic chapel, where he preached and said Mass. The excommunication pronounced against him by the Holy Office opened the eyes of many who had allowed themselves to be led astray by the selfstyled reformer, but did nothing to restrain the "misled brother" as Scalabrini continued to call him. He declared himself a bishop, called a Synod, began to confirm, beatified Savonarola and composed a grotesque Mass in his honor. He asserted that he belonged to the Old Catholics, and went through a mock episcopal consecration, having sent for a certain Villatte from America, who "claimed to be a bishop."[73] He then put on another sacrilegious parody, ordaining as a priest a poor youth, who later received not only forgiveness from Scalabrini but also the most charitable assistance as well.

At this point, the civil authorities, who at first had laughed at the Bishop and were quite content to fish in the troubled waters,[74] were confronted by Scalabrini with their responsibilities. They closed the chapel and forbade Miraglia to wear episcopal insignia or robes. The Court of Appeals confirmed the judgment of the Court of Piacenza that he was guilty of libel and other charges. The Catholic press[75] had been quick to repudiate the slanders and expose the trickery involved. The liberal newspaper La Libertà, the only one that had supported Miraglia, was caught in a scandal in which Miraglia had involved a young countess related to the managing editor. With all these chickens coming home to roost, Miraglia decided to flee to Switzerland.

For a good five years, this demagogue had turned the heads of his "unforgettable and most ardent" followers, who at the end numbered about four hundred. There was in addition a political Masonic and newspaper campaign that can be explained only in the context of the passionate and petty anti-clericalism of the end of the century[76] and by the rather submissive and passive character of the Piacentini, if we are to judge from the testimony of the time, and the stories in the local press.

For the Bishop, these were five years of agony.

"That unfortunate priest is plaiting a veritable crown of thorns for me...but I must say that until now, at least, the Lord has given me so much strength that I almost do not feel the sharp and constant pain. I see that He governs me with a Providence full of mystery, and I feel, or at least I seem to feel, disposed in every instance to repeat: Yes, Father, for that is what it pleased you to do. (Matt: 11:26) You who are so zealous, obtain for me the grace of perfect conformity with the wishes of heaven."[77]

Thus he wrote to Bonomelli at the beginning of the schism. Bonomelli replied that he believed there was sectarian activity behind Miraglia and added words of comfort.

"May God bless and reward you generously for sharing my sorrows. The Lord is truly scourging me and He has a thousand reasons for doing so. He grants me, however, a singular calm and tranquillity. Am I not to drink the cup that the Father has given me?" (John, 18:11)[78] A few months later Scalabrini wrote: "That wretched Miraglia unfortunately persists in his rebellion. God will provide. As for me '...in peace is my bitterness most bitter' ." (Is., 38:17)[79]

The peace and tranquillity cost so great an effort that his health suffered as a consequence.

"Doctor Luigi Marchesi, the Bishop's physician and our family doctor, has told us many times that the Miraglia scandal was the start of his heart ailment. In fact, the way he failed was striking evidence of his indescribable suffering: he had become a shell of his former self."[80]

"He suffered immensely and I have often seen him in a state that moved one to pity."[81]

"Many times I saw him weep and prostrate himself before the Most Blessed Sacrament to implore the mercy of God on that poor unfortunate and the salvation of the souls entrusted to him."[82]

In the long hours he remained before the altar[83] he found the resignation, comfort, renewed commitment to charity at all costs, and support for that "forebearance, which was unique in this world."[84]

"I have never heard him say a word or seen him make a gesture that would indicate any impatience, rancour or irritation toward the unfortunate apostate. And in fact, if one of his household uttered a hostile word against Miraglia, he reminded him of the obligation of Christian charity."[85]

"Only God knows what Bishop Scalabrini was suffering, and I do not hesitate to say that it was the greatest trial God imposed on his faithful servant. God, meanwhile, was opening the eyes of the right-minded and inspiring a strong current of opinion favorable to the Bishop. I remember, in fact, an occasion when I was pastor in Pianello and Bishop Scalabrini came on a pastoral visit. He was enthusiastically welcomed by all the people, except for one poor wretch who shouted 'Viva Miraglia'. The Bishop then performed an act of great humility. He first of all took no notice of the disturbance. He assisted, smiling, at the catechism examination, and when he had distributed the little rosaries I had given him for the children, he turned to me and said: 'will you give me one too?' When I said yes, he took the rosary, kissed it and put it in his pocket."[86]

His intentions for Spiritual Retreats belong to those bitter days:

"I must always consider crosses, tribulations, humiliations and scorn as so many precious means for sanctification and never complain, become sad or be discouraged. I must offer all things in union with the sufferings of Jesus Christ. *Fac me cruce inebriari!*...I should never become excited or disheartened over bitter experiences (and there are so many of every kind!) but humble myself and repeat from the heart, 'It is good for me'. (Ps., 118:71)[87]

Divine Worship

Scalabrini's apostolate was also marked by zeal for the proper conduct of the liturgy.

"He was jealous about everything that touched upon the honor and glory of God. He was not only most observant in matters of the interior life, but also most scrupulous with respect to the sacred ceremonies and proper performance of the rites. Nor was he content to be most correct himself, but he required it always and from all his priests...During the spiritual retreats he used to attend the explanations of the ceremonies and took a lively part in the discussions."[88]

He instituted courses on the liturgy in the seminary, and he required the students to demonstrate, in practice, that they had learned to conduct the services with an attention, devotion and seriousness that would be edifying for the faithful.[89] All who had seen him officiate at any liturgical function are agreed that his manner was so dignified and recollected as to be edifying and to inspire admiration as well.[90]

For him, music had an important function in the liturgy:

"It can become a kind of sacrament, that conceals profound and sublime mysteries...Music is one of the greatest, strongest, and most beautiful expressions of religious feeling...It raises us to God...If it does not, this is the fault of the listener, and perhaps also of the one who is performing the music."[91]

To remedy abuses that had crept into sacred music, he established the "Commission of St. Cecilia." This was to see to the observance of the directives promulgated by Leo XIII and the second diocesan synod.[92] In the latter there are details that seem quite minute, but they occur again in the *Motu Proprio* of Pius X and the Decree on the Liturgy of Vatican Council II: to be eliminated were secular elements, repetitions and alterations of the sacred text, theatrical floruishes, solos, long drawn out passages. Music must serve the text, not the text the music. The organ is to serve the Mass, not the Mass the organ. The words must be intelligible, the melodies such as to inspire devotion. If the organists do not obey, they are to be fined "five lire" to be given to the Institute of St. Opilio.[93]

He gave preeminence to Gregorian chant, "the most apt, if properly done, to inspire in the hearts of the faithful sentiments of Christian joy, compunction and devotion."[94] He directed that it be taught in the seminary, and that there be a final examination in it at the end of the school year.[95]

When Pius X's *Motu Proprio* was issued, he formed a commission to carry out its directives,[96] communicated them to the diocese and recommended that pastors introduce their parishioners to Gregorian chant, "patiently teaching them to take a more active part in the Mass and in Vespers on holy days, as used to be done in former times," and as some parishes do "with most happy results."[97] He sent three priests to Rome to study, with the Benedictines, the best methods of teaching authentic Gregorian.[98]

With respect to "sacred art" his views were that "we know art has its rules, but the Church which has created and re-created the arts and whose influence favors and nourishes them, also has its rules."[99] He counseled his pastors to see to it that the faithful had images that inspired devotion but that at the same time respected historical truth and beauty.[100]

"In one rectory he saw an oleograph, very popular at the time, of a soul in adoration before Jesus in the Blessed Sacrament. The soul was represented by a young girl in a flowing white robe and with an abundance of blond hair streaming over her shoulders. Scalabrini who had a decided antipathy for certain over-sentimental forms of devotion, turned to the pastor and said: 'Do you think its proper to have the Blessed Sacrament adored by a young woman in a nightgown with hair all uncombed?' "[101]

We have noted how during his pastoral visits, he was concerned about the smallest detail regarding vestments and sacred vessels. He donated these himself to the poorest churches, so that nothing might detract from the dignity of the ritual. He also reformed the diocesan "proper" of the breviary.[102]

There are numerous evidences of Bishop Scalabrini's deeply felt zeal for the House of God: the over two hundred churches which he personally consecrated,[103] the generous subsidies he granted for repairs and redecoration, the reduction of the number of parishes in the city, something which had been tried three times in vain by his predecessors. There were thirty of these churches, one for every thousand persons. Some were veritable holes in the wall and were kept open with great difficulty.[104] Despite this, the Bishop had to overcome stubborn resistance and even to have recourse to Rome. But he was not the man to be intimidated when he was convinced of the rightness of his cause. Having obtained the support of the Holy See he reduced the number of parishes in the city to fourteen.[105]

He was also active in restoring the more beautiful of the churches of Piacenza, such as the medieval churches of St. Euphemia and of St. Savino and the renaissance churches of the Holy Selpuchre and St. Peter. His name is inseparably linked with the restorations in the Duomo, a magnificent Lombard-Romanesque structure of the twelfth century, whose authentic Gothic-Romanesque lines had undergone successive alterations in the intervening centuries. It was restored to its ancient splendor, "to that harmony of the parts and the whole, that majesty and elegant simplicity, that air of solemnity and mysticism... for which the monuments of Lombardy are famous, and ours among the first."[106]

The work of restoration, which was both daring and difficult, was finished thanks to the energy of Bishop Scalabrini, who besides furnishing the original impetus and constant encouragement, also contributed a large sum of money, which he personally collected, quite unashamed to beg for the House of God.

His zeal for the liturgy and his love of art were not his only motivation, however:

"I must also mention another very different reason, but one which should also carry great weight (as it did in inducing me to assume the responsibility of this undertaking) with all those for whom the suffering of the workers is not merely a simple and easy subject for speech-making but a grievous fact, which each of us must try to remedy within the measure of his own possibilities. The economic depression, which is serious throughout all Italy, is most serious here...It therefore gives me a lively pleasure to think that the money we donate to this great work, will be turned into so much bread for a great many families."[107]

The architect Luca Beltrami commented on the works of restoration:

"Many could think, with some justification, that the size of the project and the multiple difficulties involved in carrying it out would delay or seriously compromise its achievement. Bishop Scalabrini, however, followed the encouragement of his words with his no less authoritative example. The episcopal palace was joined to the transverse nave...and the Bishop unhesitatingly decided to tear down the part of his residence that disfigured and partially hid the Duomo. Since this meant sacrificing the direct and private passage between the Bishop's residence and the cathedral, there were those who thought the personal sacrifice too great. Bishop Scalabrini would reply: 'Why should the bishop mind having to walk among his people in order to get to the church?'...Anyone seeing the Duomo today, only three years after the work of restoration...was begun, cannot help being surprised...Every part of the church is being transformed; it is being stripped of all the accretions which have no sense and no artistic value. One might say that the structure is coming to life again and speaking a language that could have been thought lost."[108]

In 1901, on the occasion of his silver jubilee, Bishop Scalabrini was able to enter the restored cathedral with the "emotion of the Priest who could finally offer his Mystical Bride a house...made more beautiful and resplendent by pure artistry."[109]

This was in a sense a kind of culmination of Scalabrini's concern to safeguard the artistic treasures of the diocese. From the beginning of his episcopate he had directed that the greatest care be taken to preserve buildings, paintings and sculpture of artistic merit; he had forbidden any remodeling without his consent, which was given only after consultation with competent artists; he also forbade, under pain of ecclesiastical penalties, selling or giving away any objects of art or sacred vessels, "the glorious witnesses of the devotion and greatness of our ancestors."[110]

The Liturgy

Zeal for the beauty and dignity of religious ceremonies would be meaningless, however, if they did not nourish Christian life. Religious observance was at the heart of the Bishop's intention, and all his efforts of persuasion and action were devoted to inducing his flock to keep holy the Lord's Day and to participate in the sacramental and liturgical life of the Church. He never tired of urging on his clergy and his people the importance of frequent attendance at Mass.[111]

"To keep holy the Lord's Day," he said in one of his last pastorals, "is a first and fundamental law of religion...Observe Christians on that day. They meet in the church. Joy shines on every face, there is peace in every heart. Liberty, equality, fraternity are not empty words for those people but a consoling reality...They all meet within the arms of the same Mother, they raise to heaven the same prayer, they kneel with the same sense of adoration, they hear the same words of truth, they profess the same faith, they offer the same sacrifice, they partake of the same mystical meal, they long for the same fatherland...Fathers and mothers, old and young, rich and poor, all of you here, masters, servants, workers, I repeat to you again with hands joined: By all that is sacred to you in heaven and on earth, sanctify, sanctify, the Lord's day."[112]

He returned to this subject in the pastoral of the following year:

"Some think that attending Mass is a good work, but more or less as good as saying rosary, giving alms, saying the Stations of the Cross. These pious practices are all good and holy, there is no doubt; but Holy Mass surpasses them in infinite measure, for it is of infinite value."

He invariably stressed the human and social value of keeping the feastdays holy, and warned masters against putting obstacles in the way of their workers:

"Industry! Commerce! Most fine and noble things without doubt and they will ever expand and multiply, but they must never, nevèr, expand and multiply at the expense of holier and nobler things, such as human dignity and freedom...To multiply your own enjoyments, to increase production for your own profit, would you make a slave of a man, a beast of burden? You are barbarians! Are you unaware perhaps that in that body bronzed by the sun, in those limbs hardened by labor, there lives an immortal soul equal to your own? Do you not know that with respect to Christian Faith and knowledge the worker is in everything, except in his material circumstances, equal to the most noble of princes, to the most powerful of monarchs? Precisely in fact because he is a workingman he is the clearest reflection of the divine Artificer who gave being and form to all things and of the divine Artisan of Nazareth who, by his example, ennobled poverty and labor."[113]

He continually urged his priests to preach often on the preeminence of the Mass and the necessity of attending it. He encouraged the confraternity which recommended daily Mass to its members. He recommended the closest participation in the Mass itself, with reception of Holy Communion, or at least through spiritual communion. For him the parish church was the family home of the faithful, the compendium of religion, the homeland of the Christian (in this he was following St. Charles) and he could not grant that anyone should go to Mass in another parish because he did not like his own pastor. He attached fundamental importance to the liturgy of the Word, almost as much as to receiving the Eucharist.[114]

The Eucharistic movement Bishop Scalabrini inspired will be treated in the next chapter. We have noted the zeal with which he heard confessions. He was equally zealous in administering the sacrament of confirmation. He often expressed the desire to be summoned when a small child lay dying so it might not be deprived of the grace and quality of this sacrament.[115] During his visits to emigrants in America, he made himself generously available to officiate at confirmations despite all his other engagements. "In the last five days I confirmed five thousand persons...Just imagine; on Saturday I confirmed 2153 persons without feeling the least bit tired."[116] He was over sixty-five years of age, but he was still animated by the ardor of youth when it came to exercising his pastoral ministry.

Neither danger nor fatigue deterred him. During the Socialist uprisings of 1898 he was seen to walk through the crossfire in the streets to administer the last sacraments to a fatally wounded youth.[117] Nor did he hesitate to respond when called to the bedside of a child suffering from petecchial typhus.[118] Only twenty days before his own death, he went to visit the grandfather of one of his priests, although to do so he had to climb a staircase that was "steep and difficult even for those in good health."[119]

During his pastoral visits in the mountain towns, despite the wearying duties these entailed, he administered the sacraments without any thought of time.

"I arrived up here safely," he wrote to Bardi. "The weather is stormy and cold, but fine and very warm for the spirit. I went to the church at five in the morning and stayed there until two in the afternoon, giving communion to several thousand persons from twenty-three parishes, who had walked here on pilgrimage despite the terrible weather."[120] And on another occasion he wrote: "I spoke with feeling, and then went to hear confessions until eleven at night."[121]

During a pastoral visit to Gropparello, he gave two sermons, celebrated Mass, distributed general communion, performed two hundred confirmations, and inspected the church and the vestments and sacred vessels. He had just returned to the rectory when he heard of a poor woman who lay dying. Despite the steep descent to her house, he insisted on going to her, heard her confession, gave her Communion, recited the prayers of the dying, and stayed to speak words of consolation and hope to the members of her family before climbing back up to the church.[122] If he demanded greater zeal from his priests, and complete availability for administering sacramental grace, he spurred them on far more with his example than with exhortations or synodal dispositions. It was said he "left no one in peace," but that included himself.

He was even reproached for not leaving the saints alone.[124] Bishop Ranza had recommended that his successor try to authenticate the various relics preserved in the diocese. Bishop Scalabrini started on this immediately, confident that it would contribute to greater devotion, especially to the patron saints of the diocese, and convinced that this type of devotion was an important means of sanctification.

He established a commission of experts, composed of archeologists, hagiographers, chemists, physicists, physiologists and theologians. The first relics to be authenticated were those of the patron of Piacenza, St. Antoninus, a martyr of the Theban Legion, and of St. Victor, the Bishop. This was celebrated with solemn ceremonies and the subsequent systematic and scientific research produced a list of 158 relics which had previously been questioned or had given rise to the charge that the Piacentini were a credulous lot.[126]

He himself was devoted to these "diocesan" saints[127] and he also renewed interest in the patron saints of the various parishes, whose feast days he desired to be commemorated with all the solemnity of former times.[128] His aim was always the same. Just as the feast of the Holy Patrons of 1880 had brought about a "great awakening of faith and an extraordinary reception of the Holy Sacraments,"[129] he hoped that throughout the diocese "the unbelieving would open their eyes, the sinners would be converted, the erring would return to their father's house."[130]

He personally had great devotion to St. Joseph, whose help he sought during spiritual retreats and to whom he dedicated his Institute for the Deaf and Dumb, his patron St. John the Baptist, St. Charles Borromeo, after whom he modeled his own ministry "and whose footsteps," he said, "he wished to follow as closely as possible"[131] St. Francis de Sales, "whose picture he kept on his desk...because he said he was both gentle and strong,"[132] and St. Louis Gonzaga, to whom he prayed as a boy and the tercentary of whose death he celebrated with special ceremonies.

"In short, he used all the means at his disposal and all that his own enlightened zeal suggested to do good to his people and his clergy."[133]

He had made a spectacular beginning and there were many who predicted that he could not go on like that, for he was only a man after all. Instead, at the end of his life, everyone was saying: "He is incredible." The witnesses who testified for his beatification agree that he was faithful to his program with a consistency that astonished his priests first of all, with heroic constancy, and in fact with a cresecendo that reached its peak in his last years when his vigor and health began to fail.[134]

"The salvation of souls? It is our life, our only reason for being, and our whole existence must be a constant search for souls. We must not eat, drink, sleep, study, speak, and not even amuse ourselves except to do good for souls, without ever, ever growing tired."[135]

"His own large diocese was not enough for his zeal," Don Orione said.[136] When he dedicated the bust of Bishop Scalabrini in the Church of San Bartolomeo in Como, Cardinal Ferrari, recalling the inscription on the memorial to Alexander Volta — "To Volta, the Fatherland" — exclaimed: "To Scalabrini, the world."[137]

One newspaper declared that he had renewed the example of St. Charles Borromeo and St. Francis de Sales, with whom he could repeat, after the

Good Shepherd and St. Paul, "I have not held my own life more precious than the souls of my flock."[138]

He sought no other happiness: "To make one soul happy is much more than being happy!"[139]

CHAPTER VI

Scalabrini As Administrator

Prudence

"The practical ideal of the apostolic priest, anxious in all things to lead all men to Christ, is not without its dangers. Zeal can border on fanaticism — an extremely hardworking man may seem and even become intrusive. Perspicacity can fall into cunning and intrigue. Two things saved Bishop Scalabrini from these dangers...The integrity of his intentions was above suspicion and he possessed rare practical prudence. He was a true priest, *homo Dei*, who sought only the interests of the Lord...and on earth the well-being of everyone. Equal to his integrity was the prudence of his judgment...He summed up in his personality the talents that make a good administrator, born to success, to effective authority. In whatever group he entered he had a natural superiority — his fellow bishops could well have confidence in him and, in fact, quite willingly accepted and often asked for his advice..."[1]

In his eulogy, on the occasion of the solemn transferal of Bishop Scalabrini's body to the cathedral, Cardinal Nasalli Rocca said:

"Piacenza had been wisely guided even before his episcopate, but the changed times demanded a new vigorous life. He worked with the delicate tact of the administrator inspired by God. He certainly could not be understood immediately. He was sympathetic with those who did not understand while remaining as firm as necessary to have his ideas accepted. This is why his actions irked certain persons who then made absurd charges against him. Today emotions have simmered down. As we stand before his coffin, we can declare that Bishop Scalabrini steadfastly clung to the principle, 'Ubi Petrus, ibi Ecclesia'. If he sought to draw everything and everybody to himself in order to win all for Christ, there can be no shadow of suspicion that he deviated even for an instant from the directives set forth by the Supreme Authority of the Church."[2]

Bishop Scalabrini lived in a time of profound political and social change, marked by restless pioneering, even subversive, movements and equally determined conservative trends. His diocese and priests were bitterly divided on philosophical and political lines and about the educational systems in the different seminaries, while a good part of the clergy was ultra-conservative and stuck in routine. The bishop had to be able to reconcile.

"...a burning anxiety for renewal and a great prudence in achieving it gradually, through evolution, not revolution. Wisdom is reconciling, at the crossroads of history, the immutable with the contingent, clothing the certainty of principles with the splendor of throbbing reality; intuition with tact in affirming the presence of a lively Christianity working in a world in which — between the incipient modernism of some Catholics with their stubborn worship of change, and the unrealistic integralism of others, with their rockbound loyalty to form — the necessary solution was what we today call Christian humanism. Over the arguments for a break with the world or for submissive adaptation to it, there had to prevail, for the supreme interests of the Kingdom of Christ, the case for participation in the secular in order to permeate society with the Christian leaven, to transform it and to save it."[3]

"He was born to govern," the noted Father Serafino Balestra, his professor and later his colleague in the Seminary of Como, said of the young Scalabrini. Scalabrini was universally so recognized for his sense of balance, his prudence and tact, his captivating, intelligent and gentle manner, and for practicing himself the recommendation he repeatedly gave his colleagues and pastors: fortiter et suaviter.

"He knew the art of governing. In fact, he governed his diocese with extraordinary prudence, thereby succeeding in preventing conflicts and settling dissensions."[4] — "He was very skillful in blunting the differences that could give rise to conflict."[5] "His episcopacy was one of fine administration marked by a sense of balance, so that he successfully prevented divisions among his people,...and with his unwavering justice he greatly tempered the divergent trends among his clergy, creating almost a new era."[6]

His particular blend of authority and fatherliness, of justice and gentleness caused even his adversaries to exclaim, "What can we do? With that man, we always have to give in."[7]

Natural talent is perhaps not enough to explain his success, especially when we consider the difficulties and anxieties of his tenure as bishop. He added, and this was an exercise in virtue, serenity and confidence in God. Prudence, calm, trust in God were what he often counseled in his letters before adding those other elements of his apostolic activity: courage and firmness.

"Before beginning battle, I reflected, I weighed all the difficulties, and I convinced myself I could withstand all the forces of our enemies. Prudence, care, but above all courage and firmness."[8] So he wrote as a young man, and this remained his approach throughout his life.

"He used to say that in every occasion it is necessary to see, foresee and provide."[9] He thought and rethought before acting, he weighed his words and measured his strength,[10] but above all he prayed, with a confidence that reflected the evangelical faith and simplicity with which he turned to prayer. There is extant a letter from a priest whom Scalabrini advised to place under the corporal during Mass the letters or documents that required a particularly serious decision. He called it the "corporal system."[11]

The Bishop himself often confidently announced, after saying Mass, a decision about which he had been quite perplexed the night before. He did not, however, fail to seek competent advice.[12] He appealed often to the Holy See, not only on the most difficult questions, but also when he could have proceeded on his own authority. He made numerous journeys to Rome, "to seek the opinion of his superior." The Holy See recognized his prudence and also used his advice in some of the most delicate matters.

Various Cardinals and many of his brother bishops sought his counsel,[13] much in the spirit of Bishop (later Cardinal) Riboldi of Pavia, who wrote, "keep your precious friendship for me, to correct me and help me to be least unworthy a bishop as possible."[14] In very important cases, Bishop Bonomelli used to say, "We must hear what the Bishop says," meaning Scalabrini.[15]

During the diocesan exploratory process, witnesses were asked whether Scalabrini, in his relations with Bonomelli, had always been prudent, "so that he had incurred no responsibility for the unpleasant things that befell that eminent prelate." All replied that if Bonomelli had taken his friend's advice he would not have been involved in the incidents which brought upon him painful warnings...from the Holy See.[16]

Bonomelli himself said: "Our friendship, although intimate, did not affect our freedom to think and act in our own way on different points. Bishop Scalabrini gave me repeated and truly noble proof of this when times were difficult."[17]

He was singularly prudent, charitable and patient when he was obliged to take severe measures, a fact all the more noteworthy "since he was inclined by nature to be somewhat impulsive."[18] He himself suffered as well: "He called me and was moved to tears as he told me the painful measure he had to take...I know that the Servant of God promised to help...and in fact he later sent financial aid."[19]

In such cases, he would move slowly, with the most careful investigation. He would find extenuating circumstances, "he would always try to mitigate the blame and soften the punishment,"[20] he would seek advice and, above all, he would pray. Then, as we have seen, after a first kindly warning, a second stern one, he would at last take vigorous action.[21]

"A Superior," he used to say, "must correct those under him but not discourage them. Respect for their Superior is a great source of strength for them. Let us be gentle in judgment. Who does not have any defects? Those who act are the ones who make mistakes. Criticism is much easier than action."[22]

Fortitude

When the honor of God and his ministry were involved, or the good of souls, obedience to the Holy Father, the laws of the Church, or justice, then Scalabrini did not weigh obstacles, labor, sacrifice or any adversary however powerful. Nor did he ever yield to the temptation to win favor with his superiors at the expense of justice or what he deemed his rightful duty.

"We need fortitude more than anything else in this age of cowardliness, in this age in which there are so many milksops," he said in his 1881 Pentecost Sermon. A soul filled with the Holy Spirit does not fear the world, he continued, "because he does not belong to it in any way; he is indifferent to its judgments; its gossip and its raillery make no more sense to him than a tinkling cymbal; he is proud of virtue before those who scorn it; he is guided by truth alone, he has none of that timid compliance that brings so much harm to religion."[23]

He was a Christian and a Bishop who practiced the proverb of the Saints: "He who loves does not fear."[24]

"He gave proof of his strength in the way he held true to his purpose — provided it was a question of the honor of God and the salvation of souls — regardless of the opposition, whatever its source. He, too, endured his Calvary."[25]

"He was fearless and gave proof of exceptional courage, particularly in the various tremendously stormy times that marked his episcopate...

especially in confronting the Masons and the arrogant civil authorities who were conspiring against religion and morals, for example in his vigorous defense of religious instruction in the schools and his efforts to keep divorce from shattering family life, working *toto pectòre* so that the Piacentini would reject the proposal to legalize it."[26]

For these reasons and because "he dared to fish for souls in the sea of free thought," the Masons hated him. But "threats never kept him from doing his duty," Don Orione affirmed. "I remember that he once received a letter with a black hand drawn on it and the words: Five more days. He paid no attention to it, and in fact pursued with even greater energy his fight against the enemies of the faith."[28] The opposition exploded in a virulent newspaper campaign against the Bishop. Gregori records some interesting minutes of a meeting of a Masonic Lodge:

"The most powerful enemy of our society in Northern Italy is Signor Scalabrini, the Bishop of Piacenza. With his generosity, his winning manner, his talent, he is popular with everyone, and they all follow him blindly. Three of our brothers died profaned by the rites of the Church through him, and he shamelessly prevented us from honoring them with our own. The Lodge of Piacenza, once so flourishing can be said to be ruined now thanks to his tricks. We must fight with every means the work of this formidable enemy and demolish him in our Masonic sense of the word."[29]

It was, in its way, a tribute to his fearlessness.

Unhappily he was also constrained at times to display the same courage in matters affecting the clergy. At the beginning of his episcopate, he was obliged to undertake a radical reform in his seminary: "I am convinced that we must not tolerate anything or anyone that is not in willing accord with the Bishop."[30]

Toward the end of his life, when the first indications of modernism were surfacing, he was worried about the intolerance of certain priests: "The plague of insubordination on the part of some of the clergy is unfortunately, as in all the dioceses, a great danger for the future. It is to be feared that it will spread if the Bishops' hands are not strengthened and a sound lesson is not administered."[31] Convinced of this danger, and grieved by it, he did his best to obviate it.[32]

The "Rocca Case"

These anxieties explain the actions he took from the very beginning of his episcopate against the elements that were undermining harmonious relations and obedience, both from within and without the diocese, in the name of the "philosophical question." In reality the matter was one of discipline.

Notwithstanding the care he took to ensure in his seminaries the Thomistic orientation desired, and later imposed, by the Holy See, he was suspected and accused, at least indirectly, of being a Rosminian.

At that time "the climate was very hot on both sides," so that "when two intellectual factions confront one another with passion and partisanship rather than calm or strictly scientific reasoning, the results are always unexpected."[33] But another characteristic of the polemics of the period was the confusion between the cultural and the political, or in any event, the practical elements. In other words, the cultural argument became part of the political debate between the transigents and the intransigents, fought principally around the Roman Question.

Without going into the merits of the debate, it is clear that the accusations against Scalabrini were unfounded. In his case, the controversy revolved around the political aspects of the Roman Question (to which we shall return later), but its cause really lay in two different but closely related facts: the dissension between the Urbano Seminario (Seminary) and the Collegio Alberoni and the dismissal of the rector of the Seminary.

When Scalabrini became bishop of Piacenza, the Urbano had about thirty-six pupils. The rector was a poor administrator, with hazy notions about the obedience due the bishop, and its debts were enormous. Even greater was the tension created by the conflict between Thomists and Rosminians that had absorbed as well the old differences between the Urbano and the Alberoni, the latter being accused of excessively favoring Rosmini. The Bishop's directives did not have immediate effect — for example the naming of Thomist professors[34] for the Seminary, the adoption of Thomistic texts for the Alberoni and the founding of the *Divus Thomas*. Celebration of the feast of St. Thomas was restored, a chair of Thomistic philosophy was established, and the seminarians were required to conduct periodic academic exercises on Thomistic themes. Scalabrini's Thomistic reform is all the more conspicuous in view of the fact that at the beginning of his episcopacy there were a good two hundred Rosminians among his clergy. Hence his anxiety to eliminate causes of dissension among them.

Soon after the appearance of *Divus Thomas*, however, articles attacking it began to appear in the *Osservatore Cattolico* of Milan, and a little later others criticizing the bishop for opposing the Seminary rector, who was presented as "the victim of the pressures used in some dioceses by the Rosminian faction to capture the chair of philosophy in the Seminaries"[35] in order to "demolish the cause of the Pope," and "promote Rosminian doctrines, which are the science and the substratum of liberal Catholicism."[36] Herein lay the misunderstanding.

Scalabrini denied that he had done anything to persuade the rector to interpret St. Thomas according to Rosmini, "while everyone knew that as early as October 1876, anticipating the wishes of the Holy Father, in a special decree greatly praised by the Sacred Congregation, I prescribed for the two diocesan Seminaries and the Collegio Alberoni, the doctrines of St. Thomas, precisely according to the authors whom the Holy Father later proposed as the authentic interpreters of the Angelic Doctor."[37]

The witnesses at the diocesan exploratory process related facts, from which it appears that the Bishop dismissed the rector for disciplinary rather than doctrinal reasons:

"From a personal incident I had proof that Canon Savino Rocca was in conflict with Bishop Scalabrini. Rocca asked me to give him (the Bishop) an envelope and to get a receipt for it. Unaware of its contents I brought it to him and asked for the receipt, but he said to me: 'Keep the envelope: I will not give you a receipt.' He did not, however, add any word of resentment or disapproval, but maintained a calm, serene manner. It was said that Rocca regularly spoke ill of the bishop, and that he went so far as to censure publicly the bishop's actions and some of his documents. It was for this reason that he was removed from the rectorship of the Urbano Seminary."[38]

"The Servant of God, seeing that the Rector through his notorious intransigence...was giving a wrong direction to seminary training from a disciplinary, not a doctrinal point of view, let him know in various ways that he would welcome his resignation, and meanwhile named him Canon Theologian of the Chapter of the Cathedral. But Rocca turned a deaf ear, for he wanted the Bishop to dismiss him explicitly, which the Servant of God did for the good of the Institute. Rocca's suspension from giving the theology lectures to the Cathedral canons was due to the fact that at the end of the lesson he would make obvious allusions to those he considered his enemies, beginning with the bishop, as I myself heard him do."[39]

Monsignor Francesco Torta, who was then a seminarian, stated: "Canon Rocca could not bear Bishop Scalabrini's attitude; he considered him a liberal and repeatedly spoke ill of him to the clergy that came to the Seminary. This created a difficult and dangerous situation. The Servant of God tolerated this state of affairs for a long time, but he was finally constrained to take action and he dismissed Rocca."[40]

Monsignor Giuseppe Dodici, on the other hand, was from the Alberoni: "I was then in the Collegio Alberoni. I remember that the affair made a great impression on me because I thought that Rocca's position was unshakeable and his dismissal took a heroic act of courage on the part of the bishop. When I thought over what Rocca said and did against the bishop, however, criticizing and discrediting him with us seminarians and openly accusing him of Liberalism with such subtle and seductive skill that we were caught by him (for we placed more credence in Rocca than in the bishop) then I realized that the action of the Servant of God was just and opportune, and I had proof of his great courage, since he had done something everyone considered heroic."[41]

All the other witnesses are in agreement with this version of the affair, and even those who tended to favor Rocca could not help characterizing him as "lacking in the balance necessary to direct a seminary."[42]

Cardinal Nasalli Rocca testified that the seminarians "certainly were not being trained to have respect for the bishop. As for the theology lectures he was suspended because, though he had been warned, he continued to indulge in unseemly personalities from the pulpit."[43]

The testimony is also in agreement with what Bishop Scalabrini himself said on the subject:

"The clergy were certainly not unaware of Rocca's poor administration of the Seminary and they knew that he was one of the principal if not the only source of the dissensions that disturbed them. The indignation of the more sensible among them was both great and legitimate. Since I had perhaps a little too much patience, some of them intended, I was told, to submit a petition to the Synod. When they learned, however, that I not only would not accept it, but that I also disapproved of the idea, they did not present it. I had already decided upon Rocca's dismissal, but I delayed precisely so that I would not seem to be yielding to pressure. It did not take place, in fact, until ten months after the Synod, and was generally welcomed with true satisfaction." Recalling that he had even named him Censor for the *Divus Thomas*, he continued, "When it became known that he had written the unfortunate articles in the *Osservatore Cattolico di Milano* and the *Eco di Parma*, it naturally became necessary to replace him."[44]

Before appealing to the Holy See, which later in a formal trial took away the benefice attached to his office and recognized the justice of the Bishop's action, Rocca had asked help of the Milan paper, which continued to accuse the bishop of lies and calumnies and the Piacentian clergy of Phariseeism and Jansenism. Bishop Scalabrini endured all this patiently, while the accusations were merely insulting. But a more worrisome danger was emerging:

"The confusion of tongues is truly frightening. If things go on like this the diocese will become ungovernable...In this sad state of things I pray God every day that he will grant me and all my colleagues patience, calmness, tranquillity, confidence in his divine help, without which we shall all go crazy."[45]

The Bishop of Piacenza clearly saw the dangers in the confused dissensions of the time and the threat they represented to the hierarchical order and to the good of souls, which was his supreme preoccupation.

"I frankly confess that the miserable state of our dioceses, thanks to the troublemakers and scandalous controversies, is the most painful sorrow of my life and afflicts me so much that it affects my mind. When I went to Rome, I spoke quite clearly, perhaps even too bluntly, to the

Holy Father, of the deplorable things that are taking place among us, and of the impossibility of governing our dioceses."[46]

When Scalabrini dismissed Rocca, Milan's *Osservatore Cattolico* indirectly accused him of calumny, of being an exponent of Rosminianism as a doctrinal justification of Catholic Liberalism, of tricks and deception. It then moved to a direct attack on the Bishop with a distorted version of a disciplinary measure of the Ordinary of the diocese.

"We are thus in a period of anarchy," the *Osservatore* editorialized, "and at the point where the direction of the Seminary, this seed-bed of Faith and Piety, is falling into the hands of a sect. Thus an act of weakness could ruin the work accomplished through so many years by so many excellent men, it could ruin a whole diocese. Young seminarians, turn your eyes to Rome, to the Pope, and listen there to the voice that will save you. Do not yield like cowards to the suggestions of teachings that invite you to disobedience, that weaken your hearts and make your minds rebellious. Obey to the death the Vicar of Christ; respect those who have raised you in unbounded devotion to the Pope."[47]

This was too much even for the long patience of Scalabrini. It was interference in the administration of his diocese and tantamount to charges of immorality and heresy against him as bishop and against his clergy. It was systematic use of calumny as a journalistic weapon and open incitement to disobedience. He could no longer keep silent and he published the following protest:

"We protest above all against the offenses...to our divine authority, as well as to that of our beloved and venerable brother bishops, considering ourselves to be one with them, since the Episcopacy is one and undivided. We protest against the serious contempt, shown by that newspaper, for the Supreme Pontiff, as represented in our humble person...against the insults cast upon our venerable clergy, labeled *Jansenist* more than once in its columns...We protest against the unwarranted interference of that paper in matters concerning our diocese. We are directly responsible to the Supreme Pastor of the Church, and we are ready to give an account to him for the reasons which led us to this or that directive; but to those who try to dominate and sacrilegiously subvert the hierarchical order established by Jesus Christ — we owe no accounting whatever, ever. We protest against that paper's malicious insinuation that the organization of studies in our diocese depends on this or that individual...against its distortion of facts, its gratuitous and malicious assertions...Finally, we protest against the insubordination preached by this newspaper and against the new kind of liberalism it is injecting into the hearts of the youth called to serve in the Church's militia and which can give rise only to religious anarchy in the dioceses and in the Church. To conclude this painful expression of our duty, while we are ready and firmly resolved to censure whatever member of our clergy authors articles offensive to the Ecclesiastical Authority, we also declare before Jesus Christ that we forgive, from the heart, the insults and offenses directed against our humble person. We fervently pray meanwhile that the spirit of union, charity and peace will at last pervade the hearts of all, and retemper them in true, perfect and sincere obedience to the Roman Pontiff."[48]

The protest was supported in a statement signed by 119 priests of the city, that is almost all of them, by nine-tenths of the priests outside the city, by the various religious communities and many lay personalities. A counter-statement, on the other hand, garnered only eight signatures.

Before publishing the protest, Scalabrini had written to the Pope informing him of certain points which reflect both his own sincere attitude toward the episcopal mission and toward the Pope, from whom the mission derives and to whom alone account must be rendered:

"The factions which latch on to one pretext or another to undermine the Episcopacy little by little and to mold Catholic public opinion according to their own way of thinking are becoming increasingly bold, to the point at times of rendering it impossible for the Bishops to exercise their sacred Ministry...Holy Father, I am not the only one to complain of wounds...; many, many Bishops much wiser and more noteworthy than I grieve over these things in their hearts and do not dare to speak out but anxiously await from Your Holiness a prompt and effective remedy. Holy Father, you know my frankness of spirit, you know the sacrifices I have made for the glory of the Church and to give witness to what I feel myself to be, entirely in Your service and for Your cause, which is the cause of God. Therefore, prostrate at Your feet, I ask only one favor: call to order this extra-hierarchical element — and especially the journalists..., who protesting devotion to the successor of St. Peter, a devotion they do not have, offend the high authority of the Bishops, dishonor the Church, and render it contemptible to serious persons by their violent and scandalous polemics. And they disrupt that wonderful union among Pastors that has been until now one of its finest glories..."[49]

After this letter Scalabrini remained always in close contact with the Holy See. He candidly expressed his own opinions but complied with the judgment of Rome. As soon as the protest was published he sent a copy to the Secret Chamberlain, Monsignor Gabriele Boccali, for transmittal to the Pope. He also wrote to the Cardinal Secretary of State, requesting that he forbid the Milan paper to interfere in the administration of the dioceses and to accept for publication letters on internal diocesan affairs which were not approved by the respective Ordinaries.[50]

Rome directed the newspaper to publish a statement[51] which turned out as follows: "We declare that though it was far from our intention to sadden with our judgments any high ecclesiastical authorities, nevertheless we withdraw what — due perhaps to hasty preparation — has caused some distress."[52]

In view of this weak statement, Scalabrini asked the Holy Father for a public retraction in the interests of his sacred ministry and his clergy, which had been publicly and unjustly defamed:

"It must not surprise you, Holy Father, that I speak of revolution and revolutionary maneuvers against the Church of God...If she were fought only by unbelievers, there would be little to fear, but when Catholics and priests, I say this with great sorrow, raise the standard of rebellion within the Church and under fine appearances corrupt the Christian sense of the young clergy and the people, the Bishops cannot and must not keep silent; nor will I keep silent. I have been suffering under these evils for years, Holy Father, and I bitterly deplore them. It is now impossible to ignore them any longer...After having prayed at length I have decided to confront this arrogant party which is trying to gain the upper hand and is the source of so much spiritual ruin...The destructive and rebellious work of the new liberalism, believe me, Holy Father, will not stop until some clear public action is taken in support of the authority of the Bishops. I hope that You will understand and listen to me. Yet if God should deprive me of even this consolation, my deep veneration and filial affection for Your Sacred Person and the Holy See would be no less. I would always have the consolation of never having failed to speak the truth to anyone, of having fought the good fight and kept the faith, in the hope of the crown that the Just Judge will one day grant me. I will not close this letter, Most Blessed Father, without first declaring that I am and always will be ready to obey not only Your commands but also Your wishes, so that if you think I should keep silent, I shall maintain a calm and tranquil silence, out of respect for you, entrusting everything to the hands of God, and to You, who are his agent."[53]

We learn the tone of Rome's reply from a letter of Scalabrini:

"Here is a copy of my letter to the Holy Father, who had Boccali write me to be patient, because if the gentlemen in question refuse to heed the admonitions they have received, more severe and effective measures will certainly be taken. The fact that the Holy See took the measures mentioned above, however, is already a source of satisfaction..."[54]

Scalabrini was patient, kept silent, and took no action against the *Osservatore*. In short, he obeyed as he had promised, although the silence cost him a great deal. At the same time he did not stop talking where he could and should, namely, to Rome. He soon wrote again to Bishop Boccali, so that he would report to the Pope, along these lines:

"We must not mistake lack of courage for prudence. There is a time to keep silent, and I kept silent for a good six years. But there is also a time to speak, and I have spoken as I felt it my duty to speak. Please assure the Holy Father, Excellency, that the effects of my having done so have been more widespread and salutary than could have been expected, both within my Diocese and beyond it. The depressing silence of the entire Hierarchy, either frightened or humiliated by the constant attacks of a press that claimed to hold it, and especially the Holy See, in profound veneration, was already viewed, by more serious and thoughtful souls, as evidence of extreme weakness and connivance with the disorders that resulted from it. It became necessary for some one to make his voice heard, and circumstances ordained that I should be that person. And here, dear Monsignor, I would point out one thing. An extremely simple and private act was distorted into a Rosminian question, and that is the secret of all the noise that was stirred up. But what could be more untrue? I do not follow the philosophical system of Rosmini; I state this frankly. I would loudly declare the opposite if it were true. My few writings and the educational measures I took in my Diocese long before the admirable Encyclical *Aeterni Patris* appeared, speak for themselves only too clearly. I declare, however, that I esteem, respect and love, in the charity of Christ Jesus, all men of good will, who work with pure intentions for the holy cause of God and his Church, whatever the opinions which they profess and which the Church allows to be discussed...On the other hand, I would ask, why should anyone wish to turn the yoke which Jesus Christ called sweet into a tyrannical burden? Why not leave minds that honest freedom that the Church accords them and has always jealously guarded? Calm, serious, dignified discussion, in complete charity whatever the clash of differing opinions, this is what we must desire. Is this not what the Supreme Pontiffs have always recommended, as well as our illustrious Holy Father in that most wise Brief to the Archbishop of Malines? Oh, how I wish that he be listened to!"[55]

The Holy See finally decided in favor of Bishop Scalabrini.[56] It was slow in doing so because in the meantime an ecclesiastical trial against Albertario was instituted in the curia of Milan and Rome did not wish even to seem to be interfering in the slightest. In addition to various private replies, which in substance recognized that the Bishop was right, the Pope intervened with a first, solemn official act, the Letter Cognita Nobis of January 25, 1882, addressed to the Archbishops and Bishops of the ecclesiastical provinces of Milan, Turin, and Vercelli. The document was an obvious defense of Bishop Scalabrini and deplored certain attitudes assumed by the press:

"It is also necessary that they (journalists) avoid anything that can reasonably offend an honest man, and that they always use moderation... But above all the Catholic press must hold as sacrosanct the name of the Bishops, who are to be respected because of the high office to which they have been raised in the hierarchy. And with respect to decisions taken by the Bishops in the proper exercise of their ministry, private individuals are not to think it is permissible to sit in judgment on them, for this undoubtedly would give rise to serious disorders and intolerable confusion."

The Holy See intervened a second time the following year with a public, though indirect, acknowledgement of Scalabrini's fidelity to pontifical directives with regard to the "philosophical question." This was the Brief in which Leo XIII expressed satisfaction with the "most opportune" initiatives taken in Piacenza — the *Divus Thomas* and *Il Catechista Cattolico* — which were most "acceptable" because they "fully correspond to the desire" of the Pope for the reestablishment of sound philosophy and Christian catechesis.[57]

Meanwhile, however, the director of the *Osservatore Cattolico* had exceeded all limits with the anonymous publication of a pamphlet attacking the Archbishops of Turin and Milan and the Bishops of Lodi, Cremona and Piacenza. Scalabrini asked:

"Must we allow ourselves to be destroyed? This matters little for ourselves, at least for my totally insignificant person. What about the souls under our care, the Church and the interest of Jesus Christ? Dear God! How far has this gone! Personally I believe we must defend ourselves against these intrigues with moderation in every pastoral act, by preserving leniency in our hearts, but being firm in what we say. We must defend ourselves publicly, too, but as far as possible without accusing anyone."[58]

On March 15, 1883, he took the decisive step and sent to the Cardinal Secretary of State a long, thoroughly documented statement in which he rebutted each one of the accusations, calumnies, and distortions. He pointed out in particular two flagrant and deliberate falsifications and all the tricks with which he knew "very well the Rev. Albertario inverted the truth, making the persecutor the persecuted, the calumniator the calumniated, the aggressor the victim," and he concluded:

"It will be claimed that I want to destroy the *Osservatore*: quite the contrary. As I already wrote last year to Bishop Paolo Ballerini, I do not make common cause with anyone, I have no hostility toward that paper and much less toward the persons who write for it. God is my witness. My sentiments are still the same as those I had occasion to express personally in 1878 in their regard to His Eminence, Cardinal Franchi of beloved memory. It is not true that at that time I 'pleaded their cause'...It is true, however, that when I was asked whether or not I thought the *Osservatore* should be suppressed, I answered...*convertatur et vivat*, hoping that it would really change...Despite all the fine promises, despite repeated protests and despite various admonitions, it went ahead if not with greater disloyalty, certainly with greater culpability...In any case, as I wrote before, I am ready to be a friend again with the journalists of the *Osservatore* if they will reread the back issues of their paper and recognize that I in no way slandered them, that I did not charge them with faults they did not commit, etc.; and if they will openly and publicly declare that they were misled by their correspondents with respect to matters in Piacenza and therefore acknowledge that my protest is justified, my stand — let them also state that it expresses my views — was not aimed either against the paper in general or against the principles it championed, but only against what was inaccurately stated therein on the basis of reports from persons they believed to be sincere and non-partisan. On this condition, and provided they return to and stay within their own field of action, I will be very happy, I repeat, to restore to them my full confidence and my friendship."[59]

When he later saw that "one of those half measures which achieve nothing"[60] was emerging and that the journalist in question had in fact reissued the libelous pamphlet and was publishing that he had nothing to retract,[61] Bishop Scalabrini sent the Cardinal Secretary of State the most indignant protest of his life:

"Now I must absolutely justify myself or be justified. To advise me to keep silent in this instance is adding insult to the injuries of that sacrilegious slanderer. It would be like saying that it does not matter at all that episcopal authority is thrown into the mud; it would be giving credence to the rumor that one is afraid of the hidden control of certain unprincipled men and that we are powerless to defeat them. A doctor of the church would cry woe to religion if bishops are forced to keep silent!...Am I in error, Your Eminence? Then tell the Holy Father to correct me and he will have, as always, a submissive and most obedient son in all things. But if, on the other hand, I am on the side of truth, justice and right, then how can a bishop, even the least and most unworthy of bishops, be permitted to be dragged publicly before the judgment of a priest, who has nothing of the priest about him but his cassock and the semblance of priesthood? To conclude: I again most fervently appeal for that favorable affirmation I believe it is my right and my duty to ask for. I request it and I expect it. Forgive me, Your Eminence if I seem importunate, but believe me it seems much more bothersome to me to be forced to bother you again. I trust that you will deign to grant my request this time so that, undisturbed by this matter, I may attend quietly and calmly to much more important things and direct all my weak energies to the salvation of the souls entrusted to me and to the defense of the sacred rights of the Holy See, which are the two subjects dearest to my heart. Have the kindness, Your Eminence, to bring this my second protest to the attention of the Holy Father..."[62]

Scalabrini's judgment on Father Albertario is a serious one. It should be noted, however, that it was not published but stated in a personal letter to a Superior and it should be viewed in the context of the virulent campaign against a man who loved truth and charity above all else and defended the rights of the Holy See and of the Hierarchy over and beyond every personal interest. The full, unconditional forgiveness he granted Father Albertario, the charity he showed him on the occasions when the "champion of Catholic journalism" had really to suffer for the cause of the Church, and by no means least Scalabrini's sincere submission to the judgment of his Superior, even when this meant heroic obedience, all these give us the true dimensions of this moment of indignation. The letter had immediate effect. The charges were, in fact, examined by a commission of six cardinals, who recognized that they were "unfortunately" well founded and decided that "Father David Albertario, editor of the paper L'Osservatore was to publish a full retraction,"[63] in a form decreed by the Holy See, thus preventing any attempt to reduce it to a simple letter of excuse.[64]

On July 25, L'Osservatore Cattolico published the following:

"Naples, June 17, 1883. Illustrious and Most Reverend Excellency, obedient in mind and heart to the injunctions of the Holy Father, I reprove and unconditionally and in most explicit manner retract the articles published in the Osservatore Cattolico which constitute an undue and subversive interference in Your Excellency's administration of your diocese. — And so for this, and for any other offense I have personally committed against Your Excellency, I humbly ask forgiveness. Kneeling to kiss the holy ring, I am, Your Excellency's devoted servant, Rev. David Albertario, Editor, Osservatore Cattolico."

Piacenza's Catholic paper published the retraction with a comment remarkable for its restraint and discretion, considering all that had happened:

"The above documents, which, as the Osservatore itself remarks, inspire admiration and edify its readers with the obedience and dutiful submission of their author, redound at the same time to the praise of our illustrious Pontiff, Leo XIII, who with strong and provident wisdom, watches over the preservation of the Catholic Hierarchy and the principle of authority. They are also of great comfort to the venerable Clergy of Piacenza, who with great devoted affection were and are honored to be united to their Bishop, in the knowledge that only through union with their Bishop can they be united with the Pope."[65]

What trace did all this storm and stress leave on Scalabrini? Only the offer of pardon and the desire for reconciliation. We have already noted how patient he was with Canon Rocca. If some persons attached any blame to him it was for having been too patient and lenient. Free as he was himself from any malice or falsehood, it was difficult for him to see them in others, and it was all the more painful for him when he had to accept them as facts. He was also tempted to be depressed,[66] but he always returned to the considerations uppermost in his mind: to strive for holiness, to prepare for death, and to be concerned with safeguarding the dignity of the episcopal office. It is true that we find very strong expressions in his confidential correspondence with Bonomelli. But this is quite understandable given the intimate friendship between the two bishops involved in the controversy, and the typical Lombard frankness that characterized both of them, their love of truth and hatred of double dealing, and their profound sense of authority, understood as service to the Church, so that for them silence was a sin.[67]

When Leo XIII put an end to the controversy between L'Osservatore

Cattolico and the bishops of Piacenza and Cremona, Scalabrini summed up his motives this way:

"If the Bishops do not stand on their own feet with all the strength of divine authority, all is lost as far as obedience and diocesan government is concerned. It is necessary to be energetic, especially with the Seminaries. I have taken very serious measures and I thank God for them...When the well-known paper has given proof of sincere amendment of its ways it will have the good wishes of all the Bishops."[68]

Apart from the reasons that forced him to defend the truth and the episcopal ministry, what were his personal feelings?

"You speak to me of a cross. Oh my God, this is our lot, and the Church makes us wear it of gold on our breast while it often turns to rough iron that tears the soul. How many times I clasp it to my heart, and raising my eyes to heaven I pray with the ardent desire to be heard: *Fac me cruce inebriari.*"[69]

Relations with the Civil Authorities

Prudence and fortitude marked Scalabrini's relations with the civil authorities also. Such relations were far from easy with representatives of a State, the position of which vis-a-vis the Pope, the direct superior of the bishops, was to be considered illegal in many respects.

Each bishop, it might be said, was caught between the civil authorities, ready to accuse him of civil disobedience and antipatriotism, and the partisans of the Church, jealous of the rights of the papacy and therefore prone to accuse of "liberalism" anyone in the least conciliatory toward the "usurper."

A passage in Scalabrini's first Pastoral produced far more repercussions than he could have imagined. In tones either of praise or recrimination, he was called a "liberal" (to be understood in the political context of the time) bishop. The passage is as follows:

"Nor will we cease to pray for our most august King Victor Emmanuel and for all those invested with power, and for the magistrates of the city and diocese of Piacenza, so that God may grant them the wisdom to assist them in their respective offices and may this wisdom aid them in achieving the true happiness of the people, to the comfort and adornment of the Catholic Church whose sons they are, and in defense of the holy religion in which may they be reborn to God and Jesus Christ."

Much later Scalabrini had to clear himself to the Holy See of a charge of Liberalism based on this very passage. He replied:

"It is my unwavering principle to feel always and in all things with the Pope. I sacrifice everything to this principle and I hope to conform to it, with divine help *Vesque ad extremum vitae spiritum.* It is true that in my first Pastoral Letter I used the phrase: *Rogate etiam pro Rege nostro Victorio Emanueli,* but I added *ut laboret ad populorum felicitati veraciter consulendum* (that the king may sincerely endeavor to provide the happiness of his subjects). I used the phrase in the sense currently given it in Lombardy without thinking of different meanings it might have in other regions. It was a pure and simple oversight and it was so considered by most people."[70]

The Bishop's sentiments were clearly evidenced in 1878 on the occasion of Victor Emmanuel II's funeral.

"The representatives of the City, who had decided on an official, solemn memorial service for the king in the cathedral, had asked Bishop Scalabrini, to grant them the use of a church and also whether or not they could count on his presence. The bishop who had received a circular letter from Cardinal Simeoni prescribing complete abstention from such ceremonies on the part of the bishops, answered in general terms. He said he would have liked to reconcile the duties of conscience with what had been asked of him but, subject to the directives of his rightful superiors. Two days later, however, a new communication from Rome granted permission for a memorial mass to be said in any church, but preferably not the cathedral. Use of the latter was to be granted only in case of formal insistence on the part of the civil authorities, but the bishop was not to participate personally in the service. Bishop Scalabrini consequently followed this directive, although, as he later had occasion to tell Volpe Landi, he was disposed to grant the use of the cathedral if it were not for the possibility of disorders. But in the absence of the acting mayor, in whom the bishop had some confidence, the mounting tension went unnoticed. Although it would have been possible to agree on a plausible reason to use a church other than the cathedral, the representatives of the city council and of the provincial delegation immediately reacted with hostility. The bishop was accused of being completely negative and this was also carried in the local Liberal paper."[71]

On the evening of the day set for the memorial service, a group of citizens went to meet Scalabrini, who was returning from a pastoral visit, "in order to persuade him not to enter the city, where a demonstration hostile to him was being organized. The Servant of God, though saddened by the news, remained calm and continued his journey, saying he had confidence in the goodness of the Piacentini."[72] "Instead he was attacked by the mob who not only hurled irreverent epithets at him but made him the target of a thick barrage of stones...His life was saved that day by the coolness and skill of his coachman...who made the horses rear up on their hind legs and so opened a way through the crowd, and the carriage was able to reach the palace and take the bishop home in safety."[73] Witnesses praise the composure and serenity with which the bishop faced the danger. Until permission came from Rome nothing could move him from his obedience to the Holy See: "Let them say and do what they will! If I do not have a directive from Rome,

I will not move; I will do nothing about it." A few days later, in a letter to the Diocese, he declared that no maneuver whatever would induce him to disobey the Roman Pontiff, and it was not right that he should be vilified for not betraying his mission, to which he would be faithful at all costs...[74] When permission was granted, he personally said the requiem Mass.

"I took part in the services," Msgr. Torta recalls, "and I remember that his first public statement (on the matter) was one of forgiveness for all those who had caused him grief in any way."[75]

"When Pius IX learned of the facts, he sent him a gold chalice as a token approval for the firmness and prudence he had shown on that occasion...It was the last and therefore the most precious gift of that holy Pontiff. It was sent in fact on the sixth of February. On the seventh, Pius IX left this life amid the universal mourning of the Catholic Church."[76]

Meanwhile, thanks to the bishop, peace had been restored. Two days after the requiem Mass for the king, the Mass for the Pope was attended officially by all the civil authorities and a great crowd of people.

Masons and anticlericals, however, kept watching for the slightest pretext to cause trouble in pursuit of their sectarian aims. Unfortunately the authorities either belonged to that faction or were influenced by it, since that was the official climate of the time.

The apostate Miraglia, for example, was supported for some time, at least indirectly and through inaction, by the authorities. Bishop Scalabrini protested to the Minister of Justice:

"How can one presume that people should remain calm and indifferent when faced with these constant, persistent and provocative acts. Prudence is all very well, and I am the first to counsel it, and heaven help me if I did not use it. But in the end prudence cannot be exercised to the detriment of justice...Temporizing in cases like these I believe is very dangerous, and may God grant that I be mistaken. Forgive me, Excellency, if I speak frankly, for in any case you will be glad of it. I close, demanding that prompt and vigorous measures be taken..."[77]

The measures were delayed, as it would seem from this strong letter the Bishop addressed to the Prefect of Piacenza:

"After the truly inexplicable behavior of Your Excellency in this ugly matter I can no longer keep silent. I have been patient until now in the hope that the wise instructions of the Government and your own repeated promises would be finally translated into action, but in vain. The evil continues...And I can assure you that many, in fact the majority are convinced that you are beginning to favor the unfortunate man who is the author of these lamentable disorders. I do not believe this at all, but I do not hide from you that I am tempted to believe it in view of certain facts...Is there or is there not a government in Italy? I have no recourse but to present again to Your Excellency this request which only a sensitive regard for Yourself keeps me from making it public. With the intention, however, of bringing my repeated protests to public notice in a forth-coming document in order to avoid any misunderstandings, relieve my conscience and also protect the public welfare, I am, etc...."[78]

A few days later the Prefect finally gave the order to close the schismatic chapel.

The Bishop took equally vigorous measures against the anticlerical administration of Bedonia, which was obstructing the local seminary in every possible way;[79] against the construction of a crematorium in the municipal cemetery;[80] against efforts to legalize divorce, against which he went to Rome to argue with certain Ministers who favored it;[81] against the Zarnadelli Law which included articles damaging to the freedom of the Church. In this latter case, he was entrusted by neighboring bishops to draft a "strong, dignified" protest.[82]

He always took action, however, with such prudence and tact that he almost always achieved his end. He was able to act as intermediary with the government, for example, to obtain the restoration of the Committees for the *Opera dei Congressi*, not only for his diocese but also for others. He always spoke with Christian candor. He did not hesitate to greet Zanardelli with "Keep in mind that we are enemies of the sects," or the mayor of Piacenza with the words "I want to see you carrying a candle in procession,"[84] even though he had shortly before refused to accept the mayor's card of good wishes because his attitude was one of opposition to the bishop.[85]

After all, he maintained that the "principle of obedience to the constituted authority we consider to be inviolable," and the authorities themselves acknowledged his loyalty and his prestige as a bishop. To cite only one of many examples, at the official banquet commemorating his episcopal jubilee, the Prefect was seated on his right and the mayor on his left — "a thing that would not have been possible a few years ago in Piacenza...Who would have thought it eight or ten years ago when there were threats to pelt the city officials with rotten apples only because they were courteous and kind, in the best interests of Piacenza, with the Ordinary of the diocese?"[87]

Gregori who quotes this comment, adds:

"There is something that is high...and conquers all partisan quarrels and political competition. It is the work of one who, forgetful of self and animated by ideals that transcend all human calculations and egoisms, goes on his way unmoved, spreading about him nothing but good,"[88] and peace. 'If you want my opinion, let us keep going. An ounce of peace is worth more than a hundred pounds of victorious issues,' Bellarmine said."[89]

The Synods

Bishop Scalabrini's administrative talents were evident also in the organization of his diocese, to which he gave an organic legislative structure. He had encountered the need for this during his first pastoral visitation, and even before finishing it he convoked the first diocesan synod in 1879. A hundred and fifty-six years had elapsed since the last one.

His first synodal constitution reaffirms the obligation to profess the faith, to manifest it externally as well, the duty to defend it from the dangers of the time — rationalism, progressivism, indifferentism, communism, nihilism and spiritism. The antidote for such errors is obedience to the Church, religious instruction, avoidance of the corrupt press, and especially preaching the Word of God and the catechism. Curious details in the constitution reflect the importance he attached to the full, constant preaching of the Word of God: the pastor was to give religious instruction if only one child showed up for it; and if no one came, he was to wait in the church, with the doors open, for at least a half hour.

Other prescriptions in the constitution recommended frequent reception of the sacraments; children were not to be confirmed before they were seven years of age; those who condemned frequent communion were deplored; Mass was to be celebrated with devotion or the sermon would do no good; the sanctity of marriage was to be assured by the free choice of the spouses and premarital education.

The second synod took place in 1893 at the end of his third pastoral visitation. The pattern is the same as that of the first, since he wished to bring the previous rulings up to date after the practical experience of fourteen years and his direct observations during the pastoral visits. This second synod, therefore, was the result of experience, was extremely practical, and was admired and imitated by many other bishops.[90]

The third synod, held in 1899, had a special character, concentrating on the Eucharist. It was a testimonial to Scalabrini's devotion to the Blessed Sacrament.[91]

Co-Workers in the Apostolate

Scalabrini always considered his priests as his natural co-workers, for they shared in his priesthood. His most thoughtful care was devoted to them from the time they entered the seminary. "It is better to have a few who are good priests than many who are not."[92]

The many letters to rectors of the seminary of Bedonia reflect his preoccupation for a careful, and even exacting selection of candidates. Sometimes an ordination was postponed for some minor inadequacy. The strictures might seem excessive to us today. He, however, deeply felt the need to form a clergy for that time that was serious and obedient enough for every trial they might meet.

"It is certain that something serious against the Church is in the making...Let us pray and let us strive for holiness; the clergy has not corresponded to God's design, they have breathed deeply of the world's atmosphere of disobedience and minimal submission, and so we must expect what we have deserved."[93]

He required written reports, at least every three months, on the progress of each seminarian, and he received one a month on the students of the Seminario Urbano. The affection with which he reviewed them is reflected in words like these: "The time I spend in spirit with my seminarians is the happiest, and you give me the same happiness, teaching them in my name to be devout and diligent."[94]

His solicitude, however, extended beyond ordination.

"He watched most carefully over his flock, and especially his Clergy. With admirable constancy he was anxious for their sanctification, using every occasion to inculcate in all the obligations of duty, he himself leading the way with his example."[95]

"In this regard, I have a personal recollection. When I was pastor in Mareto, while the new church was being built, I found myself in trouble at various times because of some disagreement with the people. I discovered from my colleague in San Bassano that he often asked about me, concerned above all for my spiritual welfare, and whether or not I was fulfilling my personal and pastoral duties...He loved his priests, but he wanted their behavior to be edifying, and he wanted to know if they went to the sacraments. One day when I was complaining that my parishioners gave me no help for the building of the church, he asked me if I had forgiven them and he insisted on an answer."[96]

"He was most attentive where his priests were concerned, and I remember his saying that when he was not sure that a priest attended to his daily spiritual duty he would observe him with greater attention, and during the pastoral visit, as soon as he had a free moment, he would invite him to say the Office with him, asking to use his breviary. He thus would note whether the breviary was well used and how far the priest had gotten in the Office of the day."[97]

His was a deep and fatherly affection for his priests, concerned for their devoutness and their zeal and especially for their unity — unity among them in a diocese troubled by various currents of thought and educational trends, unity with the Bishop. This was his "oldest and most fervent prayer." He had more than one occasion to praise their devotion:

"I am proud of my priests, my religious, of my holy communities, all of them most dear to me without distinction...This is the conviction that has comforted me so that I never lost, thank Heaven, not even for an instant, the serenity that should shine, like the smile of God, on the Bishop's face, no matter what the storms...May the Church always be proud of you, venerable priests and religious, who are and always will be, I hope, my joy and my crown!...There is no purer or holier joy than to understand each other completely, to communicate with each other...O my friends, wherever you are may you always be one in heart and soul with your Bishop...In this union lies the strength of good and therefore the guarantee of victory."[98]

His last words, as he lay dying, reveal the place his priests held in his life: "And my priests? Where are my priests? Let them enter. Do not keep them waiting."

It is no wonder, then, that he was able to achieve so much from his priests. "He could present things in such a way that one felt it necessary to agree with him. And I know this from personal experience, for he made me go where I did not want to, and yet I always ended being glad of it."[99] This talent he combined with a gift for choosing as his closest co-workers "persons outstanding for their virtue and knowledge, among whom several were elevated to the episcopal dignity,"[100] for example, Bishops Vinati of Bosa, Dallepiane of Iglesias, and Archbishops Bruni of Modena and Sidoli of Genova.

Relations with the People of the Diocese

It would have been difficult for a bishop like Scalabrini not to win the affection of his people. Even the most restive finally yielded to his disinterested zeal. He himself said:

"God governs the world and especially mankind with a Providence that is most mysterious, but always loving. Sad happenings are followed by joyful ones; joy is followed by sadness. He uses, however, both one and the other to achieve, in ways impenetrable to us, his adorable designs for the glory of His Name and the sanctification of souls. It is a web of joys and sorrows, and more of these latter, that leads us to our end. Such, for those who keep their eyes fixed on the faith, is the life of every Christian, every priest, every bishop. After the anxious worries and bitternesses of the past, here are the joys of the present hour, which you, my Brothers, in union with your faithful, have given me with so much affection."[101]

All this was symbolized in the numerous gifts he received on his jubilee as a bishop, in June, 1901, and summed up, as it were, in the chalice:

"I know that our Illustrious Prelate, in the days of sorrow — and they were not a few — used to pray during his Mass, 'O Lord, this chalice is very bitter indeed, but I drink it gladly for love of you and for the love I bear all my children.' And now all his children, with one mind and heart, were saying, 'Father, you offered to God for us the chalice of your sorrows. Now accept from us, with our gratitude, the chalice of joy and exultation'."[102]

On this occasion Leo XIII sent him an Apostolic Brief, Cardinals and Bishops throughout the world sent him messages of congratulation and affection, and the celebration was attended in person by Cardinals Ferrari of Milan and Svampa of Bologna, and the bishops of Modena, Cremona, Como, Crema, Forli, Rimini, Perma, Alessandria, Reggio Emilia, Cervia, Borgo San Donino, Pontremoli, Bobbio, Sarsina, Bertinoro, Carpi, Faenza and Tortona. Queen Margherita sent a personal representative and a gift of precious vestments. All the political and military authorities were present along with representatives of the Government. But he was moved most of all by the sincere and enthusiastic participation in the event in one way or another by his priests, his people, the workingmen, the prisoners, and the peasants who flocked in from the countryside and the mountains.

"Given the spontaneity of these tributes and felicitations, the great value and number of gifts, the participation of all the members of the diocese to make the jubilee celebration as solemn and impressive as possible, then we must say that our Bishop is truly beloved of his children."[103]

Less impressive, perhaps, but warmer and more affectionate, were the demonstrations to comfort the Bishop in the bitterest hour of his life, during the Miraglia schism. At Easter in 1896, on his way back to his residence after celebrating the pontifical Mass:

"The people pressed around him to kiss his ring, while crowds of others waited for him at the exits, along the stairs and halls. When he appeared they burst into long and loud applause and cheers, that followed him into the main hall. Another such filial demonstration, even more impressive and enthusiastic, took place after Vespers. The crowd poured out of church and into the courtyard of the bishop's residence, where they repeated the cheers and the 'vivas' with an insistence and crescendo such that the Bishop, despite his weariness, was obliged to come to the window to thank them. It was a fine thing to see that dense crowd, composed largely of high-spirited youths and distinguished citizens, with one mind and heart, waving their hats and handkerchiefs toward their Father, who, deeply touched, gave them his blessing."[104]

Two months earlier, they had given him a mitre to demonstrate that the more attempts were made to trample his authority, the more they accorded it recognition. The Bishop, still convalescing from the illness triggered by the scandal, replied:

"My children, I thank you for this new pledge of your affection. I accept it because it redounds to the glory of Christ, whose humble representative I am among you. When I was consecrated I prayed on the tomb of Peter for the grace to sacrifice myself for my people, and I feel I have fulfilled my mission. Today you have given me great comfort. Bless you, Bless you, Bless you!"

And again we read, "overcome with emotion and with tears in his eyes, he said that perhaps he had not known how to show us all the affection he had for us, but that he had loved and still loved us very much, that he would love us always in every circumstance no matter what the sacrifice; that he loved the faithful, and he also loved those who had caused and were causing him grief. When we saw how he could not continue for the fullness of his affection, we should have had hearts of stone not to be moved to our very bones."[105]

There were many other spontaneous demonstrations of affection in similar circumstances. For example, after the insults following the requiem for King Victor Emmanuel II in 1878, after his illness and the virulent attacks of the Masons in 1884, when it was rumored he would be promoted to the patriarchate of Venice, on his return from his journeys to the Americas, etc. Sincerely moved, he accepted the devotion and the praise both gratefully and without false modesty. He was generous toward those who had offended him. He himself found in these occasions only another reason for humility:

"Notwithstanding, therefore, my personal unworthiness, my nothingness, I am, beloved Brethren, the representative among you of Jesus Christ, the preeminent and legitimate continuator among you of His mission, the shepherd, the bishop of your souls. From this viewpoint, I do not wonder at these demonstrations. It would be false modesty on the part of an ambassador to refuse the honors intended for his sovereign... My years as bishop, however, which in your faith and goodness you find a cause for celebration, are for me a source of fear and trembling. Today more than ever I feel the formidable burden that weighs on my shoulders. I think of all the various, remarkable, extraordinary, special graces which, with constant cooperation on my part, would have brought me to a high degree of perfection, and I am afraid. I think of the great accounting I must render the Divine Judge...; and if the future terrifies me, the past makes me deeply humble and disturbs me: I can say with St. Augustine, *terret quod vobis Episcopus sum* (that I am your bishop makes me tremble). I am humbled and disturbed by the thought of all the good I might have done you with a more dynamic will, a more enlightened zeal, a more industrious virtue."[106]

The affection evidenced by people and clergy alike ("I would think it a small thing to give my life for him," Bishop Sidoli said) tightened the strong bonds that now united Bishop Scalabrini inseparably to the diocese of Piacenza: "Every year is another line in the chain that binds me to you, a chain forged in mutual charity, a chain which, far from eroding with time, grows ever stronger and becomes unbreakable."[107]

"In the thirty years of his episcopacy, he had an unchanging affection for his diocese, his clergy, and his people. He always spoke of them in this sense, as I had occasion, especially in Rome, to hear him, in his conversations with prelates and other personalities. He never complained of the dissents, the oppositions, the lack of understanding for his work and his initiatives. I consider this truly heroic, given the fact that time brings with it a certain weariness, and given his Lombard nature, characteristically very active and full of initiative."[108]

In 1901 the rumor spread that Bishop Scalabrini was to be named archbishop of Ravenna. To the dignitary who wrote him this, he replied:

"I really would not like to accept, and if Your Excellency can help me, if it is necessary, I shall be most grateful. To change dioceses at sixty-two years of age, with all the matters in which I am engaged, while my excellent Clergy and my dear people are preparing, with so much affection, the celebration of my jubilee, no, no, it is not possible. To live, to strive for greater holiness — and it is time! — and to die in Piacenza. This is the intention I renew every year during my Retreat. And God always hears such intentions..."[109]

He confided only in Bonomelli, whom he told he was no longer giving the matter any thought when Msgr. Piacenza received from an authoritative source in Rome the confirmation that his appointment as Cardinal Archbishop of Ravenna was certain. But then nothing came of it. "If there was such an idea, it was put aside; I shall have nothing but bother over all this, and it's just as well."[110]

Three years later the rumors were more insistent. This time they concerned the succession to Pius X in the patriarchate of Venice.

"I shall stay in Piacenza," he wrote, "I have great need to prepare myself for death. I am not at all interested in all the rest. This is also a grace of God, and may I make good use of it."[111]

To a reporter who interviewed him a few days later he repeated:

"Here I have bound my heart; here I have readied my tomb. I have never thought or desired to leave here. Here I am certainly not necessary, but perhaps I am useful."[112]

During the restoration of the cathedral, he had a niche prepared at the base of the altar of the Blessed Sacrament. During his Retreat in 1896, he wrote:

"I must promptly discard any ambitious thought of changing my state, rejoice sincerely in the advancement of others, think of winning God's favor in the post in which I must sanctify myself and die." And in 1900: "No longer be interested in these rumors concerning me. Here I must live and die. Sanctify myself as the Bishop of Piacenza. The rest does not exist for me."[113]

Finally in February 1904 he could announce the end of "this new kind of martyrdom":

"Yes, my crisis is happily ended. I have just received a letter from a Cardinal, who writes: 'Saturday I had a long conversation with the Holy

Father and we also spoke about you. His Holiness told me now and again that Your Excellency is dear to him, a very dear friend, and that he had given up the proposal of Venice because it was too painful to you and your Piacentini.' "[114]

Cardinal Agliardi had indeed mentioned the cardinalate, and Pope Pius X had promised him he would make Scalabrini a cardinal when he returned from Brazil. On his arrival home, several already congratulated him for his coming elevation, but he answered: "Even if it were true, I would not accept, because I cannot leave Piacenza."[115] God "who always hears these intentions," had indeed heard his prayer. He died as Bishop of Piacenza, which remembers him as its special bishop. Cardinal Samorè recalls that when he was a young seminarian, twenty years after Scalabrini's death, "when the priests spoke of Bishop Scalabrini they used to say 'the Bishop.' In their speech, as in their memories and their hearts, he had remained the Bishop *par excellence.*"[116]

CHAPTER VII

Social Works

"To say civilization is to say Catholicism; to say Catholicism is to say priesthood. They are synonymous. Question history and you will find a priest at the head of every social movement; you will find him at the head of all intellectual progress, all moral progress, all civil progress... As for works for the poor, the disinherited, the blind, the deaf and dumb, the workers, there are so many foundations of Christian charity, so many forms of refuge open to all sorts of poverty and misfortune, and organizations and institutions that have grown up under the aegis of religion. The priest is not only·the man of the Church, the man of God; he is also the social man *par excellence.*"[1]

There is in these lines a certain echo of romanticism, of the concept of "religion as civilizer." For Scalabrini, however, the social question, and the unique contribution which the Church brings by right to its solution, were to be viewed in the context of the coming of the kingdom of God, the salvation of souls. It might be said that he viewed social action in terms of apostolic action, without, however, any lessening of sincere and deep solicitude for man's material as well as spiritual well-being.

His first foundation was the one still known as the Istituto Scalabrini per Le Sordomute (Scalabrini Institute for the Deaf and Dumb. In his first pastoral letter he had recommended to his priests the religioius instruction of the deaf and dumb, an indication of the important place they held in his concern. In 1880 he wrote a pastoral specifically on "the instruction of the deaf and dumb," perhaps the only one of the time, in which he declared that he felt it to be, more than a duty, a need to do something for them: *"charitas Christi urget nos"* (2 Cor., 5:14).

"The deaf-mute," he said, "is deprived of that marvelous instrument through which harmonies enter the soul, the dearest expressions of family affection are heard, the noblest sentiments of faith are nourished and the doors are opened, so to speak, of one's inner shrine where conscience is sovereign. The word, this power which is co-created with thought and reveals ideal worlds, this mysterious bond which unites the intangible with the physical, intellect to intellect and heart to heart, strikes against his ear, but with no effect, like an arrow shot against stone."

In this pastoral Scalabrini announced that he had established an institute for deaf and dumb girls, and he declared it was now everyone's duty to aid it. It was the duty of the priests, who mindful of the fact that "there had not yet been established an institution for deaf-mutes without the effective cooperation of the clergy," and in obedience to the prescriptions of the first Synod, were "to become, in the phrase of Holy Scripture, the tongue for their muteness, the ear for their deafness." It was the duty of the civil authorities, who, having made education compulsory and having declared that the right to education was to be safeguarded, had the grave obligation "to provide, with all solicitude, for the education of the deaf and dumb, aiding them not with sterile compassion but with active and effective love, restoring to them the privileges of men, enabling them to take their place in society, and to be useful to religion no less than to their country." And it was the duty of the rich, who had the strictest...obligation to help the unfortunate and the needy." It was, in fact, the duty of all the faithful, in whose midst Providence had placed these disadvantaged brothers.[2]

Scalabrini was moved by a delicate human perception of the personal drama of the deaf and dumb, which he viewed within a supernatural context. For some time he had had "broad, perhaps too broad" desires to aid them.[3] His affectionate concern found expression in the Seminary of Como when he discussed with his former professor and colleague, Father Serafino Balestra, methods of educating the deaf-mutes and the two of them stimulated each other to action.[4]

Balestra, whom Scalabrini dubbed the "apostle of the word," introduced into Italy the method known as lip reading. He conducted a vigorous campaign on their behalf, which went beyond Italy, and together with the Scolopian Father Tommaso Pendola and Father Giulio Tarra of Milan he organized the first international congress on "special education" for the deaf and dumb, which was held in Milan in 1880 at about the same time that Bishop Scalabrini published the pastoral quoted above.[6]

Scalabrini had characteristically moved from theory to practical action and had become the catechist and spiritual director for the deaf-mutes in the school run by the Canossian Sisters in Como. He himself recounted his last visit with them on the eve of his departure for Piacenza, marked by deep sadness on both sides and his promise to them to promote this special education for the deaf and dumb throughout his diocese.[7]

He kept the promise. During his first pastoral visit he learned that there were about three hundred deaf-mutes in the diocese. In 1878 he had a survey made and in his first catechetical pastoral and at his first Synod, he exhorted his priests to consider the religious instruction of deaf-mutes a serious duty in conscience. In 1879 he found occasion to start the work he had dreamed of, not as large as he wished, but at "least a humble refuge...for deaf and dumb girls who, being more exposed to danger, had need of prompter assistance."[8]

A married couple, both artisans — Giuseppe Rossetti and Dorina Azzali — donated a house, which the Bishop offered first to the Sisters of Charity, and after a few months to the Sisters of St. Anne,[9] who took in the first deaf and dumb pupils. They lived together as a family and earned their living with work they did, especially for the churches. The oldest among them were able to learn little, but for the young ones it was possible to organize a complete system of education and religious instructions. Their annual presentations before the civil authorities and their benefactors never failed to move the audience to tears and admiration, and their success inspired further contributions from both public and private sources.[10]

Pope Leo XIII, when he learned of the Institute, paid the expenses for one girl.[11] The government of Canton Ticino sent a number of girls from that district to the Institute and paid their fees.[12]

The Institute was organized in three groups: the first comprised the older girls, who had more difficulty in learning, and returned to their families after a relatively short course of instruction; the second included the girls who could take the regular curriculum; and the third was composed of orphaned girls who decided to dedicate themselves to "a kind of religious life, although they were always free to leave." They lived in the Institute, forming a kind of Third Order of St. Anne,[13] and devoted themselves to adoration of the Blessed Sacrament and to their work.

The Bishop often visited the Institute and spent some time among the students, especially the little ones, "even teaching them to knit; and they had great affection for him and trust in him, and they called him their 'papa'."[14] After his death, the Superior General of the Sisters named the institution in his honor, the *Istituto Scalabrini*.

He was also concerned for the deaf-mutes among the emigrants, whom he always warmly recommended to his missionaries. During his travels in Brazil he "was sadly impressed by the lack of a school for the deaf and dumb in the capital of the important state of Sao Paolo, and he soon thought about providing one, with all the ardor that he had for every good work, and he immediately assigned one of his priests to prepare himself for this function of exquisite charity."[15] He wrote to his secretary to ask the Superior General of the Missionary Sisters of the Sacred Heart to make available for this work in Brazil two Sisters trained at the Institute in Piacenza.[16] "He was not able to see the completion of his plan, but his sons did not abandon the project, and it is now a fact, although of modest proportions."[17]

During his brief stay in Buenos Aires, "he recalled with affection the noble personality of Balestra," who had founded an institute for the deaf and dumb in Argentina and he declared that "he desired to promote the foundation of similar institutions throughout the Americas."[18]

Above all he wished to parallel the Institute for girls in Piacenza with a similar one for boys. He mentioned this in the pastoral (1880) quoted above as a "wish that we have had for some time and that we hope to be able to realize one day if Providence comes to our aid."[19]

"During the previous winter," he recounts, "a deaf-mute was found lost in the snow in the country around Carpaneto and almost dead from the cold. He was brought to the city, and after his frozen hands and feet had been cared for, the authorities did not know where to put him, and do you know where they did? In prison, where he remained for several months. A magistrate of that time read my pastoral about the deaf-mutes and immediately came to tell me about the case and to ask if I could do something about it. Yes, Sir, I answered. I shall keep him with me in my house. And I kept him in my house for some time. He did not know anything, he did not understand anything, he was already of a certain age and could not learn easily, and so he did not profit very much from the little time I could spend in instructing him."[20]

The Prefect of Piacenza wrote to the Bishop that he had informed the Minister of the Interior of his charitable act, and the Minister had replied, "It is welcome news that the Bishop of your city assumed the care and support, at his own expense, of the unknown idiot arrested in Carpaneto and I beg Your Excellency to thank that Prelate for his kind action on behalf of this Ministry, assuring him that a search will be made to find the unfortunate man's parents and home town."[21]

It is an interesting letter in that it shows the attitude of the authorities of the time toward cases of this kind. The poor deaf-mute in question died soon afterwards before the search was completed.

In 1885 the Bishop continued to cherish his project and expressed a desire to start a print-shop in order to provide work for deaf-mutes.[22] This was realized thanks to one of his priests, the Servant of God, Father Francesco Torta,[23] who wrote:

"When I told him my desire to open an institute for male deaf-mutes, he embraced me affectionately, with tears in his eyes, and, with the enthusiasm of his noble heart, he invoked the highest blessings of God on the new work, which, he said, fulfilled a desire he had nourished in vain for so long a time."[24]

The Bishop announced the new institution to the diocese and to the Prefect of Piacenza, and encouraged its founder to have full confidence in God's help:

"God will be with you; good people who will cooperate with you for the success of this work will not be wanting; and the day will come when you will also be able to provide for the blind, as you desire."[25]

"When mention was made to Bishop Scalabrini of the need to provide for the education of so many blind persons, who could be seen wandering through the city and the countryside, he would say confidently, 'The day will come for the blind, about whom I am very much concerned.' But death came for him while so many good and holy works were still expected of him, and several blind persons, for whom he provided as a loving father, were sadly left without aid."[26]

In 1910, Monsignor Torta, who felt always that the Bishop's blessing was working in his institutions, was finally able to found an Institute for the blind next to the one for the deaf-mutes.[27]

Scalabrini also took thought for the institute for those ill of scrofula (Istituto Scrofolosi) which had been founded by his chancellor, Msgr. Giuseppe Pinazzi. With his usual courage, he supported the latter, defended him from the slanders against him related to the Sacred Congregation of the Council, and during the controversy continued to help the institution secretly.[28]

On July 4, 1903, at the annual meeting of the Catholic associations, Bishop Scalabrini made a proposal supported by Bishop Pasquale Morganti of Bobbio. This was to set up a committee to study the problems of the migrant ricepickers in order to set up some permanent agency to help them. The idea was welcomed and many clerics and lay persons of the dioceses of Piacenza, Bobbio, Lodi and Pavia offered to cooperate.[29]

Men and young women migrant workers came especially from the provinces of Liguria and Emilia. Every year about 170,000 men, women and children moved to the rice fields of Piedmont and Lombardy for harvesting and transplanting the rice. They were neglected or forgotten, although they were burdened with difficulties and sufferings, which they endured only because their poverty forced them to.

"In fact, those poor unfortunates encounter many very serious dangers and evils, moral and physical dangers and evils it is easy to imagine. It is urgent to find remedies, it is urgent to take measures so that they will not fall victim to greedy speculators, so that they will be able to observe the Lord's Day, so that they will be protected from immoral designs, so that they will be better paid for their labors, in short, so that far from their families, they may find defense, protection, comfort."[30]

To gather the necessary statistics, a questionnaire — unusual for that time — was sent to all the parishes. Along with the moral-religious preoccupation it also reflected a practical and effective social interest characteristic of Scalabrini. Questions regarded the conditions of work, such as salary, hours of work, Sunday holiday, food, lodging, sanitary conditions. They asked for the names of the principal recruiters who often did not differ very much from the "traders in human flesh" who were so active in the field of emigration. Also requested were comments on negative aspects noted when the migrants returned to their own towns.

To be noted especially is the importance given to Catholic lay organizations, both in the meetings held to discuss the problem, which were attended by the most qualified representatives of the *Opera dei Congressi* and associations of Catholic workers, and in the gathering of statistics as well as in practical action. The attorney Giovanni Baroni of Lodi was elected president of the executive committee of the movement.

When the necessary data had been compiled, an inter-diocesan meeting *Pro Mondarisi* (for the rice-pickers), was held on November 16, 1903. It was chaired by Scalabrini and attended by the Bishops of Tortona, Bobbio, Modena, Guastalla, and Pontremoli, representatives of the bishops of Lodi, Pavia, Milan, Turin, Genoa, Vercelli, Vigevano, and officers of the diocesan associations of Catholic Action. The following agenda was adopted:

1. — To establish in the dioceses of Bobbio, Genoa, Lodi, Milan, Novara, Piacenza, Pavia, Tortona, Vercelli, Vigevano a foundation to be called *Opera dei Mondarisi* (Rice-Pickers Institute), with headquarters in Piacenza and affiliated to the *Opera dei Congressi* in order to organize and protect the material and moral interests of the migrant workers in the rice fields through the establishment of diocesan "labor offices" and parish or inter-parish teams to see to the placement of workers and group contracts.

2. — To name an inter-diocesan Commission composed of a representative of each of the above-mentioned dioceses, which will develop the practical means to achieve the above as soon as possible.

3. — Meanwhile, it is proposed that the following measures be taken:

a) a compilation of statistics to determine from which towns and in which areas respectively there is the greatest contingent of workers and their occupation;

b) in each parish from which migrants go to the rice fields, the Pastor is to keep in touch with competent persons who can supervise the migrants, protect their interests, inform the Pastor of their destination and indicate the persons to whom he can refer for information and clarifications;

c) before the rice-pickers leave, the Pastor is to gather them together in some special religious celebration and give them the information and advice he thinks best;

d) in the principal areas where the migrants are working it is proposed that special hostels and kitchens be built for them according to their needs and convenience."[31]

At the meeting of January 11, 1904, the Executive Committee of the *Opera dei Mondarisi*, chaired by Bishop Scalabrini, decided to sent the Ministry of Agriculture and Commerce and the Labor Office in Rome a Memorandum documenting, with specific data as to the actual facts and the laws, the miserable conditions of the migrants. It addressed to the Labor Council a number of proposals for changes in the laws, then under review, covering the work in the rice fields. The main suggestions were these: to recognize for the "associations of rice-pickers" the right to collective bargaining and to be legally represented by their president; to guarantee the minimum daily ration, to be prepared by a woman chosen by each team of rice-pickers; to oblige the employers by law to provide the necessary diet for those ill of malaria, to furnish gratis quinine, as preventive for malaria, and the necessary treatments for eczema and psoriasis; to fix the schedule for regular and over-time work; to have the weekly rest day fall on Sunday; and to make the pass book issued by the public health authorities obligatory.[32]

"The Labor Council invited the Committee to meet with the Government Commission of Inquiry dealing with the areas concerned, and welcomed the information it offered."[33]

"In establishing the *Opera dei Mondarisi*, Bishop Scalabrini sought to safeguard the material and spiritual well-being of all those unfortunate people. The problem was complex and full of difficulties. Competent men were needed, capable of carrying out, promptly and wisely, duties of an economic as well as moral nature. It was necessary besides to ask the government to intervene with compulsory measures when the warnings and solicitude of the *Opera* were unable to prevent brutal exploitation on the part of the employers. Bishop Scalabrini entrusted this mission to Toniolo, and with tenacity and discernment he set about to eliminate the multiple difficulties in the way. With his numerous contacts, the prestige of his vast and deep scholarship, he interested those among his friends and admirers who could, through their social or civic position, support the institution vis-a-vis the Government. Thus began the deserving *Opera dei Mondarisi*, which has done so much good in the fifty years of its existence."[34]

CHAPTER VIII

The Labor Problem

Scalabrini's Social Thought

In a tribute to Scalabrini after his death, Bishop Bonomelli said he always felt small in relation to his friend:

"Providence placed me in contact with many men in high position in the Church of God because of their office, their learning and experience, their knowledge of society. I can affirm in all sincerity, however, that I never met anyone, or very few, who knew as he did our true social and religious conditions and the real needs of our time. He would have gathered all into his great heart, provided for all, sacrificed himself for all, forgetting himself completely."[1]

Bonomelli, who was bishop of Cremona, had himself a keen perception of the times and so the tribute has a special significance. It suggests, too, the four pillars, so to speak, of Scalabrini's apostolate: wisdom, an energetic will, charity, learning.[2]

We have already noted the interest Scalabrini took in the working man while he was a pastor in Como.[3] Before discussing his principal work, aid to emigrants, we may note his thinking and action in the social field in general and the labor sector in particular.

"The social question, essentially an economic one, becomes in its immediate consequences a question of political and religious morality." The same must be said of socialism, which is per se an economic question but in order to be realized, "must wound humanity in its most intimate and essential constituents...,religion, the family, the individual freedom."[4]

Such a system therefore compromises essential elements of the faith and Christian morality. The Church, then has the right and duty to become involved in the social question and at the same time, recalling men to the observance of the Gospel precepts, she performs a work of social defense.[5]

The intervention of the Church against socialism is legitimate, necessary and efficacious, for socialism claims to resolve the social question by overthrowing the foundations of society itself through violent revolution and by destroying the Gospel and religion. The Church must intervene against the irrational fear of those who would suppress socialism by force, and against the blameworthy inertia of those who view it fatalistically as a phenomenon that must be left to run its course.[6]

The Church's intervention in defense of the rights of the workers is legitimate and necessary and already "enjoined in strong words and thought"[7] by the Scriptures and Tradition. The Church supports many of the demands put forth by socialism: limitation of the hours of work and wages fixed by law, the right to work, the right to strike, the institution of arbitration procedures, pensions for those incapacitated, protection for women and children, healthy working conditions: these are sacrosanct rights of the workers. At the same time he warns "the ingenuous against the facile seductions of too easy promises" and restrains the impatient who want the instant achievement of all rights at the risk of endangering the very interests of the workers themselves.[8]

The intervention of the Church is urgently necessary. "Socialism, which is trembling with impatience to fall upon its prey...is the voice of Heaven warning us that the hour for action has struck."[9] — "Shall we then wait until this activity, aimed at wooing the masses from virtue and religion, is successful and spread throughout the countryside? It is time, it is time to rouse ourselves."[10]

Ours is the time for deeds not words. "We must act and give encouragement and help to those who act...A cerebral speculative Catholicism, a neutrality on the part of religion while the most vital questions are being hotly debated by society, is an absurdity if not a kind of betrayal. Between hiding one's faith and losing it there is only one step."[11]

Action taken by Catholics is to be primarily religious, then economic, but without any political aims. "It is not our purpose to engage in politics, as our adversaries would have people think. We wish above all to work for a moral rehabilitation, and to provide for the economic needs and legitimate aspirations of the working class especially. The exploiters of the poor have made magnificent promises up 'til now, but they have kept none of their promises. They have promised bread and justice, and today the people lack justice and bread. Now it is our wish to organize, precisely for these people, helpful institutions, to expand mutual aid, favor the development of industry and commerce, and develop the charitable works that are most suited to our time."[12]

It is a broad view of social action that begins with a fundamental and indispensable religious recovery in order to heal the economic and social order. It is Christian social action. Scalabrini would have called it Christian socialism if he did not sense contradiction between Christianity and "socialism" in the historical meaning of the word: "demagogic socialism will not be defeated...except by another socialism..., a Christian sociology that can cure society of its present malady."[13]

To rechristianize the workers is to rechristianize the world and save society.[14]

Scalabrini's perspective ranged far beyond the limits to which Catholic social action was reduced both by Marxist historiography which viewed it merely as competition with the bourgeois State for economic ends only, and Liberal historiography, which attempts to explain it as political action taken in opposition to the Liberal State.[15]

Bishop Scalabrini follows, in fact, the teaching of *Rerum Novarum*. Charity predominates among the remedies proposed against socialism, against individualism, "the only goal of an atheistic and materialist society,"[16] and against capitalism, "the well-fed idleness of the few and the penury of the workers."[17] The principal antidote to social evils lies in religious renewal, both as Christian charity and as social justice based on the equality and brotherhood of men before their common Father and geared to eschatological justice.[18] There is also in his thinking a concern to forestall socialism by preempting Marxism of its just demands,[19] and a desire for the clergy to act as "substitutes," so needed, at the time, for the legal protection of workers' rights that was lacking then. There is too the apostolic *motif*. He views socialism as the enemy of religion: the enemy not of the priests, but of souls.

Scalabrini does not neglect economic remedies. He wants a greater share in the profits for the workers, the right to work guaranteed by law, healthy working conditions made compulsory, life insurance and health and accident insurance, compensation for those incapacitated, and old age pensions.[20] He asks that the worker be given time to get more education or training, that an age limit be set and the number of working hours reduced, and that a minimum wage be fixed by law. The last two measures he thought should be brought about gradually so that neither industry nor the workers dependent upon it would lose out to competition.[21]

For Scalabrini, violent revolution is contrary to the Gospel[22] but he considers resistance licit "when the exercise of our rights is impeded or lessened and the law gives us no means of defense."[23] The right to strike is one of the postulates which in theory "are good and do not conflict with either divine or human laws."[24] It is a "corrollary of freedom," but it becomes a "crime when the strike is imposed with violence, limiting the freedom of others."[25]

Among the social remedies he suggested were trade and craft unions,[26] mutual aid and "provident" societies, producers and consumers cooperatives, insurance, rural credit unions and Catholic banks.[27] There is mention, too, of scientific progress, limited however to agriculture, such as the use of the newly discovered chemicals and agricultural training for both people and clergy.[28]

Action by the Clergy

Scalabrini's first appeal is addressed to the clergy. They are to be prudent, serene, calm in judgment, with a balanced knowledge and awareness of what they must oppose and what they must concede. Priests are to renew their studies so that they will be able to refute — by speaking the same language — the sophisms with which lecturers, books and newspapers of socialist propaganda are saturating the minds of the workers and peasants.[29]

But the priests are to act as well; they are to promote mutual aid organizations, cooperatives, insurance societies, Catholic banks and rural credit unions created to combat usurious interest rates. They are to persuade landowners to improve the contracts for their tenant farmers and to eliminate "the customs and burdens of other times."[30]

"During these last twenty years I have seen many parish properties in my diocese, formerly uncultivated, transformed into vineyards and fertile fields through the praiseworthy initiative of the pastors, and following their example whole tracts of land recovered and made productive by more intense and more rational cultivation. I should like to see this work, done by a few, become everyone's work in the future. To this end I have instituted courses in agriculture in my Seminaries so that the young clergy will have the necessary knowledge to give the people entrusted to their care bread for their bodies as well as their souls."[31]

We must not be afraid of progress; rather we must greet it with joy, because it can only resound to the glory of God.[32] Neither must we be disinterested, afraid of struggle, detached or inactive. "Let us not delude ourselves. If we do not act others will act without us and against us. Let them accuse us of ulterior motives and worldly aims. The charge was made long before us against Jesus Christ, who, although he taught them to render to Caesar the things of Caesar, was accused of seducing the people. To do one's duty and remain at peace with everyone is impossible..."[33]

"What we men of the Church are asking is that the Gospel be invoked to guide these economic and industrial changes, that the sincere practice of its law may purify and ennoble material progress, so that it will not arouse brutal instincts in the various classes and thus become the cause of fratricidal discord and conflict. I would like all the members of my clergy to understand this. In our day it is almost impossible to lead the working class back to the Church unless we are in constant contact with it outside the Church. We must go out of the temple...if we wish to exert a salutary influence in the temple...And we must be men of our time. Certain forms of new, or new-old propaganda must not frighten us. We must live the life of the people...Let us fight prejudices with lively zeal, but let us just as warmly support and second the legitimate interests and aspirations (of the people), being careful, however, not to feed them with illusions nor to excite them to contempt for themselves or their employers. After the example of the Catholics of other countries, let us master the modern movement and lead it, working instead of standing aside and grumbling. My dear friends, the world is moving forward and we must not stay behind because of some formalistic difficulty or the dictates of a mistaken prudence."[34]

These lines would hardly set Scalabrini among the churchmen who wanted to restrain Christian social action. He did not rest on positions of defense or fear, but fought the conservatism of one current[35] and the formalism and simplism of its opposite. He marked out a practical road to follow, convinced that the Liberal State could not solve the problem of the proletariat; in fact it was wasting time fighting the Catholics as "enemies of the fatherland" while the Church had the authority and capacity to make an effective contribution. Even before the publication of *Rerum Novarum*, he declared:

"After the bad government they have given our poor country, usurping the privilege of being its great lovers, it takes a big dose of insolence to call us our country's enemies when we have fought against all the exactions, abuses, injustices, plundering and crimes which have reduced it to the present state of misery...We feel all the more worthy of the name of good Italians the less we have had to do with the actions of those who have betrayed and ruined Italy."[36]

The Bishop of Piacenza was certainly not an "ally of the enemy" but neither was he alienated. The evidence of his whole life confirms the following statement:

"The love of religion and the love of country are most holy loves...But the generous impulses of the one must not suffocate the sublime aspirations of the other. Justice cannot be extinguished by patriotism. The fortunes of a country we must one day leave cannot prevail over the immortal destiny that awaits us, nor can this destiny be pursued without the necessary means that society has to provide through observing the laws God has given men for their present and future well-being."[37]

It is a genuinely Christian view, and for that time an exceptionally clear view, of the relations between Church and State, between Religion and Fatherland, between our eternal destiny and temporal action, between the religious and the social order, distinct but united, with rights that must neither be confused nor hindered, because all becomes one in the name of Christ.[38]

The Duties of the Laity

For Bishop Scalabrini the cooperation of the laity was both necessary and effective:

"If the time when our misled society will return to the straight way seems far off, you alone, my good lay people, whom social apostasy disgusts and horrifies,...you can hasten the longed-for hour and dispose the minds of your brothers to reform" through the witness of your lives, your words and your actions — "by professing your faith before all, proud of your Christian character, by redoubling your activity and counting it an honor to be able to serve the Lord, to be able to glorify him in the various encounters of your life. You can accomplish much because, as a famous journalist said, 'you are not old age moving to the sunset but youth at the dawning'. It is up to you to take hold of society, to remake it Christian, working with broad vision and firm purpose so that the Catholic spirit will permeate everywhere and infuse everything that is a part and an element of the intellectual, moral, and often even the physical life of the world."[39]

It is an invitation to the *consecratio mundi*, in which lay persons in many cases can do more and better than the priests:

"How many teachings which through lamentable prejudice become suspect when spoken by the clergy make a profound impression when spoken by lay persons! How many doors which stay closed in the face of the minister of God are thrown open before the man of the world!...How many opportunities you have to approach the faithful, to undeceive them, to speak worthily of Christ and his Church in your daily relationships, opportunities which the priest does not have or finds very rarely! What an apostolate in society could be yours, beloved friends, and what a fruitful one!"[40]

"The secular church of Satan must be opposed not only by the forces of the priesthood but also of the laity in the Church of Christ. It is to these two forces united together that God in all ages has reserved the victory...The Church in its full meaning, the Church as the Mystical Body of Christ, is not composed of 'priests alone...but of the Pastors together with the faithful." By the very fact that every Christian through baptism has been incorporated in the Church, "it is clear that every Christian, whether priest or layman, in his own circumstnces and according to his own abilities, must contribute to the safety and well-being of the Catholic Church."[41]

For Scalabrini the apostolate is the direct consequence of baptism, and in fact he does not hesitate to speak of the priesthood of the laity:

"All of you as Christians have a kind of apostolate."[42] — "If that spirit truly lives within you, my dear friends, it cannot help giving signs of life, moving into action. From your soul it must pass to other souls, to your family, relatives, friends, students, fellow citizens, to the whole great and small world that surrounds you. This priesthood, this lay apostolate was always a duty and a glory; today, it is an absolute, supreme and urgent necessity."[43]

The Catholic laity must act where the priests are unable to act or are prevented from doing so;[44] they must move beyond useless complaints and prepare a better future, because "the realities of one epoch ordinarily have their roots in the one which preceded it...actions follow ideas.[45]

The field for Catholic lay action is very broad:

"To promote, aid, and diffuse good publications; to unite in Catholic Committees and Societies and to organize them where necessary; to press insistently for religious instruction in the schools and for Sunday rest; to join, as far as it is licit to do so, in public affairs through participation in elections to public office;...to put out of office, when the occasion arises, the domineering and the cowardly types in the town governments who dare at times to offend the most delicate feelings of the people, allowing their faith to be outraged, their most sacred rights and dearest traditions trampled upon; to gather the young in Sunday youth centers and Christian schools, protecting them from the corrupting influences in secular society; to come to the aid of the august poverty of our Common Father with the offering of filial love; to provide new priests for the Church by offerings to benefit needy seminarians; with credit agencies to root out usury and help the working class especially in their needs; through legal means to seek the true, real freedom and independence of our Holy Father, calmly, prudently, but firmly and bravely, without hesitation..."[46]

He made a special effort to arouse people to energetic action in a milieu little given, traditionally, to enthusiasm or initiative:

"Energy...that is what most people lack today..., energy which is strength of soul and will..., which is the virtue that conquers...Energy above all in our convictions...Be energetic in your struggle against passions. Even these can be effective instruments for good if we know how to restrain and direct them through our energy of will...Be energetic in the apostolate, for every Christian must in fact be an apostle..."[47]

Energy, however, must not work to the detriment of order and charity:

"Let us work with purity of intention, sacrificing all our personal feelings to the triumph of the great cause; let us work with firmness but with charity; let us above all be disciplined and united, in our work."[48]

To this end it is necessary to organize:

"Association is an eminently Christian idea. It has its origins in the heart of Him who said: *You are all brothers; where two or three are gathered in my name, there am I also in their midst.* Association is collective life...It has a hidden power that cannot be measured solely by numbers but must be judged above all by the dynamic and reciprocal influence of the members thus placed in contact with one another."[49]

Scalabrini, having instilled new life into the clergy at the first Synod, moved immediately to organize the Catholic laity, convinced of the undeferrable necessity of lay cooperation with the hierarchy:

"It is time, it is time to rouse ourselves...In every country of the world, the sons of labor comprise the great majority of the population. To inspire in the workers the essentially peaceful and salutary spirit of Christianity is to save society...Catholic association and action: these are the characteristics of the true sons of the Church in our day; association and action which must have as their aim to support in all things the wishes of the Vicar of Jesus Christ, to restore to the Church and its Head the necessary freedom, and to restore greatness, peace and prosperity to Italy by making families Christian again, communities Christian, schools Christian, laws Christian, the people Christian, and above all the workers Christian."[50]

Undertakings on Behalf of the Workers

Bishop Scalabrini showed great interest in the *Società Operaie*, or workingmen's societies, and favored their establishment in every parish or at least in the principal cities of each vicariate.[51] He attached particular importance to all organized forms of Christian social action and insisted that their freedom be respected:[52]

"Every care must be devoted to the societies, varied in form and in purpose, which are flourishing among us, so that the spirit of association may increase and strengthen the bonds of brotherhood, so that it may provide what the weakness of the individual cannot and remedy the unexpected blows of misfortune. A brother helped by a brother is like a fortified city."

He urged his clergy, therefore, not to oppose but to promote the "new spirit of association which is spreading and penetrating everywhere," to support and champion "all the provident and mutual aid societies...two modern ways of doing good to one's neighbor, which combine the advantages of charity and education. Those who are benefited share in the process and acquire the habit of thinking of the future and being both provident and foresighted." Here he quoted the following from Ketteler: "In the past the rich endowed the Church with convents and public charitable institutions; today, they could do something more pleasing to God by taking the lead in organizations of workers, producers, consumers, cooperatives, in order to improve the conditions of the workers."[53]

In 1893, Father Luigi Cerutti, who had founded the Catholic rural banks, suggested to Scalabrini that there be a campaign throughout the diocese for "rural savings and loan banks."[54] The Bishop gladly supported their establishment in various parishes[55] just as he supported the educational programs carried out by the *Cattedra Agraria* and the *Consorzio Agrario* of Piacenza.[56] He promoted cultural events and lectures, inviting to participate the most outstanding exponents of Catholic Action: Toniolo, Paganuzzi, Tovini, Rezzara, Crispolti, Meda, Mauri, Longinotti, DeMoiana, Arcari, Cavazzoni. Among the ecclesiastics who took part we may note, besides Father Cerutti, Msgr. (later bishop) Giacomo Radini Tedeschi and Father Davide Albertario.[57]

Among the various initiatives promoted by Bishop Scalabrini, mention must be made of the *Circolo Operaio S. Antonino*, which flourished for a long time;[58] the Committee for the defense of the *Opere Pie* (Works of Religion), chaired by Count Carlo Radini Tedeschi, which later became the *Comitato Centrale per l'Alta Italia* (Central Committee for Northern Italy);[59] the Banca S. Antonino, established primarily to support Catholic works;[60] the *Oratorio S. Giovanni* (Oratory of St. John), which besides providing a number of vocations to the priesthood, trained many lay persons[61] and confirmed the confidence the Bishop had in young people[62] and in the lay apostolate; the dairy cooperatives; a communal oven "which fixed the price list and at the same time ensured the quality of bread"; a kind of trade union of dressmakers and salespeople, which succeeded in having the shops and dressmaking establishments closed on Sundays and holidays.[63]

During the last years of his episcopate, Socialist pressures became ever more threatening. In the meeting of the deans he reiterated the immediate need for action by Catholics and deplored the lack of a Catholic paper that could defend Christian principles against subversive currents. He then invited Giovanni Ghisola, director of the Central Labor Office, to come to speak; the latter had already agreed to visit the diocesan associations. Ghisola proposed guidelines for organizing autonomous unions of peasants and landowners who would meet in mixed arbitration committees, charged with fixing rates stipulating agreements and farm contracts, and settling disputes between capital and labor. With his personal contribution, the Bishop started the subscription opened by the Diocesan Committee to establish an office for the protection of labor in Piacenza. Ghisola also suggested the publication of the weekly newspaper dealing with social questions, *Il Lavoro*, a suggestion which was immediately adopted and executed.[64]

In 1901 a *Circolo Scalabrini* for social studies was founded in Piacenza in commemoration of the bishop's episcopal jubilee. Its purpose was to instruct the workers in Christian sociology "by supporting and anticipating action by workers and farmers in defense of their rights against capital,...by promoting associations of an economic and above all a professional nature, and most especially, by educating the workers through conferences held in various parts of the Diocese."[65]

The *Circolo Scalabrini* was affiliated to the *Opera dei Congressi*, to which belonged, according to the 1897 statistics, six youth organizations with 460 members, eight rural banks and eleven *Società Operaie*.[66]

Finally, we must note the action taken by the Bishop of Piacenza during the conflicts and disorders of 1898. He succeeded in settling the strike at the button factory, amid the plaudits and blessings of the citizenry.[67] When riots broke out in Piacenza on May 1st, as in many other cities of Italy, in which one person was killed and several were wounded, He went to the spiritual and material aid of the victims and their families, worked on the authorities to take measures to calm the people and addressed to the faithful a letter overflowing with grief and love:

"I have wept and prayed for all in these days: I wish I had been able to come to each of you, to help you in your needs, to comfort you with the word of hope and faith, and to restore to your spirits the calm which your sufferings and the excitements of the moment have made you lose! The difficult economic situation, the rise in food prices, the lack of work have taken from you the serenity which has always been the boast of our city: and in those evils you have an excuse."

He announced the measures already taken and those promised by the authorities, and urged them in the name of God not to aggravate the situation by a resistance which would produce the most painful consequences for the workers themselves. He appealed to them to restore harmony "which is the means to remedy a state of affairs that all of us concur in deploring."[68]

At those times "it seemed the workers were his favored sons: they always had access to him personally...and to his purse."[69] When as a consequence of the riots the State suppressed the revolutionary movements and took occasion to suppress the Catholic movement also, Scalabrini protested:

"The Liberal conservatives live on prejudices and fears and do not realize that by obstructing Catholic organization...they not only flagrantly belie their own liberal program but hurt the most powerful and legitimate of the remedies for the (social) order."[70]

Statements like these, however, were not to be interpreted as supporting the idea that Catholic action was reactionary:

"The civil authorities are wrong if they continue to think that the clergy are cherishing regressive ideas and are not aware of the ineluctable and destined forward movement of society — preordained by Christian principles to limitless perfectibility — toward higher forms of civic community." Much less should Catholic activity be considered subversive: "Italian society is sick, there is no doubt, and its collective functioning does not always correspond to principles of good and right. Nevertheless I again assert that the clergy cannot be an instrument of subversion. This is a sectarian slander..."[71]

Bishop Scalabrini's balance and realism were not belied. He saw evil where it was and how far it reached, but he never assumed the partisan posture of those who saw only disorder, illegality, the kingdom of Satan in the legal system then in force in Italy:

"Fanaticism, besides offending reason and intelligence, is often suspect. It seems to hide some ulterior motive less worthy than the glory of the Church."

His attitude remained eminently pastoral:

"I avoid political gossip. I should like to ignore it if that were possible and my ministry permitted me to. Quite different problems claim the whole-souled attention of the Pastor...Note that I do not use the word socialism in the pejorative sense that you might think. I am speaking of the socialist *fever*, namely, the phenomenon which is profoundly anti-Christian because it is purely materialistic and destructive, and not of the critical, rational and just postulates which political socialism uses as a front. More than anyone else we priests have the duty to face the causes that determine collectivist proselytism: painful and formidable causes of human discontent for which too many injustices are a constant tinder box. And when leaders fail to carry out the remedial works of faith and Christian duty, they become powerful accomplices in the injustices."[72]

Bishop Scalabrini and the Opera dei Congressi

At this point it is natural to ask what Scalabrini's relations were with the *Opera dei Congressi*, which was at that time the strongest organizing force for Italian Catholics in a field that was at once religious, social and political.

He inaugurated the Diocesan Committee of the *Opera* in April 1881.[73]

"In the great hall of the Episcopal palace...were gathered priests and nobles, townsmen, workers...His Excellency the Most Reverend Bishop invited to the dais the Marchese Giambattista Volpe-Landi, the president, the Rev. Pietro Giacoboni, the ecclesiastical moderator, and the other distinguished members of the Diocesan Committee. He then addressed to the crowded audience a magnificent and eloquent disocurse on the opportunity and importance of lay action in cooperation with the Clergy, and he sketched briefly the way, throughout the centuries of Christianity, this work produced the happiest results for religious and civic well-being."[74]

The Marchese Volpe-Landi was soon succeeded in the presidency of the Diocesan Committee by Count Carlo Radini Tedeschi, father of Bishop Giacomo Maria Radini Tedeschi.[75] But in the Catholic movement Volpe-

Landi was closer to Scalabrini; he may be considered a founder of the *Opera dei Congressi* and from 1873 on he was one of the first promoters of the "Workers' Circles" which he conceived as having an economic, moral and religious goal on behalf of the poorest classes and which were coordinated by a committee under the Ordinary of the diocese.[76]

Every year the Bishop met with the representatives of all the Catholic organizations in the diocese to coordinate their activities and to urge them to concrete and effective action.

At the meeting held on April 11, 1886, he again declared the absolute necessity for Catholics to organize and to act subject to the hierarchy, urging the observance in practice of the papal directives, of which the Bishop is the legitimate interpreter. In reply, Attorney Casoni reaffirmed the complete dependence of the Committee on the authority of the Bishop and Count Carlo Radini Tedeschi concluded with the words: "For the Pope and with the Pope through the closest union with one's Bishop."[77]

In the accounts of other diocesan committees it is not easy to find so explicit an affirmation. Bishop Scalabrini was inflexible on these points: obedience to the Bishop, the legitimate and natural mediator between the Pope and the faithful, and cooperation between clergy and laity. These were the principles on which he required Catholic action to be based. He returned many times to this theme, which was quite controversial in the historical context of his time as he did for example, in his address to the second regional meeting of the Catholics of Emilia, in 1899, organized in Piacenza by the *Opera dei Congressi* and attended by G. B. Paganuzzi, president of the Permanent Committee.

"Bishop Scalabrini observed that the greatest difficulties in the development of this action lay with the clergy, which in general is not aware of the usefulness of our Committees. Hence the necessity to make Pastors and Clergy understand that our Committees have no intention of imposing themselves on them to interfere with or hinder their work, but have a practical aim and activity. It is necessary, the Bishop said, to do away with the dislike that exists for our Committees."[78]

In reply, Paganuzzi explained, a little laboriously perhaps, the relationship between the various Catholic organizations and the diocesan committees, claiming for the latter a certain autonomy "coordinated with absolute obedience to the Bishops and the Pope."[79] There followed addresses by the Bishops of Modena, Perma, Borgo San Donnino, by Attorney Casoli and Father Albertario. Bishop Scalabrini gave the closing address: "he stressed the necessity of organization and action to defend the freedom of the Church, the Pope and the Christian conscience. He added that we must be united and steadfast, that we must proceed with charity, which should characterize all our actions, and that, where truth is concerned, we must be not only intransigent, but most intransigent."[80]

He had "always gone along with the forms that Catholic Action was gradually assuming although he was not always completely satisfied with them."[81] He kept hammering on the idea that it should be much more subject to the hierarchy like all the other types of pastoral organization. It should be subject to the Holy See, yes, but through the bishops:

"As early as 1886, in a letter to Cardinal Jacobini about the Permanent Committee of the Opera dei Congressi, which had issued guidelines to be followed in the elections, he stated bluntly that this made the bishops, in their direction of the consciences of the people subject to a handful of laymen, and although he recognized their respectability he found the situation *more than unseemly and not even in conformity with the divinely instituted order of the ecclesiastical hierarchy.*"[82]

Bishop Scalabrini was in fact following the directives of Leo XIII, who was trying to strengthen the spiritual authority that had been shaken by the events of the period. The Pope wished the "associate apostolate" to be under the direction of the hierarchy:

"Christians must consider it a duty to be directed, governed and guided by the authority of the bishops and that of the Apostolic See."

They should also remain above political partisanship.

"To involve the Church in political questions and presume to use her support in order to win more easily over one's opponents is an imprudent abuse of religion."[83]

And again in 1895 the Pope warned:

"The bishops and all the clergy have the principal task, the laity a secondary one. The latter in fact can aid the apostolic efforts of the clergy."[84]

Pius X held the same view and in 1904 placed the diocesan and parish committees of the Opera dei Congressi directly under the supervision of the bishops. On that occasion Scalabrini was heard to observe: "It seems the era of bishops in top hats is over."

Encouragement of Catholic Committees

In 1896, Scalabrini issued a pastoral letter on Catholic Action in which he emphasized the religious commitment to restore the balance of the human edifice, "placing as its foundation Jesus Christ." The purpose of Catholic Action is "to promote, through an organization relevant to the needs of the times, this movement, which is affecting the consciences of all honest people, to bring Jesus Christ back into the school, into our customs, into the family, into society." Given the manifest urgency of Catholic Action, he does not exhort but commands his "co-workers in the salvation of souls" to set up a committee immediately in every parish and to make it efficient.

"We must be quite convinced that what was enough at one time is not at all enough today. For new times, new industries; for new wounds, new remedies; for new methods of warfare, new systems of defense. Today, as I have said to you before, it is truly necessary for the priest, and especially the pastor, to go out of the temple if he wishes to have a salutary influence on the times."[85]

At the interdiocesan meeting in Bedonia, July 1896, Scalabrini blessed the banner of the "Workers' Society" of that city, numbering 800 members, in the presence of the representatives of the Catholic movements of Piacenza, Parma and Borgo San Donnino. Paganuzzi was represented by Father Luigi Cerutti, and Father Albertario was also a participant. On that occasion, Scalabrini declared: "If it is not possible to establish a parish committee, even with only a few persons, at least three, then such a parish would deserve to be suppressed."[86]

Such a statement proves that the extraordinary growth of the Catholic movement in the diocese of Piacenza was due principally to the constant pressure the Bishop put on his pastors. He was even heard to exclaim: "I don't know how a pastor can say Mass if he does not have his parish Committee."[87]

In 1883 at the Sixth Catholic Congress, the Committee of Piacenza was judged the most active. From 1892 onwards, as the Bishop had predicted, the renewal was slow but steady. Piacenza's activity, like that of Modena and Reggio Emilia began to gather momentum.[88] According to the report presented to the Milan Congress in 1897, Piacenza was in second place, with 227 parish committees comprising 6,164 members in 365 parishes. Only Milan was ahead with 260 parish committees numbering 5,319 members in 776 parishes. The statistics are eloquent, especially in comparison with those of the other dioceses.[89]

Bishop Scalabrini, however, did not attach great importance to the number of members. At that very time he was writing to a pastor:

"Have you notified Count Tedeschi, President of the Diocesan Committee, that your Parish Committee has been established? If anyone wishes to withdraw, let him; it is not necessary to have many members; it is better to have few who are good ones, true Catholics."[90]

He always tried to be present at the inauguration of Catholic organizations, to inspire enthusiasm and courage:

"A limp, homely, or negative good which is fond of impossible reconciliations is no longer enough for our day when our enemies sweep into the piazza to abduct all, and...feel stronger by our debility."[91]

His call to battle was constant but it accorded with St. Augustine's motto, *Diligite homines, interficite errores,* and the weapons he recommended were prayer, action, sacrifice, courage.[92] At the same time, he stressed another virtue indispensable to the effectiveness of Catholic Action, namely, harmony guaranteed through union with the Bishop:

"Catholics must above all seek agreement and unity in action. And both these conditions will be achieved if each one holds as law the directives of the Apostolic See and is obedient to the Bishops whom the Holy Spirit chose to govern the Church of God...In the struggle we are now fighting for things of the highest importance, it is absolutely necessary to quell all internal discord and partisan competition. Everyone must, with the same purpose and spirit, direct his efforts to the common goal, which is to save the things of great religious and social concern."[93]

This advice, quoted from the Encyclical *Immortale Dei* and addressed to journalists, recalls Scalabrini's views on the need for a Catholic press:

"He who was himself esteemed as a writer...and who so often felt the uproar in the Masonic and anticlerical press directed against him, was a convinced apostle of the press at the service of an idea, and in particular of the Catholic paper. The Catholic paper in the Piacenza diocese at that time was *L'Amico del Popolo* (Friend of the People), and it is easy to imagine with what malice and with how many pretexts attempts were made to silence its voice, which irritatingly unmasked errors, proclaimed aloud the rights of freedom and duties toward the authority and refused to bend with partisan winds...It was the Bishop who courageously defended the paper, and in 1897 at personal sacrifice made it a daily instead of a biweekly."[94]

The year before he had founded a weekly called *La Voce Cattolica* (The Catholic Voice) to counter the errors and calumnies spread by the review, *Gerolamo Savonarola,* published by Miraglia. A few years earlier he had condemned a paper called *Il Penitente* (The Penitent), which carried gross atheistic propaganda.[95] The following excerpt from the letter of condemnation is noteworthy for its advice to the Catholic press.

"I warmly recommend to you the support and diffusion of a good press, there being today no more opportune method to stem the tide of errors which are being spread everywhere by a lawless and shameless press. In this connection the Holy Father teaches all of us to be serious and temperate in what we say, to reprove errors and defects but without bitterness and with respect for the persons concerned. Great and very wise counsel...How many evils would Christians avoid if everyone followed this advice! How much more good would be done for God's cause! Sarcasm, insults, scorn, these are not the weapons needed by him who is strong in the truth; let us leave them to its enemies and let us always be guided, dearly beloved, by the dictates of that evangelical charity which, motivated only by divine love and the welfare of others, always gentle and temperate, always generous and helpful to everyone, works to win everyone to Jesus Christ."[96]

L'Amico del Popolo abided by these directives. But in 1898, along with the Catholic organizations, it was caught up in the storm brewed throughout Italy by Liberal and Masonic intrigue. Bishop Scalabrini decided to suspend the publication of the paper temporarily and thus succeeded in having the investigation of the Catholic organizations conducted with some moderation. He was also able, as a result of the esteem in which he was held in high places, to obtain from the Premier permission to reestablish the Committees in Piacenza[97] and to support the reconstruction being carried out by Paganuzzi and Rezzara, who at that time "did not take a step without first asking his opinion."[98]

When, in fact, they noticed that the Bishop of Piacenza could get such good results, "Bishops and Diocesan Committees constantly appealed to him to support their requests, a thing he did very gladly...But what he wanted was for the Government to eradicate all the repressions emanating from the provincial authorities." He worked hard at this, keeping in contact with President Pelloux, and the Minister of Internal Affairs Di Rudini until, with the amnesty of 1899, the skies cleared again over Catholic Action and he could devote his energies "to making it flourish in his Diocese, recalling to action the associations that had been disbanded."[99]

The facts and figures are eloquent, and so it is difficult to explain the puzzlement or reticence of certain witnesses in the Diocesan Process and of those historians of the Catholic movement who picture Scalabrini as being somewhat cold or quietly skeptical about the lay organizations. When he said, "The Pope wants it and this is enough!" did this mean that he supported Catholic Action only through obedience and not from conviction?

We have already noted that he was not entirely happy about the forms Catholic Action was then taking because of the principles that animated all his own activity: submission to the Bishop *(nihil sine Episcopo)*, a clearcut distinction between religious activity and political action, unity and harmony among all Catholics.

We have no wish to undervalue the fact that the *Opera dei Congressi* made a unique contribution to the involvement of the Catholic laity in fostering a Christian spirit in the temporal order. Anyone familiar with the history of the Opera and the men who were its principal exponents admires their courage and zeal but also knows their uncertainties about the right way to proceed, the political implications of certain activities, the various changes in direction, unclear relationships with the hierarchy, internal conflicts, the laborious search for a line of political action and the ambiguity between political and religious activity, and the difficulty in quickly finding, at that time, laymen adequately prepared for the delicate task entrusted to them.[100]

Above all, there was the frequent tendency, supported by one or another current, to bypass the bishops. And Scalabrini was not the man to tolerate this especially when it was a question of religious activity, for which he felt responsible in his diocese:

"I do not disregard the cooperation of the laity, but in strictly religious matters I do not care for lay initiators because it is difficult for them to be free of ulterior motives which are basically political. Was there not loud criticism of the bishops in top hats? I love justice and consistency in all relationships. The older I become the more convinced I am that true good is done when everyone keeps to his own work."[101]

It should be noted that he is not referring here to the intransigents but to certain so-called "Liberal" Catholics with whom Bishop Bonomelli was dealing in order to establish his program for the emigrants. Scalabrini was not in fact moved by any sense of partisanship. His attitude was the logical result of his premise: it is urgent to be united; peace is necessary for unity; peace requires that each one keep to his own work.

When Pius X in 1904 clarified what is today called the "order of the apostolate," Bishop Scalabrini discarded all his reservations and embraced the cause of Catholic Action. With even greater enthusiasm he would have welcomed the long desired directives in the Encyclical *Il Fermo proposito*, published ten days after his death.

In any case, the reservations and criticisms he did not hestiate to express concerning certain aspects and personalities of the *Opera dei Congressi* should not obscure the facts, which reveal an activity that was neither limited nor lukewarm with respect to lay cooperation.

Bishop Scalabrini and Christian Democracy

Perhaps the need to act and to act quickly ("the evil is so serious that it seems to be dictating the conditions; we do not face it with the necessary efficacy") explains Scalabrini's hesitation and reservations with regard to the young Christian Democratic movement. He was certainly not opposed to it in principle. The premises that gave rise to Christian democracy in France coincided perfectly with the principles Scalabrini set forth.

"In France Christian Democracy was first under the guidance mainly of the clergy, who had responded enthusiastically to the Pope's call to social action and for acceptance of the Republic (and they often quoted an address by Bishop Radini Tedeschi to a congress in Fiesole in which he urged the clergy to come out of the sacristy). They were clearly aware of the dechristianization taking place and they already regarded France as a 'mission country'. In their view the people no longer knew the Church and therefore the clergy had to come out of the sacristy and seek more effective methods for theapostolate without opposing authentic social, political and cultural progress either through laziness or selfishness."[102]

Scalabrini held similar concepts. Speaking of preparing young seminarians to face "the great common peril" he declared:

"For some time the system in our seminaries has been improving rapidly in this direction. In the annual bishop's meetings the subject has been treated in depth. In fact I was chosen by the bishops of Emilia as the rapporteur for this important theme. The Seminary in my Piacenza is producing good results and it is my care and my love. My young priests, as you can see from our host, Father Bardi, have had a fitting preparation for their great new duties. And it is urgently necessary that this be so. The socialist idea wears an illusory, fascinating face, and unfortunately the indifference, obstinacy and anti-Christian improvidence of others is transformed among the blind masses of the poor into a kind of compendium of all the legitimate claims of the proletariat. Hence difficulties increase at every turn and the flood tide keeps spreading unavoidably. Our young pastors must come out of the churches and sacristies to confront the enemy tempter. But active practical works are necessary and a strong organization."[103]

In 1896-1897 there arose a serious conflict within the Catholic movement throughout Italy over the term "Christian democracy," which many Catholics and a good part of the hierarchy did not like.[104] At the time Scalabrini was accused of having fired "a triple volley of applause" for the Letter of the Bishop of Fossano by declaring, "The Christian idea has nothing in common with the Christian democracy now being propagated through Italy." Scalabrini explained that someone had used one of his visiting cards to write on it — without his knowledge — the above sentence, which was reported in the *Italia Reale* of Turin. He requested *L'Amico del Popolo* to publish the correction, saying that while he admired the courage of the Bishop of Fossano, who had affirmed certain truths despite the fact that they would be resented, he himself "would not have agreed, without reservations, to all that was said about the democratic movement of today."[106]

When Toniolo defined the meaning of Christian democracy, identifying it with the Christian social movement, that is, a Christian democracy that was not political-social but ethical-social, Italian, and papal and obtained the Pope's authorization to use the term, Bishop Scalabrini accepted it precisely because it meant popular, Christian, social action. Leo XIII, in the encyclical

Graves de communi of 1901, erased any political meaning from the term "Christian democracy" and gave it a purely social meaning: *actio benefica in populum.*

Scalabrini, therefore, held the position defined by Leo XIII and Toniolo. He did have reservations, however, about the current known as "young Christian democrats" which was gradually becoming a political party in the true sense of the word. These reservations were not so serious with regard to the group led by Meda and Albertario, which respected the authority of the hierarchy also in political action, as they were in the case of the group led by Murri, which held out for autonomy.

"I disagree with this youth movement, or rather I do not approve of it. Within it there are young men of great intelligence and fine knowledge, but they seem to be on a dangerous route. Their teacher — Professor Toniolo — has a great, balanced and original mind. It is also an organizing mind. While inductively and deductively he defines the limits and basic procedures of his teachings, he creates solid, rational, intellectual structures. But, alas, this same teaching, scattered among many untried and impulsive heads, gives rise to bold and reckless actions and spreads great confusion. I think that these zealous Christian democrats, whose aims are so vast and noble, would do better to engage in some practical action first, that is, to create programs of renewal reconstruction and Catholic resistance among the erring or forgetful multitudes and then permit themselves the joy of generalizing the canons of their teaching. Otherwise one observes their propaganda not without some disquiet."[107]

Scalabrini's reservations about the *autonomy* championed by the Murri group were due to the fact that at that time the Catholic movement, of which the Christian democrats remained a part in accordance with the Pope's wishes, still claimed to be a preeminently religious activity, and religious activity was to be directed by the hierarchy. In 1900, when Scalabrini expressed the view cited above, the distinction between religious and political action was far from clear, even in Murri's thinking.[108] The "reckless actions" and the "confusion" Scalabrini feared were probably disobedience toward the Pope, disunity among the Catholic forces, collusion with socialism, and confusion between the terms "social" and "political." It seems that he over-estimated these dangers. He did not, however, share the too rigid posture of Paganuzzi[109] — "Let these young ones have their head a bit," he would say in his Lombard dialect — and at the same time he did not have much confidence in Murri. "Let's see how he will end," he observed. When Murri came to give a lecture in Piacenza at the invitation of the Worker's Circle of Sant'Antonino, the Bishop had him as his guest but did not permit him to address the seminarians.[110]

When the Holy See condemned the activity of the "so-called autonomous ones" Scalabrini published the March 1 (1905) pontifical letter to the Archbishop of Bologna and again recommended obedience to the papal directives.[111] At the same time, in a letter to its president, Count Radini Tedeschi, he congratulated the Diocesan Committee of Piacenza which had always functioned in complete obedience to the hierarchy.[112]

Scalabrini's Relations with Toniolo and Other Lay Leaders

Despite certain differences of opinion, the friendship between Scalabrini and Toniolo remained constant. Toniolo admired the Christian social activity of the bishop of Piacenza and in 1889 offered him his cooperation.

" 'Excellency, I am presuming to write to Your Excellency although I do not have the honor of knowing you personally. Forgive me, through that gentleness which is characteristic of you.

From the beginning I have naturally been an admirer of your most fortunate work for the emigrants, prompted in this sentiment by my studies, as professor of Social Economics in this university, through which I daily experience the importance, in fact the urgency of a doctrinal and practical movement of good and educated Catholics in the field of social action.'

"The famous Professor goes on to express the wish that an association of the laity for Italian emigrants be established, if one did not already exist. To this end he hopes to meet Bishop Scalabrini soon...! Bishop Scalabrini, who held Toniolo in high esteem, was happy to receive this letter and answered him at length. He informed him that a lay organization for the emigrants (Società di Patronato degli Emigrati) already existed, working side by side with the Society of Missionary Priests, but it was not in very flourishing condition since the Catholic laity did not fully understand the problem. Toniolo's cooperation therefore could be both precious and effective. 'Without knowing each other personally' Scalabrini wrote, 'there is a meeting of minds and affection between us.'

"He went on to invite his new friend to come soon to Piacenza, where a friend of Toniolo's, Marchese Volpe-Landi, was doing useful work. From this time on their friendship grew ever closer. Knowing that Scalabrini often went to Rome, Toniolo showered him with invitations, saying what supreme joy it would be for him to kneel before so worthy a prelate. But the Bishop of Piacenza had always had too much to do to stop over in Pisa. So the Professor during his own travels would stop off for an hour or two at the station in Piacenza where Scalabrini would almost always be waiting for him.

"For these two holy men, these were moments of spiritual and intellectual joy. With both wisdom and humility they discussed the most difficult problems of the time, and the most evident Catholic needs. And it was during these conversations that Bishop Scalabrini invited Toniolo, among other things, to support his institute for the rice-pickers.

"...Bishop Scalabrini had the joy, at least once, of returning the many visits of his friend. It was in 1891-1892, when the Apostle to the Emigrants was traveling throughout Italy urging people to help these brothers of ours and to organize local committees...Professor Toniolo wrote to him that his city too would like the honor of having him as its guest...The good bishop was moved by his friend's insistence...and his own deep feeling of friendship, and in view also of the possibility of some good results for the institute, he went to Pisa. His arrival gave Toniolo great joy. He was among the first, together with Archbishop Capponi, to greet him at the station, and he was beside him throughout the day, also at the Bishop's request. When Bishop Scalabrini spoke to a large and select congregation in the great church of the Knights of St. Stephen, the professor sat in the front row with shining eyes. The Bishop's words moved everyone, but especially Toniolo, who proposed to become a simple but active member...of the local Pisan committee for emigrants. Scalabrini wanted to make him chairman, as undoubtedly the most worthy, but he would not accept, both because of his scholarly commitments and his deep humility, which retreated before a new honor. The Honorable Emilio Bianchi was elected chairman instead, and the Committee in Pisa was among the best in Italy, thanks principally to the constant and intelligent work of Toniolo."[113]

Bishop Scalabrini's relations with the most representative laymen of the Catholic movement — Paganuzzi, Rezzara, Medolago, Albani, Olivi, Crispolti, in addition to Toniolo — were in general very cordial. We have already noted Marchese Volpe-Landi, who became the Bishop's right hand in the St. Raphael Society for emigrants. As president he insisted that this be affiliated to the Opera dei Congressi, from headquarters on down to the parish committees. Secco Suardo observed in this connection, "It is to be noted that Volpe-Landi always had close personal and active relations with the Opera dei Congressi and with Paganuzzi, even if Scalabrini, who never belonged to the intransigent current, was somewhat reserved about them although he very much appreciated certain of their activities."[114]

This judgment on Bishop Scalabrini, which is common to some students of the political and social action of Italian Catholics after 1870, should be revised in the light of the facts reported above and the relations between Scalabrini's programs for the emigrants and the Opera dei Congressi. It is enough to note that cooperation was neither easy nor effective. It is likely that Scalabrini, quite apart from his views on the politics of the Opera, felt that the lack of incisive practicality, for which he criticized the Catholic movement, was reason enough to fear that any concrete help for his projects would stay in the limbo of good intentions, given all the other numerous sectors of activity contemplated by the Opera dei Congressi.

Without faulting anyone, we can see that the polemics that divided Catholic Italians had crept in here also. In one of his letters Toniolo observed that Scalabrini's works "here in Italy leave the Catholic party a little cold and suspicious because of certain personal ideas of their promoters who were rumored to be 'transigent' conservatives."[115] But Scalabrini was not the man to be put off by difficulties of that kind. In the field of emigration, he pressed incessantly for action that was authentically social for it dealt with the workers, Italian because it served the country's most unfortunate sons, which she could not feed, and above all Christian. It was a concrete realization of the commandment of charity.

A German sociologist, Romano Maerker described Bishop Scalabrini as the Ketteler of Italy in a certain sense, saying he hoped a detailed biography would be written of him like that of the pioneer of Christian sociology. "It could be of great use to Italian Catholic Action."[116] It is an aspect of his life and personality that has been somewhat neglected until now.

CHAPTER IX

The Emigrants

"I knew His Excellency Bishop Scalabrini personally from the very beginning of his initiative on behalf of our emigrants," wrote Toniolo. "I consider this an honor and my good fortune, for which I thank God. For if I compare the first concepts and efforts of the religio-social institution which the enterprising bishop was about to establish with the events that later accompanied the expansion of Italian emigration...I am forced to exclaim: this man had an intuitive sense of the future, which is characteristic of superior minds and great hearts, or rather of those whom the Lord calls to be special and timely instruments of His profound and merciful providential designs for the world!"[1]

The Christian sociologist's description of the "Apostle of the Emigrants," the "Holy Bishop of Piacenza," as he was wont to call him, is very apt.

"The salvation of the emigrants was an early anxiety for the apostolic zeal of Scalabrini. When he was Prior of San Bartolomeo's (1870-1876), in an attempt to avert the dangers his parishioners who were emigrating might encounter, he allowed none of them to leave without a letter of recommendation to the clergy where they were going to settle, and this had good results.

As bishop, and as early as his first pastoral visit, he came to learn even ·more about the evils accompanying emigration and the dimensions the problem of the salvation of the emigrants was reaching. Twenty-eight thousand persons emigrated from the diocese of Piacenza alone. At the end of the visit, in the diocesan Synod of 1879, he immediately set about interesting his clergy in the problem, including among the decrees a relevant article 'whose observance,' Scalabrini himself said, 'as I was able to note in my second Visit has yielded no little spiritual fruit.' "[2]

The Synodal decree is based on the following concepts:

"The first means to prevent the harm to the emigrants should be the zeal of their pastors in combating the trend toward emigration and in trying in every possible way to persuade their parishioners not to leave their country. But unfortunately, in the majority of cases this does not succeed and it is necessary to suffer this emigration as a painful necessity. *To steal* or *to emigrate*, this is the terrible dilemma I heard repeatedly from the lips of our poor artisans and peasants. The pastor in these districts must not let anyone leave without giving him a letter of recommendation to the clergy of the place where he is going to live."[3]

The bishop, whose charity one diocese could not exhaust,[4] viewed the phenomenon of Italian emigration in all its complexities: human, social, and above all religious.

"In Milan a few years ago I witnessed a scene that left me with a sense of profound sadness.

"As I walked through the station, I saw the vast waiting room, the porticoes at the side and the adjacent piazza filled with three or four hundred individuals, poorly dressed and separated into various groups. Their faces, bronzed by the sun and marked with the premature wrinkles drawn by privation reflected the emotional turmoil agitating their hearts at that moment. There were old men bent with age and labor, young men in the flower of manhood, women leading or carrying their little ones, boys and girls — all united in a single thought, all heading to a common goal.

"They were emigrants. They belonged to the various provinces of Northern Italy and they were waiting with trepidation for the train that would take them to the shores of the Mediterranean Sea, from where they would embark for the far-off Americas where they hoped to find less hostile fortune, a land less unresponsive to their labors.

"They were leaving, poor souls, some sent for by relatives who had preceded them in this voluntary exodus, others without knowing where they were heading, drawn by that powerful, instinct that impels the birds to migrate. They were going to America, where, they had heard many times, there was well paid work for anyone with strong arms and good will.

"It was not without tears that they had said good-bye to their native village, to which so many tender memories still bound them. But they were getting ready to leave their country without regret, for they were familiar only with two of her hateful aspects, military duty and taxes, and because for the disinherited the fatherland is the country that gives them bread, and there far, far, away, they hoped to find bread less scarce even if it meant no less labor.

"I left there deeply moved. A host of melancholy thoughts pressed on my heart. Who knows what accumulation of misfortunes and privations makes so painful a step seem sweet to them I thought...How many disappointments, how many new sufferings is an uncertain future preparing for them? How many will emerge victorious in the struggle for existence? How many will die mid the turmoil in the cities or the silence of some uninhabited plain? How many, though they find bread for their bodies, will have no bread for their souls, which is just as necessary, and in a totally material ambience lose the faith of their fathers?

"Ever since that day my thoughts have often turned to those unfortunate people, and that scene always reminds me of another, no less desolate, which I have not seen but which it is possible to glimpse in the letters from friends and the reports of travelers. I see the poor wretches landing in a strange land, among people who speak a language they do not understand, easy victims of inhuman exploitation. I see them wet the unyielding ground with their sweat and their tears, ground that exudes disease-bearing miasmas. I see them, broken by labor, consumed with fever, sigh in vain for their distant fatherland and the old poverty of their native home, finally dying without the consolation of their dear ones, without the word of faith that points out the reward God has promised the good and the unfortunate. And those who win out in the cruel struggle for existence, alas! Isolated, they forget all supernatural concepts, all precepts of Christian morality, day by day lose all religious sense, for it is not nourished by pious practices, and allow brutal instincts to replace more noble aspirations.

"Faced with this lamentable situation, I have often asked myself: how can it be remedied? And every time I find in the papers some government circular warning the authorities and the public against certain speculators who carry out veritable slave raids to propel these unfortunates, blind instruments of greed, far from their native land toward a mirage of large and easy profits; and whenever from letters of friends or travelers' accounts I see that the pariahs among all emigrants are the Italians, that they do the meanest kinds of work — if indeed there is meanness in work — that the most abandoned and therefore the least respected are our own countrymen, that thousands upon thousands of our brothers live defenseless in a distant country, objects of exploitation that is often unpunished, without the comfort of a friendly word, then I confess that I blush with shame, I feel humiliated as a priest and as an Italian, and I ask myself again: what can be done to help them?

"Even a few days ago a distinguished young traveler brought me greetings from several families from the mountains of Piacenza now living in camps on the banks of the Orinoco river: 'Tell our Bishop that we are always mindful of his counsels, tell him to pray for us and to send us a priest, because here we live and die like animals...!' That message from my far-off children struck me as a rebuke..."[5]

The rebuke was not in vain. Bishop Scalabrini felt again the missionary urge that had attracted him as a young priest, and he immediately began to prepare himself intellectually and spiritually to tackle the problem.

Italian Emigration at the Time of Scalabrini

The great increase in Italian emigration coincided with the unification of Italy. From 1869 to 1878 the numbers who emigrated permanently remained fairly steady at about 20,000 a year, while seasonal or other temporary emigration amounted annually to 80,000. In 1879 the numbers doubled. In 1881 the exodus reached the striking figure of 135,832 persons, most of whom left for permanent residence in the Americas.

From the beginning, public opinion had been disturbed about the phenomenon. In the early parliamentary debates (1868 and 1872) the government seemed to pour the blame on the capitalists and entrepreneurs accusing them of not having created enough jobs. In actual practice, it would seem from the measures restricting the freedom to emigrate (1868 and 1873) that the government was allowing itself to be manipulated by the landowners who, hit by increasingly heavy taxes, were trying to get theirs back from the farm hands and wage earners and were now fearful that the loss of manpower would result in their having to pay higher wages. For many years the government continued a policy of repression rather than protection, favoring the interests of the upper classes rather than the peasants and emigrants, even when measures were taken to combat the fraudulent practices of the "recruiting agents" and prevent the consequent "artificial" emigration. In reality, these measures did not go to the heart of the problem. The agents were merely speculating on an already existing evil. For too many Italians, and especially the peasants, there were only two alternatives, either to emigrate or to starve to death.

The new Italian State, partly because of the exigencies of the situation, partly because of a policy that was too liberalist and paternalistic, brought no benefits to the lower classes. It was in debt through the creation of infrastructures (i.e. administrative and railroad systems) and overly concerned about its prestige (i.e. heavy expenditures for the army and navy). It did not know how to cope with the crisis that hit the rural areas, particularly in the Veneto and the South, when the bottom fell out of the European market for agricultural products and commercial relations were broken off with France. Nor could it cope with the distressed circumstances of the working class, burdened with low salaries, inhuman working hours, and the exploitation of women and children.

The landowners clamored for laws "protecting" and "supervising" emigration in order to protect the low cost of farm labor. There were also some economists who opposed free emigration (i.e. the Marchese di Cosentino in 1872-1874 and Florenzano in 1874). On the other hand some Southern conservatives exposed the landowners and promoted free emigration and the interests of the emigrants (See *Rassegna settimanale,* Franchetti and Sidney Sonnino, 1879).

Leone Carpi (1871-1878) and Jacopo Virgilio (1873) publicized the advantages of emigration and began to call it the "safety valve" for overpopulation. They were perhaps secretly on the side of the landowners or shipbuilders, but in any event did not document their views with facts. More solid studies were produced by Sidney Sonnino in 1876, and by Stefano Jacini in 1884, that is, after the agrarian survey that had revealed the deep roots of the social unrest. In their view emigration would help to create a class of small landowners and merchants as a kind of intermediary between the large landowners and the peasants. It was necessary therefore that emigration be free and at the same time regulated. This concept was not very far from that of Italy's nascent socialist movement, which, however, viewed emigration as a weapon with which to fight capitalism on legal grounds (See *La Plebe,* 1876-1877).

The landowners, who carried great weight in parliament, continued to inveigh against the recruiting agents, but certain outstanding economists (Sonnino, Zanelli, Ricasoli, Del Vecchio, Fortunato) accused them of trying to cover up their own mistakes, namely, their neglect of their dependents, their absenteeism, the backwardness of the system, the inadequate wages or compensations they paid, latifundism, and the scant circulation of capital.

Behind the phenomenon of emigration, some saw the specter of socialism. Others, more rightly, saw in it a social protest against the Italy of the land rich *signori.*

At the same time, due principally to the great exodus, a colonial mentality began to develop. Some envisaged free or economic colonies, others political colonies. The latter idea gained increasing popularity despite the warnings of the more astute economists, who maintained the time was not ripe for political colonization since the domestic situation was still in disarray.

Meanwhile, as we have noted, the numbers emigrating reached unexpected totals: 290,736 in 1888; 307,482 in 1896; 352,782 in 1900. The typical liberalist mentality began to consider it, almost fatalistically, as an inevitable phenomenon, the result of natural laws and outside the competency of the State. This was the attitude of Agostino Depretis, who thought the only useful measures were charity and private aid committees. Similar attitudes of withdrawal saw only the need for a new law for public order, but not a special law for emigration (1883). Crispi took a much more active interest in the problem, but amid many uncertainties and even contradictory policies. For Crispi the problem was not one of internal order (i.e. the police) but of foreign policy. To give the emigrants a little prestige he promoted Italian schools and patriotic celebrations abroad, but these were in any event sterile efforts. He supported, even financially, the *Missioni d'Oriente* and Catholic schools abroad but from a nationalistic motive. At the same time he regarded with disfavor the *Associazione per soccorrere i Missionari Cattolici italiani* (Association for Aid to Italian Catholic Missionaries, of whom we shall speak later) and Bishop Scalabrini's institute for the emigrants because they did not submit to government control.

This was the state of affairs in 1887 when Crispi finally proposed a law establishing free emigration, restrictions on emigrant recruitment, obligatory government licensing and bonding for recruiting agents, and penalties for clandestine recruiting operations. Rocco de Zerbi's "more liberal" counter-proposal was designed to establish freedom to emigrate and to have others emigrate; in other words, it protected the recruiting agents. Unfortunately it was this counter-proposal which was adopted with some amendments.[6]

1887 was also the year in which Bishop Scalabrini, moved by quite different concerns, felt he must do something about the problem.

Scalabrini's Views on Emigration

In 1887 Scalabrini wrote a pamphlet entitled *L'Emigrazione Italiana in America* (Italian Emigration in America), which went through various printings and was widely diffused. In the following year he published *Osservazioni e Proposte* (Observations and Proposals) as an open letter to the Under Secretary for Finance, Paolo Carcano. It was in fact another pamphlet, of sixty pages, called *Il Disegno di Legge sulla Emigrazione Italiana* (Proposal for a Law on Italian Emigration). In 1891 he published the report he had read at the Exposition in Palermo, entitled *Dell'Assistenza alla Emigrazione Nazionale* (Aid to National Emigration). His lecture in 1899 at the General Italian Exposition in Turin was published under the title *L'Italia all'Estero* (Italy Abroad).

He became intensely active giving lectures, talks, etc., especially in the two-year period, 1891-1892, in an effort to finally arouse public opinion, which was kept in the dark about the realities and extent of the migration phenomenon. His talks stirred considerable response in the principal cities of Italy and in the religious and political press. "Contrary to what contemporary social historiography seems to imply, which considered Scalabrini simply an activist,"[7] he had worked out a clear and complete theory on the emigration problem, he had studied its causes, effects and the development of its various elements, and he had outlined directives for its solution, not only with respect to its religious aspects but also its social, economic, legal and political aspects.

To the question whether emigration was good or bad Bishop Scalabrini answered its cause was a misfortune that should be prevented with all possible effort, but the phenomenon itself was inevitable. "In almost all cases it is not a pleasure but an inescapable necessity."[8] Therefore it is a right. As for its effects, "it can be a good thing or a bad thing depending on the way it is carried out. It is undoubtedly a good thing both for those who go and those who remain, a true safety valve, relieving the country of excess population, opening new avenues for commerce and industries, blending and perfecting civilization, broadening the concept of fatherland beyond physical boundaries, making the world man's country. But it is a very grievous evil, from a personal and patriotic viewpoint, when it is allowed to take place without laws, limits, direction, or effective protection. This represents not lively and intelligent forces organized for the good of the individual and society, but forces in conflict, often destroying one another in turn. It means activities exploited to their (the emigrants') loss and shame, and to the harm and shame of their country of origin."[9]

On the consequences emigration can have for social progress and human solidarity as well as for evangelization, his statements are extraordinary for his times.

If emigration is a natural right and can be a good thing when it is voluntary, "being one of the great, providential laws that preside over the destinies of peoples and their economic and moral progress,"[10] can the State intervene to limit this right? At the time, there was no longer any discussion about the right itself, but rather the question of regulating it. If the citizen has this right, Scalabrini said, it is the duty of the State:

"To defend the freedom to emigrate, but it is also its duty to oppose freedom to cause one to emigrate. It is the duty of the ruling classes to provide the proletariat with a useful occupation for their skills, to help them pull themselves out of penury, to help them in the search for paid employment, but it is also a duty to keep their good faith from being betrayed by greedy speculators."[11]

The State, according to Scalabrini, should act in three ways. The first is to remove the causes for the painful necessity to emigrate, providing employment within the country as far as possible. Consequently it should favor internal migration, "the ideal form of emigration, which is most useful and for us easy to accomplish...Let us establish colonies within the country, free all Italian territory from malaria, intensify agriculture and render it more productive. All that can be done along these lines will be an excellent thing. But let us have no illusions. Let us colonize as much as possible but, to avoid disappointments, let us realize it is not so easy as it seems at first sight, and it certainly is not possible to the extent necessary to meet the rapid increase in our population."[12]

Hence, though he considered internal migration the best form, Scalabrini did not minimize the practical difficulties in the way of rationalizing agriculture and achieving the necessary industrialization to support a population of 50 million inhabitants. How can our nation, he wrote, find room "for the growing population, which, given the average rate of growth in the last twenty years will reach about 100 million in a century."[13] He made this projection in 1899, and his calculations have proved to be correct if we consider that, despite the gradual decline in the growth rate, the descendants of the 30 million inhabitants in the Italy of his time now number 80 million, including, of course, the Italians living abroad and the descendants of the emigrants.

Therefore, it was necessary for the State to assume the second alternative, namely, to direct the migrant flow to the most advantageous outlets. Italy was not and could not become a colonial power,[14] and, on the other hand, there could be no illusion that emigration was a temporary phenomenon instead of "the genuine expression of a permanent state of things."[15] Therefore, instead of limiting itself to obnoxious and counterproductive police measures, "which are motivated more by the interests of the well-to-do who remain than by the needs of the poor who are constrained to leave,"[16] the State should adopt measures for protection, guidance, and the prevention of abuses.

"Without promoting ruinous campaigns for conquest, Italy could find in America a vast field for the development of her colonies," which would be agricultural and commercial, a kind of peaceful penetration. "If politically they did not depend on the mother country, like the English and French colonies, they could nonetheless be of great advantage in developing trade and the legitimate spread of influence."[17]

But it is indispensable to guide them, protect them, act as guardian through special agencies such as so many other nations have provided. Italy has done nothing, or almost nothing like this; she has sent her children into danger. The Government has contented itself "with a great deal of talk flavored with a little rhetoric."[18] In fact, the measures it has taken have only served to worsen the situation. Private efforts, "with the best intentions in the world have accomplished little or nothing."[19]

The third type of State action, Scalabrini suggested, was the adoption of effective laws accompanied by vigorous action to prevent "instigated" emigration, which was deplorable in all its aspects. It diverted the migrants from more advantageous and less dangerous directions and instead of meeting their real needs it appealed to a desire for quick riches or a mistaken spirit of adventure, thus creating a greater number of those displaced and disappointed.[20] Above all it turned the emigrants into merchandise at the mercy of recruiting agents, true "traders in human flesh," unfortunately so licensed by the law of December 30th, 1888. In 1899 Bishop Scalabrini mentioned about 8000 "licensed recruiters...misery's parasites."[21]

He had opposed the law with a study that documented, with the pitiless eloquence of facts, the villainies of the recruiters.

"Citing incidents and observations drawn from the records of the Brazilian parliament and of the Commission of Inquiry on Immigration of the United States, as well as from the national and foreign press, Scalabrini describes, for about twenty pages, all the devices through which recruiting companies speculate with the misery and ignorance of our poor peasants, how they drag them overseas with infinite promises, and how they then condemn them to unsafe and underpaid drudgery when they don't abandon them altogether in order to proceed to the exploitation of other poor deluded wretches."[22]

De Zerbi, the sponsor of the law in question, had called it one of the most liberal in Europe. The Bishop replied "it is not so important for a law to be liberal as it is for it to be good," that is, just.[23]

He was not listened to but future events proved his foresight correct. Legalization of emigrant recruitment, which the Bishop of Piacenza called "intrinsically evil" became in the period from 1888 to 1901, one of the most painful evils in our emigration phenomenon.[24]

Scalabrini strongly supported other proposals: information centers in Italian and foreign ports; resettlement centers in the debarkation ports; cooperation between the Italian and American governments to coordinate resettlement policies; protection of the emigrants during their voyage; the establishment of Italian schools in the communities abroad taught by seminarians who wished to become missionaries to the emigrants; a true volunteer "social service" for five years instead of three years of military service;[25] and finally protection of the emigrants' savings in banks controlled by the government, to keep the money they sent home out of the hands of fraudulent or, at the least, usurious money-handlers.[26]

The Situation of the Emigrants

Scalabrini cites abundant figures on the emigrant flow which demonstrate, in addition to the vast extent of the phenomenon, its steady continuation and the transition from individual departures to the emigration of whole families and entire villages. His writings transform the arid language of statistics into a moving description of the odyssey of the Italian emigrants, revealing his complete empathy and compassion as a man and as an apostle. His words express all the poignancy of the documented reality which weighed upon him, and which he had already decided to remedy, beginning with his own personal involvement.

"From separate accounts and facts reported from time to time in the papers, I note that our countrymen abroad are the least protected, that they are often the victims, either through ignorance or good faith, of contemptible speculation, and that they are the least likely to have recourse to the consular authorities to establish their rights or when they are in need. This may all be due to a spirit of independence or to the fact that the Italian is not used to seeing the government of his own country as his natural and effective protector. But it may also be a grave indication of mistrust, the product of the habitual negligence and impotence of our authorities, so that our countrymen have found it better to get out of their difficulties as best they can themselves rather than wait for a tardy and ineffectual defense from their distant fatherland."[27]

After being fleeced at the embarkation point by the "traders in humanity," they are "stowed into the ships worse than beasts, in numbers much greater than the regulations or the capacity of the vessels allow, they make the long uncomfortable voyage literally crowded together in heaps, with what damage to their health and morality can easily be imagined. And when they arrive at their destination, their painful Iliad is far from ended. Often cheated by clever tricks, dazzled by a thousand promises and forced by necessity, they bind themselves in contracts that are a veritable form of slavery, their children led from begging to crime, and the women thrown into dishonor."[28]

Scalabrini recounts many shocking incidents taken from official reports or from letters of emigrants. One example comes from a proposal for a law brought before the U. S. House of Representatives in 1886 to "abolish the importation of Italians or other slaves or laborers, contracted and kept in forced servitude in the United States of America..."

"We quote Article 3 in its entirety because it shows to what extremes of barbarity we have descended:

'Sec. 3 — That any Italian padrone or his manutengolo (accomplice), or whatever other person or persons who shall bring to the United States, the territories thereof, or in the District of Columbia any man, woman, or children of either sex from Italy or elsewhere and use them as organ-grinders, street-musicians, dancers, mountebanks, sham blinds or infirms at the corners of streets and churches, beggers, or as gatherers of rags, waste paper, decayed meat, bread or other rotten food, or in any other vagrant, low, and degrading trade, vice, work, performance, or profession or shall contract them individually, or by squads, or en masse, to work on the railroads, canals, reservoirs, or museums at a low price, and shall compel them to pay to the padroni or his manutengoli (accomplices), or to any other person or persons two-thirds of or any portion of their earnings, shall be deemed guilty of a felony and, upon conviction thereof, shall be imprisoned for a term not exceeding five years, and shall pay a fine not exceeding five thousand dollars.' "[29]

From among the numerous examples he cited only a few that showed:

"How wet with tears and how bitter to the taste was the bread of the emigrant, of those unfortunate souls who, attracted either by vain hopes or false promises, found an Iliad of woes, abandonment, hunger, and not rarely death, where they had believed they would find a paradise. They saw an Eldorado, brightened by the mirage of need, without remembering that the violent wind of reality scatters in an instant the enchanted cities of dream! Unhappy ones! Exhausted by work, the climate, the insects, they fall disconsolate to the soil made fertile by their labors, on the edge of the green forests they have cleared, not for themselves nor for their children, shaken by the gentle and fatal sickness of nostalgia, dreaming perhaps of the home country, which could not even feed them, calling in vain for the minister of the holy religion of their ancestors, who calms the terrors of the agony of death with the immortal hopes of faith. Gentlemen, it is not a happy picture, but it is the true story of thousands and thousands of our fellow countrymen who have emigrated, and I have put it together from the reports of my Missionaries and from what has been told or written to me by those who witnessed and shared these most distressing exoduses. I do not wish to be misunderstood, however, or to be considered pessimistic. The sad happenings I have mentioned are not true of all our emigrants. Very many of them have found in hospitable countries an adequate living, many a comfortable one, and some have even found wealth. They form colonies of which the motherland can be proud. But there are also very many who are miserable, and in great measure this is due to their ignorance and to our neglect."[30]

What caused the Bishop most anxiety was the lack of religious care. Economic and social assistance is mainly the concern of civic society, although the Church can help to supplement it.

"What a vast field is opened for the work of the clergy and laity in these simple words: direct and protect the emigrants! Direct and protect them, both by promoting intensified governmental and legal action on their behalf, and by making up for the inevitable deficiencies of both."[31]

The mainspring of Scalabrini's apostolate, however, is religious:

"The poor peasants who emigrate, when they don't die along the way or succumb to privations and heartbreak at being trapped by deceit, are left, it may be said, without a shadow of religious assistance. Their state is more easily imagined than described."[32]

The local priests cannot help them effectively because they do not understand the language and because the emigrants are dispersed in various places.

Therefore the Italian who lives in America is almost constrained, generally speaking, to live a life that is worse than pagan, without Mass, without Sacraments, without public prayers, without worship, without the word of God, so that it is saying a great deal if the children born there are baptized. Now it is evident that such a state of affairs must imperceptibly lead to a frightening indifference toward religion and a dehumanizing materialism."[33]

Does the evil derive from a superficial faith? No: "to be deprived of spiritual bread, not to be able to make one's peace with God, to lack encouragement for good, has a most disastrous effect on the morale of the people." If even the educated man runs the risk of weakening faith without the "signs," how much greater is the danger for the ignorant, whose "concept of religion is inseparable from that of the church and the priest. Where there is no visible religious instrumentality, he gradually becomes unmindful of his duties to God, and the Christian life in his soul weakens and dies."[34] In America, furthermore, "if on the one hand all support of religion is lacking, the dangers to the faith abound," because of intense and omnipresent Protestant or Masonic propaganda.[35]

Bishop Scalabrini looked to a future when:

"Those little settlements of cabins, spread now in a kind of desert, will become flourishing towns and cities, both through the natural increase in population and because of this tide of emigration that rises higher, so to speak, every day. Then what will happen? It is easy to foresee that in a few years we shall have in the vast plains of the Americas a new Italy, perhaps rich in material goods but poor in the riches of the spirit, or more precisely, we shall have a society conforming to the direction given it at the start. The first impressions are also the most persistent and lasting, and the first traditions are the ones that give a family, a city, a settlement its special characteristics...The religious and moral future of our settlements in America, therefore, will depend on how much religion and morality is preserved by these first centers of population. Will they be inspired by civic and Christian sentiments? Will their descendants be civil and Christian and those who later join them from Italy who will have to adapt more or less to the traditions of faith and piety they find there? Shall they be abandoned instead? They will grow up like savages and even those who arrive afterwards will soon become savages. The tendency of our emigrants to settle together, furthermore, is a fact that should not be overlooked and which will make it less difficult to reach them. To neglect them now that it is a question of choosing the site of the future cities and giving them the religious and Italian character on which their prosperity and future importance must depend would be an unpardonable error. That character must be given them immediately. Any delay, I believe, will be fatal."[36]

"If there is long delay, the harm will be irreparable. Lack of belief, heresy, and above all freemasonry, which is very powerful in America, will be active in capturing the minds and hearts of the emigrants. If, then, it is a matter now of reclaiming neglectful Catholics deprived of religious assistance, soon it will be a matter of working to convert unbelievers, heretics, freemasons, atheists. And those same unfortunates, who from poverty or for other painful reasons had to abandon their native land, pray and plead for us to come to their aid. An Italian gentleman, back from a long journey of exploration in America, told me that he met groups of families from the mountains of Piacenza. They wept and asked him for news of their Bishop, whom they begged him, through this traveler, not to forget them in his charity but to send them a priest, if only for a few months. It was very moving, the gentleman said, to hear those poor people mourn their lost happiness, recall their feastdays, their little church, their ceremonies. As for them they were ready to make any sacrifice to pay for the priest's voyage. 'If he is not moved to pity for us', they said, 'we shall become worse than the pagans, and very many of us, which is much worse, will die without being able to make our peace with God.' These simple words bursting from hearts still filled with faith, are a living statement of the extremely sad situation in which almost all the emigrants find themselves. The urgency to provide for them is clearly evident. Oh let it be done! Let it be done!"[37]

The Remedies

Bishop Scalabrini carried on a steady campaign to arouse the Government and public opinion so that a body of law and effective action would be provided for the protection and guidance of the emigrants. He was convinced, however, that the adoption of the desired measures would only partly obviate the troubles and meet the needs of "the wandering misery of the country," especially in the moral and religious field.

"Laws are not enough to heal the wounds that afflict our emigration, for some are inherent in the very nature of emigration, others are due to remote causes outside the reach of law. Even with the best laws in the world, therefore, and with numerous perfect agents, we would not succeed in rooting out those evils."[38]

Consequently he proposed to establish immediately two practical mechanisms: an association of sponsors and a congregation of missionaries.

"The needs of our emigrants are of two kinds, moral and material, and I should like an *Associazione di Patronato* to be organized in Italy, which would be both religious and lay and so would be fully responsive to this double need."[39]

The Association was intended to protect the emigrants from the speculators and exploiters by setting up committees at the principal embarkation and debarkation points to receive them, take care of them, advise them and protect them. The Association was also to establish resettlement centers at the ports of arrival, in cooperation with the Italian government and the various American governments. It would provide emergency help in case of disasters or illness during the voyage and after landing. It was to wage a relentless war against the agents of this traffic in persons, reporting it to the police and keeping public opinion informed. And it was also to make sure that religious assistance was provided both during the journey and in the countries of immigration.

It was this last function "that especially concerned the Servant of God. But to carry it out the *Associazione di Patronato* was not enough. A troop of generous men was needed whose sole purpose was the religious ministry to the emigrants and would therefore be united in a society organized essentially for that purpose. This could only be a congregation of priests who, free from all other duties and ties, found in a supernatural motive, in a mission received from above, the sacrificial energy to serve those unfortunate people. As soon as he began to study the emigrant problem from the viewpoint of salvation, and especially of moral well-being, therefore, Bishop Scalabrini's first thought was to establish an institute of priest missionaries. He says this himself in the first letter he sent to His Eminence, the Cardinal Prefect of the Sacred Congregation of the Propagation of the Faith on February 16, 1887. "Would it not be opportune, Your Eminence," he wrote, "to think about an association of Italian priests for the spiritual ministry to the Italian emigrants, who would watch over their departure and arrival and would provide for their Christian future, as far as possible."[40]

"Given the urgency of providing this assistance and the impossibility of establishing immediately a permanent corps of missionaries Bishop Scalabrini proposed to send priests on temporary mission assignments, who would also have the duty to prepare the way for future missionaries. They were to go among our countrymen abroad, conduct 15-20 day 'missions' and gather all the information that would be useful in organizing the spiritual ministry. From one of Bishop Scalabrini's notes it would seem that the flying missionary mentioned in this plan was to be an integral member of the *Associazione* in its final form. It reads: 'two kinds of priests, permanent and temporary missionaries; the former to stay where they are assigned and the latter to travel about giving missions.'

"The idea of flying missionaries, as we shall see, was included specifically in the pontifical documents approving the Institute, but during the lifetime of the Founder it was only partially realized for lack of funds...Priests from Italian dioceses who applied for membership in the *Associazione* were accepted provided they were known for their zeal and piety and had exercised the sacred ministry for at least three years. Missionaries who were to remain abroad at least a year were governed by the norms which the *Propaganda Fide* used for the priests under its jurisdiction, and in the exercise of their ministry they were to be under the jurisdiction of the local bishops... In order to make a good beginning, Bishop Scalabrini planned first of all to address an appeal to the Hierarchy and Clergy of Italy in order to interest them in this serious problem and to set up Committees, especially in the seaports, which would help the missionaries by raising funds and by directing the emigrants to them. He then suggested that a Circular Letter be sent to the

American bishops, inviting them to set forth the needs of the Italian emigrants and to say what provision would be made for the Missionaries once they were sent out. It was also suggested that they take up collections to establish a seminary in some American city in order to train an indigenous Italian clergy which would serve only the Italians."[41]

Bishop Scalabrini in Rio Grande do Sul, Brazil with (from right to left) his missionaries Fr. Antonio Serraglia

CHAPTER X

Missionaries for the Emigrants

Foundation of the Order

On June 26, 1887, Cardinal Simeoni, Prefect of the Sacred Congregation of Propaganda Fide reported to Leo XIII its decisions regarding Scalabrini's project, and the Holy Father approved them. This general approval was followed by specific approbation in the audience granted Bishop Jacobini, Secretary of the Congregation, on November 4, 1887.

The proposals the Holy Father approved were those on which the Secretary and Scalabrini had agreed upon to improve the original plan. For example, in order to belong to the Missionary Society "it was decided that members should promise to remain in it at least for five years instead of one, as in the original proposal. There was a provision that in the future the Institute could accept, in Piacenza, young Italians, sons of emigrants, who gave indication of having a vocation. Also approved was the proposal to build a motherhouse for the Missionaries in America, so that they could take care of the so-called 'flying' missions among those emigrants who resided at some distance from any others and for whom therefore it was not possible to provide a priest in permanent residence. It was agreed that the Institute would be approved in a Pontifical Brief addressed to the Bishop of Piacenza and that the notice of its foundation would be communicated to the Bishops in the Americas and to the Papal Representatives."[1]

The Apostolic Brief, *Libenter agnovimus*, approving the Institute, was sent to the Bishop of Piacenza on November 25, 1887.

"Having received the approval and blessing of the Vicar of Christ, the Servant of God, Bishop Scalabrini, immediately set to work to establish this work so dear to his heart, and, as the first Chronicle of the Institute relates, 'on November 27, 1887...he sent for the Right Reverend Monsignor Domenico Costa, pastor of the famous Basilica of St. Antoninus Martyr and explained to him that he wishes the new Institute to be established near the tomb of the Glorious Martyr St. Antoninus, the patron saint of the city and diocese of Piacenza. The said Provost, a man of truly apostolic zeal, gladly acceded to the Bishop's wish and in fact placed his rectory at the disposition of His Excellency as the temporary residence of the student missionaries. The Bishop accepted his offer and at the same time appointed him Rector of the new Institute.' The following day, 'at about 11 o'clock, the above-mentioned Reverend Rector together with two Reverend Priests, Father Giuseppe Molinari of Piacenza and Father Domenico Mantese of Vicenza were received by the Bishop, who had the following provisory rule read to them:

"In the Name of Our Lord, Jesus Christ —
'Basic rules:

1. Absolute obedience to the Roman Pontiff, the Vicar of Christ.
2. Obedience and submission to the Bishop, Founder, Protector and Head of the Institute.
3. Obedience to and respect for the Rector.
4. All prayers and good works, both public and private to be directed to the glory of God, the salvation of souls, and especially to the development of good and holy Missionaries.
5. The student Missionaries will strive to maintain among them always a spirit of harmony and mutual charity'."

"These rules were followed by several specific prescriptions and the daily schedule of studies. At twelve o'clock on the same day, the Servant of God led the little group of first students to the church of St. Antoninus and on the tomb of the Holy Martyr he received their first profession."[2]

In a letter dated December 16, 1887, addressed to the Cardinal Prefect of the Sacred Congregation of Propaganda Fide, the Bishop was able to write:

"The undertaking to which the Lord deigned to inspire us for the benefit of our poor countrymen who have emigrated to America can be said to be well begun, with the help of God...I am very pleased with the three priests who have already been accepted; they manifest a real vocation and I hope they will do very well...["3]

"As soon as it became known throughout Italy and abroad that Bishop Scalabrini had established an Institute for the spiritual ministry to the emigrants, messages of praise and encouragement were sent to the Founder from everywhere, and also financial assistance. From both North and South America came letters from bishops and emigrants requesting that missionaries be sent from Piacenza. Archbishop Michael Corrigan of New York, in a letter to Scalabrini dated February 10, 1888, wrote:

'The Lord be praised a thousand times! Now I can breathe easy. Now there is good hope that something can be done for these dear souls, who are being lost by the thousands. Up to now I could find no way to save them!...Now I am happy and assured...I commend to you my neglected Italians. I should like, if possible, two missionaries immediately.'

Requests from priests ready to dedicate themselves to the work were not slow in coming. To provide for them, Scalabrini planned to acquire a home for the Institute which he intended to name for "him who brought the faith and civilization to America, Christopher Columbus."

"On January 27, 1888, His Eminence, Cardinal Simeoni, Prefect of Propaganda Fide, expressed his pleasure at the encouraging development of the work and authorized Bishop Scalabrini to start proceedings for the purchase of a new building, which could be registered, as he wished, in the name of the Sacred Congregation of Propaganda Fide. The plan, however, could not be carried out immediately and the Institute had to move temporarily from the Rectory of St. Antoninus to the *Pio Ritiro Cerati* (Cerati Rest Home for priests), a former Carmelite monastery. The move took place on March 5, 1888. On March 7, Bishop Scalabrini installed the new Superior of the Community, Father Bartolomeo Rolleri,"[4] who had been "an intrepid and most zealous" missionary as well as the secretary of Bishop Comboni.[5]

"The Prefect of Propaganda Fide received the following telegram from Piacenza on July 11, 1888: 'First team Institute Missionaries for Italian Emigrants about to leave America send grateful respects to You their Superior, Benefactor, Father. Praying God to keep you for their affection, good of the Church, advantage to Missions, imploring blessings. Rolleri Superior.' The group was composed of seven priests and three lay helpers. Two of the priests and one layman were to go to New York, two priests and a layman to Santa Felicidade a suburb of Curitiba (Paranà, Brazil), while the other three priests and the third layman were assigned to the State of Espirito Santo, also in Brazil."[6]

The departure ceremony took place on the following day in the Basilica of St. Antoninus. Bishop Scalabrini celebrated Mass on the tomb of the Martyr and the missionaries made their profession to him, taking the vows of poverty, obedience, and chastity. He blessed them and gave each of them a crucifix which was to be "the inseparable companion of their apostolic journeyings, their unfailing comfort in life and death."

He then sent them forth with these words:

"The field that lies open to your zeal is limitless. There are churches to erect, schools to open, hospitals to build, orphanages to establish. There are numberless sufferings to which the beneficient influence of Christian charity must be brought. How to provide for all this? Go: *ite!* Divine Providence, which with motherly tenderness watches over the works it inspires will solve the difficult problem, but you must be careful to respond to its counsels. Act so that everyone will know and love Jesus Christ, so that his kingdom will spread ever more and more widely... Never furl, never lower to the level of worldly interests the sacred banner of religion: hold it high and unstained always and everywhere. And beside the standard of religion, let the flag of our country, of this Italy, fly glorious and revered, for here is the heart of the Church; it is here God willed to establish the center of religious life, the See of his Vicar...I know that labors await you, and dangers, opposition, struggles and sacrifices; but it is precisely this that should assure you of the rightness of your enterprise and give vigor to your spirit. May the cross be your comfort, your guide and your surest defense."[7]

After being embraced by the Founder, the missionaries walked to the door of the Basilica while the *Benedictus* was sung. Waiting outside were the carriages of the first families of the city, which had vied with one another for the honor of taking them to the station. A few minutes later the seven who were headed for Genova and thence to Brazil departed and soon afterwards the three who were to embark at Le Havre for the voyage to New York.

"In the following September Bishop Scalabrini already had news to communicate to the Propaganda Fide about the first encouraging results achieved in New York and Curitiba and the difficulties encountered by the missionaries who went to the State of Espirito Santo. Other departures followed, one after the other, for both North and South America. And if the Propaganda had not considered Bishop Scalabrini's request inopportune, there would have been other missionaries sent to the Italian possessions in Africa."[8]

Characteristics of the Scalabrinian Congregation

The new "Rule of the Congregation of Missionaries for the Emigrants" was approved by Propaganda Fide on September 19, 1888 *ad experimentum* for a five year period, under the jurisdiction of Propaganda Fide, which named its Superior General. The purpose of the new Congregation is defined as follows: "to preserve the Catholic faith in the hearts of our countrymen who have emigrated and to lead them as far as possible to achieve their moral, civil and economic well-being."

The activities which Scalabrini outlined for the institution reflect a broad vision and envisage a wide field of apostolic work.

"The Congregation will achieve its aim (1) by sending missionaries or teachers wherever the needs of the emigrants require them; (2) by building churches and chapels in the various centers in the Italian colonies and establishing houses for missionaries, from which they can carry out their civilizing activity through visits to the outlying communities; (3) by establishing schools where with the first rudiments of the faith, the children will learn our language, arithmetic and the history of our country; (4) by sending for studies leading to the priesthood the young men who give indication of having a vocation to the priesthood; (5) by organizing committees at the embarkation and debarkation points to assist, direct and counsel the emigrants; (6) by accompanying them during the sea voyage, both to exercise the sacred ministry for them and to assist them, espeically in cases of illness; (7) by favoring and promoting those associations and activities that will be judged most appropriate for preserving the Catholic religion and Italian culture."[9]

The Rule was an ascetical-pastoral guide rather than a body of laws. Special importance was given to pious practices and community life, "in order to preserve the spirit of the Congregation."[10] It was essentially an exhortation to spiritual preparation and to the exercise of the ministry among the emigrants. The fundamental elements of the juridical part of the Rule were merely sketched in.

"Given the urgency of providing for the salvation of hundreds of thousands of emigrants who were without religious assistance, the primary concern was to have many priests immediately who were inspired by true apostolic spirit and were disposed to accept sacrifice. Hence the greater weight given in the rule to the ascetic-pastoral part than to the juridical-constitutional."[11]

Scalabrini's thought is reflected in a letter to one of his missionaries in the United States: "A certain Saint, who founded a religious order, used to say that Providence had from the beginning sent him men of great heart, but that sometimes when they undertook projects which exceeded their possibilities and were frowned on by their more prudent colleagues, they seemed to be plunging blindly along; in the end, however, he had to admit publicly that without those men his work would have been born dead, or almost dead."[12]

The 1888 Rule underlines the two basic characteristics of Scalabrini's institution: it is a missionary and a religious congregation. Its missionary aspect is its specific purpose, and the religious character modifies the missionary: "All those accepted in the Institute must be thoroughly imbued with the idea that for five years they are promising to live as true religious, animated by zeal for the salvation of souls."[13]

In a letter to his missionaries the Bishop of Piacenza thanked God for their zeal, which "given the immense difficulties it must have encountered in the beginning, had truly accomplished miracles."[14] Very much remained to be done but it was not impossible if the missionaries were moved by the same spirit as the Apostles, if they remained in close union with Christ through constant prayer, and united among themselves, this last being a requisite for apostolic efficacy. Their motto must be obedience to their superiors and especially to the Pope.[15] He had then some wise advice with respect to the delicate problem of the relations between the emigrants and the local population:

"Continue to use all the talent and strength you have for the religious, moral, and civil well-being of our countrymen, and while you try to keep alive their love for the mother country, be careful not to instigate among them anything that can separate them from their new fellow citizens or alienate them in any way from other believers. It is up to you to see to it that there will be no reason for the Italians to stand out except in greater respect for authority, more exemplary behavior, greater industry, more faithful observance of their duties and a livelier attachment to the faith of their fathers."[16]

St. Charles was named the patron of the Congregation,[17] and the missionaries were to emulate his virtues: fearless constancy, generous patience, ardent charity, and enlightened, tireless, and magnanimous zeal, a thirst for souls. According to their Founder they were to be:

"Men of action, who are never hesitant or divided among themselves and who never retreat; who throw into every act the whole strength of their conviction, all the energy of their own will, their whole personality, all of themselves, and win."[18]

In July 1892, the young community was able to take possession of the former Capuchin Monastery on the street now named for Msgr. Francesco Torta. The modest 17th century building, with the church of St. Charles next to it, became the Motherhouse of the Congregation and was named for Christopher Columbus, the discoverer and first evangelizer of America.

A new building was added in 1896 to house the young student missionaries who were attending classes at the neighboring Seminario Urbano. The philosophy and the theology students had classes within the Motherhouse, where they were given special training in addition to the customary subjects. They studied meteorology, architecture, hygiene and medicine; the languages spoken in the Americas, the problems presented by anti-Catholic propaganda, and the pastoral and legislative norms relating to emigration.

Bishop Scalabrini's missionaries, then, were to be men of apostolic spirit and evangelical detachment, whose principal aim was religious. At the same time they were to know how to treat not only souls, but men, the whole human person; soul, mind and body. They were to respond directly or indirectly (e.g. through the *Società del Patronato*) to man's three great needs: for a priest, a teacher and a doctor.[19]

Scalabrini's Order, then, was "a Congregation of Missionaries whose principal aim is the spiritual well-being of our emigrants," and which "achieves its purpose by establishing churches, schools, orphanages, hospitals, and by priests united as in a family by the religious vows of poverty, chastity and obedience, ready to hasten wherever they are sent — apostles, teachers, doctors, nurses, according to the need."[20]

In 1895, Bishop Scalabrini issued the new "Rule for the Congregation of the Missionaries of St. Charles for the Italian Emigrants." This was more juridical in content but still entirely consonant with the ascetic character of the preceding rule. The most important new element was the introduction of perpetual vows, which the Bishop had been considering for some time, anxious as he was to assure "better and better trained personnel" for the missions[21] and greater stability for his Institute. He had sought advice on this matter from the Jesuit, Father Rondina, who was the spiritual guide of the infant Congregation, and he then announced his decision. The young students greeted the news with enthusiasm and he felt sure then of having established the Order on a solid foundation: "It is the first time that I have felt deeply consoled and completely confident of the future."[22]

This statement proves that the preceding structure of the society had been shaped by the urgency of the need. The concept behind the institution could not be completely realized unless it was both a "missionary" and a "religious" Order. Scalabrini's intention is all the more evident from the fact that he insisted on retaining the perpetual vows despite the contrary judgment of the Commission of Propaganda Fide for the Examination of the Rules or Constitutions of New Institutions, whose opinion was supported by the famous theologian and canonist, Father (later Cardinal) Alessio Lépicier, and was based on the belief that emigration was a temporary phenomenon.[23]

Scalabrini took a longer view and understood more clearly the nature and the needs of the migratory phenomenon. He wrote to the Cardinal Prefect of Propaganda:

"As for the observations of the Commission for the Approval of the Rules, I reserve the right to deal with them either in writing or in person. For the moment I would note only that I should be extremely sorry to change what has brought about true development of the

Congregation. In any case, when I have explained my reasons, I shall always be devoted and obedient to the directives of my Superiors."[24]

It appears from documents of ·the following years that he explained his views in person to the Prefect of Propaganda Fide and obtained an oral approval of the Rule in 1895. In fact, up to the time of his death he insisted that it be followed, particularly with respect to perpetual permanent vows.

Time proved him to have been right, for the emigrant flow continued and still continues to a significant degree, nor is the end in sight unless there is recourse — as Scalabrini observed — to means such as birth control or war.

"Emigration is a natural and providential fact. It is a safety valve God has given to this troubled society. It is a factor of conservation much more powerful than all the moral and physical means of compulsion dreamed up and adopted by legislators to protect public order and the life and property of our citizens...It is an inescapable necessity...To prevent it is to violate a sacred human right...Human rights are inalienable,...therefore a person can go and seek his well-being where it best suits him."[25]

Scalabrini's words and foresight found still later confirmation in the teachings of Pius XII, who on more than one occasion defended freedom of emigration and the need for it. He also recognized the permanency of the phenomenon and declared that the provision of spiritual assistance to the emigrants should be written into the law.[26]

Still another proof of Scalabrini's wisdom and foresight is the renewed growth and development of the Society of St. Charles since 1934, the year when perpetual vows — which, together with temporary vows, had been replaced in 1908 by a simple promise of fidelity — were again made obligatory.[27]

The Spirit of the Founder and of the First Missionaries

Though Scalabrini could not himself become a missionary, he remained faithful to this vocation which had so appealed to him in his youth and he communicated his own enthusiasm to his missionaries:

"I feel that faith has made my heart beat more vigorously, more strongly...the infinite charity of God fills my breast, my mind is exalted with the prospect and desire of the apostolate. As I clasp to myself the gold cross of Bishop, I gently complain, almost, to Jesus because he has denied to me the wooden cross of the missionary, and I cannot refrain from expressing to you, my young apostles of Christ, my deepest respect; I cannot help feeling a holy envy of you."[28]

On his way to Brazil in 1904 he wrote:

"We are sailing past the coast of mysterious Africa. For hours at a time, almost motionless and prey to mysterious sadness I keep looking at those once flourishing lands. I think of the vigorous Catholic life in the early centuries of Christianity, of the celebrated churches of the Carthaginian Province, of Numidia, and Byzantium, of the great men who made them famous with the splendor of their apostolic virtues and their learning — Cyprian, Augustine, Fulgentius, etc. I think of the Councils attended by up to 270 African bishops. I think, in short, to what these lands were and what they are, and I am tempted to weep...Oh, why do we priests not run to evangelize these peoples and to sow with our blood the fertile seed of Christianity!..."[29]

When he arrived in Brazil, the President of the State of Paranà asked him to take an interest in the extensive parish of Tibagy, which numbered among its 20,000 souls Brazilians, Indians and Italian emigrants. Scalabrini immediately accepted and expressed the wish to meet the chief of one of the Indian tribes.[30]

Fogazzaro's account of the meeting is somewhat romanticized, although he heard about it from the bishop himself.[31] An eyewitness wrote as follows:

"Scalabrini confined himself to visiting the nearest villages although he wanted to go more deeply into the country...I remember that on this occasion the chief of the tribe gave him two metal cruets for the Mass, which had belonged to the Jesuit missionaries the Portuguese government had driven out, cruets which the Servant of God brought as a gift to the Holy Father Pius X. This tribe was very pleased with the visit of the Servant of God, and its chief asked the Servant of God to have the Great Priest (the Pope) send them some missionaries."[32]

Father Marco Simoni was sent to the Mission at Tibagy. A few months later he sent the Bishop a report, the language of which was sprinkled with Portuguese and Guaranì expressions. We quote it in part as an example of the spirit Scalabrini inculcated in the pioneers of his missionary Order.

"I give you news of Tibagy and the Mission of our poor, unhappy Indians. I have begun the Mission. I have been in a veritable beehive of Indians, who were very gentle and mild, and I stayed with them three days. I said Mass every day and they were all present. I spoke to them of God (Topè), of the life to come, and of the absolute necessity of Baptism to enter Paradise. I also spoke a few words in their language and it seems they understood me, because on the second day, at the end of Mass, all of them wanted to be baptized and I took advantage of their good will and the grace of God and baptized fifty-one of them at one time. I heard confession and married three of the best couples. This time I slept in their houses. To do something to please me they fashioned a bed of small poles set one next to the other on the ground in a corner of the house, which is open to the four winds...For three days I ate their food with them, I attended their dances and singing, and since I enjoyed being among them they could not do enough for me they were so pleased.

When I started to leave they did not want to let me go...It is not hard to find even among the clergy those who say these people have to be taught the catechism at gunpoint. Now I have drawn up a petition to the government, asking for 6,000,000 (reis?) a year (6000 lire) to take care of my expenses. I also asked for a large tract of land just for the Indians so that I can teach them to cultivate it...I have extreme need of a priest to work with me; I am so far away that I have to walk for four days to get to confession, and I have not been for four months...While I was visiting the Indians I also visited some Brazilian settlements; I heard 240 confessions, gave First Communion to more than a hundred persons, varying in age from twenty to fifty, distributed 176 communions and baptized 279...”[33]

Four years after the foundation of the order, by the end of 1891, forty-eight missionary priests and thirty-eight Brothers (catechists) had crossed the ocean and established eleven missions in North America and five in South America.[34] The number grew rapidly in the early years. In the same year, at a lecture in Rome (February 8), Scalabrini gave an account of the first three years:

"At various times, 33 priests have gone out and are now working in the field; they were accompanied by 27 catechists, or young laymen, also bound by religious vows, who, according to their abilities, are to take care of the houses, the Churches, and the Schools,[35] brothers rather than companions of the missionaries with whom they live. At the present time there are about 300,000 Italians entrusted to their care."[36]

"I hope later this year to be able to realize a dream I have had for some time of a College or Seminary for the sons of our emigrants who wish to embark on a career in the Church."[37]

At the end of the same year, in the report presented at the Exposition of Palermo, he wrote:

"In the Christopher Columbus Institute, which is maintained by charitable contributions, there are now forty-two students — priests, seminarians and laymen. Among them are several young men from Italian families who have settled in America and who are preparing themselves for mission work among their emigrant countrymen."[38]

"I shall respond to the insistent and very moving requests that constantly come to me from overseas by sending out the Priests I have gathered in the Institute in my Piacenza, praying that God will send me saints and heroes."[39]

Providence did send him many vocations and, through benefactors, the means to support them. It can be said without exaggeration that God also sent him some saints and heroes among the first Scalabrinian missionaries.[40]

Early History of the Congregation

The Congregation continued to grow throughout its early trials, especially the difficulties arising from the outbreak of the first World War. At the untimely death of its Founder, while it was still in the process of being organized, it went through a period of anxiety, but St. Pius X reassured the missionaries and confirmed their aim in the person of the new Superior General, Father Domenico Vicentini, who was elected in Piacenza on Sept. 28, 1905.

After a visit to the North American missions, Father Vicentini asked the Holy See to modify the Rule so that it would be "practical, responsive to the circumstances of the Missions and the same for all of them."[41] At the request of Propaganda Fide, therefore, he prepared a new Rule, which was approved with the decree of October 5, 1908. The Missionaries of St. Charles were thus given a new juridical framework. Instead of perpetual vows, stability was ensured by a perpetual promise to persevere. Thus the Congregation again became a religious order in the broad sense, that is, "a community without vows."

In 1910 Father Vicentini transferred the Generalate to Rome (Via di Ponte Sisto, 75) and was reelected at the Society's first General Chapter, which began on September 23 of that year. In 1912 he laid the cornerstone of the Apostolic School (Scuola Apostolica) in Crespano del Grappa (Treviso). In compliance with Pius X's *Motu Proprio* of 1912 — *De Catholicorum in exteras regiones emigratione* — the Society, on February 20, 1914, came under the jurisdiction of the Sacred Consistorial Congregation, in which the *Motu Proprio* had established an office or section for the spiritual ministry to Catholic emigrants of the Latin rite. The internal regulation of the Order continued to be governed by the Sacred Congregation for Religious.

The first World War produced a crisis both for the emigrant flow and the Society of the Missionaries of St. Charles. The Second General Chapter, held in Rome August 20 to 29, 1919, elected as Superior General Father Pacifico Chenuil of Valdosta (1869-1931). To remedy the lack of personnel due to the war, he embarked on an active campaign among the Italian clergy and was thus able to provide about forty priests for the missions. This did not, however, solve the internal problem of the small number of students or applications. This falling off in membership prompted the Holy See to name an Apostolic Visitator, Father Serafino Cimino, OFM, who, however, conducted his mission through written reports and correspondence. His report to the Consistorial Congregation suggested that the Society should be allowed to close down. The Scalabrinian priests would then function under the same conditions as the missionaries sent abroad by the Pontifical Institute for priests who volunteer to serve the emigrants.[42] In other words, he advised that the Society be suppressed.

When the Secretary of the Consistorial Congregation, Cardinal De Lai, reported the decision of the Consistorial Cardinals to Pope Pius XI, it was decided instead that the Society should come under the direct jurisdiction of the Consistorial Congregation itself; its Cardinal Secretary thus became *de jure* the Superior General of the Society (March, 1924).

Cardinal De Lai "immediately sent to the Motherhouse of the Society in Piacenza, his Assessor, Bishop (later Cardinal) Raffaello Carlo Rossi, who was later to play so large a part in the rebirth of the Institute as to earn the title *alter parens*.[43] His visit took place in April, 1924, and was truly providential."[44]

Bishop Rossi's visit as well as the tour of the Missions conducted by Bishop Amleto Cicognani (then substitute secretary of the Consistory, later Apostolic Delegate to the United States and then Cardinal Secretary of State) proved that the situation was quite different from that reported by Father Cimino. "When one is on the spot one sees that many things were badly reported." — "I now see that the decision of their Eminences to keep the Institute alive has been most wise."[45] In Piacenza Bishop Rossi had found an excellent spirit among the seminarians and a "supreme desire" to keep the Institute alive. The little community was taken in hand by Father Francesco Tirondola,[46] an intuitive man of creative and open mind, who had a talent for organization and achievement.

"These two names are associated with the opening of the splendid seminary in Bassano del Grappa in 1930; the Scalabrini-O'Brien Institute in Cermenate in 1939, the gift of Auxiliary Bishop William O'Brien of Chicago; the Scalabrini-Bonomelli Institute in Rezzato in 1947; the Nursing Home in Arco in Trent, 1947; the additions to the Generalate and the Motherhouse; the establishment of seminaries in the United States and Brazil for sons of Italian emigrants; and many other works that marked the rebirth of the Order. The work was spreading even beyond Italy. In 1936 the first Scalabrini Fathers left for Paris and began the collaboration with the Bonomelli Missionaries that was to bear so much good fruit in the future. Between 1941 and 1943 we find the Scalabrinians in Germany and Switzerland to serve the contingents of Italian laborers. In 1946 they are also in Belgium and Luxemburg.

"The reason for so much vigor and this degree of expansion is to be sought in the spiritual order, and the historian of the Society will inevitably find it in a measure of supreme importance taken by the unforgettable Cardinal Rossi in 1934. That was the restoration of religious vows, which restored the Society to the spirit of its beginnings."[47]

The Society again became a religious Congregation, properly so-called, on February 10, 1934, when Pius XI approved the introduction of simple, temporary and perpetual religious vows.

The new Constitutions were approved by the Consistorial Congregation on August 15, 1936. The rapid development of the Society then gave rise to new requirements, which were met by changes in the Constitutions approved by Pius XII in the audience granted Cardinal Rossi on August 7, 1948, and consequently published by his successor, Cardinal Adeodato Piazza on January 17, 1949.

The latter, who was secretary of the Consistorial Congregation from 1948 to 1957, convoked the third General Chapter of the Society (July 5-14, 1951), which elected Father Francesco Prevedello as Superior General. The Scalabrinian Congregation thus regained its autonomy and full status as a religious congregation "ad norman iuris communis."[48]

The following year Scalabrini's goal was realized when the Church officially assumed responsibility for emigrants with the publication by Pius XII of the Apostolic Constitution Exsul Familia, which codified the Church's concern up to that time for emigrants and refugees.[49]

In 1957 the fourth General Chapter elected Father Raffaele Larcher as Superior General. He was succeeded in 1963 by Father Giulivo Tessarolo, who was elected by the fifth General Chapter. The Scalabrini Missionaries, meanwhile, had extended their activities to France (1936), Switzerland (1939), Argentina and Germany (1940), Belgium and Luxemburg (1946), Australia and Chile (1952), Canada (1953), England (1954), Venezuela (1958) and Uruguay (1961).

In 1967, eighty years after its foundation, the Congregation was divided into nine Provinces and two delegations under the direct jurisdiction of the Superior General. It numbered 575 missionaries working in 15 countries, five major seminaries with 218 students, 11 minor seminaries with 818 students, three novitiates with 55 novices, 93 territorial parishes, 46 national parishes and 51 other missions. Mass was assured in 766 chapels or mission centers, and the Order was responsible for 98 social-recreation centers, 111 parish schools, 100 kindergartens, 50 evening schools, 4 orphanages, 4 shelters, 9 parish hospitals or chaplaincies, 3 radio stations broadcasting 94 religious programs a week. It was also publishing 200,000 copies of missionary or parish publicatioins, had organized two Centers for Migration Studies, and was reaching with its ministry 2,043,600 persons.[50]

Bishop Scalabrini on the ship "Liguria" before departing for North America.

CHAPTER XI

The Two "Pastoral Visits" to the Emigrants

The United States

The zeal that took Scalabrini through the five pastoral visits in his diocese naturally kindled his desire to visit those distant sons who were also his charges and who, even more than those at home, called for their Father's presence. The missionaries had repeatedly asked for a visit, and this was also greatly desired by the emigrants. A few years earlier, Leo XIII had encouraged him to undertake a journey to the Americas, but in Rome Scalabrini had the impression that a trip to the United States might offend certain sensibilities of the American hierarchy.

The bishops of the United States feared that the immigrants would be withdrawn from the jurisdiction of the local hierarchy and they had reacted vigorously to an idea put forth at the International Congress of the Raphaelsverein in Lucerne in December of 1890. The delegates of the St. Raphael Society had sent a petition to the Pope the preceding spring, in which they stated, among other things, that:

"It would be desirable, whenever it was deemed possible, for the

Catholics of the different nationalities to have in the Hierarchy of the country of immigration a bishop of the same national origin. In this way it seems the organization of the Church would be perfect. Every immigrant people would be represented, and their needs defended in the assemblies of the Bishops."

This type of proposal, which was later adopted by Vatican Council II,[1] was one of those ideas that, as Scalabrini noted, were hopelessly slow in gaining acceptance. In the United States the relation of the Bishops to the immigrants was rather delicate because basically the country was composed of multiple immigrations. Hence it is understandable that the proposal, quite misunderstood in that extremely sensitive atmosphere, was suspected of being directed against the bishops of Irish origin and seemed an unwarranted foreign interference in the Church in the United States. Actually, the suggestion was for a *de facto* not a *de jure* representation in the Bishops' meetings; there was no intention whatever of asking for "national" bishops with jurisdiction over the groups of immigrants from their respective countries of origin. The violent reaction in the American Catholic papers, which spread to Protestant and then political circles, prompted a letter of clarification from Cardinal Rampolla to Cardinal Gibbons, the Archbishop of Baltimore, dated June 30, 1891:

"The Holy See, having carefully studied this plan, found it to be neither opportune nor necessary and does not consider that changes should be introduced in the practice followed up to this time...Therefore the Holy Father has charged me to appeal to Your Eminence not only to advise you not to approve or foster that movement, produced by unfounded fears, but also to ask you, in agreement with your colleagues in the Hierarchy, to work to restore calm in the certainty that the august head of the Church is not disposed to accept any proposal that can cause the least disquiet, while assistance to the Catholic emigrants in the various countries can be provided by the national clergy, as has been the custom."[2]

These events explain Scalabrini's hesitancy, for he was always careful to respect the rights of the local hierarchy. But his hesitancy was overcome by Father Gambera of the Boston mission, who sounded out the ecclesiastical climate, found it favorable, and left for Piacenza with the intention of having "His Excellency Bishop Scalabrini come next year to visit these Missions. The Apostle, or better the Father of the Italians in this land has the right and the duty to visit his children at least once."[3]

Father Gambera brought the letters of the American Bishops to the Prefect of *Propaganda Fide*. The Congregation approved and encouraged the trip, and Leo XIII blessed the Bishop on his departure.

On July 18, 1901, Scalabrini embarked at Genoa on the *Liguria*, the use of which was given him through the courtesy of Senator Piaggio. He immediately went down to third class to see the emigrants, who gathered around him, confused and deeply moved by his presence.[4] Twelve thousand more emigrants boarded the ship in Naples. Scalabrini was happy to act as their ship's chaplain, and a young American priest, who embarked at Naples, became his secretary, confessor and friend.[5]

The notes Scalabrini kept on the trip and sent to his secretary, Father Mangot, reveal the inner spirituality and apostolic commitment of his priestly life. To quote at random:

"July 21. I celebrated Mass on the deck, overlooking the sea, which was perfectly calm. All the passengers were present. It is Sunday...I cannot describe what I feel...they are impressions of heaven, of the divine. At the Elevation of the Host, they were moved to tears...

"July 24...I am making my usual monthly retreat.

"July 28. I officiate at First Communion and Confirmation for several children of our emigrants. The altar is on the open deck and 1200 persons attend the services. Before Mass I preach the sermon. Many weep. We are on the high seas...Every day from four to five I explain the catechism to a number of young boys; this is a great consolation.

"July 31. I keep very well. I eat, sleep, pray, study, meditate on the same schedule I do at home.

"August 1. Yesterday I heard quite a number of confessions and this morning I was to repeat Sunday's ceremony; but there is a rather strong gale blowing and so it had to take place inside in the salon, which was crammed with people. I spoke before giving Communion and again before the Confirmation. Three young boys were confirmed today. One becomes eloquent, even if one is not. We are drawing near American soil...How grateful I must be to God who has brought me this far with so many special blessings and to my dear priests and people in Piacenza who have prayed for me!...I am up on the bridge and contemplating...the vastness of the Ocean...How one feels here the greatness of God! Benedicite nomen Domini...

"August 2. What a great consolation it was to celebrate the Mass of St. Alphonsus this morning! How moving it was to give Communion to the men who had come to confession yesterday!

Nine o'clock. Te Deum Laudamus! We have arrived safely...So I must close and I do so with regret...I found so much comfort in talking with you and my sons across the Ocean even if only in my thoughts!...I embrace you, I bless you all...I embrace and bless my priests and my people, whom I love with a great love..."[6]

He landed on the morning of August 3rd. The missionaries and Italian authorities had prepared a royal welcome for him. Sixty carriages accompanied him in procession to the first Scalabrinian church, the parish of St. Joachim.

"The bishop, in warm and affectionate terms, addressed the faithful, exhorting the Italians to remain united in the memory of their distant fatherland, to win respect in this strange country and to obey its laws... Immediately afterwards Archbishop Corrigan of New York arrived and offered the hospitality of his residence, but Bishop Scalabrini, thanking him for his solicitude, remained with his Missionaries."[7]

On the 7th he visited the "splendid centers for other nationalities established by the St. Raphael Society"[8] and admired the arrangements made for the Irish and German immigrants. He went to Ellis Island, where he watched the arrival of 600 Italians. According to one newspaper account he marveled at the speed and organization with which the officials processed those great numbers of passengers of various nationalities and languages and quietly sorted them as to whether they were to be admitted or detained on the Island.[9]

But Scalabrini had a much more profound reaction to the scene, as he himself later told President Theodore Roosevelt:

"The Italians have seen themselves scattered throughout the world for some time, without any protection or defense and subjected to the disdain of others. Hence they have been forced to defend themselves. They have done wrong, but one must also consider how they have sometimes been treated. While I was visiting Ellis Island I myself saw a guard order an emigrant to hurry. The man could not hasten his step because he was carrying two large suitcases and because his way was blocked by the crowd in front of him. The guard then hit him such a terrible blow in the legs with a huge stick that I thought he had broken them. The Italian, without saying a word, set down his suitcases, turned and slapped his tormentor sharply twice, and then mumbled: If I had had a revolver I would have killed him. Certainly that would have been an evil thing; but why do some functionaries have to be so cruel to these workers who come in peace and instead of giving them on their arrival a little confidence in their new country treat them like beasts or worse?"[10]

That afternoon he took a boat trip around the harbor.

"It is astonishing. Four million persons engaged in feverish activity, with elevated trains, etc. Here indeed new and grandiose ideas are fermenting."[11] "From this incessant, rapid, feverish motion, the numerous riches of this land, I can now understand the inventiveness and mental effervescence and at times the eccentricity of this people."[12]

Church and School

On the 9th, Scalabrini inaugurated and blessed the *Casa San Raffaele*, which the missionaries had established to aid Italians on their arrival. Along with his advice on aid to the immigrants, he noted the lack of unity that weakened Italian assistance activities.

"Oh, if only our settlements in the United States, unfortunately divided
in bits and pieces by the hundreds of provident societies and societies
of persons from the same town of origin, followed Bishop Scalabrini's
plans, how many works of mutual benefit could be easily carried out to
lift them to the level of other foreign settlements! But little or nothing
can be done because their forces are completely dissipated...Those who
accomplish something truly good, practical and disinterested, motivated
by pure love of Religion and Country, are the Missionaries of Bishop
Scalabrini's order, and not only in their churches, at the doors of which
disastrous regionalism disappears and Northern and Southern Italians
enter and sit down together as brothers,...but also with the St. Raphael
Society, which on Ellis Island helps, comforts and advises the poor
Italians detained there."[13]

Scalabrini expressed a similar thought to the President:

"A great future is opening up for us Italians, provided we are united
and work together and are guided by our faith. This is what I told
President Roosevelt. The Italian element, provided it stays together and
above all keeps its religion, can become one of the mainstays of the
American structure...United and faithful to religion, that is all."[14]

On August 11th, he visited the second Scalabrinian church built in New
York, dedicated to Our Lady of Pompeii.

"I am pleased at what I find," he wrote. "Our Missionaries do a great
deal of good; they enjoy universal esteem and many of the clergy, even
American priests, go to them for confession. The Bishops are very
satisfied with their work and express their great approval to me,
observing only that there is need of more priests."[15]

And again: "I continue to hear the greatest praise for our Missionaries.
Yesterday the Bishop of Harrisburg said to me, 'Your Missionaries are
admirable priests; we prefer them. They live where they can and make
the best of what they have, in order to provide for the needs of their
countrymen. We have only one complaint; you send us too few. All the
Bishops who have Italian colonies earnestly desire to have them'." —
"All the Bishops seek to keep the Missionaries they have. The Bishop of
Cleveland, as soon as he saw me, exclaimed, 'If possible, I forbid you to
take away any of my Fathers.' So be it, I answered."[16]

From August 15th to the 18th he visited the Italian communities and
missions in Jersey City and in Newark, New Jersey. From the 19th to the
24th he preached a retreat to sixty Italian priests.[17] But then he was obliged
to take a rest for a few days.

"The weather was not favorable; the heat was suffocating and it was
so damp the doors were warped and could not be closed. The food was
horrible, all American style, and every one got sick, myself included.
However, I continued the *opus Dei* to the end."[18]

On September 1st he was in New Haven, Connecticut, where he was welcomed with typical Southern Italian enthusiasm, fireworks and brass bands from the various Italian societies with a strange assortment of names: Brotherhood, Garibaldi, St. Anthony, St. Mary Magdalene, Victor Emmanuel III, Children of Mary. The religious ceremonies were "Beautiful and moving... great attendance at Communion, more men than women; Confirmation ceremonies recollected and devout."[19]

In an interview with a correspondent of the *New Haven Union*, he underlined the problem of the Catholic, or Italian parish school:

"It is striking fact that the Italians are the only Catholics in this country who are without a parochial school system...The bishop long ago conceived the idea of starting a movement in favor of Italian parochial schools in this country, and that is mainly his purpose here at this time..."He said that the system of parochial schools which he would have established among the Italians here differed not at all from those in existence among Irish and German Catholics. The only reason why these schools have not been started among the Italians is that they are a very poor class, and in their struggle for a lifelihood have neglected this most important phase of education. The bishop feels that the time is now ripe to start parochial schools among Italians."[20]

Nationalism as an end in itself, however, was entirely foreign to Scalabrini's thinking. In the preservation of Italian culture — as an ethnic not a political reality — he saw a means of preserving the faith which the immigrants, unfitted for religious independence for the most part, had learned in the cultural environment of their native country. He was anxious to create the same vital environment for them but at the same time he encouraged them to enrich their lives with the new culture in which they had to live:

"Naturally I believe in a good education in English. But the Italian citizen in the United States should learn both languages. There is no reason why, in studying the life and customs of his adopted country, he should forget the land of his birth."[21]

Studies on the migration phenomenon and Vatican Council II have renewed the concept of acculturation — of the harmonious living together of various cultures for mutual enrichment and the development of a more universal man. This concept and the question of Italian parish schools, Scalabrini stressed repeatedly. The ideas expressed in his writings on emigration were now confirmed by experience. To the Italians in St. Louis he said:

"Observe the customs of the country that has received you; conform to them as much as possible. Learn to speak English but do not forget your own beautiful maternal tongue. Send your children to school; help the parish schools where they have been established. Above all go to church."[22]

According to *The Italian Herald* his journey was "from beginning to end an act of justice to our country, an omen for a better and closer union between our people and the American people, a vindication of our immigration in answer to those who do not understand it or know it only superficially, or fail to appreciate it out of prejudice."[23]

In an address to the Catholic Club of New York on October 15th, Scalabrini spoke of the benefits that would accrue to humanity and the Church from the vital interchange among the various cultures:

"I think the religious and moral greatness of the Italian emigrant cause and the political and material greatness of this hospitable country...are destined to be fused and to unveil to the twentieth century the secrets of a new era, which will lack neither the blessings of God nor the conquests of civilization...This land of blessings will give rise to inspirations, develop principles, unfurl new mysterious forces that will come to regenerate and revivify the old world, teaching it the true economy of liberty, brotherhood, equality, showing it that people of diverse origins can very well keep their own language and nationality while being politically and religiously united, free of the barriers that divide and cause envy and without armed forces to dominate and destroy one another. And thus, by America and through America, the great promise of the Gospel will be fulfilled: One flock and one Shepherd."[24]

At the reception tendered him before his departure by the leaders of the Italian colony, Scalabrini confessed that one constant disturbing thought he had had about his visit was the fact that the Italians did not seem to care about preserving Italian culture for their children who were born or educated in America. Their indifference and neglect, however, he felt was due to the lack of Italian schools. He therefore warmly seconded Father Gambera's proposal, which was to stop waiting for action on the part of the Italian government and to have the missionaries take the initiative despite their limited means.

"Begin, begin, even in a small way. The colony will recognize the value of your work before you think they will; the government of your fatherland will recognize it and perhaps will subsidize it."[25]

He had admired, with a certain envy, the position the Irish had earned for themselves though they "were poor when they arrived and looked upon with disfavor," but he was sure the new Italian immigrants, protected according to the law of 1901, would soon reach the same level in American society. "Two things are necessary, however, the Church and the School."[26]

Opportunities and Prospects

On the evening of September 5th he arrived in Boston, where he was given a tremendous welcome. "It is not possible to describe the enthusiasm of our colony, which numbers more than 40,000 persons. Processions, bands, lights and decorations that cannot be described."[27] The colony had indeed prepared a welcome that combined characteristic American "bigness" with the colorfulness of Little Italy. But on the evening of September 7th, came the news that President McKinley had been shot by an anarchist, and Scalabrini requested that the festival prepared in his honor be cancelled. His gesture was greatly praised in the American press.

While in Boston he visited the Polish mission, which was headed by the Scalabrinian Father John Chimielinski.

"With my permission he has dedicated himself for years to his Polish fellow countrymen and he has succeeded in building a fine church with a good rectory...I said Mass and had Father John say what I could not tell them. They understand only their own language. I was deeply touched by this function, which was for me a silent one."[28]

On the 12th he left for Utica, New York: "This morning when I left the church after Holy Mass, the people wept as they said goodbye, so that it was heartbreaking to see them and to hear the names they showered upon me, angel, savior, etc."[29] On the 14th he confirmed 900 children in Syracuse and on the 15th he returned to Utica to lay the cornerstone for the Church of Our Lady of Mount Carmel.[30]

On the 17th he wrote from Buffalo:

"I am going to visit our schools and this evening I will speak in the church to our colony, which numbers as many as 20,000 persons. Two more Missionaries are needed: *rogemus Dominum messis* and all that follows. The Bishop (Bishop Quigley) is a modest, cordial man, who is truly apostolic and admirable. If they were all like him, full of respect and affectionate solicitude for the Italians, our colonies would soon advance and would soon acquire a very important status."[31]

After a brief stop in Canada, he arrived in Cleveland on the 18th, and on the 21st he was in Detroit. A twenty-three hour journey by train took him to St. Paul, where he again met with his friend Bishop Ireland, who had come to greet him on his arrival in New York and had promised to send him a special train in order to have a visit from him.[32]

After another twenty hours by train, he arrived in Kansas City[33] on the 28th, and on October 1st he went to St. Louis.

"I was very pleased with my stay in St. Louis. After twenty years of quarreling and sterile complaints, I have managed to purchase the church they were renting. They are all satisfied, and have quietly accepted my proposals."[34]

The reference was to the usual disagreements, typical of the Italians, which so worried Scalabrini.

On October 6th Scalabrini wrote from Cincinnati, Ohio:

"I should like to be on my way, but unfortunately I have to postpone my departure until early November. If I had to accept all the invitations who knows how long I would have to stay here. But I feel the need to return; this will tell you whether I could have accepted the responsibility the papers were talking about, rashly as always, perennially given to disturbing other people's peace."[35]

He was referring to the appointment as Apostolic Delegate to the United States, but the story was not unfounded for Cardinal Rampolla had mentioned the matter to Scalabrini's friend, Bishop Agliardi.[36]

He arrived in Columbus, Ohio on October 7th and in Washington, D. C. on the 9th. He visited the Apostolic Delegate and called on the new American President, Theodore Roosevelt, who acknowledged, though from a somewhat utilitarian viewpoint, the merits and the sacrifices of the Italian immigrants.

"He told me that our immigrants are worthy of respect and that our laborers are needed where there is difficult and dangerous work to do because their intelligence and their persistence are without comparison."

The President also praised the intelligence of the Italian boys who were carrying off all the prizes in school. But Bishop Scalabrini led the conversation to the painful subject of crime, for he was anxious to correct the ugly reputation of knifers that weighed indiscriminately on all Italians. He noted that in the latest statistics on crime, Italians were at the bottom of the list. He deplored the behavior of some but led the President also to deplore the way in which Americans frequently treated the immigrants, pushing them until they reacted by taking the law in their own hands or resorting to crime.[37]

On October 11th in Baltimore he had a friendly visit with Cardinal Gibbons. On the 13th he returned to New York, where he confirmed 750 young Italians, and on the 15th at the Catholic Club he gave an address, "vibrant with faith and prophetic inspiration," which was published in the metropolitan newspapers. He thanked those Americans who had given sincere evidence that disdain for the Italians was beginning to disappear and that there was growing recognition of the benefits they contributed to American society through their hidden heroism, often with an abundant offering of blood. But he went on to enlarge upon the perspectives of faith and Christian hope, on the Christocentric vision of history, on the providentiality of emigration as an event in the history of the salvation and unity of the human race.

"Once again I have admired, with a deep and enthusiastic joy, God's great design for America...It is a principle of faith that God has done all things and does all things through His Word, Jesus Christ. Therefore all that He has done for the American continent He has done through Christ, and Christ does all things through His Church. America then is the patrimony of Christ, the promised land of the Catholic Church![38] Here, therefore, if inertia, ignorance of the ways of God, complacency over laurels won, and differing aspirations do not deviate the people from the divine plan, one day all the nations will have here numerous descendants, rich, happy, moral, religious who, while retaining the characteristics of their respective nationalities, will be closely united... I hope this, yes, I hope this, Gentlemen. For while the world is dazzled by its progress, while man exults over his conquests of matter and lords it over nature, disemboweling the earth, yoking the lightening, cutting isthmuses to mingle the waters of the oceans, eliminating distances; while nations fall and rise and renew themselves; while races mingle, spread and fuse; above the roar of our machines, above all this feverish activity, over and beyond all these gigantic achievements and not without them, a much vaster, nobler, more sublime work is developing; the union in God through Jesus Christ of all men of good will."[39]

In Providence, Rhode Island, on October 19th, he blessed the church and again stressed the need for schools. On October 27th he returned to Boston to administer confirmation in the Polish Church and to greet again the sizeable Italian colony in the city, to which he wrote:

"I shall pray for all of you because I hope that this Colony in Boston will be the most flourishing and the most religious in the United States. But to obtain this grace, you must keep alive the idea of an Italian School and Sisters."[40]

At the end of the month he preached the retreat for the four deacons he had had come from Piacenza and on November 3rd he ordained them. Among the four there was another Pole, Father Stephen Duda. In the afternoon he visited the Italian colony in Brooklyn:

"My reception was something quite extraordinary and moving. I was deeply touched by that rare explosion of Italian faith, which on every occasion shows up with such vigor in those who have not lost it. For the dangers to the faith here are many. The Protestants use every means to lure the Italians especially and I return to Italy with much greater apprehension on this score than I had when I arrived here."[41]

The last stop on this great "pastoral visit" was Newark, New Jersey, on November 11th, where Scalabrini dedicated an orphanage for Italian boys.

"He preserved a very deep and pleasant memory of this last function on American soil. When he carried the Blessed Sacrament out of the church to bless the people crowded in front of it, the whole throng dropped to their knees as one person in so great a demonstration of faith that the mayor of the city, a Protestant, when he later congratulated the bishop added: 'If I see another spectacle like this I shall lose my own faith and become a Catholic.' "[42]

On November 12th he blessed and embraced his missionaries, said his goodbyes to the authorities and to the crowd that had come sorrowing to see him off, and started on the journey home.

"He was in the United States for three months and ten days, and in that short time he gave 340 talks, confirmed thousands of children, traveled night and day for thousands and thousands of miles, sleeping in trains, changing beds, food, climate, and habits, and yet in the midst of all that work he was always happy and always, thanks be to God, in good health. An evident sign that the Lord wanted him in America to do a great good for the poor Italian immigrants. And he did it. We must thank the Lord from our hearts because Bishop Scalabrini's brief stay in America greatly boosted the morale of the Italians and everyone, without distinction, recognized in him a true apostle, a saint, filled with zeal for the salvation of souls."[43]

The "independent" paper of the Italian colonies, *Cristoforo Colombo* carried a tribute to Scalabrini:

"Bishop Scalabrini's order is *providential*. Let laymen, or the skeptics or in any case the opponents of the Bishop of Piacenza establish one themselves that is equal or better than this. If they succeed in doing as well or better, they too will have a right to the admiration of the public. But as long as Bishop Scalabrini, with his missions, is the only one to take thought for the immigrants and to provide for their welfare, his institution is above criticism. To him and him alone encouragement and praise is due, and it is right, in fact it is patriotic, to give the Apostle of the Italian immigrants the reverence and gratitude which are the right of the true benefactors of humanity."[44]

Scalabrini landed in Naples on November 26, 1901. Leo XIII received him on the 29th and listened with great interest to his report. We do not know how he was received in the Secretariat of State, which had been surprised at the enthusiasm shown by American Catholics, who were rather cool to the papal representatives.[45] He conferred with *Propaganda Fide* and Foreign Minister Prinetti on the emigrant situation and the protective measures his observations·recommended before returning to Piacenza on December 4th.

He was greeted by such an impressive demonstration of affection on the part of the people and the clergy and of respect from all the civil authorities, that when the *Te Deum* was ended he could hardly speak.[46]

On the wearisome journey that he had accomplished so successfully, his characteristic comment was: "The consolations were far greater than my modest efforts."[47]

Brazil

"Are you planning on taking another trip?" he was asked.

"You go too fast. I have just arrived home and I have to reckon with my age. I am sixty-two years old!"[48]

Meanwhile, despite his age, he plunged into a period of feverish activity to make up for lost time.[49] He undertook the fifth pastoral visit, during which long rides on horseback aggravated the illness that was later to cause his death and he himself made mention of a certain sense of physical weakness and lack of spirit.[50] Yet how could he speak of lack of spirit when he was planning to go to Brazil where he knew the only means of transportation was a horse or a donkey? The missionaries and the emigrants were expecting him. Pius X had repeatedly told him he would like to see him repeat in South America the beneficent results of his first journey. Above all he felt the need to settle on the basis of experience the definitive form of his Congregation, and the training to be given his missionaries, for he confessed he had not yet formed a clear concept of this despite the copious correspondence he carried on with the missions in Brazil.

Many of his friends, when they learned of it, tried to dissuade him from making this second journey; his brother Angelo who was familiar with Brazil tried especially hard.[51] But Bishop Scalabrini turned a tin ear. For him there were only two voices, that of charity and that of the Pope, and these were the voices of God. During a difficult time at sea he wrote: "I am here for Him, and for Him I will carry out the program He inspired in me, even at the cost of my life if necessary."[52]

Having learned Portuguese in a few months, drawn up his will and said goodbye to his friends and people, he left Piacenza on June 13, 1904. The following day he was received in audience by Pope Pius X, who was awaiting detailed information on the emigrants' situation before issuing the decrees already drawn up on their behalf. The Holy Father was visibly moved as he affectionately embraced his old friend. He invoked God's blessings on him and the six missionaries accompanying him and promised him that everyday at seven o'clock he would "send" him his blessing. On the 17th, Scalabrini set sail from Naples.

"On board, June 17, 1904. This morning, united in spirit with the dear people of my diocese, I celebrated Mass here in Naples on the tomb of Blessed Paolo Burali, my glorious predecessor in the See of Piacenza, and I experienced a deep emotion and a great tranquillity of spirit. I seemed to hear his voice saying: 'Go where God calls you; I will take your place during this time and care for the people who once were mine...' Toward the hour of the Ave Maria the ship sailed out of the harbor and my journey began. May God be with me and help me."[53]

On board ship he kept to the same schedule he had at home. Every day he practiced speaking Portuguese with a Brazilian colonel and with his missionaries. He chatted with the passengers, and often went down into third class to visit with the 500 emigrants, of whom 100 were Turks of the Maronite rite. But this time he left the duties of ship's chaplain to his young missionaries. He needed to rest before taking on the rigors of the land journey.

"He is always busy on board, he is never idle a minute, and he is satisfied and content, he says, because he is now leading a relatively quiet life. The work, the sacrifices will come later for him, there in the land of Santa Cruz in the vast country of Brazil."[54]

Whatever the winds and storms at sea, his diary reveals a great sense of interior peace and tranquillity, which he attributed to the daily blessing of the Pope.[55]

Throughout the crossing, he devoted himself to the usual duties of the ministry:

"June 19, Sunday. Today our mission may be said to have begun. The ship seemed converted into a monastery. I celebrated a Pontifical Mass and spoke to the 500 travelers, and we were all very much moved...Many received Communion...At three o'clock there was Christian doctrine for the children and the adults. We have enrolled those who will make their First Communion or be confirmed within the next two weeks. We will have catechism for both groups every day to prepare them.

"June 28...We priests have heard confessions until quite late. I am a little tired tonight but nothing more...

"July 1...at one o'clock a poor crewman had the misfortune to be hit on the head with an iron bucket. He was taken immediately to the infirmary with a badly fractured skull. I went to visit him...He was a pitiful sight! He went to confession as well as he could, since it was very difficult for him to speak. Now it seems there is some hope of saving his life. May God will it!"

Two hours later a fight broke out between an Italian and a Turk. The Bishop's servant, Carlo Spallazzi, gave this account on his return:

"I was dozing and jumped from my berth and ran to look for the Bishop, for I did not know the cause of all the uproar; and I found the Bishop in his cabin guarded by a group of Italian emigrants, ready to defend him from a possible rebellion of the Turks...The sailors ran toward the fight and threw anything that came to hand at the two violently struggling men. When they were patched up the captain put them in irons, and they were released only through the intercession of the bishop...When we passed the Equator, the weather was terribly hot and damp, depressingly sultry. The Bishop nevertheless said Mass on deck, and often went down among the emigrants and helped a great many of them."[56]

On July 3rd, after a stormy night during which he spent himself comforting the terrified passengers, Bishop Scalabrini said Mass, though with some difficulty, and preached holding on to the altar with one hand and the railing with the other. He gave First Communion to fifteen youngsters, and two days later on July 5th, he confirmed twenty.

He landed in Rio de Janeiro on the 7th and was welcomed by the Archbishop, to whom he spoke of the need for aid for the Italian emigrants at the port, and also a church for them. He decided to proceed by ship to Santos, and from there he reached Sao Paulo on July 9th, traveling by a special train placed at his disposal. All the civil and ecclesiastical authorities were waiting for him on his arrival, with the Bishop "in full ceremonial regalia as if he were receiving the Pope,"[57] a great crowd of Italians, and bands from the Salesian schools and the Christopher Columbus orphanage. The band from the latter had gone to greet "their" bishop on the train itself some miles earlier. Among the six missionaries accompanying Scalabrini were two who had been brought up in that same orphanage.

In Sao Paulo

Scalabrini was careful to avoid in Rome and Rio any contacts that might cast the least shadow of political intent on his journey. He soon realized that his prudence was justified. In an interview carried in the *Fanfulla* of Sao Paulo, he stated:

"I have no mission whatever from any government. My mission is essentially religious...I sought out no officials in Rome and none sought me...A political mission, so to speak, would have compromised my work and given rise to envy. Even if one had been offered me I would have refused it. I have too many things to do...My program can be precisely summed up in these words: to do all possible good without inconveniencing or troubling anyone, while seeking to keep alive the Italian language and traditions of our people. And to do this with strict respect for the laws and customs of the countries where our countrymen go to live...And to develop this program to strengthen the faith and to increase the number of our schools...I insist very much on education. During my long trip through North America I told our countrymen over and over again: 'the Italian language; this is the key to your strength and your unity...' While a man speaks *his own* language, he does not lose his faith."[58]

At this point we might ask ourselves if all Bishop Scalabrini's ideas would be considered valid today, or if he himself would hold the same views if he were living in our time. But the question is irrelevant. What is important to note here is the strictly religious and missionary spirit which inspired him and the goal for which he used the means which at that time and that moment in migrant history he considered the most useful:

"As for me and my missionaries, we lay no claim to scholarly research nor do we offer easy solutions. Our desire is that the Italians who go overseas preserve their religion and a feeling for their fatherland. It is the faith...which sustains us through the misfortunes of life. To preserve it and to have a common language means being united in thought and in feeling. The faith cannot nor should it exclude what is Italian...For me the *trait-d'union* of the Italians overseas must be the faith..."[59]

He chose to stay at the Christopher Columbus Orphanage, declining the invitation the Benedictines pressed upon him. "It's a poor dwelling, but I am with my children,"[60] and his "children" gave him great consolation:

"Our fine missionaries enjoy esteem and respect from all classes, from both the Clergy and the laity. The two orphanages are truly worthy of admiration. It is edifying to see the devotion, goodness, and good manners of these 260 little orphans...These two houses have already educated and placed 810 young people. Yesterday many of them gathered here, blessing this 'holy house' as they call it."[61]

"I am glad I came. In Sao Paulo our missionaries have a tremendous amount of work to do; more than 3000 *fazendas* to visit regularly. I followed them on their rounds to get an idea of it. It is crushing work. The six priests who came with me stayed behind there, but others are needed to carry out the programs I arranged with that good Bishop."[62]

He agreed with Bishop José de Camargo Barros of Sao Paulo to take over the parish of Sao Bernardo, in which there were 40,000 Italians; and to establish two missions in the interior of the state to assist the Italians on the *fazendas*.[63]

During the month he spent in Sao Paulo, besides visiting the colonies or *fazendas* where the Italians were working,[64] he preached retreats for his missionaries and for the Sisters, and often gave lectures in Portuguese in the Seminary and in the schools of the Benedictines and Salesians.

On August 2nd he left Sao Paulo, and made a brief stopover in the states of Espiritu Santo and Rio de Janeiro. On the way from Rio to Santos, August 12th, he ran into a storm so violent that at one point he feared for the life of his servant, Spallazzi. From Santos he journeyed by coastal steamer to Paranguá, where he began the trip to Paranà. The Bishop and the civic authorities prevailed on him to stay a few days in Curitiba, and on August 19th he finally arrived at the humble wooden house of the missionaries of Santa Felicidade.

"They say this is the best colony in Brazil. The Church is very beautiful and can hold several thousand persons. Here there are Sisters, schools, frequent attendance at Mass and reception of the Sacraments as in the best Italian parishes. Within a radius of about forty miles there are many Italian colonies: Agua Verde, Campo Comprida, Timbituva, Caratuba, Ferraria, Rondinha, Campinas, Umbarà, Santa Maria Novo Tirolo, etc., all of which I visited greeted by indescribable demonstrations. Each colony had its own chapel, attended at regular intervals by the Missionaries...This territory had been a forest, the refuge of thieves and assassins, and now it is a garden in every sense of the word."[65]

On September 3rd he took the steamer at Paranaguà and on the 10th he arrived in Porto Alegre, the capital of Rio Grande do Sul, "the most beautiful of beautiful cities."

"Here they were worried about me because a real hurricane blew up, uprooting trees and ripping the roofs off houses, etc., and there was fear of a fierce storm on *Lagoa dos Patos* not far from the city. Instead we felt nothing, and the terrible Lagoa was as smooth as oil. The same thing happened to me my first time in Paranaguà. Oh, the prayers of my good Piacentini and the blessing of the Holy Father."[66]

In Rio Grande do Sul

Now came the most difficult part of the journey, the visit to the colonies in the luxuriant but trackless state of Rio Grande do Sul. The trips here took eight to ten hours on horseback and the illness he had contracted during the pastoral visits must have made this extremely painful.

"Whoever has seen these places can understand the discomforts of the trips undertaken by the Servant of God, who because of a certain ailment could not ride horseback. And when he could endure it no longer, they had him mount an improvised cart drawn by two or three horses. Imagine therefore what the Servant of God suffered, given also the winter season and the constant rain."[67]

Scalabrini left Porto Alegre the 12th and went up the river to Lageado, from where, after a seven hour ride on horseback, he reached Encantado.

"In the morning the horses sent from Encantado were ready, along with a goodly number of settlers to accompany him. The Bishop immediately understood what a rough journey he was to make, or better the torment he was about to endure from the means of transportation provided him. He was already suffering from the ailment that afflicted him, and he asked more than once if there really were not some vehicle, even any ordinary little cart. When he heard there wasn't, he said, 'let us go, *in nomine Domini*,' and he set out. It meant about seven hours on horseback for him."[68]

Three hundred horsemen escorted him the last few miles. After seven hours of martyrdom, he went directly to the church and preached, arousing, if possible, even greater enthusiasm among all those good people who had given him a clamorous and joyous welcome, complete with firecrackers and mortar shots.[69] He remained in Encantado for ten days to receive the immigrants who were pouring in daily by the thousands from the most distant colonies.

Bishop Rinaldi[70] recalled that Scalabrini spent himself "in constant, tiring work all the more exhausting because of the climate and the state of the roads...But he adapted to everything and was always smiling, in good humor, even at meals contenting himself with whatever the cook, who was the undersigned, had prepared...Our meals were quite frugal and hurriedly prepared, since he insisted that I stay with him instead of taking care of the cooking."

September 22nd found him in San Lourenço de Villas Boas:

"I left Encantado, on Thursday, the 22nd, and arrived here after five hours on horseback; I was not expected. They had expected me the day before, but the rains had ruined the trails. As soon as they saw me, the various groups shot off cannon and rifles and were amazed and moved by my courage."[71]

He confirmed 1500 persons and then went on to Comde d'Eu, and from there to Alfredo Chaves, a journey of 36 miles in a subtropical downpour.[72]

He visited Capoeiras and pushed on as far as Nova Bassano, about 200 miles from Encantado. On the way back to Alfredo Chaves, still tireless, he visited the missions entrusted to other orders, for he considered "his" all those dedicated to the service of the immigrants.[73]

"The activity of the illustrious Bishop of Piacenza, given his advanced age, is truly remarkable. Suffice it to say that in only four days, besides visiting the houses of his missionaries, the fazendas, etc., he confirmed a good 5000 persons, going sometimes on foot sometimes on horseback (over often terrible roads) from one place to another, receiving innumerable visitors everywhere, blessing marriages, churches, cemetaries, laying the foundation for other useful works, hearing confessions, preaching two, three, five times a day...To hear him and receive his blessing many — as in Caxias — spent the night in the church square and on leaving asked God's blessing on this holy Prelate."[74]

After stopovers in Bento Gonçalves and Comde d'Eu, Scalabrini arrived in Caxias on October 12th. This was the last town he visited. The fact that the crowd, who had traveled long distances to greet him on his arrival, spent the night in the square in order to attend his Mass the next morning is some measure of the warmth of the welcome they gave him.

"In the five weeks he spent among the Italian colonies he confirmed no less than 15,000! It seems incredible when one considers the difficulties and discomforts of the journey and the exertions it entailed."[75]

On October 27th he departed from Porto Alegre and on the 29th stopped in Rio Grande to await the steamer that was to take him to Buenos Aires.

"In Porto Alegre I had to wait almost eight days; and here, how long must I wait? It is a great trial...I have come for the Lord, and for love of Him one must endure everything, everything."[76]

He did not reach Buenos Aires until November 9th, and there he was able to greet his brother Peter, whom he had not seen for forty years, and who was now director of the National Museum and professor at the university.

Together with the auxiliary bishop and the Salesians, who had been zealously working for many years among the numerous Italians in Argentina, Bishop Scalabrini planned the establishment of the St. Raphael Society in Buenos Aires. He left on the 11th and landed in Genoa on December 5th. The next day he sang the *Te Deum* of thanksgiving in his own cathedral. His people welcomed him with outpourings of affection, and the Holy Father congratulated him in a letter bearing his personal signature and accompanied by a large gold medal. Pius asked to see him as soon as possible.

For a French newspaper, Bishop Scalabrini summed up his impressions thus:

"Politically our emigrants are tolerated rather than protected. Economically their situation varies with the regions...Each group has built its own chapel dedicated to the patron saint of the town they came from, and they gather there to pray. For the liturgical functions they go to the church. A railway will cross the country (he speaks here of several valleys transformed by the Italians). The French engineer in charge of laying it told me with emotion that in the humblest homes he had found two pictures, that of the Pope and mine. I found strong religious devotion. I confirmed 40,000 persons. I preached in Italian, in French and in Portuguese...and I was always listened to with respect. Our missionaries are in turn apostles, doctors, farmers, artisans, counselors; that is the secret of their influence. They know personally each one of their sheep."[77]

A missionary who was at that time in Brazil wrote:

"During that difficult trip and his sojourn among the Italian colonies, Bishop Scalabrini had lost some weight and seemed pale at times, but he appeared to be completely restored during the sea voyage. In looks and conversation he gave no evidence of being tired and much less worn out. Enriched by new experiences and pleased with the results achieved by his Institution, he was dreaming...of greater things. Who would have thought that within six months the illness which had been consuming him for seven years would bring him to his grave? It is the general view that he himself contributed to this sorrowful disaster by the exhausting strains he endured on that trip. I do not know; but if that was the case we would have still another reason to salute in Bishop Scalabrini the Apostle and Martyr of the Italian emigrants."[78]

CHAPTER XII

The St. Raphael Society — Emigration Laws

The First Committees

Among the institutions for aid to emigrants he proposed, Bishop Scalabrini assigned an important role to a Benevolent Society *(Associazione di patronato)*. This was to be composed of both religious and laity and was to assist the spiritual and material needs of the Italians on both their departure and their arrival.[1] "The establishment of an entirely ecclesiastical Institute would be inadequate for the provisions necessary for full assistance to our emigrants."[2]

The proposal for such a society was presented to the Sacred Congregation for the Propagation of the Faith,[3] and on June 26, 1887, at the audience granted the Cardinal Prefect, Leo XIII approved the following:

"1. — Establishment in three or four of the principal Italian ports a committee of priests and laymen who would supervise the embarkations and give aid and encouragement to the emigrants.

2. — Establishment of a central committee in Rome to which these committees could address their correspondence and from which they

would receive instructions and necessary information.

3. — Establishment, in the principal ports of North and South America, counterpart committees composed of priests and laymen who would aid the emigrants with encouragement and advice."[4]

A month later, in July, a provisional Emigration Committee was already set up in Piacenza.[5] We do not have a clear picture of this during the first two years of its activity. At times it seemed to be a committee of the *Associazione nazionale di soccorso ai Missionari Cattolici* (National Association for Aid to Catholic Missionaries), founded in Florence in 1887 by Augusto Conti and Ernesto Schiaparelli.[6] At other times it seemed to be part of the Christopher Columbus Institute, or the Scalabrinian Congregation, which in the beginning was called *Associazione missionaria* or *Associazione di Assistenza* (Missionary Society or Aid Society). From newspaper accounts of July 11 and 14, 1888, we learn that at the departure of the first group of missionaries there was present "a large representation from the Piacentian Committee of the National Association for Aid to Italian Missionaries."[7] In an article of the following November, Marchese Volpe-Landi, the first president of the St. Raphael Society, wrote that Bishop Scalabrini spoke of the "laymen, led by the worthy Association for Aid, etc."[8] Elsewhere, however, he speaks of the Benevolent Society established in Piacenza by Scalabrini.[9]

The provisional Committee gradually disentangled itself from the confusing connections that could have proved inhibiting and developed a clearer identity more in conformity with the ideas Scalabrini had outlined in 1887.[10]

The Society was officially established on May 1, 1889. The announcement read:

"Noting the innumerable sufferings of the emigrants Bishop Scalabrini appealed for civic and legal aid among others to meet the urgent needs of the emigrants, and especially to protect them from being exploited... We, the undersigned, encouraged by the favorable reception generally accorded the generous appeal of the Bishop of Piacenza and reassured by the support of prominent citizens from every part of the country, we have accepted the summons and have decided to organize ourselves as the Central Committee of a Benevolent Society to assist the national emigrant movement..."

There followed the signatures of Marchese Volpe-Landi, Count Giuseppe Nasalli, Count Calciati, Attorney Calda and a dozen other personalities prominent among the laity of Piacenza.[11]

The Society's constitution, published four days later,[12] comprised five articles setting forth the directives the Society would follow to achieve its goal. This was:

"To cooperate to keep alive in the hearts of the Italian emigrants, along with their faith, their sense of nationality and their affection for their fatherland, and to bring about the best possible state of moral, physical, intellectual, economic and civic well-being for them."

Moral-religious assistance was already the specific activity of the Scalabrinian Congregation. In this field the Society envisaged for itself a role of support and cooperation ranging from financial help, both to the Congregation and for the erection of "churches, chapels, Mission stations," to make sure that the emigrants did not lack religious care during the sea voyage. In other, secular matters, the Society exercised greater autonomy. Its activities included medical services during the voyage; the establishment of schools and other institutions for the preservation of Italian culture; legal aid and social assistance in matters involving contractual and legal obligations whether with private citizens or the authorities, and especially legal protection against speculators; a clearing-house of information to help emigrants make a better choice of working conditions and places to settle and to aid them through the first difficulties encountered in adapting to their new environment.

The Benevolent Society had both sustaining and active members and was organized with a central committee in Piacenza and local committees in the ports of embarkation and debarkation as well as in those Italian cities which contributed the most or evidenced the greatest awareness of the migrant phenomenon. The first president of the Central Committee was Marchese Volpe-Landi, whom we have already met as one of the pioneers of the *Opera dei Congressi* and of social action on behalf of the poor. He therefore corresponded to the aims of Bishop Scalabrini whose devoted and active collaborator he was, not only as president of the Benevolent Society but in various other fields of lay activity. In particular, he was the intermediary in the delicate relations between the Bishop and the *Opera dei Congressi*.

Relations with the Opera dei Congressi

In the period 1887-1889 Volpe-Landi insisted that the Society's activity be connected with the *Opera* from the Central down to the parish committees.[13] As early as 1882, Count Acquaderni, during the preparations for the Third Catholic Congress (Naples, 1883) had proposed that action be taken for the "protection of the emigrants abroad through the establishment of the St. Raphael Society."[14] In 1888 Count Stanislaus Medolago Albani raised the question of whether the second section of the *Opera dei Congressi*, concerned with Christian socio-economics, should indeed be doing nothing with respect to the "two great social movements we are witnessing; the abolition of slavery[15] and the protection and regulation of the migrant movement. The Second Section should decide to become involved in these two movements immediately and as actively as possible."[16]

In 1889 Volpe-Landi asked Toniolo to have the union for Social Studies, which he had founded a few months before, take an interest in Bishop Scalabrini's work. Toniolo spoke of it also to Medolago Albani, who promised to do all he could.[17]

In 1892 Scalabrini sent greetings to the First Congress of Social Sciences, organized by Toniolo in Genoa on the occasion of the Columbian anniversary celebration.[18]

At the 13th Catholic Congress (Turin, September, 1895) Volpe-Landi "spoke on the subject of emigration, and proposed the extension of the work of the St. Raphael Society through Catholic committees for the protection of the emigrants."[19]

Finally the 16th Congress, which met in Ferrara April 18-21, 1899, acting on a proposal of Radini Tedeschi, dealt explicitly and at length with the emigration problem, with Bishop Scalabrini as the main speaker on the subject.[20]

"I have always keenly desired Italian Catholics to deal in...these meetings with emigration," he declared, "both because this would shed new light on this serious problem and because new blessings would pour on the work of the Catholic Congresses of Italy, which is already so highly deserving."

Three laws were about to be proposed to Parliament. Scalabrini urged the participants to establish an emigration section within the *Opera di Congressi* to amend and eventually plug any loopholes in the laws.

"Everyone knows that governments and their agents are bound by certain international customs and concerns, and they either cannot take some measures or if they did take them they would only exacerbate the wounds they are trying to cure. It is here, Gentlemen, that the work of the ruling classes must begin, here where that of the laws and governments stops. How? First by studying and discussing the great emigration problem and integrating within the activity of the regional, diocesan and parochial committees (and this is the prayer I address to the leaders of the Catholic movement) action directed to the religious, economic and civic good of all our unfortunate brothers, by collecting financial aid for them, by vigorously counseling against emigration when this would have disastrous consequences, by defending emigrants from fraudulent contracts, in short, by surrounding the migrant flow with all possible religious and civic assistance in order to strengthen it against enemies, and to present a united, I would almost say, invincible front; for the safety of each in this case becomes the safety of all. Yes, Gentlemen, wherever the people work and suffer, there also is the Church, for the Church is the mother, friend and protector of the people."

"Scalabrini's address was greeted with prolonged and enthusiastic applause and his proposals were unanimously adopted. It is significant that the 16th Catholic Congress in Ferrara was the first congress to adopt a series of resolutions and definite decisions on the subject of emigration. It was Father Luigi Gerevini, a member of the intransigent, democratic group, who in the name of the entire assembly voiced complete support for Scalabrini's ideas. He first expressed satisfaction that the *Opera dei Congressi* was thus opening a new field of endeavor for its members and creating within the second Group a new section which, in cooperation with the St. Raphael Society established by Scalabrini, would work to protect the interests of the emigrants. He then read the following conclusions, which were adopted with applause:

"The 16th Italian Catholic Congress...

"convinced that it is the duty of Christian and patriotic charity to counsel and protect the emigrants;

"commending the action taken to date on behalf of the emigrants through the initiative of the Most Reverend Bishop;

"invites the Permanent Committee of the *Opera dei Congressi* to establish within the Charity and Christian Socio-Economic Group an appropriate section which, in union with the St. Raphael Society, will promote the work of counseling and protecting the emigrants, indicating the practical and effective means of achieving this noble goal; and it expresses the hope that Catholic economic institutions, in distributing their earnings, will take due account of this work"[21]

"The Section has been set up," Volpe-Landi wrote later, "and it is composed of representatives of the St. Raphael Society and the Charity and Christian Socio-Economic Group. Now it is necessary for the local affiliates of the *Opera dei Congressi* — that is the Diocesan Committees — to take on, directly or through associated or member organizations the task of representing the St. Raphael Society, in view also of the role assigned to private initiative in the bill on emigration soon to be discussed in Parliament."[22]

Medolago, chairman of the Christian Socio-Economic Group, also told Bishop Scalabrini that the next Congress, to be held in Rome, would discuss protection of the emigrants and asked for his "orders and advice" as well as information on what the Bishop "intended to do with respect to both permanent and temporary emigration."[23] The report on the question at the 17th Congress in Rome was given by Father Cevenna. Section IV of Group II, in charge of emigration matters, was headed by Bishop Scalabrini's old friend, Father Giuseppe Alessi.

On the agenda of the 18th Congress, which met in Taranto in 1901, there was a proposal for a Secretariat of the People, which, among other labor problems, was to consider assistance to emigrants and their families. The committees of the *Opera* were to place themselves at the disposal of the Bishops according to the directives of the Holy See, in order to make action on behalf of the emigrants more effective.[24]

The *Opera dei Congressi*, therefore, was not insensitive to the serious emigration problem. If the results did not match the expectations, this was due in part, it would seem, to the crisis the *Opera* was going through at the time and in part to the excessive burden of activities which the committees had gradually been assuming.

Scalabrini's Campaign

While appealing and hoping for the cooperation of the *Opera dei Congressi* Scalabrini could not delay. He himself started the principal local committees of the St. Raphael Society and carried on an intensive campaign throughout 1891 and 1892.

He began in Genoa where a committee had been in existence for a year. It was the city where abuses in signing up the emigrants were most widespread and he published a lengthy documentation on the subject. He stimulated the local Committee to greater activity and secured the valuable cooperation of the Port Inspector, Captain Malnate; and he defended the interests of the Italians before the Representative of the Brazilian government.

A few days later he gave a talk in Rome in which he criticized the De Zerbi law for its exclusively police character and deplored the absence of an information center. Many deputies were present, among them the Hon. Carcano, Count Soderini, the biographer of Leo XIII, and Commander Bodio, general secretary of the International Statistical Institute and later Commissioner General for Emigration. Scalabrini's lecture was criticized by the *New York Herald*, which took the side of the exploiters, and by the review *Diritto*. The government paper *Riforma*, however, agreed with it and underlined particularly Scalabrini's reference to industrial and agricultural development as a factor that could facilitate the solution of the migrant problem.

In the month of March the Bishop gave a lecture in Florence, attended by Cardinal Bausa, the first patron of the Scalabrinian Congregation, and gave still another address in Turin. During April, despite the opposition of the Masons, he spoke in Milan in the church of St. Alexander and to the Circolo Manzoni. In April, 1892, he was in Lucca and in May he was making his appeal in Palermo in the presence of the Archbishop and many other bishops of Sicily, which was sending a large number of emigrants especially to North America. A lecture planned for Livorno was not given, however, because of the opposition of the Prefect who feared disorders. In October of the same year he spoke in Pola and Treviso, where he won the friendship of Professor Luigi Olivi, one of the most prominent personalities of the *Opera dei Congressi* and an admirer of the Bishop of Piacenza. And finally in December he was speaking in Pisa, where, in the large audience of members of Parliament, professors and university students the leading figure was Giuseppe Toniolo.

The first result of the campaign was the establishment of local committees of the Benevolent Society for Italian Emigrants in all the cities where the Bishop had spoken. His lectures shocked public opinion and finally exposed the tragic realities which the Government was covering up.

Another consequence was Scalabrini's indirect contribution to the improvement of legislation on emigration. But he was not content with this indirect influence on the numerous deputies, senators and journalists who attended his lectures. He wanted to bring pressure directly using, to this end, the Benevolent Society, which by this time had taken on a definite character. In 1894 the general assembly of the Committees decided to rename it the Saint Raphael Society because its beginning and structure were similar to the German society of the same name; founded in Magdeburg in 1871 and approved by Leo XIII in 1878.[25] Much more important was the decision to give priority to the moral-religious aims of the Society and to place it under the direction of the Hierarchy in order to guarantee its stability and its apostolic character.

This was consistent with Bishop Scalabrini's concept of lay action, namely, that its goal was essentially religious, without political implications, and was to be pursued under the authority of the Bishops. The Archbishop of Genoa, in a circular letter to the bishops of Northern Italy, dated November 6, 1894, stated:

"At the same meeting it was also decided that the Society is to direct its activity principally to the realization of religious and moral objectives, with the cooperation of the Missionaries, and, in order to manifest this more clearly, it is to place its work under the aegis of the Bishops, especially those from whose Dioceses there is the greatest flow of emigrants. The latter Bishops are to name an ecclesiastical representative to membership on the Committees. Through the Bishop of Piacenza, the writer was asked to inform the Most Reverend Ordinaries of Northern Italy of these deliberations and at the same time to invite them to accept the work under their patronage and to establish, where they consider it appropriate, Committees in their Dioceses, naming to membership those persons they deemed most suitable and ensuring for them the enlightened and zealous cooperation of the parish clergy, especially in rural areas."[26]

The Committee in Genoa and Father Maldotti

The St. Raphael Society's program, as conceived by Bishop Scalabrini, is best illustrated by the committee in Genoa, which was the most important. First proposed in April of 1889,[27] it was established January 20, 1890. It was the first concrete, organic realization of the desires of the Holy See, which as early as 1883, had urged the Archbishops of Naples, Genoa and Palermo to attend to the needs of the emigrants at the ports of embarkation. The committees formed as a result of that appeal had been impractical, had lacked coordination and perseverance, and so had been short-lived. Scalabrini surmised that to sustain the good will in these committees and to ensure their stability a priest was needed, and specifically one who was both "specialized" in aid to emigrants and was completely dedicated to the work in a missionary spirit — in short, one of his own missionaries.

In 1891 he assigned to this difficult mission Father Francesco Zaboglio. He was succeeded in 1894 by Father Pietro Maldotti, who was the heart and soul of the Genoese committee.

In four years of sharp and painful experiences in the port of Genoa, Maldotti could touch with his hands, as it were, what Bishop Scalabrini had correctly foreseen in 1888 when, in his famous Open Letter to the Honorable Paolo Carcano he opposed legal recognition of the agents and sub-agents of emigration...

"Father Maldotti, assisted by another young missionary from Valdosta sent to Genoa by Bishop Scalabrini, Father Theophilus Glesaz, took up his stand in the railroad station and met every incoming train. He tore the hotel addresses from the hatbands of the emigrants and stirred up an indescribable ruckus among the vested interests. He had no mercy for those guilty of abuses and swindles, and he denounced them to the police, getting fines imposed and instigating lawsuits almost every day.

"One day, in the square in front of the Piazza Principe station, which had been overrun by more than two thousand emigrants, Maldotti became involved in a scuffle with one sharpy — out of the many — who had robbed an emigrant from Cremona of all his belongings.

'Then and there, with no preambles,' wrote Maldotti 'we got into a pretty lively fight, and if I collected a good dose of punches, I can say I landed a few like mad myself.'

"The fact that a priest was single-handedly and openly opposing, in fact challenging, the mass of shady dealings going on roused the speculators to put an end to his activities. Maldotti was described to the Prefect of Genoa as one of the usual troublemakers who had landed in Genoa to interfere with the development of trade and small industries. There was a flood of anonymous letters. Maldotti was even threatened with death. He sought the advice of the Port Supervisor, Cavalier Malnate, and then got in touch with the newspapers of the city, offering to give them the facts.

"The next day, February 1, 1895, the *Caffaro*, echoed by the rest of the city press, came out with the sensational headline: 'Vicious exploitation of the emigrants in Genoa.' For twenty nights, Maldotti continued to distribute the documentation he put together on the situation and for twenty days the papers kept the city stirred up with account of unbelievable skullduggery, until finally the authorities intevened. The first ones attacked by the newspapers were the agents and sub-agents, and the guides or porters in the harbor. Next came the innkeepers and hotel managers and the money changers.

'We were threatened with lawsuit after lawsuit,' wrote Maldotti in his 1898 Report, 'but we kept on washing the dirty linen in public. And a flood of lawsuits fell, not on me, but without warning on both big and little exploiters caught in the net. The Prefect immediately changed his tune and from Rome came the Ministerial decree we wanted so much, which compels Companies and Agents to bring the emigrants to Genoa only the night before their departure, and to lodge and feed them gratis until they embark.'

"The Ministerial order cited by Maldotti, which was later embodied in the text of the 1901 law, was not the only result of the campaign the missionary fought in defense of the emigrants. On February 20th the *Caffaro* published a circular from the police which cancelled the licenses of the provincial sub-agents. On the 8th of March the Genoese Committee for the Protection of the Emigrant approved Father Maldotti's proposal to collect clothing for the neediest emigrants, and especially for the children. In less than a year more than two thousand articles of clothing were distributed.

"Maldotti also carried on a persistent campaign for the erection in Genoa of a hostel for the emigrants, which was the only basic solution to the recurring problem of chicanery on the part of hotel managers and the need to provide clean and safe lodgings. The new decree obliging Companies and Agents to bring the emigrants in only on the eve of departure did not solve everything. They lodged and fed the emigrants on board the ship that was leaving the next day. How disastrous it was to pile thousands of people on board before medical inspection it is easy to imagine. The epidemics that broke out on the high seas (the ship *Parà* registered thirty-nine deaths from measles in a single crossing) were due in large measure to this pernicious practice.

"Among the first to realize the urgent need for a Shelter in Genoa and to propose its establishment was Scalabrini himself, who did so in the lecture he gave in the Church of the Maddalena in Genoa on January 25th, 1891. Between 1891 and 1895 the proposal to build a Shelter was put forward repeatedly by the Society for the Protection of the Emigrant and was repeatedly accepted with promises of action by the authorities of the Prefecture and the harbor but with no results...

"Maldotti did not confine himself to making suggestions for improving the aid given the emigrant before his departure. Two voyages to Brazil, which he took in 1896 and 1897, were enough to give him a clear picture of the most urgent changes needed in the maritime and health regulations then in effect. Among the principal modifications Maldotti suggested —

later embodied in the new emigration laws — were a speed of twelve miles an hour, an increase in the sanitation and health care facilities and the appointment of government personnel on board ship to make sure the rules were followed...

"On his first trip, from April 12th to August 2nd, 1896, he confined himself to the rural areas of Minas Gerais, to Rio, Sao Paulo and part of the Goiaz. On his second journey, from May 18th to December 12th, 1897, he went to all the other states in Brazil as well as to the capitals of Uruguay and Argentina. To get a clear picture of the conditions in which the emigrants were living, he traveled incognito through the various *fazendas*, like an ordinary explorer, accompanied by a doctor from Piacenza, M. Galluzzi. 'I traveled 6000 kilometers by train and 500 on horseback,' he wrote Msgr. Mangot on August 6th, 1896, 'preaching, hearing confessions and writing with pencil in my diary, I was the victim of interviewers, who pursued me, and of the telegraph wires, used to spy on my every move, so that I was forced to get myself up as a brigand. I shall bring you a picture taken of me by an old friend, who I met in the virgin forest for the first time in twenty years.'

"Maldotti's principal conclusion at the end of his journeys was that it was necessary to create a special group of functionaries to work with the consulates, consular agents and correspondents, whose duties would be exercised within special limits and definite areas and would be directed mainly to the aid and protection of our emigrants."[28]

The St. Raphael Society in New York

Father Pietro Bandini of Forlì (1853-1917) founded the Mission and the St. Raphael Society in New York.

The emigrants who landed there were victimized by speculators who "took possession of them, stowed them in foul lodgings and boarded them until they had milked from them whatever small sums they had left on arrival. And when there was nothing more to be wrung from them, they loaded them on the first train bound for the place they were to work and turned them over to their colleagues in rascality. Here there was another network of vampires. There was the *boss* or general contractor who ruled and exploited a crowd of smaller entrepreneurs. They got theirs back by exploiting the laborers, on whom fell the burden of everybody's exploitation. Each of these secondary entrepreneurs had a wooden barrack that functioned at one and the same time as a store, wineshop, cookhouse, and dormitory, and which sometimes became the scene of savage fighting, when, that is, the tension reached the breaking point and the slaves rebelled against the whip-cracker. Tragedies developed silently but were fierce and terrible, and were always followed by a premeditated fire that consumed the proofs of the crime."[29]

The boss system often swallowed up 90% of the laborers' earnings, cynically exploited child labor and sometimes employed children as beggars. An even worse lot awaited the women. The chain of tragic circumstances had to be broken at the beginning, and that was the port where the emigrants landed.

There was another serious wound to be healed. The new arrivals had to pass inspection on Ellis Island. Many were detained until relatives or friends came for them, while others had not received the means to continue their journey. Those who had fallen ill were hospitalized but were among strangers and without comfort or hope for the future. It was necessary to come to the aid of these detainees, to help them trace their relatives, assume responsibility for them with respect to the authorities, shelter them until they could be relocated, comfort the sick, and help the many who were forced to return home.

The Archbishop of New York appealed to Bishop Scalabrini, who sent Father Bandini to organize the work. In 1890 it was possible to found a St. Raphael Society for the Italians similar in spirit and purpose to that already in existence for the Irish and German immigrants. Bandini soon captivated both the authorities and the people, working with a courage and self-sacrifice equalled only by his ability.[30] Without getting involved in the actual contracts, he defended the emigrant and made sure the terms were implemented. Anyone wishing to engage a laborer was required to give references, guarantee the type of labor to be performed as well as an adequate salary, and provide transportation expenses to the place of work. In its first year the New York St. Raphael Society helped more than 20,000 emigrants. Father Bandini was authorized to conduct his work in the Immigration Office on Ellis Island in 1891, three years before the Italian Government succeeded in getting permission from the U. S. government to set up an information office there. In fact, he was invited by the U. S. Secretary of the Treasury to be a member of a commission that was to go to Italy to study various aspects of the Italian emigrant flow to the United States, and particularly to seek ways to eliminate the underworld organization of agents and contractors and direct the Italians to agricultural settlements.[31] These were the first steps toward the 1894 agreement between Italy and the United States, which had always refused to assume any serious responsibilities for the protection and settlement of immigrants from other nations as well. Part of the merit must be attributed to Father Bandini, who with the St. Raphael Society and without funds, did all that was possible and whose example was followed by those who succeeded him, Fathers Gambera, Moretto and Secchia.

"The St. Raphael Society has done an immense amount of good among the Italians...While the Commissioner for Immigration, Mr. Williams, had occasion to rebuke and even to dissolve other societies and committees for the protection of the immigrants, he not only respected our Society but praised it highly, calling it to the attention of the United States of America and pointing it out for recognition."[32]

President Theodore Roosevelt, during a visit to Ellis Island, congratulated Father Gambera and expressed high praise of Bishop Scalabrini, calling him a philanthropist and bishop of signal merit.[33]

Contribution to Emigration Legislation

The character and work of men like Maldotti and Bandini underline the determining influence of Bishop Scalabrini and his missionaries and the contribution they made to the creation of legal and social protection for emigrants.

In his first work on the subject, the Bishop of Piacenza wrote with some bitterness that it would be futile to search "in our legal code for a law or in our Country for an institution" which took account of the facts, statistics, studies, and proposed legislation that had been submitted to the Government up to that time to regulate the emigrant flow or at least to lessen its harmful consequences.

Scalabrini urged the suppression of the traffic in persons and a condemnation of emigration "by contract" or "pledge" whereby the emigrant pledged to reimburse through his labor the advance given him for his travel expenses — a repayment that was too heavy a burden for the emigrant in the first, and most critical, period of his sojourn in a strange land and made him practically a slave to his boss. The Minister of the Interior, Francesco Crispi, who realized that public opinion had been shaken by Scalabrini's book and the institutions he was establishing, and who feared perhaps that the Church was about to "steal" the initiative from the Government, introduced a law in the Chamber of Deputies in 1887. This, as noted above, was reviewed by a Parliamentary Committee, which formulated a counter-proposal introduced in turn by the Honorable Rocco De Zerbi.

The Bishop studied both proposals and entered the debate with an Open Letter to the Honorable Carcano, Under-Secretary of the Treasury, who had been his classmate in the Volta Liceo in Como.

"I am addressing you publicly, not to garner vain attention, which I shun on principle and by nature, but because the question I am raising is one which needs to be discussed, and I have found no other means to attract the notice of an indifferent and heedless public which does not read unless it is led to do so at least by a title which arouses its curiosity. I thought an open letter from a Bishop who is concerned with social questions and proposals for legislation, addressed to a Deputy, might present a title capable of shaking up the unwholesome indifference of the public, and be reason enough, at least once in a while to spark discussion of a law, which might be tiresome but also productive, instead of the usual items."[34]

Crispi was allied with the southern landowners, and Scalabrini criticized his proposal for its unlawful restrictions on freedom to emigrate and the exclusivist nature of its police measures. The Parliamentary Commission represented the liberal Southerners, led by Nitti. Scalabrini answered them with relentless documentation setting forth the evils resulting from legalizing emigrant recruitment. The phrase, "freedom to emigrate, but no freedom to cause anyone to emigrate" effectively summed up Scalabrini's criticism of both proposals.

Furthermore he proposed, as noted earlier, the establishment of Italian schools abroad and a kind of "civil service" for the seminarians who intended to become missionaries to the emigrants.

The Government reacted vigorously to both these suggestions, for fear that they would give the emigrant flow a religious character which it should not have and would produce a "contradiction of the very name of Italy"[35] as a nation. Unfortunately, despite Scalabrini's appeals to various members of Parliament, De Zerbi's law was adopted in December of 1888 without the amendment of the Honorable Bonafadini suggested by Scalabrini which would have eliminated the legalization of recruitment.

Twelve years later, the deputies Visconti-Venosta and Luzzatti, in reporting the new bill which became law in 1901, acknowledged the correctness of Scalabrini's position:

"All of us erred in 1888; and we did not understand at that time the need for economic and social measures, not only or principally for police measures."[36]

The 1888 law had some positive aspects, however, such as an obligatory written contract for transportation, the declaration that any agreement whereby an emigrant was pledged to work out the equivalent of his transportation was null and void, and the establishment of the first penalties for abuses in matters dealing with expatriates. The following year, the new Zanardelli law introduced the "crime of fraud" committed by "anyone who, for profit, induces a citizen to emigrate, deceiving him with statements of non-existent circumstances and false information." This was a provision that Scalabrini had repeatedly called for.

Later, after he had established his own activities on behalf of the emigrants, Scalabrini returned to the charge in the interests of achieving a just emigration law, and this time he used the facts reported by his missionaries and the experiences of the St. Raphael Society.

At the request of the president of the St. Raphael Society, Father Pietro Colbachini, a missionary in Brazil, compiled a report on the social, economic and religious situation of the Italian immigrants in that country.[37] His report written in 1892 and published in 1894, aroused so much interest in government circles that the Minister of Foreign Affairs, Baron Blanc, asked the author for a copy, which he presented in 1895.[38] In 1896 Father Maldotti also addressed a memorandum to the new Foreign Affairs Minister, Visconti-Venosta. Thus two Scalabrinian missionaries effectively contributed to the action finally taken by the Foreign Ministry, under whose jurisdiction and competencies the emigrant problem fell for obvious reasons.

In two monographs, Father Colbachini denounced the vicissitudes undergone by Italian emigrants, from the disastrous journeys to reach the *fazendas*, to the lack of proper food and the brutalizing effect of the real slavery imposed by systems that recalled, in even more repugnant forms, the customs of ancient serfdom. This was in fact the status of Italians contracted to work for a wage in the large *fazendas* of the capitalists. Not much better was the situation of those who were resettled by the government. On the other hand, the economic and social situation of the private and independent colonies established by the Italians themselves in Paranà and Rio Grande do Sul was much better.

According to Father Colbachini, therefore, who faithfully mirrored Scalabrini's thinking, the Italian Government should intervene to direct the emigrant flow to private and independent settlements. For this purpose it should control the emigrant societies and set up pertinent labor offices. Furthermore, it should, in agreement with the Brazilian government, intervene in the drawing up of contracts for labor on the coffee plantations and insist upon their implementation.

"In a long seventeen page commentary on Colbachini's Memorandum, the January 10, 1899, issue of *Civiltà Cattolica*...underlined the complete identity of viewpoint between the principal ideas in the proposal of the Hon. Canevaro and the ideas expressed by Colbachini in 1894.

"This similarity has an important significance. As we know the law proposed by Visconti-Venosta and Canevaro, resubmitted with some modifications in December 1900, later became the Italian emigration law of 1901, the principal measures of which are still in force.

"In the preparation of the final draft proposals of the law, which led to the formulation of the final text, there figured the activity of another Scalabrinian missionary, Father Pietro Maldotti."[39]

Maldotti became in 1894 Scalabrini's most valued collaborator in his contacts with the Government to promote a new emigration law.

The Law of 1901

"Three particularly important documents published by Maldotti between 1896 and 1899 attest to this: the Memorandum sent to His Excellency the Minister of Foreign Affairs, Visconti-Venosta in November, 1896, drawn up in collaboration with Marchese G. B. Volpe-Landi, the Report on the work of the Mission of the Port of Genoa from 1894 to 1898 and on two voyages to Brazil, and finally the report on 'The Italians in Brazil' given in Turin in 1899."[40]

With the same fearlessness with which he acted against those exploiting the emigrants, Maldotti pursued the authorities to persuade them to enact practical measures. In order to achieve more solid results, Scalabrini suggested to Maldotti and Volpe-Landi they approach the Foreign Minister, Visconti-Venosta. The latter suggested that they set forth their requests in a memorandum. The Memorandum, which was written by Scalabrini with the cooperation of Volpe-Landi and Maldotti,[41] deals with the protection of the emigrant before his departure, during the journey and in the country of immigration. It restates the urgent need to do away with sub-contractors and underlines the necessity of broadening the definition of "emigrant" to include not only those whose emigration was paid for or subsidized but also those who went at their own expense, at the cost often of all they possessed. It recommends the establishment of hostels in the principal ports, proposes modifications or additions to the laws already promulgated and insists on the need to consult a Commission made up of competent and practical persons before formulating any new law.[42]

Many changes suggested in the Memorandum and Maldotti's other two writings were subsequently included in the new emigration laws, namely, the speed limit for the ships, an increase in the space allotted to sanitation and health facilities, the appointment of government supervisors during the voyage, the establishment of information bureaus and of employment offices in the ports of debarkation.[43]

The zeal of Scalabrini and his missionaries inevitably collided with the slowness of Parliament. In 1899 in Turin the Bishop observed:

"Gentlemen, in this survey I must repeat observations and cite facts that I have already stated here and elsewhere, but it is not my fault if these observations and recommendations have not yet been translated into law. After all, it is well known that the progress of ideas is marked by frustrating slowness, especially when they conflict with interests and passions, but it is a constant progress when the ideas set forth are just and of genuine use. We keep persevering, therefore, since all slow progress reaches its goal provided its champion is not overcome by weariness along the way."[44]

Earlier pessimistic predictions had come true. The law of 1888 had worsened the condition of the emigrants. Now there was hope that the new law proposed by Visconti-Venosta would remedy the serious abuses and repair the lacuna that was "filled with dangers."[45] Scalabrini's lectures (September 26-27) had been preceded by private meetings in which scholars from various places and of different orientation discussed the proposed law. The chairman was Senator Lampertico and the future president of the Italian Republic, Luigi Einaudi, then 24 years old, acted as secretary.[46] The latter supported the recommendations of Scalabrini and Maldotti — "men whose aim in life is the good of others" — with respect to protection for the emigrants before, during and after their voyage.[47] Almost all of them were included in the text adopted January 23, 1901, and so was the proposal Scalabrini repeated in Turin to modify the law on military service with respect to the emigrants, their children and the missionaries. The latter were exempted up to 26 years of age if they were students, and indefinitely if they were abroad.

A counter-proposal to the Visconti-Venosta draft was submitted by the Hon. Pantano and the far Left, which wished to maintain emigration agents in order to forestall a monopoly by the shipowners.[48] Maldotti and Malnate urged the Bishop of Piacenza to intervene.[49] He must have done so immediately and effectively if Maldotti was able a few days later to announce the good news from Rome.[50] The law was passed on December 21, 1900, by the Chamber of Deputies, but serious difficulties were foreseen in the Senate where the emigration agents had organized a strong opposition. Bishop Scalabrini sent Maldotti to Rome to keep him informed on what happened in Parliament. Soon, in fact, Maldotti and Hon. Luzzatti alerted the Bishop to urge all the senators with whom he had any influence not to be absent from the chamber. During the voting they were not to get the flu, and the preventive was a good dose of letters from Scalabrini.[51] The law was passed by the Senate on January 29, 1901. A few days later, another law for which Scalabrini and his missionaries had long been arguing, was promulgated on the protection of the savings and remittances home of Italians abroad.

Scalabrini thus saw his efforts triumph. Maldotti called it "our law." The Bishop, more of a realist and always reaching for complete organization, was anxious to achieve the coordination of all the forces in play, frankly cooperating even with the State. He sought what united not what divided.

"We are not playing politics, nor do we wish to do so; (aside from all the questions which later may possibly divide us) we desire and hope for everyone's agreement with our program...If all were agreed, how much good could we do for so many of our brothers, and how much good to our country, keeping so many distant sons linked with their fatherland as Germany and England have succeeded in doing. The new emigration law is a good one (if it is not spoiled in its administration). But it will remain a dead letter, a blunt instrument, without the constant, disinterested, and loyal cooperation of pastors, mayors and all good citizens."[52]

He expressed the same thought after his first journey to America: "I have been convinced *de visu* of what we must do, all of us, priests, the Government, citizens, legislators."[53]

"The main lines of what should be done were described by Scalabrini, as soon as he returned from New York, at a meeting he had in Rome with the then Foreign Minister, Hon. Prinetti. Death did not permit the great Apostle to the emigrants to carry out his beneficent plans."[54]

This last observation — already expressed many times — might seem naive or at least useless if what Bishop Scalabrini succeeded in achieving and what was vital in his ideas and institutions was not more than sufficient testimony to his intuition, genius for organizations and especially to his apostolic zeal. But it is the fate of great organizers not to have equally great successors. In the Missionaries of St. Charles, Scalabrini did have men who continued his apostolic spirit and work, if not his organizing talents and achievements. The Bishop of Piacenza had launched a number of ideas. Of those he did not have the time to carry out, many were finally realized as we shall see. Others, perhaps the more grandiose, did not always find the necessary person, means, or the opportune moment for their actualization. It is said that Bishop Scalabrini was born fifty years too soon. This is too human an observation which underestimates the providential nature of his work at that specific historical time. But it does indicate his extraordinary qualities, which are now better understood and therefore even more deeply appreciated.

CHAPTER XIII

For the Emigrants of All Nations

In the religious field, one of Scalabrini's proposals to come to fruition was the establishment of a central body in the Holy See which would provide impetus and directives for aid to emigrants of all countries, taking into due account the different nationalities and places of resettlement.

"After his voyages to America, he sent a Memorandum to the Secretariat of State in which he wrote: 'The emigration, or rather the emigrants of various nationalities, given the dangers to their faith, need the vigilant and maternal care of the Church.' Further on, after observing that the Italian emigrants, through intolerance or misunderstanding were sometimes 'badly served even in the churches,' he added: 'The same is said of the Poles, the Ruthenians and the Germans.' "

"Bishop Scalabrini's horizons therefore embrace all emigrants and for them he seeks an organism of the Roman Curia in order to render aid to them more effective. This can only come from the Holy See. He appeals to the Cardinal Secretary of State of St. Pius X to establish a commission or even a Pontifical Congregation 'pro emigratis.' "

"But let us proceed chronologically: On February 28, 1905, he wrote about this for the first time to Cardinal Merry del Val, asking him to speak to the Holy Father. On March 19 he received an encouraging reply from Rome:

'I wished to give more thought to this serious question which truly concerns me very much. I do not need to add that I have spoken of it many times to the Holy Father. It would not be difficult or unacceptable to the Holy Father to address to all the emigrants of every nation the words of comfort you indicate; but it seems to me that this message should be given when it can be followed up with care and with effective provisions...We may name a Commission '*pro emigratis catholicis*' and then what?...It is necessary to find competent persons and then draw up a plan of action, defining the apostolate and the means it will have at its disposal as well as how these will be employed in practice...See, Bishop, if you can study the question and prepare the necessary elements for effective action, which, I believe, should begin within modest limits and without too much fanfare. A *granum sinapis* would be best which later, with the Lord's blessing, could continue to grow.'

"A few days later, Bishop Scalabrini replied to the Cardinal Secretary of State assuring him that he would do what he wished. In fact, in May he sent to Rome a long Memorandum, from which we quote only the more important parts:

'After describing the serious consequences of the spiritual neglect of the emigrants, he wrote, I believe that the first remedy, as I mentioned above, lies in a wise organization of the work to be done...And this should come from the Holy See, an authority not only undisputed and indisputable among the entire Catholic clergy, but universal in nature and embracing, therefore, all the nationalities...In addition to the providential institution of *Propaganda Fide,* therefore, it is necessary to create, as I have already stated in an earlier communication, a special Commission *pro emigratis catholicis* that will study and provide for the protection and preservation of the Faith among Catholic emigrants... Isolated instructions and measures, however good they may be, are not enough, since it is only human that both count very little without an organism that ensures their implementation and keeps them alive.'

"How should this Commission be organized? Bishop Scalabrini's answer is precise:

'It should be composed, I believe, of representatives of the various nationalities which produce the greatest emigrant flow...These representatives should be chosen by competent persons who are knowledgeable about the conditions and needs of their respective fellow countrymen...'

"What should be the purpose and task of this Commission or Congregation?

'The purpose should be to provide spiritual assistance to the emigrants, especially in the Americas and thus to keep alive in their hearts the Catholic faith and Christian sentiment.'

'Its task:

— to study the complex and serious problem of emigration...

— to promote the establishment of Catholic committees, while respecting the praiseworthy private initiatives already active in this field...

— to stimulate, through the Bishops, the zeal of pastors on behalf of these committees and to suggest practical means of aiding them...

— to reply to questions which might be asked in relation to the measures adopted...and to take care of the difficulties that might arise...

— to ensure above all that the emigrants are accompanied by priests during their voyage...and also that the various settlements are also provided with good and zealous missionaries.'

"Bishop Scalabrini concludes with the observation that this Commission would be extremely effective because of the authority it would have from the Apostolic See and would 'increase (its effectiveness) with wise provisions which would certainly bring great benefit to the mass of Catholic emigrants.'

"It is not difficult to find in this Memorandum the concept of an Office of the Holy See for emigrants and also the proposal for a 'Supreme Council' for emigration composed of competent persons from various nations, like the present 'Supreme Council' established by the Apostolic Constitution, *Exsul Familia*. An Office of the Holy See could not be set up during Scalabrini's lifetime. His last letter is dated May 17, 1905, scarcely two weeks before his death. There was no time for him to receive a reply. But the idea was not abandoned. Seven years later, St. Pius X, with the *Motu Proprio, Cum omnes Catholicos*, dated August 12, 1912, set up in the Consistorial Congregation the *Sectio de emigratione;* its purpose was to study *et parare omnia* for the religious care of emigrants of the Latin rite.

"Another work on behalf of emigrants is due to the great heart of St. Pius X. It corresponds, if not to the specific measures, certainly to the broad concepts set forth by Bishop Scalabrini. He, in fact...had proposed to Leo XIII that 'one or more Institutes of Priests be established in Italy.' For some years the Scalabrinian Institute was the only one, and then through the initiative of Bishop Bonomelli, encouraged by Scalabrini, the Missionary Institute for emigrants in Europe was founded. Finally, St. Pius X, with the *Motu proprio, Jam pridem* of March 19, 1914, established in Rome the Pontifical College of Priests for Italian Emigration and asked the Scalabrinian Missionaries to take charge of it. The latter could not accept at the time; but in September, 1949, on the invitation of His Holiness Pius XII, Bishop Scalabrini's Missionaries took over its direction and gave new life to this work begun by a Saint, which melds so well with the broad program of Bishop Scalabrini."[1]

Other Initiatives

Scalabrini also had thought of creating diocesan centers for emigration. These were to be under the jurisdiction of the Bishop, who would thus guarantee their effectiveness, stability and well organized activity. The diocesan committee or center was to be composed of influential persons from among the clergy and laity. It would see to the organization of subcommittees in the minor centers and act as intermediary between the pastors and a central office in Rome. The duties of the diocesan centers were envisaged as follows: issuing "emigrant passes" that would assure assistance from the St. Raphael Society in the ports of departure and arrival; announcing the departure of ships that carried a missionary on board; keeping a register of departures and repatriations, addresses, destinations; informing the League for the Protection of Girls about the young girls who were emigrating; prodding the pastors to observe the norms issued by the Holy See regarding the orientation to be given the emigrants, the maintenance of a flow of correspondence with parishioners abroad, and seeing that the repatriates returned to the practice of religion.[2]

Again it was Pius X who promoted the establishment in Italy of Diocesan Committees and Aid Societies for Emigrants.[3] These were later the subject of recommendations in the Apostolic Constitution *Exsul Familia*, which lays stress on the duty of pastors to give special catechetical instruction to parishioners preparing to migrate, to remain in constant contact with them after they are resettled and to issue ecclesiastical identification cards.[4] There is now in Italy a Bishops' Commission for Emigration, established by the Conference of Catholic Bishops and under the direction of the Central Office for Italian Emigration (UCEI). Under the Commission in each diocese there is a Diocesan Migration Committee, which in turn has charge of sub-committees or parish "Nuclei," the entire network reflecting Bishop Scalabrini's proposals both in its structure and its functions.[5]

He was also the founder of the National Emigrant Day *(Giornata Nazionale dell'emigrante)* which he proposed in order to raise funds for the Commission *pro emigratis catholicis*. The Day was established for all of Italy by the Consistorial Congregation in 1914[6] and became a world day at the suggestion of *Exsul Familia*.[7]

The Creation of the Office of Prelate for Italian Emigration also corresponded to Scalabrini's proposals. This was a bishop "who, endowed with the necessary faculties and free from diocesan duties, would have the time to dedicate himself to the spiritual needs of the Italian emigrants."[8] Benedict XV appointed Bishop Michele Cerrati to this office.[9]

Scalabrini's solicitude for the exercise of a spiritual ministry for migrants during the sea voyage has been noted several times. This was one of the purposes both of the Scalabrinian Congregation and the St. Raphael Society. But Scalabrini himself understood from the beginning that it would be difficult to find priests who would devote themselves permanently to this activity, however necessary. To remedy the situation, he enjoined his missionaries — who were needed most in the areas of resettlement — to act as chaplains during their journeys to and from their mission stations. He added to the actual missionaries a category of "external" missionaries, priests who agreed to take even one trip as chaplains to the emigrants.

One of the first of these "external missionaries" was Father Giuseppe Marchetti, pastor of a parish of 210 souls in a suburb of Lucca, who had decided to emigrate en masse. He accompanied them to Genoa, protected them, with the providential intervention of Father Maldotti, from the agents who had swooped down on them like vultures, and saw them safely settled on board. His parishioners seemed more grieved at not having a priest with them than they did about leaving. The shipowner noticed that Father Marchetti looked worried and taking him by the hand said: "I bet you would be glad to go with them to America!" The look in Father Marchetti's eyes was answer enough, and the shipowner continued, "Fine; I want all my ships to have a chaplain not only this time but always. If you agree, there will be a cabin ready for you tonight."

Marchetti thanked God, for he saw in this resolve an answer to one of Bishop Scalabrini's most ardent prayers. He called Father Maldotti and then accepted the proposal. But he had neither passport nor the permission of his bishop, so he was obliged to wait for the next sailing. A few days later, on October 15, 1894, he was enthusiastically welcomed on board a ship headed for Santos.[10] We shall see how, on his second trip, Providence placed the young priest in a position to save a widower from despair and to take charge of an orphan, the first of the thousands sheltered in the Christopher Columbus Orphanage in San Paulo.[11]

Father Marchetti's example was followed by other priests, but Scalabrini and the St. Raphael Society did not succeed in providing a chaplain for each ship. At some periods there were as many as fifteen sailings a week.

A month after Scalabrini's death, the president of the Antislavery Society, who had served as chaplain during one voyage to America, founded the Society of the Missionaries of St. Anthony of Padua. This was approved by St. Pius X and recommended to the Italian hierarchy in 1908 by Cardinal Merry del Va.[12] The new society's principal aim was to aid migrants on board ship. Thus the Ships' Chaplains came into being. This institution suffered during World War I but was reorganized in 1920 and entrusted temporarily to the Superior General of the Scalabrinian Missionaries[13] until in 1923 Pius XI set it under the jurisdiction of the Consistorial Congregation.[14] Cardinal Ferretto, who was then the Assessor of the Congregation, asserted "Today there are 28 Italian ships plowing the seas and the oceans, each with a permanent chaplain on board; a silent but incomparable record!"[15]

The Problem of Pastoral Care for Migrants

Bishop Scalabrini's conception of pastoral care for emigrants deserves a much longer treatment. Only its general premises and basic assumptions are mentioned here, without going into the details, which in fact have only a relative value. He had no illusions about the obstacles implicit in this new apostolate, no less difficult than those encountered in the regular mission fields.[16] He therefore prayed to God to send him missionaries who were "holy and heroic."[17] "It is certainly an enormous undertaking for anyone," he acknowledged, "but especially for me...lacking as I do both means and capability."[18]

Since 1887 he had been carefully studying the migrant problem, but he did not have time to work out a systematic pattern of pastoral care, for this could only grow out of the experiences of his missionaries. He had gained a certain basic experience during his trip to the United States, which he followed with his journey to Brazil in the hope of giving the Congregation he had founded its definitive organization and orientation. But death overtook him while he was translating into practical terms the insights he had gained in his visit to the Brazilian missions.

The context in which Scalabrini observed the migrant phenomenon must also be kept in mind. It was an essentially historical as well as social phenomenon and does not lend itself easily to theoretical evaluations that transcend the particular historical and social contexts in which it took place. Consequently, Bishop Scalabrini, being a realist, was much more concerned with outlining what he considered the essentials, knowing full well that their practical application would be determined by specific needs in specific circumstances.

"The changes in the social situation and in men's attitudes make it necessary to change our strategy for the care of souls."[19]

He expressed a similar thought in relation to the laws:

"A law must not be a dogma, nor an affirmation of absolute principles, and...it is not good in itself or in its application if it does not fill a real need, if it is of no usefulness, if, in a word, it is not a law for its time."[20]

In fact, the Bishop of Piacenza saw the first stages of Italian emigration as a mass phenomenon. The great exodus had just begun, and the emigrants of his time were the first generation, with the second barely on the threshold. It was a period of gradual detachment from the mother country and the first uncertain efforts at assimilation with the people of the host country. It was the most delicate and difficult moment so far as religious ministry was concerned. This first generation of migrants, abandoned by the mother country, turned in protest to cut the secular ties which had linked them until then with their native soil, and, on the other hand, their new environment was inhospitable and regarded them as intruders. Bishop Scalabrini often deplored the fact that in most instances the emigrants stood alone in defending themselves both against their country of origin and the country of adoption.

All this constituted a crisis in the emigrant's psyche, which included as well his religious faith. In fact, the latter was perhaps the first to suffer. The practice of religion in strange circumstances is difficult, for it demands more than anything else, an inner and personal strength. In reality, for the great mass of our Italian emigrants it was too strongly linked with their native environment. It has beeen noted above that Scalabrini clearly understood this situation, which was due especially to the lack of religious instruction but also to the fact, proved by experience, that "to be deprived of spiritual bread, to be unable to reconcile oneself with God, to lack all stimulus to good," not only "has a most disastrous effect on the morale of the people," but also endangers the faith of even the educated man.[21]

Other social and religious factors of the period should also be kept in mind. The emigrants preferred to gather in their own "communities" when they settled in the large American cities, or in "colonies" when they went in for farming. The local hierarchies had already made some provisions for the religious care of the immigrants but not in a systematic or stable way, and in the United States, the establishment of national parishes had been allowed. In addition, many Italian priests, following the same mirage as their countrymen, had settled in the Americas. The Bishops therefore had adopted an attitude that was sometimes favorable, more often unfavorable, according to the positive or negative experiences they had so far encountered, and they were influenced besides by their particular mentality, educational background and nationality. Bishop Scalabrini had to take all these elements into account.

In fact, he approved of the national parish for the city settlements and of the territorial parish for the colonies in rural areas.

"Catholic agricultural colonies would be an immense advantage...like those already established in the United States for the Irish and the English. It seems these colonies are nothing but a kind of Catholic parish, with Catholic priests and schools, to which they send their countrymen instead of letting them depart like sheep without a shepherd. The emigrants would then find themselves almost at home among Catholics and benefit from at least the basic religious support."[22]

Culture as the Safeguard of Faith

For Bishop Scalabrini, however, the formulation of a particular type of pastoral ministry was of relative importance. His principal concern was dictated by the urgent necessity to preserve the faith and the practice of religion in the specific historical period in which he began his work.[23]

The fact that he laid so much stress on preserving the Italian identity of the emigrants is explained by the need to preserve their religion. Scalabrini deeply loved his country not as a chauvinist but as a Christian and an apostle. If he worked so hard to prevent the loss of the emigrants' national character, it was because he saw the inescapable need to preserve, as far as possible, the original complex context in which the religious sentiments of the Italians had been born and nurtured. Scalabrini's sense of being Italian was rooted chiefly in the Catholicism of his country. For him Italy's greatest glory was the faith, her greatest privilege to be the seat of the Vicar of Christ. For him, Italian history, civilization and culture was great because it was Christian. To preserve Italian culture, therefore, was to preserve the Catholic faith. To conserve Italian customs helped to safeguard Christian morality.

"To keep alive in their hearts the faith of our fathers, and, reviving the immortal hope of life after death, to educate and elevate their moral sensibilities, for, we must not forget, the one ethical tract of our people is still, fortunately, the Ten Commandments."[24]

Today the situation of emigrants, or rather of the children of emigrants in countries of permanent settlement is quite different from that observed by Bishop Scalabrini, and his ideas might seem quite nationalistic. But even in the period following his death, there is evidence confirming the basis of this idea. Bishop Francis Kelly, president of the Catholic Extension Society, in an address (August 17, 1915) carried in *The Catholic Mind* of September 8, 1915, stated that there is only one way to solve the religious problem of the Italians, and that is through the schools. Of all the emigrants who come to the United States, he noted, the Italian is the least likely to preserve the language and the traditions that bind him to what was best in the fatherland. If an emigrant people loses its mother tongue too quickly, this could mean that it is beginning to feel contempt for its ancestors and the faith of its fathers. The emigrant should be taught his own language and should be encouraged to maintain it.[25]

Protestant evangelizers tended to promote or complete the process of detachment from the native soil:

"The Protestants deliberately detach young men and boys from the family environment, encourage them to forget the customs and traditions of their parents, especially their religion, and to disdain everything Italian." And when it was pointed out to an "eminent Protestant, who was very much engaged in social action, that in this way the psychology and religion of the Italians was being totally destroyed, he replied that this was precisely what the Protestants were trying to achieve among the emigrants."[26]

A little later, in 1924, The Scalabrinian Father Manlio Ciufoletti drew up a kind of balance sheet on the experiences of the Italian national parish in the United States, in which he showed how the pastoral approach adopted by the Scalabrinian missionaries responded to the real religious and social needs of the Italian communities.

"How many difficulties our Missionaries encounter from both men and milieu and how much indifference even from those from whom they had a right to expect protection and help! It is through these pioneer priests especially that the necessary contact between the Italian Catholics and the Bishops of America is established. When the more populous centers in New York, Boston, Philadelphia, Providence, etc., were more or less organized, it was decided to give each of these cities its own Italian church. As soon as the news is spread, there is a general movement of consent and action among the people which draws the emigrants of the entire city together in this noble common enterprise. And thus the Italian colony is gradually being consolidated.

"Before we had separate groups, composed of people from the same town or province groups which often regarded each other with little sympathy and sometimes with stupid and chauvinistic rivalry. We had little Calabrias, Basilicatas, Campanias, Abruzzis and Sicilies overseas, not little Italies overseas."

"With the erection of churches, the superior air with which the emigrants from Northern or Central Italy — particularly the Ligurians and Tuscans — were wont to regard their compatriots from the South has begun to disappear...The Church is a strong factor of convergence and community. Social life is developing; mutual aid societies are formed; banks, pharmacies and shops are opened, professionals set up their offices among them."

"In this movement of people and things, the most intelligent and active among them have the opportunity to get to know one another and to become known, and thus from among the emigrant mass the future political and economic leaders of the people begin to emerge, some of whom, unfortunately, will take advantage of their position for their own personal aims and interests. The fact that all are called upon to contribute to the building of the church has in itself also a great social value. Since it is a community enterprise, the good parishioners become in a certain sense activists..."

"And now we are in the third stage of the history of the parish, namely, its functioning and progress."[27]

It is also the third stage in the emigrant flow. Bishop Scalabrini — as noted — was mainly concerned with the first two, but he never lost sight of the third. His was a long range vision which took in all the dimensions of the migrant phenomenon, from its international character to the problems of the future. He took an active interest in the emigrants of other nationalities, in fact, and wanted his missionaries to include them in their work.[28] He studied the problem of religious ministry to the emigrants of all nations on the part of the whole Church,[29] and his views on the way to the final assimilation of the emigrant and his children in the life of the host country are today more valid than ever: no forced or violent assimilation, no destruction of the rich culture and traditions of each group, but a "living together" of each culture and their mutual enrichment.[30]

Father Ciufoletti's report gives a picture of how Scalabrini's ideas were worked out in practice:

"And now we are in the third stage in the history of the parish, namely, its functioning and progress. The local press now speaks of the Italians not only as a large but also as an active ethnic group in the community, that has its own priests to guide it, that, in competition with other nationalities, makes sacrifices for its own institutions and is proud of having established them and of maintaining them not only as means of religious and moral uplift but also as a proving ground of civic virtue and wholesome Americanization."

"The local Catholics...appreciate them and consider them brothers in the faith. The others admire their strong attachment to their own religious and civic traditions and feel they augur well for the good of this Republic, which will always have in them an element of conservation and order...And the emigrant benefits from this more favorable public opinion in his regard and is able to participate increasingly in social life..."

"The educative efficacy of the Church has had and has a great influence in persuading our emigrants to become American citizens... Besides, the Church is a bridge between the Fatherland and its distant sons. It is in church that they most often hear, in their mother tongue, echoes and memories of their native villages and the popular and religious festivals that were so great a part of their simple country life. When they enter their Church — in Chicago, New York, San Francisco — they are at home. In the statues, the paintings and sometimes the architecture, they recognize the church of their youth, full of tender memories, which consecrated the most important events in their lives and those of their dear ones..."

"Up to this point I have confined myself to the influence which the Church exercises in its establishment and development among the emigrants who came as adults. But it is for their children, born and raised here, that the church and the parish school have a special value and significance, even from the social viewpoint. In fact, it is only in these institutions that the moral continuity that should exist between parents and children is respected and strengthened. Both go to the same church, they have the same pastor and priests as their guide, they take part in the same recreational activities in the parish hall. In the parish schools and catechism classes, the religious traditions — and these are almost always the same as the civic traditions — of the country of their parents, are spoken of with respect and even with admiration, and the simple, devoted faith of the parents is respected..."

"Through these and other relationships with the parish — in addition to the purely religious — the young people born here are in constant contact with the national church, which thus takes on the semblance of a huge Italo-American family. And while the first immigrants are moving toward their final rest, the young are growing up with sentiments of gratitude and devotion to the glorious land of their ancestors, as well as with intense love for their great country. For them and in them, Columbus and Washington, Italy and America, join hands in friendship across time and space, in a pact of brotherhood and progress. From a religious viewpoint the young Italo-Americans represent the great stream of glorious Italian religious traditions merging its pure waters in the calm, safe ocean of the American Catholic Church."[31]

Scalabrini's Insights Confirmed

Bishop Scalabrini's insights seem to find confirmation in our own day. In an address to the Sons of Italy in 1965, Cardinal Krol of Philadelphia deplored the fact that in the past there was the attempt to obliterate the cultural and religious patrimony of the various ethnic immigrant groups:

"More than a hundred years ago, some budding sociologists advanced the theory of total passive assimilation of the various cultures of the people in our country. They proposed a process of intensive purification and purgation of the dross of foreignism and the consequent emergence of the 100% pure and unadulterated American and American culture... Their prime targets were the foreign-language immigrants; their culture, traditions, and even their religion. It is a fact that in a blighted era of our great city's history, Catholic churches were set on fire."

After a summary of the evil consequences of such attitudes in all fields, he expressed complete agreement with the ideas Scalabrini set forth eighty years ago regarding religious ministry to the immigrants and the presence of their religion in the broader spectrum of social life.

"The spiritual life of the immigrants, in fact, is far from being a negligible factor, even from the economic viewpoint, for religion is a social good par excellence. In our own city Bishop Neumann took pride in mastering a number of languages. He invited the first groups of Italian immigrants to his own chapel and instructed them in their mother language. He established the first national parish in this country for Italians. Throughout the United States, Bishops established foreign language parishes and schools. They encouraged immigrants to preserve their cultural heritage. They encouraged the preservation and propagation of the rich diversity of racial and ethnic cultures and gifts for the sake of giving the individuals pride of ancestral roots, and for the sake of enriching the culture of our American society. They acted with the conviction that a man who denies an alien origin and who ignores his ancestral heritage is a man without roots; a man who does not respect his own past admits his own inferiority and will not gain the respect of others. The social philosophy of the Church accepts the principle of integration of cultures rather than assimilation by a melting process."

In conclusion he acknowledged the truth of the wish expressed by Scalabrini in his 1901 lecture to the Catholic Club of New York:[32]

"With others you constitute that pluralism from which the strong unity of this Nation is formed...May God bless you and keep you and may He prosper your good works for your mutual wellbeing and that of the community and the Nation."[33]

Another of Bishop Scalabrini's assumptions, which was variously disputed in the past, has recently been confirmed, namely, that it is necessary to preserve the religious ambience of the place of origin during the period of adjustment in the new environment.

Pius XII refutes those who deny the profound and providential social value of religion:

"Man, as God wills him and as the Church enfolds him, will never feel firmly rooted in time and space without a fixed territory and without traditions...The long experience of the Church as the educator of peoples confirms this. She therefore takes care to link religious life in every way with the customs of the fatherland, and she is particularly solicitous for those whom emigration or military service keeps far away from their native country. The ruin of so many souls provides tragic justification for this maternal anxiety of the Church and leads to the conclusion that a permanent territory and fidelity to ancestral traditions, which are indispensable for the health and wholeness of the human personality, are also basic elements for the human community,"[34]

John XXIII, in an address to the emigrants and refugees on pilgrimage to commemorate the tenth anniversary of *Exsul Familia*, declared:

"The emigrant, in fact, in the first period of transition especially, may be said to have suffered an expropriation — of family love, as well as of his home parish, and his native country and language...He needs to be able to confide in friendly persons, to pray and to receive religious instruction, at least at first, in a church or chapel that meets his particular state of mind."[35]

While no one denies that the individual's religion must be increasingly a matter of inner conviction and spirituality, it must be kept alive before it can grow in perfection. Scalabrini was certainly concerned with the process of interiorization and strengthening of religious observance, as evidenced by the catechetical instruction which he prescribed for emigrants and which he considered the essential part of every apostolate. But at the same time, he was realistic enough to note when remedial action was urgent. If the religious life of the Italian emigrants was to improve, the spark of faith had first to be kept alive.

The Creation of Religious Structures in Certain Dioceses in Brazil

For Brazil, Scalabrini preferred the territorial parish supported by "flying" missions. Even in that field he and his missionaries were ahead of their time.

"It can be said that Scalabrini was an exponent *ante litteram* of the objectives which today mark the program of the Pontifical Commission for Latin America and the various Ecclesiastical Institutions under its jurisdiction. From its founding the Scalabrinian seminary in Piacenza, established by Scalabrini in 1887, was characterized by the spirit and aims of what are today the seminary of Our Lady of Guadalupe in Verona, the College pro America Latina of Louvain, and the college for priests of the OCSHA in Madrid.

"With the formation of his religious congregation, Scalabrini aimed in fact to assure for the new immigrant populations on the American continent a sufficient number of priests who in new geographical areas would continue the work of catechetical instruction and administering of the sacraments that they had carried out in their home regions. His objective was to create in this way parish structures among the emigrants. This institutionalization required the presence of a priest, and it was through the presence of the Scalabrinian and other missionaries especially that the Italian communities in southern Brazil succeeded in forming communities of religion, first around a chapel, and later in administrative parish units..."

"The remarkable number of brick chapels, built by the immigrants for the expression of their common religious life, in places where there were no priests to celebrate the mysteries or to evangelize is a surprising fact frequently remarked upon in the reports of the Royal Consuls or in the accounts of private visitors at the end of the 19th and the beginning of our century, wherever there were strong centers of Italian immigrants..."

"It was the insistence with which the Italian communities asked Bishop Scalabrini to send them a priest that the chapels, which they built in their free time, were gradually provided with missionaries.[36] At the present time, within the geographical limits of the Scalabrinian parishes, which are often quite extensive, there are 566 chapels, many of which will sooner or later become local parishes."

"This is one of the most precious contributions of the Scalabrinian Congregation to the development of the organization of the Church in Brazil, a work comparable to that which in the economic field is indispensable to regional economic development, namely, the creation of 'infrastructure.' It is a work evidently geared (like that of economic infrastructures) to long range results."

"If today we can honestly say that infrastructures of parish life in several areas where Italian farmers first settled in Brazil exist and are functioning, we maintain that this is due in large measure to the activity of the 'flying missionaries' Scalabrini sent to the south of Brazil at the end of the last century."

"The Italians were not the only ones to benefit from this assistance. It may be a surprise to many to learn that the flying missions of the first Scalabrinian Missionaries were not limited to the Italian settlers but often included various ethnic groups of European origin as well as the indigenous inhabitants of the locality. In this connection it is interesting to read the report this publication received in March, 1904, from Santa Felicidade (Parana) on the mission carried out in the parishes of 'Cupim' and 'Prudentopolis' by Father Natale Pigato and his lay catechist and coworker, Angelino Slompo, a twenty-two year old Tyrolese, among the Polish, German and Brazilian residents of the region. The mission lasted two months. The importance of this international opening out of the Scalabrinian apostolate was underlined in the report at that time:

" 'This time, we may frankly say, the Mission was somewhat original, somewhat extraordinary in various ways. And in truth it was not limited to Italians alone as on other occasions but was extended to include the Brazilians, Poles and Germans living in the above-mentioned parishes,' which in territorial size can well be compared to our diocese of Piacenza.' (Monthly Publication of the Congregation of the Missionaries of St. Charles, a.2, n. 4 April, 1904)."[37]

A letter from Father Natale Pigato to Father Brescianini gives us some idea of the hardships of those two months of missionary life:

"We are in the midst of these woods, or rather in wild forests which I do not think civilization or morality has yet penetrated. Here people live like animals in every respect. We have found shelter in the house of a Pole, and we have been half sick for four or five days because of the drenching we took on the way with no means of getting dry and without anything to eat, and we are so embarrassed we do not know what to do. This time we are, so to speak, between the devil and the deep blue sea, and we can't escape. It would not do to turn back because we have already come a long and difficult journey, and we are afraid to go on because we do not yet have the strength to do so, and meanwhile we can only weep and pray. In truth never in all our lives have we suffered so much, never has anything made so deep and gloomy an impression on us. Father Superior, pray and have prayers offered so that we may soon be able to continue our journey. We hope to see you again. Meanwhile, good-bye and give our regards to Angelino's family."

The results of this trip verify the Gospel saying that "some sow and others reap":

"This is what Father Natale has been able to do in almost two months of mission work. After having traveled back and forth between those two parishes and after having suffered every possible discomfort and inconvenience by day and by night — and his Sacristan has suffered as well so that the health of both of them has been affected — he was able to solemnize only ten marriages, baptize 92 babies, and hear the confessions of and give Communion to only 335 persons. He was able to arrange for the building of four new chapels, and to designate the site for three new cemeteries, for which he blessed the crosses. This is the spiritual fruit we culled in that vast territory."[38]

The immediate visible harvest was certainly not cause for great satisfaction from a human viewpoint. It was the painful time of the sowing. Those humble chapels were the germ of future parishes.

The Diocese of Santo Andre, formerly part of the Archdiocese of Sao

Paolo, was created in 1954 on the territory of a former Scalabrinian parish, and provides a significant example of the humble and generous contribution which the Scalabrinian missionaries, following the footsteps of their founder, made to the development of the Church in Brazil.

"In 1904, the Servant of God, Bishop Scalabrini, while on a visit to his missionaries in Sao Paulo, obtained from His Excellency Bishop Jose de Camargo Barros the Parish of San Bernardo. This was an old Brazilian parish, which had been going through a period of revival since the end of the last century when the first nucleus of Italian settlers established themselves there. They had also established their customs and traditions, especially the religious ones, so that the presence of an Italian priest was necessary.

"The township of San Bernardo, which took in all the territory of the present new diocese, then had about 10,000 inhabitants. Other groups of Italian settlers were established at Pilar di Ribeirao Pires and Sao Gaetano, while a few years later, with the opening of the first factories, groups of workers — especially Italians — began to live in the area of the ancient Santo Andre, which had been colonized by the Portuguese Joao Ramalho even before Sao Paulo was founded."

"In 1911, the Curia of Sao Paulo separated from Sao Bernardo the new parishes of Ribeirao Pires and Santo Andre, to which was annexed the village of Sao Gaetano. These three Scalabrinian parishes provided the religious ministry throughout the territory which forms the present diocese until 1922, when, with the increase in population, it began to be subdivided into other parishes which were gradually entrusted to other Religious Congregations and to the Diocesan Clergy."

"To meet the needs of the increasing local developments the Scalabrinian Fathers multiplied their activities and built new churches, schools and orphanages everywhere. Their work in the lower part of the parish of Santo Andre was impressive. There they built all the structures necessary for the new parish, which they then handed over to the Archdiocese and where the Church of Our Lady of Mount Carmel became the new Cathedral; there they built the priests' residence, the Bishop's residence, the building to house the parish activities, the chancery building, the parish school, and the Episcopal College..."

"Thus the Scalabrinian Missionaries repaid the gesture made fifty years before by the Bishop of Sao Paulo, who gave them a parish, offering him in exchange an entire Diocese."[39]

This may be taken as a symbol of the realization of Bishop Scalabrini's dream when he began this work:

"It is a new, marvelous, consoling awakening which the Church is stimulating on behalf of the have-nots and the disinherited, and whoever can help her in this work for religious and social renewal is blessed a thousand times. It is the time, as the Apostle proclaims, when if one member rejoices all the members rejoice, and if one member suffers, all the members run to help him."

"If the past was sad, if until yesterday our brothers were left to their own resources...Christian charity and modern civilization enjoin us to put an end to such a deplorable situation, unworthy of a great and generous people."

"The fight I am recommending to the thought and the action of the Italian clergy and laity is a great one, noble, untried and glorious, and in it the widow's mite and the rich man's offering, the humble action of more quiet souls and the generous impulse of the most zealous spirits have equal worth and dignity."

"Religion and country, these two supreme aspirations of every good heart, are interwoven, and they complement each other in this work of love, which provides protection for the weak, and are fused in wonderful harmony. The wretched barriers erected by hatred and anger disappear. Arms are outstretched in a fraternal embrace, hands are pressed with warm affection, and lips are curved in smiles...; with the disappearance of every distinction based on class or party, men reflect that phrase which is so beautiful in its Christian splendor: *Homo homini frater.*

"May my poor wards be the seed of wonderful works which will rebound to the glory of God and of His Church, for the good of souls, the honor of our country, and the relief and comfort of the unfortunate and the disadvantaged."[40]

CHAPTER XIV

The Heart of the Church

"A man of the Church, a man of God," were epithets often applied to Scalabrini. Both are aspects, as he himself said, of the priesthood, for the priest "represents the universal Priest and the eternal Christ Jesus"[1] among the people of God; as the "personification of the Christian people he offers to God the sacred things of this world; as the personification of Jesus Christ, he bestows on the world the sacred things of God."[2] The ecclesiastical mission of the priest is essentially fulfilled in the Eucharist, which in turn is the heart, the center of the Church.

"The Eucharist is the center of the Church, the substance of divine worship, the tree of life within the Church. It is the ferment which Incarnate Wisdom has hidden in this sacrament...and it makes man spiritual. And this leaven, which through the Church penetrates the various social situations by means of the priestly ministry, will give flavor to the world, which before was flavorless...and it will gather together all the various peoples into the one body of the church."[3]

"The Eucharistic sacrifice, while it is an offering in which Christ through the Holy Spirit offers Himself, an Immaculate Victim, to God, is also an oblation in which the whole body of the Church offers itself with

Christ, so that the whole Christ *(Christus totus)* is at one and the same time the one who offers and the victim offered."[4]

Without the Eucharist the Church would be "a religion without sacrifice, an association of utopians, a house built on sand: Christ himself would be a fable, a myth."[5] "On this sacrament is the Church established, and all its riches are summed up in the bread and wine."[6]

For the evils of his time Bishop Scalabrini found no remedy more efficacious than devotion to the Eucharist, which he understood as a reawakening of the ecclesiastical spirit. While he admired scientific progress, he felt men could not close their eyes to the fact that its goals are exclusively material and that it carries with it the temptation to forget man's eternal goals. Nor could they, in his views, be blind to the sectarianism which had taken over the reins of society, or to Marxism, with its thrust toward a universal conspiracy.

For the people of Piacenza, the schism caused by Miraglia was an open wound, a symbol as it were of social apostasy. What was needed was a return to union in Christ, which flourished at the birth of the Church in the Eucharist, the sacrament of unity, the center and *raison d'etre* of the Christian community at the time of the Apostles, the bread of the brave and of virgins in the era of the catacombs. The Church lived in the Eucharist; in it she found the source of life, the nourishment for her growth, the strength for her victory.[7]

For these considerations came the idea for the third diocesan Synod, which was held on August 28-30, 1899.

The Synod on the Eucharist

Scalabrini had but recently completed his fourth pastoral visit, during which to his great "consolation and joy" he had been able to observe the zeal and obedience of his clergy in carrying out the directives of the two previous synods. He was convinced that a synod was the best preparation for a pastoral visit, and so before embarking on his fifth such visit he called an assembly of the clergy for June 6, 1899. In the words of St. Charles this was to be "a kind of general visit," the "salvation of the Church, the terror of her enemies, the nervous system of the body of the Church." The third synod was to have a particular theme and tone; at the end of the 19th century and the beginning of the 20th, it was to be the particular contribution of the Church of Piacenza to the chorus of homage and consecration that was rising to the Redeemer, the Lord of the centuries, from all over the world. The synod was to be a stimulus to union and harmony in "the sign of unity, the bond of charity, the symbol of concord, which is the Sacrament of love, the gift of gifts."[8]

On the morning of August 28, 1899 the synod was opened with a pontifical Mass in the Basilica of Saint Antoninus, at which the Bishop addressed the first of three discourses to his priests. At this distance in time we still admire the wisdom and organization of the synodal arrangements, which are still considered substantially valid today. But even more impressive are the three *orationes*, which are filled with so much doctrine, so much Biblical, patristic and liturgical background. They reflect the holiness, devotion and zeal which he wanted to inspire in all his priests, so that clearly he was speaking from the fullness of his heart.

The following excerpts deal with the Eucharist as the key to priestly holiness and ministry.

Devotion to the Eucharist was the first and principal devotion in the history of the Church.

"Thus it was in the Church at its beginnings. Now we see that times have changed and other devotions have partly replaced faith in and love for Christ, namely, prayers to the Saints and the filial devotion due the Mother of God. I do not say this...to deplore or to belittle in the slightest degree these devotions. There is no partisanship in my words. I enthusiastically praise these manifestations of piety. In fact I make every possible effort so that they will be accepted and be ever more widely practiced...Nevertheless it is necessary to be careful that the imitation of and devotion to the Saints does not lessen perhaps our faith in and love for Christ."

Devotion to the Eucharist purifies us from our sins, increases virtue, gives nourishment, strength and protection to our spiritual life, enriches it with charisms, and makes us sharers in His divinity. The celebration of the Mass leads naturally to "a gentle inclination to recollection, a stronger instinct for prayer, a secret sweetness in the contempt for self, a desire for perpetual immolation, the choice of the hidden life in Christ, the wonderful ascents of the soul to God."

The Eucharist is the principle of the priestly vocation, the *raison d'etre* of the priesthood, the foundation of the Church and the treasure of priests. They must enrich themselves and others with it. It is a deposit entrusted to the ministers of God, a deposit of grain which cannot be kept hidden: "he who hides the wheat will be cursed by the people."

The Eucharist is the guiding star of priests. It appeared to them as children and led them to Christ; it governed their adolescence and guided their youth. It justly constitutes the power, the stability, the support and uplift, the light, health and vitality of their adulthood. "All that you are and all that you have comes from the Eucharist...The priest is fortified on all sides by the Eucharist; he is marked in all things by the signs of the Eucharist." He must measure his ecclesiastical spirit by his devotion to the Sacrament which is the "center of all our faith, the synthesis of divine works, and, so to speak, the compendium of the Word."[9]

In his second discourse, Scalabrini stressed the need and efficacy of preaching about the Eucharist:

The faith is spread and it is conserved through preaching. But there is a strict relationship between the revealed Word and the Incarnate Word, present in the Sacrament and the Sacrifice. Preaching is empty and sterile if it does not relate to the Eucharist, just as the recollection of the Passion would be ineffective without preaching: "Do this in memory of me. In reality Christ united his preaching with his sacrifice; the sacrifice alone would be ineffective, and the sacrifice without preaching would stand in isolation."[10] Only the word makes sacramentally clear the relation between the Sacrifice on Calvary and the Sacrifice on the Altar.

If today mensa Domini despecta est the reason is that God's gift is little known. Priests are not to lay the blame on the wickedness of the times, the publicity given error and scandal and the loss of faith — all evils that derive from inadequate preaching. In particular, the subject of the Eucharist is neglected or at the most is treated like any ordinary item of Christian doctrine. Instead, it should be preached constantly, and every opportunity seized to bring it into the discussion, whether of fine weather, the rain, the summer, the winter, or all man's labors and problems, as Christ and St. Paul did.

If the priest is to offer the faithful abundant nourishment of the divine word, this presupposes constant study of the Scriptures, the patristic writings, the Summa of St. Thomas and modern writers. Do not be frightened off, the bishop told his clergy, by the scarecrow of little understanding on the part of the faithful. Understanding the divine mysteries is above all a matter of divine grace, of the light of faith, not of natural intelligence. And then, very often the faithful do not understand because the priest keeps treating them as children and never helps them grow to adulthood; he keeps feeding them milk, never solid food. The Eucharist is at one and the same time the milk of infancy and the food of the strong, the bread of the hardy. Do not be content, he admonished, with preaching the story of Christ. Preach the presence of the living Christ, the present reality of His sacrifice, the continuity of His dwelling among us.

Christ continues to praise the Father in the Church, but he does so with your voice, with your preaching, and with the Eucharistic banquet which you prepare.

As always, Scalabrini's vision is fixed on the future. The blacker the day, the rosier the sunset, with a promise of a splendid tomorrow. — Lift your eyes and see how the fields are golden with the harvest...The poor shall eat and be filled and they will love forever...The future generation will be named "of the Lord," for the heavens — that is, the priests — will proclaim the holiness of the people about to be born, formed by the Lord. It will be the people of the most Holy Sacrament; the twentieth century will be called the century of the Eucharist.[11]

The life of the priest and of the Christian people in the Eucharist is the theme of his third discourse. A summary follows:

The rectitude and the holiness of the priest are the best means to accomplish the mission which the Lord has entrusted to him.

What is an upright heart? It is a heart that seeks only God, a simple, pure heart, the source of all virtues, the root principle of the priestly life. An upright heart is achieved through meditation on the divine law, through continuous conversation with God in prayer. Through meditation the priest will acquire *innumerabilis honestas;* without prayer, *desolatio desolationis,* a barrenness of all good works. Priests cannot pursue their divine mission if they are submerged in external affairs throughout the day, if they can find no time for meditation in the morning, if they relegate saying the divine office to the end of the day as if it is the last of their concerns. Then it becomes tiresome to talk to God because one loves Him so little. Love grows and is nourished through meditation. Meditation is the daily ration of wood that keeps the fire of priestly love alive. The *secret of success* for the priest is mental prayer, and above all meditation on the Eucharist. There he finds rest, security, happiness, fullness to ecstasy, the fulfillment of the heart, the live charity of Christ: thus does he achieve an upright heart.

Once a priest has acquired this richness of heart and life he can communicate it to his people, he can be an example to them and this is essential if his preaching is to be effective. If the good example of the priest is lacking the people go astray. If a plant withers, the trouble is in the root.

Priestly example requires a spirit of adoration and faith, and familiar conversation with Christ in the Eucharist. Priests are angels who adore Christ, who becomes present through their ministry, they offer him to be adored by the people. And they must conduct themselves as angels whenever they are in church. The faithful will discern in their behavior the living expression of faith, and they will be edified when they see in their priests persons who bear the invisible within them as if it were visible.

Visits to the Blessed Sacrament are a necessity for the heart, which hastens and lingers there where its treasure is. Christ in the Eucharist is the treasure, the wisdom, the counsel, defense and strength of the priest. If Christ no longer speaks to him through the Sacrament it is a sign that his faith is declining, that the fervor of his early years has evaporated.

The priest should make his meditation early in the morning, if at all possible, and before the tabernacle. He must allow ample time to prepare for Mass and to make his thanksgiving afterwards. Some, hardly allow Christ a scant quarter of an hour and immediately hurry out "impatient only with God, *solius Dei impatientes.*" The people, on the other hand, must see the priest often before the tabernacle saying his Office, making his examination of conscience, greeting the Lord on leaving the house and on his return, and sometimes also enriching his studies and "flavoring" his occupations with a conversation with Christ.

Pastors must be diligent in cultivating devotion to the Eucharist among their people. Let them go into the streets and bring them into the banquet. Let them invite the rich and the powerful, let them seek out the poor and let them do violence, as it were, to the recalcitrant. They are to prepare their sermons before the Blessed Sacrament, and thus allow Christ to suggest the appropriate words to them. At the tabernacle they must kindle the fire which is to illumine and warm the people, as Moses and the prophets did, and as the Apostles did who went out from the Cenacle "*praedicaverunt ubique Domino cooperante.*"

Children and young people must be the first object of their zeal. *Sinite parvulos venire ad me.* Then the mothers, who only with the knowledge and in the love of Christ in the Blessed Sacrament can give their children a solid Christian upbringing, and the fathers, who must learn from Christ true solicitude and watchfulness over their families.

Parents should be persuaded to offer a Mass three or four times a year, if they can, for the well-being of their children. All should be exhorted to pay a visit to Christ on the evening of Sundays and holydays, and those who live close by should be urged to do so every day. Frequent visits to the Blessed Sacrament make Christ real to us as king and lord, master and friend, brother and spouse. Christ must have first place in the family as in all things.

This is the remedy for the evils of the present time: the heart of Christ. Knowledge of his love will lead to love. Imitation of his universal charity will conquer selfishness and class struggle. The example of his obedience will restrain the spirit of anarchy and insubordination. The sign of his humility will successfully overcome the mania for social and economic advancement, which, detached from the desire and hope for spiritual advancement, produces "a great number of persons filling jobs for which they are unsuited and creates as a result the misfortunes and oppressions of the masses as well as the instability of society."

The Eucharist will be the leaven that transforms and uplifts the world, the sign that will gather all peoples into the one body of Christ, that will shake individuals out of their inertia and make them energetic workers of virtue.[12]

Prescriptions for Ritual

For the doctrinal part of the Eucharistic Synod, Scalabrini drew on the Council of Trent, the Roman Catechism, the teachings of the Fathers of the Church, papal teachings and Thomistic theology. The norms he outlined draw upon the jurisprudence of the Decretals and the replies of the Sacred Congregation of Rites and are greatly influenced by the Provincial Councils of St. Charles Borromeo, who was Scalabrini's model in this field as well. If the long series of prescriptions seems a harvest of minute detail this is due in part to Borromeo's example and in part to Scalabrini's personal devotion to the Eucharist. He never tired of telling his priests:

"Since in the Mass there is nothing superfluous, nothing idle in the Eucharistic devotion, but all is divine, all is capable of arousing in the people devotion to Jesus in the Sacrament, so everything, however small it may seem, is to be always the object of your careful solicitude."[13]

He therefore indicates examples the priests could use to explain the meaning of transubstantiation, tells how the genuflection should be done as a sign of faith and adoration, indicates where the children should be placed for Adoration so that they will be near the Lord who loves them. He also goes into details about creating an atmosphere of reflection during the Forty Hours, by shading the windows and keeping directions about preparations distance from the church, and he gives specific directions about preparations for the procession, such as cleaning the streets, adorning the houses and having persons ready to invite the spectators to genuflect. He also directs how the Sanctuary lamp is to be kept burning, suggests the organization of little festivities on the 25th and 50th anniversaries of First Communion, and explains how the sickroom is to be made ready for the Holy Viaticum. And the guards are to remember to "present arms" when the Blessed Sacrament is carried past one of the barracks — which were quite numerous in Piacenza.

He makes practical suggestions for verifying which parishioners had made their Easter duty. Soldiers, migrant workers, the sick are not to be neglected, and he held that the Eucharistic fast was not obligatory for them — a probable opinion at that time. He insists on the purity of the bread and wine that is to be used, suggesting that if possible they be prepared by the priests themselves or by Sisters assigned to that task.[14] He invites families to offer wheat and grapes for the Eucharist according to the ancient custom, through which they "would participate more intimately in the sacrifice, thus drawing from it abundant graces."[15]

He quotes in its entirety the Tridentine Decree *de observandis et evitandis in celebratione Missae* and directs his priests and seminarians to learn it by heart. He censures the priest who *a profanis occupationibus vel e lecto surgens, accedit ad altare*, and praises the one who *depositis, non proiectis in sacrario vestibus*, abstains from any idle chatter and hastens to kneel down and make his thanksgiving.

The most scrupulous cleanliness is recommended, one might say, on every page. Neatness, cleanliness, decorum are words that recur again and again in connection with the church itself, the altar, the vestments, furnishings, sacred vessels, and especially the celebrant himself. In this connection, it is enough to recall that he branded the use of tobacco before Mass as indecent, *sive attritum trahere, sive addensum adspirare, sive dentibus mandere*. He set forth a schedule for the annual, monthly, weekly and daily cleanings of the church down to the smallest detail. In this he is only reproducing the norms set forth by St. Charles. He explains that he does not emphasize cleanliness for its own sake but as homage to the Eucharistic presence, a sign of the purity necessary for approaching the sacred mysteries, and also a necessary condition for preserving the artistic treasures of the Church. He threatens the severest ecclesiastical punishments for selling or otherwise parting with sacred objects of artistic value.

The details seem a little curious now perhaps, but they witness to his great love for the Eucharist. Naturally, he gave due emphasis to the more important aspects of the devotion to the Eucharist. We may note here the themes that are the most significant either from the viewpoint of that period or for the manner in which he develops them.

Frequent Communion

It is interesting first of all to note Scalabrini's thinking on frequent and daily Communion several years before St. Pius X, the Pope of the Eucharist, caried out the reform that was to bring about a resurgence of Eucharistic devotion in the Church.

The Synod goes back, as Pius X will do later, to the decrees of the Council of Trent, which admitted the possibility of and in fact recommended sacramental Communion as the most efficacious participation in the Eucharistic sacrifice and as a response to the love of Christ, who willed to gather us all together in this sacrament of unity. But the Jansenist heresy had intervened after Trent. Scalabrini does not hesitate to label as "agents of the devil" those who allowed themselves to be influenced by the cold wind of Jansenism and thus inhibited the thrust of the soul toward Christ.

"If Christ ardently wishes communion it is evident that we can do nothing more pleasing to him than to respond often to such love in order to strengthen ourselves to fight the battles of the Lord."[16]

Those who persist in requiring extraordinary purity before granting permission to receive Communion are confusing the disposition necessary for receiving the Sacrament with the result which only frequent reception of the Eucharist can bring about. *Non est opus valentibus medicus, sed male habentibus.* The Eucharist has been instituted for men, not angels.[17] All priests and especially pastors must on every occasion and with all diligence exhort the faithful to frequent Communion. And suiting their actions to their preaching, they must always be "happy and ready" to serve souls by administering the sacraments of Penance and Communion.[18]

The question of daily Communion was then being debated, and the Synod appealed to the instructions of Innocent XI, who taught that the matter was to be considered on a case by case basis, and that in general one should neither refuse nor oblige persons in the matter of frequent reception of the Sacrament. It was much more necessary and appropriate to be careful about the preparation for its reception. Scalabrini therefore adopts the rules of St. Alphonsus. Frequent Communion — that is, more than once a week — may be permitted and even counseled to those who, though they might fall at times into venial sin, repent and strive not to fall again. Daily communion may be permitted those who are making progress in virtue. The sole judge is the confessor. It is necessary therefore for priests to be ready to hear confessions every day, and if possible, at any hour of the day, remembering that, as St. Francis de Sales said, the martyr's crown belongs not only to those who confess to God before men, but also to those who confess to men before God.[19]

It is clear that Scalabrini wished to facilitate for the faithful as much as possible the preparation necessary for the proper disposition so that they would receive Communion ever more frequently and, in fact, every day. Two years later, in the Lenten Pastoral of 1902, he returns to the subject with an ardor that bespeaks his earnest desire to see a complete return to daily Communion.

The processions, the external celebrations, the joyful feastdays[20] in honor of the Blessed Sacrament are praiseworthy, but "devotion to the Eucharist requires much more. It requires that in each parish a sizeable number of persons receive Communion several times a month, others several times a week, and others every day. Where this frequency is lacking, the most essential part of Christianity gradually declines because it is deprived of life."

He does not seem able to find words adequate to praise the fruits of Communion:

"If in the Incarnation of the Word, God personally took on human nature, in Communion he partakes even more of our personality. In this way he makes divine our essence, he Christianizes, I may say, our individual being, and his union with us has as a sign the same union which transforms the food into the substance of the body which is being nourished." Thus in those who are nourished with the Bread of angels, He does everything in all of them, and they no longer live in themselves; it is the Word of God who lives in them."

"But if these are the fruits of Communion, what must we say of those confessors and spiritual directors who, instead of exhorting the faithful to frequent, perhaps daily, Communion keep them from it under the pretext of zeal for the honor and reverence due Jesus in the Sacrament? This is the result of an arid, cold, misunderstood piety; perhaps they are still in the throes of a niggardly, hypocritical and utterly severe teaching" which is contrary to the example of the early Church, the teachings of the Council of Trent and of the most eminent Fathers, doctors and theologians, and to the will of Christ, who chased from the banquet only those without a wedding garment, that is, without sanctifying grace. "Why then must be required of the faithful an extraordinary purity of mind, heart, and deeds before admitting them to this banquet? Is not frequent Communion precisely the best disposition for worthily approaching the Eucharist?"[21]

The Synod fixed nine or ten as the age for making one's First Communion, and it would be made even earlier given the proper disposition: *cognitio et gustus*.

"It is of the greatest importance in fact that Christ our Lord take possession of the hearts of the children before the passions are awakened. In fact, their innocence and ingenuousness more than make up for their lesser knowledge, provided this is sufficient."[22]

Preparation for First Communion should last a year, and be intensified in the last month. It should end with spiritual exercises conducted morning and afternoon for three days. Scalabrini condemned the custom, then in vogue in many areas, of postponing the second Communion to the anniversary of the first. He appeals to the sincere love of souls to evoke from pastors the gentle charity that is kind and patient. Even Christ had to reprove the Apostles who wished to keep the children from him with the pretext of not disturbing the Lord...If they were in danger of death children were permitted to receive Communion even before the age of seven as soon as they showed they understood Whom they were about to receive.[23]

Scalabrini's admonitions to priests to be prompt and zealous in bringing the Viaticum to the dying are stressed with a vigor that might seem excessive if we did not remember his own zeal and self-sacrifice, which led him more than once to risk his life rather than deprive the dying of the last comforts of the faith. Priests are to remember that they are not the "owners but the dispensers of the mysteries of God."[24] During the epidemics they are to ignore the danger of infection.[25] They are not to fail to be an example to the faithful. Priests who are ill are to receive Communion at least once a week to avoid, among other things, the scandal of dying without the Sacraments, which unfortunately had sometimes happened.[26]

Perpetual Adoration

Both in his prescriptions and his addresses at the Synod, Scalabrini repeatedly stresses the importance of good example on the part of the priests, who are to be models for the faithful in Eucharistic devotion. To this end he urged his priests to enroll in the Society for Perpetual Adoration.

Through this, the priest, the visible angel of the Church, joins the heavenly angels of God in the worship and constant honor offered to Christ...Thus the priest resembles Christ the mediator, *semper vivens ad interpellandum pro nobis...*[27]

At a Eucharistic Congress, Scalabrini was prevailed upon to address the assembly:

"My proposal is that perpetual adoration of the Blessed Sacrament by the clergy be instituted in every diocese." He cited the example of one diocese where "it seemed the hand of God lay heavy on the priests. Their bishop who, like all other bishops, carried in his heart the sorrows of all his flock and especially the sorrows and misfortunes of his priests, was profoundly grieved. He prayed and had prayers offered; he realized that God wanted something out of the ordinary and he established perpetual adoration by the clergy...This produced an immense good in that great diocese. The scourge that had led to its institution disappeared. Several of the first members, who had been faithful in the practice and very zealous in promoting this devotion, died with signs of certain predestination. The parishes who possessed a treasure in these priests flourished. When one of them was sent to a parish in need of renewal he spent his regular hours at the feet of Jesus in the Blessed Sacrament like an adoring angel. During the night, between midnight and one o'clock one of those who called themselves free thinkers was walking past the church. On seeing the light he immediately thought of thieves. He approached softly, looked in and saw his good pastor prostrate in adoration. He was rooted to the spot at the sight and his eyes filled with tears. His mind was illumined, and he was reconverted and is now a fervent Catholic. The pastor, who was faithful to the practice of adoration, transformed his people and when their Bishop fell seriously ill, the entire parish kept watch before the Blessed Sacrament for three nights and obtained the answer to their prayers."[28]

Scalabrini's hope was that the example of the priests would lead their parishioners also to the practice of perpetual adoration. He felt the habit should be acquired in the seminary. When the Rector asked permission to have theatrical presentations during carnival time, Scalabrini answered:

"During the days when God is so offended, I would much prefer to see the Exposition of the Blessed Sacrament, and the young men in turn offering adoration of reparation. It is necessary to accustom them to enter according to the times into the spirit of the Church."[29]

And on the subject of adoration of the Eucharist, he repeatedly said:

"With respect to anything in relation to the Eucharist, never let your lips say the foolish words, this is impossible. Impossibility in this case does not exist except for those who avoid self-denial and sacrifice."[30]

Throughout the diocese there was not to be a single hour when Christ was not being adored in the Blessed Sacrament in order to make reparation with daily worship for the daily offenses against the love of Christ and in order to obey the law of love, through which the faithful of the diocese, which is one body and one family, must continually, and for another, render thanks to God and beseech his mercy.[31]

Scalabrini never tired of stressing the fundamental theme of love, of which the Eucharist is the Sacrament. On the days assigned to them for adoration, the confraternities of the Blessed Sacrament of one parish must invite those of neighboring parishes, in order to promote, ever increasingly, mutual love.[32] During the period of adoration they are to bestow on the dying the charity of prayer, that they may die in holiness.[33] Within the confraternities, the members must ever exercise mutual charity. If one falls ill, he is to be visited and given material and spiritual assistance. It is even more incumbent on them to have a care for the health of a soul, offering fraternal admonition when necessary.[34] Here too the priests must give good example, helping one another on the days of adoration, in order to offer the people an abundant banquet of grace. And those who refuse to participate in the great encounter of the Christian community in the procession of the Blessed Sacrament are even threatened with suspension.[35]

The theme of unity in love and in the Sacrament is reflected again in Scalabrini's keen sense of the parish community.

"The parish church is the home of all the faithful, because it is the house of God in which he has pitched his tent in the midst of our tents... It is, as it were, the epitome of the religion and the family of the Christian. There, in fact, he is born spiritually, there he grows spiritually, is nourished by doctrine and then by the more solid sacred food."[36]

Therefore he "prays and implores" his people "through the bowels of the mercy of Jesus Christ" to attend Mass in the parish Church at least on Sundays so that they may be nourished by the pastor into whose charge they have been entrusted, instructed in Christian doctrine, prepared to receive the Sacraments more worthily, and enkindled to zeal by his exhortations, and in order also that they may always be well informed on all the dispositions, observances, rites and means to grace, set forth by the sacred hierarchy...[37] If one does not attend his own parish church and wanders about to other little churches and chapels, he often remains ignorant of the principal elements of faith and morals. It leads to neglect of worship, good works, Christian education, and the family and diminishes the effectiveness of the pastoral ministry.[38] The Religious who are exempt are to arrange the schedule of their Masses so as not to interfere with attendance at the parish Mass.[39]

Devotion to the Eucharist

Besides the above mentioned perpetual adoration societies for priests and laity,[40] Scalabrini initiated numerous other means to create throughout the whole diocese a deep Eucharistic movement, such as the renewal and promotion in all parishes of the Confraternities of the Blessed Sacrament for men and women, and the society for daily Mass. Especially to be noted among them were Tabernacle Institute for poor churches,[41] the founding of the order of Deafmute Sacramentine Sisters,[42] and the creation of the Pious

Society of Pages of the Blessed Sacrament. Champion of the latter was Father C. Molinari, who presented it to the Pope of the Eucharist seven days before Bishop Scalabrini's death. In an autographed Brief, Pius X bestowed his blessing on it and expressed the hope that it would spread to other dioceses. On that occasion also he gave evidence of the concern with which he was following his friend's illness, when he told Father Molinari that Scalabrini had undergone surgery on the previous day and expressed his joy that — as he had been informed — the operation had been successful.[43]

From the testimony of witnesses at the informative process and from all other available evidence, we must conclude that the most effective contribution to the spread of Eucharistic devotion in the diocese of Piacenza was the example of the Bishop himself.

"He was truly filled with enthusiasm when, in the presence of the Blessed Sacrament, he spoke of it to the faithful whether in public or in private. He gave the impression that he could actually see the Lord with his bodily eyes."[44]

But his most convincing sermon was the way he celebrated the sacrifice of the Mass. He himself was convinced that the most important act of the priest's day was without question the Mass. Therefore it held first place among all the activities of the ministry. He prepared for it zealously with a period of intense mental prayer.

"In preparation for Holy Mass," he noted in his own resolutions — "if only I could first make my meditation: What a preparation! Courage! Get up in time! Dear Jesus in the Blessed Sacrament, help me! *Hoc fac et vives.*"[45]

Again, when making application to keep the Blessed Sacrament in his private chapel, he wrote: "Before Mass, I will go to my chapel and make my meditation."[46]

Those who attended his Mass were unanimous in evidencing the great devotion with which he celebrated it and the edifying effect this invariably had on everyone present. According to one priest, he became so fervent that "a kind of warmth seemed to radiate from his person, which made a great impression on me since I am not easily suggestible."[47]

Still another wrote: "I have attended his Mass many times and I remember that at the Consecration he was transformed and his eyes shone like two suns."[48] And again we read: "His voice, recollected attitude, and the ceremony itself reflected a spirit absorbed in contemplation of the divine mysteries."[49] "It seemed to me that he could really see the Lord."[50]

He devoted at least a quarter of an hour to his preparation for Mass and another quarter hour to his thanksgiving. "His long personal thanksgiving, after the liturgical one, was extremely edifying."[51]

Whenever he could he heard a second Mass, even on days when he was especially busy. "In this connection, I remember seeing him in the church in Agazzano attending Mass, kneeling on the bare floor."[52]

It is not to be wondered at that such great faith and devotion were accompanied by an absolute confidence in the Lord, one tangible evidence of which was Scalabrini's habit of placing under the corporal the documents requiring the most binding decisions and the list of priests' appointments. The swift transition from perplexity to decision he and others always attributed to the special enlightenment God grants in the intimate contact of Communion when the evangelical conditions of faith and hope are present.

"At those times he was transfigured. It was clear he was communing with the Mystery, made tangible to him by the gift of God. It is no wonder, then, if afterwards he took extraordinary decisions, declared innocent without question persons on whom the severest disciplinary measures were about to be visited, and in conversation read what was in your heart."[53]

"A priest of Piacenza had been accused of very serious offenses and action was to be taken against him; the Bishop was being pressured to condemn him. Bishop Scalabrini answered: 'At the moment, I do not feel up to it. Wait until I say another Mass.' After the Mass, he said: 'There is nothing to be done. That priest is innocent.' And his innocence was proven by the facts."[54]

"He very often consulted his confessor and he implored spiritual enlightenment not only in the ordinary way, but in long periods of prayer, especially before the Blessed Sacrament. And he used to say that after a visit to the Blessed Sacrament, he felt certain about the decision he was to take."[55]

"It seems to me that you have half an idea to become a priest," he said to a young man from Milan whom he met for the first time. — "Yes, Excellency; in fact I need to talk to you about this." — "Fine, fine," the Bishop replied, "but it is better to pray first; wait until I have said Mass tomorrow morning and then we shall talk about it." The next morning he confidently encouraged the young man: "Go ahead," he said, "the Lord will bless you."[56]

With the simplicity of holiness, he believed that others were granted a similar gift.

"I would like you to read this letter before the Holy Tabernacle," he wrote one priest. "There you will receive the light and the strength to carry out my advice."[57] And in letters to others we read phrases like these: "Kneel for a moment before the Blessed Sacrament and then give me your answer; I will resign myself to the will of God and accept it."[58] — "Prostrate yourself before the Tabernacle..."[59] — "Be of good heart and do not be caught up in vain fears. Do your duty with prudence, but openly. Why be discouraged? Do you not have Jesus Christ in the Tabernacle who keeps saying to you *quare dubitasti?*[60]

He suffered most keenly when he was constrained by force of circumstances to omit saying Mass. The journal of his voyage to the United States is full of expressions of joy or regret depending on whether or not conditions at sea permitted him to celebrate the Holy Sacrifice.

"July 22 (1901). Clear sky. Quiet sea. I say Mass in the grand salon and to my great consolation I hear that of the Canadian priest, Father Louis Rodier."

"July 26. It is the feast of St. Anne, a beautiful day, but I cannot say Mass today either. I am grieved. I was hoping that the Saint would assure me the grace of being united with Blessed Jesus, but I did not deserve it...The sea continues rough and the altar is too unsteady... Patience! Tomorrow."

"July 27. A magnificent day; the sea is calm. I say and I hear a Holy Mass. *Deo gratias.*"

"July 31. I say Mass and after me, as always the priest acting as my secretary. I could not truly have greater good fortune..."

"August 2. How much consolation it was to me this morning to say the Mass of St. Alphonsus!"[61]

In the journal of Scalabrini's voyage to Brazil, the Mass again has the most important place:

"June 20 (1904). I say Mass, not without difficulty, surrounded by a great crowd of people."

"July 2. The terrible weather continues. Violent rollings even during Mass. One of the Missionaries holds the chalice, another the missal and another keeps the altar steady. I keep my balance as best as I can."

"July 3. I say Mass with great difficulty, and give First Communion to about fifteen boys. As I speak to them, I have to hold on to the altar with one hand and to an iron railing with the other."

"July 4. The poor ship is being battered by the waves. I say Mass nevertheless, with difficulty, but to my great consolation."[62]

Immediately after Mass he liked to spend time in adoration of the Blessed Sacrament. God alone knows how many hours he spent "prostrate before the Tabernacle," in joy or in tears, by day and by night.

"He used to spend long hours prostrate in a gallery of the Episcopal palace that had a view of the Blessed Sacrament altar in the Cathedral. And many times I heard some member of the household urge him respectfully to sit down, at least, and he always asked not to be disturbed."[63]

When the Cathedral was restored and the passage to the Episcopal palace was done away with, he requested insistently and was granted permission to have the Blessed Sacrament in his private chapel, where he went whenever his duties permitted. Every morning he knelt there for a quarter hour of meditation,[64] he prayed late into the night,[65] and he often awoke from sleep and went back there to pray.[66]

In adoration of the Eucharist, he lived the Communion of the Saints and the mystery of unity in Christ:

"Adoration! It is no little comfort to me, I confess, when before the Tabernacle I think that all those whom I have loved here on earth are adoring with me the same God — they face to face, I under the mystic veil. Members of the Church Triumphant and the Church Militant, we are kneeling before the same Redeemer, the same Father. My prayer rises to melt into the hymn of love which my dear ones beyond the tomb are lifting around the throne of the Lamb in their eternal dwelling. I meet them again in this sacred assembly."[67]

The thought of the Sacramental presence of Christ in the Tabernacle was always with him. There was no danger that he would ever forget the Divine Guest, the Master of the house, as he used to say, when he went to visit a parish or a seminary. The first visit, the first greeting was always for the Lord, not a quick, routine visit, like a bow to convention, but a long conversation in faith and love. This constant awareness of Christ's presence often led Scalabrini, who was universally admired for his strength, to what seemed naive or childlike expressions of tenderness. For example, he like to pick the flowers to decorate the altar. When he was about to leave on his sixth pastoral visit he insisted on saying his good-bye to the people of the diocese by personally giving each of them Communion. And finally, there was his hope that he could again say Mass on the day of resurrection.[68]

His most beautiful sermon on the Eucharist he gave on his death bed.[69] Was this perhaps the moment of the dream with which he ended his Eucharistic Pastoral of 1902?

"When the Lord, in His infinite goodness and mercy, shall grant that I see devotion to the Eucharist deeply rooted in my beloved diocese, then there will be no more for me to do but to exclaim with the prophet Simeon: 'Now thou dost release thy servant, O Master, in peace because my eyes have seen the Savior thou hast given us loved, thanked and venerated by those who are in the time and shall be in eternity my joy and my crown!' "[70]

The Viaticum seemed to revive him and the doctor, who was an unbeliever, almost thought he was seeing a miracle. It was not a miracle, however, but a sign of the beatitude which the Lord must have allowed him to foretaste in the long hours he spent in adoration:

"This joy of the pilgrim soul, this tranquillity filled with confidence, this restfulness filled with consolation, this harmony filled with sweetness, this peace, full of love, this is in truth the most beautiful example, the truest image of heavenly beatitude."[71]

Bishop Scalabrini with his brother, Prof. Angelo Scalabrini, and his secretary, Msgr. Camillo Mangot.

CHAPTER XV

The Mother of the Church

On Pentecost Sunday in 1900, Bishop Scalabrini crowned the statue of Our Lady of the Miraculous Medal in the basilica of San Savino in Piacenza. Set in the crown was a ring that had been given him by Leo XIII. This gave him the opportunity to speak on one of his favorite themes: Mary is the Mother of the Church; devotion to Our Lady cannot be separated from devotion to the Pope and love of the Church.

Mary's prayer in the Cenacle, he explained, helped to make the descent of the Holy Spirit richer in grace for the Church.

"It is precisely on the day of Pentecost that Mary began to exercise on earth the spiritual motherhood to which she was raised at the foot of the cross. For as the Holy Spirit in Nazareth consecrated her as the Mother of God, in the Cenacle He consecrated her the Mother of the Church."

The Pope's gift had a particular significance: "Honor the Virgin, but do not forget that to honor her worthily you must be united, united in mind and heart to the Vicar of her Divine Son. Remember that the Roman Pontiff is the visible head, the visible foundation, on which Jesus Christ erected the immortal edifice of his Church...In the Cenacle, the image of this Church was Peter, the prince of the Apostles and the vicar of Christ; and it was Mary, the queen of the Apostles and the mother of Jesus. And what does this mean? Through Peter the prince we belong to the Church, through the Church to Mary's Son, and through Mary's Son to the true and living God who communicates with us through the Holy Spirit...Without question, God, Jesus Christ, the Virgin Mary, the Catholic Church, the Roman Pontiff are all links in the mysterious chain that binds time to eternity. Woe indeed, and woe threefold to anyone who breaks even one of these links."[1]

His homily on the Feast of the Assumption in 1882 was devoted to Our Lady as the type model of the Church. Thus, he declared, "the two most noble loves in our hearts, the love of the Church and the love of Mary, will be fused."

"The entire life of the great Virgin, the mysteries fulfilled in her, the graces that adorn her, the good that was spread through her were, in the words of St. Ambrose, a vivid type, an image, almost a prophecy of the Catholic Church: *Maria figuram in se gerebat Ecclesiae.*" Directly bound to the life of the Son, become one with Christ, Mary lives by His Spirit, celebrates His glory and loves Him with a perfect love..."In all the Sacraments which the Catholic Church administers, her divine motherhood is reproduced and extended...through the virtue of Christ. *Caro Christi, caro Mariae;* the blood of Christ is the blood of Mary. The various images in Scriptures (the genealogy of the Woman, the Ark, the Tabernacle, the Temple, etc.) prefigure both Mary and the Church. The events in Mary's life parallel those in the life of the Church. At Christmas the very first believers — the Church in embryo — gather about the Mother of Jesus. The flight into Egypt marks the first step in the evangelization of the Gentiles: it is Mary who carries Christ beyond Israel. In the episode in the Temple, Mary "keeps" the words of Christ just as the Church is the depository of the Divine Word, At Cana, the Virgin brings human needs to Christ and asks Him to provide for them, and thus begins the series of His miracles. On Golgotha, Mary becomes the mother of John, that is, of all humankind and therefore of the Church. On the day of Pentecost, the intervention of Mary's prayers was necessary just as her "fiat" was necessary — the latter for the birth of the Redeemer, the former for the birth of the Church. The parallel necessarily extends to the Assumption. To Mary's victory over death, there corresponds the victory of the Church over the persecutions and errors that threaten it with death. "Mary was assumed into heaven for the good of the Church!"

Even Mary's death has a parallel in the history of the Church. Our Lady is dead: "the Church achieves a victory most often by losing." Our Lady died of love; the Church is persecuted because it loves, because it is faithful to its Spouse. If it betrayed Him, if it came to terms with the world, it would no longer have any enemies. It suffers for its love and becomes weak, but its weakness is transmuted into strength. "Assailed by thousands of enemies, despoiled of its possessions, drenched with opprobrium, weighed down by insults it seems about to succumb at every moment, and at every moment its life is doubled." The Assumption of the Virgin is a guarantee that the Church will conquer and that the secret of victory is love.[2]

The Divine Motherhood and the Immaculate Conception were the two aspects of Marian devotion dearest to Scalabrini and he considered them inseparable even from a dogmatic viewpoint. In his pastoral Letter of 1879, on the 25th anniversary of the pronouncement of the dogma of the Immaculate Conception, he set forth the theological basis of the Christian tradition and demonstrated that the truth of the Immaculate Conception derives from the dogma of the Divine Motherhood, as he had previously pointed out in his lectures on the Vatican Council.[3] His treatment of the historical-dogmatic importance of the definition of the dogma, however, is significant in the context of the doctrinal and practical errors of the period. In Mary Immaculate Scalabrini saw the reconciliation between God and the world: "As the Incarnation of the Word was the outpouring of the forgiveness and love of God toward the world, which had completely forgotten Him, so Mary, in the framework of the 19th century, represents humankind regenerated, returning to the arms of its God."[4]

The 19th century is dominated by a heresy, Scalabrini went on, the denial of the supernatural. Scientific progress had given man the presumptuous notion that he "knows everything, can do everything, is sufficient for everything," and he consequently denies the existence of a transcendent order, the impairment due to sin, the redemption and eternal life.

"For him the reason is faith, science is revelation, nature is his divinity...His one preoccupation therefore is to conquer matter, to transform matter, to see nothing, desire nothing, hope for nothing, admit nothing outside of matter." Hence the divorce between the Church and the world, he concluded, between faith and science, between nature and grace. "Who will heal this horrible wound of our unhappy century?... The compassionate Mediatrix of Peace and pardon between nature and grace, between God and the 19th century will be the one who is precisely the most beautiful miracle of nature, the most perfect work of grace, the one in whose person nature and grace, the natural and the supernatural, science and faith are united and interwoven in the highest degree, in the most marvelous manner: the one in short who alone can be called the Immaculate."[5]

He repeated the same concepts in his sermon on December 8, 1904: "A proud rationalism which denies original sin, magnifies man's natural forces, makes them the criteria of truth, the standard of good and the source of all human happiness: this is the capital sin of our era." The doctrine of the Immaculate Conception, he said, reaffirms the truth of the supernatural elevation of man, of original sin, of the need for the redemption, of the authority and infallibility of the Pope: this is the historical significance of the definition of the dogma in 1854. "Certainly after the pronouncement of this most beautiful dogma...the Church has endured severe trials. But we must not have a false idea of what constitutes victory. The Church on earth is and always will be militant. Its strength and its greatness do not reside in the absence of struggle and persecution. The triumph of the Church lies in the reawakening of the faith and the exercise of virtue, in the restoration of all things in Jesus Christ. Was not the age of martyrs a golden age?"

The gains made by the Church in the past fifty years, Scalabrini concludes, are due to Mary Immaculate:

"And who can count the inestimable gifts God has bestowed on his Church through the intercession of Mary Immaculate in the last ten decades? Oh! If souls have not been overwhelmed by the flood of errors, if so many of our brothers could rise, even in this period of time, to the most heroic acts of virtue; if despite all the forces of godlessness the faith has been so widely spread through the world; if the Church has been defended by so many generous sons and daughters at the price of their own future, their own substance and even of their own lives; if she has been able to demonstrate again that all the powers of the abyss will never prevail against her; if the Church through all its difficulties has witnessed so many distinguished conversions, so many peoples returned to the fold; if she vigorously animates and nourishes in these our times all the initiatives of the spirit, the vast network of works that envelops society, the numerous troops of heroes and heroines of charity whose ranks keep swelling despite the world and who constantly offer splendid proof of her vitality, the great flowering of religious devotion, pilgrimages, and various organizations, the abundance of miracles; if the Church has been able to achieve new glory through the admirable unity of the Hierarchy, the timeliness of her definitions of dogma, the canonization of her saints, the greatly increased moral influence of the papacy, the mysterious movement of peoples toward Rome, the providential longevity and singular wisdom of her Supreme Pontiffs and thousands of other manifestations of religious life which I pass over for reasons of brevity, from whom must we say all these things flow? Is it not the Immaculate Virgin, glorified in the mystery of her immaculate conception?"[6]

The Bishop carefully prepared the jubilee celebrations and announced them to the diocese before his departure for Brazil. In a letter from Bento Goncalves dated October 12, 1904, he exhorted the people of the diocese to hurry with the preparations. He himself arrived home barely in time for the closing of the jubilee year. On the 8th of December, despite the weariness and sufferings that had increased during his journey, which had ended only three days before, he was as usual the soul of the celebration. His homily at the Pontifical Mass was a hymn to our Heavenly Mother vibrant with love and emotion. One priest recalled that the Jesuit Father Trussardi, near whom he was sitting, exclaimed at the end of the sermon, "That is the way the angels speak!"[7]

On many other occasions he manifested a special devotion to Mary Immaculate.[8] He began his first pastoral visit on her feastday in order to place it under "the strong protection of the Immaculate Mother of God...: as source of special consolation and filial trust."[9] From the beginning of his episcopate he tried as much as possible to have the principal events coincide with the feastdays of Our Lady. He wanted to end his journey in Brazil with a discourse in Portuguese on Mary Immaculate at Niteroi: "it would be a fine thing to end my pilgrimage with a tribute to our beloved Immaculate Madonna and then leave."[10]

"He had so much confidence in Her that he was sure it was impossible to be in difficulty for very long if one was devoted to Her. One of his priests...had become a Protestant. He was very upset by this, but he said 'That priest will not perish because his holy mother has brought him up in love for the Virgin; She will save him.' And that is what happened. On the feast of the Immaculate Conception, the poor man was invited by the Protestants to deliver a talk against the dogma and he adamantly refused...And this was the beginning of his reconversion, which took place soon afterwards."[11]

At the time of a public disaster Scalabrini invariably had recourse to Our Lady. One pastoral letter is entitled, "Let us have recourse to Mary. Let us help the poor victims of cholera."[12]

Through all the various aspects of his apostolic activity, there invariably runs a dominant theme, so to speak, a kind of necessary return to its original basic context. Even in this devotion to Mary, for example, there is emphasis on the religious education of the young, which was ever the primary concern of this Apostle of the Catechism. An illustration of this is his institution of the "Society of Prayer for the good education of children through the intercession of Our Lady," which had its headquarters in the church of St. Mary in Cortina where the Childhood of Mary was venerated.

"How can we hope for the right direction in education without special divine help. And how can this special help be obtained without prayer? Without prayer strengthened through the intercession of our Blessed Mother?"[13]

The Patroness of Piacenza

The Feast of the Assumption was also a special day for the Bishop of Piacenza since Our Lady under the title of the Assumption was the patroness of the city and the cathedral was dedicated to her. In 1884 he insisted on delivering the sermon despite his ill health, but his strength failed him in the middle of it and he had to leave the pulpit.[14]

There are extant sixteen of the homilies — probably there were twenty-seven in all — which he delivered on the Feast of the Assumption. It was not easy to speak on the same theme year after year, but he managed to do so always with some fresh doctrinal insight or new approach to devotion.

"I remember in this connection that my uncle, Count Giuseppe Nasalli, a man of culture and a good Christian, was always surprised and edified at the way he treated this theme every year so fluently and effectively."[15]

Bishop Scalabrini and the whole diocese were thrown into consternation when, on the night of January 9th, thieves broke into the Cathedral and stole the two precious crowns with which, in the 17th century, the Piacentinians had crowned the statue of the Madonna del Popolo. The people reacted as if it were a personal loss, and in generous response to the appeal of the Bishop and of the Cathedral Board of Trustees they donated two new crowns. On the second anniversary of the theft, Scalabrini, desiring that "grace should abound there where a great wickedness had taken place," invited all the people of Piacenza to an act of reparation, "not attracted by unaccustomed pomp and ceremony and extraordinary solemnities, but in a spirit of compunction and devotion coming to the Sacraments of Confession and Communion." In fact on January 10, 1893, although it was a weekday and the thermometer had fallen to 12 degrees about 20,000 received Communion, to the inexpressible joy of the Bishop, who could not conceive of Marian devotion as separate from that to the Eucharist.[16]

On August 12, 1894, he blessed the new chapel of the Madonna della Bomba, which Monsignor Franceso Torta had had built to enclose a popular image of Our Lady painted on a house on Facsal Avenue.[17] The first to contribute to the new chapel had been the Bishop. On the morning of the dedication:

"in his formal robes, he was completely at ease in the midst of the great crowd of people, enthusiastic in their faith, who were making up to him for the bitternesses occasioned by the dominance of the Masons and the burning 'Roman question'. But even more radiant was the face of the thirty year old pastor of St. Brigid, drawn though it was with the weariness of sleepless nights and work-filled days. He later wrote in his diary: 'In 1894 I was finally able to fulfill my vow to the Madonna della Bomba'...That morning the Bishop spoke seven times in such moving fashion that all the people assembled wept. Among other things he said that in that·little shrine, Mary had appeared especially as a powerful Mother who loved the Piacentinians. His words were proved true. The little chapel was like a seed from which later, in 1903, came the Institute for Deafmutes, in 1910 the Institute for the Blind, in 1921 the Congregation of Sisters of Providence for Abandoned Children (Suore della Provvidenza per l'Infanzia Abbondonata)."[18]

Scalabrini's constant recourse to the intercession of the Blessed Virgin and his confidence in her patronage are reflected also in his correspondence with the Rector of the Seminary in Bedonia, at the side of which is the shrine of Our Lady of Consolation, called Our Lady of St. Mark. Among the dozens of letters and notes, there is not one in which he does not ask for prayers to

Our Lady.

"Pray for me to Our Lady, and have me prayed for to her; I have so much need of her help."[19] — "I appeal to our beloved Lady in everyone's prayers."[20] — "Make a visit to our Most Beloved Mother...and all for me, for I have very great need. Ask her to teach me love of God, love of the Cross, holy abandonment to the divine will, death to the world, oh then I would be truly happy."[21] Or simply: "Grant me the usual charity of saying three Hail Marys for me."[22]

He entrusted his seminarians and missionaries to the special care of Our Lady: "Pray and have prayers offered to Our Lady for me and for the work of the Missions. Monday I leave for Rome to discuss matters relating to the Missionaries, who are doing an immense amount of good."[23] — In referring to a seminarian who was ill, he wrote to the Rector, "Tell him that I was very glad to have his letter, and that Our Dear Lady will cure him."[24] In a letter of recommendation for another seminarian he added, "May the air there and his closeness to our dear Lady of St. Mark bring him great benefit!"[25]

When decisions were difficult he invariably turned to Mary's intercession: "One is never mistaken to imitate the patient governance of God and to hope against hope. You will endanger his soul if you reject him, and endanger others if you accept him. Place the matter in the hands of our beloved Lady. Make a triduum, and afterwards whatever you decide will be well decided."[26]

"On one of his visits to Bedonia a poor boy came to him and begged his help so that he could study for the priesthood, to which he felt strongly drawn. Before giving his answer the Servant of God went to pray before Our Lady of Consolation, venerated in the shrine at Bedonia. He returned to the youngster, his face radiant, and gave him an affirmative answer, telling him that he would have a fine future. The youth was Francesco Sidoli who forty years later became the Archbishop of Genoa. Not infrequently, before installing a new pastor in a parish he sent him to say the rosary before the statue of the Madonna del Popolo."[27]

In 1889, as an act of devotion and gratitude to Our Lady of St. Mark, he decided to conduct a solemn crowning of the statue. This was also intended to stimulate greater devotion to Our Lady.

"Yes," he wrote to Monsignor Natale Bruni, Rector of the Seminary of Bedonia, "let us make a great celebration of the crowning of Our Lady; send me immediately the measurements for the two crowns. But, understand, it is to be a celebration that will be pleasing 'up there.' First there must be a good mission, which can be attended by all the surrounding towns, where the people are so devoted to Our Lady, general communions, etc., etc....Please, we must not let the feast of Our Lady turn into a bacchanal. Fine to have the distinguished personalities, etc., etc., but nothing inappropriate to a distinctly Catholic celebration."[28]

In his desire to render homage to the Virgin commensurate with filial love, he sublimated his love for his own mother in his love for her.

"All right, take care of it, but make sure that everything tends to the glory of God and of Our Lady and the good of souls. I have seen the design of the crowns; they will be beautiful. I want precious stones, real ones. They are expensive, but I want to offer Our Lady, to whom I owe everything, a gift that is in no way unworthy of her, according to our poor, limited ideas."[29]

But the most important stones in the crown were his mother's. He wanted them set there to express the "feeling a loving son cherished in his heart for his heavenly Mother, to whom, through the supernatural phenomenon of grace which perfects nature without destroying it, he gave all the tender affection that he had felt and still felt after so many years for his earthly mother."[30]

The crowning was set for July 8th but the Bishop arrived in Bedonia on June 27th in order to attract with his example as many as possible to the preparatory Mission. The day of the crowning was, as he desired, a "great feastday" that must have been pleasing "up there." There was a great outpouring of faith and devotion, general reception of the sacraments, and a solemn high Mass attended by several bishops (from Parma, Fidenza and Bobbio) and by people from the whole valley, whom he addressed in an outdoor ceremony, his hymn of praise to the Virgin so beautiful that "he seemed to be inspired by an angel."[31]

During the procession, as at other times, "a violent storm broke...over Mount Pelpi, which rose behind the shrine, and which was white with rain. Now while a murmur ran through the crowd and everyone was starting to leave, the Servant of God shouted: 'Do not go, it will not rain (here) today.' And it was possible to go on with the procession to the great satisfaction of the crowd of faithful assembled."[32]

Manifestations of Popular Devotion

At the shrine of Bedonia there was another enthusiastic manifestation of Marian devotion in July of 1896 on the occasion of the Seminary's jubilee celebration. This ended with a procession in honor of the Virgin and the rain was pouring down as it was about to begin. The Bishop refused to cancel it, however, and had everyone wait in the church, praying and singing until the weather cleared. Toward dusk, the procession was finally able to get under way, with eight or ten thousand persons taking part in it.

"...our Bishop, although worn out by all that he had done and all the sermons he had preached...could not refrain from addressing still another eloquent word to that great multitude of people that filled the square and the nearby woods and spilled over into the neighboring streets. His strong voice, vibrant with emotion, seemed at the time, amid that shimmering sea of people and in that deep silence, to be coming from heaven...He had never spoken more effectively or more movingly. A great, shattering and prolonged applause burst from the crowd with cries of *Viva Maria! Long live our Bishop!* And the applause and the shouts continued late into the night."[33]

At Bettola, at the ceremonies in honor of the Beata Vergine della Quercia (the Blessed Virgin of the Oak) in October of 1896, the rain, which had been heavy since morning and had prevented many from the mountain parishes from coming, again threatened to drown out the procession.

"But the more enthusiastic participants prevailed, and the venerated image was carried out of the church right behind the canopy under which the Bishop was walking. The rain stopped then, and by the time the procession had crossed the long square, wound around the town and climbed the hill to the place where the apparition had occurred, the sun was shining more brilliantly than ever, its rays sparkling on the multicolored crowd that stretched from the old convent all the way down to the first houses of the village. It was a moving spectacle, and when His Excellency turned to bless the people, he could not contain the fullness of his emotion; in a voice that seemed double in strength he gave a short and moving homily...As he ended his sentences from time to time with *Viva Maria,* the cry was taken up by thousands of voices...to echo throughout the surrounding valleys...And the cry of *Viva Maria* was followed spontaneously by the shout of *Long Live the Bishop, Long Live Bishop Scalabrini...*It was the sense of brotherhood, of a community of ideas...His Excellency was well aware of this as, after each shout, he took up his discourse again, speaking with ever greater emphasis and affection. Finally, he deplored the fact that there was no longer a church dedicated to the Vergine della Quercia and exhorted them all to emulate the faith of their ancestors and to compete with one another in contributing to the erection of a new one. To spur them on he said: 'I will make the first offering, I will give what I can'...New shouts of *Viva* greeted the end of his short but splendid sermon...while his Excellency standing there on the hill at the foot of the statue opened the list of subscribers to the new church."[34]

A few months later he went back to lay the cornerstone and again aroused the liveliest enthusiasm for the Virgin among the people.[35]

Similar enthusiastic manifestations of Marian devotion inspired by the Bishop's eloquence were not rare. It is enough to recall the jubilee celebrations of the Immaculate Conception[36] and the pilgrimage to the shrine that was dearest to him after those in his own diocese — the shrine of Loreto.

"He promoted various pilgrimages to Loreto. On one of these his preaching was so eloquent and the enthusiasm he inspired was so great that at a certain moment they all burst out with the shout of *Viva Maria!* And everyone was greatly moved."[37] This occurred during the pilgrimage of June 10, 1895, which the Servant of God had prepared with great care and joy: "I am anticipating the joy of those solemn moments when I shall have the opportunity to offer the great Sacrifice there for all the beloved people of my diocese, to give the Eucharistic Bread myself to all those fortunate to be present and to speak to them from my heart."[38]

There were seven hundred pilgrims from Piacenza, a number considered extraordinary at that time. From the mention the Bishop made of it on the Feast of the Assumption, we may understand something of the character he gave to these manifestations:

"Who does not remember with lively pleasure the pilgrimage just made by hundreds of our people to the Holy House in Loreto? Who can speak of the consolation found there, the tears of joy that were shed there, the emotion with which we left those holy walls, the prayers, hymns and *Vivas* that echoed everywhere the enthusiasm with which we took leave of the blessed House and the miraculous image of our Mother? Hail Holy Queen *(Salve Regina)*: this was the last shout we raised to Her, voicing the feelings of all of us: Hail Holy Queen, Mother of Mercy *(salve Regina, mater misericordiae)*."[39]

In May, 1882, he accepted Bishop Bonomelli's invitation to attend the celebration of the nine hundredth anniversary of the apparition of Our Lady at Caravaggio: "I am at your disposal for the celebrations in Caravaggio; under Our Lady's mantle we cannot fail to be well."[40] — "But I should like to ask a favor of you; if you will dispense me from preaching I shall be grateful, for I should like to come with no other thought in mind but to pray to Our Lady and to be given the last seat, the only place I should have. In addition, I do not know the exact story of this shrine, I do not have the time to read up on it or to write, and therefore I would not be able to say any but the most banal things!"[41] Nevertheless he did find the time to prepare a sermon that was rich in quotations and historical references to Marian devotion in Italy.

On the invitation of the Bishop of Cremona he was in Castelleone near Crema, September 12-14, to take part in the crowning of Our Lady of Mercy. On October 10th he consecrated the Marian shrine in Roveleto.

In 1886 he attended the crowning of Our Lady of Grace in Brescia. "I was also among those fortunate to be present and I wept with emotion with you. I recall your devotion, illustrious citizens of Brescia, the ardour of your faith." On the tenth anniversary of this event, in 1896, he was asked to give the sermon on September 6th. It was an impassioned and vigorous discourse, worthy of "devout Brescia, strong and contemptuous of every base thought. Brescia, never second to any other city in works of religion has also been distinguished always for its strong and tender devotion to Mary."[42]

Dr. Giorgio Montini (father of Pope Paul VI) spoke for the whole city in thanking the Bishop of Piacenza when he wrote "your greatly desired presence and your eloquent words added great solemnity to our celebration."[43]

Bishop Scalabrini also took part in the meeting of the Catholic Associations, speaking after Giuseppe Tovino and before Cardinal Ferrari. More than sixty years later we heard the venerable Bishop Ernesto Pasini, Vicar General of the diocese of Brescia, recall Bishop Scalabrini's sermon with admiration and quote several passages from it.

In the same year he attended the centenary celebrations of the "Madonna Greca," venerated in the shrine of Santa Maria in Porto in Ravenna. We had been there the year before with a pilgrimage of many Piacentinians, and his devotion had been remembered with admiration.

"In this place, away from the world, Your Excellency has warm admirers, and your presence among us is a propitious event. I do not exaggerate, for many, many people are asking me whether we shall have a sermon from Bishop Scalabrini at our centenary."[44]

Among the many other celebrations in which he took part, we mention only those of Our Lady of Guastafredda in the city of the "Madonnina" in Bardi, the Madonna del Carmine in Borgotaro, the Madonna del Popolo in Castelsangiovanni, and Maria Bambina in Fino Mornasco.

Marian Devotion

Scalabrini was greatly attached to the daily recitation of the rosary, a habit he had had since childhood. He recalled his childhood memories and impressions in a sermon at the crowning of the Madonna of Saint Savino in 1900.

"How dear is the memory most of us have of the unbreakable habit the piety of our parents fostered with so much love during the tender sweet years of our childhood! Amid the general happiness there sounded an hour at which, at a nod from mother, all work and joyful chatter stopped and the whole family knelt before the antique image of the Blessed Virgin. The Holy Rosary was the affectionate tribute we paid her every day."[45]

He vigorously supported Leo XIII's efforts to promote the devotion of the rosary and became its apostle in his own diocese. He called it the prayer:

"most pleasing to Mary, the one that recalls the titles dearest to her, and her highest merits...When we repeat that prayer all we do is send back to Heaven, as it were, what Heaven has let fall among us...Love, it has been well said, has only one word, and in saying it we never repeat ourselves...The rosary is a summary of the Christian religion, the most engaging picture of what Jesus Christ has done for our souls; it is a memorial reminder of the most stupendous miracles; it is the noble mark of Catholic piety."[46]

Therefore, he recommended that his priests do "everything fine and holy you can think of in relation to your own devotion. What we ardently desire is that you warmly urge your parishioners to try to faithfully say the divine devotion of the rosary either in public or in private, each in his own house and with his own family, without ever neglecting the practice."[47]

Thus, as the Pope issued each of the encyclicals on the rosary, Scalabrini hurried to publish them throughout his diocese, exhorting his people to respond to the wishes of the Holy Father, who attached particular importance to this Marian prayer to remedy the serious religious situation of the time.

"There is one thing only about which I love to remind my dear children in Jesus Christ, the family recitation of the rosary. This dear and pious custom of our elders, never completely forgotten among us, has, thanks to the affectionate urgings of the Supreme Pontiff, taken on new vigor.

"It is necessary now to make the practice as universal as possible, so that no family fails to follow it...The family rosary is a sweet balsam, a symbol of union, a messenger of peace."[48]

The rosary, Scalabrini declared, is the prayer of the Mystical Body, of the whole Christ.

In the rosary, "Jesus Christ himself prays in us and with us, Mary prays with us, the angels pray, the saints pray, all of paradise, I might almost say, prays with us. And all these prayers, all these praises, these canticles, these *vivas* alternate, interweave and are repeated in the rosary in uniform variety and varied uniformity so that their efficacy and value is multiplied a thousand times."[49]

At all three Synods he recommended the daily rosary to his priests[50] and "in order that his prescription about the recitation of the rosary in Church during October would carry more weight, he gave good example by reciting it publicly himself in the Cathedral."[51]

The rest of the year he was faithful to the daily rosary, saying it in public or privately, and to the Angelus, thus keeping the resolution he renewed during his monthly day of recollection.[52] When he took time for a little walk or outing, he always had the rosary in his hand.[53]

The depth and tenderness of his devotion to Mary is attested by many eyewitnesses[54] as well as by the brief sentences in the few but revealing pages that remain as documents of his inner spiritual life:

"Great, true devotion to the dear, most sweet Mother Mary. *Ora pro me peccatore: nunc et in hora mortis meae. Amen.*"[55] "I dedicate myself with greater care to devotion to Our Lady: throw myself at her feet, into her maternal arms every day!"[56] — "Constant and tender devotion to Our Lady: she is my Mother, and she will obtain all things for me if I am truly and sincerely devoted to her!"[57]

Every morning he renewed his consecration to the Blessed Mother in the prayer of St. John Berchmans, which he had copied in his own hand, signing it *Joannes B. Ep. miser peccator.*[58]

The best informed witness, his biographer Monsignor Gregori, summed up his impressions thus: "From his sermons and also from the notes he jotted down after his annual retreats and his monthly days of recollection it is clear that his soul was dominated by the thought of the divine motherhood and of Mary's motherhood for all men."[59]

"We are the children of her cooperation in the redemption."[60] Mary is *sicut lilium inter spinas:* "just as the weight of the blossom binds the lily plant gently toward the earth, so all esteem bestowed on Mary turns her heart toward us."[61]

Two themes recur in Scalabrini's writings and sermons:

"Ah, she loves us as the children of her grief!" — "She is not like people on earth, who, as soon as they rise to a high post in the world, almost look down upon their equals. No, no. The more sublime the post she occupies in Paradise, the more she shows us her compassion."

His last talk in honor of the Madonna was given at Rivergaro on May 7th, 1905, when he led the first pilgrimage to the Blessed Virgin del Castello. It was only twenty-five days before the end of his own earthly pilgrimage, and his sermon made an extraordinary impression.[62] Ever since he had consecrated the shrine three years before, it seemed to replace the shrine at Bedonia as his favorite.

We are told that "one day as he was crossing the Trebbia near Rivergaro, a flash flood (due to torrential rains in the mountains) threatened to swallow the boat. A terrified shudder ran through the crowds pressed together along the banks. The Servant of God fixed his gaze on the Shrine that rose behind them and landed unperturbed. The crowd shouted it was a miracle and accompanied the Servant of God to the Shrine of the Castello to thank Our Lady for his escape from danger."[63]

The pastor of Rivergaro, on the third anniversary of Scalabrini's death, had this to say:

"This church, which he solemnly consecrated three years ago, speaks eloquently of his devotion to the Most Holy Virgin. Eloquent testimony also was the precious gift with which he adorned the Virgin's statue, which he crowned in the public square among the general jubilation of the people. He always spoke of this Shrine with pleasure, so that often in private and in public he expressed the wish to have a humble grave here. And for us May 7, 1905, will always be memorable, the day on which, with His Excellency Archbishop Morganti of Ravenna, he inaugurated the first diocesan pilgrimage. On that occasion he spoke of the Virgin of the Castello with so much fervor and affection that the parishioners were saying to one another: 'We have never heard our bishop speak like this. Just as the flame about to die sends forth its liveliest and brightest rays, so our pious Bishop, nearing the end of his life, displayed an extraordinary love for the Mother of God and our Mother.' It seemed as if from this high hill...he raised his eyes and like the swift dove tested the wind in order to fly straight to Paradise to bless the heavenly Queen he had always invoked with filial tenderness."[64]

In the crown of the Virgin of Castello, he had set the last of his mother's gems and the precious stones from his pectoral cross, which he replaced with colored glass.

There is various testimony as to his desire to be buried in the shrine of Rivergaro, so there can be no doubt about it. Was this in conflict with his other desire, which is also attested,[65] to be buried near the altar of the Blessed Sacrament in the Cathedral? Or was this merely one uncertainty of a heart almost torn by three loves, the Eucharist, the Virgin and the Church, which in the end formed only one great love?[66]

CHAPTER XVI

Devotion to the Church and to the Pope

An Act of Courage

Just as Scalabrini devoted his life wholeheartedly to the Head of the Church present in the Eucharist and to the Mother of the Church in the invisible order, he was as wholeheartedly devoted to the Pope and the Church in the visible order.

The publication of his lectures on the Vatican Council (*Conferenze sul Concilio Vaticano*[1]) was considered an act of courage. In fact the climate was seething with political complications over the emerging Roman Question and the flood of calumnies and prejudices poured out against the Church by the "liberals," the Protestants and even by governments. Many Catholics had been shaken by all this; they were either confused or preferred to keep silent out of not very commendable human respect.

It was the intention of the young Scalabrini to "clarify the thinking on the essential truths of the Catholic faith, which were being distorted and adulterated every day by a petulant and unbridled press, by the perfidy of certain apostates, by the incredible empty-headedness of certain weak Catholics without strong convictions, and especially by the diabolical conspiracy of those wretched 'old-Catholics' who are going about everywhere inciting an angry and violent rebellion against the holy Vatican decrees."[2]

Many of his confreres, he said, could surpass him in style and elegance of phrase, in frank and confident reasoning, in knowledge of doctrine, but no one could outdo him in "the most simple and unlimited submission to the Successor of Peter, the true Vicar of Christ, Father and Doctor of all Christians, infallible Teacher of Truths."[3]

"In the great sadness of these times and amid the fearful caution of the good, I frankly confess to you that I am most happy to be the first to speak to you of those glorious gifts, which, while they form the glory of the Father, are also the glory of the children."[4]

As in his later writings, certain of the principles that shaped his life and activity are reflected in the lectures on the Vatican Council. It is not difficult to discern them for he lived them so intensely they were uppermost in his mind. At the same time, in style and method of reasoning, based on theological arguments rather than on rational and juridical proofs, it is the man of faith and the apostle who is evident.

The Pope is the shepherd, kind, universal father, supreme judge, the one to whom all have the right to turn for help, and indeed do turn for help, he declared. "The Church is the sheepfold of Jesus Christ and the Bishop of Rome is its shepherd. He must of necessity and by the will of God have freedom of communication with his flock, otherwise he could not feed or govern it. The Church is the house of the children of God, and the Bishop of Rome is the common Father of all. Wherever there are Catholics he must be able to exercise his spiritual authority. The Church is the kingdom of Jesus Christ and the Bishop of Rome is its ruler. In order to carry out his divine mandate he must be free to command everyone and direct everything in order to maintain the unity of faith and of the kingdom. The Father...is never a stranger to his children, wherever they may be or whatever the level of their station in life."[5]

Freedom to communicate with all the faithful is "a divine right, for by heavenly dispensation he has the right to all without which he could not carry out his apostolate among the peoples...The See of Peter may be attacked, deprived of its splendor. The noble successor of Peter may be betrayed, stripped, imprisoned, go wandering in search of asylum, return to the catacombs if need be. But the wishes, the prayers, the hearts of all Catholics will follow him everywhere, and wherever he is, in whatever condition, he will be greeted as Father, Teacher, King of the universal Church, Vicar of Jesus Christ. His voice, free and independent of every earthly power will always be lifted to attack injustices, to denounce legal cruelties, to comfort his children during the ill-omened days that are being readied for the Church of God."[6]

Papal Infallibility

According to Scalabrini the greatest accomplishment of the Council was the definition of papal infallibility, which "exalts the Head of Religion, it magnifies and makes him illustrious and *in him it exalts the entire Catholic Church,* but the greatest advantage of this definition is all ours and that of our brothers."[7] He sees in this doctrine a sign of the unity "whereby, with all the reservations of the Gallicans and Ultramontanes abolished forever, the Church could see all her children bearing *one name only,* that of Catholic Christians, and all gathered under a single standard."[8] He viewed infallibility above all in terms of the charisma and service of the Church. It was necessary for Vatican I to define it in order to strike with the swiftness "of the Angels and of God" the errors which were spreading with "the speed of lightning."[9] He insists at length on the timeliness of the definition and the reason is evident. The few French, German and Italian bishops who opposed the declaration of the dogma did so, it seems, not because they doubted the truth of faith but because they intended their abstention as an opinion on the timeliness of the proclamation.[10]

Let us consider precisely what Scalabrini's concept of infallibility was: it is a divine prerogative. Just as God communicates His power to the miracle worker and His knowledge to the prophet, so He transmits His infallibility to the Church. The principal reason is that given by Bossuet:

"The Church is Jesus Christ. But Jesus Christ, could never approve, nor do, nor keep silent about anything that is contrary to the faith."[11]

Hence the infallibility of the Church is not only the consequence of the fact that Christ created it as the depository of His truth, to be handed on in all its purity and integrity. It is postulated not only on the unity of faith. It is rooted much deeper in the very essence of the Church:

"Jesus Christ is the Head of His Church, which is His body, His spouse to whom He is indissolubly bound. He is the head and spouse of this virgin, without stain or blemish, always holy and immaculate. He is her honor, her protection and defense, so that error may never prevail within her and that she may be in every time the *Church of the living God: foundation and column and mainstay of the truth.*"[12]

In addition to the infallibility of the "teaching Church, composed of the Bishops in union with their head, the Roman Pontiff," Scalabrini mentions also the infallibility of the "Church taught." He refers to it according to the Scholastic tradition as passive infallibility, but stresses the fact that "its witness is one of the bases on which rests the definitions of the teaching Church," and he thus gives due weight to the *veneranda traditio* and the *prepetuus Ecclesiae sensus.*[13]

To be noted is the insistence with which Scalabrini sets forth the infallibility of the Church with regard to *dogmatic facts*:

> "(The Church) the infallible witness of the sacred deposit received from Christ and the Apostles, must also be the infallible judge in resolving controversies, the infallible teacher in pointing out the life-giving pastures and keeping her children far from the lethal poison hidden in the writings of the enemies of God and of the truth. To take away the infallibility of the Church in these matters is to destroy a venerable tradition, one of the foundations of the faith, which in reality is nothing other than an aggregate of dogmatic facts."[14]

Among the moral facts woven through revelation, "in which it is also necessary for the Church to be infallible," the future Apostle of the catechism spent some time on the problem of education, which evidently held priority among his concerns even in his youth. The Church — he declared — is infallible "when it praises or reproves certain educational systems with respect to their religious or irreligious content, and according to whether they promote or are opposed to the spiritual well-being of the Mystical Body of Jesus Christ, of the salvation of souls."[15]

Also reflected in this first work of his is another dominant theme in Scalabrini's life, and this is love of country, understood and lived in purely Christian terms. In this he was never deflected by political or sentimental considerations and was governed only by his love for the Pope. He was disturbed to see Italy moving to ruin precisely because she was rebelling against the Supreme Pontiff:

> "Would the time ever come when the threat of Jesus Christ must come true for this country of ours: *the kingdom of God will be taken from you and given to a people who produce its fruits?*... With humility of heart we beseech the Savior not to transfer elsewhere the mystic vine He Himself has planted, His infallible bride, our dearest Mother. Let us swear eternal and filial obedience to her, mindful that it is on the Church and not on us that the power of enlightening human minds has been conferred, that she alone can guide us to salvation, that he who does not have the Catholic Church as his mother on earth cannot have God as his father in heaven."[16]

This passage is to be interpreted in the context of the difficult problem of the relations between Church and State at a time when for an Italian Catholic, the test of obedience to the Pope was also the "matter of conscience" created by the Risorgimento.

Relations Between Church and State

The goal of the Church is "to lead all men to greater moral perfection, and therefore all questions in which Religion and morality are involved necessarily fall within its domain."[17]

In Scalabrini's time this concept inevitably led to the question of how the temporal power of the Church could be part of its ultimate goal. His answer was this:

"The Church, writes a modern apologist, uses a throne, too, for its necessary freedom and independence, but its love does not rest on the thrones of this world nor the miserable rights of such thrones. It wants only those temporal things which are necessary or useful to promote, in freedom and independence, the diffusion of the things of heaven."[18]

As for the relations between Church and State, he had this to say:

"(The Church) is completely independent. The Church welcomes and blesses all forms of government, because all...are in themselves equally legitimate...She does not desire to be the arbiter in all the vicissitudes of the social order," but she has the right to require that the State "not offend against her laws, that it not repress her teaching, that it not think it can do without God." It would be usurping the rights of the State if the Church intervened in political, economic and administrative questions, but it is entirely within its rights when it judges that "alliances made to usurp others or to oppress the weak are unjust; that partisanship, favoritism and corruption in the administration of justice are wicked; that to teach errors and evil doctrines to the young is treason; that excessive taxation on business, industry, labor, property, is a burden and a serious tragedy for the people"; that perjury, rebellion, divorce are crimes..."The Church, it is true, is not all knowledge or all human progress, all civil policy, but she has always a germ, a fertile breath of life for all human things, and he who repudiates her repudiates life." Above all, the Church demands freedom, "which is her natural daughter." — "Freedom for her altars and her feast-days,...not only within the enclosure of the sacred walls, but also out in the sunlight; freedom for the ministry and evangelical preaching; freedom of the holy hierarchy...; freedom to aim for Christian perfection...; freedom to own property...; finally the great fecund liberty of Christian teaching and Christian education."[19]

This was Scalabrini's position with respect to the Italian government's policy toward the Church at that time. The "liberal" State was confident it could overcome Catholic resistance and impose its unity on the Italians with coercive power. Scalabrini warned that "pastors and priests will always do more good with the catechism alone than all your best organized politics and all your most formidable armies!"[20]

He, too, pondered one of the most delicate questions of that period for Italian Catholics: given the anti-Catholic posture of the State, should they take a position of protest, of abstention from politics and the administration? His answer was a logical one: if the Church, even though political, economic and administrative activity is not its province, has the right to judge this in terms of morality and to demand that her rights be respected, then it is not possible to be content with sterile protests; it is necessary to act.

"Today...it is not permissible to remain lazily within our houses, sighing or weeping, when the fire of unbelief is spreading and threatening to destroy...the ark of faith throughout our countryside. Let us, therefore, go out from our tents, and above all let us remember that we have no weapons let us enter public life, without regard to political parties, accordingly as the laws of our Catholic conscience permit, ready to die rather than come to terms with what is false or unjust. Let us enter public life, not as enemies of the constituted authority but as tireless adversaries of evil wherever it is found. Let us enter as men of order, who can, after the example of Christ and His Church, tolerate evil but who can never approve it or commit it...We must participate in public life striving in all licit ways for the triumph of truth and justice."[21]

The examples Scalabrini sets forth are the recommendations Leo XIII gave Catholic Action: against the assemblages of the enemies of the faith, set Catholic associations; fight the bad press with a good press, the corruption of youth with Christian education, hatred with love, cold philanthropy with evangelical charity, the violation of ecclesiastical property by renewing the generosity of our ancestors — in short, not by faith alone but by faith and works.[22]

Given the concrete problems and the polemics of the time, how did Scalabrini view the obedience due the Church in those matters that did not fall directly or indirectly within the province of her infallibility?

"We accept with our minds and our hearts all the doctrinal teachings and all the practical norms set forth by the religious Authority. Thus we do not intend to be or to be considered 'transigent' in our religious or politico-religious faith. Among the teachings of the Roman Pontiff we declare that we recognize and adhere specifically to those which relate to his temporal power. We desire that the Pope be powerful, morally great, sovereign and free, the sole judge of the form, extent and amount of freedom necessary for him in governing the universal Church. *In the present conditions there is no other means to provide for his autonomy except real and effective Sovereignty.* Otherwise, in the exercise of his primatial rights, the Pontiff will have to be subject to other authority as the experience of these last few years has shown."[23]

"Even though dogmatic infallibility covers only revealed truths, nevertheless it is to be expected that the Providence which *penetrates and shines through the universe,* will in a very special way spread its wings over the Papacy, which, therefore, in the universal government of the Church and in indicating to the faithful the way to follow in defending or claiming its rights, is certainly immune from errors which would be tragic for the cause of Catholicism."[24]

One Pope is not to be compared unfavorably with another, Scalabrini continues. Pius IX had the right to choose one direction and Leo XIII has an equal right to choose another. Otherwise we would still be stuck in the Council of Jerusalem discussing circumcision and the eating of strangled animals or blood.[25] The Catholic Church is not immobilistic: it stands "firm, like the tower that does not fall, on its divine element," but it displays a vigorous youthfulness, an ever exuberant vitality in whatever is variable.[26] In accord with this vitality, "we prefer, for our part, a dynamic policy to a static one," in order to avoid the inertia that results in the loss of souls,"[27] and we consider obedience to the authority of the Pope as the "basic criterion for our activity."

"In questions which are matters of opinion and there is freedom for human debate, we choose the most rational solutions and those which best serve the religious and civil advantage of the people. Our motto has been to follow the direction which the Pope, in his enlightened knowledge and with the particular assistance promised him by Christ, deems best suitable for the well-being of the Church. And when we learned that some view we held did not meet with the approval of the ecclesiastical authority, we were able to make the sacrifice of our convictions and our self-love in homage to it and on the strength of our principles."[28]

"But, some one will say, must we listen to the Church even on matters that do not concern it? Yes, without doubt, for anyone who wants to be a true sincere Catholic...Whether her laws are organized for the protection of her independence, or are related to the accomplishments of her multiple functions, whether they derive directly from other precepts of divine law or whether they fall exclusively within the realm of ecclesiastical law...whether they refer to the faith, to customs, or only to questions of discipline, it is Catholic teaching that these laws bind the conscience before God."[29]

The Concept of Church as Society

Scalabrini leans always toward the Christological content of theology, and so places special emphasis on the doctrine of the Mystical Body. He favors the definition of the Church which underlines Christ's intimate union with her:

"The Church is a society, a natural society entirely different from all others because it is an earthly-heavenly society, the true image, therefore, of its Founder, Man and God at the same time. It may be defined as the incarnation of Jesus Christ on earth, the continuation of His mortal life, his perpetual manifestation among men."[30]

Because of this nature, and because it is the Sacrament of Christ, it follows in the footsteps of the Savior: it must suffer, it is the object of wrath and persecution, of calumny and betrayal, just as, on the other hand, it is called to share in the resurrection, and the triumph, the light, the grandeur of the glory of the Lord.[31]

Scalabrini's practical conclusions may be summed up as follows:

(1) All Catholics have the duty to cooperate for the greatest good of the Church, because the "state of the body, whether good or ill, is common to all the members"; (2) the body must be united with its head in order to stay alive: "thus we must remain closely united with the Church if we wish to live the supernatural life of grace, which is diffused through it by its invisible Head, Jesus Christ";[32] (3) as there is a diversity of functions in the body, there is a diversity of functions among the members of the Church: a visible Head, with "supreme and universal power to govern"; the Bishops, "subordinate" to the Roman Pontiff, but supreme rulers of a part of the Church, who might be called "eyes of this body"; the Priests and other ministers represent the arms; the faithful represents its totality and its completion;[33] (4) obedience is necessary: whoever wishes to belong (to the Church) with sincere affection and as salvation requires must remain intimately united with it, subject and obedient to its legitimate Shepherds."[34]

In discussing the Church as a perfect society, Scalabrini leaves aside the juridical aspects to concentrate on the mystical. "The primary and essential condition of a true and perfect society...is firm unity," he says.[35] But unity is achieved only through a hierarchical order. Christ has given the ecclesiastical society "a principle of supreme, central, ruling authority," Peter. "To him he associated other shepherds as brothers, namely, the Apostles, and he invested these also with his authority," conferring on them doctrinal that is, teaching authority, sacramental authority, i.e. that of the ministry, and legislative authority, namely the authority to rule.

"This threefold power of the Apostles was transmitted to the bishops who succeeded them, as divinely instituted, in the government of their individual churches. They are Shepherds joined and subordinate to the Supreme Pontiff...yet true Shepherds nonetheless, each ruling his own particular church and all together assisting the Pope in governing the universal Church. In this way, for the things of the soul, the faithful are united with their pastor, the pastors to their Bishop, the Bishop to the Pope. Thus a chain is forged that reaches from the Pope through the hierarchical order down to the lowliest of the faithful."[36]

This is not a strictly juridical hierarchy, however, but rather a fact of life that is the essence of Christianity:

"Thus all who believe form one vast family, one compact united body, wonderfully articulated through the connecting links and levels of the hierarchy, the invisible head of which is the same Divine Author, Jesus Christ. And from Jesus Christ, as from the head through the members of the human body, the moral person of the Church derives its strength, its beauty, its movement, its life, the life of grace on earth, the life of glory in heaven: *Crescamus in illo per omnia qui est caput, Christus.*"[37]

Hierarchical unity is defined as the "body" of the Church; the union in grace as its "soul." Just as the union of body and soul is necessary for human life, so the union of life and grace with Christ is not possible without hierarchical unity. In fact, Christ himself in the hypostatic union, is the image of the Church. The Church is the "extension of the Incarnation down through the centuries." Just as divine nature and human nature, though distinct, are inseparably joined in the Word Incarnate, so the Church is at one and the same time a visible society and a spiritual society. Jesus saves, but "through the bodily and perceptible forms of the Incarnation." He continues to save in the Church through worship, the magisterium, the sacraments. It may therefore be said that there is a spiritual part in the Church that is called *soul*:

"It is what vivifies, informs and governs all the mystical members and places them in communication with the Divine Head and with one another, and works that blessed exchange of merits and spiritual riches that is called the Communion of Saints...It includes all that is internal and spiritual in the Church: faith, love, hope, the gifts of grace, charisms, the fruits of the Holy Spirit and all the heavenly treasures that come to it through the merits of Christ the Redeemer and His servants."

The rest is the *body* of the Church, namely, "all that is visible and external, whether in the assemblage of its members, the ritual of worship and the ministry of teaching, or in its external organization and regime." The unity of the two parts is achieved by Christ through love.[38]

The union of the faithful with the Church is achieved through sanctifying grace, which unites us with the *soul*, and through union with the hierarchical priesthood, to which Christ has entrusted the task of preserving the unity of faith, of communion, and of rule (unity with the body).[39]

Whether the Church is viewed as the Mystical Body or as a society, Scalabrini concludes that its vital unity is achieved through the hierarchy; without this there is no union with Christ in grace.

"To be a Christian and to be saved, it is not enough to be baptized, it is not enough to profess faith in Jesus Christ, it is not even enough to partake of the Sacraments, but it is necessary, absolutely necessary to obey the legitimate Shepherds; that is, to obey the Pope, to obey the Bishop, to obey those who are placed in charge of our souls by the Pope or the Bishop. Whoever, therefore, does not obey the Pope, the Bishop, the Catholic Priest, can be anything whatever but not a Christian, not a Catholic certainly. He is proud, a hypocrite and nothing else; he is outside the Church."[40]

This is the only path to salvation:

"Certainly Jesus Christ, through his divine power, could have saved men without using other men, but in his infinite wisdom he did not choose to do so. And so, in the order of grace, as in the order of nature, he created intermediate and secondary causes. Between men and

Himself he placed His Priests, in whom He deigned to continue Himself, and in His prayer to the Father He recognizes as His disciples only those who have believed through them. The Gospel in fact always mentions three: God, the Priest and man. Whoever excludes the Priest removes the link and breaks the chain; he destroys the bridge and creates an abyss."[41]

At a time of heated doctrinal polemics and political change, Scalabrini's writings evidence not only the purity of his doctrine but also his dedication and consecration of self in love for the Vicar of Christ and for our common Mother.

The wish he expressed to the faithful was in fact his own action program:

"May it one day be said of each of us what the divine Poet said of himself — *Pius in Christum, pius in Ecclesiam, pius in Pastorem* — he loved Jesus Christ, he loved the Church, he loved the Pope. May these be, beloved, our greatest loves, our strength, our consolation and the glory of our whole life."[42]

Considering the time in which it was published, it is not surprising that this first work of his produced such a favorable impression in the Vatican as to influence his promotion to bishop at such a young age. In all probability, on the basis of this book he was pointed out to the Holy See by Bishop Lucido Parocchi of Pavia and St. John Bosco as a candidate of certain "Roman orientation" — as the saying was at the time.

"At that time Bishop Scalabrini also approached Don Bosco. He said he came to the Venerable to ask him to read his book on the infallibility of the Supreme Pontiff. Don Bosco, having read it, approved it and advised him to have it published. He remembered this when the occasion arose to nominate new Bishops and he proposed him for the See of Piacenza."[43]

His tenure as bishop began under similar auspices. Pius IX had noted with pleasure the "noteworthy devotion to the Supreme Pontiff and the Apostolic See" so eloquently manifested by the author of the *Conferenze sul Concilio Vaticano*:

"Amid this most serious conspiracy of impious persons seeking to snatch the soul of the faithful from the obedience and reverence due the Apostolic See in order to drag them more easily into the dark snares of error, it was very pleasing to our Blessed Father that you employed your devoted efforts to spreading the light of Catholic truths and devotion and obedience to the supreme See, without which Catholic unity cannot be preserved."[44]

Very much the same thing was said in the Brief in which Pius IX named Bishop Scalabrini a Domestic Prelate and Assistant at the Pontifical Throne and a Papal Count just two days after his consecration:

"It is the custom and habitude of Roman Pontiffs to honor with special benefits and graces those who greatly distinguish themselves for their fidelity and obedience to this Apostolic See...Therefore that intense attachment that you, Venerable Brother, display toward this See, which We have noted and appreciated..., together with your other clear and exceptional virtues, constrains Us, so to speak, not only to number you among our Domestic Prelates, as if you were always present in our Mother City, but also to confer on you, with pleasure, the rank of Episcopal Assistant to the Pontifical Throne."[45]

Bishop Scalabrini and Pius IX

Scalabrini never forgot his first audience with Pius IX.

"The Pope? As often as I see him I seem to be seeing him for the first time, that real first time when I was received by Pius IX just after being named a Bishop. One always feels so little in his presence!"[46]

The Pastoral he addressed to the diocese on the day of his consecration set union with the Holy See and obedience to and love for the Pope as basic elements in his program as Bishop.[47]

At his first Synod in 1879 he mentioned among his reasons for calling it the desire and exhortation of the Holy See, which he respected as commands,[48] and the unhappy situation of the Church at that time, when she was "oppressed by difficulties and persecutions on every side and her Supreme Pastor was unworthily held in outrageous imprisonment."[49] The first synodal Constitution firmly underlined the Vatican Council teaching on the primacy and infallibility of the Pope and inculcated reverence and obedience to the words of the Roman Pontiff as if to the words of Christ Himself, of whom the Father said: 'Listen to Him.'[50] So that his priests would always keep them in mind, Bishop Scalabrini had the decree on the profession of faith, the Syllabus, and the Vatican's dogmatic constitutions on the Catholic faith and the Church of Christ included in the documents of the Synod.[51] An appropriate Constitution was dedicated to the Holy Father:

"Speaking now of our most Holy Father, the Supreme Pontiff, it is with a joyful mind and with all my heart that I take this precious occasion to express the sentiments of veneration, homage, devotion, obedience and filial love which all individuals but especially the ministers of the Church must feel and manifest, even publicly, whenever the occasion arises to defend, with all due prudence, the authority of the Pope against the insults of the ungodly, and to inspire these same sentiments in others, so that they may not seem like dumb dogs when the honor of the Holy Father of the Christians is at stake."[52]

After quoting numerous passages from the Fathers, the Constitution prescribed veneration to the Pope, for whom more than for any other father the Fourth Commandment is binding; voluntary, complete and generous obedience, which is a matter of life and death for the ecclesiastical society not only in the case of *ex cathedra* definitions but also in those matters in which non-observance or a difference of opinion involve no heresy or excommunication. It enjoins love for him who is the true Father of all Christians, for without true, courageous and active filial love it is not possible to speak of the honor or the obedience which God requires for His Vicar. One Sunday a year is to be devoted to instructing the faithful on this subject. They are to form the habit of praying and fasting for the Pope and helping to alleviate his poverty with Peter's Pence.[53]

As was the custom at every meeting over which Scalabrini presided, the Synod had begun with sending a telegram to the Pope, in which the Bishop and priests expressed their gratitude to him "in unity and concord" for the admirable encyclical *Aeterni Patris* and solemnly pledged their devotion, loyalty and undying filial affection. The telegram ended with a letter, signed by all the participants in the Synod, in which they renewed their promises of loyalty and obedience to the Supreme Pontiff and to the Bishop.[54] Leo XIII's reply congratulated Scalabrini for having resumed the practice of holding a Synod — after a lapse of 156 years — and for having revived the close union between priests and their Pastor.[55]

The second Synod, held in 1893, recalled the deliberations of the first one and added a regulation which is somewhat unique though without any particular doctrinal or disciplinary importance. It does seem to have been prompted by sound pedagogical sense and sensitive filial love:

"Since today especially it is a sign of no little esteem and love to have in the house photographs of the persons dearest to us through ties of blood or because of kindnesses received, no house should lack a photograph of the reigning Pope, as a profession of faith in the Vicar of Christ and the infallible Teacher of the Church."[56]

Parents are invited to cooperate in inculcating this *sensus Ecclesia* by "inspiring in the young minds of their children, sentiments of devotion" to the Pope.

"They should abstain from anything he does not approve of or judges inappropriate *(non expedire)*; they should love him with a filial devotion, defend him from the slanders of the impious, and assist him, insofar as they are able, with the subsidies established by the first Synod."[57]

All the parishes were to commemorate the annual anniversary of the election and coronation of the Pope. Pastors were to announce these on the preceding Sunday and exhort the faithful to join in prayer with all the world, to attend Mass and possibly to receive Communion, promising God "always to show to His Vicar on earth the obedience of subjects, the docility of disciples, and the affection of sons."[58]

The third Synod (1899) was devoted entirely to the Eucharist, but Scalabrini could not fail to speak of the Pope.

"All of you, associate yourselves, as Jerome says, with the See of Peter, that is, with the Supreme Pontiff. As members of one body we must not only obey the august head of the Church, but it is absolutely necessary that we unite with him in one will, one thought, one feeling as if, without will of our own, we seemed to think, speak and act through him. In a matter as important as this, we must abhor all sophisms, cavils, temporizing, and arbitrary interpretations, for they are unbecoming in a priest and are a foretaste of defection."[59]

He lost no occasion, then, to teach, orally, in his writings and especially through his example love and obedience to the Vicar of Christ. It is enough to cite as examples his lectures at the centenary celebration of Blessed Gregory in February, 1876, and his sermons on Epiphany and Pentecost in 1877; two pastoral letters in the same year — La Chiesa e la societa presente, and In occasione del giubileo episcopale di Pio IX — five pastorals in 1878 — Per il secondo anniversario della sua elezione, Per la morte di Pio IX, Gesu Cristo capo invisibile della Chiesa, Per l'annuncio della elezione del nuovo Pontefice, Communicazione della prima Enciclica di Leone XIII.

He continued the custom introduced by his predecessor, of sending a message of homage from all the priests together with Peter's Pence to the Pope at the end of each Retreat, which he preferred to make with his clergy. Pius IX, in a brief dated September 25, 1876, expressed his thanks and his appreciation for the obedience and devotion of the Bishop and clergy of Piacenza to the Holy See.

"We congratulate you, therefore, and especially because...you have openly declared your opposition to all errors and in particular to that sect full of deceit and falsehood which calls itself liberal-catholic."[60]

On March 1, 1877, Scalabrini announced that Pius IX's jubilee, June 3, was to be celebrated in all the churches and he especially urged the reception of Communion for the Pope. He directed public prayers in the month of May and the taking up of the Peter's Pence collection, and arranged that a special delegation was to take to Rome the expressions of homage and congratulation from the diocese. Since this was a solemn pilgrimage he led it personally and was received, together with the delegation by the Pope on June 7. Pius IX gave him a pectoral cross as a sign of affection and added: "The Bishop's cross is precious, but even more it is heavy."[61]

This was not the only gift or token of affection Pius IX bestowed on the young bishop of Piacenza, and it is not surprising that Scalabrini responded with love and devotion. It is true he loved the Pope as Pope, "proof being that he demonstrated the same affection for Leo XIII and Pius X"[62] and that he taught this same transfer of affection to the faithful, on the basis of the universal love and obedience due the Vicar of Christ apart from any personal reasons.[63] But there were personal reasons as well for his affection for the Pope he had venerated from childhood, who had made him a bishop and had given him evidence of his own affection for him.[64] His grief at his death was understandably intense:

"It is with a heart filled with anguish and grief that we announce to you, Beloved, the greatest misfortune that could befall the Church and the world: Pius IX is dead! Alas, what a good Father we all have lost! He is dead! We have been used to say his sweet name, to admire his heroic virtues, to take inspiration from his noble example, to take fire from his holy words, and now we shall see him no more here below."[65]

He directed that the entire diocese pray and celebrate memorial Masses for his soul. There was a solemn high mass in the cathedral with an impressive number of clergy, people and civil authorities in attendance. On May 13th, he appointed a committee to decide on a monument to the Pope's memory in the cathedral, and the most famous sculptor of the time, G. B. Dupre, was chosen to execute it. He completed it in two years and on May 29, 1880, at the opening of the celebration for the identification of the relics of Sts. Antoninus and Victor, Scalabrini, accompanied by four other bishops, unveiled the statue.

He "exalted the virtues of the great Pius and noted the love of Piacenza for this Pope and for the Roman Papacy, and the predilection both showed for Piacenza...The modesty, in fact the humility, of our Pastor, did not permit him to say more. But all hearts were united in thinking at that moment that among the wonderful favors Pius IX had bestowed on Piacenza, within the orbit of whose diocese the noble Mastai had had him home in early times,[66] there must be numbered the gift of so pious, charitable, learned and virtuous a Father and Pastor as Bishop Scalabrini."[67]

The following year he voiced a sorowful protest against the insult to Pius IX's memory when a group of fanatic anti-clericals tried to throw his body into the Tiber:

"We are speaking...of that terrible crime which stained our country on the ill-omened night of last July 13. Is there any well-bred person who was not filled with horror and shame? A cry of indignation immediately arose from every corner of the world from millions and millions of hearts, and we too felt it our duty to place our humble protests at the feet of our common Father, both as a Bishop and as an Italian, thus interpreting your sentiments, Venerable Brothers and Devoted Sons, for you gave so many proofs of your devotion and affection to the immortal Pius IX and his most worthy successor. We exhort you, Beloved, not to rest in this regard but rather in fact to summon up in yourselves the spirit of action, sacrifice, zeal and courage which is so necessary in these days for the defense of the sacrosanct rights of the Church and of her August Head."[68]

Bishop Scalabrini and Leo XIII

On February 20, 1878, the bells of Piacenza announced that the difficult but glorious burden of Pius IX had fallen on the shoulders of Leo XIII. Bishop Scalabrini issued a pastoral letter on the same day and three months later went to Rome to present his homage and that of the faithful of the diocese to the new Pope. The Holy Father asked him to carry a special blessing to the writers of the modest but pioneer publication *Il Catechista Cattolico*:

"We know that the most benign Holy Father received him with particular kindness, that he kept him in cordial conversation for more than an hour, and that he expressed to him his complete satisfaction with this humble publication, which he praised and blessed in a completely special way. He then dismissed with an affectionate embrace our noble Prelate, who was visibly moved and in wonder at so much kindness and consideration."[69]

Leo XIII followed with interest, approval, blessings and praise, the various apostolic activities and charitable enterprises of Bishop Scalabrini. In 1879, as soon as he learned that the latter had established the Institute for Deafmutes, he sent him his blessing through Cardinal Nina, the Secretary of State, and contributed the maintenance for one of the children.[70]

In 1880, in reply to a communication from Cardinal Moretti and fifteen other bishops who had taken part in the celebration for the solemn identification of the relics of Sts. Antoninus and Victor and who wished to express their gratitude for the encyclical *Aeterni Patris*, Leo commended all the signatories to the letter but especially the Bishop of Piacenza for the love, devotion and sincere will of obedience to the Holy See which he manifested.[71]

On March 3 Scalabrini communicated to the diocese the encyclical *Arcanum* on Christian marriage.[72]

On April 18, 1881, he inaugurated the Diocesan Committee for the *Opera dei Congressi* and thus was one of the first to respond to the Holy Father's wishes. He prepared for his first *ad limina* visit knowing "from experience that after seeing and hearing the Pope, one takes courage for great initiatives and the holy battles of duty, and one returns from his presence rejuvenated in spirit and with joy in one's heart...We shall set before him our doubts and our troubles. We shall beseech his advice."[73] In Rome "he received the most flattering welcomes from eminent personalities and from the Holy Father, to whom he presented 8000 lire as the Peter Pence offering from the diocese. He had two long audiences, the second of which was requested by the Pope, who talked with him at length and showed him great affection."[74]

In September of 1881 he presented to the Holy Father the members of a pilgrimage from Piacenza who, this time also, offered a gift of eight thousand lire and a list of eighty thousand signatures to a protest against the conditions the Italian Government had imposed on the Holy See together with a pledge of filial adherence to the teaching and authority of the Vicar of Christ.[75]

By the end of the year Scalabrini's correspondence with Leo XIII had greatly increased because of the polemics with the *Osservatore Cattolico*, and it was characterized by great forthrightness.

"I beg you, Excellency, to make known my views to our Holy Father, since I do not wish to conceal from him, as sons should not do, the slightest inclination of my mind. Thus, if I am mistaken in anything, he can correct me, and I always accept his corrections with the same joy and the same gratitude with which I would accept his approval, for He is my Pastor, my Father, and I am his most affectionate son."[76]

Despite the difficulties, he continued to educate the clergy and the faithful in obedience and affection to the Holy See. None of the encyclicals, discourses and important addresses of the highly productive magisterium of Leo XIII escaped the attention of the Bishop, who communicated them to the diocese in pastoral letters and other messages explaining the significance of the papal documents and applying their teachings to the practical needs and activities of the diocese.

It seems unnecessary to list here the commemorations, pilgrimages, Peter's Pence collections, and other manifestations which had certainly an importance at the time and in which the diocese of Piacenza was second to none. Rather it is Scalabrini's teaching that is of interest here.

In his message on the encyclical *Diuturum*, which clarified Catholic teaching on political authority, Scalabrini deplored the offense committed against the corpse of Pius IX and then took occasion to preach open and courageous devotion to his successor. He refuted the claim that the common sentiment among Italians was one of hostility to the Pope, and stressed the significance of the pilgrimage to Rome, which was tantamount to a profession of faith and loyalty.[77] With the encyclical *Etsi nos* he finds occasion to restate that Italy's truest greatness is linked with the civilizing and enlightening work of the papacy, and that the country can be saved only by a bold and active faith that is to be jealously protected from atheistic propaganda. Practical measures were membership in Catholic associations, promotion of a "good" press, whose mission it is to teach the truth and also charity,[78] and support of the seminaries. And then comes a most timely directive: "At this moment in which We speak to you, there is presented to us the first number of a paper published here in Piacenza with the title *Il Penitente* (The Penitent)," to support the atheistic propaganda of those Piacentinian "progressives" who are afraid to seem backward in comparison with the "democratic" organizations in other cities. As a result of the Bishop's prompt condemnation the Penitente was stillborn.[79]

The encyclical *Supremi Apostolatus* marked the beginning of an initiative which seconded a desire of the Holy Father, namely, the daily recitation of the rosary in all families.[80] In distributing the encyclical *Humanum genus* directed against Masonry, Scalabrini not only deplored the sect's activities, and it was truly powerful at the time and dominant in political affairs, but he urged that the Pope's suggestions be carried out: religious organizations, charitable institutions, Christian organizations of workers and business men, and especially the Società Operaia Catholica — or Catholic Labor Society — the establishment of which he recommended "at least in all the major parishes of the Diocese," and finally religious instruction of the young. "Catechism, therefore, We shall not cease to shout, Catechism."[81]

In 1885 he distributed Leo XIII's discourse to the pilgrimage of French workers, as being "most important, beyond measure." This afforded him the opportunity to again promote the growth and diffusion of Catholic organizations, especially among the workers, in order to forestall the increasingly threatening Marxist thrust toward organizing them. He again stressed the importance of parish committees of the *Opera dei Congressi*, as he had already done in two above mentioned pastorals and his Lenten pastoral of the previous month.[82]

The encyclical *Immortale Dei* Scalabrini greeted with such enthusiasm that he wrote a long letter of thanks to the Pope and hastened to communicate it to the diocese, directing the pastors to explain it in a series of sermons and to give special instruction on it so that all might be informed on the Church's teaching on the constitution of States. They were to emphasize particularly the necessity of relying on the judgment of the Church in matters concerning acceptance of "modern liberties," the need for courage, for Catholic participation in administrative and educational fields, for unity among Catholics, with no compromising with error, without equivocations, and without making liberalist distinctions between public and private life, but with respect, however, for the opinions of others and the need finally to work to "end internal discord and party struggles."[83]

For Scalabrini, in *Immortale Dei* Leo XIII "opened to the world the treasures of the Church's wisdom," and in *Quod auctoritate*, which announced a special jubilee, he offered the riches of grace — a precious opportunity to throw off indifference, which generates hatred of religion, and to better society through the individual. Again he urges courage against the enemies of the faith, who are also adversaries of civilization, and stresses unity among believers.[84] In the same year, in response to the appeal of the committee headed by Count Acquadernis,[85] he began to prepare for Leo XIII's jubilee, which was to be celebrated in December, 1887. It was to be a world demonstration of faith and love for the Pope. In announcing it, Scalabrini took occasion to refute again the refrain of the Liberals and the Masons, who were exploiting the political situation to accuse the Pope of being an enemy of Italy:

"In his great heart as Priest and Italian (Leo XIII) will never do anything to cause sorrow to his country...History will rightly recognize for his pontificate the glorious title of peacemaking. He has already given all the nations of Europe certain proof of his singularly mild and conciliatory character...And would some have us believe that it is only to the Italian nation that he is indifferent, and worse still, hostile? Who ever dares so say, We repeat, is lying...As soon as his pardon and his help is requested, Leo XIII, like the first Leo, will join his Italy in stemming the rushing tide of demagogic anarchy, and without causing a single drop of blood to be shed he will save Italy's honor as a nation and as the inviolable seat of the Papacy."[86]

There was intense activity in the Piacentinian diocese in preparation for the jubilee. The Bishop directed that beginning with January, 1887, there was to be a special monthly Mass in all the parishes, and he arranged for a solemn high Mass for the Pope to be celebrated the last Thursday of every month in the basilica of St. Antoninus, which was attended by all the ecclesiastical organizations and the Catholic societies. When it was not possible to invite another bishop, he celebrated it himself and gave the sermon.

A committee was formed to promote prayers for the Pope, organize commemorations, collect gifts and Peter's Pence, which were then presented to the Holy Father by the pilgrims led by the Bishop in December. On the first of January in 1888 the sacrifice of the Mass was offered in all the parishes at the same hour at which Leo XIII was celebrating his jubilee Mass. Bishop Scalabrini decided that the new chapel of the diocesan Seminary in the city should memoralize the jubilee celebrations. He dedicated it to the Piacentinian deacon, St. Opilio, and had the figures of three popes represented in the stained glass windows: St. Sylvester, who sent the first bishop, St. Victor, to the city, Pius IX and Leo XIII.

In 1888 the Bishops of Emilia asked him to write the Protest against the Zanardelli law, the episode in the sectarian fight against the Church, which had grown more bitter after the hopes of conciliation in the previous year.[87] With Bishop Bonomelli he also tried privately to influence some of the more important members of Parliament, but to no avail.

In the same year he distributed to the diocese the encyclical *Libertas*[88] and the papal decree *Post obitum*.[89] His Lenten Pastoral in 1889 dealt with Christian education and also communicated the encyclical *Exeunte jam anno* on Christian life.[90] A few months later he directed that the encyclical *Quamquam pluries*, on devotion to St. Joseph, and the papal allocution protesting the monument to Giordano Bruno be read and explained to the people. He had already joined with his colleagues of Bobbio, Parma and Borgo San Donnino in addressing a petition in this regard to the Holy Father, who was very pleased with it.[91] He exhorted the faithful to demonstrate in every way "as Catholics and Italians, how the sectarians in a thousand ways made it clear that they were impious and enemies of Italy's true welfare." He urged pastors, "while scrupulously observing the laws of charity and carefully avoiding offending the legally constituted authorities, nevertheless to raise their voices against all violations of the law of God and of His Church." And finally he had a Mass of reparation said in all the churches.[92]

In 1890 he communicated the encyclical *Sapientiae christianae* on the duties of Christian citizens and the relations between Church and State. Then came the encyclical *Dall'alto* addressed "to Italians on the war being carried on against the Church," which Scalabrini called the "cry from the Pope who loves his children with a unique love and desires to protect their faith; the cry of an Italian who loves his country with a true love and loves not only its salvation but also its greatness and its glory."[93] In addition, he based one of his most important pastorals, *Unione, azione e preghiera*, which we have quoted several times, on the Holy Father's discourse to the Italian pilgrims on May 11. Similarly his pastoral of December 25, 1890, on the freeing of slaves in Africa[94] was based on the encyclical *Catholicae Ecclesiae*.

Among the various expressions of esteem the Holy Father gave Bishop Scalabrini, who was one of the few who boldly and sincerely told him *verbe veritatis*, we find a particularly affectionate audience which took place in 1891:

"The Pope received me immediately and with extraordinary cordiality. I found him well and in a happy, even witty mood. Imagine — at a certain point, noticing my snuffbox he said with a smile, 'Give me a pinch of your snuff, Bishop, Then I shall see if you have a good nose for this also.' We spoke of America, and our conversation turned almost entirely on this subject and especially on the need to protect the people of various nationalities in those countries. The Pope was convinced and asked me to draw up a memorandum on the subject, which I have already very gladly begun to do."[95]

In 1893 the long-lived Pontiff was to celebrate the fiftieth anniversary of his consecration as a bishop and his fortieth anniversary as a cardinal, and another jubilee therefore was in preparation. Beginning in October, 1891, Scalabrini issued directions for papal commemorations in the diocese and recommended a concrete way to respond to the Holy Father's wishes, namely, joining in the Holy Hours of Reparation of the Catholic nations, which had been instituted in the Church of St. Joachim, built in Rome in memory of the preceding jubilee.[96]

In 1892 Bishop Scalabrini established the *Opera di Sant'Opilio* for financial aid to poor seminarians and as "a perpetual memorial of Leo XIII's jubilee anniversary as a bishop."[97] In 1893 he dedicated to the Pope his Lenten Pastoral, a synthesis of the teaching he had been giving for years on the subject, on all possible occasions and circumstances.[98] The jubilee year was a period of intense prayer for the Pope and celebrations in his honor, which culminated in the pilgrimage from Piacenza to Rome and the special commemorative function held in the cathedral on February 15.

Scalabrini transformed into a tribute to the Church and the papacy the commemoration of the 800th anniversary of the First Crusade, announced by Pope Urban II in 1095 to the Council of Piacenza. His sermon, on April 21, 1895, went from a historical synthesis, at which he was a master, to a comparison between the peacemaking efforts of Urban II and that of Leo XIII for the union of the churches. The Pope thanked him in a brief, which cited the conclusion of the Bishop's discourse:

"Having prayed for peace for all the nations, We have firmly worked and We still employ all our efforts — and you, Venerable Brother, noted this in your discourse — so that all people may arrive at that harmony which is the only source of prosperity and consists in this, that all enter the same fold and that all be governed by one Shepherd."[99]

Leo XIII sent him another brief on September 19, in which he expressed his particular pleasure at the homage given him in filial love at a time of "deep and extraordinary sorrow."[100] In his communication on the encyclical on the rosary, *Adiutricem populi*, Scalabrini had added:

"We are about to see the 25th anniversary of the occupation of Rome, and there is the intention to celebrate this event, which produced so many troubles for Italy and is the cause of so much grief in the Catholic world, with sensational festivities, despite the fact that men of proven political good sense consider this inopportune. As Catholics and Italians we consider them ill-advised and harmful, as all things are ill-advised and harmful which sow discord, foment partisan conflicts and exacerbate the destructive dissension between the Church and the State."[101]

In 1900 the Bishops' Conference of Emilia asked Scalabrini to draft their joint pastoral *I diritti cristiani e i diritti dell'uomo* (Christian rights and human rights), on Christian education, the sanctity and indissolubility of marriage, the liberalist legislation that was heading toward atheism and communism, and on the corruptive influence of the press. The 1900 joint pastoral on Peter's Pence was also given Bishop Scalabrini to write.[102]

With the turn of the century came the 25th anniversary of his consecration as bishop, and he desired to open the year with a special blessing from the Holy Father — "one of those blessings that renew one's life, comfort the soul and render it superior to itself." Examining his conscience on his fulfillment of his duties over the 25 years, he wrote to the Pope:

"If I look at what I have accomplished amid incredible difficulties, I have great reason to be happy. But if I probe within my secret soul I find only regret for all the good I did not do or for what I have not done well. Of one thing only I can assure you, most Holy Father, and that is that I have never had any aim but the glory of God and the salvation of the souls entrusted to me. Now I intend to consecrate the little life that God may still grant me entirely to the good of the Church, the defense of your sacrosanct rights, and to drawing ever closer to Your August Person my beloved flock."[103]

Leo XIII sent the blessing on the anniversary day in a Brief, in which, noting the by no means small evidences of his good will toward the Pontiff, he expressed congratulations on the fruits of twenty-five years as a bishop, produced amid griefs and difficulties, and reaffirmed his "very great affection."[104]

In communicating the encyclical *Fin dal principio* in 1902 on the education of the clergy, Scalabrini invited his priests to organize a pilgrimage to Rome in April, 1903, when Leo XIII would have "fulfilled the years of Peter." He also presented to the Pope an album containing the signatures of all the members of the diocese.[105] The Pope's jubilee was marked by general participation of the faithful in prayer and reception of the sacraments, "thus imitating the first followers of the cross, by whom *oratio fiebat sine intermissione ad Deum pro eo.*"[106]

A few months later the Bishop had to ask the faithful to pray and offer their communion for the repose of the soul of the great Leo XIII and to invoke the Holy Spirit in the election of his successor.[107]

Bishop Scalabrini and Saint Pius X

A few hours after the election of Pius X, Bishop Scalabrini sent the circular of announcement to the diocese. In it he repeated that, more than personal qualifications, what one was to see in the pope was the mission and the authority of the Vicar of Christ. But the letter also reflected his own personal joy, for his friendship with Pius dated from the time when the latter was Bishop of Mantua. In fact, Pius said he had known Scalabrini when the latter was a pastor in Como.[108] Scalabrini's friendship foresaw Pius' election as pope:

"Yes, I saw Cardinal Sarto as pope and I told him so many times. And he would reply: 'Then I will do this and that.' And I would say, 'You are joking, but I am serious; we shall see.' My wish for him was a bad one, for who knows what sorrows await him now that he is Pius X. But Heaven has its secrets, and may God, who guides the Church with mysterious but ever loving providence, inspire and help him."[109]

Scalabrini expected much from Pius X in the religious field but not so much in the political.[110] He was happy to have to change his mind:

"Pius X, may God assist him! It is certain he is changing the old system. He answered me with a letter in his own handwriting on the occasion of an address I directed to my clergy gathered together for the spiritual exercises. Does he intend to break the sovereign traditions defended in the past with so much rigor? Enough; the beginnings are good; the rest will be what God wills."[111]

After his first *ad limina* visit, his hopes increased:

"The other evening I left the audience with the Holy Father, which had lasted an hour and a half, completely satisfied. He is still Cardinal Sarto, with the same friendliness, the same simplicity. It does your heart good to be near him. Among many other things, I touched upon the present state of affairs and spoke with utter frankness. From his replies I am convinced again that Pius X is and intends to be above all a spiritual Pope, that he will be concerned with politics only insofar as it is necessary to safeguard the rights of the Holy See, and that he will not cause any embarrassment to the Government. Oh, if only there were men of talent and character in the government! I believe much could be done. As for the elections, there is no change for the present, but I believe a change will come."[112]

When he communicated Pius X's first encyclical, Scalabrini repeated the main principles of his relations with the popes:

"Let us take care especially not to reduce the greatness of the Catholic cause to the paltry dimensions of our private judgments. In all matters that may be the object of discussion among us, let us think as the Pope thinks, let us judge as he judges, each of us working for the common good with those means and in that degree which He is His wisdom prescribes, working always with that uprightness of intention, with that perfect union of mind and heart which alone can invoke the blessings of God on our labors and render them fruitful for the most holy purpose indicated to us by the supreme Hierarch. Let us not be frightened by persecutions and difficulties, mindful always of the divine promises which ensure victory for our faith."[113]

With affectionate interest, the Holy Father blessed and followed Scalabrini's journey in Brazil. In fact, there developed a kind of spiritual communication between them, to which the Bishop attributed the special divine help he received during the long months of unstinting labor:

"The blessing of our most beloved Holy Father, the memory of his sublime simplicity, his magnificent goodness, his face, and smile and words, are sweetly moving and sustain me...The waves come rolling and roaring and tossing black foam. I say Mass not without difficulty. Many communions. I feel the effect of the special blessing of the Holy Father and of the prayers of my good people of Piacenza and my friends...When I say that Peter is living in his successor Pius X and that every day he sends me and those traveling with me a special blessing, it is a moment of unutterable emotion. I receive this every day on my knees in my cabin, and it fills me with a sense of security, a calmness and serenity which I did not feel during my other journey."[114]

Bishop Scalabrini also attributed to the Pope's blessing the perfect health he enjoyed throughout the time he spent in America despite the hardships and illnesses that threatened him. The newspaper, El mensajero, of Buenos Aires recounted that the Bishop had a headache on only one day and he wrote to Pius X and asked him if on that day he had forgotten to send him his blessing.[115]

The Holy Father's feelings for Scalabrini are reflected in the following autographed letter which he sent him on his return from Brazil:

"Most Illustrious and Reverend Bishop,

"With my first affectionate greeting as soon as you set foot on the Continent, I should have liked to present my congratulations on the great good that You have accomplished on your apostolic visit to Latin America, especially to our poor Italians. But because of the many preoccupations of recent days your kindness anticipated me. And while I thank you with all my heart for the productive work you carried out there entirely for the glory of God I pray the Lord for abundant rewards for you. I shall gladly see you whenever you can come to Rome without any serious inconvenience to yourself to share with me your precious advice, and your holy suggestions for improving the standard of living of our doubly beloved children."

"Meanwhile I thank you for the offering and send you in exchange my wishes for the Holy Season desiring the greatest consolations for yourself and for your diocese, with the Apostolic Blessing which I impart to you from the fullness of my heart."

"From the Vatican December 22, 1904.

Pius PP.X"

The Pope received him in long and cordial audiences at the end of January to hear his report on his Brazilian journey and his proposals for a central organization of assistance to the emigrants of all nationalities. Scalabrini also assisted Pius in the consecration of Bishop Radini Tedeschi of Bergamo, and these were the last occasions on which these two great souls met. Four months later, the Holy Father spent anxious days over the sudden illness of the Bishop and asked to be kept informed daily of his progress. He sent him a special blessing which was given him during a brief moment of wakefulness on the night before he died. And when Monsignor Bisleti, Maestro di Camera, gave him the sorrowful news, he wept and exclaimed, "We have lost one of our best bishops." He sent condolences to the Bishop's family and had a letter sent to Msgr. Mangot asking him:

"To express to all the relatives and friends of the lamented Bishop Scalabrini his sentiments of profound grief at the loss of the Venerable Prelate, toward whom he had always felt special esteem and affection. Esteem and affection that live even beyond the tomb, and keep before him the memory of this blessed soul in the celebration of the august mysteries."[116]

The Conference of Bishops of the Emilian region, meeting in Bologna, sent the Pope a message in which they expressed the "sorrow beyond measure that the loss of an excellent and most dear Brother has deprived us of the most helpful aid of his authority and prudence which we experienced many times."

Pius X replied:

"If a Brother, no less remarkable for his wisdom than for his goodness, has been snatched from your consultations, this has been for Our soul, as for you, a bitter and most painful loss. May Our Lord receive into His glory this diligent and most zealous prelate to pray in heaven for you and your dioceses."[117]

CHAPTER XVII

Obedience to the Pope and the Church

Declarations and Actions

When public opinion turned against Bishop Scalabrini for obeying the Pope on the occasion of the funeral ceremonies for Victor Emmanuel II, he declared:

"Above all we taught you, in our talks and in our writings, complete submission to the Vicar of Christ, and we Ourselves gave you the example of unlimited and filial obedience to his orders, his words, his teachings and even his wishes...If We did not feel confident and strong enough to fight to the end for the cause of obedience...we would not hesitate a minute to beseech Him who raised us to this most noble See to permit us to leave it and withdraw to a cloister to repent of Our weakness and Our sins."[1]

The following quotations seem among the most significant of the declarations he frequently made to the Holy Father from the beginning to the very end of his episcopate:

"To obey you and love you unto the death, this will be our ambition, the sweetest comfort of our life, and we shall make every effort to win as many souls as possible to obey and love you."[2]

"We call upon heaven and earth to witness that we shall make every effort, with our whole heart and our whole soul, to deem and respect Your words as the words of the Lord, Your judgments as the judgments of God, Your explanations as the judgments of Jesus Christ."[3]

"For Us, Most Blessed Father, it is a reward, a glory, every time We have occasion to support even the least of your desires. Given Our lowliness we can do little, but that little is all for You, who are our loving Father, our infallible Teacher, our living law."[4]

"It will always be our boast to think as He does, always and in all things, to judge as He does, to feel as He does, to work as He does, to suffer with Him, to struggle with Him and for Him;...we would consider ourselves fortunate to be able to give our life's blood for His cause, which is the cause of God."[5]

"Holy Father, speak and it shall be our boast to obey you; guide us and we shall obediently follow you; teach us, and your teachings will be the constant, invariable norm of our conduct, for we well know that You alone have words of eternal life, that he who is not with you is against Jesus, and that our eternal salvation depends upon our union with you."[6]

"With my clergy and my people I press close to your cathedral, for I am sure that through it and with it I thus remain close to Jesus Christ."[7]

"To the Pope, then, the eyes of the mind, the affections of the heart. Only in him and through him and with him can we all be as one and go forward to battle as a well ordered army, certain of victory...Let ours not be a homage of sterile admiration, dearly beloved. Let us love him, Oh, let us love the Pope, let us venerate him, let us seek new ways to show him our devotion; with our own boundless obedience let us make compensation to him for the bitterness which disobedient and ungrateful sons do not hesitate to pour out for him."[8]

The sincerity of his declarations was evidenced by his actions. He displayed similar clarity and sincerity, however, in those matters left to free discussion, true to the maxim: *in necesariis unitas, in dubiis libertas, in omnibus charitas*. He made a clear distinction between obedience always and at any cost, and freedom where differences of opinion were permissible. He seems to have achieved a happy synthesis between the obedience of faith, proper to the Christian, and the autonomy, correctly understood and proper to the human person, in matters not the object, even indirectly, of the infallibility of the Pope and of the Church.

His acceptance of his nomination as bishop was for him a painful test of obedience.[9] Another example, at the very beginning of his episcopate was his behavior when permission was granted for the *Exequatur* of the papal bull carrying his nomination. He scrupulously observed the Holy See's directives, and, unable to take possession of the episcopal residence, which was then in government hands, he lived for a year and a half in an apartment loaned him by the Marchesa Fanny Anguissola Visconti di Modrone. During this time he was supported by the charity of the faithful, who made up for the part of the income legally assigned for the bishop's maintenance, but which also had been taken over by the government.

"I well remember," Monsignor Mondini attested, "that his attitude on being named Bishop was one of fearless fortitude with respect to the Freemasonry that prevented him from obtaining the *Exequatur*. He entered the Diocese and made the best of his lodgings in a private house."[10]

In 1877 the Holy See decided that all the bishops should request the *Exequatur* from the government, and only then did Bishop Scalabrini request and obtain it in the royal decree of April 24, 1877.

We have already noted the spirit of sacrifice and obedience he brought to the controversies over the "philosophical question" which had been stirred up, in the majority of cases, by intemperate journalism.[11]

In 1885, the Pope addressed to Cardinal Guibert, Archbishop of Paris, a Brief deploring the imprudent open letter of Cardinal Pitra in which the latter expressed his views on the Liberal Catholics in very strong terms and declared several of the intransigents were unjust victims of papal measures. He thus implicitly criticized Leo XIII's policies, comparing them unfavorably with the glories of the pontificate of Pius IX.[12] The Pope clearly warned those Catholics "who, not content with the role of subjects in the Church, think they have also a part to play in its government," interfering with the exercise of the magisterium which is proper to the teaching Church:

"That the ordinary faithful should assume authority and claim to be judges and teachers, that subordinates in the government of the universal Church should prefer or seek to have prevail a direction different from that of the supreme Authority, is a reversal of order; it causes confusion in many minds and falls into error." The same is true of "those who, while claiming to be concerned for the power and prerogatives of the Supreme Pontiff, do not respect the Bishops united to him or do not give due account to their authority, or whose interpretation of their actions and intentions is hostile, rendering their judgments ahead of the Apostolic See."[13]

Scalabrini found in the Pope's words both comfort and support for his own line of action: "You have dispersed the mists blown up by the spirit of the abyss to cloud the Christian horizon. You have defeated that entirely new liberalism spreading increasingly from the last ranks of the Catholic army. You have, so to speak, redeemed the Episcopate and freed it from a hidden, illegitimate power which, with most astute maneuvers was attempting to yoke it to its own cart."[14]

Above all he played an important role in countering the attempt to confuse public opinion which occurred at the end of August or the beginning of September with the appearance of a libelous pamphlet, printed in Basilea and published in Milan with the title: "Letter of Cardinal Pitra. Commentary. The Pope's Word."[15] The pamphlet was gaining widespread distribution in Northern Italy including the diocese of Piacenza. The Bishop wrote to inform the Cardinal Secretary of State, and told him he had cautioned his clergy about it.

"Would it not be opportune to make a public statement? Personally, I confess that when I see the Holy Father so ill served by certain so-called Catholics and think of the pain he must feel, I shudder and would do anything at all to mitigate it. On the other hand, I do not want to be carried away by the ardent love I bear him and thus do something that would not meet with his full approval. If, with your customary kindness, Your Eminence would give me your advice on what to do in this regard, I shall be very happy to abide by it."[16]

Cardinal Jacobini replied that he knew about the pamphlet and agreed with Scalabrini's suggestion.

"And since," he added, "a learned priest had already made several judicious comments on this unpleasant incident, please accept to include them in your booklet; to this end I have arranged to have them edited and adapted to your publication. These notes, however, need to be enlivened and illumined, and this is entrusted entirely to your skillful and learned pen."[17]

Scalabrini set to work immediately and for the most part retained the above mentioned notes, adding little of his own. He sent the draft to Cardinal Jacobini, who replied:

"I have given the manuscript of the Pastoral to the Holy Father...It has been read and reviewed and I therefore return it herewith so that it may be published."[18]

He therefore published the Pastoral, in which he first dealt with various points in the Pontifical Letter to Cardinal Guibert. He then deplored the actions of those who, while cloaking themselves in the banner of loyalty to the Pope, persisted at the same time in supporting ideas only recently condemned by Leo XIII, thus resowing the seeds of discord among Catholics. Under the vague label of liberal clergy, he said, they lumped together priests and prelates accusing them of connivance with Freemasonry and undermined the principles of unity, charity and hierarchical order at their very roots.

The following excerpt from among Scalabrini's additions to the comments is of particular interest because of the direct, if unofficial approval it received from the Pope:

"We are more than convinced that there are very, very many persons of noble spirit who suffer ineffably from the accusation that they are rebels against the Church, for the defense of which they would gladly give their last drop of blood if it were necessary; that very, very many of distinguished intellect, both clergy and laity, who are the target of every base insult and are covered with mud simply because they profess opinions left open by the wise moderation of the Holy See, would humbly submit to the sacred authority recognized in their baptism and would gladly break their pens in obedience to whatever decisions of the Pope, although they refuse, and rightly so, to submit to those who usurp the role of the Pope."[19]

Scalabrini's Pastoral pleased Rome, and its spectacular national and international success astonished its author:

"The Holy Father had Cardinal Jacobini write to me for fifty copies and to tell me that this *excellent work is completely in accord with his views*, wonderful words which I tell you in confidence since I would not like for them to be made public.[20] The Lord be blessed and thanked...The truth meanwhile is being sown and will grow, and despite the snares that will be stretched about it, it will cut through them on its royal way."[21]

The Pamphlet "Transigents and Intransigents"

Scalabrini's prophecy had to await a distant future for its fulfillment, for shortly afterwards there occurred the most famous episode in the controversy then raging. The Bishop of Piacenza was seemingly defeated but at the same time the affair demonstrated to an uncommon degree the confidence the Holy Father placed in him and the purity of his obedience and devotion to the Chair of Peter.

On November 3, 1885, he left for Rome to ask Leo XIII's advice about a new publication he was preparing at the direct invitation of the Pope himself. The latter was then intensifying his policy of reconciliation, evidenced, for example, by the establishment of relations with Germany and the naming of three "transigents" as cardinals: Battaglini, Capecelatro and Schiaffino. The last two were close friends of Scalabrini and their ideas on conciliation were even more advanced than his. To test the water, so to speak, Leo XIII chose a man on whom he could count not only for the soundness of his ideas and his sense of balance and restraint but also for his unfailing loyalty.

Scalabrini told Bonomelli about the publication in roundabout but significant terms:

"A Bishop friend of yours is publishing a pamphlet entitled *Transigents and Intransigents, Observations of An Italian Bishop*. It will cause a great deal of talk, but the author is a secret and there is complete understanding between him and His Holiness *(inter nos tantum)*, who has read and approved the work. I hope it will be good and clear away many misunderstandings."[22]

Scalabrini's pamphlet was published anonymously in December, 1885. The Preface set forth the author's purpose, namely, to develop the concepts in the Pastoral on the Letter of Cardinal Pitra in order to disprove the mistaken notions that arose from the use of the terms transigent and intransigent. This is basic for an understanding of what Scalabrini himself understood by transigence and of the real meaning of the phrase, too freely used, that Scalabrini was a "transigent."

"In politics as in law," he says, "the concept of compromise not only does not involve any concession with respect to principles but by its nature excludes it. In fact, jurists are unanimous in asserting that it is not possible to allow compromises that are offenses against the law, and only facts (not principles) may be the subject of compromise. Similarly in politics, to be transigent or intransigent does not in itself involve any concession or cession whatever in the matter of doctrine and rights. Hence the alleged antithesis in this regard is entirely false. The true difference between transigents and intransigents is a factual matter, since the latter remain locked in a negative attitude of absolute struggle and condemn the former, who, in contingent matters, consider what is relative and temporary rather than what is absolute and perpetual."[23]

Having thus clearly defined the terms of the question, the author declares that he accepts with his mind and his heart all the doctrinal teachings and practical norms set forth by the religious authority and in particular those which pertain to its "civil jurisdiction." The sovereignty of the Pope must be real and effective. He alone is to establish the form, degree and extension of the liberty he deems necessary. "Therefore we reject the charge that we are 'Liberal Catholics,' for these are transigent with respect to principles and therefore are in essence rejected by our program."[24]

This posited, he proceeds to rebut the intransigents — not all those who "represent a past which was in many ways worthy of respect and which they rightly regret and evoke its return," but only those who "represent the most extreme and complex form of intransigentism," the party which "arrogates to itself the mandate to impose its program on the Catholics and to condemn anyone who is not disposed to follow it."[25]

Turning then to concrete political facts and realities — since in the last analysis that is where the whole problem lay, while the theological and philosophical questions were only pretexts and smoke screens for the extremists — the author rebukes these extremists for "trying to destroy the great contemporary realities, which are but the consequence of previous facts, and to try to destroy them with a sweet-do-nothing, or rather with a systematic a priori opposition."[26] Leo XIII was providing a completely different example through his new policies with respect to France and Germany, and this was all to the good of the Church and of souls. "What results have the intransigents achieved with their program of immobility and abstention? By removing oneself from contemporary society, placing oneself outside the laws and public life, can one really hope to arrive at any practical results? Does it perhaps accord with one's duties as a Catholic and a citizen to let everything go to rack and ruin — religion, morality, country — rather than extend a compassionate hand to prevent the loss of souls, the corruption of many youths, the approval of a law contrary to religion? Perhaps political systems are superior to the rights of religion or should the interests of the former bow before the supreme rights of religion? It is very easy and comfortable to settle into the passive policy of inertia and await the cataclysm which, by some unknown law of history, will drag the world back to prehistoric times."[27]

The transigents, the pamphlet continues, do not seek to impose any particular program but remain "in the field of hypothesis and discussion," and with respect to debatable issues are ready to obey the decisions of the Pope. Next came the prickly question of elections, and it is precisely in this regard that this trial balloon of Bishop Scalabrini, or rather of Leo XIII, was sent up.

"It was our conviction that competition in well ordered elections would contribute to the legislature a contingent of Catholic Deputies" who would be able "to prevent the presentation or approval of laws opposed to the Church." This conviction was supported by the example of Belgium and Prussia where Catholics had obtained permission to enter the political arena and had obtained excellent results, although they did have to collaborate with anti-Catholic or agnostic Governments. "But when we were given to understand that, for reasons of the highest order, the only elections in which, for the present, it was permissible for Catholics to participate were the municipal ones, we reverently accepted the august statement and withdrew from the discussion of a hypothesis considered to be inexpedient. We gave constant and diligent attention, however, to the municipal elections, and tried to have elected to the city Councils, at least in large numbers, those citizens whose religious faith was unquestioned or who at least were certain not to attack it. Our candidates could not always prevent an evil but they often succeeded in mitigating it at least in its consequences. And certainly the present and future generations ought to be grateful to them for having seen to it that religious instruction was retained in the elementary schools."[28]

In conclusion, the pamphlet declared: "Do not suppose that these pages were inspired by resentment or prompted by Partisanship. You certainly have offended us in all that we hold most dear, our faith and our honor. You have accused us of being 'Liberal Catholics,' traitors, Judases, only because we tried to come to the aid of our country, to offer some remedy, to pour oil and wine in her wounds, like the Good Samaritan, not vinegar and bile. We forgive and forget the personal insults. But on your part stop sowing the seeds of discord, draw close around Leo XIII, follow his admonitions obediently. Away with anger, away with hatreds, away with attacks "among those whom one wall and moat contain." If charity and unity once more reign among us, oh then clear days will shine again and the dove carrying the olive branch of peace will joyfully return to Vatican hill."[29]

This was then Scalabrini's "transigence." Even though he placed himself among the "transigents" when he defined the meaning of the term, he knew very well that the terminology was dangerous.

"I do not know what value the adjectives transigent or intransigent have with respect to the character of the faith. Either we are Catholics or we are not. The rest has to do with a conventional terminology which is very doubtful and dangerous."[30]

It is not names, however, but facts which define a man. And here the fact is of decisive significance in evaluating the character of Scalabrini, namely, the fact that the thesis he expounded in the famous pamphlet was the Pope's thesis, for, in a certain sense, it can be said that the Pontiff was much more its author than the Bishop of Piacenza.

Part of the Catholic press attacked the pamphlet with incredible violence.[31] When Bonomelli asked Scalabrini why he did not reveal himself,[32] the latter calmly answered:

"I am answering your letter of yesterday right away to send you a million wishes for the New Year, and for many, many years, all filled with every success as you well deserve. As for the pamphlet you mentioned, I am as calm as oil. Do you really believe that I am the author? If you knew the story of that little work, you would be astonished, dumbfounded. When you were here, I could not tell you because the Bishop of Nancy, was always present, a wise and excellent prelate but a Frenchman. I cannot therefore tell you in all truth: I am the Italian Bishop and I am answerable not to you but to the Pope...The dominant theory down there now is good, but the practice is such as it is...There must be some rag or other to throw to the mob, and if I am to be that rag, *sit nomen Domini benedictum!* What would you? My very dear friend, I am so happy and read with much pleasure the blasts of certain people that I often laugh and say to my Secretary, either I am a saint or a philosopher; but unfortunately I am neither the one nor the other."[33]

When Bonomelli insisted that he ask the Pope "to show his hand a little,"[34] Scalabrini, who began to be distressed that his colleague of Cremona was the subject of increasingly open attacks as the supposed author of the pamphlet, decided to tell him the origin of the writing that was eliciting so much incrimination.

"You are right not once but a thousand times; but it seems you have not yet understood the high level origin of that poor pamphlet. It was given me only to edit its form; for the rest there was little to be done and I did it. But the one who gave it to me to edit and then take to Bologna, do you know who that was? The Pope. Precisely the Pope, who said that he had initiated it and was in fact its author. Do you understand now the reason for my silence and my incomprehensible *apatheia*?"[35]

Scalabrini is even more explicit in a letter to the Pope, a draft of which is extant: "If you will permit me, Holy Father, I would make bold to offer some observations on the pamphlet you deigned to entrust to me in order that I might have it published and distributed."

He suggested certain modifications and asked for guidance regarding the imprimatur and the format of the publication.[36] In another note he calls it "the pamphlet dictated by Your Holiness."[37]

Another noteworthy detail underlines Scalabrini's prudence and personal disinterestedness, his readiness to be the rag tossed in the air. After the attacks in the press, the Pope had given him permission to reveal the name of the author — that is, Scalabrini, of course — but at the same time he indicated his desire that he do not do so:

"Whenever, because of the persons involved or for other reasons, you think it well to reveal your name, you may do so freely, while giving due weight, in your wisdom, to how much that is disagreeable would result from this revelation."[38]

Scalabrini understood the Pope's wish and remained silent. The Pope comforted him indirectly in a Brief in which he said that the Bishop's good wishes had renewed the joy he had experienced in conversing with him because of the excellent sentiments he had expressed in his recent audience. He praised his magnanimous spirit and the zeal he manifested in all that concerned the well-being and glory of the Church, and he assured him he followed with benevolence his ministry of love and devotion, reaffirming his affectionate regard for him.[39]

Two documents of Bishop Scalabrini refer to the pamphlet. In a letter to the Pope, the draft of which bears no date but is to be placed at the end of 1886, he writes:

"I am sending Your Holiness a clipping from today's *Osservatore di Milano*. From it Your Holiness may learn the fruits of my sacrifices and my obedience...In other past issues the *Osservatore* had insolently declared that the one who had denounced the intransigents, referring to Your Pastoral, had disobeyed the commandments of the Pope. The Pastoral and the Pamphlet,[40] herein lies the secret of the whole plot against me which succeeded in creating the belief in Rome that I had proposed candidates for the legislature! I do not complain about those people, Your Holiness, for they are capable of anything, but I must deplore, respectfully but with all the energy of my soul, the fact that I am abandoned by the One who ordered me to do what caused so much strife. Fortunately, Holy Father, my faith rests on much deeper foundations than human wisdom. I must therefore place my cause in the hands of God. He, the Just Judge, will be able to vindicate the honor, violated and allowed to be violated, of a Bishop like the undersigned, who in his actions never did anything but obey the One who had every right to command him."[41]

In a letter to Cardinal Schiaffino about the "famous pamphlet" we find another outburst:

"One does generously and for love of the good alone what one is permitted or advised to do, but not only do they abandon the first scouts they sent out but they join with the enemy to beat and if possible crush them, and good night! What do you think of this, Your Eminence? For my part I was not surprised at the maneuvers, tricks and calmunies of the well known party; but I deplored, and strongly even, to the Holy Father the fact that they had been listened to there where they should have been treated with contempt. I had in mind to defend myself, and so I wrote the short Pastoral attached herewith. I sent it to the Holy Father, and it is evident from the red marks that he sent it to some one or other for review and then sent it back to me with a request that I do not publish it. A truly heroic sacrifice was imposed on me, which I accepted solely, I admit, for love of God."[42]

With respect to the honors offered him by way of compensation as well as to the exasperation expressed in the letters cited above, it is well to recall what Scalabrini wrote to the Cardinal Secretary of State, right in the middle of the controversy:

"I do not aspire to any honors, nor is it my own most lowly self that I seek, God is my witness. I exert myself and know that I am working for a much higher purpose and a far more noble and holy cause."[43]

He was indignant when he knew and saw — and no one else could know better than he, — that the ideas which were indeed his through deep conviction but also those of the Pope were being contested. After being charged to make them known and then to be abandoned could mean, therefore, that they were no longer the Pope's views, and he found himself in a situation he feared and abhorred the most, that of being in disagreement with the Holy Father. It became a drama of conscience for him. His indignation is evidence of his sincerity, and proves that he wasn't just saying words when he spoke of heroic obedience.

The Elections of 1886 and the Non Expedit

We come now to 1886, the year of the elections, which were the touchstone of obedience for the so-called "transigent" Catholics. What was Scalabrini's conduct on the "level of facts" — as he said — when it was a question of the principle of authority and not a question of arguable opinions?

Since 1880, the diocesan paper of Piacenza carried stern rebukes and warnings to Catholics who had participated in the elections[44] contrary to the decree of the Sacred Apostolic Penitentiary which in 1874 had declared *non expedit*, it was not expedient, for Catholics to take part in the elections and they were not permitted to participate in the Parliament of the Kingdom of Italy. In 1881, Scalabrini insisted to Bonomelli that it was necessary "to leave the solution of such extremely serious questions entirely to the Holy Father," namely, participation in the elections and the "Roman question."[45] In 1882, the new electoral law of May 7th raised the number of voters from 600,000 to 2,000,000. Leo XIII submitted to the Bishops of Piacenza and Cremona six questions on the *non expedit* given the situation in Italy and the new electoral laws: was it useful to insist on the prohibition, or was it better to revoke it immediately, or to wait; what was to be the attitude of the clergy; what suggestions did they have to ensure that the prohibition was observed or, on the other hand, to prepare the faithful for its revocation.[46] Both bishops replied in favor of abolishing the *non expedit*.

Bishop Scalabrini had already presented the case to the Holy Father:

"I beg you, Blessed Father, to enlighten me soon with regard to a subject closely related to the good government of my diocese as well as all the dioceses of Italy, namely the participation of Catholics in political elections. While awaiting the new electoral laws, is it licit for them to participate? I confess, Blessed Father, that I have been asking myself this question for some time, and having closely examined before God the arguments on both sides of the question, it seems to me the time has come to try something in this regard, but I must not forget that it is up to you alone to decide. The reason why I feel obliged to inform Your Holiness, is the fact that in my Diocese all the landowners without exception (and there are many), the managers of shops, factories, etc., have had all their workers registered on the voting lists, and so I greatly fear that the *non expedit* of the Holy See, which was not observed very much in the past, will be even less so in the future, with great harm to individual consciences and to the detriment of the very authority of the Church."[47]

Scalabrini answered the six questions cited above during his *ad limina* visit at the end of September. He was given to understand that there was no intention of abolishing the *non expedit*. Instead he had received from the Holy Office an affirmative answer to the following inquiry concerning, not the general question, but particular cases in point: "If, given the not infrequent case that in a given electoral list there are several competing candidates, some of whom are well-known Catholics determined to defend in every possible way the cause of the Church, and the others are more or less hostile to it, could it be approved, or at least tolerated, that voters devoted to religion take part in the voting with complete peace of conscience in order to ensure the victory of the Catholic candidate."[48] In those particular instances, therefore, it was permissible to vote and naturally also to run as a candidate. Otherwise the affirmative answer would not have made any sense. Besides, the reply also contained the explicit injunction to "write afterwards to the Cardinal Prefect of the Holy Office to obtain for the Catholic elected permission to take his seat in Parliament."[49]

In 1886 elections in Piacenza turned out as Scalabrini had foreseen. It was a question of keeping the radical-socialist candidates from winning, which they would do if the Catholics abstained from voting. Bishop Scalabrini was asked his advice. He could have used the reply he received in 1882, but he chose the side of prudence and wrote to the Pope again. The latter replied through Msgr. Boccali, making a distinction between the general question and particular instances: "Nothing was changed with respect to the conduct Catholics were to follow," but in the particular cases set forth in the request, "Your Excellency may, as in 1882, use the confidential response you received from the Sacred Apostolic Penitentiary."[50] A week later, Msgr. Boccali explained further: "the replies given by the Holy Father are valid for the guidance of the Bishops in some special case that arises: therefore it is not appropriate that they be published."[51]

On the same day that the Holy See said these confidential replies were not to be made public, the diocesan paper L'Amico del Popolo emphasized the general prescription of the non expedit.[52] On the other hand, the Bishop told some persons individually and in strict confidence and for special reasons, that although the non expedit was still in force it was not illicit in itself to take part in the elections. He gave no advice either for or against their doing so; they were to act according to their conscience.[53]

On May 8th he left on his pastoral visit to the vicariates of Centenaro, Rompeggio, Bedonia, and Varsi. The Catholic paper announced that the Bishop would be absent from the city until the 9th of June, since all these places were quite far from Piacenza in the Parmesan Appennines. As soon as he left, the few candidates who had spoken with him privately informed one another of what he had said, since they all belonged to the same party, the moderate Unione Monarchica. Since they had all received the same reply they decided it was permissible to stand for election and distributed a brief circular to that effect. At the same time, a Canon published, on his own responsibility, an article in the Amico del Popolo in which he expressed the personal opinion that the Catholics would do well to go to the voting booth in the particular, concrete case of Piacenza in order to prevent the victory of radicals like Cavallotti and Priario who were notoriously and blatantly hostile to the Church.

The abstentionists, for their part, took to the Amico del Popolo to publish a communication in which they set forth the fact that the "Circular in question was sent to each of the Parish Committees without the Bishop's knowledge...We stand by the non expedit as it has been explained to us by him who alone has the authority and the right to explain it to the Faithful."[54]

Immediately afterwards the paper became completely reticent on the subject, by order of the Bishop, who in reply to a letter from his secretary, wrote from Brugneto on May 11th as follows: "Here is the negative reply as expected. The greatest prudence is necessary, also on the part of *L'Amico*. Not a word in support of the elections."[55] The abstentionists put out a flyer entitled *I Cattolici alle urne? (The Catholics at the Polls?)* in which they stated that the Bishop was "completely outside" all the maneuvers engaged in by the "interventionists." A group of "dissident Catholics" published their point of view in the liberal newspaper *La Libertà* on May 17th, but they also maintained that the Bishop had always told anyone who asked him that the *non expedit* was still in force.

The radical Masonic newspapers, *Il Progresso* and *Il Piccolo* got into the fray with an entirely new campaign, to teach Catholics their duty to obey the Pope and to follow the *non expedit*. They thus unwittingly underlined the special reasons that had led Bishop Scalabrini to permit the exceptions allowed by the Holy See.[56]

There was, therefore, great confusion. Then the fact that the candidates of the *Unione Monarchica* won with the support of the Catholic vote infuriated the papers that championed the "progressives" along with others who should have been pleased with the election results, evident proof that, as Scalabrini said, principles were not involved. It was all a matter of politics.

In this atmosphere, molehills became mountains. Both the intransigent and Masonic press hurled accusations at the Bishop, one of the more specific charges and one cited as documentary evidence in the denunciation presented to the Holy See was a note that contained only the following words: "Give my regards to the Marquis Federico Landi; tell him I have received his very welcome letter and that I thank him very much."[57] This innocent note was transformed into a letter of praise and congratulation to Landi, one of the chief "interventionists" for the victory won by his candidates. And that was the way it was presented to Rome, evidently without any documentation. Yet Bishop Scalabrini, who knew that every act of his would acquire exaggerated importance during the election period, thought he had used all possible prudence. Landi had written him about some family matters. The Bishop, who was on his pastoral visit in Bedonia, in the province of Parma, did not want to answer personally, and told his Secretary Msgr. Mangot, to give Landi the message personally. Instead Mangot wrote a note quoting the Bishop literally.[58]

Another false charge, which was retracted with bad grace by the *Piccolo*, attributed to the Episcopal Curia, or the Bishop or the Vicar General, the circular published by the "interventionists." Here also there was not the slightest documentation.[59]

The following document, however, seems clear enough. It is the second letter still extant from the period during which Scalabrini was absent from Piacenza on his pastoral visit to the Parmesan Appenines:

"Bedonia, May 22, 1886

"Dear Don Camillo,

A short note just to tell you that I arrived safely yesterday in Bedonia and despite the very tiring aspects of the journey I am in excellent health. By the time you receive this the noisome fracas over the elections will, I hope, be all over. But the greatest prudence must be used to clarify in the paper that the ecclesiastical authority, while maintaining the *non expedit* for general cases, gave private individuals the advice he could and had to give in directing their consciences in particular instances. I have just received your two letters. Everything is fine; but maintain the greatest reserve. I do not think I need to answer Count Calciati[60] at this time. You could let him know that I am on a visitation, that I thank him very much and that when I return to the city I shall send him the letters sent to me, etc., etc. My regards to Marchese Federico Landi and *tell him* that I have received his very welcome letter and I thank him. On June 1, your signature as Episcopal Delegate will be authorized. Before signing anything, however, examine it closely and where you have doubts set the matters aside until my return. With my blessings and affectionate..."[61]

The date of the letter, May 22, is sufficient to disprove the calumnies built on the alleged congratulations to Landi for his victory in the elections, which took place on May 23rd. The letter is even more important for the proof it gives of the Bishop's conduct in that particular circumstance, conduct that would not longer be licit four months later when the Holy Office declared that the *non expedit* was to be interpreted as a genuine prohibition. But in May of 1886 the Bishop's actions could not be considered as violating the obedience due the Holy See, according to the interpretation given the formula by many bishops, some of whom were interpreting it much more broadly than the bishop of Piacenza.

When Scalabrini returned to the city he was surprised to find the following letter from Cardinal Monaco La Valletta, Secretary of the Congregation of the Holy Office:

"It has been reported to this Congregation that Your Excellency not only stated and had it stated that it was permissible to participate in the elections, but that you even promoted it, making use of the Pastors in this regard. However incredible this may seem, since the directive of the Holy See in this matter is known to everyone and is the only rule to be followed, nevertheless the newspaper *L'Amico del Popolo* which is said to be directed by your Curia, and Your Excellency's letter to one of the promoters of an election committee congratulating him on the success of several candidates, which is said to have been circulated throughout the city, have given rise to serious apprehension among their Eminences the Cardinal Inquisitors, my colleagues, on whose behalf I beg you to give me all the information necessary to restore their peace of mind. It is unnecessary to add that your alleged conduct does not correspond to the replies, however specific and private, given you at other times and of which there is no trace in the Acts of the Holy See."[62]

In his reply Scalabrini denied the charges and set forth the real facts. To counter the implication that he had invented documents of the Holy See, he transcribed the letter of Msgr. Boccali, quoted above, which could be easily verified since it had been sent only a few weeks before. He also wrote to the Pope, protesting the malicious interpretations and direct accusations that had appeared in certain newspapers and stated he had to defend himself, at least before his own people.

He received an answer from the Secretary of State, saying that the praise he had received from the Holy Father the previous year should compensate him for the attacks in the press, which were censurable insofar as they struck at the person and dignity of the Bishop; but the latter was not to be surprised if the directives given, even indirectly by the Curia of Piacenza, were disapproved, because they fell outside the general policy lines prescribed by the Holy See. It was not considered opportune, therefore, that he defend himself publicly.[63]

Scalabrini's reply is interesting for its sincerity, consistency and Christian fortitude. The following are the essential points in his letter:

"I like to speak the truth openly and clearly, and I like others to speak the truth to me openly and clearly. I therefore thank Your Eminence from the bottom of my heart, for your venerable letter of July 11, on which, however, I beg leave to offer some observations...It grieves me deeply that there persists the belief in the Vatican that I did not strictly observe the norms set by the Holy See with regard to the elections. But in the name of God, what proofs are adduced? No, a thousand times no, Your Eminence...Neither directly nor indirectly did this Curia give out suggestions contrary to those norms. Why is no attention paid to the published denials of this, denials which no one has contradicted? It is true that certain laymen, imprudently but in good faith, distributed certain circulars in which it was stated that the ecclesiastical Authority had said it was not illicit to participate in the elections in our case (and these are perhaps the facts which Your Eminence states cannot be erased) but it is also true that I disapproved those circulars even publicly as soon as I learned about them. What blame do I have if a generalization was drawn from a counsel given in a particular case? Your Excellency will perhaps say that this advice should not have been given. But then why did the Vatican reply that, given the circumstances, it was permissible, or at least to be tolerated, that in certain specific instances Catholics could participate in elections?...Have I failed in some way, unwittingly? I stand ready to be corrected and another time I shall be the first to declare publicly that the *non expedit* is in force, if this disastrous formula is still in existence. Kindly inform the Holy Father of this also. Kindly assure him also that out of respect for his wishes, I completely renounce my intention to publish my defense, and that I leave my case entirely in his august and paternal hands. Certain expressions which I used in the letter I sent him recently, Your Eminence, are to be interpreted in the spirit in which I dictated them, that is, with profound respect and at the same time sincere love of the truth. In any case, I beg Him to forgive me if in some way I have been the occasion, unwittingly, of causing displeasure to His most noble heart, and as a pledge that He has deigned to hear my prayer may He grant the Apostolic Benediction which I humbly beg of Him through Your Excellency."[64]

A month later the above mentioned decree of the Holy Office appeared. *L'Amico del Popolo* published it on August 7, adding the following: "Now that the legitimate Authority has declared the meaning of the *non expedit*, in full obedience to it,...we are happy that now all ambiguity and cause of discord among Catholics is removed."

Since the attacks against Scalabrini in the press gave no sign of abating, the Bishop prepared a circular in his own defense and sent it to the Pope for review. This time, also, he was requested not to publish it and obeyed.[65] Leo XIII then reassured him, through Msgr. Galimberti, that he could "always count on that esteem and that confidence" "special proofs" of which had been given him.[66] With his usual tact and depth of meaning, the Pope then confirmed his confidence in and affection for the Bishop of Piacenza, to whom he was always grateful for a service he would have welcomed from everyone but received from very few,[67] namely, plain and candid speech. Given that particular moment when every word tended to engender confusion, he rightly preferred not to make an explicit gesture, but instead sent the Bishop as a gift a beautifully bound copy of his poems with an affectionate dedication.

It is useful here to note the results of the Informative Process with respect to Bishop Scalabrini's behavior in the circumstances.

"He was always faithful to the orders of the Holy See in matters relating to the *non expedit* although before the declaration that the term *non expedit* meant *non licet*, he personally preferred that Catholics participated in the religious-political struggles in order to prevent the victory of Freemasonry over the Church."[68] — "The charge that he was a Liberal, that is, in opposition to the Holy See in political matters, was absolutely without foundation. He was so respectful of the Supreme Hierarch of the Church, that even in things of little importance and of a non-obligatory nature, he always sought information regarding the directives and desires of the Supreme Pontiff. With respect to the charge of Liberal, certain in his own conscience, he changed nothing in his own conduct, although it grieved him that he might seem to be a disobedient son to the Holy Father in the eyes of the people of his diocese, not so much because this was personally distasteful to him but rather because it could be the cause of scandal to the faithful."[69]

"He was so obedient to the dispositions and directives (of the Holy See) that he not only accepted and followed them himself, but required that others do so also even when he himself had different views. He used to exclaim: 'It is a command of the Pope! That's enough!' "[70]

"Bishop Scalabrini was broad-minded and of generous spirit. He stood always and absolutely with the Pope and for the Pope and, as he used to say, he would have cut off his head for him twenty times, and for this reason he sometimes declared that the intransigents certainly were not with the Pope."[71]

"From what my late father and I understood," the son of Count Carlo Radini Tedeschi testified, "while Bishop Scalabrini maintained strict obedience to the Holy See, we had the impression that he personally favored participation in the elections. He never, however, took a positive stand but neither did he support the leaders of abstentionism."[72]

"If Bishop Scalabrini held views that were then considered liberal (for example, the suitability of conciliation between the Kingdom of Italy and the Holy See and of Catholic participation in the elections), he nevertheless always tried to act in accordance with the thinking and the dispositions of the Holy See. And whenever he published anything on the above mentioned questions, he did (so far as I know) with its consent, for it rightly had confidence in his prudence, his ability to maintain secrecy or confidentiality, and his readiness to sacrifice himself when it was necessary. The Servant of God confined himself to invoking the judgment of the Holy See when he was accused of Liberalism, and renounced defending himself any further when love for the Church and the country required this."[73]

"As for the question of the *non expedit,* although he thought gentlemen should participate in the elections in order to make Italy Christian and to arrive at an honorable solution of the Roman question, and although at the beginning, on the basis of special faculties received from the Holy See, he very prudently gave permission for such participation in individual cases, nevertheless later, that is when Rome declared the opposite position, he held strictly to the latter despite his own personal views, adding: 'We, the Clergy, are like an army; woe if indiscipline triumphs; the General speaks...it is necessary to obey.' "[74]

"There were two reasons why he was accused of Liberalism. The first was that he openly favored a reconciliation between Italy and the Holy See and a resolution of the Roman question. The second was that he was convinced, as he often told me, that abstention from voting in the political elections was harmful to the religious interests of the nation. 'How do you expect good laws,' he exclaimed, 'if you don't send good representatives to Parliament?'...And he used to add: 'If we keep on with this legislation that is so hostile to the Church, we shall be very lucky if after many years we have anything left on which to rebuild.' However, when it came to the method for resolving the Roman Question, he relied entirely on the judgment of the Holy See...He observed and had others observe, as much as he could, the directives from Rome and requested the obligatory authorizations in specific cases."[75]

We might be tempted here to discuss how foresighted he was, not so much in political as religious matters, from the testimony briefly quoted of Cardinal Nasalli Rocca, but we shall confine ourselves to the moral judgment on the Bishop's conduct, which carries no doubts whatever.

When it came to ideas, we know how resigned he could be to the desperately long time it takes for some to come to fruition[76] and how he believed in their ultimate triumph. Precisely with respect to participation in public life, we find the following sentence in a famous letter from Bishop Bonomelli to Pius X, dated October 1, 1911:

"Judgments and opinions are condemned which now seem audacious and erroneous, but in twenty years they will be common. This was said to me many times by Bishop Scalabrini, whose merits you greatly appreciated."[77]

After the declaration of the Holy Office on July 30, 1886, just as he had accepted difficult exploratory assignments at personal sacrifice and had courageously taken up avant-garde positions, Bishop Scalabrini, good soldier that he was, now fell back into the ranks with the same generosity of spirit, hoping meanwhile that for the good of souls and only for that, the "high reasons" which imposed abstentionism would soon cease to exist.

"Do you see?" Blessed Luigi Guanella used to say to the nephew of the Servant of God, "The Church is an army; some belong to the advance guard, some to the rear guard. Now Bishop Scalabrini belongs to the advance guard, but always with the Pope."[78]

Some years later, in an interview widely carried by the Italian press, Scalabrini reasserted the position he had consistently held. He disapproved the action of a priest of Cremona who had disobeyed the *non expedit*, he maintained the absolute necessity for obedience, but at the same time he declared that the *non expedit* was not a dogma and therefore its opportuneness and effectiveness could be discussed in private.[79]

The Roman Question and Conciliation

Before expressing them to anyone else, Scalabrini had expressed his views on the Roman question to the Pope himself. In November 1885 he had submitted a memorandum on the subject so that, he said, "you may know how I think and, believe me, how very many persons think who sincerely love the good of the Church and who perhaps do not always have the courage to say what they think."[80]

Having first declared that he adheres "scrupulously to all that the Church has stated many times regarding the need for temporal power, that he condemns and maintains all that the Church condemns and maintains," and that he is considering only the application of the principles it has proclaimed to the degree that this is possible given the present situation in Italy, he proceeds to examine the actual state of the question.

"Apart from a miracle, restitution of the temporal power as it existed before September 20, 1870, can be achieved only through physical or *moral* force. The first does not exist in Italy and cannot be expected from foreign powers. But even if this last were possible, the day that it became a reality would be a most unfortunate day for the fate of the Church and of the Holy Father in Italy. The country would rise as one man to defend its independence, and if it won, it is easy to see what the situation of the Church and the Catholics would be. If it was defeated, all the resentment over the defeat would fall upon religion and the Pope, who would be blamed for the destruction of the nation. The Pope, having become once more a temporal Prince, would have a moral desert around him and would constantly hear around his throne the mutterings of the revolution waiting to overthrow him. The social catastrophe which the intransigents foresee, would be a catastrophe precisely and above all for the Church. Since physical force is out of the question, there is nothing left but to hope in moral force."

"This," he continues, "does not exist in Italy to the degree necessary for the purpose. Therefore, it is necessary to increase it. Nor is it impossible that after a few decades the Italians, even the non-believers, will understand that the Pope cannot be a subject and therefore must have some form of principality whatever it may be."

"What can be done," he continues, "to get out of this truly intolerable situation which, if it lasts much longer, will mean a fearsome future for the Church and for society? It is not a question of recognizing what has been done, and not even of undertaking dishonorable actions on behalf of the Holy See. It is a question of finding the means for a long term but certain preparation for a better future. After developing the argument that 'it is necessary above all to persuade the Italians that the Pontiff in no way desires the return of the foreigner and the old divisions in the nation' he proceeds to suggest several means: 1. not to oppose elections with a broad program geared to the moral and religious well-being of the country; 2. work for recognition that Catholics desire to act loyally on legal grounds and are seeking only the common good; 3. allow responsible men to participate in the Senate in order to increase the number and the strength of those already in it.

"He returns to the idea that the indestructible strength of the Papacy is completely moral, that it is still great and even greater than in the past. 'Try,' he says, 'to increase this influence throughout the world, and thus prepare the restoration of its material position, which can come about in whatever form will be possible according to the times.'

"He concluded: 'to desire temporal power now, in its entirety as it was formerly, is simply impossible and places Catholicism in Italy in serious danger: temporal power is but a means, and the means must not imperil the end.'

'Once hatreds have been laid to rest, mistrust dissipated, even its enemies will understand the strength of the Papacy and that the welfare of Italy requires that the Pontiff again be an independent prince in fact. It is well to hope that, persuaded of the advantage to themselves, they will voluntarily grant him the degree of temporal princedom that will make his situation tolerable.'[81]

"He ends the memorandum with these words: 'You know these things incomparably better than I do, but I have wanted to set them forth to show what I think and also to dispel some suspicions that may be raised in my regard. Finally, I have wanted to say them, not to give advice (God forbid) but to obey my conscience, which in any case will hold Your word as its undeniable rule.' "

It should be noted that Scalabrini was much more cautious than many other conciliationists, foreseeing as he did the need for several decades of preparation. He did not believe in any immediate or miraculous solution to the problem, but he was anxious that some first steps be taken before it was too late, and precisely through Catholic participation in political life. For this reason we find only unenthusiastic mention of the wind of conciliationism that blew through Italy in 1887. The ardent hope did not die nor could it be dampened, but an expectation of a solution in the relatively near future was given a mortal blow in 1886 when the *non expedit* became a *non licet*.

After the famous papal allocution of May 23, 1887, which had fed the hopes of the ingenuous, the *Opera dei Congressi* promoted a Catholic petition to Parliament, inviting it to accept the Pope's words and make peace. Scalabrini remarked:

"This is truly an odd performance! Catholics must stay out of Parliament and then they promote and support petitions to Parliament. If this is consistency, I do not understand it."[82]

But when he later learned that the Pope wanted the petitions to be supported, he told his pastors, in a tone of command rather than advice, to collect as many signatures as possible and urged the bishop of Cremona do the same.[83]

"Rome, Italy and Reality"

For some months Bishop Bonomelli had been thinking about what was to become of the most famous of his writings, *Roma e l'Italia e la realtà delle cose* (Rome, Italy and Reality). He had told Scalabrini about it in March, 1887, and sent him the outline of the work and had asked his advice.[84] Scalabrini preferred first to test the water in Rome:

"If I have not yet answered your dear letters it is because I was waiting for an answer from down there. But until now I have waited in vain...What to do meanwhile? I have thought and thought about you many times and I am of the opinion that you must do *ad mentem, et mens est,* that you write out the entire pamphlet as planned, that you issue it in completely private edition, and that you send copies to the Pope, the principal Cardinals and Bishops, and also to the King. Thus you will test the terrain and a great deal of trouble, will, it seems to me, be avoided."[85]

But Bonomelli had for some time been feeling quite compulsive about the matter[86] and could not bring himself to accept the prudent steps suggested by Scalabrini, who, however, kept cautioning him: "Go slowly, my friend; be careful not to take a wrong step. Times are changing, but I do not think they are quite ripe enough for this yet."[87] Besides, the Pope had given him to understand during an audience, that he wanted Rome returned to the papacy.[88]

Bonomelli's mind was made up by this time, and Scalabrini's last warning came from Rome too late, namely, the need to face another reality, the fact that the tension between the Vatican and the Italian Government was too high at the time.[89] While Scalabrini was still in Rome, there appeared anonymously in the March 1, 1889, issue of the *Rassegna Nazionale* the article entitled *Roma e l'Italia e la realtà delle cose. Osservazioni di un prelato lombardo.* Scalabrini found himself in an embarrassing position. At first he advised his friend to maintain his anonymity, even when he learned that the Pope had disapproved the article. This he did in the letter *Gratam scito* to Bishop Corna Pellegrini of Brescia, who had written Rome a protest against the article.

"I have this minute learned, with some sorrow, from the *Cittadino* of Genoa that the *Osservatore Romano* is publishing a letter to the Bishop of Brescia in which the Pope is expressing his disapproval of the famous article. For heaven's sake, advise the author again not to reveal himself, not to be carried away by an excess of piety and throw himself into the hands of his enemies...It would ruin everything. In any case, after an act of that kind I begin to have hope for the future. This evening I shall read the document. Courage, keep calm, be prudent, and go on."[90]

The following day, however, he agreed with the decision Bonomelli had taken after reading the papal letter and before he had received Scalabrini's note. On April 4th, (the date of Scalabrini's letter) he had written a statement of submission to the Pope and on the following day had sent it to the Bishop of Piacenza saying that he was willing to send it immediately to Rome but would do what Scalabrini suggested, e.g. would it be better to publish an anonymous statement of submission in the *Rassegna,* or go to Rome, which he was not very much inclined to do.[91] Scalabrini replied by return mail on April 5th:

"I have read everything and have given very serious thought to your reasons, and I am finally persuaded that there is no point in hesitating. I shall send your very noble statement on with a letter of my own. It will revive the glorious examples of the greatest Bishops and will crown you with glory. The article will not die and the truth will triumph in the end...Let us be of good heart; God will take into account the rightness of our intentions."[92]

Meanwhile, however, Bishop Bonomelli had had second thoughts, and decided to postpone sending his signed submission to the Pope. He gave his reasons in another letter, namely, that if he revealed his authorship it would make the administration of his diocese difficult and would attract the strong support of the Liberals. This would place him in an embarrassing position and would create difficulties for him especially with the Pope. Besides, it would worsen his position vis-à-vis the Government, which disliked him anyway[93] and would add fuel to the politico-religious struggle (this last was probably the one most puzzling to Bishop Scalabrini).[94]

When he learned of Bonomelli's change of mind,[95] through his secretary whom he had sent to Cremona, Scalabrini agreed that *for the moment* an anonymous statement of submission could be sufficient.[96] He suggested that Bonomelli not reveal himself for the time being but that he send him his reasons, for keeping silent and he (Scalabrini) would find a way to bring them to the attention of the Pope.[97] Bonomelli did so in his letter of April 13th, summarized above; his views were to be given to their mutual friend Msgr. Agliardi and through him to the Pope, but Bonomelli asked Scalabrini not to reveal his authorship even to Agliardi. The latter wrote from Rome on the 17th that the Holy Father had been satisfied with the anonymous statement but at the same time would be pleased if the author would make himself known. On the 20th, as soon as he learned this, Bonomelli wrote to Piacenza: "Now what must that person do, now that you have sent him that news? He wants peace of conscience at all costs. Find out for certain what he must do and he will do it immediately..."[98]

Bishop Scalabrini answered him on the same day, telling him again to keep silent and he would find out what he could from Rome. But just as he was closing the letter, he learned that the article had been placed on the Index the preceding day, "still another reason for not coming forward."[99] He still held in general with the "highly prudent reasons" Bonomelli had communicated to him. The latter, however, who was of a generous and ardent nature, suddenly swept aside all these considerations, especially when he learned that the newspapers in Brescia were printing hateful accusations against him and that many priests and laymen in Brescia had no doubts about the identity of the author of the controversial article. Thus there arose the danger that further silence would be interpreted as a sign of disobedience to the Holy Father, and he preferred instead to provide a heroic example to the contrary.[100]

Bonomelli learned of the condemnation on Holy Saturday. On the following day, April 21st, after delivering the Easter homily with his usual quiet eloquence, he read his famous public retraction. It was his most celebrated gesture, but entirely in keeping with the characteristic magnanimity of his sentiments and intentions.

On the same day he sent his secretary to Piacenza with a copy of the retraction and a letter setting forth the reasons for his sudden decision, and requesting Scalabrini to send the retraction to the Pope with an explanation of the reasons for the delay.[101] Scalabrini immediately sent a telegram to the Holy Father:

"Hasten send consolation Your Holiness. Today Bishop Bonomelli at end of homily from pulpit of Cathedral crowded with people declared himself author of condemned pamphlet and read act of perfect submission to Apostolic See, amid great emotion of congregation and sent me noble document through his secretary with request I send it immediately to Your Holiness as I am doing. Beseeching the Apostolic Blessing on me and most Venerable Colleague, worthy of all admiration and praise."

At the same time he sent the document to Msgr. Boccali with a note explaining why Bonomelli had not sent immediately the act of confession and retraction.[102]

On Easter Monday, Scalabrini received a reply from the Holy Father, which he communicated right away to his friend:

"Reply herewith: the Holy Father heard with great pleasure the news Your Excellency communicated to him by telegram yesterday and gladly imparts the requested blessing to You and to the Bishop of Cremona. Cardinal Rampolla.. Affectionate regards. Bishop Giambattista."

Before receiving Cardinal Rampolla's telegram, Scalabrini had that morning sent Bonomelli his congratulations on "the truly heroic act," the news of which had "stunned" him.[103] On the Tuesday after Easter he sent him the reply of Msgr. Agliardi, to whom he had communicated the news:

"Yesterday evening I received your esteemed letter, and later your telegram. This morning I sent both to the Holy Father, who, however, had previously received another telegram on the same subject,[104] and notwithstanding this he expressed great satisfaction at the confirmation mine brought him. He had words of praise for Bishop Bonomelli's noble act, which was truly worthy of a bishop. He was also pleased at the part you have played in all this. This morning the College of Cardinals will meet with the Holy Father and His holiness will circulate the telegram privately so that their

Eminences will take note of it."[105]

A few days later, a reporter for the *Corriere della Sera* badgered Bonomelli for an interview and received a short reply: "I am a soldier of the Pope, and when he commands I obey and will always obey." On these exact words the reporter stitched a long "interview" which made it appear that Bonomelli had submitted for political reasons. Rome turned up its nose and Cardinal Schiaffino wrote to Piacenza saying that a clarification was desired from the Bishop of Cremona. Scalabrini defended Bonomelli's good faith, which was evidenced by the fact that he did his best "to stop the distribution and prevent further editions of his unfortunate pamphlet" and had in fact succeeded in withdrawing many copies from sale. He did not consider it opportune for the Bishop of Cremona to make another declaration after the solemn and explicit Brief he had received from the Pope,[106] and he added:

"Nevertheless, since you desire it I shall write today to our mutual friend to encourage him to do what you suggest. He is in a state of great physical and psychological exhaustion and I, too, will have to use a great deal of tact."[107]

Bonomelli, after the first few days of tension, had in fact been prostrated. Without mentioning the Cardinal's letter, Scalabrini gently advised him to publish the Brief, communicating it to the people of his diocese with a few lines of explanation which he (Scalabrini) himself suggested; he added words of comfort and urged him to be patient.[108] Bonomelli assured him that he was not pessimistic nor desperate about the situation but that he was depressed and suffered greatly at the turn for the worse which things had taken:

"It tears at the soul. People are plunging into unbelief; and are being lost by the thousands and not a thought is even given to this! The temporal power is everything, and all the rest, the souls of the faithful are nothing...Sects flourish, partisan conflicts are refueled. My heart is heavy and I dream of a cell in the desert where I could not see so many evils. God alone can save us. Write to me..."[109]

It is in this context that we must consider a letter of Scalabrini's which evoked a certain criticism. Instead it is to be read as a brotherly expression of comfort, based on convictions which in no way prejudice his obedience and devotion to the Holy See, but do reveal certain intuitions about the future:

"So you have certain ideas about becoming a friar...I know very well that you do not mean them! A cell in Egypt indeed! Let those who are the cause of so much desolation go and bury themselves there[110] not a Bishop like you who has spoken, written and done so much to prevent it. Come, come! God has set you on the battlefield and you must stay there, even though enemy bullets rain down from every side. You are gloriously wounded. After all, ideas move forward. They are ideas of truth, charity and peace. Draw back and let them march forward. They cannot fail to conquer and you will be able to say that you opened the way for them."[111]

Reconciliation, An Apostolic Exigency

Given the futility of all efforts to change the course of events, Scalabrini dedicated himself completely to work "with facts," as he preferred, for the reconciliation between Religion and Country, the two ideals with, in a synthesis of Christian charity, inspired his work for the emigrants: "a practical means," he stated in 1888, "a beginning of that calming of consciences which is one of my most ardent desires."[112]

Scalabrini had no pretensions about influencing the Pope's conduct nor did he substitute his own judgment for that of the Holy See in matters that belonged to its competence, thereby prejudicing its freedom and this is abundantly clear from the proposals he made to the Holy Father. After all, if it is true, as Giuseppe dalla Torre maintains,[113] the intransigents' decision to abstain from political life at first and their later decision to enter it preceded and therefore prompted the Vatican directives. Scalabrini, who had suggested this latter attitude several years before cannot be suspected of disobedience or scant respect for the Holy See.

Recent historians now argue that the question is not one of doctrines and principles, but concerns the timing of the two groups into which, generally speaking, the Catholics were divided, too few of them, unfortunately, taking any interest in these problems. From the point of view of good timing and the good consequences hoped for, we know that the Catholic deputies of Giolitti's time carried practically no political weight, so that Don Sturzo seems to have been the only one who was not seduced by the "moderationism" of that liberal statesman. We would perhaps be tempted to wonder whether for many years, in times not yet ripe according to the prevailing view, it had not been Scalabrini's idea that Catholics should enter political life while the battle was raging, with a clear stance repudiating dogmatic liberalism, opposing any more or less legal attempt whatever to "de-Christianize" the people, and moving toward a gradual solution of the Roman question. In his view, such a solution would have achieved in the Italian mind the separation of the cause of religion from the political cause of Italian unity, and would thus have cleared the anticlerical prejudices from the field for the apostolate.

He spoke of collaboration in view of what he called "conservation," by which he did not mean political or social conservationism, but preservation of the religious and social order which was threatened by socialism: "the rebel against the laws of the State," as he called the socialist, "is always and more fiercely so against those of the Church."[114] We have no direct evidence of how he measured the danger of social conservationism, which was feared as a consequence of the abolition of the *non expedit*.[115] His thinking is indirectly revealed, however, in his social action, which, as we have seen, was one of the most open and complete of the time and was also one of the most free, in a Christian sense, vis-à-vis the liberal State, as evidenced by his works for emigrants.

Certain current judgments should be re-examined, therefore, but this involves an evaluation more or less of the political wisdom and foresighted intelligence of the man. We are interested rather in the fact that we do not find in him any inclination to reform the ecclesiastical structures on the basis of ideological assumptions, which at that time were called "Rosminian." His desire and action to achieve Conciliation were inspired only by the need — for him undeferable — to respond to concrete religious necessities: the salvation of souls. It is his only motive. We have seen it repeated innumerable times both in his pastoral and his private writings, in his letters to the Pope and to his friends, in his homilies and in his conversations.

We also believe it is not necessary to go digging deeply for theoretical or ideological assumptions at the basis of Scalabrini's activities. Apostolic concern and his realism as a man of action inclined him inevitably, given his character, to conciliationism. People were being alienated from the Church in increasing numbers, because, among other things, only the anticlericals were allowed to act. While the Catholics protested, the others "did" and they were "doing" in an Italy that was liberal in the worst sense of the word and anticlerical. The consequences have lasted to the present time. Italy cannot be considered a Catholic nation and one reason, certainly not the last, recalls the prophecy of the Bishop of Piacenza: "if we continue with this legislation which is hostile to the Church, we shall be extremely fortunate if there is anything good left on which to rebuild."[116]

After 1887, when he founded the Missionaries for the emigrants, he naturally continued to foster the desire for Conciliation, keeping the hope for it alive and expressing his wish, publicly as well, that the great dream would come true. There are innumerable references to Conciliation in his writings and lectures on emigration where they take on a particular significance. The first of these, for example, seems to sum up the hope expressed in all the others:

"May these humble words of mine be the seed of wonderful works that will resound to the glory of God and of his Church, the good of souls, the honor of our country, and the relief of the unfortunate and the disinherited. May Italy, sincerely reconciled with the Apostolic See, emulate her ancient glories and achieve another lasting one by setting her far-off sons on the bright paths of true civilization and true progress."[117]

And the last:

"Religion and Country! Gentlemen let us all unite around this sublime ideal which, in the work to protect our emigrants, takes on shape and form, we might say, and we shall be able to hope for better days for our Italy, we shall be able to hope that in the not too distant future God's plans for her may be realized."[118]

It might be well to underline that these public appeals for Conciliation and for cooperation between Church and State had the full approval of the Pope even after 1887:

"I had occasion to approach several highly placed persons in ecclesiastical Rome and in all of them I found an unexpected moderation in language and a more lively desire than ever for concord and peace. And, yes, Crispi was still in office. If I am not mistaken, it would seem they are beginning to understand the realities. Let us hope. Two signs that confirm me in this idea are the following: when the Pope expressed the wish that I give a lecture on emigration in Rome, I pointed out that I would necessarily have to speak about our country, about love of country, of Italy, etc., and that in fact I expressed the hope that Italy would be reconciled with the Holy See and that therefore...'But yes, but yes,' the Pope interrupted, 'everywhere but especially in Rome these things must be said.' However, since I remembered the episode of Father Agostino, I wanted more assurance and I read the strongest passages to the Pope, who approved them almost with enthusiasm..."[119]

Given the difficulties that blocked the way to the realization of the dream, it is easy to understand now that Scalabrini's attitude was neither naive nor stubborn opposition to the wishes of the Holy Father. On the contrary it accorded much more concretely than many others with the apostolic desires of the Pope:

"And Conciliation? It seems to be moving forward slowly, slowly, but as inexorable as fate, and then? He who was wrong will be right. So be it. So be it."[120]

It would be unfair to his contemporaries, and especially to the priests and laity who knew him best, if we did not mention that almost all of them understood and admired in him that deep and sincere integration of love of religion and love of country, which involved no surrender on principle and no effect on his feelings and duties as an obedient and affectionate son of the Church. The following are answers of witnesses to the fortieth question on the Promoter of the Faith in the preliminary or informative process: "Did the Servant of God love his country? And with what kind of love? Can the witness tell whether the Servant of God was accused of liberalism by anyone because of a mistaken and exaggerated love of country?"

"The Servant of God had a great love for his country, but it was the kind of love that desires the true good of the nation, not only in the material sense but more especially in the spiritual and moral sense. The dissension between the Church and the State was a source of great sorrow to him and he looked forward to its end whenever the subject arose, not only (when he was speaking) with simple peasant folk but also with eminent personalities, as for example at the dinner at Cardinal Agliardi's...When the conversation turned on the Roman Question and the Minister expressed the view that the Pope should make the first proposals for peace, the Servant of God did not hesitate to point out to him that it was up to the sons to present themselves to the Father, whom they had offended and despoiled."[121]

"The Servant of God greatly loved his country, but with a holy love, and the reconciliation between the State and the Church, without prejudice to the rights of the latter, was always uppermost in his thoughts, because he saw in such an accord a great advantage for both of them, although he was well aware that his statements in this regard were given a sinister interpretation by various elements, among whom there were also several priests held in no little esteem, almost as leaders of a party."[122]

"Certainly he loved his country, and how very much! But it was a love motivated by charity, which sought the true good for it...The charge of liberalism against the Servant of God was occasioned particularly by his relations with the authorities and many dignitaries: but his purpose was to win them over and turn these relationships to the good of the Church."[123]

"There is no doubt that the Servant of God loved his country. It is also true that at that time whoever loved the Country seemed to be failing the rights of the Church and of religion. It was the intransigents who considered it essential to restore Rome to the Pope in order to solve the Roman question. And among them was a certain Father Costa, pastor of Vigolo Val Nure. In an audience with the Bishop, when this subject came up, he saw the latter become serious and say: 'I know that I have come into a land of dreamers.' "[124]

All witnesses affirmed the rectitude and religious sentiment of his love of country. Some give a clear enough picture of the times with respect to the "matter of conscience" for Catholics of the last century. Others furnish small details that add color to the difficulties of the time, for example, those who give a certain importance to the funeral services ordered by the Bishop for those killed at Dogali, or the indulgence granted the prayer composed by Father Semeria for the Italian soldiers who were leaving for China, or the prayers and good wishes for the soldiers being sent to Ethiopia: all of them "strange and unusual things" in those years...[125]

Cardinal Nasalli Rocca recalls the Bishop's opposition to the stone commemorating the plebiscite in Piacenza which the civic authorities wanted to insert in the wall of the chapel of St. Francis, "stating that he could not give his approval to recording purely political facts on sacred edifices."[126] We might also note that unlike many other bishops, who were considered "intransigent," Scalabrini never went to pay his respects to the king, who passed through Piacenza several times,[127] out of scrupulous fidelity to the directives of the Holy See, nor did he ever permit himself any "benign" interpretations of the latter. Thus he also always refused the honors the Italian Government wished to confer on him for his work on behalf of deaf mutes and the emigrants,[128] and he kept his brother Angelo, as noted earlier, from presenting his candidacy at the elections.[129]

Lastly we might note Scalabrini's attitude toward the action brought by Abbot Stoppani against the *Osservatore Cattolico* in 1887.

The Abbot's lawyers declared they could not do without the testimony of Bonomelli and Scalabrini, but at the same time Stoppani himself made it clear that the Bishops could argue that it was impossible for them to appear in a civil court. His lawyers wanted to request a hearing at home, and in case the court did not grant this they said they would renounce having the testimony of the two bishops.[130] Scalabrini — as well as Bonomelli — immediately answered that the abbot should give up "absolutely" the idea of a hearing in domicile.[131] Two weeks later both received a letter from the Cardinal Secretary of State: the Holy Father had learned with displeasure that they had been subpoenaed as witnesses in a civil trial and he did not intend to give them permission to appear in court.[132]

This time Scalabrini answered in no uncertain terms. After repeating that he deplored, and had said so many times, Stoppani's action in having recourse to a civil court, he noted that he had received the subpoena several days before. Elementary prudence and knowledge of canon law — "which one cannot fail to assume a Bishop possesses without seriously offending him" — would have prompted him to notify the Holy See immediately if he had not already decided to reject it. Therefore "it was perfectly useless to write me that the Holy Father does not give me permission to appear in civil court. A bishop, who is neither a child nor an imbecile, asks for the faculties that are necessary to him, and he is always pained by a negative response to things he has not asked for."[133]

Evidently the new Secretary of State, Cardinal Rampolla, had been misinformed. Bishop Scalabrini was surprised that who ever had hurried to advise the Holy See of the subpoena did not at the same time inform it of his immediate flat refusal to appear. He considered the whole matter a maneuver of the defendants. A man who hated maneuvering as much as he did could not tolerate especially that such dealing be brought to the Vicar of Christ: "It has seemed most important to me to bring the truth about this dispute directly to the Holy Father, knowing that this is an attempt to keep him completely in the dark about anything that could prejudice the case of those gentlemen."[134]

CHAPTER XVIII

Integrity, Love, Obedience

Consequences of a Concept of the Episcopacy

The Stoppani episode, although something of an extreme example, underlines Scalabrini's characteristic attitude in his role as intermediary or bridge between the Pope and the faithful. Frankness, sincerity, fidelity to the truth, whatever the circumstances, not only flowed logically from his own forthright nature, but were also the consequence of a precise concept of the episcopal ministry and an authentic love of the Church and of the Supreme Pontiff.

In his pastoral *Cattolici di nome e cattolici di fatto*, ("Catholics in name and Catholics in fact") he repudiates the liberals who call themselves Catholic although they do not obey the Church, and he groups with them the "liberals of new mintage" whom he rebukes thus:

"It is anything but a true Catholic spirit when such persons meltingly protest their attachment to the Pope and at the same time dare to be wanting in the respect due to the Bishops united to Him, opposing their rule at least indirectly or distorting their acts and intentions; identifying themselves, so to speak, with the Holy See..."[1]

This type of conduct, Scalabrini considers to be subversive of the divine institution of the episcopacy and the hierarchical order:

"What then? Will it no longer be licit for a Bishop to speak or write as his conscience, his right, and, more than his right, his duty command him without having persons, despite several warnings, try to oppose him?...Will the Bishop, placed by the Holy Spirit to govern the Church of God, called upon to share in the pastoral care of all the churches, be unable to set forth his views in all candor to our common Father concerning the dangers threatening men's souls without hearing himself called the cause of ruination and scandal?...Have they become so arrogant as to condemn actions with which the Supreme Pontiff was pleased? Have they become so presumptuous as to condemn, even if in veiled terms, what he asserts is *fully in conformity with his wishes?* Good God! What have we come to? And where are we heading with such a system? Alas, we say with a holy Father, alas for the Church when the Bishops are forced to keep silent!"[2]

To understand this discourse better, we must go back to his pastoral of October 15, 1885, *Sull'Opuscolo "Lettera dell'E. mo Card. Pitra. I commenti. La parola del Papa,"* that had aroused so much interest. In this, after quoting several passages from Leo XIII's letter to the Archbishop of Paris, Scalabrini adds:

"Remember that in the Church of Jesus Christ every extra-hierarchical mission was excluded...; that no one can set himself up as a teacher in the school of Jesus Christ except those who were placed there by the Holy Spirit...Let no one among you, dearly Beloved, allow himself to be caught in the unfortunate illusion, which penetrates and misleads some minds today, even though they are neither wicked nor ungenerous, namely, the belief that anyone can be truly united with the Pope when he breaks the divinely established and necessary bond of the hierarchical order, when he is not united in obedience, respect and charity with his own Bishop and with him and through him to the Pope; of when, under the banner of zeal and an exaggerated devotion to the Pope, he fails in the obedience and respect due his Bishop, and on the basis of his own arbitrary views, makes a judgment as to whether or not he (the Bishop) is being faithful to the papal directives. Without doubt this would be preempting the judgment of the Apostolic See, an attack on the divine constitution of the Church, a step in the direction of the most subtle and pernicious liberalism. The faithful united to their pastor, the faithful and their pastor united with their Bishop, the faithful, their pastor, and their Bishop united with the Pope who is the center of this union — this is what is truly Catholic."[3]

We must remember that this pastoral was written according to the outline and notes sent him by the Cardinal Secretary of State, who, in fact, had shown the manuscript to the Holy Father. The latter had made two observations, the second relates to "the final part, which the Holy Father would like to be more concise and therefore more telling." The Cardinal Secretary of State had also assured the author, when the pastoral was published, that the Pope had found it to be "a perfectly fine work and in accordance with his views" and had requested fifty copies.[4]

In complete accordance with the views of the Pope, therefore, must be the conclusion:

"To consider the Church as an inorganic mass that must be stimulated by an omnipotent hand, with no one able to enlighten her nor submit to her his humble and pious reflections, is the greatest harm that one can do her."[5] He then repeats a thought already set forth in the *Conferenze sul Concilio Vaticano*: the Pope is infallible, but he is also obliged to act with prudence and to take into account the advice of experts: "Infallibility has two distinct parts, the *divine part*, which is the *inspiration*...the *human part*, which includes the scientific elements and necessary research in relation to Tradition and the Scriptures, as well as the most suitable way to make known the truth to the people."[6]

In fact, the infallibility of the Pope is not something apart from the infallibility of the Church, "as if his faith were separate from the faith of the Church." The situation cannot arise in which the Pope is on one side and the Bishops on the other in the case of two irreconcilable doctrinal positions, because in a living body the head cannot be separated from the other members.[7]

The candid attitude of the Bishop of Piacenza toward the Vicar of Christ is based on these theological principles, on a spirit of obedience free of hypocrisy, on a love nourished by deeds, and on a clear conscience. There were some who, with the best of intentions and though worthy of respect for their many qualities, did not understand Bishop Scalabrini and caused him a great deal of suffering because of his stance vis-à-vis the Pope. At this distance in time we can now clearly discern, not their intentions, but the different levels on which they moved. His frank, plain speaking might have scandalized those who had different political views but can ony elicit admiration and approval in those who have a truly sacred and authentically Christian concept of the Pope and the Church, such as that held by Scalabrini.

In the pastoral inspired by the Vatican, which Leo XIII judged to be "fully in accordance with his views," he had repeated the cry, "Alas for the Church when the hierarchy is constrained to keep silent!"[8] And he acted accordingly, deeply convinced that a Bishop fails in his duty when he does not exercise his right to speak plainly to the Pope.

"We are too outgoing and sincere," he thought, "that is very true, but I do not think this is bad. There is also a time to speak and I think it has come, when and where, of course, one can speak and considers it opportune, since the silence of the entire hierarchy has been of powerful assistance to the increasing boldness of the liberals."[9] — "I follow my own road, deeply convinced that the faithful and obedient Bishops are not those, who out of some misguided respect, foster certain deceptions and perhaps make use of them, but those, and they are few, who sacrifice their peace, their future and their all, in order that the Holy Father may be aware of the deception and that the Church may be free from the disastrous consequences of the errors."[10] — "It is a duty of our ministry to let the Pope know the true state of things in order that we may save what we can."[11]

We may conclude that the candor of this Bishop, who failed none of his responsibilities, was the most difficult, dangerous and therefore the most trying manifestation of an unqualified devotion to the Vicar of Christ and the Church.

The Signs of the Times in the Light of the Gospel

We have been considering a simple provincial Bishop in his encounter with three great Popes, and particularly one of great stature, Leo XIII. There might be some uneasiness about the direct confrontation that often took place between the two.

Scalabrini's love for the Pope and the Church, his fidelity to doctrinal and moral principles are above question, even when it came to heroic renunciation and to silences stronger than words and deeds. Some might not like all the positions he took vis-à-vis the Holy See. They might consider his frank speech lacking in respect, his protests against specific administrative systems as something less than perfect obedience; his insistence on a more rapid solution of the "political" problems, which were rapidly becoming very serious spiritual and pastoral problems as well, may have seemed to some a pretext to impose his ideas on the Pope. And then, how must we answer another question: how did it happen that there were so few bishops who thought as Scalabrini did or at least showed publicly that they shared his views?

A fair evaluation of a person who has been above all a man of action because of his apostolic vocation cannot fail to take into consideration the historical context in which he lived. The last part of the 19th century was such a confusing and difficult period for those who lived with the complex, emotionally charged problems and heated polemics, that not even the Holy See was able to make a clear straight choice of the means best suited to carry out the directive — which was definite and constant — to safeguard its rights vis-à-vis the State, which had achieved its unity with juridically unacceptable means and was trying to justify itself with an ideology that was more sectarian than liberal.

Scalabrini always kept the controversial questions on the "level of fact": the solutions he proposed looked to the Conciliation between Church and State. Catholic participation in politics was a means of slow preparation for the Conciliation.[12] The decision as to "how much civil princedom" was necessary to guarantee his sovereignty and therefore the complete liberty of the head of the Church was to be made by the Pope alone. It was up to the Italian State, therefore, the party in the wrong, "to take the first step" and to ask for "pardon and help." It was impossible to return to the "status quo" and at the same time it was realistically possible to renounce, without harm, those claims that would compromise the unity of the new State. These were the solutions Scalabrini championed and were precisely those gradually adopted by Pius X, Benedict XV and Pius XI.

Now if we believe that history is the living relationship between the past and the present, we cannot but admire the men who suffered and labored, often in danger and struggling against the tide, to prepare a better present. They acted and suffered, in the last analysis, for the truth discovered in the present.

History tells us that Bishop Scalabrini was right on many counts, and Vatican II underlines this. For example, he propounded a broader and pre-eminently pastoral view of the problems of the Church and foresaw a more spiritual conception of the Church even in relation to temporal values, and a prestige deriving solely from "moral force." He maintained the necessity of giving absolute priority to the good of souls, mindful that everything else is merely a means to be adopted according to whether it is necessary or useful to that end. He urged greater unity between the Pope and the Bishops, with respect both to the more spiritual conception and the moral prestige noted above and he himself sought this unity through those "things which unite and not those which divide." He promoted greater intellectual freedom and believed in a discipline that sprang from a deep sense of the Church, not one fragmented in juridical minutiae.

On other more "political" matters, many historians do not agree with Scalabrini's ideas. With respect to the "Catholic movement" we have already noted the "fundamental ambiguity in an organization which on the one hand carried on 'Catholic action' and on the other took on the functions of a Catholic party...When, for example, Catholic militants were counseled not to break the unity of the Catholic forces in order to promote particular political opinions, there was the danger of imposing a unanimity of political thought on the basis of religion. Then when Catholic action was required to be absolutely obedient to the Bishops and all other ecclesiastical authorities, a standard of conduct proper to religious societies was imposed on an organism that was also political."[13]

Pius IX and Leo XIII, as we have seen, strengthened the central authority of the Church. Contributing to this was the fact that the Vatican Council was able to discuss and approve only the eleventh chapter of the schema *De Ecclesia Christi*, which dealt with the primacy of the Roman Pontiff. The interruption of the Council prevented the discussion of the other fourteen chapters. Therefore the pronouncement on the immediate and universal jurisdiction of the Pope was not completed by the pronouncement on the divine rights of the bishops, which had already been discussed in the ecclesiology of the time.

By coincidence another important influence was provided by the emergence of the laity, which was called upon to make common cause with the Pope for the defense of the rights of the papacy. Its organization required a unitary, supradiocesan direction, and this contributed another element toward centralization, in order to avoid the dangers exemplified in the actions of the anti-Roman bishops who leaned toward the separatist policies of their respective governments.[14] These realities seemed to put the authority of the bishops in second place and to inaugurate an era of "bishops in top hats," namely, laymen, and even priests without a specific mandate from their bishops who, because of the above mentioned ambiguity, began to take over "the direction of consciences" from the Bishops, as Scalabrini noted.

There is always a conflict of rights at similar times of structural transition. Only time eventually clarifies the distinction between the new graft and the old stem. In the beginning it is not hard to confuse ancient principles, which are immutable, with the structures in need of renewal. Nor is there immediate comprehension of which new principles have the right of citizenship in the Church, in the name of the vital progress of the "people of God," and which undermine the divine constitution of the Church.

At such times, we do not admire the foresighted so much as those who have remained faithful to their mission. For Scalabrini it was an inescapable duty of conscience to conduct his episcopal functions as ecclesial responsibilities, namely, with a sense of "corresponsibility" with the Pope. If he insisted on the "divine strength" of the episcopacy, it was not with a mistaken sense of autonomy. On the contrary he was concerned to safeguard hierarchical unity, which in its turn is inseparable from the community of grace. We repeatedly meet in his writings the name of St. Ignatius Martyr, whose thinking is summed up in the phrase: "Every bishop composes the unity of his flock."[15]

We know that many Fathers of the first Vatican Council were opposed to the concept (of corresponsibility) and as a consequence little attention was paid to Leo XIII's reminders of the true and proper mystical unity of the Church. And so we consider it possible to speak of foresightedness in

Scalabrini's case, in view of his insistence on the essence of the Church, the Mystical Body, as opposed to 19th century individualism and the incipient manifestations of a false collectivism, just as he constantly stressed the need for unity and a fullness of life within the Church. There was too much said about the defense of rights and too little about the duty of the individual to make continual progress in the conquest of the truth. There was too much apologetics and too little theology (how much the Apostle of the catechism contributed to transforming it from apologetics to theology!). The zealous Catholic was too often mistaken for a complete Christian.

Bishop Scalabrini believed in the Church. For this reason it never entered his head to debase it as an instrument for human or political ends. Faith and the zeal for souls were the bases on which he made his judgments and the motives for his actions. He feared sins of omission. St. Paul's *opportune importune*, which he quoted frequently, encouraged him to be fearless even at the risk of displeasing some and of being misunderstood by others. He did not feel bound to an epoch, which was ended in any case, whatever its many merits had been. But he did feel part of the process of transformation his time was experiencing, and he neither avoided its problems nor fought shy of new ideas and initiatives. He did not run from battle because he lived and believed in the Church, in the fertility of its faith. He did not reject what he believed to be his vocation nor did he consider that any risk dispensed him from taking action he deemed necessary and undeferable while at the same time he forced himself to "remain perfectly serene with regard to all that happens through divine disposition, not only where oneself is concerned but also with respect to the Church, working on her behalf according to the divine command."[16] His unwavering faith and his attachment to hierarchical tradition produced no bitterness, scorn or aridity in him. He reproved certain *a priori* "intransigents" for identifying the Church with themselves, for with him it was a case of identifying himself with the Church.[17]

Some have criticized Scalabrini for impetuousness and impatience. These are common faults of those ahead of their time. They are to be judged as precursors. Historically we cannot view them apart from today's realities, which were not suddenly produced through spontaneous generation but were born from yesterday's long travail.

"It is the law of the philosophy of history," Scalabrini himself wrote, "that great events..., as they are effects of other events which preceded them, are also causative in relation to the events which follow them. Therefore this chain of causes and effects represents the principle of causality in the historical order. Providence has ordained and directs the threads of this chain to its own ends. From this it follows that to be presumptuous enough to destroy great contemporary realities, which are but the consequence of those which preceded them, and to try to destroy them either through *a dolce far niente*, or through a systematic *a priori* opposition is hardly rational to say the least...For if on the contrary, taking into account what the times have brought about, one distinguishes between good and evil and one tries to lead mankind back to the laws of morality and justice with those arguments which converted the world at another time, then one can hope that the events, having entered the domain of history, will be purged of the dross that covers them and will be directed to the true good of the human race."[18]

This was the rod with which he measured his present time, and it is this same measure which should be used in judging him. He was a Pastor who examined the signs of the times, who was all the more admirable for being so solitary, who was one of the few with vision and acted accordingly, without hesitation over the cost to himself personally.

He fulfilled in fact the duty the Church has always had "of scrutinizing the signs of the times and of interpreting them in the light of the Gospel *("those arguments which converted the world at another time")*. Thus, in language intelligible to each generation she can respond to the perennial questions which men ask about this present life and life to come, and about the relationship of the one to the other *(the "case of conscience" of the Catholics of his time, viewed by the Servant of God solely as the "fever of souls")*. We must therefore recognize and understand the world in which we live *(this is the realistic view of the times which was characteristic of Scalabrini)*, its expectations, its longings and its often dramatic characteristics."[19]

It is in this context that we must view his pastoral achievements, in his diocese and beyond it in the Church: the catechism, his apostolate to the workers, and his apostolate to the emigrants.

He was a child of his time, with its limitations, but also a precursor of our time, because he was an authentic son of the pilgrim Church always in step with the "destined progress of society, preordained on a principle of unlimited Christian perfectibility."[20]

CHAPTER XIX

A Life of Faith

"Make Me Holy!"

The Biblical Jacob's ladder figured in Scalabrini's episcopal coat-of arms. A play on the meaning of "scala" or ladder (in his name), it was a symbol of the reaching upward of a heart that yearned for God and of a life that was, in fact, a continuous ascent.

For a Bishop who possessed such a profound sense of the dignity of the priesthood and of the office of bishop, the need to strive for holiness was logical. If he considered holiness inseparable from being a Christian, so much the more did he consider it inseparable from the priesthood. If the vocation to faith, he used to say, means a vocation to holiness, so much the more must the priest be holy, for he is called not only to personal holiness as every Christian is, but also to the duty of sanctifying others. Christ must be brought to the faithful not only through the sacramental administration of grace, but also through a living model of holiness which is, in turn, an imitation of Christ. Sharing the priesthood of Christ is not limited to its ministerial aspects. It must also represent the holiness of the Redeemer.[1]

Since he was a practical man, Scalabrini's concepts of holiness were clear and simple. He often exhorted both priests and faithful not to be led astray or to be discouraged by vague or mistaken conceptions of holiness:

"He is holy who firmly believes all the truths of the faith, who places all his hope in God, and who loves Him above all things else." Holiness "consists in keeping the commandments of God and of the Church, and in faithfully fulfilling the duties of one's state in life."[2] — "It was not some extraordinary gifts that shaped the most illustrious Saints, or rather the only Saints recognized by the Church...; it was the faithfulness, the vigilance, the precision with which they constantly fulfilled the duties of their state, and they fulfilled them in the sight of God. This is the true, the essential character of holiness."[3]

He unceasingly urged his clergy to strive for perfection. He is perfect, he told them, who does not commit grave sins and tries to avoid even venial sin; it is he who runs untiringly along the path of virtue. He outlined three means to achieve holiness: an ardent desire, a true hunger and thirst for perfection; the perfect fulfillment of the duties of one's vocation; the constant attempt to imitate Christ every day.[4]

This is precisely the same simple outline of Bishop Scalabrini's own ascetics: hunger and thirst for justice, a constant yearning for perfection; a fidelity to his pastoral duties, which was defined as heroic both by the unanimous testimony of the witnesses at the diocesan informative process and by the testimony of his entire apostolic life; and imitation of the Crucified Christ.

The sincerity of this desire was matched by the intensity of his efforts. He constantly repeated to himself the admonition: *tantum proficies, quantum tibi ipsi vim intuleris.*[5]

"In all his actions the Bishop must be moved by the Holy Spirit, the secret mover of the most holy humanity of Jesus Christ. He must do violence to himself to achieve holiness."[6]

"Remember always that the bishop must be virgin, confessor and martyr. Virgin in the purity of his life; confessor in patience; martyr in zeal and charity. A formidable burden — necessary sufferings — powerful graces."[7]

"*Deus honor omnium dignitatum* — and especially of the episcopal office. And I must take account of this by uplifting myself, by ennobling and purifying myself, by seeking to partake of the divine. *Episcopus est homo Dei et post Deum terrenus Deus.* It is necessary to be serious, irreproachable, modest, firm, gentle, strong, great and noble in all things."[8]

Mention must be made here of his constant effort to imitate Christ and to identify with the Crucified Christ:

"All our thoughts, all our words, all our actions, all our desires, all our inclinations, all our sufferings must be so many strokes of the pen that shape and express in us some aspect of the life of Jesus Christ, in order to make us, so to speak, so many copies of him. This will come about...when we judge all things as Jesus Christ had judged them; when we love all that He loved...; when in our hearts we have the same sentiments and dispositions which He had in His heart."[9]

"It is not enough therefore to do good, to be upright..., to struggle and suffer in any way whatever...It is absolutely necessary to do all this with one's eye on God; with one's intentions focused on Jesus Christ, with the submission, with the love and with the spirit of Jesus Christ. Jesus Christ must be the beginning and the end of all our activities, the soul of our soul, the life of our life."[10]

"Without the light that radiates from Him, all is darkness and mist; without His work, the order of nature and of grace, man and the world, the past and the future are a book sealed with seven seals."[11]

"A coin must bear the image of the Sovereign, otherwise it is valueless and cannot be used; and the works of the Christian must bear the imprint of Jesus Christ, for otherwise they have no value in securing Heaven, while nothing is pleasing to His Eternal Father if it does not bear the image of His Son and does not in a certain way reflect His character."[12]

"The sacrifice of Jesus Christ and our sacrifice are two equally necessary sacrifices; they are two sacrifices that do not placate Divine Justice if they are not inseparably joined together; Our sacrifice, if unaccompanied by the sacrifice of Christ, is unworthy of God. The sacrifice of Christ, unaccompanied by our sacrifice, is useless to us."[13]

Holiness is "purity consecrated to God in sacrifice."[14]

Imitation of Christ Crucified

The imitation of the Crucified Christ seems to have been the pivot of Scalabrini's asceticism, the basis of that *"fac me cruce inebriari"* which we find written on every page of his life.

"Fac me cruce inebriari! God educates us through tribulations, through humiliations, through sufferings, through the irritations of the ministry, of the audiences. He protects us, He enlightens us, He makes us great. Therefore love the crosses, the cross. Love it; unite it to the sufferings of Jesus Christ. Hold the pectoral cross close to your breast and repeat often, *fac me cruce inebriari!*"[15]

"God has been particularly good to me; how many extraordinary graces he has given me for my sanctification, how many crosses! The crosses were inseparable from God's designs...And I have never gone lacking for them!...But God be blessed! *Te Deum laudamus!* I sang this a little while ago in the cathedral. Thanks be to God, and courage in the Cross of Jesus Christ Our Lord."[16]

"Consider the crosses, the tribulations, the humiliations, the scorn one receives as precious means for sanctification. I must not complain, not be sad, not discouraged: I must offer all things in union with the sufferings of Jesus Christ. *Fac me cruce inebriari!...*"[17]

As if the crosses and privations arising from his pastoral ministry were not enough, Bishop Scalabrini never failed to impose other penances and physical mortifications on himself. He often used flagellation and the hairshirt.[18]

Members of his household stated that he was scrupulous in his observance of the prescribed abstinences and fasts, and in fact was sometimes more rigid in this respect than the obligation itself.[19]

"When someone objected that strict abstinence was troublesome he used to exclaim: 'If oil makes you sick, skip the meal!' And that is what he did himself, taking nothing more than a little chocolate even when there were several days of strict abstinence in succession."[20] His servant recounted that on one Good Friday he had taken nothing but a slice of polenta.[21] Another example of his strict observance of the laws of fast and abstinence took place on his return from Brazil. His brother Angelo gave a reception in his honor, in Rome, to which many distinguished personalities were invited. Among those present were the Minister Carcano, the undersecretary Fusinato and the newspaperman Belcredi. As soon as he entered the room, the Bishop saw that the meal prepared did not observe the Friday abstinence. He calmly dispensed all the guests from the Church precept, but said he did not feel dispensed himself. And no matter what they said or did, pointing out the rigors of the journey he had just completed and his delicate health, he remained unmoved. "I am a Bishop," he answered, and took only two eggs and a little milk. Nevertheless his action occasioned no embarrassment among the guests. He was a jovial table companion and all admired his firmness and his spirit of sacrifice.[22] He used alcoholic beverages very sparingly[23] and in fact preferred to drink milk. If he was offered a bottle of wine, he drank barely an ounce or two.[24] One day when he went to return a visit of Count Radini-Tedeschi, he was served from a bottle of old wine. The butler had not taken the precaution of tasting it first. Instead of being a precious wine, it was pure vinegar, but the Bishop sipped through the whole glass, keeping up the conversation meanwhile, and giving no sign of the unpleasant taste.[25]

He was always extremely frugal and never ate more than was necessary.[26] He never ate between meals, and even in America, despite whatever inconvenience this caused him, he always ate what was being served.[27]

Nevertheless he always said that the "priest's hairshirt must consist above all in the exact fulfillment of every one of his duties and in resigned acceptance of the many crosses and great sacrifices encountered in the ministry."[28] He never wanted for lack of understanding, or physical and mental sufferings. These at certain times assumed in fact such seriousness as to frighten less stalwart souls. But he was prepared for them. In the intimacy of his daily meditation, his life was a constant encounter with Christ, and from Him he learned to endure his own cross with patience.

In letters to friends in trouble of one kind or another, he always mentions Christian patience. To a priest who was ill he wrote:

"I should like to see you healthy, happy and content. But the Lord guides us through ways that are mysterious but secure, and to those who follow the ways of Providence with humble simplicity *omnia cooperantur in bonum.* Let this illness and the internal and external crosses be a powerful means of sanctification, for a true follower and still more a minister of Jesus Christ cannot and must not be without them."[29]

To still another he wrote, "I am deeply sorry to learn of the illness affecting your eyes and wish I had the gift of miracles to work just one for you. But knowing how to do the will of God as you do is a much more precious treasure than one's sight."[30]

Even in a letter to a Cardinal, who was his friend, we find the same exhortation to faith in God and Christian patience:

"Providence is leading Your Eminence along uncommon and almost incredible paths, and this is a cause of joy for your true friends and should be for you also. Reason and faith teach us, and we sense this in our intimate souls, that all that happens is willed or permitted by God, who is Infinite Love, and that sometimes, through the gentle designs of his mercy, He permits his servants to be humbled but not confounded, and they must meditate with joy on the divine depositions, and always thank Him and accept with joy every tribulation. Even our inner sufferings cast a salutary bitterness over the present life, detach us imperceptibly from all that is mortal and bring us the inestimable gift of recognizing the nothingness of greatness, and there is no finer grace than this. But the eternal wisdom of God, Your Eminence, has truly arranged all things with firmness and gentleness, and if for a time He gives us a chalice of bitterness to drink, He then offers us the cup of the greatest joys. It is a mysterious chalice, whose contents alternate, and blessed is he who can bring it to his lips with unshakeable fidelity, in intimate union with God."[31]

"The hour of suffering came also to Bishop Scalabrini," his successor, Bishop Pellizzari said, "and he endured it with a resignation truly worthy of a holy Bishop and with that generosity in forgiving which is characteristic of great souls...And you saw him in those days of grief drag himself to the altar and there offer the twofold sacrifice of the Divine Victim and of his own heart."[32]

In 1884, when the local Freemasons attacked him furiously, he wrote:

"This year the Lord has deigned to visit me with physical pains and moral anxieties. May His holy will be done in all and for all! What was written in the *Piccolo* — the local Masonic publication — and who writes it I do not know...For my part I assure you that I have paid no attention to it whatever, and that I am continuing on my way, blessing the holy name of God in the midst of this tribulation of words, in the hope that He will draw some good out of it."[33]

Meanwhile, however, the mental anguish caused by the campaign of calumny was undermining his health. A few months before he had written:

"My health seems to be good, but I fear I am no longer what I once was. On the Feast of the Assumption, I almost fainted in the pulpit. At one point in the homily I felt so ill I had to stop. What can be done? We must adore the judgments of God and supplement our physical weakness with holiness. And I have so little of this! Pray a little for me therefore."[34]

Then came the collapse and he had to undergo tiresome treatments:

"Now, thank God, I really feel quite well...The doctor assures me that if I continue this way for another month, I shall be completely cured and I do hope so, but it will be what God wills. *Sicut Domino placuit, ita factum est; sit nomen Domini benedictum.*"[35] — "Continue to pray for me so that I may in and for all things accomplish the Divine Will, not only with resignation but with joy."[36]

With each year there were new sufferings, but he never lost heart:

"If you only knew the weight of this cross...How true it is that the Bishop is a sign of contradiction — Truly the life of a Bishop is a martyr's life."[37] — "As for me, thank God, I maintain a perfect serenity of spirit and I know that one *Blessed by God* (as my St. Francis de Sales used to say) uttered amid trials and troubles is worth more than a rosary said in prosperous times, and I accept all these troubles from the hand of God, who permits or ordains them, and I try to accept them with love. Are they not precious bits of the Cross of Jesus Christ?"[38]

With Miraglia's schism, as we have seen, his anguish became even deeper:

"The Lord has willed to visit me this year with all kinds of tribulations, but I do not think I have ever lost my spirit of resignation nor my calm. I kept in mind always that *omne gaudium existimate cum in tribulationes varias incideritis* and I was even joyful about this. Oh! the sublime philosophy in those words, true love of the cross."[39]

Suffering for Christ was by now at the heart of his activity. Nothing diverted him from the increasing desire to embrace the Cross. When he received letters or articles criticizing him personally or his actions, he placed them under the crucifix on his desk.[40] They were his contribution to the Passion of Christ. It was in this context that he viewed every happening and every undertaking.

"Your Institute will not fail," he told the Sisters Apostles of the Sacred

Heart, "because it was born at the foot of the Cross, and I would not have taken it under my protection if I had not realized this."[41]

In the letters of his last years, there are expressions that reveal complete detachment from all things and a close acceptance of God's will:

"My crosses," he wrote to Cardinal Agliardi, "follow one upon another with such rapid frequency that they cancel each other out, and now, thank God, I have little interest in the things of this world and I seek to occupy myself more and more with those of the future life."[42] — "It is a period filled with crosses and bitterness, these, too, a gift from the hands of God, who governs his shepherds with a Providence full of mysteries. If only I could thus sanctify myself and sanctify all the souls committed to my care."[43] — "I bless God in all things and I feel a lively joy in suffering with resignation all the troubles and contradictions He sends me. I receive these difficulties from the hands of God, who permits or ordains them for our improvement, and I believe that I thus do some good for souls. For my part I desire only the glory of God and the greater good of souls, even though these must be won with the greatest sufferings. *Ita Pater quoniam sic fuit placitum ante te.*"[44]

Asceticism

Bishop Scalbrini was not spared the cross of temptation. He was zealous in his dedication to chastity, one might be tempted to say scrupulously so if it were not for some of his private notes that reveal glimpses of his temperament and the battles he fought to dominate it: "What is nothing to others, is fatal for me."[45]

"Be quick to cast out every impure thought...otherwise I will perish...I will perish."[46] — "I shall go to confession as soon as I perceive a temptation, immediately, right at the beginning, or when I shall have unwittingly exposed myself to some danger. Throw myself before God and weep for my miserableness and confess my sins."[47] — *Potius mori quam foedari*...Strict custody of the eyes...Be quick to cast out temptations with disgust. Every day (at Holy Mass) and after Mass a prayer to Christ, *Virgo, Virginis Filius, Rex et caput Virginum*, that he may strengthen me, protect me, defend me..."[48] I must purify myself at all costs, with divine help, from this capital weakness, oh my Jesus: promptly erase from my mind any thought that can harm me; be careful about the custody of the eyes."[49] — "I must then strenuously fight this evil that disturbs my existence."[50]

Witnesses at the Process variously described him as "angelic," a "spotless being," a "pure soul." All noted how this purity of heart and soul radiated from him.[51] No one could have any doubts about his virtue,[52] and in fact those who lived close to him were convinced that he had maintained his baptismal innocence until his death. He had such a horror of sins of impurity that he did not speak of them unless it was absolutely necessary, and then the terms he used were expressive of his repugnance.

He never spoke a word that could even remotely offend virtue[53] nor did he allow others to use any such terms in his presence. The slightest indelicacy irritated him,[54] he severely rebuked priests who used double meanings even in joking[55] and he was disturbed if he was constrained to listen to any scandal.[56]

He always kept the thought of death in mind, and not only in his later years. As early as 1882 he had declared that his principal care was to prepare himself for death.[57] He plunged into his monthly day of recollection as if he were to die that very night.[58] A part of his hour of daily meditation was devoted to preparing himself for a good death.

Almost as a reflex, he reminded his people of death at the beginning of each year[59] and he never missed an opportunity to cause his priests to reflect on it on the most solemn occasions as for example, during his synodal allocutions:

"How many of us will be here at the next Synod? Therefore — and this is the inevitable conclusion — let us run toward holiness with all our strength, without respite, with our eyes fixed on Christ, who is the author of our priesthood and our holiness, who has called us to holiness, and as he is the source of our holiness so is he its reward."[60]

The practice of the harsher forms of traditional asceticism may be surprising in a person of Scalabrini's mentality and scope of activity. This is what he himself says about this:

"When Cardinal Agliardi was visiting me, my brother said to him: 'Although the Bishop is a well-balanced man, for some years now he has been practicing an excessive asceticism.' And the Cardinal answered: 'Just think I myself have been suspecting this, etc.' I smiled sadly and thought to myself that if the Lord had not given me the grace of a little asceticism, in tempore opportuno, I do not know how I should have made out...If I could only become holy! Hoc est omnis homo."[61]

Those familiar with his writings, like those who knew him intimately, are struck by this aspiration to holiness, this constant tension toward perfection. The witnesses at the informative process asserted that Bishop Scalabrini practiced virtue to a heroic degree, both in the extraordinary nature of his virtuous actions, and the exceptional constancy of his daily practice.[62]

"His life, which was methodically regular and of exemplary virtue, convinced me that Bishop Scalabrini was constantly striving for perfection."[63] — "I have always believed that he was completely absorbed in the Lord, in his clergy, and in the souls entrusted to his care. And I might add that this constant attitude of his made an enormous impression."[64]

A Man of Faith

The essential fact of a man's life is the nature of his personal relations with God. This is not difficult to discern in Scalabrini. "His holiness equaled the greatness of his works."[65]

That he was a man of God, a man of faith, is the only explanation of his life:

"The supernatural was the life of his life. It shone from his eyes, from his face, from his words, from his whole person. It was enough to approach him to feel it and to understand that he was constantly guided from on High."[66] — "He had a sense of the divine, which constantly guided him."[67]

"From its splendid beginnings to the end of his glorious tenure as bishop I think he revealed himself particularly as the man of God who seeks God in the ardors of study, God in the zeal of his apostolic labors, God in his conversations with the great and the small, God alone and God always."[68] — "I remember hearing him speak these words...: 'Nothing is more natural than the supernatural.' It seemed impossible to him that anyone should doubt the supernatural."[69] — "He was a man who lived by faith and tried to transfuse it into the souls of others."[70] — "I have never known anyone who reflected a more ardent faith."[71]

His great faith is revealed in his spirit of prayer and his apostolic zeal. A great part of his writings are devoted to prayer, "to this mysterious power that could be called the law of laws of the universe," "the identity card of the true believer," "the complete profession of Christianity." The tone of his exhortations derives from St. Alphonsus. The following excerpts from his last pastoral *La preghiera* seem to be the clearest reflection of his spirit:

"He who does not pray has no soul, or no understanding, or no feeling, or no love."[72] — "Prayer is the chain that binds all of humanity. However vast the distances, however insurmountable the barriers that separate people from one another, prayer draws them all together; it unites all things. It is prayer that folds the living together in its embrace, and the living with the dead. It binds the family on earth with the family in heaven. It forms between the militant, the suffering, and the triumphant Church that constant interflow of prayers and intercessions that theology calls the Communion of Saints. Transcending all obstacles whatever, prayer is like an electric current that flows from brother to brother and, passing through the heart of God, the center and source of love, it forms of all hearts one heart, as it were, of all families one sole family."[73] — "This conversation above is called praise, ecstasy, love, beatitude, eternal happiness. Here below it is a little of all these things and is called prayer. Therefore on earth it is the prelude to immortal life...There are two great things that I admire in heaven and on earth: in heaven the power of the Creator, on earth the power of prayer...Prayer, when it is humble, not only equals but, I might almost say, surpasses the very power of God. *God is all powerful, says the Prophet, and who can resist Him? Prayer*, I answer."[74]

He filled his day with prayer; with it he established a conversation with God; through it he sought strength and enlightenment for his episcopal duties. He made a voluntary vow to meditate a half hour every day, was faithful to the Divine Office, to the rosary and to all the other pious practices, and in fact took time from sleep in order to pray. On one occasion when Fogazzaro, his guest, was about to retire he asked the bishop at what hour he would get up the next morning. Scalabrini answered, "at five o'clock." — "And will you say Mass right away?" Fogazzaro asked. — "No," Scalabrini replied, "First I must pray for those who don't pray."[75]

A Christian View of History

Scalabrini was profoundly Christian in the sense that he lived completely in Christ, on whom his mind, heart and will were concentrated. He was so absorbed in the Christian experience that he viewed everything from this perspective — history, progress, human victories and defeats, the sufferings and triumphs of the Church. For him nothing happened by chance, because he saw Divine Providence governing all events as one sole, great protagonist.

"In the order of nature as of grace," he declared, "all is guided by the hand of God, and the wishes of Heaven are sometimes revealed in certain small circumstances that at the time escape the human eye but in time shine with a light clear enough to those who observe them carefully."[76]

It was with the eye of faith that he viewed the past:

"Christ conquers, Christ reigns, Christ triumphs...," he exclaimed in his address at the centenary commemoration of the Crusades. "Amid the greatest cataclysms in history, midst the shattered fragments of crowns and scepters, between the birth and death of human institutions, the rise and disappearance of all heresies, above the agitation of prophets in the raging storm, stands the Cross. The Cross is the beacon of indistinguishable light, the tree of our salvation, the glorious trophy of Him who reddened it with His Divine Blood: *Stat crux, dum volvitur orbis.*"

After outlining briefly the somber moral, religious and socio-political state of the 12th century, he praised the great men who rose up at the cry, "God wills it," and he asked, "What would Europe be now if it had fallen under the domination of the Turks?" But Providence was watching over Europe and used Italy in a special way to save the continent. In his view it had a particular mission in history:

"The initiative for the Crusades came from Italy, just as the impetus for every holy and useful undertaking. This means that if Italy has received a privileged, cosmopolitan mission from Providence because it has the signal honor to house the center of the Catholic faith, it has the obligation to protect and religiously cultivate this faith. Now why do people not see or do not want to see that as our country draws away from this sublime mission, social unity is crumbling, anarchy with all its execrable activities is making progress, and we are regressing toward barbarism, which can very well exist side by side with steam engines, the telegraph and all the marvelous inventions of science?"

He concluded with a vision of a new history, which directed and governed by Providence, advances toward Christ:

"While the world busies itself, dazzled with its own progress, while man exalts himself from his conquests over matter and his mastery of nature, disemboweling the earth, changing the lightning, cutting through isthmuses to mingle the oceans, eliminating distances; while peoples fall into decline, rise again and renew themselves and the races intermingle, expand and are melded; across the tumbling of our machines, above all this feverish activity and these gigantic undertakings and not without them, there is coming into being a vaster and more sublime epoch, the union in God of all men of good will. The servants of God who labor unaware of his designs are numberless in every age, but in periods of great renewal there are many more than we know or think. Therefore be sure that the ultimate goal of humanity fixed by Providence is not the conquest of matter through the progress of science, nor the formation of new peoples who from one time to another seem the incarnation of power, wealth or learning — not at all. It is the union of souls in God through Jesus Christ and his visible representative."[77]

Mention of the supernatural was frequent with him, and every one of his letters offers an example of this:

"We have lost one of those priests who are the blessing of the community and the presence of Christ in the Church. May God's will always be done!"[78] — "Truth will find a way to be known. Let us thank God for it!"[79] — "God desires to punish us. He is taking away the best supports of the Church...Let us adore his counsels and let us pray."[80] — "While awaiting the hour of God, live with the Sisters, live entirely in Him, with Him, and for Him, and He in His mercy will help us in the great work we wish to undertake."[81] — "Love God and His Church very much. Love souls and the good and do not try to penetrate matters that by nature transcend our limited minds, but which nevertheless form part of the always adorable designs of Heaven."[82] — "It is necessary to know how to keep silent, to pray and to adore. What to our short human sight seems disharmony, is part of the harmony of the designs of God."[83]

All for God and the Good of Souls

His constant work and preoccupation, the often vexing worries made him feel more keenly the need of union with God.

"The bush born from the earth," he wrote in his personal diary, "finds its nourishment in the earth; the soul which has its origin in Heaven can find nourishment only in what comes from Heaven."[84]

He formed the habit of withdrawing often into himself and of seeking the enlightenment necessary for action through concentration of all his faculties on God.

"Certainly the administration of a diocese is a holy thing which comes from the supernatural and leads us to it," he wrote to a fellow bishop. "But one is often distracted...Every day I feel more keenly that in order to carry the episcopal burden in our external life without falling under it, an interior life is necessary in which we can find the consolation, strength, and internal nourishment, the light and peace which sustains us, the *manna absconditum*."[85]

His writings are eloquent in this regard. Following are excerpts taken from his letters. When he was being maliciously attacked by his opponents he wrote:

"...No, dear friend, we are joined as a target for the arrows of these poor blind men, and we must oppose their insane attempts without losing our calm, or the purity of our intentions, seeking only the glory of God and of the Church, and the salvation of souls."[86] And again: "Let us adore the judgments of God and take this occasion to work always with greater rectitude and perfection."[87]

"To pretend that we suffer no troubles at our age is a little too much. The body is wearing out, and we are moving with long steps toward the last step of all. Meanwhile, we speak, we preach, we write, we go on horseback, we travel about and sweat and work to win at last the favor of the Lord...For my part, I now live only for my Diocese, and if I am not indifferent to the great happenings taking place, neither do they interest me a great deal."[88] — "It is truly something that tears the soul to see good and holy works opposed by those who boast that they are champions of the faith. You are still young; prepare to see even worse things. I know the world and I know what I am saying. I am increasingly convinced that one must do good for the sake of good, only for the love of God, without seeking the approval of others nor paying attention to their disapproval."[89]

During his trips to America, Scalabrini's thoughts were also concentrated on the glory of God and the salvation of souls.

"I am here for Him, and for Him I shall carry out the program He has inspired in me even if it should demand the sacrifice of my life."[90] — "Despite the discomforts of these interminable voyages and exertions of every sort, my health has always been excellent and I trust that God, for whom I have come, will keep me so."[91] "Here it is as if we were out of the world...; I see no newspapers...I know nothing about anything. And yet I feel very well, working for Heaven and for souls!"[92] "We work only for God, with God and in God, and all will be crowned with success."[93]

"All his prodigious activity was motivated by the principle he used to keep repeating: — 'Let us save souls and for the rest let come what may.' "[94]

Both his sermons and his conversations touched the hearts of those who heard him, especially because of the "impression he gave of a soul inspired and alight with the liveliest faith."[95]

Scalabrini was quite aware of the temptations to vanity. So much more admirable then was his effort to direct to the glory of God and the good of souls a work that would have been more than sufficient to satisfy ordinary human vainglory. During his journeys in America, he often made mention of great suffering, not only physical but psychological, because of the "obstacles put forth by his opponents, who maligned both his works and his intentions. He endured all this with heroic patience for the love of God, to whom alone, he looked for his reward, not to men as his illwishers insinuated."[96] Some, in fact, whispered that he had gone to America on a hunt for money and honors, but then "he was not the man to seek *lucrum* but souls."[97]

"This is evidenced by the fact that he did not accept the usual offerings for conferring confirmation and other Sacraments. And I know the American bishops were greatly edified and pleased by this fact."[98] — "He was not a man to go begging for honors: the only thing he sought was souls."[99]

Many witnesses spoke of Scalabrini's catechetical apostolate as the principal proof of his great faith, and rightly so. For they might have cited other motivations, such as his human, or social or patriotic sensitivity, along with the principal motive for his charitable and social initiatives. But in the catechetical movement which he promoted there is no other motivation but love and zeal for the faith.

We might apply to him the explanation he himself gave for the life of the saints:

"Only, therefore, because they lived the faith and in accordance with the dictates of the faith, the saints all became such...men of apostolic labors, of marvelously fruitful activities, men of prayer, of penance and of sacrifice, men who...proved themselves angels in the flesh, a sublime mirror of all noble virtues, dead to the world and alive only to the grace of the Lord, taking little thought for the present and always anxious for the future."[100]

Such was Scalabrini's own life: to relate "the Gospel to everyday life so that our actions are always the external reflection of the inner light that quickens and illumines the spirit."[101] His faith was "strong in heart, courageous in speech, effective in action."[102] It was not an abstract concept, or idealism, much less sentimentalism. For him it was school, worship, morality, life, grace,[103] a faith that was simple, humble, serene, in which he felt a spiritual communion with the people whom he loved:

"To you artisans, workmen, pious women, children of the people, I have a most consoling word to say...In the simplicity of your faith you are most secure and most happy. The great truths of religion, the ineffable joys of the faith, which at times have cost so many learned men the most tormenting studies you possess and enjoy in tranquillity and in a comforting certainty of spirit. Oh, blessed be God who keeps these high things hidden from the proud and reveals them to the humble...The greatest philosophers, the greatest thinkers, the very Fathers and Doctors of the Church, after so many investigations and so much reasoning, after so many sublime flights of thought, end up coming back to where you are, and with faith, humility and devotion they say with you and like you: I believe in God..."[104]

CHAPTER XX

Hope

Trust in God

Scalabrini's complete and simple faith prompted him to "see in all events, whether sad or joyful, the compassionate hand of God who orders all things for our good."[1] He therefore abandoned himself confidently to the hands of God: "I must have an inexhaustible confidence, unchangeable in all things, right up to the end."[2]

For his part he neglected no means at his disposal, and especially prayer. He took into account all the considerations prompted by his own prudence and that of others. He exerted himself to be worthy of divine help, and then he entrusted himself to the omnipotence of the Father who is in heaven.

"It is true in fact that *omnia possum in eo qui me confortat* and this is verified when we are worthy."[3] — "Our work is certain to be blessed by heaven if we render ourselves worthy of it by the holiness of our lives and complete trust in God."[4] — "Let us lift up our eyes to heaven and foster a lively confidence in the Lord, *qui non deserit nisi deseratur*. When we are worthy through holiness and in the true spirit of Jesus Christ, He will come to our aid, never fear."[5]

Zealous as he was for the salvation of souls, he suffered keenly to see that many were lost, and he was disturbed the more because he felt the cause lay in the time wasted discussing secondary matters instead of approaching people with the necessary love. No right, he maintained, can silence the supreme duty of the Church's mission, which is the salvation of souls. Yet however deep the grief he suffered, he was never discouraged. He was always in the forefront of the struggle, and he never ceased his efforts no matter how bleak the outlook.

"Unfortunately things are going very badly. Everyone sees this and no one is giving any thought to a remedy. There is truly no hope but in God. Now that not even the loudest trumpets can waken the sleepers and blow away the last illusions, let us leave things to Him. We continue calmly on our way and try to save as many souls as we can."[6]

"After so much hope and so many efforts," he wrote to one of his missionaries, "the Church of St. Mark will not be opened! Let us adore the judgments of God and let Him provide for all those abandoned souls...Let us not force the gates. We seem near the time when they will ask us, and we, forgetting all other things, will be mindful only of Jesus Christ and of the souls He redeemed."[7]

"Bad news follows bad news with great rapidity. What to do? Lose heart? No. God wishes to test us in the fire of tribulation and God be blessed now and always, by everyone. Let us ponder often the text: *recogitate eum qui talem sustinuit contradictionem ne fatigemini animis vestris deficientes*. Courage, calm, and trust in God."[8]

And there is the characteristic conclusion to many of Scalabrini's letters that "calmness, patience and trust in God are omnipotent weapons,"[9] that to adore His judgments and to conform in all things to His will, is the secret of peace and of victory.[10]

"It can be said that Bishop Scalabrini hoped against hope. Though fully aware of all his responsibilities,...he never wavered, but abandoned himself to the hands of God, especially in the most difficult and turbulent times of his episcopate."[11] — "He felt his responsibility to an extraordinary degree, but at the same time he abandoned himself completely to the dispositions of Divine Providence."[12] — "At no time was he ever disheartened; in fact he seemed seized with even greater zeal."[13] — "Amid all the conflicts, difficulties and sufferings that marked his episcopate...he never lost his spirit of complete trust in God. And that is evident also from the letters he wrote when circumstances were at their worst and which he invariably ended with expressions of complete concordance with the will of God and unlimited confidence in His help."[14]

We have already noted the resignation and hope he displayed during the episode of Miraglia.[15]

"Even at times of greatest trouble, and in particular during the painful Miraglia period, even though I saw he was deeply saddened, I never heard him express any disquiet, discouragement or lack of confidence."[16]

It was in those years, in fact, that the difficult lesson of the Cross penetrated his soul:

"This year that is ending has been full of crosses for me, but perhaps it has also been the most productive, thanks be to God. It is really true that *in Cruce vigor, in Cruce robur.*"[17]

To one of his missionaries who at the time had written him a "desolate" letter he replied:

"All you have to do is ask God for the grace to conform completely to His will. The sufferings that accompany your career are either willed or permitted by Him to achieve His providential plan for us. It is through sorrow that God calls us close to Himself; grief is a law of love, a powerful stimulus to all great things, to all heroic efforts for souls like your own, which are capable of the most noble sentiments."[18]

In these lines Scalabrini unwittingly revealed the secret of his own activity: grief for him was the most powerful stimulus for all great, heroic things. The Cross formed the essential matrix of the living designs of "Providence, full of mysteries but always loving." These expressions recur throughout his correspondence.

It was through his Christian hope that he overcame his natural inclination to a kind of pessimism:[19]

"Pessimism always or almost always comes to those past sixty. The *laudator temporis acti* is always present in man, with all its consequences. But the world has always been the same more or less, and so has the life of a Bishop. Therefore let us keep a serene mind and a tranquil heart. A little asceticism, fine asceticism at that, is the panacea for all black humors...Thus in the midst of trials of every sort, I have suffered, and I continue to suffer for the well known reasons, but only a little, for I do all that I can and place in God's hands the final outcome of all matters."[20]

And there is the confidence with which he undertook his many apostolic works despite all kinds of difficulties:

"When he encountered opposition he used to say: — 'This is a good sign; the devil does not want this work to succeed; that means it is willed by God, and so forward ever!' "[21]

"After having thought and deliberated over a matter he used to say: 'Let come what may. We must go forward because God wills it.' And this was his attitude even in the midst of the struggles and conflicts that were never lacking throughout his episcopal ministry...In fact he maintained that it was usual for God's work to be resisted by men."[22] —

"He was a man of singular hope in Divine Providence; I have never seen him waver a moment, even in the most difficult circumstances."[23]

Awareness of Providence

It was his awareness of Providence that gave him courage in the financial difficulties with which he always had to contend. He would never permit a good work to be abandoned or interrupted for fear money would be lacking. If he had been prudent in a too human sense, he would never have carried out or even begun his many apostolic activities.

"If we concentrate too much on the difficulties," he used to say, "without taking other considerations into account, we shall end by accomplishing nothing."[24]

"He had a most lively hope in God with respect to the means to carry on the works he hoped to see realized: great works and even bold ones for that time."[25] — "He used all the human means at his disposal; then he placed all his confidence in Divine Providence, which never failed to help him, as is proved by the survival of his enterprises, no one of which has failed."[26]

The people in Clermont-Ferrand attributed a noble ancestry to him, placing in his coat of arms, in addition to Jacob's ladder, the figure of a crusader who had been the first to scale the walls of Dimyat for they believed he was descended from a French family that bore that heraldic symbol. The Bishop declared he never knew he was of noble birth, but if carrying out great works with few human means and with only great hope in God was a sign of nobility, then he could consider himself very noble indeed.[27]

Nevertheless there was no presumption in him.

"He had great trust in Providence, but he never gave in to quietism. He did not tempt God, for he, on his part, did all that he could."[28] — "He worked with his brain and his purse and he was extremely active."[29] — "He never neglected to use all the means that prudence and wisdom suggested, especially when he was initiating works that carried serious responsibilities. In fact, he never failed to consult experts, form committees, draw up financial estimates and plans, as for example in undertaking the extensive restorations of the Cathedral and in establishing his various Institutes."[30] — "He was a man of great vision and of great resourcefulness, and it was characteristic of him to base and place all his trust in God. Therefore he was far from being presumptuous. He concentrated all his remarkable energies and the prestige, which he prudently used as a reserve, to his initiatives and undertakings."[31] — "He was not a man to wait for Providence to come in through the window, but in all his undertakings, he did everything he could himself."[32]

When he was certain in conscience that he had not overlooked any available means and was convinced that the project would redound to the glory of God and the salvation of souls, he was stopped by no obstacle whatever.

"I begin a work and then I place it in God's hands, and He takes care of it."[33] — "I am never discouraged for I know that Divine Providence watches over the works it has begun with a mother's tenderness and is indeed able to bring them to term. I touch this fact, I might say, with my hands every day. And then, did not Our Lord say this very clearly?"[34]

"He was a great judge of persons, and skillful in finding funds...On one occasion in Turro, where Signor Govanni Celli...known for his wealth and philanthropy also happened to be, the Servant of God tactfully suggested that he spend his 72nd year for the Church."[35] — "The esteem in which he was held in his Diocese always obtained the necessary funds for him, both from his own people and from wealthy persons not of his diocese...I myself witnessed a contribution of 100,000 lire, a truly extraordinary sum for those times."[36]

We have seen how he sought the help of the Duke of Parma. Among his papers there are notes of offerings from the industrialist Francesco Rossi di Schio, a wealthy lady of Pegli, and other benefactors from various parts of Italy, prompted to contribute by his courage and his faith.

At the same time, however, his faith in Divine Providence was so great that he believed the best way to ensure its intervention was to spend all one had and then throw oneself into the arms of the heavenly Father. "If we give ten to the Lord, He will make a hundred available."[37] He exhorted the Ladies of Charity "not to keep any money, but to give all that they had, because Providence never fails. And he said it with moving conviction."[38] He used to say, "We can do nothing with credits, but with debts we accomplish something,"[39] and "we must not cease carrying out good works for fear of not being able to meet expenses, but always with prudence and economy...To be able to give, we must save. That — he used to say — is the way to obtain God's help in doing good."[40]

His confidence was rewarded at times in ways that seemed miraculous.

"He often told me that Divine Providence had intervened in a thoroughly unexpected way to help him meet urgent needs...One day, I went to remind him respectfully of the bill for 17,000 lire for restoration work in the Church of St. Peter, and when I entered his study, he tossed me the bank book of the Cassa di Risparmio, and without moving from his desk, exclaimed: 'The Lord has provided. Take the dirty stuff.' The bank book registered a deposit of 33,000 lire."[41]

"I was in Bishop Scalabrini's study one day, and the conversation turned on Divine Providence, a favorite subject with him. With the liveliest satisfaction he told me that a few days before he had been visited by a gentleman who...at the end of their conversation handed him an envelope. As soon as he had left, the Servant of God said he had hastened to open the envelope, guessing that it must contain something providential. And in fact, he found the sum urgently needed to meet a binding obligation."[42] — This fact is narrated by many witnesses, who cite the sum of 25,000 or 30,000 lire,[43] nor is it the only example. "A second time (and I verify this of my own knowledge) when he was in serious need, I gave him a purse containing a large sum of gold money offered to him by an anonymous donor who wished to remain unnamed."[44]

The foundation of the Missionaries of St. Charles was an act of trust in Providence. When a certain priest asked to be admitted to the Congregation, but asked if it would last, Scalabrini replied:

"Will the Institute last? Will it not last? It will last as long as God wills...It is in the hands of God. To trust in Him with all simplicity is much more effective than to look for any guarantee in moral, economic and stable situations."[45] — "You ask me," he wrote to a benefactor — "what means I have to provide for my foundation. The means that Providence furnishes me from time to time."[46]

His reliance on God was without reservations:

"If it is a work of God, it will live; if it is not a work of God, I do not want it either." — "First of all we make plans; when we are sure that they are truly useful, and better still necessary, we carry them out. When the work is done, we pay if possible; if it is not possible we wait for Providence to send us the means, and it never fails." — "It is certain," he told a journalist, "that one needs faith for these undertakings; and we have it, and we have never been disappointed. The day before my first missionaries were to leave for America, just think I needed 25,000 lire and did not have them. Day came, and I received a package from Genoa. I opened it and found twenty-five big bills, precisely the sum I needed. — 'And who had sent it to your Excellency?' — How do I know?..."[47]

He taught others to have the same trust.

Sister Candida Quadrani, Superior of the Instituto Sordomute...told me that when she ran out of money she used to go to the Bishop, who comforted her and urged her to place her trust in God, saying: — 'Do not worry; God's help will not fail.' — And in fact, God's help never did fail, for at the end of every month she always had the wherewithal to pay her debts, and this for a period of over thirty years."[48] "He used to say that when one works for the Lord, His help cannot fail. And he taught this to us young priests when he sent us up to the mountains to begin our sacred ministry, saying in the good dialect of Como — 'Take along a little pot and pan, and then the Lord will provide.' "[49]

His confidence in God was rewarded in the most enviable of all ways when he suddenly found himself facing death, but with the calm serenity of one who had set above all other aspirations his desire for the kingdom of the blessed: "How desirable are your tabernacles, oh Lord, and how fortunate are they who dwell in your house! Oh dear and holy country! Oh when will it be granted me to be one of your citizens!"[50]

He loved his earthly fatherland, but he never spoke of it without adding: our true fatherland is heaven. He never for a moment stopped laboring on earth, but "whenever anyone asked him when he was going to rest, he always gave the same reply: — 'We shall have plenty of time for that after death.' "[51]

And when time came to weigh the anchor of hope for his last journey he could say, with the simple faith of the just man: "Lord, I am ready; let us go."[52]

Bishop Scalabrini at the Emigrants' Villa of San Paolo. At the right of the Bishop is his brother.

CHAPTER XXI

The Principal Virtue

Pope Benedict XV, who was his friend, considered that among Scalabrini's "most noble virtues" the principal one was charity.[1] His whole life was eloquent testimony of this, but here it might be useful to recall certain evidences, such as his hatred of sin and his generosity in forgiving.

Hatred of Sin

His love of God, lived with devotion, especially to the Eucharist, and with faithful meditation, was parallelled by his hatred of whatever offended the Lord.

A priest to whom he often went to confession stated:

"His love of God was ardently demonstrated especially in his inplacable hatred of mortal sin, particularly sins of impurity. He hated deliberate venial sins as well and sought the grace of God to avoid them through his devotion to the Most Holy Eucharist and to the Blessed Mother."[2]

"That the Servant of God was constantly afire with extraordinary love for the Lord was apparent not only in all external acts of worship but also in all the expressions of his life, so that whoever came near him, as I had the fortune to do, understood that his mind was fixed on God, and whatever the subject under discussion, his ardent love of God was so evident that it had a holy and edifying effect and often immediately inspired the least observant in the faith to salutary thoughts...He had a most delicate conscience, and to have a confessor always at hand, chose one among the priests who lived nearest the episcopal residence; he used to say many times that he often felt the need to be reconciled and he sought this; he did not avoid going to confession to young priests and even to those who worked with him...He used to say that the Bishop, who is burdened with such heavy responsibilities and has so many occasions in which he can fail, needs often to purify his soul."[3]

To newly ordained priests, he used to say:

"The finest wish your Bishop can make for you at this moment is that you will never in all your life celebrate the Holy Mass in a state of mortal sin."[4]

During his pastoral visit, "he often went to confession and preferably to priests he himself had ordained."[5] He was strict in requiring his priests to give proof of their weekly confession to the rural deans, and he himself furnished an example by regularly sending his own certificate to his Vicar General.[6]

Many priests recall the impression the Bishop made when he spoke to the seminarians, to whom he urged the avoidance of the slightest fault in terms so impassioned that they could only reflect his own extremely delicate conscience.[7] His priests also underlined his punctuality in carrying out even his smallest duties, and his invariably edifying manner.[8]

"On all the occasions I had to observe him I have never noticed in the Servant of God anything that could be considered a serious sin and not even a deliberate venial sin."[9]

The only fault commented on was his tendency to outbursts of impatience:

"If at times he did not restrain some first expression of irritation, he quickly corrected the bad impression this might have made with a smile that bespoke his humility and kindliness."[10]

The blamelessness of his life prompted not only the average persons but the most qualified witnesses to speak of saintliness:

"I have always had the impression that Bishop Scalabrini led the life of a saint: but more than my personal impression, I am happy to report that his assistant secretary, Father Francesco Sidoli, who later became Archbishop of Genoa, also shared this conviction. More than once he spoke to me of the Servant of God with such admiration as to be speaking of a man of most virtuous life and the highest perfection."[11]

This was the impression he made on the persons who knew him best. His secretary declared, like a true child of his time, that the Bishop would never be canonized because he was often seen to be friendly with "non-practicing" persons, although this was only in order to accomplish some good. At the same time he himself was personally convinced that he had lived for twenty-nine years in the company of a saint.

"His life throughout his episcopate was always extremely virtuous, a life of devotion, modesty, charity and zeal. This impression constantly grew on me, and now I can and do attest in fact, calling on God as my witness, that given the circumstances, and the men and affairs of the time, his was a truly heroic life, the life of a truly saintly Bishop...When he died, I had the conviction that a saint had died, so much so that I prayed to him, and I still tell him my needs, and I am convinced that I have received special favors and have been spared in many dangers."[12]

His servant, Carlo Spallazzi, expressed the same conviction:

"I can say that the Servant of God practiced the Christian virtues in what was, to me, an extraordinary manner. I can say that only those who had the good fortune to know him intimately as I was able to know him as his personal servant, can know the degree of perfection to which he practiced the Christian virtues and that I myself could never have imagined."[13]

His Master of Ceremonies, who enjoyed a close relationship with the Bishop in the last eleven years of the latter's life, especially during the pastoral visits, affirmed that through long habit the Bishop had always practiced the theological and cardinal virtues, "often in a truly extraordinary manner, and sometimes to a heroic degree. In general I can say that I never saw him do anything contrary to the above mentioned virtues, although his was a very sensitive temperament."[14]

"His contemporaries of every class and even those of a different religion had the highest opinion of the Servant of God both as a man and as a bishop; they had great esteem for his intelligence, his learning, and his extraordinary administrative ability, but especially for his holiness, which radiated from his every word and his every act."[15]

This was how those closest to him felt about him. While they loved him deeply, there is no reason to assume that their affection would blind them completely to the imperfections that constant familiarity inevitably exposes.

The general opinion of others not so close to him may be gathered from the following:

"I can with conscience attest that the Servant of God had the reputation of sanctity among the people. As for the Clergy, I am able to state that there were very many among them who not only esteemed him but admired him for his exceptional virtues and that in general he was considered a true man of God, motivated only the desire for good...This does not mean there were not some...who criticized him, but not even the saints were immune from this."[16]

The *ex-officio* witnesses gave the same testimony:

"I am convinced that Bishop Scalabrini practiced virtue to a heroic degree, particularly faith, charity, poverty and chastity."[17] — "By heroic virtue I mean that which is practiced to a greater degree than is common, and not only in the sense that it is evidenced in extraordinary acts, but rather that it is clear in the constant fulfillment of one's duty whatever the sacrifices this requires. Now I am convinced that the Servant of God exercised the theological virtues in the manner mentioned above, his devotion and his zeal being truly edifying. He displayed also a special heroism."[18]

An exceptional witness *ex-officio* was Don Orione, who testified as follows:

"Ever since I heard that his Cause of Beatification was being introduced, though others were a little surprised, I did not consider it at all unexpected, and I gladly declare that I desire his Beatification because then he would continue to do in death what he did in life, namely, edify, display his apostolic fire, and remind us that in the heart of the Priest, even in the darkest hours, there is always ardent love of country as well as zeal in bringing honor to the Catholic hierarchy."[19]

Forgiveness

Scalabrini's yearning for holiness was essentially love — love of God and love of neighbor become one love in practice, with his desire to imitate the goodness of Christ, of whom he said: "his every word was mercy, his every step a comfort, his every miracle a grace."[20]

"He was truly in love with God, and he impelled us toward God with the remarkable examples of his deeply fervent devotion. But if he spoke to us about God, he spoke to God about us. If he warned us against the dangers of evil, he defended us in every misfortune, he was at our side in every grief. Whoever had a more compassionate heart, a more gentle soul...? His chief adornment was his kindness...Most strong in giving support, he was at the same time weak, tender and gentle in suffering with those who suffered; he combined within himself a compelling authority and an engaging gentleness, a strict attitude toward sin and a maternal compassion toward the sinner, a steadfastness that would choose death rather than betray a soul and the invincible patience that can be excoriated without complaining...He resolved all the most difficult problems with kindness...He pushed his kindness to the farthest limit he could without offending the tranquillity of his own delicate conscience."[21]

With respect to some incidents, there is the inclination to think the Bishop gave in a little too much[22] especially in the most painful situations, as in the case of Miraglia.

"He kept silent! All the most valid reasons were overcome by the fear that anything else might be interpreted as revenge...It is easy to say and to write these few words, but the generosity of these actions God alone can measure, and they form a halo that does not diminish with the passing of time!"[23]

His silence when he was insulted by the excommunicated Miraglia shows that he had learned the lesson of the Cross, and he could tell his people:

"It is a comfort, in fact a sweet balm, to know that one suffers for justice, that one suffers without hatred, but rather with love for him who persecutes us so that he may be converted and have life. And is it not another source of comfort to know that our persecutors are rods of correction in the hands of God? While we would deserve much worse for our sins, He, the most merciful God, has so ordained things that all that is happening seems a test rather than a persecution."[24]

The Bishop had spoken out more against those who appeared to be wavering or inclined to the apostate than against Miraglia himself. "He who loves, fears," he used to say, and therefore he was at pains to explain the severity of the measures he took:

"Does anyone think some reproach I have made is too harsh? I would be very sorry because, believe me my children, if I detest evil I do not bear the slightest shadow of resentment against anyone...I love you, and precisely because I love you, I am angry at anyone who causes scandal for you and seeks to betray you, I embrace you all in Jesus Christ, and I would like to hold you all within my heart. I would give my life and would gladly become anathema for each of you if I could thus bring you to salvation. No, to me there is no friend or enemy among you, for you are all children of my one family."[25]

In announcing that Miraglia was excommunicated, Scalabrini exhorted the pastors to have the same charitable feelings toward those who were "more deluded than evil" and had allowed themselves to be caught in the web. They too were brothers, for whom they would be accountable to the Lord. They were to approach them with mercy and compassion, rather than with all the trappings of zeal, to make them understand that the Church was always ready "to be disarmed by repentance."[26]

We have noted the wonder aroused by his kindness to two persons who, in the same period, cause him acute sorrow.[27] One was the young Sicilian who had accepted the mock ordination from Miraglia and presented himself as a priest. When he repented he was not only pardoned but helped by the Bishop who found him an honorable occupation.[28] The other case already cited was even more painful because the apostate was a priest. "When he spoke of him, Bishop Scalabrini used to say: I am sure he will come back, because he had a good mother who is praying for him now in paradise. — And his words came true when the above mentioned priest made a solemn act of abjuration, and was not only pardoned but showered with paternal attention."[29] In fact, Scalabrini immediately received him back in the diocese, hastened to ask the Holy See to restore his faculties and allowed him to "be assigned to a parish endowed with the rights of lay patronages."[30] Bishop Giovanni Radini Tedeschi informed Scalabrini of the priest's abjuration on April 20, 1898. Three days later the prodigal returned home and wrote to the Bishop:

> "It is impossible for me to express in words the immense joy I felt at having Your Excellency address to me that sweet salutation, 'dearest son!'...Nor can I ever tell you all the graces, light and holy energy brought my soul by the very special blessing that Your Excellency deigned to send me through Bishop Radini Tedeschi."[31] The same priest later said: "I knew the Bishop was extremely kind, but I would never have thought that he would welcome me with so much fatherly affection."[32]

Two other priests caused Bishop Scalabrini great suffering. We have already noted the episode of Canon Rocca, with whom the Bishop tried every possible means of reconciliation, so that he was tempted to reproach himself for an excessive indulgence that lasted until Rocca's death.

> "Unfortunately he died without being reconciled to the Bishop, although the latter went to visit him and give him his blessing. It was said that Rocca did not receive the Bishop because his presence would have made too great an impression on him and would have wakened the memory of a too painful past. And this was also the interpretation of the Servant of God."[33]

This was an extremely charitable interpretation, according to one of Rocca's friends:

> "At my suggestion, Rocca went to an audience of the Bishop and returned, I well remember, deeply moved and enthusiastic. Thus I can testify that the Servant of God, although he knew that for my studies and for reasons of friendship I frequented Canon Rocca, he never remarked to me about this and, in fact, when occasion arose he always spoke of him with esteem and without saying a single bitter word: and this aroused great admiration in me."[34]

Another canon, a friend of Rocca's, had been suspended from his teaching duties in the Seminary because he used his lectures in theology to make bitter personal attacks against the Bishop. In addition, he continued to promote an opposition movement against Scalabrini and had inveighed against him during a sermon to the great scandal of the faithful. When this canon, who had been carried away by his own impetuous and hot-tempered nature, realized how wrong he had been, he begged forgiveness of the Bishop, who even at the height of their conflict had shown him exceptional kindness. Father Calzinari, who was a young seminarian at the time and train-bearer at the pontifical masses, recounted the following:

"One day, when we had returned from the Cathedral to the episcopal palace, Bishop Scalabrini, having dismissed the others, detained Canon Rossi, and to my surprise embraced him affectionately and murmured a few words in his ear."[35]

Then, with "fatherly solicitude he absolved him and afterwards held him as one of his most distinguished and dearest priests, and made use of his work."[36] In fact, after a few years he wrote letters of recommendation for his promotion to the rank of Domestic Prelate:

"Your Excellency has responded to the many serious displeasures I caused You with a gesture of kindness so unusual that if on the one hand it confounds me on the other it shows me the greatness and generosity of your truly paternal heart."[37]

The charity displayed in similar cases by the Bishop, who restored the repentant to their functions, placed complete confidence in them and in fact showed them special warmth, gave rise to both admiration and criticism.[38] He replied that this is what the Gospel taught and that in any case he always sought the approval of the Holy See.[39] He was so forgiving, in fact, that it used to be said that to win his love it was enough to offend him:

"And here I beg pardon of your noble soul, Oh Great One, because I myself who am now speaking of You have thought and said many times that the surest means of obtaining favors and graces from You was to become blameworthy through offending you, because your heart responded to those who repented and generously showered benefits on them."[40]

"Not Adversaries But Brothers"

Perhaps the best known example of Scalabrini's generosity is his reconciliation with Father Davide Albertario after a long and bitter series of polemics. He summed these up precisely when he was asked to send Albertario his blessing on the occasion of the latter's jubilee as a priest and anniversary as a journalist:

"I would be happy to be able to send him without reservations a cordial 'evviva' but he has too much sense and there is too much lombard blood in his veins to accept this from me without a word or two to make things perfectly clear. I have always praised and still praise his fierce battle on behalf of the freedom of the Church, the true and real independence of her august Head, his complete obedience to the word of the Pope, our Leader and Supreme Teacher, for the pure Roman doctrine has held against everything and everyone. On this ground we have always been of one mind and one heart. It is true that in the past I had occasion to complain of him, but now all that is forgotten in the charity of Jesus Christ. You remind me of the conversation I recently had with Albertario in Turin. I am happy to assure you that I too was completely satisfied with that conversation because it was frank and open and helped, I think, to clear up many things. There remained no doubt that in the field of action as well as principle, Catholic journalism must be the energetic champion of the Hierarchy, the valid auxiliary of the Bishop, the faithful echo of his teachings. I heartily unite with my venerable colleagues whom you have mentioned, therefore, in sending Father Davide, on this happy occasion, sincere good wishes for a long and prosperous life and I beg God for every choice blessing for him."[41]

They had been reconciled two months before, at the Eucharistic Congress held in Turin in September, 1894.

"He permitted one of his fellow bishops to say to his opponent: Bishop Scalabrini has forgotten everything, because he never harbored any rancor. He embraces and kisses not adversaries but brothers, who have offended him through error."[42] — These words were reported to Albertario and encouraged him to go to Scalabrini. It is said that when he entered, he knelt before him and asked his forgiveness. There is no doubt that the Bishop welcomed him with the fatherly affection with which he welcomed all who repented and which led us to say that in order to enter his good graces it was necessary to have first committed an error."[43]

For the anniversary of Albertario's ordination to the priesthood Scalabrini publicly sent good wishes and blessings, writing to the chairman of the anniversary committee:

"I, too, bless Father Albertario and rejoice with him on this happy occasion, and I wish him with all my heart a long and prosperous life, rich in every noble virtue, productive of holy works, and deserving of the crown that God reserves for those who worthily battle for the triumph of truth and justice."[44]

Albertario went to Piacenza in December of the same year. Bishop Scalabrini had received Bonomelli's assurance that he too would pardon him[45] and he welcomed him warmly and read him the reply from the Bishop of Cremona.

"He listened not only with pleasure but with great emotion and told me he would go to Cremona to do his duty. I believe he will do so. Meanwhile, caught up perhaps in his work, he has written you and you answered him as a good and generous Bishop. I read this in the Osservatore. That word 'generous' I believe means that you have forgiven him."[46]

Albertario in fact had chosen to make his first approaches to Bonomelli by letter and had so informed Scalabrini, who was acting as intermediary:

"After You read me the letter from His Excellency Bishop Bonomelli, I would have failed in my respect for Bishops if I had kept silent. To what I told Your Excellency I added a letter which I sent to Cremona setting forth my wish to show that Most Reverend Prelate the sincerity of my desire to make my peace with him...I extend to Your Excellency my lively thanks for the kindness You have shown me as a Bishop, a Father, and, if I may say so, a friend."[47]

Albertario later attended the regional meeting of the *Opera dei Congressi* held in Piacenza in 1897.

"When Father Davide rose to speak a stir ran through the large audience which was familiar with the events. But the athlete of Catholic journalism, who immediately understood what was happening, spoke these exact words: 'Some people will wonder on seeing me in this Episcopal See, on seeing that I can speak among you. I must justify my presence in this place. Well, I have just one justification — the great heart of Bishop Scalabrini...' Afterwards I went up to Father Davide, as he came out of the meeting covered with sweat and was making his way to the rooms in the residence, and shaking his hand I said: Bravo. Those words of reconciliation do you honor. — 'Oh,' he answered almost in tears, 'Bishop Scalabrini will perform many other miracles.' "[48]

Following the riots instigated by the Socialists in the next year, Father Albertario was arrested and unjustly condemned to three years in prison. As soon as he heard of the arrest, Bishop Scalabrini asked General Genova di Revel to use his good offices with the military governor, Bava Beccaris, so that Albertario would not be brought to trial. The general answered that the military court had decided on a summary trial and not even Bava Beccaris could stop it, notwithstanding the approaches he had made to him on the Bishop's recommendation.[49]

After the verdict, Scalabrini tried as hard as he could to get the king's pardon for Albertario as is evident in his correspondence with Paganuzzi and Rezzara. He informed the latter that he had enlisted the interest of the Attorney General Pelloux, who, however, had replied: "If he is set free too soon it can be interpreted as a slap at the military court and it has been decided to postpone the matter until there is an occasion for amnesty." Scalabrini suggested drawing up a petition to be presented to the King and the Minister of the Interior, saying that he himself would sign it.[50] Meanwhile he has asked Minister Pelloux to try to obtain the King's permissioin for Albertario (detained at Finalborgo) to say Mass and to resume clerical dress,[51] and he persuaded Bonomelli to write for the same purpose to the King and to Zanardelli.[52] Four days later Pelloux assured the two bishops that he had given orders for Albertario to be permitted to say Mass every day.[53]

To his "numerous persistent recommendations on behalf of Father Davide," Scalabrini received — on October 29, 1898 — a "very confidential reply," which said that within a few days the first decree of amnesty for those arrested would be published, and that "on May 14th all the others would be freed, including, of course, poor Father Davide."[54]

And precisely on May 14th, 1899 Albertario wrote to Scalabrini:

"Most Reverend and Illustrious Excellency:

"I am using the only paper I have at hand at the moment. I am just out of prison and I cannot delay in fulfilling my duty to Your Excellency. My sister has told me of your comforting words and your letters of fatherly affection. May God repay your compassion for those who suffered with blessings on You personally, your diocese, all those whom you love and all for whom you pray especially to the Lord. I was also told that Your Excellency had requested the Minister — as I did last August — that I be allowed to celebrate the Holy Mass in prison; I am grateful, Your Excellency for this solicitude. The Holy Mass was my life...Now my freedom has been restored. I shall wait some time before I start work again. I need rest after all the agitation I have suffered. If the moment presents itself when I may pay my respects to Your Excellency, I shall be able to tell you things that I shall never reveal to anyone else. I express again my most heartfelt thanks, Excellency, for all the kindness you have shown my family and myself. The Lord cannot but love him who wipes away the tears of the unfortunate."[55]

Albertario kept his promise to visit Bishop Scalabrini, "who had him come to the Seminary where he was given a festive welcome."[56]

Thus the troubled relations between Scalabrini and Albertario were resolved in the light of charity. The last act in the episode illumines and interprets Scalabrini's previous attitude, due to his sense of duty to speak against interference in diocesan administration and offenses against episcopal dignity. In fact, some of the strong expressions Scalabrini used in speaking of Albertario are found only in letters addressed to his Superiors and to those involved in the same situation; they never appeared in public documents or interventions. Neither did he allow the heat of the polemics to be talked about in private conversation, where it could have become backbiting. Two witnesses who were close to the Bishop tell us the following:

"The only time I heard him speak of his relations with Albertario was the day I happened to be at dinner with the Servant of God at Bishop Bonomelli's. The conversation turned casually on some of the things that had happened a few years before...The Servant of God was calm and serene, and merely skimmed over the subject."[57] "I must say," Cardinal Nasalli Rocca affirmed, "that I have never heard him say a bitter word against this priest journalist."[58]

It was one of the characteristics of his love to help his offenders, toward whom he made every effort to show special kindness.[59]

After the insults hurled at him during the riot that erupted at the funeral ceremonies for Victor Emmanuel II,[60] He issued a broad pardon:

"Our prayers in these days were and shall be especially for those who, not out of ill will certainly but through thoughtless emotion, went so far as to heap abuses and insults on us. We can in fact assure you that in the calm and tranquil spirit of one who knows that at a time of great trepidation for good men he has conscientiously done his duty, We pardoned their offenses, recommended them to God and blessed them with all Our heart, grieving only for the offenses committed against Jesus Christ in Our poor person."[61]

He did not stop with declaring a general pardon. In fact, "when he came to know most of the leaders of this reprisal, he treated them with the greatest kindness and in fact helped the son of one of them."[62] — "He also placed in the Ospizio Maruffi and helped a man nicknamed Tredici, who had shouted insults at him during the riot...and, it is said, had spat on him."[63]

There are numerous similar examples of the solid virtue Scalabrini achieved, and it seems that in his later years, sensitive as his nature was, he was no longer upset by like offenses. There is the following little incident that happened in New York:

"In the midst of all the festivities, a rascal threw a potato at Bishop Scalabrini...Instead of being offended, he turned and blessed the boy. The episode aroused the indignation of those present who wanted to give the youth a lesson but the Servant of God intervened immediately and forbade that any measure be taken against him."[64]

"You have such a kind heart, and imitate so well the gentleness of the Eternal Shepherd," a priest wrote to him who was desolate "for having caused grief to so loving a father." The priest quoted from St. Francis de Sales, the Doctor of gentleness, the eulogy of meekness acquired after heroic sacrifices. It is easy to understand why Bishop Scalabrini always kept before him on his desk the picture of St. Francis next to the Crucifix, under which, as we have seen, he used to place "writings or articles opposed to his works or to him personally."[65]

"As for myself," he used to say, "thank God I kept perfect peace of mind...For the rest, if I do not deserve to be offended by what they wrote, perhaps I deserve it for other things. Perhaps my detractors see my defects better than I see them myself, and those who love me do not see them. I know and confess that I am not above reproach, nor am I a saint. But even if I were, were not the saints exposed to opposition and insults? And what was not said of Our Lord, who is perfection itself?"[66]

Scalabrini
toward the end of his life.

Photo used for
his North American visit.

CHAPTER XXII

Humble and Poor

Humility

Love of Christ Crucified, who forgave as he died, presupposes humility. However dignified, Scalabrini's manner was always affable and humble:[1]

"While he treated the noble and the rich with great courtesy, he flattered no one."[2] — "If he showed any preferences, these were for the children of the poor."[3] — "He never avoided contact with persons of humble station; in fact, this aspect of his virtue might be summed up by saying that he stopped the poor to speak with them, while he allowed the others to stop him."[4] — "He did not hesitate to wait on the poor on occasional meals, as for example that given on Holy Thursday after the washing of the feet. He treated everyone equally in a fatherly manner, mixing with the poor and those of humble station. The peasants enjoyed this and felt honored by this friendly treatment."[5]

He asked for the prayers of the faithful and of his priests, declaring that "he felt increasingly every day an immense need of them."[6] When he suffered some humiliation he liked to repeat the verse of the psalm: *Bonum mihi quia humiliasti me.*[7] With the same humility he accepted the observations and even the ridicule of his inferiors.

"He had by nature a quick temper which he was able to control through humility. In this connection I remember that during the ordination ceremony held on December 23, 1893, the new priests were somewhat confused in following the sacred rite. Bishop Scalabrini, noticing this, made a gesture of impatience. But at the respectful reminder of the master of ceremonies, Canon Armelonghi, the Servant of God folded his hands and remained immobile, waiting with humble attitude for the ceremony to continue...When I was in Veano, where the Collegio Alberoni is, several priests along with myself used the presence of the pastor of Denarolo, who had a talent for perfectly mimicking the voice, words and gestures of others, to get him to imitate the Bishop, who we thought had gone to bed. His performance had reached a high point when suddenly the shutters were thrown open and Bishop Scalabrini appeared in the window. Far from being offended, he was laughing heartily and exclaimed: — 'For heaven's sake, stop it; I am dying of laughter.' "[8]

These are little anecdotes but they do confirm the modesty of the Bishop, who had any number of reasons to grow proud, surrounded as he was by universal esteem and affection. Yet he "maintained a most humble concept of himself."[9]

"He abhorred honors, praises, and always considered himself a poor sinner."[10] — "His refrain was: it is necessary always to be afraid of oneself."[11] — "I have never heard him say a word that could be interpreted as self praise."[12] — "He never said anything that could elicit the praise of his listener."[13] — "In all the times I was with him, and these were very many, I never heard him speak of himself, nor boast in any way. In fact, it was his custom to repeat that we can do nothing of ourselves, and the more things turn out well, the more we must recognize that this is due to nothing on our part."[14]

One day he interrupted a program organized in his honor by the students of the Collegio Alberoni exclaiming, "I have to leave, for you are making me lose my humility," and with that he led the boys off to chapel where he gave them a sermon on that virtue."[15]

"Though he appreciated their deep spiritual significance, he regarded with holy indifference the reverent and affectionate demonstrations given him so often. For him, as he said, they were a form of torture..."[16]

"For some idea of the opinion others had of Bishop Scalabrini, and his own idea of himself," a liberal journalist related, "I am happy to recount an episode that took place in the last years of his life and which I faithfully reported in the *Progresso*. A certain poor woman had been ill for six months, confined to her bed because she could not move her legs. She insisted that her husband get Bishop Scalabrini to come and visit her, placing great hope in the efficacy of his visit. The Bishop came to know of her desire, and at the request of the husband he went. When he stood at her bedside, the Servant of God asked the woman to try and move her legs. She replied that she could not. But the Bishop insisted, and she did try to move them, and after a few moments she got up from the bed. Both the woman and her husband began to exclaim that it was a miracle. But Bishop Scalabrini said: 'No, no, it is not a miracle, because it is the saints who work miracles and I am not a saint. This may be a form of hysteria.' (He perhaps said this so they would not spread the news about in praise of him.) This showed his humility. I am not here to judge whether or not it was a miracle, but merely to recount the matter as it actually took place."[17]

Scalabrini took pains to hide what could be turned to his praise — the letters of thanks from those he helped, for example — and even to disguise his own modesty.

"I have always been convinced that the Servant of God possessed the virtue of humility to a heroic degree and that he often acted very casually and paid no attention to certain little things in order to cover up his own virtue."[18]

A New Kind of Martyrdom

For a man as humble as he was, and who was besides "an enemy of publicity as a matter of principle,"[19] it must have been "a new kind of martyrdom"[20] when from time to time the word was spread that he was to be honored in some way or promoted to a higher office.

"I never knew anyone as indifferent, as adverse to honors as Scalabrini," Bonomelli attested. "His talents, learning, and extraordinary activity, his practical touch, the works he accomplished and the high virtues with which he was endowed destined him for the highest honors in the Church. He never said a word or made a single gesture that could smooth the way to attain them. Rather he often spoke and acted in such a way as to show that he did not want them, and he declined them."[21]

After the publication of the pamphlet *Intransigenti e Transigenti* in 1886, it was rumored that the Bishop of Piacenza was to be named Nuncio to France, and he received a number of letters of congratulations, from French bishops among others. Scalabrini called it "exhilirating news...Am I really destined to become a world legend?"[22] But the rumor was not unfounded. It has not been possible to find confirmation of Soderini's statement that the Pope wanted to make the Bishop a cardinal in compensation for the sacrifice he made in not defending himself against the attacks to which he was subjected because of the pamphlet he had published at the wish of the Holy Father. According to Soderini, Bishop Scalabrini replied that "It was repugnant to him to have honors lavished on his person while the ideas to which he was completely dedicated were condemned."[23] Monsignor Mondini relates:

> "The Holy Father proposed that he make him Nuncio to Paris at a difficult time, and the Servant of God told me...that His Holiness had deigned to insist that he accept. And he added that he had not accepted, declaring that he did not have the qualifications, that he felt called instead to the pastoral ministry rather than to the diplomatic life and that he preferred to avoid the worldly ambiences in which those who held such office were constrained to move."[24]

In 1901 Catholic papers carried the news that Scalabrini was to be transferred to the metropolitan see of Ravenna, traditionally held by a cardinal. As noted above,[25] he did everything he could to ward off the promotion, and he laughed heartily at the "fantasy" of Bonomelli who already saw his friend "mounting the throne of Peter and beginning a new age." And he did not communicate the proposal even to his faithful secretary, "for 25 years the inseparable companion of my few joys and my many sorrows."[26]

Toward the end of 1903 and the beginning of 1904, the news spread throughout Italy that he was to succeed Pius X as patriarch of Venice. The rumor was due to an indiscretion on the part of the mayor of Venice, Count Grimani, who must have been told by the Venetian deputy Macola about the negotiations under way to obtain the *Exequatur* from the government.[27] The Bishop was deeply grieved that the news was so widely circulated and disturbed by the congratulations pouring in from everywhere. He called it "an annoying, troublesome, crazy rumor, a true persecution,"[28] and he hastened to avert the danger.[29]

Cardinal Agliardi wrote him that the Holy Father had listened to the wishes of his "dear, very dear friend," and so had abandoned the plan to promote him to the Venetian patriarchate, because this was "not commensurate with your activity and was prejudicial to your interests, and too painful to your heart and that of the Piacentini who adore you. Since, however, I insisted that he satisfy the desires of your friends and, let us say also, of the Italian Catholics, by granting you, too, the honor of the purple, the Holy Father agreed with me on this but added that he would wait to bestow this promotion after your new voyage to America."[30] Scalabrini immediately expressed a sense of relief and liberation to Bonomelli who had both congratulated him and expressed regret that nothing had come of the original plan and who had praised him for "the great example of evangelical spirit" he had given at a time of "such feverish vanities and ambitions."[31]

"Yes, the crisis is happily terminated...For if the new kind of martyrdom the newspapers have put me through can produce the magnificent result that you say, then God be thanked."[32] — "What does it matter whether one is first or last," he thought. "When one works for God, with God and in God, the last place is dearer than the first."[33]

The Bishop's nephew, Msgr. Attilio Bianchi, who was then a member of Pius X's private secretariat and later became a Camaldolese monk, confirmed the fact that the Holy Father had decided to make him a cardinal at the Consistory which then was held shortly after Scalabrini's death. The latter, however, replied to everyone who offered congratulations and good wishes:

"What red hat! I am thinking of death."[34] And again: "We must not think of getting dressed up in red, but rather of going to the cemetery."[35]

Poverty

Scalabrini was now quite detached from the goods of this world. His meditation often concentrated on the theme of poverty:

"What can be more precious here below, more noble, greater and worthy of more esteem than that which has the esteem and the honors of a God?" he exclaimed. "When a king wishes to ennoble a poor child of the people so that all will respect her, what does he do? He seeks her out among the obscure people where she is hiding, makes her his bride, and invites her to sit on his throne; he places a crown on her head and a sceptre in her hands...This is what Jesus Christ has done with poverty, choosing it as his inseparable companion from his cradle to his tomb, and from that day forward poverty began to receive a queen's honors among Christians."[36]

He wanted to be poor after the example of the Master. His love of poverty was reflected in his whole way of life, in his sparsely furnished room, in the barely sufficient heating he used in winter, in his linens.[37] He usually had no money in his pocket. He had charged his servant to distribute whatever charity to the poor who approached him, while he himself spoke some word of comfort or encouragement.[38]

And yet enormous sums often passed through his hands. In fact, many benefactors of the Diocese, since they had great confidence in the Bishop, used him as a channel for their own charities. "But whatever came in, the same was given out again," for "he was completely detached from money."[39] There was a rumor current that he had torn up "a will that made him heir to a spectacular sum in order not to deprive the relatives of the deceased of their inheritance, since they were living in great poverty." He persuaded the Marchesa Fanny Visconti Anguissola di Modrone not to make him her sole heir, the money to be used in works of charity, preferring instead to receive from her relatives "some help through their kindness."[40] All the money that was entrusted to him through public subsidies was used for the poor and for the diocesan institutions.[41] As for himself, he took care that no attachment to money should enter his soul. An episode recounted at the *Process* confirms this spirit of evangelical poverty.

"One day he told me that during his meditation the devil had tempted him to keep a bank book with a deposit of three thousand lire, left over from the allotment for the Bishop's support, as an initial fund to be increased with later savings. To offset any danger, he called me, explained what had happened, and handed me the bank book, and had me take it immediately to the Institute for the Deafmutes."[42]

His living quarters were simple, his furniture belonged to the episcopal palace. He wanted no rich draperies, and only when he had special guests did he permit the use of the silver tableware which had been given him.[43]

His dress, too, reflected his love of poverty. He used no silk and, in fact, his underthings were often mended.[44] He was never negligent in dress, however, and negligence in others he found offensive. "Clean up a bit," he said half in earnest half in jest to the virtuous Bishop of Parma. At the second dicoesan synod, he issued strict dispositions in this regard:

"Priests are always to conduct themselves in a manner that reflects a clean simplicity and a simple seriousness. Therefore they are to be greatly reproached who take excessive pains with their hair, and so are those who go uncombed and this applies also to those who spend too much on their own persons as well as those who do not give enough thought to the necessary cleanliness. Pastors, whose consciences we bind on this point, are not to allow priests who are dirty and thus betray the clerical dignity to say Mass or perform the other sacred functions."[45]

Neither over-refinement nor carelessness, therefore, but dignity and detachment. This was the norm he had chosen for himself and recommended to his priests, to whom he was fond of repeating an anecdote about St. Charles Borromeo. The latter was brought, almost as if it were a relic, the beretta of a priest who had died in the odor of sanctity but who had left a sizeable inheritance to his nephews. St. Charles threw the beretta into the fire, exclaiming, "But then, he was not a saint!"[46]

"The vow of poverty was not being observed very perfectly in a certain religious house in Piacenza. Bishop Scalabrini was disturbed by this *coram Deo* and had not failed to make some fatherly observations in this regard. But the evil continued. One day he was asked to visit that particular religious house. As he did so he was met by the entire community in tears. 'See, Excellency, what this night's fire has done to us!' His reply was: 'Light the candles in the chapel right away; we shall sing the *Te Deum*. This is no reason to weep but to bless the Lord who with this fire has healed your house.' "[47]

In his will Scalabrini wrote:

"I came to Piacenza a poor man and I leave the world a poor man; the little that really belongs to me will be enough to pay my bills and the expenses of my funeral, which I wish to be a very modest one."[48]

His spirit of poverty was matched by temperance. To do away with certain rather unedifying customs that had crept into the "fraternal agapes" of the clergy, he was constrained to set forth detailed norms which were to be observed under pain of ecclesiastical censure.[49] When he himself was present he required that the rule be observed without any special exceptions because "of the Bishop" and if the rule was forgotten he reacted vigorously.[50] He either turned his plate over and refused to accept anything else to eat[51] or he left the table and went for a walk in the courtyard.[52]

On the other hand, when he visited a poor parish, where he was not expected and the pantry was therefore quite empty, he was never disturbed, but thankfully took whatever was set before him.[53]

At Montecanino, the old pastor, who was a very casual type, had set before him only a couple of eggs and some fish of very poor quality. The Bishop not only did not complain but acted very satisfied.[54]

On another occasion, in the middle of summer, he arrived at a mountain parish, Scopolo, very tired from the long ride on horseback. Nothing was ready in the priest's house, and with difficulty they managed to get a little soup in the nearby inn. The priests who were accompanying the Bishop were annoyed and began to complain, but he told them to be quiet and had only compassionate words for the poor pastor who had not expected them and so was unprepared.[55] Finally, at Centenaro, the housekeeper made excuses for the frugal meal, observing that in the mountains one did not have the same conveniences as in the city. The Bishop replied with great simplicity: "Is there milk? Is there butter? Are there any eggs? Well, then, that's enough."[56]

He was never upset by the discomforts, or mishaps and bad weather encountered on his pastoral visits. He was always patient and serene, and never lost his good humor.[57]

He himself laughingly told how in one parish of upper Val Nure he had slept in a tiny room that had evidently served as a chicken coop. One may imagine therefore the company that kept him awake all night. And as if that were not enough, as soon as it was dawn, he was regaled by the crowing roosters and cackling hens that were in the next room, separated only by a thin wall.[58]

He slept only the minimum he needed, spending the other hours of the night either working or praying.[59] He ususally slept about seven hours, but shortened his rest when he was to officiate at solemn functions.[60] He loved to rise early; he was up at five in the morning,[61] and he would open the window and bless the city. Even during his pastoral visits, although he heard confessions late into the night, he was always up early in the morning.[62]

CHAPTER XXIII

His Memory is Blessed

Death

As he grew more and more detached from this world, the more serene Scalabrini became in a growing union with God, who was his frame of reference for every human event and in whom alone he sought his peace.

"As we have already noted, the thought of death was a very familiar one to the Servant of God."[1] — "He had been preparing himself for death for quite some time; he went to confession more often, and he prayed more and with greater fervor. He mortified himself and spoke often of death; according to him, one had to think of death."[2]

In the last year of his life he seemed to sense that his encounter with Christ was drawing near. On New Year's Day, 1905, he gave "a most moving sermon" in the Cathedral and "he chose certain expressions almost as if he foresaw that his own death was near, so that some said it seemed a last will and testament."[3]

"In this dizzying passage of time there is an impenetrable mystery that moves us in spite of ourselves. The days we have lived, the sufferings and the joys that now are no more than memories, the griefs that broke our heart and have faded in the distance like all the rest, the years that pass so swiftly, what a strange and mysterious thing these are, what salutary reflections they inspire. For the modern man, the first day of the year is merely a pretext for new diversions, new amusements. For the true Christian it must be something quite different. The first day of the year should call to his mind the image of the world that is passing, that melts into the distance and disappears; the grace of God that follows him and to which he must respond at all times throughout his life, and finally the day of God that is drawing near and for which he is obliged to prepare himself. Yes, the image of the fleeting world...The first day of the year reminds us of the great day of eternity. Life's journey will not go on indefinitely; like all journeys it will come to an end. Now this end, which every human life must encounter, is not annihilation, but eternity."[4]

"The sufferings and sacrifices which the Servant of God endured during his journeys, and especially the second one (in Brazil) were certainly many and grave. I remember that soon after his return he came to my parish to bless the bells, and I found him to be very worn out; he was no longer himself! I remember, too, the emotion his sermon aroused in me, especially the conclusion when he spoke of the bell-note for death. His words and his tone gave the impression that he foresaw his own death was not far away."[5]

The hydrocele caused by a riding incident during his pastoral visits and which had been bothering him for many years had grown worse in Brazil. His valet had for some time been trying to find out the reason for the spots of blood he had noticed on the Bishop's undershirt and finally, when he was straightening out his room in Sao Paulo, he came upon a hairshirt. He hid it, but then had to put it back where he had found it when he realized the bishop was looking for it. The latter had guessed what the servant had done and said to him jokingly: "You have hidden that instrument and the Lord has sent me another, much more painful...Patience for love of Him!"

On May 21, 1905 he went to the parish of Borghetto di San Lazaro Alberoni for a pastoral visit and to bless the cemetery. After the ceremony he suddenly fainted. The pastor rushed to his aid, throughout the day "he kept referring to death, saying that he felt his end was near."[6] On his way back to the city he met a funeral procession...As was his custom, he got out of his carriage, blessed the coffin and recited the De profundis. On resuming his journey he tapped his master of ceremonies lightly on the knee and said, "You will soon be reciting that for your Bishop."

"As soon as he arrived home, in fact, the Servant of God was forced to take to his bed. The doctor was hastily summoned, and for the first time he saw the nature and seriousness of the illness and the urgent need for surgical intervention. This news was a surprise and a cause of grief for all the members of the bishop's household, and they joined with the doctor in trying to persuade him to undergo surgery. But the Servant of God was very reluctant because of the nature of the operation itself. When his brother and sister, who had been called to his bedside, finally convinced him, with tears in his eyes he exclaimed: 'Dear God, do you wish this humiliation from me too; thy will be done.' "[7]

Saturday, May 27th, he went to confession, asked that everything be in readiness in case it became necessary to administer the Last Sacrament, and he personally prepared the oil stocks during the night before the operation — "a night which he spent in prayer and in adoration in his private chapel, as I had seen him do many times," his servant recalled, "because I, too, did not sleep all that night."[8]

On Sunday, May 28th, Dr. Carle of Turin, assisted by Doctors De Orchi and Marchesi, performed the operation. "He did not permit me to remain in the room while he was being prepared for the operation," his servant continued, "and when I insisted that I be allowed to stay, he replied: 'You, my boy, stay outside. If I need you I will call you.' While he was being prepared he fainted, and I believe this was caused by the repugnance he felt at being exposed to five doctors. When they called me in, I jumped on the bed to raise him a little and he said to me: 'I feel very bad; I feel bad enough to die.' The doctors then suggested postponing the operation, but having revived somewhat he asked that the operation be performed, even though he was unhappy that it should be done on the Sabbath day. Then he added: 'The will of God be done always.' At this the doctors had him carried from his bedroom, where he had been prepared, to the room in the corner of the episcopal palace where the table had been made ready for the operation. While he was being carried there, past the little chapel where the Blessed Sacrament was kept, he looked toward the altar with an expression that spoke all his faith and devotion. When they arrived at the operating room he asked Dr. Carle: — 'Listen, doctor, is the operation dangerous?' And Carle answered: — 'No, Your Excellency, it is not a serious operation. I never perform it; I always have my assistants do it. Within four or five days you will be able to take a walk in your garden.' — And the Bishop added: — 'Whatever it is, I have for some time been prepared for death. The Lord's will be done. I have prepared everything for the sacraments, even the oil stock.' "[9]

"The patient had been anesthetized with chloroform, and after the operation he remained very drowsy. When he awakened now and then and some one asked how he felt, he answered: — 'Quite well.' And this continued through the next day, Monday. Then he began to grow worse and his heart beat slowed down considerably. During Monday night, the constant attention of two doctors was necessary, but by Tuesday morning the danger seemed to be over. Instead, that evening, he grew worse again; his breathing became difficult and he was given oxygen. This continued throughout Wednesday, the oxygen being administered alternately with injections of various stimulants. Throughout his illness, he did not utter a single moan, nor the slightest complaint."[10]

On Wednesday morning (May 31st), when his condition grew much worse, "he himself asked that the Holy Viaticum be brought to him solemnly as the Synod and the *Ceremonialis Episcoporum* prescribe. He himself requested that the windows of the palace be draped, that the room in which he lay be well prepared. He asked that his rochet, mozzetta and the pectoral cross given him by Pius IX be placed on him and ordered that a tabernacle for the Blessed Sacrament be set on the little table facing the bed; he then asked that beside it on another table there be placed the little urn containing the relic of Saint Savino. When the Blessed Sacrament was brought in from the parish church as he had requested, he welcomed it with the most edifying devotion. He said the prayers of preparation for communion, recited the prescribed solemn profession of faith, and followed the prayers suggested by the priests who were present."[11]

"Then turning to those around him he said in a calm and serene voice: 'I am close to appearing before Christ the Judge; I ask forgiveness of all and I bless all.' "[12] "He received the Holy Viaticum in full consciousness, while his love for Our Lord was expressed in fervent prayers, and his strength returned to such an extent that Dr. Luigi Marchesi, who was then in attendance, exclaimed literally: 'This is a miracle; this is a dead man speaking. And to think that I have little belief in miracles.' — The improvement was temporary, however, his strength began to fail again and he asked for Extreme Unction, which he received the same day with great devotion."[13] — "A tray was brought in on which were the cruets containing the chrism, the oil of the catechumens and the oil for the sick. The patient said: — 'Let me see, because you are all so disturbed you may have made some mistake.' — He picked up the cruet of Holy Oil and handed it to his secretary; then he motioned to them to say the prayers slowly because he wished to recite them also. When he had received the Sacrament, he embraced and kissed the Vicar General of the Diocese and the others present, saying with a smile: — 'Pray for me; my greetings to the professors and students in the Seminary... my Missionaries...good-bye, good-bye...' And he raised his right hand in the act of blessing; then he fell back unconscious. He came to a little later and seemed somewhat revived when he was told of the Holy Father's blessing at which he was greatly moved. — 'Give him my filial thanks,' he said to his secretary in a thin but clear voice. And soon afterwards, he added: 'To all the pastors and canons present here at my last suffering I give the faculty to impart to me the blessing *in articulo mortis.'* — During the day, in his few lucid moments, he had words of comfort for the members of his household and gave some directions for his burial.[14] He embraced Bishop Fiorini, who had come to visit him before going to Cremona,[15] and with a supreme effort said to him: 'My most affectionate greetings to Bishop Bonomelli...' — Then he seemed to wander and kept saying 'My priests. Where are my priests? Let them come in; don't make them wait too long.' "[16]

"Up to the end the Servant of God continued to say ejaculations, to kiss the crucifix, and to recite the rosary he had in his hands, and he kept repeating, 'God's will be done,' and asking forgiveness of those he might have offended."[17]

"Toward six o'clock, on June 1, 1905, the feast of the Ascension, after a brief agony and murmuring a prayer, he gave up his beautiful soul to God."[18]

"A Saint is Dead"

The swift news of his death produced a shock in the diocese and the Church, which frequently expressed what became the beginning of his glorification: "A saint is dead!"[19]

"The body of the Servant of God, clothed in his pontifical robes, remained in state for several days, and a steady stream of people knelt around his bier, and I would say that then there was born among the people the conviction that they were praying not only before a holy Bishop but to a Bishop who was a saint."[20] — "Because of the reputation for sanctity that he had acquired through his multiple works of charity, for several days a veritable pilgrimage of citizens and the faithful, even from the most distant areas of the diocese, filed past to gaze for the last time on the blessed features of their Bishop; a number of priests hastened to touch to his body medals, crucifixes, rosaries from among the people, to be kept as precious souvenirs sanctified by that contact."[21]

Sunday morning, June 4th, saw "real pilgrimages of peasants coming from all the towns in the diocese."[22] That evening as the body was transferred from the episcopal palace to the cathedral, the funeral procession, which took an hour and a half to wind through the short distance, became a triumphal one.

"Piacenza had never seen so great a crowd of people."[23] — "No one remembers a more solemn manifestation of mourning...a more intense manifestation of grief, a greater tribute of tears and prayers."[24]

The unity of the Church, which he had promoted day by day "with the greatest wisdom and much prudence and greatness of heart..."[25] was symbolized, as it were, in the participation of the entire population, seven hundred priests, religious communities and associations, all the civic authorities, the aristocracy, the army, and half the mayors of the province. The funeral ceremonies were even more impressive, celebrated the following day in the cathedral, which could not hold even half the crowd, a great part of which was packed in the piazza."[26]

Celebrant of the funeral Mass was Archbishop Valfre of Vercelli, present as the Apostolic Administrator of Como. Among those present were Archbishop Bruni of Modena, Archbishop Morganti of Ravenna, Bishop Conforti of Parma, Bishop Bandi of Tortona, Bishop Fiorini of Pontremoli, and Bishop Sarti of Guastalla, who delivered the eulogy. When the services were over, the procession reformed and the coffin was carried to Burriera, where at the old gate it received the last welfare of the city from the Royal Commissioner and a little deaf girl. It was given temporary burial in the capitular chapel in the cemetery.

In 1908 a statue in memory of Bishop Scalabrini was unveiled next to the Blessed Sacrament altar in the cathedral of Piacenza. The following year permission was obtained from the Government to bury him in the cathedral. Through the glass inserts in the coffin it was possible to see that the body was still intact. The ceremony of transferral, presided over by Bishop Giacomo della Chiesa, accompanied by fourteen bishops was not so much a sad memorial service as a new exaltation.

"I remember as if it were yesterday the expression on every face," an eyewitness recalled. "It was a kind of melancholy joy. There was the sadness that comes from recalling sad memories, the comfort of feeling united in affection, the consolation of seeing his mortal remains, and the inextinguishable memory of that beloved man all caught up now in an even more radiant atmosphere of veneration and admiration."[27]

"His reputation for sanctity, far from fading, kept increasing, so that when the body of the Servant of God was transferred to the cathedral, the ceremony assumed such spectacular proportions that Archbishop Giacomo della Chiesa (who later became Benedict XV) exclaimed on entering the cathedral: — 'St. Peter's in Rome could not contain the tribute of Piacenza.' "[28]

In 1910 a marble statue was erected in the church of his native town, Fino Mornasco. In 1913, Cardinal Ferrari unveiled the monument to his memory in the parish church of San Bartolomeo in Como. Pius X expressed his wish to be spiritually present with an autographed message.[29] The year before (1912), when on the occasion of the 25th anniversary of the foundation of the Scalabrinian Missionaries another statue had been dedicated to the memory of the Father of the Emigrants in the basilica of San Carlo al Corso, the Holy Father had told the pilgrims from Como: "The homage that you have rendered to your illustrious fellow citizen, I feel you have rendered to me."[30]

The Judgment of Contemporaries and of Posterity

The people's judgment summed up in the phrase, "he was a saint," was confirmed by St. Pius X who called him "one of our best bishops," "no less remarkable for wisdom than for his goodness."[31] The autographed message sent for the unveiling of the statue in San Bartolomeo in Como, contained a eulogy of his beloved friend:

"I take a lively part in the commemoration the good citizens of Como are offering the exemplary Pastor, who ensured the Christian education of his people, especially through the teaching of the catechism, the learned, strong but gentle Bishop, who even in the most difficult circumstances has always defended, loved, and inspired love for the truth and never abandoned it because of threats or flattery — the courageous Apostle, who sacrificed everything to preserve the faith of our poor brothers who emigrated to the Americas, with the mission of zealous priests inspired by his spirit; and it is my wish that the memory of this Pastor, Bishop and Apostle, John Baptist Scalabrini, be always blessed, and that his example inspire holy imitators."[32]

Another autographed message reveals the esteem which Pope Benedict XV had for the Servant of God:

"On the tenth anniversary of the death of Bishop Scalabrini, we, who as Archbishop of Bologna, took part on April 18, 1909, in the ceremony transferring his mortal remains to the Cathedral of Piacenza and could personally witness how deep and universal was the affectionate mourning of every citizen for this incomparable Prelate, join with all our heart the testimony of our own memory to the commemoration of his flock and those he benefited. In recalling after ten years of uninterrupted admiration, his most noble virtues, and primarily the principal one, his charity, which so animated him that the boundaries of his vast diocese became too narrow and impelled him to seek new flocks among the far-off Italian emigrants, we express our pleasure to the beloved priests who, imitating his zeal, continue his worthy enterprise."[33]

Pius XI attested to the great merits of Bishop Scalabrini[34] and in a letter to the bishop's nephew in 1913 he called him a saint...[35] When he received a group of Scalabrinian Missionaries in 1934 he recalled that he had had "the pleasure and good fortune to know Bishop Scalabrini personally and to speak to him." He continued, "We can confirm and attest to his spirit, which was not only pastoral and episcopal but also truly apostolic and missionary."[36] When in 1936 Bishop Ersilio Menzani of Piacenza informed him of the proposal to begin the canonical process on Scalabrini's reputation for sanctity, the Holy Father exclaimed: "I view this with favor," and he gave his encouragement in "an extraordinary heartfelt blessing."[37]

In the Apostolic Constitution *Exsul Familia*, Pius XII recalled "that apostolic man, whom we proclaimed exceptionally deserving of the Church and of the country."[38] John XXIII when he was patriarch of Venice, called him "a most pious bishop, learned, zealous, generous in the service of God and of souls."[39]

There have been many eminent men of the church who have expressed their judgment of the Bishop of Piacenza. The following seems the most significant since they come from those who knew him best.

Cardinal Svampa, Archbishop of Bologna, declared:

"I cannot resign myself to the great void left by the death of the holy bishop. Two thoughts comfort me...namely, that he has arrived at the reward he earned through so many glorious and holy works — and that in heaven he will not fail to protect us, just as he loved us so much during the course of his earthly life."[40]

Cardinal Capecelatro, one of the most representative Church personalities in the field of learning and in matters relating to the religious, social, political problems of the time, knew him intimately and thus underlined one of his principal characteristics:

"I here will mention only one of his merits, which is generally very rare in our time. He was an unusual Bishop in his Christian courage. He liked to speak the truth to everyone with apostolic candor even when it was difficult, and he did so with so much charity and charm, that most were not displeased by it. He governed his own diocese, where he had very many bitter experiences, with great charity but also with that fortitude which is born of Christian courage, which in doing good keeps its glance fixed on God alone and does not fear...In many respects Scalabrini had within him something of the Bishops of the finest eras of the Church."[41]

Cardinal Agliardi considered him the "holy glory of our country and the Church."[42] Cardinal Schiaffino called him "a gem of priceless value, a radiant torch of sound doctrine, an always living flame of love."[43] Cardinal Moretti said he was a "Bishop after God's own heart."[44] From Cardinal Ferrari we have the following:

"A good Pastor, a living Father, a splendid and most gentle figure of a man of God, with an apostolic heart...a man of profound religion, exemplary piety, unshakeable attachment to the See of Peter; a man of patient, benign charity, who seeks not his own things, who believes all, hopes all, endures all things; a man fittingly described by the phrase *vir misericors, cuius pietates non defecerunt*, neither in Piacenza nor in the other parts of Italy, of Europe, of the new world...*fama magnus, re maior.*"[45]

Cardinal Richelmy, Archbishop of Turin, "had the good fortune to know his most intimate aspirations, to constantly admire the achievements of his episcopate, to help him with his institutions on behalf of the poor Italian emigrants." Therefore, he said:

"I think that his best eulogy lies in the goodness of his heart. His motto was that of the Apostle: *Charitas Christi urget nos*...His charity knew no limits...dead to himself, he lived the life of the true disciple of Jesus Christ; and did good wherever he went...A sweet and heavenly light surrounds his name on earth, and it seems to me his spirit is to be sought among the heroes of the Catholic Apostolate, among the martyrs of charity."[46]

Cardinal Nasalli Rocca, who grew up in the shadow of Bishop Scalabrini, recalled an episode from his youth:

"I found Bishop Scalabrini with a thick manuscript in front of him. As soon as I entered he said to me, 'You know, I taught Msgr. B... a little...This book is the history of my tenure as a Bishop...Oh, if only it would be read by certain persons who pass judgment on their Bishops, who can never, or almost never, justify their actions because they are bound either by charity or prudence...' And then, with a foresight that unfortunately was proven true, he began in conclusion to teach me a little also. Now that I see and feel what the word 'to govern' means, I understand what a great governor my holy Bishop was, what consummate prudence, what a generous heart, what a clear intelligence he possessed, and what a treasure my Piacenza had in him for thirty years."[47]

Cardinal Rossi wrote as follows to the Scalabrinian Missionaries:

"If Bishop Scalabrini, according to the grave and solemn judgment of the Church, were already declared Blessed, I would not hesitate to have him say to you this exhortation of St. Paul to the Philippians: *Imitatores mei estote*...But what, short of officialdom, keeps you from praying to him and trying to imitate him...Which of his teachings and example can you not, should you not follow? To be as he was, full of faith, afire with charity, untiring zeal, eager for sacrifice?"[48]

Fifty years after his death Bishop Scalabrini was commemorated in terms that reveal how alive is the memory of his virtues and how vital his example. Cardinal Fossati saw in the Servant of God, "a personality so eminent and so apostolic that by himself he could render the apostolate of the Italian hierarchy illustrious and deserving throughout a century."[49] Particularly important are observations of two recent cardinals: Cardinal Piazza, who made a profound study of Scalabrini's life as the *ponente* of his beatification, and Cardinal Bevilacqua, an exceptional apostolic personality with a profound knowledge of contemporary church history.

Cardinal Piazza considered Scalabrini "a model bishop," a "bishop par excellence, after God's own heart," the "portrait of the *homo Dei*," an "admirable champion as a bishop, as an apostle."

"The documents and testimonies gathered and evaluated, though without an intention of anticipating, much less influencing, the authoritative and independent judgment of the Church, show us in him a perfect example of a prelate and bishop, according to the profile which St. Paul sketched in his epistles to Timothy and Titus, a match for the complex exigencies and contingencies of our time."[50]

"He ended his earthly days at the age of 66, on the feast of the Ascension of Our Lord, almost as if participating in the divine triumph. We confidently await another feast of the Ascension, on which Jesus will call his priest and faithful minister to participate in his glory in this very Church, his Mystical Body, to which he dedicated his entire apostolic and missionary ministry up to his final sacrifice."[51]

Father Bevilacqua, the future "cardinal pastor," was an enthusiastic admirer of Scalabrini: "a truly great one, a man who has covered all the roads of the world." By his very temperament he could not like the "little chapel" of liberal Catholicism:

"For Bishop Scalabrini the Church is the human cathedral, in the fourfold measure of Christ: height, depth, breadth and length...At difficult times, he suffered for the Church and for such a Church! Only because he had come to this essentiality of the Church had he learned so well when to speak and when to keep silent. And his silences were more expressive, more filled with teaching, even than his words...After having spoken out as a son of the Church, he submitted in silence to that obedience of which he was a true champion. No parishes closed in on themselves, unaware of the diocese, unaware of their cathedral. Not even dioceses closed in on themselves with no understanding of the catholicity, the universality of the Church of God! Bishop Scalabrini was aware of all the problems of his time. First problem: There was need of priests suited to the culture of the time. I do not know whether, with respect to this problem, there is another bishop to be compared with Scalabrini...He understood the true malady of our people. The people, he said, do not need to be moved, but to be instructed!...Scalabrini was the precursor of the Catholic Action of the laity, while before there had only been confraternities...He defended other Catholic organizations with unique vigor...He refuted socialism when it was still at its first, but then terrible, attack in Italy. He understood that a people are not saved with negative criticism, but with well organized social reform...He defended the constitution of the Church with great energy, with that energy that ignores diplomatic speech...If he fought it was only to bear Christ as the light of the world, as the light also of Italy...One does not love the Church if one does not fully assume its responsibilities according to the proper hierarchical order...He had the highest concept of episcopal authority, the one most genuinely in conformity with tradition. I would say that no one like Ignatius of Antioch gave us a clear idea of what a bishop is. Bishop Scalabrini, too, always believed that it is the duty of the bishop to defend the Church, to speak in its defense..."[52]

Among the numerous bishops who knew and esteemed Scalabrini, we would quote first Bishop Bonomelli, who knew him more intimately than any of the others and who shared his joys and sorrows, his worries and his hopes:

"Bishop Scalabrini's entire life is that of a model Bishop, especially for our times, which he understood perfectly. How many times on certain days, at certain times, I remind myself of the conversations I had with him, and the enlightenment, advice, and comfort I drew from them! How he understood modern society, the needs of the Church, and the means to remedy the moral and religious disasters which indifferences and misbelief go piling up."[53] — "I remember the days, the happy hours we spent together, helping each other to forget our troubles, advising each other on the means to overcome the difficulties sowed in our way, in order that we might procure glory for God and the salvation of souls; then I recall the treasury of virtues that great Bishop carried in his heart. What wisdom! What a vigorous will! What charity! What learning! I have never seen him draw back when a sacrifice was required in a case of duty, of the good of souls. He suffered, and I felt small, a nothing, in comparison to him."[54]

Bishop Pellizzari, who succeeded Scalabrini in the diocese of Piacenza, expressed his feelings this way:

"Bishop Scalabrini is one of the brightest lights in this series (of Piacentinian bishops), one of the most precious gems in this chain, one of the most glorious pages of history not only for Piacenza, but for Italy, for the whole world."[55] — "His memory will not perish, because his was a true greatness...His life became a perpetual school of devotion and virtue...A beloved Pastor, Benefactor of mankind, boast and glory of the Catholic hierarchy...a prelate who gathered in himself all the virtues and the greatness of his predecessors."[56]

Among the bishops who were Scalabrini's contemporaries it is interesting to note the comments of those who held different "political" views. Bishop Radini Tedeschi of Bergamo called him "a most venerable and unforgettable bishop, from whom I received all the Sacred Orders, along with the inspiration of examples of tireless zeal and renowned episcopal virtues." For Bishop Lacroix of Tarentaise, the death of the bishop, with whom he had wanted to make an eight day retreat in order to learn how to be a bishop, was "a great loss for the Church."[57] The Bishop of Reggio Emilia, Archbishop Sidoli of Genoa, the Bishop of Clermont-Ferrand declared him "holy and worthy of the honors of the altar..."[58]

The bishops of Piacentinian origin — Malchiodi, Prati, Bergamashi, Rossi, Albanesi, Oddi declared: "One day which we hope and pray is not too distant, the Church will confirm with its infallible judgment the heroism of the virtues of our holy bishop, who was an honor to the Italian hierarchy and the special boast of our diocese."[59]

We note later the esteem and veneration St. Frances Xavier Cabrini held for him.[60] Blessed Luigi Guanella was one of the most fervent admirers of Bishop Scalabrini, who was listed among the friends of the holy priest of Como in the decree of the latter's Beatification.[61] In fact, the two knew each other as youngsters and were fellow students at the Collegio Gallio and the Seminary of Como. Together they requested that they be allowed to become missionaries, and from that time they remained bound by mutual affection and esteem, just as they resembled each other in their boundless faith in Providence. "My dear Father Luigi," Scalabrini confided to him one day, "we are truly puppets in the hand of Providence. That is what leads us."[62]

Blessed Luigi, along with Don Orione, Cardinals Laurenti and Caccia Dominioni, Bishop Rinaldi, Commendatore Nogara and other eminent personalities, was a member of the Roman committee for the celebration of the 25th anniversary of the founding of the Missionaries of St. Charles. He had his nephew, Father Lorenzo Sterlocchi, a former pupil of the Servant of God, write his life, "for the glory not only of the Diocese of Como, which boasts it is the birthplace of that Great Man, but of all Italy, and to refute the views of those who see in the clergy nothing but selfishness and indifference to those in need."[63]

Bishop Massimo Rinaldi[64] and Msgr. Francesco Torta[65] both recalled Blessed Luigi Guanella's admiration for Scalabrini. Rinaldi heard Blessed Luigi "say many times after Bishop Scalabrini's death, that he considered him a saint."[66] Torta recalled that Guanella called him fortunate because he was a beloved student of the Bishop of Piacenza, "saying that he was a great soul."[67]

Don Orione expressed desire for the beatification of Bishop Scalabrini so that he might continue to be an example of apostolic endeavor and so that the Catholic priesthood might be exalted through him.[68]

"He left behind an extraordinary impression. It was possible to judge him in different ways, but he impressed even those who disagreed with him. And I have often had the thought that if he had lived in the early days of the Church, he would have illumined it with his learning, doctrine and even with his martyrdom."[69]

Even Father Calabria hoped that the Lord would "glorify even on earth his heroic Servant," the "great Apostle," the "great saint."[70] The Servant of God, Giuseppe Toniolo, thanked the Lord for the good fortune and the honor of having personally known Bishop Scalabrini; he numbered him among the superior minds and great hearts, among the special instruments of the merciful designs of God and called him the "holy bishop of Piacenza."[71]

The Beginning of the Canonical Processes

Scalabrini's reputation for sanctity, which spread throughout the diocese and beyond, led many to pray for his intercession.

During his lifetime there were those who credited him with miracles. An episode considered extraordinary was given in testimony in the diocesan proceedings.

"It was 1902. During the summer, Bishop Scalabrini was here on a pastoral visit, when a fire broke out in the wood-drying warehouse of the Società Candiani-Girardi and Berni. The flames spread in no time and enveloped the roof of the plant. It caused panic among the townspeople who had run to the fire at the sound of the fire bells and the plant's alarm whistle since they feared the fire would spread throughout the town because of the hundreds of quintals of wood within the warehouse itself and the thousands piled up outside it. There was an added danger in the warehouse in which the alcohol distilled from the wood was stored, situated close by and which the fire could quite easily reach...One of my sisters-in-law...was among the first to notice the fire and to alert Enrico de Thierry, executive director of the company, whose servant she was. Now on that evening the Bishop was the guest of de Thierry, whom he had converted from Protestantism. As soon as news of the disaster was given, Bishop Scalabrini ran to the scene, where the townspeople and workmen had gathered, powerless to control the fire. The bishop immediately blessed the fire and began to pray and urged the others to pray. After a few moments, not to say immediately, not only did the flames disappear as part of the roof collapsed, but inside also the fire was almost completely under control, so that after a half hour, we returned to work...I was immediately convinced that this was a miracle, as everyone was saying then, for with all that inflammable material no one could understand how the fire could suddenly die out."[72]

According to some witnesses, there were stories among the people of extraordinary graces received through the prayers and the blessing of the Bishop, but specific details about these are lacking.

After his death, his reputation for sanctity kept growing and spreading. Many attributed uncommon happenings to his intercession.

A man working on the decorations in the cathedral in Piacenza made the following deposition:

"One day, between 1909 and 1911, after the octave of Corpus Christi, I was removing the hangings from a pillar in the Blessed Sacrament chapel near Bishop Scalabrini's tomb. I was on an extension ladder about 14 meters high. As a result of a mistaken movement on the part of one of my assistants, the gear-tooth hit against the column and was released. The roller around which the metallic cords were wound began to whirl crazily, and the ladder collapsed. In no time I found myself on the floor clinging to the last rung of the ladder, about a meter and a half away from the tomb of the Servant of God. My fall was so sudden that I did not have time to think what was happening nor to say any prayer. The people in the church, about ten, fled in terror thinking I was killed. People ran up to me and when they saw I was unharmed, that is with only a bruise or two on my legs, they exclaimed it was a miracle and they attributed it to Bishop Scalabrini. I am convinced that I was truly, miraculously saved, and I am not averse to attributing it also to the intercession of the Servant of God."[73]

Msgr. Gregori tells about a youth dying of pneumonia:

"One evening the doctor gave out little hope for his life. The same evening, I and my sister, unknown to each other, were ending a triduum to the Servant of God, praying for the patient's recovery. The following morning I went to visit him and found that the crisis was happily over and the danger was passed."[74]

Sister Lucia Gorlin, a Scalabrinian, attests to the surprising and sudden recovery of three sisters.[75] Similar episodes are recounted by other witnesses at the process, and numerous other graces have been attributed to the intercession of the Servant of God after the diocesan process for his beatification was begun.[76]

As Scalabrini's reputation for sanctity grew more insistent and the desire to see his glorification became widespread, Bishop Ersilio Menzani of Piacenza suggested to Pius XI that the cause of his beatification be inaugurated, and the Pope gave his encouragement and blessing.[77] The Scalabrinian Father Francesco Prevedello was named postulator of the cause in the decree of the Episcopal Curia of Piacenza dated May 5, 1936. On June 20th the diocesan tribunal was established and the investigative process on his holiness and virtues was begun. In 1938 the tribunal to examine his writings (over 7000 pages) was formed, and in 1939 the Process de non-culto was started.

On February 29, 1940, the three ordinary diocesan processes were ended, during which, in 185 sessions, 56 witnesses were questioned, among whom were persons who had lived in close relationship with Bishop Scalabrini, for example, his secretary, Msgr. Camillo Mangot, his master of ceremonies, Msgr. Ludovico Mondini, and his valet, Carlo Spallazzi. Among the most authoritative witnesses, we might mention Cardinal Nasalli Rocca, Archbishop of Bologna, the Scalabrinian Father Massimo Rinaldi, Bishop of Rieti, and Don Luigi Orione. Almost all the witnesses expressed the hope that the Servant of God would be beatified.[78]

About a hundred letters favoring the cause of beatification were addressed to Pope Pius XII in 1954-1955 by cardinals, archbishops, bishops and superiors of religious orders and congregations. On March 6, 1940, Bishop

Menzani submitted the three ordinary diocesan processes to the Sacred Congregation of Rites. On the following April 30th, Cardinal Carlo Salotti, Prefect of the Congregation, issued the decrees for the opening of the three Ordinary Apostolic Processes. On April 3rd he had announced that the Pope had named Cardinal Carlo Rossi as the postulator. He was succeeded by Cardinal Adeodato Piazza, who, on the 50th anniversary of Scalabrini's death, declared:

"While the Holy See is carrying out the Process of Beatification, with the meticulous inquiry and strict procedures proper to it, his admirers and devotees can only await its judgment with confidence and humbly pray God to grant the happy outcome of the cause if this is in accordance with the plan of Providence. May He enlighten the judges to discern the features of a saint in the Servant of God and to overcome the eventual difficulties that may arise from certain of his energetic attitudes in the battle for the triumph of truth, the protection of the rights of the Church and of souls, and for the very dignity and freedom of his office as teacher and pastor. May the Lord make us hear the powerful testimony of miracles, which opens the way to the supreme glorification in the Church militant. Such are the aims and the content of our prayer."[79]

CHAPTER XXIV

The Human and Christian Features of Bishop Scalabrini's Personality

The Realist

As we think back over the life and work of Bishop Scalabrini we feel the force of a personality that was both complex and well-balanced, or better, integrated. His was a truly endowed nature, quick to absorb the fullness of supernatural grace.

His sense of balance permitted him to take stock of his possibilities in all the fields in which God called him to work. His objective evaluation of his own capabilities and limitations, and his honest humility led him to act as if everything depended on him and to be confident that everything depended on God. "We work, God accomplishes."[1]

The way he threw himself unstintingly into all he undertook was sometimes mistaken for imprudence.

"Oh, I understand very well," he used to answer, with the serene realism he was able to maintain along with a restless love for the Church and for souls. "But if we wanted perfection in human things, we would accomplish nothing. *Self-love seeks credit where God alone must be sought.* We work with good intentions; God will achieve the result. Too much prudence in doing good is not always praiseworthy. Otherwise the prime imprudent would be God himself, who makes the sun rise on the bad as well as the good and gives his enemies the means to offend him."[2]

Not the ideal "best" but the real and realizable "good." He reproached those Catholics who constantly deplored the evils of the time, debated the remedies and were always laying foundations, but who never got to building the walls.[3]

His way of looking at things — within the context of the existential situations and a few sound considerations — kept him from slipping into utopian or exclusively long term situations. The Gospel, the Church, the Pope, the Bishop, the salvation of souls, the catechism, harmony among disparate forces, unity in intention, these were the channels into which he poured his "aggressive impulses."

He saw with clarity the evils of his time: the accelerating deChristianization of the people and especially of the working classes; the slowness and uncertainty with which Catholic organization was coming out of the sacristy, abandoning useless recriminations and manning the breaches: "meanwhile, as faith dies, charity grows ever colder and the hatred of the laity for the clergy increases. The consequences can only be fatal, and who knows how long we shall have to endure them."[4]

If he had a realistic view of the evils, he did not waste time in lamenting them, or in the inconclusive jeremiads or polemics of *in infernum detrude* which were characteristic of most of the church oratory and propaganda of his day. Rather it found expression in a feverish anxiety for souls[5] and he demanded of himself a toll of work beyond his physical and moral strength.[6] This explains why he dared speak in these terms to the Pope: "I even told him that he would soon find himself before God, to whom he will have to render an account for the army of souls which is being lost...If we wait another year or more, it is doubtful there will be anything good left on which we can rebuild."[7]

Scalabrini's Temperament

Scalabrini seemed to be of a somewhat tense and nervous disposition, for he was of a sensitive nature and deeply concerned for the welfare of souls. Consequently he was no stranger to passing moments of discouragement tinged with melancholy that tended at times to impatience. A kind of pessimism is often noted in his correspondence[8] but never in his activity. He could perhaps be described as a Christian pessimist who sees the evil but does not hide his head in the sand, who confronts it squarely with faith, courage and energy. Any tendency to be depressed was overcome by his natural resilience, his great confidence and faith in God, and his vital spirituality, nourished by the Eucharist and meditation, by the Bread and the Word, so that what prevailed was a willed and conscious optimism which superficial observers sometimes found excessive.

It is certain he was never tempted to skepticism or apathy — "that inarticulate skepticism, namely that silent disdain, shut up in the heart, which is the wisdom of small minds and of the inordinately proud."[9]

"When I see certain even highly respectable priests who are cold, skeptical, who have no energy for anything...who would not lift a finger beyond their strict duty...I always have some doubt about their vocation. Apathy, which is a kind of skepticism, is fatal. We must sacrifice time, strength, money, health and life for the cause of Christ."[10]

He plunged into the world around him, therefore, accepted its battles and its exigencies, not to assert himself but to help his neighbor, with an energy explained by his love of the Crucified Christ, his thirst for souls and apostolic enthusiasm, and a brotherly spirit that reached the heights of Christian charity.

He was sensitive (witnesses at the process speak of this sensitivity, of occasional outbursts), but he did not react to petty irritations or lack respect or neglect due formalities. He did react against idleness and hypocrisy. He defended himself against unjust interpretations of his actions, especially his acts as a Bishop, but even then he was never rigid. He could distinguish between questions of principle and contingent questions, or to put it more precisely, he never transformed particular differences into questions of principle.[11]

Any intransigence he manifested in dealing with his adversaries was directed against ideas he considered deadly — against those who would block action, against sowing discord among those who were convinced that unity — hierarchical as well as mystical (for him one was the condition for the others, in fact they were one whole) — was the primary condition to "build the Church."

He always sought understanding and tried his best to discuss matters objectively and serenely and this at a time when partisan passions were more often the tools of combat than reasoned arguments or a practical overview. This explains the bitterness with which he used the word "party." For him there was nothing more absurd in the Church than a party which whatever its name, could be defined as political. "I clearly detest politics."[12] "The great law of unity," is the "sovereign principle" from which all apostolic effectiveness derives.[13] "Charity, the real truce of God, knows no party, and the blood of Jesus Christ makes us all brothers in one faith and in one hope, and this makes us debtors to everyone."[14]

Action and Activity

He was energetic by nature and given to tireless activity, and on this point his life has been described as "incredible." It is enough to read in his diary the record of one day's activity during a pastoral visit and to think how many hundreds of days were spent at the same pace, which he himself called "suffocating," "almost lunatic," expressions we find at the time of his fifth pastoral visit. Everyone was certain that he had learned his lesson during his first visit, but the breathless rhythm of his early days became a habit, and indeed his activity reached its greatest intensity when his energy and health had already begun to decline.

"I do not know how to be moderate, nor can I adapt to the idea of changing my ways, and yet I must do so. My years are adding up — 64 — work is getting heavier, our needs become increasingly serious, the socialist tide is rising and everything persuades and impels me to work beyond my physical and moral strength, and to go forward *in nomine Domini* as long as I can."[15]

His motives for stopping and for continuing were oddly mingled, and it was easy to see what the conclusion would be. One day he admitted, "I am tired to death," but this was on the eve of his passage from full activity to eternal rest, as rapid as the setting of the tropical sun.[16] Whenever anyone asked him when he would take some rest, he invariably replied, "We shall have time to do so after death."[17]

Work for him, however, was not an end in itself. The stimulus was his apostolic zeal.

"The welfare of souls? This is our life, our only reason for existence, and all our life must be a constant search for souls. We must not eat, drink, sleep, study, speak, nor even enjoy any recreation except to do good to souls, without ever getting tired, not ever."[18]

Neither can he be accused of "activism." His activity was geared to the problems of his day, which he tried to resolve both by study and by attempting to find first of all a general and lasting base on which to build a solution. Proof of this is the survival of his institutions, the vitality of his solutions and the way in which he tackled the religious problem of emigration. After weighing the pros and cons, seeking God's counsel, consulting experts in a given field, and having been convinced that a program was a good, useful or especially a necessary one, he took action with "courage, calmness and confidence in God." He also moved quickly, taking advantage of the moment, pursuing his purpose with tenacity and perseverance. Obstacles redoubled his energies, opposition seemed to him a sign of God's approval, and debts did not frighten him.

He surrendered only to the impossible, but this was a word he did not like, even when spoken by others and especially by priests, whom he counseled to repeat, *omnia possum in Eo qui me confortat*, not to be too quick to despair of a situation, not to expect quick results, to sow even though it fell to others to do the harvesting, to remember that ordination conferred the obligation to care for, not to heal. He was both magnanimous and forbearing, characteristics that he tried to infuse into his collaborators.

He also had a certain tact, based not on expediency but on charity and patience. He could be patient when necessary, even when he was incensed at seeing his efforts for the salvation of souls stymied.

"Let us adore the judgments of God, let us leave to Him the care to provide for so many poor abandoned souls...Let us not insist too much. Let us not force the gates, the time seems near when we shall be asked, and forgetting all else we shall remember only Jesus Christ and the souls He had redeemed."[19]

He was certainly a man born to govern, logical, intuitive, secure in his own thinking, with the flexibility characteristic of those who know how to organize and direct. He won others not so much through superiority of intellect or learning as through the "sovereignty of a mind endowed with and permeated by a sublime concept of the priesthood, from which he drew both the stimulus and the manner for his action."[20] In fact, "his magnanimity derived from the fact that he carried within himself the Church, which spoke, felt and worked within him like a living organ." At the same time, "this man, with so noble a mind, was almost unconsciously humble in his attitudes and manners, which made him utterly engaging." And this humility was rooted in his "sense of being a part of the whole," which is the Church, "ordained for the whole and sustained and carried forward by it."[21]

His awareness of authority and his humility formed his concept of a bishop, and he lived it with dignity. He had a very strong sense of what it meant to be a bishop, and this influenced all his behavior, with the Pope, his colleagues, his priests, the laity. The keenest students of his life found in him the great and austere type of Bishop of the early Church, when the concept of apostolic succession was most alive, in its purest and most genuine form.[22] Thus his concept of authority as ministry was apostolically true: "note that I say ministry not lordship; ministry not you yourselves."[23]

He never used his authority with a heavy hand. It could rightly be said of him that "he was never weak in giving up what he thought, and he never arrogantly imposed it."[24]

"There was nothing he detested more than the abuse of one's authority to the detriment of the authority of others, the wrong use of one's rights to the detriment of the right of others. And this was true in all fields, in thought as well as action, in the field of theology as well as philosophy, in the political as well as the social field, where the Church was concerned and where the country was concerned. He loved the straight road; roundabout ways, the ways invented by men...he did not like at all and he never traveled them."[25]

He loved justice above all personal self-interest, as Cardinal Agliardi wrote of him: "he was always guided by great rectitude in all he did and he lived thirsting always for what is just."[26]

Thirst for Souls

St. Ignatius of Antioch, Saint Ireneus, St. Francis de Sales, and especially St. Charles Borromeo, these were the saints he took as his models.

This is what he wrote of St. Charles:

"One of those men of action who never hesitate, who are never inconsistent, who never retreat, who throw into every act the whole force of their conviction, all the energy of their will, their whole personality, their entire selves, and they triumph. St. Charles! A marvelous example of that fearless constancy, that generous patience, that burning charity, that enlightened, tireless and magnanimous zeal, of all those virtues that make the true Apostle of Jesus Christ. He has a thirst for souls. He desires nothing but souls...and precisely to win souls for Jesus Christ, dear Lord, what did he not do, what did he not suffer, what did he not say."[27]

This is what he, too, wished to be. In this thirst for souls lies the explanation of his life, in which was reflected his constant awareness of the sacramental character of being a Bishop. He was always conscious of being a priest, without interruption or reservation. From the moment of his ordination as a priest and even more intensely after his consecration as a bishop he felt himself to be a person consecrated for and dedicated to others: a missionary priest and bishop.

This aspect of his personality meshed with his natural tendency to be outgoing. If his interior life was nourished by faithful meditation and love of the Eucharistic Christ, he was nevertheless happy in obeying the need to live in contact with others, to adapt to the milieu and to other persons, without self-interest but rather in forgetfulness of self. Yet he never violated nor intruded upon the autonomy of those who were the object of his attentions.

His sense of the sacred character and dignity of the episcopal office made clear the call of conscience and nourished his apostolic sensitivity. He was one of the few bishops of his day who went in search of the "alienated." He was never afraid of being accused of connivance or compromise — and at the time this was often a paralyzing fear because of the lack of clarity about the relationship between the spiritual and the temporal, between legalism and missionary concern. He did not confine himself to preaching that the Lord came to seek not the just but the sinners; he personally sought out the latter. To those professing to be scandalized he replied: "Let us save souls, and then come what may...I would ride on the shoulders of the devil himself if I were sure he would take me to save a soul." This is what gives the lie to the charge that he was sympathetic to the Liberals. "My liberalism is to recognize error and to fight it." Because he faced the enemy and entered his citadel, he was accused by those who fought from a distance with great fanfare but little efficacy. "His liberalism," one witness declared, "was an intense thirst for souls."[28]

Love of Truth

In Scalabrini's love of truth we find another source of the freedom he manifested in contrast to the majority of his contemporaries. The period was marked by a kind of servilism or conformity. Certainly Scalabrini rowed against the tide. He was one of the few who spoke frankly to the Pope. He considered this a basic duty of a bishop, and silence a crime.[29] To understand his intentions in speaking out it is enough to note the spirit of abnegation in which he did keep silence when this was required of him. He spoke as a son, and as a son he obeyed and kept quiet.[30]

It is in the context of his heroic obedience that we must consider his love of truth. To have behaved with reservations with respect to truth would have seemed to him a betrayal of the Word of God. For truth he was determined to fight "up to the threshold of death and death itself."

"Devotion to truth even at the price of one's blood...The greatest battle in this world is to tell the truth of Christ to our enemies as well as to our friends...without ambiguity, without shame, not with trepidation but rather with a sublime contempt for danger, which is the privilege of great souls."[31]

He was not attracted by any illusory reformist ambitions. Just as he was not called to be a monk, he did not feel called to be a Savanarola.[32] He was convinced that the Church already possessed the means and instruments to remedy the evils of the time. It would be enough to use them, if everyone had the courage and energy to use them, if all were united and in agreement in using them. His fidelity to truth was in fact a source of great bitterness to him in his relations with his colleagues in the faith, whom he would have wished to have with him as colleagues in action. But how could there be unity unless it was based on truth. And on what could truth be based except on charity? His attempts to protect the trinominal, charity-truth-unity, separates Scalabrini much more than any "political" differences from those who did not understand him and could not understand him because they were lacking in one of the three elements. St. Pius X, on the other hand, drew an accurate picture of him:

"He was a learned Bishop, both gentle and strong, who in the most difficult circumstances always defended and loved truth and made others love it, nor did he ever abandon it whether in the face of threats or flattery."[33]

Because of this fidelity to truth he encountered misunderstanding and even hostility. We have noted that when he reacted it was against the unjust interpretations of the positions he took. His love of truth, however, was always warmed by his fervent charity; he never stooped to a cold, abstraction of honesty. Even toward those who did not judge him as he thought he should be judged, he was not concerned with his "right" in the matter; he was moved rather by that charity which "forgets all things because it has never hated, which embraces and kisses not adversaries but brothers, who have offended through error."[34]

Scalabrini as Conciliator

This same sincerity guided him in his relations with the "liberals," the "democrats," the "progressives," in short with all those who claimed more or less to be anticlerical amid all the political complexities of the new Italy. He sought souls and for this reason only he was a conciliator — to express love of Christ, of the Church and of the country, to express love of man in his wholeness.

He was called "transigent." Yes, he answered (in the pamphlet that was less his work than that of Leo XIII), but only where incidentals were concerned, only in the case of ideas of the Church left open to debate, only in the case of temporal institutions and methods which, he repeated constantly, are means not an end and therefore must be changed when in the changing times, they become obstacles to the ends of the Church, namely, the salvation of souls. On the other hand, where truth, the faith, fidelity to the Church, love of one's fellowmen are concerned, he was not only "intransigent but most intransigent."

His love of truth, which made him free, his striving for unity in Christ and in the Church, his search for what unites and does not divide, his vision which, from the unity of two or three missionaries and amid the two divergent currents in the diocesan clergy, reached out to the contemplation of the Christology of history[35] — it was from these elements that his spirit of conciliation derived and it was in fact a basic element of his nature, and became — besides a search for conciliation between Italy and the Holy See — a way of life for him, an essential element of his personality.

It is easy to theorize about the "just mean," conciliation without compromise. Scalabrini was concerned with living it and making it live. Rather than a "conciliationist," we would call him a conciliator, a true "priest."

He was concerned not only with conciliation between Church and State, as we have said. He lived a true reconciliation between truth and charity, between prudence and strength, between zeal and contemplation, between calmness in decision and swiftness in action, between confidence in God and realism, between obedience to the Pope and his sense of responsibility for his diocese, between filial respect for the Vicar of Christ and frankness in speaking to him, between his sense of the episcopal dignity and his humility as a son of the Church, between his natural impulsiveness and his self-control, between his paternal feelings and his concept of authority which does not recoil from any responsibility. He conceived, too, of a reconciliation between the diocese and the world, between Religion and Fatherland, and it was in this context that he founded the Congregation of Missionaries for the emigrants, which he envisaged, among other things, as "a practical means, a beginning in bringing peace to consciences, which is always one of the most ardent desires of my soul."[36]

He called himself a "conservative," but "in his far-seeing soul there was room...for both the old which is rejuvenated in the new and the new which is consecrated in the old...One of those men who embodies the deepest aspirations of a given historical moment but foresees and foretells (and this prematurity is sometimes misunderstood by those who hear and dangerous for those who speak) what will be the safest and easiest path for the future."[37]

Totality of Love

It was said that he maintained the enthusiasm and zeal of a twenty year old. He himself used to say "what is eternal is perpetually young." And everyone recognized in him "a heart as big as the sea."

He was, in fact, deeply affectionate, without selfishness, both tender and simple in his attachments; mature in the fullness of joy they brought him and still more in the sorrow that refined them. He was easily moved, "he let himself be ruled by his great heart." He was cordial with everyone; he saw in other persons another self, he loved them as himself, he suffered with them, and he felt "shattered" at the sight of another who was sad on his account.

His love became charity, active and operative kindness, understanding and forgiveness, an offering and a consecration of his life. Strict with himself, precisely because he had renounced his self, he was open, smiling and welcoming to others, especially to children and the poor. If he uncovered the wounds and bruises of others it was to pour on them the oil and wine of the good Samaritan, to soothe and comfort them with the faith. He imposed his will on others when and to the extent his solicitude for the Church required it, but he did this through persuasion, with sensitivity, and through his great gift for convincing others. "He succeeded in getting everything he wanted," one of his priests testified. Cardinal Nasalli Rocca spoke of his "incomparable fascination."[38]

He was given to evaluating the consequences of his actions on others. This sometimes gave rise to a certain slowness in his deliberations. He feared that a quick reaction, even in situations that seemed to require an immediate and energetic response, might be interpreted as a personal vendetta. On the other hand, he used strong measures with those he loved the most and in whom he placed the greatest confidence, when he was sure that the punishment would be truly beneficial. With others, the fear of letting his personal feeling interfere with the spiritual needs of another person was an obstacle to him and only in the case of a higher interest, the good of souls, was he able to overcome it.

Charity took precedence over every other consideration. More than once he was judged weak and even inconstant because of this. In fact,

"Persecution, grief, bitter disillusionments, betrayals, complaints, calumnies, never changed his heart, which loved and loved always and which, in the name of love, illumined by the highest ideals of Christian charity, easily pardoned offenses, marked his enemies with greater favors, and carried out works which those with myopic charity might call weakness, but which the wise must admire as the results of his generous and magnanimous heart."[39]

By temperament and through grace, he looked always to the true, the profound, the essential: love of Christ Crucified and love for the beings redeemed by his Blood, became one love as divine love is one:

"God loves his Son...But that Beloved Son became man. Therefore, He loves man in Him. With one joy and one love He embraces all, body, flesh and soul. Now we are that flesh, the bones; we are that nature, we are one body with Christ and in Him and through Him we are made children of God, in fact, the very Son of God who is in us. Therefore in Him we, too, are included and embraced by the Father on one act of love."[40]

Giovanni Battista Scalabrini sought to "share in the divinity"[41] in this manner: to transform his life, thoughts, affections, words and deeds into one act of love, the love for the "whole Christ."

The First Scalabrinian Missionaries

The first member of the Scalabrinian Congregation was *Father Giuseppe Molinari* of Piacenza (1856-1900). He left for S. Felicidade in Parana (Brazil) in 1888 with the first missionary band, but two years later he was transferred for reasons of health to the United States, where he worked untiringly, first in New York and then in Pittsburgh. In the latter city he built a church for the 10,000 Italians living there, and he himself was by turns foreman, carpenter, painter — the first of a long series of Scalabrinians who became construction workers for the house of God. He fell ill and returned to Piacenza in 1894, where he became rector of the Motherhouse and Vicar General of the Institute. He was a man of constant prayer and indefatigable activity. He died at the age of 44, with a great reputation for holiness, so much so that there was some thought given to starting the cause of his beatification.

Father Domenico Mantese (1847-1891), a priest of Vicenza, made his religious profession with Father Molinari on November 28, 1887, the day the Order was founded. He had already been a priest in the diocese of Vicenza for twelve years when he decided to follow his fellow townsman, Father Pietro Colbachini, to Brazil, where he arrived in 1888 after joining the Congregation. He went to Pittsburgh with Father Molinari, and died a few months later in New York. His was the first death in the

Congregation. Like Father Molinari he lived only to the age of 44, but his memory too remains blessed. His asceticism was discovered at his death when his penitential instruments were found.

Father Giuseppe Marchetti (1869-1896) also died very young. He had been won to the cause of the emigrants when he heard one of Bishop Scalabrini's lectures on the subject in Lucca. He offered himself as a "missionary externe" to assist the emigrants during the ocean voyage. At his second crossing Providence intervened to ask his total consecration to the new apostolate.

"On the ship on which one of my missionaries Father Giuseppe Marchetti, a professor at the seminary in Lucca, was sailing," Bishop Scalabrini recounts, "a young woman died leaving behind a nursing infant and her husband, who was beside himself with desperation. To calm the desolate man, who was threatening to throw himself into the sea, the missionary promised to take care of the child, and he kept his promise. When he arrived in Rio de Janeiro, carrying the little orphan, he went to see the distinguished Count Pio di Savoia, who was then consul general in that city. All he could give the young missionary was some encouragement, but this was enough to set him knocking on door after door until he finally succeeded in placing the child with the concierge of a house for Religious. From that time on he pursued the idea of founding a home for Italian orphans in Sao Paulo (where he had been sent), and he finally succeeded at the cost of enormous sacrifices to himself. It is now fours years and 160 orphans later and we have a martyr who prays for them in heaven, for the great labors he endured cost this devoted and zealous missionary his life. Peace and glory be with him!"[1]

"There is something miraculous about the beginnings of the orphanage in Sao Paulo," Bishop Scalabrini asserted[2] and he did not exaggerate. When Father Marchetti decided to establish it and was seeking a suitable place, he asked the advice of a Jesuit, who promised to interest a charitable gentleman, Dr. Vincente de Azevedo, in the project. On the same day, Father Marchetti took a tram to go see one of the places that had been suggested to him, but on boarding it noticed he did not have the money to pay for his ticket. With courage and humility he asked one of the passengers, for the love of God, to give him the necessary amount, explaining at the same time the nature of his errand. The gentleman advised him against that particular site, since it had no water, and offered to show him another on the Ipiranga hill on the outskirts of Sao Paulo. When he saw how much this pleased the Father, he exclaimed with a smile, "Do you like it? Well, it is yours. I give it to you." It was the same Dr. Azevedo. On the following day the gift was officially registered and Azevedo added also the cost of the material to build the orphanage.

With the approval of the Founder and of the Bishop of Sao Paulo, Father Marchetti went to work immediately and found support for the first eighty orphans, traveling tirelessly through the *fazendas* of the interior, where he carried out a precious pastoral ministry and at the same time collected funds for the orphanage.

Like every true apostle, he was buffeted by suffering, calumnies and opposition. Twice he almost lost his life and was saved seemingly by a miracle. Home in Lucca on a visit, he so inspired his mother, sister and two other young women, that they went back with him to Ipiranga to help with the orphans, and thereby presented Bishop Scalabrini with the occasion to found the Congregation of the Missionary Sisters of St. Charles.

Father Marchetti set up a bakery and established four crafts and trade schools. He was waiting for a printing press and he had decided to build a separate section for girls, when during one of his apostolic journeys he contracted typhoid and died at the age of 27.

He had been in Sao Paulo only twenty-two months. But we know the secret of his lightning mission. To the three religious vows he had added another two: to be always the victim of love for his neighbor, even at the cost of his health and life; never to waste a quarter of an hour. He was a saint and a hero, just as he was in the prayers of Bishop Scalabrini.[3]

Father Marchetti's successor was *Father Faustino Consoni*, born in 1857 in Palazzolo sull'Oglio (Brescia) and a descendant on his mother's side of the family of San Vincenzo Strambi. He was ordained a priest at the age of 38 by Bishop Scalabrini, and he had been in the mission of S. Felicidade in Parana a little over a year when he received the following letter from the Founder: "I have chosen you to take the place of our lamented Father Marchetti. He was a saint and he will certainly help you from his place in heaven to carry forward the work he founded...My dear son! The Lord gives me great confidence in your work and you, I am sure, will obey me with joy and God will give you the strength to overcome every obstacle."[4]

Father Faustino merited this great confidence. As a boy he had rescued from drowning, at the risk of his own life, a woman who had fallen into the Oglio. With money he himself had collected he had bought a donkey for a poor wandering Sardinian who was in despair because his indispensable little beast had died on him. He had even tried to run away to America and was caught by chance by a relative in Genoa. He was the secretary for charity of the archpriest.

He would have liked to convert all of Brazil. Not content with working with the Italians, he dragged the Brazilians into doing good and tried to make himself understood by the Polish immigrants. His delicate health irritated him, but he never had a free moment. Two or three times he almost broke his neck while riding horseback over dangerous trails to bring the last Sacrament to the dying...He was not of the stuff to lose heart when, on his arrival in Sao Paulo, he found only a few cents in the cash box and a debt of about $16,000. A few months begging for the love of God remedied that situation. He finished the building at Ipiranga and carried out the plans for the girls' section, Villa Prudente.

It is hard to see how he found time for his priestly ministry. Yet we see him first as the chaplain of the Italians who, under the most brutal conditions, were working the coffee plantations of the state of Sao Paulo: "They have put me under a plantation foreman who would have dug the soul out of me. Forteen or fifteen hours of work a day. A few beans and some blows for payment. On Sunday, the hoe and the hatchet.

No Mass, no rosary...I did not see a priest's face in ten years. The first one I saw was Father Faustino. The administrator did not want to let him in. Father Faustino replied that he would enter through the gate of the *fazenda* even if they leveled a gun at him! 'I want to see my Italians at all costs!' He won his point. In the evening he gathered all the immigrants in a big room. Lord! How we wept. To see a priest, to hear him preach, to hear Mass...He heard all our confessions and gave us all Communion. There were more than two hundred communions, and many baptisms and marriages."

The story of this Venetian "colonist" was multiplied in hundreds of similar situations, which the Scalabrinian missionaries faced with true pioneer spirit. Riding horseback for days on end, eating when and what chance provided, sleeping on the ground and often in the open, keeping alert for thugs and for snakes, exposed to typhoid and yellow fever. This was the life Father Faustino led on his missionary journeys, in the course of which he confirmed 20,000 persons.[5]

Father Faustino was named Provincial Superior by Bishop Scalabrini, and added to his duties was the rectory of the Church of St. Anthony in the center of Sao Paulo, which became the refuge of the poor and of sinners, and also a kind of hostel for the clergy, open to all priests and Religious passing through the city. He became the confessor of almost all the clergy in the metropolitan city and the spiritual director of numerous persons. "That priest is a real trap," one doctor said. "Once you get near him, you never escape." The Bishop of Campinas, attacked by vicious calumnies, was comforted by Faustino, who, as we shall see, carried the same burden. "With that missionary, the cross is no longer a cross," he said. And St. Frances Cabrini advised her Sisters, "When you have some difficulty, and you need good advice, after knocking on the tabernacle door go and knock on Father Faustino's door. He is a man of God."

"No one can give what he does not have," Father Faustino used to say. He could give much because he had much. His holiness and his spiritual fruitfulness derived from two principal sources: the two loves he learned from Bishop Scalabrini, the love of the Eucharist (the tabernacle commands the pulpit) and the love of the cross.

The anticlericalism of the time used against him the same weapon it used against all Catholic educational institutions, a campaign of defamation and lies. During Father Faustino's absence they arranged for a little girl of eight years to disappear from the orphanage and then accused him of having killed her to hide a shameful act. The people were aroused by a scandalous hullabaloo, and he was brought to trial on charges that proved to be grossly false. But after four years he received only a humiliating acquittal on the basis of insufficient evidence.

It was the Italians especially who were shouting "death to Father Faustino." The Italian consul did not move a finger to help him; the greatest effort he made was to advise him to flee. But the answer Faustino gave him was, "The guilty run away, not the innocent."

Father Faustino kept silent and forgave, and he found comfort in the fact that the entire clergy of Sao Paulo stood by him and in the blessing sent him by Pius X, June 10, 1911, "with sincere admiration and with prayers for the heavenly consolation of the Lord in this time of grief."

He died after having literally used up all he had for "his poor," as the "brother of the poor Jesus." He left not even a penny nor any good clothes with which to bury him. Any new clothes that were given him he immediately passed on to poor priests and seminarians.

There were a number of priests who were sensitive to the anguished appeals for religious assistance that came from the Italian emigrants even before Bishop Scalabrini founded his congregation. They worked alone and were the exception, but they were all the more deserving and admirable for all that since they were inspired by pure zeal for souls. One of the first of these was *Father Pietro Colbachini* of Bassano del Grappa (1845-1901).

He had already given a beautiful example of dedicated priestly virtue in the diocese of Vicenza, where he had introduced the Society of St. Angela. While he was serving as preacher for the May sermons in the Cathedral of Feltre, a certain pastor read him some letters from emigrants in Brazil. In November of the same year, Father Peter set sail for Sao Paulo, fortified with the blessing of the Pope and the title of apostolic missionary. The coldness with which the bishops received him showed how difficult the position of the lone missionary was. But the difficulties did not discourage Father Colbachini, who rode horseback up and down the length of Parana, two thirds the size of Italy. He established sixteen chapels in eight years and built the large church of Saint Felicidade. He could not continue alone, however, and he called for help: "the field is immense; we will form one body; we will start a religious congregation... and a seminary."

At the very time Father Colbachini was writing in this vein to a priest of Vicenza, Bishop Scalabrini was launching his proposals. The missionary learned of them on Christmas Day in 1887, and that evening wrote to the Bishop of Piacenza, "I will be your faithful servant in life and death." He was immediately accepted and pronounced his religious vows while still in Brazil pending the time when he could renew them before Bishop Scalabrini himself, which he did in 1894. He had returned to Italy that year, barely escaping his enemies who were after his head. He had in fact opposed certain agitators who, at the fall of the Empire, were going through the colonies and dragging the Italians as well into their hatreds and civil strife. Because he had personally organized the escape of sixty Italians who had been forced to leave their families and their homes and take up rifles, he was marked for death. He was fortunately warned at the last moment and was able to flee into the forest where he lived for two months in a makeshift hut perched in the branches of a tree. "I have to make like a bird, but I do it gladly for our Italians." Disguised then as a settler he succeeded in reaching the port and setting sail for Italy.

On his return to Brazil, assigned to the zone of Veranopolis in Rio Grande do Sul, he headed two hundred settlers, cleared the virgin forest, divided the land among the Italians, and at the center of the settlement built a wooden church. Thus Nova Bassano was born in 1897. Father Colbachini was its founder, priest, mayor, and the general organizer of its farming, trading, cooperatives, and school as well as the builder of a new church.

When he felt his health begin to fail, he asked Bishop Scalabrini for permission to return to Italy,[6] but only four days later, just as he finished saying Mass, he felt ill and lay down on his bed fully dressed. His housekeeper helped him say the Litany of the Virgin, and he passed away saying, "I die content," and exclaiming with his last breath, "My Jesus!"

He went to confession every day, when this was possible, was most faithful to his devotions, never missed a daily hour of meditation, not even in times of the most intense work.[7]

There are numerous other founders of Scalabrinian missions in Brazil that could be mentioned. Among them:

Father Luigi Capra of Parma (1877-1920), built or rebuilt several churches, and laid the foundations of what later became the cathedral of the diocese of Sao Andre. He gave all he had to the poor. Even on the train he gave away his hat and shoes to some one who needed them; at home he still had a pair of shoes with no soles and a hat that had been touched up several times with ink. He was a real savior for his people during a diptheria epidemic. He organized the workers during a fearsome industrial crisis, settled strikes, and warded off conflicts and social disasters.[8]

Father Natale Pigato of Vicenza (1861-1926) literally gave his shirt to the poor. The settlers attributed miracles to him both during his life and after his death. *Father Giuseppe Pandolfi* of Bergamo (1862-1950), the author of prestigious mathematics and gnomonics textbooks, was extremely humble to the extent of obeying those under him, and he declared to the Bishop: "Excellency, all my parishioners are good. There is only one bad person here, and I am he." He served in the missions for fifty years, with never a vacation or a trip for recreation.[9]

Father Giacomo Gambera of Brescia (1856-1934), who had served as secretary of the first national catechetical congress, was assigned to New Orleans, Louisiana and had to use all his gifts of charity and boldness to calm the Italians there after eleven of them had been lynched. The people were hostile to the immigrants, who had to hide to escape death. Crispi threatened to send in a warship; the Americans threatened to throw all the Italians in New Orleans into the Mississippi. The immigrants gathered about Father Gambera, their only true friend, who welcomed all new arrivals and guided their first steps in exile.

He was named Provincial Superior and went to Rome to persuade the *Propaganda Fide* to give Bishop Scalabrini permission to visit the Italians in America. Cardinal Ledokowsky, Prefect of the Congregation, wept when he read the letters of invitation from the American bishops and embraced the missionary who brought them. That same year Father Gambera reorganized the Society of St. Raphael in New York, expanding its activities beyond the port and opening two hostels where the immigrants who had nothing could eat and sleep until they found work. In five years he had housed and fed four thousand of them. The Italian Government, which had long been requested to do so, finally granted a subsidy and paid the salary of the agent assigned to the St. Raphael Society. The only one who received no salary was Father Gambera: "I worked for nothing because I was living among the poor and I was to be poor among them."

He was then called to revive a parish in Chicago. His first day there, he himself rang the church bells and a few little old ladies turned up for Mass. A few years later it was one of the most flourishing parishes. In his record book we find the following statistics (and he still had several years of life and activity left): 20,000 baptisms, 15,000 first communions, 10,000 marriages, 400,000 confessions, 5,000 sermons. For one priest, involved in many other social works, these are proof of extraordinary dedication.[10]

The Venetian *Father Roberto Biasotti*, was first a traveling missionary among the emigrants in Yugoslavia, Austria, Switzerland, France, Luxemburg, Belgium, and Holland. He then served for five years in a Boston, Massachusetts, parish, and returned to his first vocation as a traveling missionary. The Archbishop of New York called him to direct the Italian Apostolate in that city, an institution designed to prepare a cadre of missionaries ready to go wherever their services as preachers were requested.

The idea of these "flying missions," as we have already noted, had been set forth in the first project Bishop Scalabrini had presented to the Holy See in 1887[11] and was adopted by Leo XIII in his Apostolic Letter, *Quam aerumnosa*, addressed to the American Bishops on December 10, 1888. It was also supported by Archbishop, later Cardinal, Satolli, then the Apostolic Delegate in the United States, and in this connection Scalabrini wrote to the Provincial Superior in the United States: "Bishop Satolli's idea is our old idea, and if funds were available, a house for traveling Missionaries would be the finest and most useful thing in the world."[12]

The pioneer in this work was *Father Angelo Chiariglione*, who devoted himself to it at the age of 65 after having established the Italian parish in Cincinnati, Ohio. He began in 1896 to travel through several dioceses, visiting every center, large or small, where there were Italians. He went from house to house, baptized babies, regularized marriages, heard confessions, reawakened Christian life. He would remain a few days or several months according to need, and then would start off again sometimes without any money and traveling on foot for miles and miles.

"One day he read a newspaper account about the epidemic of yellow fever in Montgomery, (Alabama), and offered his services to the Bishop there, who entrusted him with the care of the sick among the Italians and the French. When the epidemic was over the Bishop of Mobile asked for him and assigned him to the spiritual ministry of all the Italians and the French scattered throughout his diocese, which then comprised the whole state of Alabama and part of Florida, and set his headquarters in Daphne, Alabama, which was a healthy place but very poor. There were eighteen Italian families there, some of which wanted to pledge fifty cents a month for his support. He refused this and accepted instead the farm products they brought him, eking out his living expenses from the Mass offerings. Then every year, the Italians and Americans got together to buy him some clothing, and so he was able to say: *habentes alimenta et quibus tegamur.* One person offered him two rooms and the use of his kitchen for the bit of food he prepared for himself. He turned one of the rooms into a chapel because the church was four miles away and he could go there only on Sundays. Before his arrival, the people were able to hear Mass only twice a year. From Daphne he went visiting his..."parishioners" throughout the diocese, especially during the Easter Season...When he was in Daphne...he went every Saturday evening in turn to two other districts, one twelve miles away and the other sixteen miles. He would say Mass early and then return to Daphne to say another. The residents of the two districts, Italians and Germans, were more than happy and used to come and get him and bring him back in a two-horse carriage. He used to say the Mass for them in a room that was set up as a chapel every two weeks. In still another district he had managed to build a tiny church, but he could get there only rarely, since it was forty miles from Daphne. When Father Chiariglione reported all this to Bishop Scalabrini, he was sixty and a half years old."[13]

"With Father Chiariglione it was difficult to say whether his sufferings resulted more from his ever fervent zeal in bringing the consolations of religion to the poor, or from the voluntary penances he imposed on himself. One day in August of 1908, after a search of three days, he was found, like St. Francis Xavier, dead in a woods he was traversing by night in order perhaps to visit the next morning some one who was ill or some other poor soul he was determined to console. When his strength failed him he probably lay down or fell and could not get up again."[14]

Another great Missionary figure was *Father Paolo Novati* of Como (1865-1913). In 1892 he went to Providence, Rhode Island, where 20,000 Italians were living. He arrived without any funds but with unlimited confidence in God. He built the church of the Holy Spirit, built a second auxiliary church, and devoted all the energies of his strong character, ennobled by charity and piety, to the religious and social advancement of the immigrants. When an epidemic broke out among his parishioners he was seen moving among them day and night, indifferent to contagion, comforting the dying and bringing Christian hope and practical help to the survivors. The Bishop of Providence named him a consulator of the diocese, and Bishop Scalabrini appointed him Provincial Superior. In these two functions, he worked to cultivate in his colleagues the spirit of charity and self-denial that, according to their Founder, must be the characteristic of his missionaries. In 1910 he was named Vicar General of the Congregation and Rector of the Motherhouse. He died in 1913 after two months of agonizing suffering which he endured with exemplary resignation. His eulogy was delivered by a saint, Blessed Luigi Guanella, recently returned from a trip to North America where he had enthusiastically admired the work of the Missionaries of St. Charles.[15]

We have mentioned here some of the more typical missionaries formed by Bishop Scalabrini, and certain pastoral and social activities in order to exemplify the spirit the Founder infused in his priests and to illustrate his apostolic ideals in the hope that this will prompt a study in depth of this interesting phase in the history of the Church.

We make brief mention here only of the first Vicar General, *Father Francesco Zaboglio* (1852-1911); the first Superior General, *Father Domenico Vicentini* (1847-1927), *Father Pacifico Chenuil* (1869-1931); and *Father Bartolomeo Rolleri* (1839-1902), the first Superior of the Motherhouse. Finally, we would mention a true saint, *Bishop Massimo Rinaldi* (1869-1941), first a zealous missionary in Brazil and later Bishop of Rieti, whose cause of beatification we expect to be introduced.[16]

The encounter that determined the life Bishop Rinaldi chose he related himself at the exploratory process for the beatification of Bishop Scalabrini: "I met the Servant of God in the spring of 1900 in the church of San Carlo al Corso in Rome, where I had gone to speak with him about entering his Institute. I was already a priest, and he immediately made an extraordinary impression on me, for after we had exchanged a few words he asked me whether I had said Mass yet, and when I replied that I had not, he sent away his servant and insisted on serving my Mass himself. Then when I asked him what dowry I should bring with me, he answered, 'Your breviary and your crucifix.' In October of 1900 I went to Piacenza and was able to enter his Order...To clarify things, I should mention that I had been brought up by my uncle, Bishop Domenico Rinaldi of Montefiascone and was living with him, and that I had left without his knowledge because I had always had the idea of becoming a missionary. But then I thought that perhaps he might need me afterwards, and so I told Bishop Scalabrini that I would like to reserve the right to return to my uncle. The Servant of God accepted this condition and added: 'Fine, we are in agreement in everything and for everything.' I was surprised and could not resist saying: 'I do not even have the *celebret*; does Your Excellency trust your priest this much?' And he answered: 'Gentlemen recognize each other by their eyes.' "[17]

"He was profoundly Franciscan in spirit, a dreamer and a mystic, rough and gentle...and he chose Brazil as the place most suited to his temperament. He worked for ten years in Encantado, first as the pastor in an important colonial town, then as Provincial Superior of the Missionaries of St. Charles in the archidocese of Porto Alegre. He spent endless hours on horseback, traveling from the Taquary river to Rio das Antas, from the Carreiro to the Guapore, in rain, in mud, under the broiling sun of the Taquary plain, or at other times he and his horse, both tired to exhaustion, traveled on rafts down the river through the enchanting Brazilian night. Bishop Rinaldi is always the same, always the great classic missionary of Bishop Scalabrini, afire with spirituality and Italian identity. Teacher, defender, physician, and above all father to the Italians overseas."[18]

In 1910 he was elected Procurator and General Administrator of the Congregation, and he returned to Italy taking up residence in Rome, where for fifteen years he exercised an intense apostolate as priest and confessor in the service of the poor. During World War I his efforts were directed especially to soldiers and orphans. He also carried on a precious work as a journalist and as a student of the problems of migrants. He was the manager and editor of *L'Emigrato Italiano*.

When on August 2, 1924 he received word that he had been named

Bishop of Rieti, he burst into tears and believing himself to be unworthy he earnestly begged: "Holy Father, I am a poor missionary, I cannot be anything else…" "Well, go to Rieti anyway," Pius XI answered, "in your diocese you can be both missionary and bishop!"

Bishop Rinaldi visited every corner of his diocese, sometimes on muleback, more often on foot, always with his rosary in his hand. He could not bear superfluous external manifestations, formalities, dinners, receptions. He was interested only in confessions and communions and he spent hours on end in the confessional far into the night. Often he spent the whole night in Church. One morning he was found asleep on the altar steps. He had no fixed time for his meals or for rest. For more than forty years he slept on boards or in a chair.

The secret of his life lies in his spirit of prayer and sacrifice, in his humility. Notwithstanding his seeming gruffness he was affectionate and sensitive, and extremely tactful, especially with little ones and with orphans. In Rieti he founded an orphanage and a home for old peasant women who had been abandoned. He gave everything he had to the poor, often his shoes, his mattress, and even his trousers.

He restored the bishop's residence and the seminary. He loved the seminarians and visited them often to learn their problems and particularly the progress they were making. Above all, he loved his priests and helped them in every possible way. He wanted them to be good, in fact, holy. He always understood them and tempered any severity he might show with his fatherliness.

When he was rendered inactive by illness, he found comfort in prayer, and spent hours before the Blessed Sacrament, almost always on his knees. He had used himself up for his people; now he could only pray and suffer and he did so with serenity and evangelical faith.

He always had a special veneration for Bishop Scalabrini. On his death bed, when some one showed him a picture of the Founder, he said slowly: "That one…that one…he is truly a saint!" He died on May 31, 1941, in Rome, in the Generalate of the Congregation.

Religious Orders of Sisters for the Emigrants

In the report he presented to the Sacred Congregation of Propaganda Fide on August 10, 1900, Bishop Scalabrini summed up his ideas concerning a Congregation of Sisters to parallel the work of his missionaries.

"The work of the Missionaries would be incomplete, especially in South America, without the help of the Sisters. I have requested some therefore from various congregations, but without success. The good missionaries of Codogno, it is true, offered assistance, and I opened the doors of America to them, where they are doing enormous good; but it is not the good which is the goal of our congregation. We needed Sisters like those scattered throughout the dioceses of France, who adjust to living in a couple of rooms, and with no pretensions set up the first schools, teach the catechism, and where possible help the sick with all the precautions that prudence and experience suggest. Although the Missionaries kept insisting and indeed did violence to my wishes in order to have Sisters like these, I always opposed the idea, having a deep repugnance to taking on this new work. But after some years the accumulation of providential circumstances made me see that this was the will of God..."[1]

The first attempt, then, to give the Missionaries the support of a Congregation of Sisters was addressed to Mother Cabrini.

"The first meeting between the Bishop and the Sister took place in Rome in the summer of 1887, when the Mother needed to deal with him for the foundation of Castel San Giovanni in the diocese of Piacenza. After that the zealous Shepherd visited the new House many times, to bless it and to exercise his ministry, and on these occasions he told Mother of his desire to have her Sisters as collaborators in the work that he had initiated to assist the Italian emigrants in the Americas...Mother listened reverently, and in a spirit of faith and devotion, but her thoughts were directed elsewhere, to another mission: she desired to go to China. A pious and zealous Discalced Carmelite, Father Gerardo Beccaro, encouraged her to accept Bishop Scalabrini's invitation, but not even then did Mother Cabrini feel that she could agree. She wanted to think it over, to ask advice, to pray."[2]

Quite apart from her dream of the Chinese missions, her hesitation was due to the fear that her Institute would lose its autonomy and become an auxiliary of the Scalabrinian Congregation. Cabrini's exceptional personality required independence and freedom of action. Bishop Scalabrini was not discouraged at having made a wrong approach, and for her part Cabrini was deeply impressed by the Bishop's zeal. The latter spoke to the Pope about his idea and wrote to Archbishop Corrigan of New York. Then he returned to the attack with more practical and persuasive arguments.

On her return to Codogno and her usual occupations, Mother gave no further thought to America, but Bishop Scalabrini had not forgotten. Shortly after his visit to Castel San Giovanni he wrote to her, asking her to come and speak with him about a matter of the greatest importance... When she arrived in Piacenza, she was presented with a concrete proposal: the Archbishop of New York wanted some Italian Sisters to take over an orphanage. Bishop Scalabrini asked her to accept this invitation and to assume at the same time the direction of the schools which his priests wanted to open near the Church of St. Joachim in New York...Surprised and perplexed, she asked the Bishop for time to reflect and to pray."[3]

In December, 1888, she went to Rome: she was encouraged to accept Bishop Scalabrini's proposal by the Cardinal Vicar, L. M. Parocchi, and by Msgr. Jacobini, Secretary of Propaganda Fide, to whom the Bishop of Piacenza had already spoken, and by others.

"She had resolved to ask the Archbishop of New York for more specific information, and since Bishop Scalabrini, who had come to Rome to speed the matter up, declared he could wait no longer, Mother Cabrini asked for prayers through the intercession of Venerable Antonia Belloni of Codogno." Ten days later in a dream she saw herself with the Venerable Antonia, the Blessed Mother and the Sacred Heart, all of whom were urging her not to fear. "The next morning, on her way to the Vatican she met Bishop Scalabrini and asked him if he had had any news. The Bishop laughed and Mother Cabrini laughed with him; then she entered St. Peter's and, feeling somewhat disturbed in mind, she remained there in prayer for an hour. When she returned to Via Nomentana, she was surprised to see a carriage standing before the door of the house, and still more surprised when she saw Bishop Scalabrini coming toward her, who exclaimed: "Oh you and your dreams! Here is a letter from New York. Now you can depart."[4]

Not completely convinced, the Saint obtained an audience with the Pope, the only one who could resolve her doubts. Leo XIII, whom Bishop Scalabrini had been pressing for some time for Sisters for his missions, said to her: "Not to the East, Cabrini, but to the West. Your Institute is still young, it needs means; go to the United States, you will find them there and with them a great field for your labors."[5]

In January, 1889, Bishop Scalabrini informed the Archbishop of New York that the Sisters had decided to come. Cabrini herself wrote on February 16 to the Archbishop saying that she preferred to come right away with a group of Sisters rather than with one companion only as the Bishop of Piacenza had suggested.

"On the 18th of March, we find her in Piacenza, with the six Sisters assigned to the first mission in America, to pay their respects to Bishop Scalabrini and receive his blessing. Surprised that they were ready to leave so soon, the Bishop welcomed them warmly, gave them a short talk, eloquent with zeal and charity, in his private chapel, and imparted his blessing, promising to go the next day to Codogno for the departure ceremony 'so that all would be done fittingly and in a manner suited to the great work about to be begun with the help of God'...A solemn function was again held on the feast of St. Joseph in the chapel in Codogno. Bishop Scalabrini, in pontifical vestments, accompanied by Msgr. Serrati, went in procession to the church. After the *Veni Creator* was sung, each of the new Missionaries approached the altar in turn...; the Bishop gave each one a crucifix, as guide for the journey, a comfort in sorrow, a help in difficulty, and the inseparable companion in life no less than in death."[6]

Mother Cabrini landed in New York on the evening of March 31st. "She was cordially welcomed by the good Scalabrinian Fathers, who invited her to take part in a fraternal agape, marked by that spontaneous warmth we experience when we meet with people from our own country in a foreign land. The Sisters, who had come abruptly from the quiet of the vast Ocean to the deafening roar of the great metropolis, and who still felt the effects of the stormy crossing asked permission to retire to their own house. After a few embarrassed and evasive replies, they were told that that night at least they would have to sleep in a hotel. Whoever had written to Bishop Scalabrini with the assurance that all was ready — perhaps not to disappoint the Bishop or not to delay the Sisters' departure — had probably had recourse to a mental reservation. The house was there — but only as a desire. They were therefore taken at that late hour, in a pouring rain, through the dark narrow streets of Little Italy, to a hotel which the *Memorie* describe in grim colors."[7]

In fact, at the last moment the Archbishop of New York who did not think it a good idea to assign to the Italian Sisters the house donated by Countess Cesnola because he did not consider it opportune to open an orphanage for poor Italian children in an elegant section of the city, had written to Italy to cancel the Sisters' coming, but the letter had not arrived in time.[8]

Archbishop Corrigan advised Cabrini to return to Italy immediately, but the Saint reacted in her usual energetic fashion. "Here I have come on orders of the Holy See, and here I am staying." The Archbishop yielded on the recommendation of Cardinal Simeoni and allowed the new arrivals to take possession of the convent, which at the end of four months housed four hundred orphans. To support them, Mother Cabrini and her Sisters did not hesitate to go begging among the poor families of New York's Little Italy.

In the latter quarter, near the first Scalabrinian mission, Father Morelli fixed up a small wooden house for the Sisters who were assigned to teach (instruction was given in the church)...to conduct the *oratorio* on Sundays and to teach catechism.

These were the humble and painful beginnings of the apostolate the Saint undertook among the Italian immigrants. The "Mother of the Immigrants," having walked among the crosses with which God's road is always strewn, later thanked the Lord for having shown her the way and recognized in Bishop Scalabrini the one who gave her "the first push" and the "first impulse."[9]

Providence had evidently chosen Scalabrini for an important role in the holy Sister's life. For he was the one to persuade her to begin the hospital work which she at first did not want to do because it seemed extraneous to the aims of her Institute.[10]

The beginnings of this second work, too, were marked by a cross, the principal cause of which was Father Felice Morelli, although we do not know how blameworthy he was. The hospital which he had started for Italians in New York had been run for four months by the Daughters of St. Anne. They were withdrawn by their Foundress, Mother Rose Gattorno, who did not permit soliciting funds. Bishop Scalabrini appealed to Mother Cabrini, but she was hesitant and wrote to Scalabrini that she first wished to know under what conditions she would be working. He insisted that she accept because the need was urgent.

"She will come at the beginning of August," he wrote to Father Morelli, "she will look around and decide...We have perhaps precipitated matters somewhat. I praise and admire your generous spirit, your zeal and your desire to do the greatest possible good, but we must be sure of our road and remember that he who goes slowly, goes safely and goes a long way."[11]

"The same reasons that had made her hesitate about working in the United States...were dissuading her from accepting for her Institute a work, the direction of which would not be completely in her hands."[12] But Cardinal Simeoni urged her to accept and two other circumstances made up her mind when she arrived in New York and realized the serious financial difficulties in which the administration of the little Italian hospital found itself. In one of the wards, the Cabrini Sisters came upon a poor man, happy to have at last a kindly person read him the letter he had received three months before. Unfortunately, the letter brought the news that his mother had died several months previously.

"The poor man was inconsolable; the Sisters wept with him, and so did Mother when they told her about the incident. She seemed to feel all the pain of the total isolation in which that unfortunate person had lived for so many months. She imagined how much more painful his mental anguish was than his physical suffering, and she understood even more clearly how a hospital offered the opportunity not only to perform one of the works of mercy most dear to the Heart of God, but also to relieve much moral and spiritual suffering...And this time too she had one of her dreams. She seemed to see in a hospital ward a beautiful lady who, with her skirts tucked up and her sleeves turned back, was making up the sick beds. Recognizing the Blessed Virgin, she ran to help her, but Our Lady waved her back saying: 'I am doing what you do not want to do.' The lesson was clear. Mother did not wait for it to be repeated a second time, and sent ten Sisters to staff the hospital."[13]

Encouraged by these signs of the Divine Will, Mother Cabrini tackled the grave financial difficulties, displaying her usual energy and her exceptional charity, even toward Father Morelli, "beyond reproach in his priestly ministry and very zealous on behalf of the Italians," but "completely unsuited to adminstrative work."[14] To cut short the painful controversies that had arisen, including serious interventions against the Sisters on the part of the Curia, Mother Cabrini decided to start a hospital of her own in another building. She announced this to Bishop Scalabrini with admirable modesty, after having informed him of the good progress being made in other activities.

"Only the hospital was about to fail, but I could not bring myself to watch so useful a work fall apart in dishonor and to the detriment of the mission. With confidence in Providence, I decided to assume full responsibility."[15]

The Bishop admired her courage and wrote to Father Morelli urging him to bring the accounts with the Sisters to a close, "and to submit completely to the decision of the Archibhsop."[16] This is the last document we have bearing directly on the unpleasant dispute, which nevertheless in no way disturbed the mutual sentiments of esteem and veneration between Bishop Scalabrini and Mother Cabrini.

Mother Cabrini wrote long letters to him every Christmas and on the feast of St. John the Baptist, and not with the usual conventional expressions. Quoted here are a few excerpts which often in filial tones, reflect her sentiments and judgments concerning the Apostle of the immigrants and his missionaries:

"Pray, pray very hard in your fervent prayers for your Missionary daughters...The prayer of a Father for his children is always powerful with the Heart of God."[17] "I rely very much on the prayers of Your Excellency."[18]

"Have the kindness, Your Excellency, to bless our Missions, too. You gave them their first impetus. You are obliged, therefore, to help us a little with your prayers, don't you think so? In addition, now would be the time to recommend us to *Propaganda* so we may have a good allotment. As you see, I have recourse to Your Excellency with all the confidence of a daughter, and I feel certain that in your great goodness of heart you will do all that you can to help us get it."[19]

"I leave with no worries, confident because I know your nobly paternal and generously great heart: I know how much you love me and how you make sacrifices to satisfy me."[20]

On the occasion of his jubilee as a bishop she wrote: "I would like to show Your Excellency how much I share in these festivals of the soul, which fill me with unutterable consolation...For a long time I have had a warm veneration for Your Excellency...I recommend my Community and myself to your prayers at Holy Mass and to your fatherly charity, the greatness of which I have always experienced. Bless me, then, and may your blessing, as always, call down upon this Institute, of which Your Excellency is the benevolent Protector, the graces and the blessings of God."[21]

"Yes, God will show you every moment his love and predilection, and will ever maintain and indeed increase in you that serene and vigorous strength that you draw from the Heart of Jesus, that unshakeable calm that you maintain in every most difficult circumstance and that is characteristic of those who find in God alone the secret of their most noble and arduous virtues..." After telling him that his missionaries were reaping "excellent results in the salvation and sanctification of many souls" she added: "Oh! Who knows what a crown is reserved for you in Heaven, Your Excellency, to reward your life spent entirely in a perfect sacrifice of Self for the greater glory of God."[22]

"I am happy to see how the Reverend Fathers of Your Excellency's Mission reap good results from their labors, and how the affairs of the Mission, too, are improving. Oh! how clearly one sees the finger of God, for when a work is truly His, it always encounters obstacles and opposition, but then victory follows."[25]

"Wherever I have seen your Fathers in America, I have always found them to be zealous and active in promoting the well-being of our Missions. They do a great deal of good, and you have good reason for consolation, as one who is the first cause of it. If in my travels around our Missions I have found something to be happy about I could not help thinking of you, who gave me the first encouragement and who therefore has the first merit for the little good we do. Continue to help us with your blessing, and with your prayers, as we keep you always in ours."[24]

And here is what Bishop Scalabrini thought of Mother Cabrini and her Congregation:

"It pleases me very much to be able to say that the Missionary Religious of the Sacred Heart, whose foundress and Superior General is that holy and most active woman, Venerable Mother Frances Xavier Cabrini, are highly deserving, not only for the good they do in Italy, but also for the very great work they do in the Americas, where they have established themselves at my suggestion and with my advice. The spirit of God which animates them, their scrupulous observance of the Rule, their truly apostolic zeal, the works of charity they have undertaken in a short time, make them worthy of the admiration of all good people, but also worthy of help, of which they are in extreme need especially in order to send Religious to America."[25]

"The maternal assistance given the Italian emigrants by this strong and pious woman," wrote Cardinal Carlo Rossi on the eve of her beatification,"...is still being carried on, is flourishing, beneficent and greatly appreciated after fifty years. Alongside Mother Cabrini's Institute of the Missionaries of the Sacred Heart, other Institutes were founded or renewed through the pastoral zeal of Bishop Scalabrini and one of them is devoted exclusively to caring for Italian emigrants, but the fact remains that the first Religious to understand and fully realize the Bishop's anxiety for the health of the souls of the emigrants and to become a co-worker in the first efforts of his Missionaries of St. Charles, was the Servant of God, Frances Xavier Cabrini. The relations between her, Foundress of Missionaries, and the Bishop, Founder of Missionaries, were always holy and cordial and marked by mutual esteem and confidence, right up to the death of Bishop Scalabrini."[26]

The Missionary Sisters of Saint Charles

Mother Cabrini's Sisters did not meet all Bishop Scalabrini's plans, as he himself said. After having appealed to various other congregations, he was induced "by an accumulation of providential circumstances" to overcome his "repugnance to taking on this new work," namely, to found a congregation of Sisters to complete the work of his missionaries, and especially to teach catechism, to teach school, and care for the little children, the orphans and the sick.[27]

Apart from the various requests from other missionaries, the most decisive "providential circumstance" was the brief return to Italy of Father Giuseppe Marchetti, founder of the Christopher Columbus Orphanage in Sao Paulo, Brazil. He had come to set before Bishop Scalabrini the urgent need for Sisters to care for the orphans and the opportunity at hand of founding a congregation with the specific aim of aiding the emigrants. The Bishop answered that he had been thinking of this for some time, and at the moment was considering how to go about it. Father Marchetti's proposal seemed precisely one of the signs of God's will.

The four candidates, who became the first Missionary Sisters of St. Charles (Mother Mary Assunta Marchetti, Father Marchetti's sister and the first Superior General, accompanied by her mother and two other young women from Lucca, Sister Mary Angela Larini and Sister Maria Franceschini) "were on their way to Piacenza...to seek an audience with Bishop Scalabrini...for the purpose of placing their vows and aspirations in the hands of that illustrious Prelate, as protector and founder of their new congregation."

On October 25, 1895, in the chapel of the Bishopric, Scalabrini received from the four postulants the profession of religious vows for six months and gave them the veil, the missionary crucifix and a rule "ad experimemtum."

Two days later the little group sailed from Genoa with the blessing of their Founder: "Go with confidence, daughters; I will send you other Sisters, and you will return for further formation and to be confirmed in the religious spirit."[28]

While these first four Sisters were seeing to the urgent needs of the orphanage in Sao Paulo, Bishop Scalabrini started a novitiate in Piacenza, at 45 Via Nicolini (now Via Msgr. Francesco Torta), opposite the Instituto Cristoforo Colombo. Six candidates were accepted, who began their postulance in June, 1898, and in December were invested by the Founder in the Church of San Carlo. During their novitiate, they were instructed by the Provost of St. Euphemia, Father Carlo Molinari, and by the Bishop, who visited them frequently and encouraged their enthusiasm for the missionary ideal. "Here are the six Colombians! Work to become good missionaries."[29]

Bishop Scalabrini also preached the retreat in preparation for their profession, conducted the canonical examination and on June 12, 1900, the feast of the Sacred Heart, he accepted their simple and perpetual vows. On August 9, in the church of San Carlo in Piacenza, he gave the six Sisters their crucifixes: "You will encounter crosses without fail, but do not lose heart; look at your crucifix and say: *fac me cruce inebriari.*"

Meantime Father Marco Simoni had arrived from Brazil, greatly concerned over the urgent need to increase the number of Sisters for the Christopher Columbus Orphanage, the number of children having doubled by this time. He felt that six more Sisters should be assigned to it without delay. Bishop Scalabrini wanted to send four only and to keep the Superior and mistress of novices in Piacenza. In fact, he wanted two to come back from Brazil, as he had told them at their departure, for the complete and regular formation of the Institute. Father Simoni insisted that he had to have six.

At this point, Mother Clelia Merloni, foundress of the Sisters Apostles of the Sacred Heart, who had been helped by Bishop Scalabrini a few months earlier, came forward with the offer of help from her congregation. The Bishop hesitated for some time, then yielded to the pressures and allowed a group of Sisters to leave on August 10, 1900.

There is only one explanation for Bishop Scalabrini's attitude. He wanted to weld the two Orders into one, although he did not think the time was yet ripe for that. When he agreed to take on the responsibility for and protection of Mother Merloni's Sisters it was with the clear intention of directing their work to the emigrants in America in cooperation with his missionaries. Mother Merloni's biography confirms this:

"Bishop Scalabrini listened with lively interest to the sad vicissitudes of the dying congregation. There was no doubt: it was Divine Providence that was placing in his path these Sisters dedicated to an apostolate for good and so sorely tried by misfortune! They would become precious auxiliaries of his Missionaries of St. Charles!...Bishop Scalabrini explained to the Foundress his intention to associate the Institute of the Sisters Apostles to the Pious Society of his Missionaries for the benefit of the Italian emigrants, promising to help in every way possible the renewal of their discredited and dejected Order."[30]

It is not clear just how Bishop Scalabrini intended to bring about the fusion of the two Orders, but from the testimony at the Process it seems that he wished to bring Mother Merloni's Sisters into the Institute he founded in 1895. He had given his protection to Mother Merloni's Order on condition that it dedicate its work to the emigrants. Therefore its goal came to coincide with that of the Missionary Sisters of St. Charles. With the authority he derived from having saved the Congregation on the basis of a specific condition and having assumed responsibility for it by approving its rules for ten years, Bishop Scalabrini felt he had a right to consider himself the legitimate Superior of the Sisters Apostles of the Sacred Heart, and he was precisely that in the fullest sense of the word.

It seems in fact that he intended to call them Sisters of St. Charles. Mother Clelia Merloni wrote to him, probably in 1904, when she was already in Alexandria at the Bishop's wishes:

"The last time I came to Piacenza, I met the Director chosen by Your Excellency as our guide. To my painful surprise, I learned from him that Your Excellency intends to change the name of our Institute and to give us the name of a Saint instead of the Sacred Heart."[31]

Mother Merloni defended her rights and declared that if she had been the cause of the division because of the gossip and persecution directed against her she was quite ready to withdraw from the Institute rather than see it destroyed. There was, therefore, a conflict of rights that prevented the fusion of the two.

Bishop Scalabrini had tried an "experiment"[32] but he came to realize that in the field the two communities each maintained its own spirit and mentality. When he arrived in Sao Paulo in 1904 and heard the story from his first missionary Sisters, he assured them that they would keep their ideal and that the cross would produce for them its own joyful result. "Do not fear, daughters, you will be Missionaries of St. Charles!" One day he met Father Marchetti's sister, Mother Assunta, as she was carrying a tureen of soup to the refectory, and he addressed a few quick kind words to her which the Sisters considered prophetic: "Ah, my poor Assunta, courage, courage; you will die a Missionary of St. Charles!"

When in 1907 the Bishop of Sao Paulo made his canonical visit and saw that the two communities remained attached to their different origins, he arranged for their separation. The Missionary Sisters of St. Charles remained in charge of the Orphanage and the Sisters Apostles of the Sacred Heart took over the Umberto I (later Matarazzo) Hospital. From then on both Congregations grew and flourished.

The Constitution of the Missionary Sisters of St. Charles was given provisional approval by the Holy See in 1934 and was definitively approved in 1948. In 1936, meanwhile, on the initiative of Scalabrinian Father Francesco Tirondola,[33] supported by Msgr. Pio Cassinari, the Provost of San Savino in Piacenza, and by Ettore Martini, who had been one of the pioneers of Catholic Action in Piacenza in Bishop Scalabrini's time, the Missionary Sisters of St. Charles saw the fulfillment of the wishes of their Founder and of their own Congregation and returned to the cradle of their Congregation near his tomb. The new provincial house, next to the Basilica of St. Savino, was ideally connected with their former Motherhouse in Via Nicolini and became the novitiate of the Italian Province, established in 1948.

In 1967, the Congregation of the Scalabrinian Missionary Sisters (like the Missionary Fathers, the Missionary Sisters of St. Charles were named thus), number 73 convents, 833 professed Sisters and 90 novices. The order developed principally in the Brazilian states of Sao Paulo and Rio Grande do Sul, and later in the countries of immigration in Europe and in the United States. In Bishop Scalabrini's apostolic spirit they have in their care four orphanages, seven hostels, 34 hospitals, 83 schools, from nursery school to the upper middle grades, as well as serving in several seminaries of the Scalabrinian Fathers and in various Catholic missions and parishes.

The Sisters Apostles of the Sacred Heart of Jesus

The Sisters Apostles of the Sacred Heart had been founded in Viareggio in 1894 by Mother Clelia Merloni to spread devotion to the Sacred Heart of Jesus. The Institute flourished at first, but was on the point of being destroyed by a sudden catastrophe in 1899. The Sisters, victims of a financial swindle, were obliged to go out begging, two by two, in their determination to ensure the survival of the Order. At the beginning of that year two of those soliciting funds arrived in Piacenza where the Bishop gave them permission to solicit and inquired into their difficulties. The two poor Sisters sensed a paternal kindliness in the Bishop and told him the whole painful story.

"When Bishop Scalabrini heard their pitiful tale...he charged the two Sisters to tell their Superior that he would like to see her and also their Rule. Merloni responded immediately to this invitation and the Servant of God encouraged her, calmed her anxieties, assuring her that he would take an interest in providing for our material needs and giving us spiritual assistance.[34] He examined our Rule and on June 10, 1900 he approved it ad experimentum for ten years. Not having found a house for our use in Piacenza, since we had to leave the convent in Viareggio, he loaned us the convent of San Francesco in Castelnuovo Fogliani, until we came here in Via Borghetto, opposite the institute for deaf mutes."[35]

On June 11, 1900, Mother Clelia and the others who had survived the storm pronounced the vows of poverty, obedience, chastity and charity.

After their first journey to Brazil, mentioned above,[36] four Sisters, accompanied by Scalabrinian Fathers Francesco Brescianini and Massimo Rinaldi, arrived in Parana (Brazil) in November of 1900, and founded their Parana Province which was later transferred to Sao Paulo. The Sisters were visited by Bishop Scalabrini in 1904, who in a letter to Mother Marcellina Vigano, Vicar General and later Superior General, called them "holy women, of excellent spirit."

That same November, 1900, the Bishop of Piacenza offered the Congregation Palazzo Falconi in Via Borghetto as their motherhouse and in an episcopal decree formally instituted in Piacenza the Congregation of the Sisters Missionary Apostles of the Sacred Heart, later called Zelatrices, "the specific aim and desire of which was to render homage to the Divine Redeemer at the dawn of the new century."[37]

On May 16, 1902, Bishop Scalabrini gave the missionary cross to six of the Sisters, assigned to the mission in Boston, and spoke words of encouragement which the Congregation has treasured ever since: "God will be with you, he will fight for you provided that in all your struggles and sadnesses and dangers you ask Him for help...Do not fear...With the crucifix in hand even an idiot can perform miracles." They were welcomed by Fathers Biasotti and Barbato, and took charge of the orphanage, the school and the Children of Mary. From this activity came the first Italo-American vocations, among them that of Mother Hildegarde Campodonico, who later became Superior General, one of the numerous evidences of the religious and social advancement of the emigrants made possible by the work of Bishop Scalabrini and the other apostles to the emigrants.

In 1904, following Bishop Scalabrini's visit to Brazil and at the wish of the Bishop of Sao Paulo, the Sisters took over the administration of the Umberto I Hospital, as we have seen.

Under Bishop Scalabrini's guidance, the five-year period, 1900-1905, saw the foundation of the future growth of the Congregation which now "carries on its charitable work in Italy, Brazil, Argentina, the United States and Switzerland. It numbers 6 provinces, 5 novitiates, 7 Apostolic Schools and 215 convents, in which more than 2,000 Sisters devote themselves to the education of children and young women, to helping the sick and to caring for the aged and the abandoned."[38]

When Scalabrini died, a few days after having regularized the legal position of the house in Via Borghetto, "bitter was the grief of Mother Clelia and all her Sisters. The magnitude of Bishop Scalabrini's holiness and work seemed enormous after his death. Then the Sisters Apostles could realize in all its great fullness, the immense loss they suffered and wept for in the death of their wise and prudent Guide, the Father who had lavished with incomparable abundance the treasure of his charity on the Congregation. As co-Founder and Father he will always remain in the prayers and memory of all the generations of the Missionary Sisters Zelatrices of the Sacred Heart,"[39] who in 1967 resumed their original name of Sisters Apostles of the Sacred Heart of Jesus.

Chronology

1839 — July 8. He was born at Fino Mornasco (Como), the third child of Luigi Scalabrini and Colomba Trombetta. He was baptized on the same day by Rev. Girolamo Felli, the assistant pastor of Fino.

1840 — He received the sacrament of Confirmation at Fino Mornasco from Bishop Carlo Romanò, Bishop of Como, in the parish church of Fino.

1852 — Having finished elementary school in his native town, he attended the Liceo Volta of Como, where he completed five years of high school.

1856 — He composed a poem in loose hendecasyllable, in honor of St. Aloyisius Gonzaga.

1857 — He entered the Minor Seminary of St. Abbondio in Como and there completed his philosophical courses.

1859 — He continued on in the Major Seminary to finish his theology course while at the same time he held the post of Censor in the Gallio College.

1860 — May 15. He stood up to the Custodian of the Civic Library who had slandered the Rector, Gatti of Fino Mornasco, in the newspaper *Patriota* and took up the defense of the priest.

— June 1. He received the tonsure in the Oratory of the episcopal residence of Bishop

Giuseppe Marzorati of Como.

— Dec. 21. He received the first two Minor Orders in the same episcopal residence of the Bishop of Como.

1861 — May 24. He received the last two Minor Orders in the same Oratory of the same Bishop.

1862 — June 24. He received the subdeaconate from Bishop Pietro Luigi Speranza, Bishop of Bergamo.

— Sept. 20. He was ordained Deacon by Bishop Carlo dei Conti Caccia Dominioni, Bishop of Famagosta and Capitular Vicar of Milan.

1863 — May 30. He was ordained priest by Bishop Pietro Luigi Speranza, Bishop of Bergamo.

— Between June and November he was an assistant in one of the parishes of the Valtellina and, later, in that of Fino Mornasco.

— During those months he asked of Bishop Marinoni to be accepted into the Institute of Foreign Missions of Milan. The Bishop of Como, Bishop Marzorati, did not grant him permission: "I need you; your Indies are in Italy."

— Nov. He was chosen to be the Director of Discipline and teacher of history and Greek in the St. Abbondio Seminary.

1865 — May 4. His mother died.

— He established the Academy in the seminary.

— He was chosen to be teacher of Greek in the Castellini di Camerlata College.

1867 — During the summer the cholera epidemic broke out in the Como region and Fr. J. B. Scalabrini devoted himself to the assistance of the ill in the city and in the area of Fino Mornasco.

1868 — Oct. 6. He was selected rector of the St. Abbondio Minor Seminary.

— Rev. Geremia Bonomelli, Rector of Lovere, was invited to preach the spiritual exercises in the two seminaries of Como: thus began the friendship between Scalabrini and Bonomelli.

— He was nominated Prosynodal Examiner and Pro-Vicar General of the Diocese of Como.

1869 — May 2. By royal decree, he was awarded the Medal of Valor for the assistance he rendered to the cholera victims.

1870 — July. Selected pastor of the parish of San Bartolomeo in Como, he made his solemn entry into the parish on the third Sunday of the month.

1872 — He held a series of eleven conferences on the Vatican Council in the Cathedral.

1875 — He compiled "The Little Catechism for Orphanages."

— Nov. 20. Bishop Antonio Ranza of Piacenza died.

1876 — Jan. 28. In the Consistory he was canonically nominated Bishop of Piacenza.

— Jan. 30. He was consecrated Bishop at Rome in the Church of the College of Propaganda Fide by Cardinal Alessandro Franchi.

— Feb. 5. He took possession of the Diocese of Piacenza by proxy and nominated Msgr. Francesco Tammi the Vicar General.

— Feb. 13. He made his solemn entry into the diocese on the vigil of the feast of Blessed

Gregory X.

— Apr. 2. He addressed a petition to the Pope that St. Francis de Sales be declared a Doctor of the Church.

— Apr. 28-30. The celebration of Blessed Gregory X in the Basilica of St. Antoninus where the Blessed had been a Canon.

— July 5. The first number of the "Catholic Catechist," the first catechetical magazine in Italy, was issued.

— July 16. He gave directives for the administration of Confirmation.

— Sept. 4. His father died.

— Nov. 4. He announced his first Pastoral Visitation.

— Dec. 8. He inaugurated his first Pastoral Visitation in the Cathedral.

— Dec. 20. He appointed a Special Committee to search for documentation to authenticate the Holy Relics and to compile a critical history of the Saints of Piacenza.

1877 — Jan. 10. He presided over the meeting of the members of the Diocesan Committee for the Schools of Catechism.

— Jan. 19. He appointed the managing Commission for the Congregations of the Cases of Conscience for the city and its suburbs and presided over the first Congregation.

— Feb. 1. He inaugurated the monthly Conferences for the Catechism teachers, in St. Mary in Cortina.

— Apr. 24. He obtained the *Exequatur.*

— June 7. He was received by the Pope together with diocesan pilgrims. Pius IX gave him a pectoral cross telling him: "The Cross of Bishops is precious, but much more heavy."

— During his stay in Rome he exposed to Card. E. Borromeo his idea of revitalizing the Lombard Seminary.

— June 19. He entered the episcopal residence, freed for the first time from the *mano regia.*

— Aug. 4. At the request of the Holy See, he sent a letter to the bishops of Northern Italy to inform them of the plans to reopen the Lombard Seminary.

1878 — Jan. 19. Because he did not succumb to the pressures of the authorities to hold funeral services for Victor Emmanuel II in the Cathedral, he was attacked by the crowds.

— Jan. 23. In a letter to his diocese he justified his obedience and pardoned the offenders.

— Feb. 7. Pius IX died. Bishop Scalabrini held the suffrages and proposed the erection of a monument in the Cathedral.

— Feb. 14. Having received regulations from the Holy See, he held the funeral services in the Cathedral for Victor Emmanuel II.

— Feb. 16. He held the solemn funeral services for Pius IX in the Cathedral.

— Apr. 8. He appointed the Diocesan Commission for the erection of the monument to Piux IX.

— May 21. The first audience with Leo XIII.

— June 11. He conducted the recognition of the relics of Sts. Antoninus and Victor.

— Sept. He invited the Daughters of Chairty to open an institute for deaf and dumb girls and offered a very large sum of money for this purpose.

— Nov. 2-13. He was in Rome for the opening of the Lombard Seminary.

— Nov. 4. He celebrated mass for the seminarians of Northern Italy in the Chapel of the Heart of St. Charles, in S. Carlo in Corso, and gave the inaugural discourse for the revived Seminary.

1879 — Mar. 9. He presided over the general meeting of the Society of the Catholic Young Workers of Piacenza.

— Mar. 10. He presided over the Association of the Catholic Promoters of Good Works.

— Mar. He went on pilgrimage to Caravaggio.

— Apr. 26. He went to Alexandria for the consecration of the Cathedral and the celebration of the Lombard League.

— May 1. He announced the first diocesan Synod.

— July 21. He went to Pejo to regain his health.

— Sept. 2-4. The first diocesan Synod.

— Oct. 10. He announced the free distribution of soup to the poor. He sold his gold chalice to give food to the hungry.

— He turned the first floor of the episcopal residence into a kitchen and offered 4,000 dishes of soup a day to the poor.

— Nov. He opened, on a smaller scale, the Institute for the Deaf and Dumb, which would have a definitive form in 1881.

— Dec. 21. The Honorable Savini praised the charity of the Bishop of Piacenza in the Chamber of Deputies.

1880 — At the beginning of the year, the newspaper *La Verità* was published.

— Jan. 30. The citizens of Piacenza thank the Bishop for the charity he extended to them during the severe winter of food shortages.

— Mar. 7. This was the date of the first issue of *Divus Thomas* (though it had been previously published).

— Apr. 17-22. He took part in the fourth Lombard Pilgrimage to the Shrine of the Holy Cross in Como.

— May 29. He unveiled the monument to Pius IX in the Cathedral and inaugurated the festivities for the solemn recognition of the relics of Sts. Antoninus and Victor. The celebration, over which Card. Moretti and fourteen bishops presided, lasted until June 6.

— Sept. 8. The pastoral letter on the instruction of the deaf and dumb was issued.

— Sept. 26. He announced to the diocese the termination of the first Pastoral Visitation.

— Nov. 3. He departed for Rome for his *ad limina* visit and remained there until Nov. 23. He had two audiences with the Pope.

1881 — Jan. 6. He promulgated the new catechism for the diocese.

— He arranged for the solemn celebration of the feast of St. Thomas in the seminaries and and established a Chair for the explanation of the *Contra Gentes*, appointing to this task Canon Rossignoli at Piacenza and Rev. Giacomo M. Radini Tedeschi at Bedonia.

— Apr. 18. He established the diocesan committee for the *Opera dei Congressi*.

— Aug. 5-7. The feast was celebrated for the recognition of the relics of St. Sixtus II in the Church of St. Sixtus.

— Sept. He announced the members of the new staff of the seminary.. Rev. F. Rossignoli, Rector; Rev. C. Molinari, Spiritual Director; Rev. G. Vinati, Professor of Dogmatic Theology; Rev. G. M. Radini Tedeschi, Professor of Canon Law. He named Rev. V. Segadelli Rector of the seminary at Bedonia.

— Oct. 3. He published a protest against the *Osservatore Cattolico*.

— Nov. He corresponded with the Card. Secretary of State because of the meddling by the *Osservatore Cattolico*.

1882 — Mar. 19. He prohibited the publication of the atheist newspaper *Il Penitente*.

— Apr. 16. He initiated the second Pastoral Visitation in the Cathedral.

— May 25. At Caravaggio he gave a discourse on the occasion of the 900th anniversary of the apparition of Our Lady.

— Sept. 12-14. He participated in the feast of the Coronation of the Blessed Virgin of Mercy at Castelleone.

— Sept. 25. During his *ad limina* visit, Leo XIII asked Scalabrini his views on the political elections.

— Sept. 27. Another long audience with the Pope.

1883 — Mar. 15. He sent to the Holy See a written statement on the problems of the *Osservatore Cattolico*.

— Apr. The Pope appointed a committee of six Cardinals to examine the differences between Scalabrini and Bonomelli on the one hand, and the Milanese newspaper on the other.

— July 25. The *Osservatore Cattolico* published an apology of the Director, for the offenses hurled against the bishop and for the undue interference into the affairs of the Piacenza diocese.

— Aug. 4. He held in the Cathedral the solemn obsequies for the victims of the earthquake of Ischia and inaugurated a campaign for the relief of the afflicted families. He offered a pectoral cross given to him by Pius IX.

— Aug. 9. Leo XIII sent him through Fr. Cornoldi, his picture with an address in Distich Latin. Bishop Scalabrini thanked him and translated it into Greek.

— Sept. 9. The Sacred Congregation of Rites approved the new *Proprium* for Piacenza as reformed by Bishop Scalabrini.

1884 — Jan. He corrected the calendar for the Piacenza diocese.

— May 19. The Masonic Lodge of Piacenza singled out Bishop Scalabrini as its most powerful adversary in Northern Italy. The Masonic newspaper *Il Piccolo* launched a defamatory campaign against the Bishop.

— June 10. At Milan in the church of St. Calogero, he consigned the Crucifix to five departing missionaries among whom was Fr. Opilio Negri, of Piacenza.

— Cholic pains and exhaustion due to his excessive work load endangered the life of the bishop who went to Montecatini once the crisis passed.

— Aug. 15. He interrupted his homily on the Assumption because of physical exhaustion. He underwent a two month period of treatment, subsisting only on milk.

— Sept. 26. He promulgated the new *Proprium* for Piacenza.

— Oct. 9. He was again stricken by illness and was obliged to retire to San Polo.

— He took up the reform of sacred music by instituting the Commission of St. Cecilia.

— Nov. He appointed Fr. Natale Bruni rector of the seminary of Bedonia.

— Dec. 7. He returned to the city cured in health. The diocese gave him a crosier and a pectoral cross as a gift in reparation for the offenses hurled against him in the Masonic newspaper campaign.

1885 — Nov. 3. He went to Rome for the *ad limina* visit. He discussed the publication of the pamphlet *Intransigenti e Transigenti* with Leo XIII and presented a written statement on the reconciliation between Italy and the Holy See.

— Nov. 28. He joined in against the Protestant Conferences which took place following upon the opening of an Evangelical church in Piacenza.

1886 — Jan. 2. The first issue of *Amico del Popolo* was published. It was a bi-weekly Catholic publication (which was to become a daily in 1897).

— Mar. 14. He inaugurated in the Cathedral the Jubilee Year in honor of the fiftieth anniversary of the priestly ordination of Leo XIII.

— Apr. 11. He presided over the general reunion of the Diocesan Committee of the *Opera dei Congressi.*

— May 19. He was a guest of the Bishop of Bobbio during his pastoral visitation of the Vicarates of the Appennines which began on May 8.

— May 23. The political elections took place.

— June 7. He answered the accusations brought against him by the Holy Inquisition regarding the participation of the Catholics of Piacenza in the political elections.

— Sept. 8. He took part in the celebration of the Coronation of the Blessed Virgin of Grace at Brescia.

— Sept. 12-14. He presided over the Coronation of the Blessed Virgin of Mercy at Castelleone.

— Oct. 20. He consecrated the Marian Shrine of Roveleto.

— Nov. 6. Card. Schiaffino, on behalf of the Pope, entrusted him to dissuade Stoppani from publishing the periodical *Il Rosmini.*

— Nov. 12. He sent the Pope a copy of a circular letter which he intended to publish defending what he had done on the occasion of the elections; Leo XIII asked him not to publish it and sent him a copy of his own book of poetry.

— Dec. 18. At Como, he participated in the jubilee celebration of Bishop Pietro Carsana, Bishop of that diocese.

1887 — Jan. He organized the celebration of the priestly jubilee of Leo XIII.

— Jan. 11. He sent a first letter to Card. Simeoni, Prefect of Propaganda Fide, with a proposal to render religious assistance to emigrants.

— Feb. 3. The Sacred Congregation of Propaganda Fide accepted the proposal of Scalabrini for assistance to the emigrants and invited him to present a program.

— Feb. 16. He sent an outline to Propaganda Fide for an "Association for the purpose of providing for the spiritual needs of Italian emigrants in the Americas."

— Apr. 24. In the episcopal residence he presided over a general meeting of the Catholic Workers Association.

— Apr. 30. He advised Bishop Bonomelli not to publish a pamphlet on the conciliation, which the Bishop of Cremona was preparing.

— June 11. He declined a summons in the civil trial Stoppani-Albertario.

— June 18. He blessed the cornerstone of the new Chapel of the Seminary.

— June 26. Leo XIII gave a first vague approval to the decisions taken by the Congregation of Propaganda Fide on the project of Bishop Scalabrini regarding the religious assistance to the emigrants.

— July 9. He consecrated the restored church of Our Lady of St. Mark at Bedonia.

— He established a committee at Piacenza for the protection of the emigrants fashioned on the German St. Raphael Society.

— Aug. 1. Once again he fell victim to physical exhaustion and had to take a period of complete rest.

— Aug. 24. He participated in the celebration of the sixteenth centenary of St. Alexander, Martyr, at Milan.

— A first meeting took place during the summer with St. Frances Cabrini concerning the foundation of the House of Castelsangiovanni.

— Nov. 9. He came to terms with Bishop D. Jacobini regarding the decisions to be presented to the Pope for approval that concerned the new Institute for the Emigrants.

— Nov. 14. In the audience granted to the Secretary of Propaganda Fide, Leo XIII approved the Institute that Bishop Scalabrini intended to establish at Piacenza for the religious assistance to the emigrants in America.

— Nov. 15. The Pope published the brief *Libenter agnovimus*, with which he approved the Scalabrinian institution in favor of the emigrants.

— Nov. 28. In the Basilica of St. Antoninus, around noon time, he received the first two priests into his Institute, Rev. Giuseppe Molinari and Rev. Domenico Mantese, who took the first vows together with their first superior, Msgr. Domenico Costa.

— Dec. 18. The conclusion of the second Pastoral Visitation.

— He guided the diocesan pilgrimage to the presence of the Holy Father.

1888 — Jan. 1. In the Cathedral he presided over the celebration of the day of jubilee for Leo XIII. To commemorate the jubilee, he dedicated a new chapel in the Urban Seminary.

— Jan. 27. Propaganda Fide authorized Bishop Scalabrini to acquire a new site for his Institute.

— Mar. 5. While waiting for the new site, the Institute of the Missionaries for the Emigrants was transferred from the rectory of St. Antoninus to the Pio Ritiro Cerati.

— Mar. 6. Bishop Scalabrini presented the first temporary Rule to his missionaries.

— Mar. 21. He issued the decree *Post obitum* against Rosminianism.

— May 1. He went to Milan to visit the Emperor of Brazil and recommended the Italian emigrants to him as well as the new Institute founded for them.

— May 3. He bagan his third Pastoral Visitation.

— May 18. He urged St. Frances Cabrini to send her religious to America to assist the emigrants.

— May 24. In the name of the bishops of the Emilian Region, he sent a protest to the Chamber of Deputies against the Zanardelli Code.

— June 5. He journeyed to Rome to finalize some matters regarding the Institute of the Missionaries for the Emigrants.

— June 11. Rev. Francesco Zaboglio, the first Vicar General of the Scalabrinian Missionaries, sailed for New York to discuss matters regarding emigration with Archbishop Corrigan.

— July. The Institute of Piacenza was authorized to take the name of *Christopher Columbus*.

— July 12. In the Basilica of St. Antoninus, Bishop Scalabrini presented the missionary crucifix to the first seven priests and three "catechist brothers" who left for the United States and Brazil on that same day.

— Sept. 8. He communicated to Propaganda Fide the closing of the contract for the acquisition of the former convent of the Capuchin Sisters on Via Francesco Torta which was to become the Mother House of the Scalabrinian Congregation.

— Sept. 19. The Congregation of Propaganda Fide approved *ad experimentum* for a period of five years the Rule of the Congregation of the Missionaries for the Emigrants.

— Dec. 10. With his Apostolic Letter *Quam aerumnosa*, Leo XIII announced to the American episcopate that he had instituted at Piacenza, through the efforts of Bishop Scalabrini, an apostolic college of priests for the assistance of Italian emigrants which he himself was placing under his own patronage.

1889.— Jan. 24. A second group of eight missionaries departed for the Americas.

— At the end of Feb. he was at Rome where he tried again to stop the publication of the Bonomellian pamphlet *Roma, l'Italia e la realtà delle cose*, which was instead already printed and was issued on Mar. 1.

— Mar. 19. At Codogno he presented the crucifix to Mother Cabrini and six other sisters departing for New York where they arrived Mar. 31.

— Apr. 21. He telegraphed the Pope for Bonomelli that the Bishop of Cremona publically retracted the pamphlet *Roma, l'Italia e la realtà delle cose.*

— Apr. 24-25. He presided over the regional meeting of the *Opera dei Congressi*, convened at Piacenza.

— May 1. At Piacenza the *Associazione di Patronato Dell'Emigrazione italiana* (St. Raphael Society) was officially constituted.

— June 17. He presided over the first meeting of the Committee for the first National Catechist Congress.

— June 30. He announced ceremonies of reparation for the erection of the monument to Giordano Bruno.

— July 7. He crowned our Lady of St. Mark in the shrine at Bedonia.

— Sept. 24-26. The first National Catechist Congress.

— At the end of Oct. he was stricken by an attack of typhoid.

— Nov. 20. He presented the crucifix to another seven missionaries leaving for America.

— Dec. Msgr. G. B. Vinati succeeded Msgr. F. Tammi as Vicar General of the diocese.

1890 — At the end of May he fell ill, exhausted by the labors of the Pastoral Visitation.

— June 23. He presided over the diocesan meeting of the committees of the *Opera dei Congressi*.

— July. He spent a period of time resting at Levico and at Rabbi, where Archbishop Corrigan of New York visited him.

— Aug. 6. He returned to Piacenza.

— Aug. 15. He suspended the solemn celebration in honor of the Assumption, patroness of the city, to protest the public dances.

— He was forced to take another period of rest in the country.

— Sept. 28. The members of the Società Cattolica Operaia Piacentina went on pilgrimage to our Lady of Fontanellato to pray for the recovery of the Bishop.

— Toward the end of Oct., he returned to the city, recovered in health.

— Nov. 12-14. At Cremona he participated in the celebration in honor of Blessed Zaccaria.

— Dec. 10. In the Church of St. Raymond he presented the crucifix to eight other departing missionaries.

1891 — Jan. 10. A sacrilegious theft of the Crowns of the Madonna del Popolo took place in the Cathedral.

— Jan. 25. At Genoa, he held a conference on emigration in the Church of the Magdalene.

— Jan. 27. He went to Rome for the *ad limina* visit.

— Jan. 30. Leo XIII received him in audience and kept him for a lengthy period of time discussing the assistance to the emigrants.

— Feb. 8. At Rome he held a long conference on emigration in the Church of St. Andrea della Valle and started the Committee of the St. Raphael Society.

— Mar. 7. At Florence he held a conference on emigration in the Church of St. Giovannino and set up the Committee of the St. Raphael Society.

— Mar. 14. At Turin he held a conference on emigration and again set up the Committee of the St. Raphael Society.

— Apr. 4. The Secretary General of the German St. Raphael Society and the Marquis Volpe-Landi, Secretary of the Italian St. Raphael, visited Bishop Scalabrini to coordinate the work of the two Societies.

— Apr. 16. At Milan he held a conference on emigration in the Church of St. Alessandro and set up the Committee of the St. Raphael Society.

— June 21. The celebration of the centenary of St. Louis Gonzaga was held.

— July 7. The Sacred Congregation of the Council approved the project of Bishop Scalabrini to reduce the number of parishes of the city of Piacenza.

— Aug. 30. He participated in the feast of the Blessed Virgin of Consolation at the Church of San Bartolomeo in Como.

— Sept. 9. He presented the curcifix to a new group of ten missionaries in the Church of St. Raymond.

— Sept. 10. He presided over the meeting of the different committees of the St. Raphael Society to discuss the definitive by-laws.

— Oct. He completed his third Pastoral Visitation.

1892 — Mar. 15. In a letter to the Missionaries for the Italians in the Americas, he declared St. Charles the Patron of his Congregation.

— He inaugurated the Mother House of the Missionaries of St. Charles under the name of Christopher Columbus.

— Apr. 19. He presided over the meetings of the diocesan Committees of the *Opera dei Congressi*.

— Apr. 20. He celebrated the first monthly ceremony in preparation for the episcopal jubilee of Leo XIII.

— Apr. 25. At Lucca, in the Chiesa dei Servi, he held a conference on emigration.

— May 1. In remembrance of the episcopal jubilee of Leo XIII, he set up the Opera di S. Opilio for poor clerics.

— May 4. He presented the crucifix to four missionaries in the Church of St. Charles, next to the Mother House.

— May 8. At Palermo, he held a conference on emigration in the Church of Gesù.

— May 9. The Exposition of Palermo conferred on Bishop Scalabrini the first class certificate for the establishment of the Institute of the Missionaries of St. Charles for the emigrants.

— Aug. 21. He participated at the solemn inauguration of the monument to Christopher Columbus at Bettola.

— Sept. 30. Leo XIII named Card. Bausa the Protector of the Congregation founded by Bishop Scalabrini.

— Oct. 12. He celebrated the fourth centenary of the discovery of America with religious services in the Cathedral.

— Oct. 23. At Reviso he held a conference on emigration in the Church of St. Agnes.

— Dec. 2. In the Cathedral of Parma he read an official discourse for the celebration of Christopher Columbus.

— Dec. 11. He was invited by Giuseppe Toniolo to hold a conference on emigration in the Church of the Knights of St. Stephen, in Pisa, and started the committee of the St. Raphael Society.

1893 — Jan. 10. He celebrated the coronation of the Madonna del Popolo in the Cathedral on the second anniversary of the theft of the crowns.

— Feb. 15. He led a diocesan pilgrimage to Rome for the episcopal jubilee of the Pope.

— Mar. 1. He announced the Second Diocesan Synod.

— Apr. 16. He consecrated restored Church of St. Peter.

— May 2-4. He held the Second Diocesan Synod.

— May 4. He started the fourth Pastoral Visitation.

— June 29. He intervened against the opening of a lay recreation center of Masonic flavor.

— Aug. 12. He blessed the Chapel of the Madonna della Bomba erected by Msgr. Francesco Torta.

— Oct. 7-9. At Borgo S. Donnino (Fidenza) he participated in the centenary celebration of the martyr S. Donnino together with the Card. Patriarch of Venice.

— Oct. 28. He attended the funeral services of Archbishop Calabiana of Milan.

— Dec. 20. He presided over an extraordinary ceremony in the seminary in honor of the episcopal jubilee of Leo XIII.

1894 — Feb. 9. He launched an appeal to the diocese for the restoration of the Cathedral.

— Aug. 19. Together with 9,000 people he participated in a pilgrimage to the Shrine of Fontanasanta.

— Sept. 2-6. He participated in the Eucharistic Congress of Turin. On that occasion there occurred the reconciliation with Fr. D. Albertario.

— Sept. 7-9. He participated in the feast of St. Colombano at Bobbio and held the official commemoration.

— Nov. 6. At the suggestion of Scalabrini, the Archbishop of Genoa sent a circular letter to all the bishops of Northern Italy in which he backed the St. Raphael Society.

— Dec. 8. In the Church of St. Charles he received for the first time the perpetual vows of the Missionaries of St. Charles.

— Dec. 11. Bishop F. Mascaretti of Susa died. Bishop Scalabrini gave the eulogy in the Cathedral.

1895 — Jan. 20. He presented a new Rule to his Missionaries, including in it the necessary changes prompted by the introduction of the perpetual vows.

— Mar. 10. He announced the celebration of the eighth century of the First Crusade, proclaimed by Urban II in 1095 in the Council of Piacenza.

— Apr. 18. He presided over the general meeting of the diocesan committee of the *Opera dei Congressi*.

— Apr. 21. The centenary celebration of the First Crusade was held with the participation of twelve bishops. The discourse of Bishop Scalabrini merited the gratification of Leo XIII.

— May 5. The priest Paolo Miraglia, called upon without the required permission of the Chancery, began his Marian preaching in the Basilica of St. Savino.

— May 15. He departed for Clermont-Ferrand, where on May 17 he held a discourse in French on the eighth centenary of the First Crusade.

— May 20-31. As guest of the Lazarists of Paris, he participated in a dinner given in his honor by the Apostolic Nuncio.

— May 30. Msgr. Vinati, Vicar General, communicated to Miraglia that all his faculties in the diocese ceased. Miraglia began to preach in profane places.

— June 10. With 720 of the faithful, he led a diocesan pilgrimage to Loreto.

— July 18. He blessed the new Institute for the scrofulous which was started with the initiative of Msgr. G. Pinazzi.

— July 27. When all peaceful attempts were exhausted, he ordered Miraglia, under penalty of excommunication, to retract the complaints hurled against some priests of Piacenza.

— July 29. He condemned the Mirglia periodical *Gerolamo Savonarola*.

— Sept. 23. He presented the crucifix to three missionaries.

— Oct. 16. He celebrated the tenth anniversary of the Società Operaia Cattolica at Alseno in an extraordinary fashion.

— Oct. 25. He received the temporary profession of vows of the first four Missionary Sisters of St. Charles to whom he presented the veil and the missionary crucifix.

— Oct. 27. The first four Missionary Sisters of St. Charles departed from Genoa for Brazil with their co-founder Rev. Giuseppe Marchetti.

1896 — Jan. 30. On the twentieth anniversary of his episcopal consecration, the diocese gave the bishop a mitre and an album with the signatures of the citizens as a sign of protest against the offenses inflicted on him by Miraglia.

— Mar. 5. He directed that memorial masses be said throughout the diocese for the 500 who died in Dogali.

— Apr. 28. The Bishops of the Emilian Region express to Bishop Scalabrini, in a collective letter, the suffering caused by Miraglia.

— May 1. He announced the greater excommunication incurred by Miraglia.

— In the beginning of July he participated in the fiftieth anniversary celebration of the Seminary of Bedonia and in the interdiocesan meeting of the *Opera dei Congressi*.

— Sept. 6. At the Shrine of Our Lady of Grace at Brescia, he gave a discourse commemorating the tenth anniversary of the coronation.

— Oct. He celebrated at Bettola, the 400th anniversary of the apparation of Our Lady of Oak.

— Nov. 15. He participated in the jubilee celebration of Bishop Bonomelli and read the official discourse.

— The weekly, *La Voce Cattolica*, was published to counteract the *Gerolamo Savonarola* of Miraglia.

1897 — May 5. He was granted a private audience by Leo XIII.

— May 6. He introduced the participants in the diocesan pilgrimage of Piacenza to the Pope.

— He gave the discourse closing the centenary celebration of the First Crusade in the Basilica of the Holy Cross at Rome.

— June 11. He hosted and presided over the fourth regional meeting of the *Opera dei Congressi*.

1898 — The Episcopal Conference of Emilia commissioned him to review the text of the *Piccolo Catechismo* (Little Catechism) that was to be adopted throughout the Region and nominated him member of the Commission for the *Catechism Maggiore* (Greater Catechism).

— May 1. Even at Piacenza a riot broke out among the workers that resulted in bloodshed. The bishop went into the street to administer the sacraments to the wounded.

— May 4. In a circular letter he invited the workers to remain calm and the authorities to respect their rights.

— May 24. Following the arrest of Albertario, Bishop Scalabrini tried to get him out without being tried.

— In the month of June six aspirants of the Missionary Sisters of St. Charles began their postulancy in the novitiate which opened at Via Nicolini 45.

— July 24. He asked Minister Pelloux for the reconstitution of the Committees of the *Opera dei Congressi.*

— Aug. He took part in the centenary celebration of St. Alexander at Bergamo.

— Sept. 6. Minister Pelloux communicated to him that he had granted permission to Albertario to celebrate Mass in prison.

— Dec. He presented the habit to six novices of the Congregation of the Missionary Sisters of St. Charles.

1899.— Feb. 22. He reassured Mother Clelia Merloni that he was taking an interest in the Rules and House of the Apostles of the Sacred Heart to try to save their Congregation after the crisis of 1898.

— Apr. 18-21. He participated in the Sixteenth Catholic Congress at Ferrara and presented a report on emigration.

— Aug. 28-30. The third diocesan Eucharistic Synod was held.

— Sept. 10. At Fino Mornasco, he took part in the feast of the Child Mary. He blessed the cornerstone of the new Church of San Bartolomeo in Como.

— Sept. 26-27. On the occasion of the General Exposition at Turin, he took part in a reunion of religious, political and diplomatic personalities in order to discuss the legal regulations of emigration. In the field limited to the Missions, he gave his conference *L'Italia all'estero* (Italy Abroad).

— Oct. 11. At Ravenna he held the discourse for the eighth centenary of the Greek Madonna.

— Nov. He consecrated Bishop A. Fiorini, chosen for the see of Pontremoli.

1900 — Jan. 30. A committee began to organize the celebration of the episcopal jubilee of Bishop Scalabrini.

— June 5. He crowned the Madonna of San Savino.

— June 10. He approved *ad experimentum* for a period of ten years, the rule of the Apostles of the Sacred Heart.

— June 11-12. He received the profession of both the first Missionary Sisters of St. Charles, who duly made their novitiate and of the Apostles who made the novitiate a second time.

— June 13. The Holy Inquisition declared Miraglia excommunicated and one to be avoided.

— June 16. The Supreme Court of Appeal confirmed the condemnation of Miraglia by the Tribunal of Bologna.

— June 23. Miraglia fled to Switzerland.

— July 29. He presided over the seventh centenary of St. Raymond Palmieri.

— Aug. 9. He presented the crucifix to six missionary sisters destined to the orphanage Christopher Columbus of San Paolo. They departed from Genoa on the following day.

— Aug. 26. He left for Rome with the diocesan pilgrimage.

— Nov. Four Apostles of the Sacred Heart left for America. Bishop Scalabrini offered their Congregation a new site on Via Borghetto and granted it diocesan approval.

— Dec. 27. In the Basilica of St. Antoninus he conferred episcopal consecration on Bishop Natale Bruni, chosen archbishop of Modena.

1901 — Jan. 31. A new emigration law was promulgated which included some suggestions of Bishop Scalabrini and his missionaries.

— June 15. The first issue of the monthly *Il Giovane Cattolico* (The Young Catholic) was published. With the exposition of gifts, the episcopal jubilee celebration of Bishop Scalabrini began.

— June 16. The newly restored Cathedral was reopened.

— June 17. The Pontifical Mass of Bishop Scalabrini, with the congratulatory discourse of Bishop A. Sarti, bishop of Gustalla, was the culminating moment of the episcopal jubilee.

— July 18. He departed from Genoa for a visit to the missionaries and to the Italian emigrants in the United States.

— Aug. 3. He disembarked at New York.

— Aug. 8. He inaugurated the St. Raphael House in the port of New York.

— Aug. 15-18. He met with the Italians of Jersey City and Newark, New Jersey.

— Aug. 19-24. He preached the Spiritual Exercises to more than sixty Italian missionaries and priests at New York.

— Sept. 1. He visited the mission at New Haven, Conn.

— Sept. 5. He arrived at Boston, Mass.

— Sept. 12. He was in Utica, N. Y.

— Sept. 14. He visited the Italians of Providence, R.I.

— Sept. 16. He met with the emigrants in Buffalo, N.Y.

— Sept. 18. He visited the Italians of Cleveland, Ohio.

— Sept. 21. He was in Detroit, Mich.

— Sept. 25. He arrived in St. Paul, Minn.

— Sept. 28. He was in Kansas City.

— Oct. 1. He visited the bishop in St. Louis, Mo.

— Oct. 5. He visited the emigrants of Cincinnati, Ohio.

— Oct. 7. He stopped at Columbus, Ohio.

— Oct. 9. He arrived at Washington.

— Oct. 10. He was received by Pres. Theodore Roosevelt.

— Oct. 11. He was the guest of Card. Gibbons at Baltimore, Md. In the evening he returned to New York.

— Oct. 15. The Catholic Club of New York organized a reception in his honor. Bishop Scalabrini gave a discourse that was echoed widely in the press of the metropolis.

— Oct. 19. He visited the mission of Providence, R.I.

— Oct. 27. He returned to visit the institution for the Italians in Boston.

— Nov. 3. At New York he ordained priests, four of his missionaries after he preached the Spiritual Exercises to them.

— Nov. 11. The last visit to Italian groups in the United States was reserved for Newark, N.J.

— Nov. 12. He left New York.

— Nov. 26. He arrived at Naples.

— Nov. 29. He referred to Leo XIII his impressions of his visit to the United States.

— Dec. 4. He returned to Piacenza and was received with extraordinary enthusiasm.

1902 — He took up again the fifth Pastoral Visit of the diocese.

— May 15. In the annual meeting of the Vicars, the publication of the social weekly *Il Lavoro* (Work).

— An outline plan of the second National Catechetical Congress was published.

— May 16. He presented the crucifix to six Apostles of the Sacred Heart, destined to the missions among the Italians of Boston.

— Sept. 5. He inaugurated the Exposition of Sacred Art in San Vincenzo.

1903 — Apr. 26. After fifteen years of negotiations, he succeeded in obtaining from the government the return of the Bramante Basilica of the Holy Sepulchre for the purpose of worship and started its restoration.

— July 4. In a general meeting of the Catholic Associations which he customarily held every year in the episcopal residence, he proposed the establishment of an institution in favor of the rice workers of the fields.

— July 21. He notified the diocese of the death of Leo XIII.

— Aug. 4. He communicated to it the election of Pius X.

— Aug. 22. He invited the pastors of the diocese to compile statistics on the rice workers.

— Nov. 15. He inaugurated the restored Basilica of San Savino.

— Nov. 16. He presided over the interdiocesan meeting in favor of the rice workers and so established a basis for the religious and social assistance to the category of seasonal immigrants.

— Nov. 18. He obtained a first audience with Pius X.

1904 — Jan. 11. He presided over the meeting of the general committee of the Opera pro Mondariso.

— June 13. He departed from Piacenza for a trip to Brazil.

— June 14. Pius X gave him all necessary faculties and promised to send him a special blessing every morning at seven.

— June 17. Having celebrated Mass on the tomb of his predecessor, Blessed Paolo Burali, he departed from Naples.

— July 7. He put ashore at Rio de Janeiro and was received by the archbishop.

— July 9. He arrived at Sao Paolo.

— July 13. In agreement with the bishop of Sao Paolo, he decided to give assistance and instruction to the deaf and mute.

— Aug. 2. After having visited many *fazendas*, he left Sao Paolo, and made short visits to the states of Espirito Santo and Rio de Janeiro.

— Aug. 12. He reached Paranaguà.

— Aug. 18. He was in Curitiba.

— Aug. 19. He arrived at Santa Felicidade.

— Sept. 3. He set sail again at Paranaguà.

— Sept. 5. He went to Florianopolis.

— Sept. 7. He arrived at Rio Grande.

— Sept. 10. He was at Porto Alegre.

— Sept. 12. He set out for Encantado.

— Sept. 22. He visited San Lourenco de Villas Boas and in the following days also: Comde d'Eu, Alfredo Chaves, Capoeiras, Nova Bassano, Bento Goncalves.

— Oct. 12. He reached the Italians of Caxias.

— Oct. 27.. He left from Porto Alegre.

— Nov. 9. He arrived at Buenos Aires.

— Nov. 11. He set sail from Buenos Aires for his return voyage.

— Dec. 5. He arrived at Genoa.

— Dec. 6. He arrived at Piacenza.

— Dec. 8. He celebrated the fiftieth anniversary of the proclamation of the dogma of the Immaculate Conception in the Cathedral.

1905 — Jan. 29. St. Pius X consecrated Bishop G. M. Radini Tedeschi, bishop of Bergamo. Bishop Scalabrini was an assistant bishop.

— While he was at Rome, Pius X received him in audience twice, during which Bishop Scalabrini proposed that the assistance to the emigrants be expanded to those of all nations and submitted for papal approval the program for the second National Catechetical Congress.

— Feb. 28. He pleaded with the Pope to write a word of comfort to the emigrants of all nations. At the same time he sent to Card. Merry del Val a written statement with a proposal to set up a Central Committee For Catholic Emigrants.

— May 5. He announced the sixth Pastoral Visitation which was to begin on June 11.

— He sent to Propaganda Fide his report on his Congregation.

— May 7. He led to Rivergaro the first diocesan pilgrimage to the Blessed Virgin of the Castello.

— May 14 (?). He held a conference at Bobbio, on the Italians in America.

— May 17. He wrote his last letter to the Holy See regarding the proposed committee For Catholic Emigrants.

— May 19. He presided over the committee which promoted the second National Catechetical Congress.

— May 21. He went to Borghetto di S. Lazaro for the blessing of the cemetery and was stricken by a momentary illness.

— May 28. He was operated upon.

— May 31. He received the last Sacraments.

— June 1. Feast of the Ascension. A few minutes before six in the morning, he died in his episcopal residence.

— June 5. After the funeral services, the body was buried temporarily in the capitular chapel of the city cemetery.

1908 — June 1. The monument erected to the memory of Bishop Scalabrini was unveiled.

1909 — Apr. 18-19. The transfer of the body into the Cathedral took place.

1910 — Nov. 28. The unveiling of a monument in the Church of Fino Mornasco.

1912 — Nov. 14. The unveiling of a monument erected in the Church of St. Charles at Rome.

1913 — Nov. 11. The unveiling of a monument in the Church of San Bartolomeo in Como.

1916 — Aug. 16. A tablet was unveiled in the facade of the episcopal residence with a medallion-picture of Bishop Scalabrini on it, after whom a street of the city was named.

1936 — May 5. Bishop Ersilio Menzani, bishop of Piacenza, started the ordinary diocesan investigation for the beatification of Bishop Scalabrini.

1940 — Feb. 29. The diocesan investigation was concluded.
- Mar. 6. Bishop Menzani presented the results to the Sacred Congregation of Rites.
- Apr. 30. Card. C. Salotti issued the decree for the opening of the ordinary investigation.

APPENDIX IV

Sources and Bibliography

Principal Abbreviations

Abba. = Archivio Bonomelliano of the Biblioteca Ambrosiana of Milan.

AGS = Archivio Generalizio Scalabriniano.

Arch. S.C.P.F. = Archivio of the S. Congregazione de Propaganda Fide.

ASMC = Archivio of the Seminario Maggiore of Como.

AVP = Diocesan Archive of Piacenza.

50th Anniversary Celebrations — *Il Servo di Dio Mons. Giovanni B. Scalabrini nella luce delle celebrazioni del 50° della sua morte* (1905 - 1 giugno - 1955), Rome 1957.

Gregori = Mons. Francesco Gregori, *La vita e l'opera di un grande Vescovo, Mons. Giov. Battista Scalabrini* (1839-1905), Turin, 1934.

Processus = *Placentina Beatificationis et Canonizationis Servi Dei Ioannis Baptistae Scalabrini Episcopi Placentini Fundatoris Missionariorum a S. Carolo pro Italis Emigratis - Summarium*, Rome 1943.

Processus, cop. publ. = *Copia publica Transumpti Processus Ordinaria auctoritate constituti in Curia Ecclesiastica Placentina super fama sanctitatis, virtutum et miraculorum Servi Dei Ioannis Baptistae Scalabrini Episcopi Placentini (. . .) Anno 1941*. We cite from this *copia* all the passages not referred to by the above cited summarium.

Processus de non-cultu = *Copia publica Transumpti Processus dioecesani (...) super cultu numquam praestito Servo Dei Joanni Baptistae Scalabrini. Anno 1942.*

Trent'anni di Apostolato = A volume of documents published by the brother of the Servant of God, Prof. Angelo Scalabrini, entitled: *Mons. Giovanni Battista Scalabrini, Vescovo di Piacenza. Trent'anni di Apostolato. Memorie e documenti* (Rome, Manuzio, 1909, p. 699).

Sources

1. ARCHIVIO GENERALIZIO SCALABRINIANO
    The Archive of the General House of the Missionary Order of St. Charles (Scalabrinians) (Via Calandrelli 11, Roma) houses the major portion of the documents, published and unpublished, concerning the life of Scalabrini and the history of the Order founded by him. It houses in particular, almost all the original manuscripts of the Servant of God and correspondence addressed to him with the exception of the Bonomelli-Scalabrini and Scalabrini-Zaboglio correspondence.

2. ARCHIVIO MONS. SCALABRINI of the Christopher Columbus Institute (Piacenza), Mother House of the Scalabrini Order. Besides encompassing many printed materials referring to the episcopacy of Scalabrini and to the works of the Scalabrini Missionaries, it includes also some manuscript documents (rough drafts handwritten by Scalabrini's secretary, Msgr. Mangot, and several letters addressed to the Servant of God): presently this archive is in the process of being transferred to the Archivio Generalizio Scalabriniano hence we have referred to it as such and have thus included it in the Archivio Generalizio which is being completed and reorganized.

3. ARCHIVIO VESCOVILE DI PIACENZA
    Contains all the official acts of Scalabrini from the period 1876-1905, correspondence received by the office over which he presided (with a few handwritten remarks for the answers), the minutes of the Synods and of the Pastoral Visits, documents and minutes of disputes argued in the diocesan Tribunal, remarks or notes relating to disputes argued in the Congregazioni Romane, etc. The material is not yet organized.

4. ARCHIVIO BONOMELLIANO of the Biblioteca Ambrosiana of Milan: where almost the entire correspondence between Bonomelli and Scalabrini is housed.

5. ARCHIVIO DEL SEMINARIO MAGGIORE DI COMO: other than a few documents dealing with Scalabrini's seminary stay as a seminarian, teacher and rector. This archive contains the letters addressed by Scalabrini to the Como priest Fr. Francesco Zaboglio, first Vicar General of the Scalabrinian Order.

6. ARCHIVIO DELLA S. CONGREGAZIONE DE PROPAGANDA FIDE: many documents regarding the founding and the first years of the Scalabrinian Order can be found there. In the present work we have cited only the documents previously published in the historical-legal study of Msgr. Marco Caliaro, Bishop of Sabina and Poggio Mirteto entitled: *La Pia Società dei Missionari di S. Carlo (Scalabriniani)*, Rome 1956, pro mns.

7. THE WRITINGS OF MSGR. SCALABRINI
    a) Published:

    1873 — *Il Concilio Vaticano.* Sermons delivered in the cathedral of Como by the priest John Baptist Scalabrini, pastor and prior of San Bartolomeo. Como, printed by Carlo Franchi, 1873, pp. XXVI-308.

    — *Le glorie del Papa nel Concilio Vaticano.* Thoughts and reflections on the First Constitution and the church as explained to the people in the Cathedral of Como by the priest J. B. Scalabrini, pastor and prior of San Bartolomeo, now bishop of Piacenza IV ed. Piacenza, Tip. Frat. Bertola. 1877, p. 216. (Contains the Preface and the four sermons which make up the second part of the first edition; reprints the second edition with the title of 1874. Turin, Oratorio di S. Francesco di Sales, p. 210).

1875 — *Prezioso dono ai bambini o Piccolo Catechismo proposto agli asili d'infanzia* by the priest J. B. Scalabrini, pastor and prior of San Bartolomeo in Como. Milan, Tipografia di S. Giuseppe, 1875, p. 84.

1876 — *Epistola Pastoralis ad Clerum et populum Sanctae Ecclesiae Placentinae*, 1-30-1876. Como, Caroli Franchi, 1876, p. 10.

— *Lettera Pastorale al Clero e popolo della città e diocesi di Piacenza*, 1-30-1876. Como, di Carlo Franchi, 1876, p. 10.

— *Sull'insegnamento del Catechismo*. Pastoral letter of April 23, 1876. Piacenza, G. Tedeschi, 1876, p. 52 (with rules for schools teaching Christian Doctrine appended).

— *Regole per le Scuole di Dottrina Cristiana*. Piacenza, G. Tedeschi, 1876, p. 16.

— *Epistola Pastoralis de Exercitiis spiritualibus ad venerabilem Clerum Sanctae Placentinae Ecclesiae*, 14-8-1876. Piacenza, G. Tedeschi, 1876, p. 26.

— Circular on the occasion of the death of the father, 9-11-1876. Piacenza, G. Tedeschi, 1876, p. 4.

— *Per la Visita Pastorale*, Pastoral Letter of Apr. 11, 1876. Piacenza, G. Tedeschi, 1876, p. 20.

— *Avvertenze e postulati* to M. RR. Pastors of the city and diocese of Piacenza regarding the practices to be observed when conducting a Pastoral Visit, 11-20-1876. Piacenza, G. Tedeschi, 1876, p. 20.

— Circular addressed to the clergy regarding the Congregazioni dei Casi di coscienza, 7-12-1876. Piacenza, G. Tedeschi, 1876, p. 8.

1877 — *Il Catechismo Cattolico*. Deliberations of J. B. Scalabrini Vescovo di Piacenza. Piacenza, G. Tedeschi, 1877, pp. X-168.

— *La Chiesa e la Società presente*. Pastoral Letter for Lent, 1877, 1-29-1877. Piacenza, G. Tedeschi, 1877, p. 28.

— *In Occasione del Giubileo episocpale di Pio IX*. Pastoral Letter of 3-1-1877. Piacenza, G. Tedeschi, 1877, p. 14.

— Circular regarding conditions of worship, 4-25-1877. Piacenza, G. Tedeschi, 1877, p. 10.

— Circular on the occasion of the Episcopal Jubilee of Pius IX, 5-20-1877. Piacenza, G. Tedeschi, 1877, p. 4.

— *Ai Maestri e alle Maestre delle Scuole Catechistiche della città e della diocesi*. Pastoral Letter of 11-4-1877. Piacenza, G. Tedeschi, 1877, p. 34.

1878 — Circular Letter, *Per il II anniversario della sua elezione alla Cattedra Vescovile di Piacenza*, 1-23-1878. Piacenza, G. Tedeschi, 1878, p. 7.

— Circular letter to the clergy and the people on the occasion of the death of Pius IX, 2-9-1878. Piacenza, G. Tedeschi, 1878.

— *Gesù Cristo, Capo invisibile della Chiesa*. Pastoral Letter for Lent 1878, 2-16-1878. Piacenza, G. Tedeschi, 1878, p. 38.

— Pastoral Letter on the occasion of the announcement of the election of the new Pontiff, 2-20-1878. Piacenza, G. Tedeschi, p. 7.

— Pastoral Letter on the occasion of the promulgation of the first Encyclical of Leo XIII (*Inscrutabili Dei consilio*), 5-26-1878. Piacenza, G. Tedeschi, 1878, p. 25.

— Circular Letter on the occasion of the death of Card. Franchi, 8-3-1878. Piacenza, G. Tedeschi, 1878, p. 2.

1879 — *Sulla Religione e la Società*. Pastoral Letter for Lent, 1879. Piacenza, G. Tedeschi, 1879, p. 72 (an announcement of the encyclical *Quod Apostolici muneris*).

— *Intorno all'Indulgenza a modo di Giubileo*. Pastoral Letter of 2-20-1879. Piacenza, G. Tedeschi, 1879, p. 24.

— *Indictio Synodi Dioecesanae Placentinae*, 5-1-1879. Piacenza, G. Tedeschi, 1879, p. 12.

— *In occasione del primo Giubileo della dogmatica definizione dell'Immacolato Concepimento di Maria Santissima*. Pastoral Letter of 11-1-1879. Piacenza, G. Tedeschi, 1879, p. 32.

— *A ricordo del primo faustissimo Giubileo della definizione dommatica dell' Immacolato Concepimento di Maria Santissima*, 12-8-1879. Piacenza, G. Tedeschi, 1879, p. 30.

— *Synodus Dioecesana a (. . .) Joanne Babtista Scalabrini (. . .)* primo habita diebus II, III ac IV Septembris anno 1879. Piacenza, G. Tedeschi, 1880, pp. XXVI-396. (Besides containing Synodal Acts and legislation it also contains the bishop's address both at the beginning and at the end of the Synod, also published independently: *Allocutiones habitae (. . .) a J. B. Scalabrini*, Piacenza, G. Tedeschi, 1880, p. 26).

1880 — *La Religione e la Famiglia*. Pastoral Letter for Lent 1880, 1-30-1880. Piacenza, G. Tedeschi, 1880, p. 51.

— *Per la pubblicazione dell'enciclica sul Matrimonio cristiano (Arcanum)*. Pastoral Letter of 3-3-1880. Piacenza, G. Tedeschi, 1880, p. 15.

— *Pel solenne riconoscimento delle reliquie dei SS. Antonino e Vittore*. Pastoral Letter of 7-4-1880. Piacenza, G. Tedeschi, 1880, p. 32.

— *Intorno all'istruzione dei Sordo-muti*. Pastoral Letter of 9-8-1880. Piacenza, G. Tedeschi, 1880, p. 25.

— *In occasione del compimento della prima Visita Pastorale*. Pastoral Letter of 9-26-1880. Piacenza, G. Tedeschi, 1880, p. 26.

1881 — *Parmessa alla ristampa del Catechismo Diocesan*. Pastoral Letter of 1-6-1881. Piacenza, G. Tedeschi, 1880, p. 13.

— *Sulla Religione e l'Individuo*. Pastoral Letter for Lent 1881, 2-2-1881. Piacenza, G. Tedeschi, 1881, p. 70.

— *Pel Giubileo straordinario del 1881*. Pastoral Letter of 1881. Piacenza, G. Tedeschi, 1881, p. 19.

— Pastoral Letter of 8-15-1881 (deprecates the offenses to the mortal remains of Pius IX and announces the Encyclical *Diuturnum illud*). Piacenza, G. Tedeschi, 1881, pp. 15-XXIV.

— Pastoral Letter of Mar. 11, 1881 (concerning the speech of Leo XIII to the French pilgrims). Piacenza, G. Tedeschi, 1881, p. 12.

1882 — *Sull'Indifferenza in materia di Religione*. Pastoral Letter for Lent 1882, 2-2-1882. Piacenza, G. Tedeschi, 1882, p. 40.

— *Comunicazione dell'Enciclica* Etsi nos *e proibizione del Giornale* Il Penitente. Pastoral Letter of 3-19-1882. Piacenza, G. Tedeschi, 1882, p. 48.

— *Appello al Clero e al popolo (. . .) a favore dei danneggiati dalle inondazioni dell'Alta Italia*, 2-22-1882. Piacenza, G. Tedeschi, 1882, p. 4.

— *Pel suo ritorno da Roma.* Pastoral Letter of 10-18-1882. Piacenza, G. Tedeschi, 1882, p. 36.

1883 — *Sulla Vita cristiana.* Pastoral Letter for Lent 1883, 1-17-1883. Piacenza, G. Tedeschi, 1883, p. 51.

— *Comunicazione dell'Enciclica Auspicato,* 1-26-1883. Piacenza, G. Tedeschi, 1883, p. 26.

— *Pellegrinaggio a Roma. Obolo di S. Pietro.* Pastoral Letter of 8-1-1883. Piacenza, G. Tedeschi, 1883, p. 7.

— *Comunicazione dell'Enciclica* Supremi Apostolatus. Pastoral Letter of 9-16-1883. Piacenza, G. Tedeschi, 1883, p. 23.

1884 — *La fede.* Pastoral Letter for Lent 1884, 1-29-1884. Piacenza, G. Tedeschi, 1884, p. 48.

— Monitory letter regarding the collection of the writings of Ven. Teresa Eustochio Verzeri, 3-19-1884. Piacenza, G. Tedeschi, 1884, p. 3.

— *Comunicazione dell'Enciclica* Humanum Genus. Pastoral Letter of 6-1-1884. Piacenza, G. Tedeschi, 1884, p. 27.

— Circular to the clergy and the people (regarding the Asiatic cholera), 8-16-1884. Piacenza, G. Tedeschi, 1884, p. 8.

— *Ricorriamo a Maria SS. Soccorriamo i poveri colerosi.* Pastoral Letter of 9-15-1884 (with an announcement of the Encyclical *Superiore anno),* Piacenza, G. Tedeschi, 1884, p. 16.

— *Circolare per la cessazione del cholera,* 11-3-1884. Piacenza, G. Tedeschi, 1884, p. 3.

— *Ringraziamento alla diocesi* (for gifts on the occasion of journalistic offenses). Pastoral Letter of 12-11-1884. Piacenza, G. Tedeschi, 1884, p. 10.

— Circular against the divorce proposal, 12-31-1884. Piacenza, G. Tedeschi, 1884, p. 3.

1885 — *La ragionevolezza della fede.* Pastoral Letter for Lent 1885, 1-29-1885. Piacenza, G. Tedeschi, 1885, p. 48.

— *Associazioni Cattoliche. Discorso del Santo Padre.* Circular Letter of 3-2-1885, p. 12.

— Circular Letter of 7-2-1885 (announcement of the letter of Leo XIII to Card. Guibert, Archbishop of Paris), Piacenza, G. Tedeschi, 1885, p. 10.

— *Il Santo Rosario.* Circular Letter of 9-13-1885. Piacenza, G. Tedeschi, 1885, p. 16.

— *Sull'opuscolo* Letter of His Excellency Card. Pitra. Commentaries. The speech of the Pope. Pastoral Letter of 10-5-1885. Piacenza, G. Tedeschi, 1885, p. 23.

— *Contro le Conferenze protestanti.* Admonition of the Bishop of Piacenza to his people, 11-28-1885. Piacenza, G. Tedeschi, 1885, p. 8.

— *Intransigenti e transigenti. Osservazioni di un Vescovo Italiano.* Bologna, Zanichelli, 1885, p. 32.

1886 — *Sull'Enciclica* Immortale Dei. Pastoral Letter of 1-17-1886. Piacenza, G. Tedeschi, 1886, p. 12.

— *Il Santo Giubileo.* Pastoral Letter for Lent 1886, 2-9-1886. Piacenza, G. Tedeschi, 1886, p. 40.

— *Pel Giubileo Sacerdotale del Sommo Pontefice Leone XIII.* Pastoral Letter of 9-26-1886. Piacenza, G. Tedeschi, 1886, p. 12.

1887 — *Cattolici di nome e cattolici di fatto.* Pastoral Letter for Lent 1887, 2-1-1887. Piacenza, G. Tedeschi, 1887, p. 47.

— The proposal of an Association dedicated to ministering to the spiritual needs of Italian immigrants to the Americas, 2-16-1887, in: M. Caliaro, *La Pia Società dei Missionari di S. Carlo (Scalabriniani),* Rome 1956, appendix I, pp. 156-163.

— *L'emigrazione italiana in America.* Observations of J. B. Scalabrini, Bishop of Piacenza, June 1887. Piacenza, L'Amico del Popolo, 1887, p. 55.

— Circular regarding the petition by Catholics at the National Parliament in favor of religious reconciliation in Italy, 11-4-1887. Piacenza, G. Tedeschi, 1887, p. 1.

1888 — *La Chiesa Cattolica.* Pastoral Letter for Lent 1888. Piacenza, G. Tedeschi, 1888, p. 50.

— Announcement of the decree *Post obitum,* 3-21-1888, Piacenza, Divus Thomas, 1888, pp. IV-7.

— Announcement of the Encyclical *Libertas* and of the Encyclical *Quod anniversarius.* Circular of 8-16-1888. Piacenza, s.i., p. 6.

— *Il disegno di legge sulla emigrazione italiana.* Observations and suggestions of J. B. Scalabrini, Bishop of Piacenza. Piacenza, Amico del Popolo, 1888, p. 56 (Nov. 1888).

1889 — *Educazione cristiana.* Pastoral Letter for Lent 1889, 2-7-1889. Piacenza, G. Tedeschi, 1889, p. 42.

— Circular of 8-27-1889 (on the Allocution of Leo XIII at the Consistory of June 30 and on the Encyclical *Quamquam pluries).* Piacenza, G. Tedeschi, 1889, p. 3.

— *Atti e documenti del Primo Congresso Catechistico tenutosi in Piacenza nei giorni 24, 25, 26 Settembre 1889.* Piacenza, G. Tedeschi, 1890, p. 394.

1890 — *Scuola di Religione per la gioventù studiosa.* Pastoral Letter of 1-1-1890. Piacenza, G. Tedeschi, 1890, p. 12.

— *L'enciclica* Sapientiae Christianae. Letter of 1-27-1890. Piacenza, G. Tedeschi, 1890, p. 6.

— *Discorso del Santo Padre. Unione, azione, preghiera.* Pastoral Letter of 5-11-1890. Piacenza, G. Tedeschi, 1890, p. 18.

— Circular against public dances, 6-4-1890. Piacenza, G. Tedeschi, 1890, p. 3.

— *Comunicazione dell'Enciclica* "Dall'alto." Circular of 10-24-1890. Piacenza, G. Tedeschi, 1890, p. 3.

— *Comunicazioni diverse* (regarding the redemption of the slaves, the devotion to the Holy Family on the School of Religion and the Oratorio Festivo, etc.). Pastoral Letter of 12-15-1890. Piacenza, G. Tedeschi, 1890, p. 11.

— Translation of the catechesis of St. Cyril of Jerusalem, with introduction and notes in: *Il Catechista Cattolico,* annuals 1890/1891/1892 (already published in part in the annuals 1883-1887).

1891 — *Dell'asistenza alla emigrazione nazionale e degli Istituti che vi provvedono.* Report made at the Exposition in Palermo by J. B. Scalabrini, Bishop of Piacenza. Piacenza, Marchesotti e Porta, 1891, p. 23.

— *Centenario di S. Luigi. Enciclica del S. Padre* (Rerum Novarum). *Obolo dell'amor filiale.* Pastoral Letter of 6-4-1891. Piacenza, G. Tedeschi, 1891, p. 13.

— *Pel Giubileo Episcopale del Sommo Pontefice Leone XIII.* Pastoral Letter of 10-15-1891. Piacenza, G. Tedeschi, 1891, p. 18.

1892 — Monitory letter regarding the collection of the writings of Msgr. Antonio Gianelli, Bishop of Bobbio, 2-4-1892. Piacenza, G. Tedeschi, 1892, p. 3.

— *Il Prete cattolico.* Pastoral Letter for Lent 1892, 2-15-1892. Piacenza, G. Tedeschi, 1892, p. 43.

— *Ai Missionari per gl'Italiani nelle Americhe il Vescovo di Piacenza,* 3-15-1892. Piacenza, G. Tedeschi, 1892, p. 15.

— *Opera di S. Opilio in favore dei chierici poveri della diocesi piacentina a perenne ricordo del giubileo episcopale di S.S. Leone XIII.* Pastoral Letter of 5-1-1892. Piacenza, G. Tedeschi, 1892, p. 31.

— *Comunicazione dell'Enciclica sul Santo Rosario.* Circular letter of 8-16-1892. Piacenza, G. Tedeschi, p. 4.

1893 — *Il Papa.* Pastoral Letter for Lent 1893, 1-18-1893. Piacenza, G. Tedeschi, 1893, p. 30.

— *Indictio Secundae Dioecesanae Synodi celebrandae,* 3-1-1893. Piacenza, G. Tedeschi, 1893, p. 8.

— Circular on the youth center, 6-22-1893. Piacenza, G. Tedeschi, 1893, p. 3.

— *Lettera circolare circa l'enciclica sul S. Rosario* (Laetitiae sanctae), 9-17-1893. Piacenza, G. Tedeschi, 1893, p. 3.

— *Synodus Placentina Secunda (. . .) anno 1893.* Piacenza, G. Tedeschi, p. 446 (contains the three *Orationes* delivered by the Bishop).

1894 — *La famiglia cristiana.* Pastoral Letter for Lent 1894. Piacenza, G. Tedeschi, 1894, p. 29.

— *Pel nostro Duomo.* Letter of 2-9-1894. Piacenza, G. Tedeschi, 1894, p. 10.

— *Documenti pontifici.* Pastoral Letter of 9-22-1894. Piacenza, G. Tedeschi, 1894, p. 4.

1895 — *La penitenza cristiana.* Pastoral Letter for Lent 1895, 2-10-1895. Piacenza, G. Tedeschi, 1895, p. 36.

— *Notificazione circa la I Crociata,* 3-10-1895. Piacenza, G. Tedeschi, 1895, p. 2.

— *La Premiére Croisade.* Discourse delivered at the Cathedral of Clermont-Ferrand, Bellet, 1895, p. 9.

— *Circolare circa il periodico* G. Savonarola, 7-29-1895. Piacenza, G. Tedeschi, 1895, p. 4.

— *Circolare sull'enciclica pontificia* Adiutricem populi, 9-16-1895. Piacenza, G. Tedeschi, 1895, p. 4.

1896 — *Unione colla Chiesa, obbedienza ai legittimi pastori.* Pastoral Letter for Lent 1896, 2-8-1896. Piacenza, G. Tedeschi, 1896, p. 48.

— *Azione Cattolica.* Pastoral Letter of 10-16-1896. Piacenza, G. Tedeschi, 1896, p. 23.

— *Discorso recitato nella Cattedrale di Cremona per il giubileo episcopale di Mons. Geremia Bonomelli,* 11-15-1896. Cremona, G. Foroni, 1896, p. 20.

1897 — *La divina Parola.* Pastoral Letter for Lent 1897, 2-20-1897. Piacenza, G. Tedeschi, 1897, p. 40.

— *Comunicazione dell'Enciclica* Augustissimae Virginis. Circular of 9-16-1897. Piacenza, G. Tedeschi, 1897, p. 2.

1898 — *I diritti cristiani e i diritti dell'uomo* (collective Pastoral Letter of the Bishops of the Region of Emilia edited by Bishop Scalabrini), 1-25-1898. Bologna, Tip. Arcivescovile, 1898, p. 32.

— *Pel Clero della città e diocesi di Piacenza* (Rules and prescriptions of homiletics, prohibited books, sacred music), 2-9-1898. Piacenza, G. Tedeschi, 1898, p. 9.

— Letter to the people regarding revolutionary movements, 5-4-1898. Piacenza, G. Tedechi, 1898, p. 4.

1899 — *Fede, vigilanza, preghiera.* Pastoral Letter for Lent 1899, 1-30-1899. Piacenza, G. Tedeschi, 1899, p. 27.

— *Il Socialismo e l'azione del Clero*, 4-14-1899. Piacenza, G. Tedeschi, 1899, p. 48. II ed.: Turin Liberia Salesiana Editrice, 1899, p. 90.

— *Indictio Tertiae Synodi*, 6-6-1899. Piacenza, G. Tedeschi, 1899, p. 4.

— *L'Italia all'estero.* Lecture held in the enclosure of the Exhibition of Sacred Art in Turin. In the volume: *Gli Italiani all'estero*, Torino, Roux-Frassati, 1899, pp. 21-39; and in the periodical: *Il Conferenziere*, yr. II, n. 1, Jan. 1900, pp. 5-26.

— *L'emigrazione degli operai italiani.* Report given at the Catholic Congress of Ferrara Apr. 18-21, 1899. In the volume: *Atti e documenti del XXV Congresso Cattolico Italiano*, Venice 1899, pp. 90-100.

— *Synodus Dioecesana Placentina Tertia Eucharistica (. . .)* diebus 28, 29, 30 augusti anno 1899. Piacenza, G. Tedeschi, 1900, p. 365. (Contains four discourses of Bishop Scalabrini.)

1900 — *L'obolo di S. Pietro* collective letters of the bishops from the Region of Emilia, edited by Bishop Scalabrini), 1-6-1900. Bologna, Tip. Arcivescovile, 1900, p. 23.

— *Il Giubileo dell'Anno Santo.* Pastoral Letter for Lent 1900, 2-3-1900. Piacenza, G. Tedeschi, 1900, p. 24.

1901 — *Promulgazione del S. Giubileo. Indulto Quaresimale.* Pastoral Letter of 1-14-1901. Piacenza, G. Tedeschi, 1901, p. 30.

— *Ringraziamenti.* Pastoral Letter of 6-21-1901 (for the jubilee celebration). Piacenza, G. Tedeschi, 1901, p. 6.

— *Circolare dopo il suo ritorno d'America*, 12-5-1901. Piacenza, G. Tedeschi, 1901, p. 1.

1902 — *La devozione al SS.mo Sacramento.* Pastoral Letter for Lent 1902, 1-29-1902. Piacenza, G. Tedeschi, 1902, p. 40.

— *Per il giubileo pontificale di S. S. Leone XIII*, 2-15-1902. Piacenza, G. Tedeschi, 1902, p.. 3.

— *Comunicazione della Lettera Enciclica di Leone XIII "Fin dal principio,"* 12-15-1902. Piacenza, G. Tedeschi, 1902, p. 4.

1903 — Circular on the occasion of the pontifical jubilee of Leo XIII, 1-18-1903. Piacenza, G. Tedeschi, 1903, p. 6.

— *Santificazione della festa.* Pastoral Letter for Lent 1903, 2-6-1903. Piacenza, G. Tedeschi, 1903, p. 39.

— *La morte del Santo Padre Leone XIII.* Notification of 7-21-1903. Piacenza, G. Tedeschi, 1903, p. 9.

— *L'elezione del nuovo Pontefice Pio X.* Notification of 8-4-1903. Piacenza, G. Tedeschi, 1903, p. 8.

— *La prima lettera enciclica di S.S. Pio X.* Notification of 10-7-1903. Piacenza, G. Tedeschi, 1903, p. 9.

1904 — *Come santificare la festa.* Pastoral Letter for Lent 1904. Piacenza, G. Tedeschi, 1904, p. 43.

— *Notificazioni.* On the acquisition of the Holy Jubilee. On the 50th anniversary of the definition of the doctrine of the Immaculate Conception of the Most Holy Virgin Mary. On sacred music, 4-9-1904. Piacenza, G. Tedeschi, 1904, p. 16.

— Circular letter on the end of the Holy Jubilee, Bento Gonçalves (Brasile), 10-12-1904. Piacenza, II Monitore Diocesano, 1904, p. 3.

1905 — *La Preghiera.* Pastoral Letter for Lent 1905, 2-16-1905. Piacenza, G. Tedeschi, 1905, p. 37.

— *Alle cattoliche istituzioni e associazioni della diocesi.* Circular letter of 3-12-1905. Piacenza, G. Tedeschi, 1905, p. 4.

— *Lettera circolare per la sesta Visita Pastorale,* 5-5-1905. Piacenza, G. Tedeschi, p. 7.

b) Unpublished:

Besides the collection of letters, there remain the manuscripts — handwritten and dictated to the secretary — of the various reports to the Congregazioni Romane, and the drafts or notes of the following discourses: 22 Christmas homilies, 13 for the New Year, 14 for Epiphany, 22 for Easter, 2 for Ascension, 17 for Pentecost, 13 for All Saints, 16 for the Assumption, 3 for the Immaculate Conception, another 10 sermons on the Madonna, 17 panegyrics of Saints, 7 Farewells to Missionaries, 5 sermons on the subject of the Eucharist, 4 for inaugurations and consecrations of churches, 8 for episcopal consecrations or jubilees, 4 on the Pope, 7 on Catholic Action, 4 exhortations to the clergy in Latin, 2 commemorations of the Crusades, 2 of Christopher Columbus, 3 discourses for the deafmutes and another 20 on miscellaneous subjects.

N.B. — The published works can be found at the Archivio Generalizio Scalabriniano; at the Biblioteca del Centro Studi Emigrazione, Rome; in part also at the Biblioteca Ambrosiana of Milan and at the Episcopal Archive of Piacenza. The unpublished manuscripts, excluding some drafts are in the Archivio Generalizio Scalabriniano: actually, however, they are located at the S. Congregazione dei Riti, per i Processi di Beatificazione.

8.   DIOCESAN INQUIRY FOR BEATIFICATION (Piacenza, 1936-1940).

a) Diocesan preliminary process regarding the renowned sanctity and the virtues of Bishop John Baptist Scalabrini.
There exists a printed copy of the *transunto* of said *Processus,* including the principal testimonies and several documents (cited in its abbreviated form as: *Processus*); and the *Copia publica* which records the answers to the proposition in their entirety (cited in its abbreviated form as: *Processus, cop. publ.)* (Vedi p. 605).

b) Diocesan *Processus* information *de non-cultu.*
Of this *Processus* we cite the *Copia publica* (cited in abbreviated form: *Processus de non-cultu)* (vedi p. 605).
No above documentation is located in the Archivio Generalizio Scalabriniano.

9.   Sources other than those ennumerated above are cited individually one at a time.

Bibliography

Albertario D., *All'Em.mo signor Cardinale Ludovico Jacobini di Sua Santità Segretario di Stato.* Memorandum of the priest Davide Albertario, Milan, 1882.

Albertario D., *All'Em.mo signor Cardinale Ludovico Jacobini.* Memorandum of the priest Davide Albertario, Milan, 1883.

Albertario D., *Un anno in carcere, 2557,* vol. 2, Milan, 1883.

Astori G., *Mons. Bonomelli, Mons. Scalabrini e Don Davide Albertario,* Breacia 1959.

Astori G., *L'opuscolo di Mons. Bonomelli "Roma e l'Italia e realtà delle cose,"* Rome 1961.

Astori G., *San Pio X e il Vescovo Geremia Bonomelli*, in: *Revisita di Storia della Chiesa in Italia*, a. X (1956), n. 2, May-Aug.

Astori G., *Corrispondenza di Mons. G. Bonomelli e Don A. Stoppani*, Brescia 1959.

Aubert R., *Il pontificato di Pio IX*, first Italian edition [based] on the third French edition edited by G. Martina, Turin 1964 (vol. XXI of the *Storia della Chiesa*, by A. Fliche-V. Martin, Italian edition edited by G. Pelliccia).

Aubert R., *Aspects divers du néothomisme sous le pontificat de Léon XIII*, in: *Aspetti della cultura cattolica nell'età di Leone XIII*, Rome 1961, pp. 133-227.

Baggio G., *Gli aspetti morali dell'emigrazione*, Rome 1949.

Baraldi G., *I Vescovi Scalabrini e Bonomelli e la questione rosminiana*, Reggio Emilia 1934.

Beccherini F., *Il fenomeno dell'emigrazione negli Stati Uniti d'America*, Sansepolcro 1906.

Bedeschi L., *I cattolici disubbidienti*, Rome 1959.

Bedeschi L., *I cattolici ubbidienti*, Naples 1962.

Bellò C., *Geremia Bonomelli*, Brescia 1961.

Bellò C., *La pastorale dell'emigrazione nelle opere di Mons. G. B. Scalabrini e di Mons. G. Bonomelli*, in: *Studi Emigrazione*, IV, n. 9 (June 1967), pp. 286-292.

Bersani S., *Memorie storiche sulla origine e vicende del Collegio Alberoni*, Piacenza, 1867-1883.

Bertuzzi G., *I Piacentini Vescovi*, Piacenza 1938.

Bianchi G., *La protesta del Vescovo di Piacenza contro l'Osservatore Cattolico*, Codogno 1881.

Bihlmeyer K.-Tuechle H., *Storia della Chiesa*, vol. IV: *L'epoca moderna*, third edition edited by I. Rogger, Brescia 1966.

Bondioli P., *Bonomelli e Albertario in documenti inediti della Segreteria di Stato di Leone XIII (1881-1884)* in: *Memorie storiche della diocesi di Milano*, vol. V, Milan 1958, pp. 39-110.

(Bonomelli G.), *Roma e l'Italia e la realtà delle cose. Osservazioni di un prelato lombardo*, in: *La Rassegna Nazionale*, 3-1-1889.

Bonomelli G., *L'emigrazione*, Cremona 1896.

Bonomelli G., *Sull'emigrazione temporanea*, Cremona 1900.
   N.B. — For a bibliography of Mons. Bonomelli's works, see Guerrini P., *Saggio di una bibliografia bonomelliana*, in: *Geremia Bonomelli Vescovo di Cremona nel XXV anniversario della morte*. Miscellany of commemorative studies, Milan 1939, pp. 243-270.

Bertolucci G., *Una Rassegna dell'opuscolo di S. E. Mons. G. B. Scalabrini Vescovo di Piacenza sopra l'Emigrazione Italiana in America*, Modena 1887.

Brezzi P.-Mori R., etc., *I cattolici italiani dall'800 ad oggi*, vol. I, Brescia 1964.

Caliaro M., *La Pia Società dei Missionari di S. Carlo (Scalabriniani)*, a historico-legal study from the founding to the general chapter of 1951, pro mns., Rome 1956.

Candeloro G., *Il movimento cattolico in Italia*, Rome 1953.

Capra G., *I Padri Scalabriniani nell'America del Nord. Estratto dall'Italica Gens*, Jan.-June file 1916. S. Benigno Canavese 1916.

Caretta A., *I missionari degli emigranti nella Costituzione Apostolica "Exsul Familia,"* Rome 1957.

Carocci G., *Agostino Depretis e la politica interna italiana dal 1876 al 1887*, Turin 1956.

Castiglioni C., *Monsignor Calabiana Arcivescovo di Milano e i suoi tempi*, Milan 1942.

Cattaneo G., *Discorso in S. Bartolomeo (Como) per l'inaugurazione del monumento a Mons. Scalabrini*, suppl. to *L'Emigrato Italiano*, 9-15-1914.

Cavagna A., *Un Vescovo tra due epoche. Mons. Pasquale Morganti e i suoi tempi*, Milan 1963.

Cavanna F., *La sospensione del 4 maggio 1893 del Sacerdote Francesco Cavanna (. . .) innanzi al Tribunale della Scienza*, Piacenza 1893.

Cavanna F., *L'ulltima parola sullla mia sospensione del 4 maggio 1893*, Piacenza 1898.

Chabod F., *Storia della politica estera italiana dal 1870 al 1896*, vol. I, *Le premesse*, Bari 1951.

Cistellini A., *Giuseppe Tovini*, Brescia 1954.

Cistellini A., *I motivi dell'opposizione cattolica allo Stato Liberale*, in: *Vita e Pensiero*, Dec. 1959, pp. 933-974.

Cistellini A., *Il vescovo Geremia Bonomelli, la Chiesa e i tempi moderni*, in: *Commentari dell' Ateneo di Brescia per l'anno 1963*, pp. 25-91.

Ciufoletti M., *John Baptist Scalabrini, Bishop of Piacenza, Apostle of the Italian Immigrants*, New York 1937.

Colbachini P., *Relazione presentata a S. E. il Ministro degli Esteri intorno alle condizioni presenti dell'emigrazione italiana negli Stati Uniti del Brasile, ed ai provvedimenti opportuni per migliorarla*, in: *Rassegna Nazionale*, Mar. 1895.

Colbachini P., *Le condizioni degli emigrati nello Stato del Paranà in Brasile*. Added to the 3rd part of F. Macola, *L'Europa alla conquista dell'America Latina*, Venice 1894, pp. 423-437.

Cornaggia Medici L., *Un profilo di Mons. Scalabrini Vescovo di Piacenza*, Rome 1930.

Cornaggia Medici L., *Le caratteristiche di Mons. Giovanni Battista Scalabrini Vescovo di Piacenza. Nel 30° anniversario della sua morte*, Reggio Emilia 1935.

Cornaggia Medici L., *Il passato e il presente della questione romana*, Florence 1930.

Cornaggia Medici L., *Antesignani della Conciliazione*, Fidenza 1936.

Cornaggia Medici L., *Parole schiette. Appendice ad "Antesignani della Conciliazione,"* Fidenza 1936.

Dalla Torre G., *I cattolici e la vita pubblica italiana (1866-1920)*, Rome 1944.

Dalla Torre G., *La natura e i caratteri del movimento cattolico nell'Italia unita*, in: *Vita e Pensiero*, Dec. 1959, pp. 999-1010.

Daniélou J., *Migration et vie chrétienne*, in: *Les Cahiers du Clergé Rural*, Jan. 1963, pp. 48-66.

D. Gasperi A., *I cattolici dall'opposizione al governo*, Rome 1955.

De Rosa G., *Storia del movimento cattolico in Italia*, vol. 2, Bari 1966.

De Rosa G., *I conservatori nazionali*, Brescia 1962.

Dore G., *La democrazia italiana e l'emigrzione in America*, Brescia 1964.

Fappani A., *Pionieri d'azione sociale (Profili di sacerdoti)*, Rome 1960. (J. B. Scalabrini: pp. 168-178).

Fappani A., *Un Vescovo "intransigente." Mons. Giacomo M. Corna Pellegrini Spandre e il movimento cattolico bresciano dal 1885 al 1913*, Brescia 1964.

Felici I., *G. B. Scalabrini, Vescovo insigne, Padre degli Emigrati*, with a preface by S. E. il Card. G. Adeodato Piazza, Milan 1954.

Felici I., *Father to the Immigrants. The Servant of God John Baptist Scalabrini Bishop of Piacenza*, translated by Carol Della Chiesa, New York 1955. (Several parts in the American edition are either reedited or new).

Fermi A., *Mons. Antonio Ranza, filosofo, teologo, vescovo di Piacenza (1801-1875)*, Vol. I: *L'episcopato di Mons. Ranza*, Parte I: *Gli inizi dell'episcopato (1849-1852)*, Piacenza 1956.

Fermi A.-Molinari F., *Mons. Antonio Ranza, filosofo, teologo, vescovo di Piacenza (1801-1875)*, Vol. I: *L'episcopato di Mons. Ranza*, Part II: *L'attività pastorale: nel turbine degli eventi politici; verso una più salda unità della Chiesa; gli ultimi anni dell'episcopato: 1869-1875*, Piacenza 1966.

Fermi A., *Vincenzo Buzzetti e la filosofia in Piacenza*, Piacenza 1923.

Ferrerio G., *Mons. G. B. Scalabrini*. Commemoration held the 6-4-1906 in the basilica of St. Antonino in Piacenza in: *L'Emigrato Italiano*, July 1906.

464   SCALABRINI

Ferretto G., *Sua Santità Pio XII, provvido padre degli esuli, sapiente ordinatore dell'assistenza spirituale agli emigranti*, Rome 1954.

Ferretto G., *La Costituzione Apostolica "Exsul Familia,"* Pompei 1955.

Ferretto G., *In normas et facultates pro sacerdotibus in spiritualem navigantium maritimorum et emigrantium curam incumbentibus Adnotationes*, Rome 1956.

Ferretto G., *L'integrazione degli immigrati cattolici secondo la Costituzione Apostolica "Exsul Familia" e gli insegnamenti dei Sommi Pontefici*, Rome 1960.

Fiocchi A., *La Serva di Dio Rosa Gattorno*, vol. 2, Rome 1937-1941.

Flick M. P., *Il grande volo*, Brescia 1956.

Fogazzaro A., *Una visita a Mons. Scalabrini*, in: *Rassegna Nazionale*, 7-1-1905, vol. 144, pp. 3-11.

Fonzi F., *I cattolici e la società italiana dopo l'unità*, Rome 1960.

Fonzi F., *Dall'intransigentismo alla democrazia cristiana*, in: *Aspetti della cultura cattolica nell'età di Leone XIII*, Rome 1961, pp. 323-368.

Fonzi F., *L' "Osservatore Cattolico" e i conservatori*, in: *Humanitas*, June 1952, pp. 592-602.

Fonzi F., *I "cattolici transigenti" italiani dell'ultimo Ottocento*, in: *Convivium*, June 1949, pp. 955-972.

Frediani G., *Il Santo di ferro* (S. Antonio Maria Gianelli), Rome 1951.

Frumento G., *Un grande vescovo catechista, Mons. G. B. Scalabrini*, in: *Catechesi*, edition for the "Scuole Medie", 1956, n. 10, Oct.

Gambasin A., *Il movimento sociale nell'Opera dei Congressi*, Rome 1958.

Gambasin A., *L'Azione Cattolica e l'ingresso dei cattolici nella politica*, in: *Vita e Pensiero*, Dec. 1959, pp. 975-989.

Gianetto U.-Gianolio G., *Il movimento catechistico in Italia dal 1870*, in: *Linee per un direttorio di pastorale catechistica*, Turin 1967.

Grabinski G., *Storia documentata del giornale L'Osservatore Cattolico di Milano*, Milan 1887.

Grabinski G., *Monsignor Scalabrini*, Florence 1905.

Gregori F., *La vita e l'opera di un grande Vescovo Mons. Giov. Battista Scalabrini*, (1839-1905), Turin 1934 (abbreviated as: Gregori).

Gregori F., *In morte del P. Giuseppe Molinari Vicario Generale della Congregazione di S. Carlo in Piacenza*, Piacenza 1900.

Gregori V., *Fiori sparsi d'un gran Vescovo*, Rome 1908.

(Gregori V.), v. *XXV anni di missione fra gli italiani immigrati di Boston Mass.*, Milan 1913.

Grieco R., *The listening Heart. Life of John Scalabrini*, II ediz., New York 1965.

Groppi U., *L'insegnamento del Catechismo parrocchiale nella legislazione diocesana di Piacenza dal Concilio di Trento ai giorni nostri.* Thesis submitted to the Pont. Università Gregoriana, Rome typescript.

Guidotti C., *Il Duomo di Piacenza, Studi e proposte*, Piacenza 1895.

Jemolo A. C., *Chiesa e Stato in Italia negli ultimi cento anni*, Turin 1953.

Labò A., *In memoria di Mons. G. B. Scalabrini.* Words delivered at the trental in the Santuario della Beata Vergine del Castello, Piacenza 1906.

Lener S., *L'unità d'Italia e la conciliazione tra Stato e Chiesa, La Civiltà Cattolica*, anno 112, vol. III, 16 Sept. 1961, pp. 573-582; vol. IV, 7 Oct. 1961, pp. 14-28.

Lorit S. C., *La Cabrini*, Rome 1965.

Magri F., *L'Azione Cattolica in Italia*, vol. 2, Milan 1953.

Malchiodi G., *Il Santuario della B. Vergine del Castello di Rivergaro. Memorie storiche*, Piacenza 1905.

Maldotti P., *Relazione a S. E. il Ministro degli Esteri, Società di Patronato per gli emigranti*, Piacenza 1896.

Maldotti P., *Relazione sull'operato della Missione del porto di Genova dal 1894 al 1898 e sui due viaggi in Brasile*, Genova 1898.

Maldotti P., *Gli emigrati in Brasile*, summary in: *Gli Italiani all'estero*. Turin 1899, pp. 41-55.

Malinverni B., *Il Risorgimento, problemi e interpretazioni*, Brescia 1964.

Manacorda E., *Movimento cattolico, errori democratici e relativi doveri dei sacerdoti*, Fossano 1897.

Mangenot E., *Catéchisme*, in: *Dictionnaire de Théologie catholique*, II, 2, coll. 1895-1968.

Manzotti F., *La polemica sull'emigrazione nell'Italia unita (fino alla prima guerra mondiale)*, Milan 1962.

Martina G., *L'Enciclica Libertas nei commenti della stampa contemporanea*, in: *Aspetti della cultura cattolica nell'età di Leone XIII*, Rome 1961, pp. 597-630.

Martina G., The Italian clergy and its pastoral activity around the middle of the 19th century; the Rosminian Question during the pontificate of Pius IX; Italian Catholic liberation (Appendix I, III, and IV to the first Italian edition of R. Aubert, *Il pontificato di Pio IX*, Turin 1964, pp. 751-782; 785-788; 789-798).

Martini A., *Studi sulla Questione Romana e la Conciliazione*, Rome 1963.

Martini A., *Leone XIII e l'emigrazione temporanea italiana*, in: *La Civiltà Cattolica*, anno 105, vol. III, 9-4-1954, pp. 470-485.

Martini G., *Origine e sviluppo della Colonia Santa Felicidade*, Curityba 1908.

Menzani E., *Mons. Francesco Sidoli*, Piacenza 1925.

Miglio G., *I cattolici italiani di fronte all'unità d'Italia*, in: *Vita e Pensiero*, Dec. 1959, pp. 905-917.

Milesi F., *Mons. Scalabrini e il problema dell'assistenza agli emigranti*. Thesis submitted to the Università Cattolica del S. Cuore, Milan 1965-1966.

Milini F., *Padre Luiz Capra, Missionario de S. Carlos*, Sao Paulo 1935.

Milini F., *Le Missioni Cattoliche Italiane tra i nostri emigrati in Svizzera*, Piacenza 1954.

Moglia A., *L'episcopato italiano accusato di liberalismo*, Florence 1893.

Moglia A., *La sospensione di Cavanna esaminata da Agostino Moglia*, Piacenza 1893.

Molinari F., *Mons. Francesco Torta, apostolo della carità*, Turin 1963.

Morisi E., *Brevi cenni dell'Istituto Scrofolosi*, Piacenza 1919.

Morra O., *Fogazzaro nel suo piccolo mondo*, Bologna 1960.

Nasalli (Rocca) G.B., *Commemorazione di Mons. Giovanni Battista Scalabrini Vescovo di Piacenza letta nella Cattedrale Basilica il 19 aprile 1909*, Piacenza 1909.

Nava C., *Mons. G. B. Scalabrini Vescovo di Piacenza*. Commemoration held 8-16-1916 at Piacenza, Rome 1916.

Negrin E., *P. Pietro Colbacchini Missionario*, Bassano del Grappa 1951.

Orfei R., *La morte di Vittorio Emanuele II e i cattolici*, in: *Vita e Pensiero*, June 1961, pp. 388-398.

Ottolenghi E., *Storia di Piacenza*, vol. IV, Piacenza n.d.

Pancotti V., *Mons. G. B. Scalabrini nella luce della storia (6-1-1905-6-1-1930)*, Piacenza 1930.

Passerin d'Entrèves E., *L'eredità della tradizione cattolica risorgimentale*, in: *Aspetti della cultura cattolica nell'età di Leone XIII*, Rome 1961, pp. 253-287.

Pecora G., *Don Davide Albertario campione del giornalismo cattolico*, Turin 1934.

Pellizzari G. M., *In memoria di Mons. G. B. Scalabrini*. Funeral oration delivered in the Cathedral 6-1-1906, Piacenza 1906.

Pellizzari G. M., *Elogio funebre di Mons. Giov. Battista Vinati*, Piacenza 1917.

Penco G. B.-Galbiati B., *Vita del Cardinale Andrea Carlo Ferrari Arcivescovo di Milano*, Milan n.d.

Perotti A., *Cronologia delle opere e degli scritti principali di Monsignor G. B. Scalabrini*, *L'Emigrato Itlaiano*, 1963, n. 5, pp. 13-19.

Perotti A., *Contributo di G. B. Scalabrini e dei suoi missionari alle prime leggi organiche sull'-emigrazione*, in: *L'Emigrato Italiano*, June 1962, pp. 3-20; July 1962, pp. 3-20; Sept. 1962, pp. 5-22; Oct.-Nov. 1962 (*Scalabrini e Governo*), pp. 5-28.

Perotti A., *Documentazione sul pensiero sociale di G. B. Scalabrini sui fenomeni migratori*, in: *Problemi di storia, sociologia e pastorale dell'emigrazione*, Rome 1965, pp. 22-32. See: *L'Emigrato Italiano*, Feb. 1962, pp. 3-12.

Perotti A., *L'intervento di Giovanni Battista Scalabrini nella polemica sull'emigrazione in Italia nel periodo 1887-1892*, in: *Problemi di storia, sociologia e pastorale dell'emigrazione*, Rome 1962, pp. 48-72.

Pesci G., *Lineamenti moderni dell'emigrazione italiana*, Rome 1956.

Pio XII, *Constitutio Apostolica de spirituali emigrantium cura ("Exsul Familia")*, Rome 1952.

Prevedello F., *Cinquantenario della morte del ven. Fondatore Servo di Dio Giovanni Battista Scalabrini*, Sao Paulo 1954.

(Prevedello F.), v. *Vita e virtù del Servo di Dio Mons. Giovanni Battista Scalabrini*, Bassano del Grappa 1936.

(Prevedello F.), *Nel centenario della morte del servo di Dio G. Battista Scalabrini*, in: *Il Catechista Cattolico*, Aug.-Sept. 1939.

Rebecchi L., *Considerazioni catechistiche del Servo di Dio Mons. G. B. Scalabrini Vescovo di Piacenza*. Introduction by Sac. Silvio Riva. Letter from S. E. Mgr. U. Malchiodi, Piacenza 1956.

Riva S., *Mons. Giovanni Battista Scalabrini pioniere della catechesi moderna*, in: *Rivista del Catechismo*, IV (1955), pp. 223-229, 302-309, 466-470; V (1956), pp. 66-71, 143-148.

Rizzato R., *Figure di missionari scalabriniani*, New York 1948.

Rizzato R., *L'apostolo degli emigranti*, Providence, R.I. 1946.

Roncalli A., *Mons. Giacomo Maria Radini Tedeschi*, III ed., Rome 1963.

Rosa di San Marco (Contessa), *Il libro dell'emigrante italiano*, Milan 1923.

Rossi G. B., *Elogio funebre di Monsignor Antonio Ranza Vescovo di Piacenza*, Piacenza 1876.

Rossi G. F., *La filosofia nel Collegio Alberoni e il neotomismo*, Piacenza 1959.

Rovelli L., *Storia de Como*, vol. III, Milan 1963.

Saba A., *Storia della Chiesa*, vol. IV. Turin 1954.

Saba A., *La questione romana e il movimento unitario italiano*, in: *Vita e Pensiero*, Dec. 1959, pp. 892-904.

Sacchetti G. B., *La posizione di Mons. Scalabrini di fronte allo stato unitario risorgimentale nella storiografia contemporanea*, in: *L'Emigrato Italiano*, 1963, n. 5, pp. 3-11.

Sartori G., *L'emigrazione italiana in Belgio: studio storico e sociologico*, Rome 1962.

Scalabrini A., *Relazione sulle Scuole italiane all'estero a Sua Eccellenza il Comm. Giulio Prinetti, Ministro per gli Affari Esteri*, Rome 1901.

Scoppola P., *Crisi modernista e rinnovamento cattolico in Italia*, Bologna 1961.

Scoppola P., *Dal neoguelfismo alla Democrazia cristiana*, Rome 1963.

Scoppola P., *Chiesa e Stato nella storia d'Italia*, Bari 1967.

Secco Suardo D., *I cattolici intransigenti*, Brescia 1962.

Secco Suardo D., *Da Leone XIII a Pio X*, Rome 1967.

Semeria G., *Monsignor G. B. Scalabrini. In memoriam*. Commemoration held July 9 at Piacenza, Piacenza 1905.

Soderini E., *Il Pontificato di Leone XIII*, vol. 3, Milan 1932-1933.

Sofia G. B., *Massimo Rinaldi Missionario e Vescovo*, Rome 1960.

Sofia G. B., *Il Servo di Dio Giovanni Battista Scalabrini e l' "Osservatore Cattolico,"* pro mns., Rome n.d. (AGS).

Spadolini G., *L'opposizione catolica da Porta Pia al '98*, III ed., Florence 1955.

Spadolini G., *Giolitti e i cattolici* (1901-1914), Florence 1960.

Squeri L., *I cento anni del Seminario di Bedonia*, Parma 1964.

Sterlocchi L., *Cenni biografici di Monsignor Giov. Battista Scalabrini Vescovo di Piacenza*, Como 1912.

Stoppani A., *Gli intransigenti alla stregua dei fatti vecchi, nuovi e nuovissimi*, Milan, 1886.

Tagliaferri L., *La Cattedrale di Piacenza*, Piacenza 1964.

Tamborini A.-Preatoni G., *Il Servo della Carità Beato Luigi Guanella*, Milan 1964.

Tessarolo G., *Exsul Familia: The Church's Magna Charta for Migrants*, Staten Island, N.Y., 1962.

Testore C., *Catechesi, La catechesi nei secc. XIX e XX*, in: *Enciclopedia Cattolica, III*, coll. 1111-1112; *Catechismo, Dal Concilio di Trento ai nostri giorni*, ibid., coll. 1123-1124.

Toniolo G., *Opera omnia*, a cura di G. Anichini, Series VI, *Epistolario*, vol. 3, Rome 1952-1953.

Torta F., *Cenni storici intorno all'Istituto dei Sordomuti alla Madonna della Bomba, con appendice sul nuovo Istituto dei Ciechi*, Piacenza 1915.

Traniello F., *La questione rosminiana nella storia della cultura cattolica in Italia*, in: *Aevum*, a. 37 (1963), pp. 63-103.

Urbani G., *La Chiesa e l'Italia*, in: *Vita e Pensiero*, Dec. 1959, pp. 860-873.

Vercesi E., *Il movimento cattolico in Italia* (1870-1922), Florence 1923.

Vercesi E., *Don Davide Albertario*, Milan 1923.

Vian N.,*Madre Cabrini*, IV ed., Brescia 1946.

Vicentini D., *L'Apostolo degli italiani emigrati nelle Americhe*, Piacenza 1909.

Vistalli F., *Monsignor Conte Giacomo Maria Radini Tedeschi*, Milan 1935.

Vistalli F., *Mons. Guindani nei suoi tempi e nella sua opera*, vol. I, Bergamo 1943.

Vistalli F., *Giuseppe Toniolo*, Rome 1954.

Volpe Landi G. B., *Emigrazione, sue cause, suoi bisogni, suoi provvedimenti*, in: *Atti del I Congresso Cattolico Italiano degli Studiosi di scienze sociali*, vol. I, Padova 1893, pp. 236-238.

Volpe Landi G. B., *Il problema dell'emigrazione*, in: *Rivista Internazionale di scienze sociali e discipline ausiliarie*, vol. XIII (1897), pp. 500-520.

Zerbi P., *Il movimento cattolico in Italia da Pio IX a Pio X*, Milan 1961.

Aspetti della cultura cattolica nell'età di Leone XIII. Proceedings of the meeting held at Bologna Dec. 27, 28, 29, 1960, edited by G. Rossini, Rome 1961.

Atti e documenti del Decimoquinto Congresso Cattolico Italiano tenutosi a Milano nei giorni 30-31 agosto, 1, 2, 3 settembre 1897, part I: *Atti*, Breganze 1898; part II: *Documenti*, Breganze 1898.

Atti e documenti del Decimosesto Congresso Cattolico Italiano tenutosi a Ferrara nei gironi 18, 19, 20, 21 aprile 1899, part I: *Atti*, Breganze 1899; part II: *Documenti*, Breganze 1900.

Chiesa e Stato. Studi storici e giuridici per il decennale della Conciliazione, vol. 2, Milan 1939.

Comitato Romano. Venticinquesimo anniversario dei Missionari di Mons. Scalabrini per gli emigrati italiani. Ricordi, Rome 1912.

Italian Episcopal Commission for Emigration. *Direttorio di pastorale per le migrazioni*, under the direction of UCEI, Rome 1965.

Costituzioni della Pia Società dei Missionari di S. Carlo per gli italiani emigrati (Scalabriniani), Rome 1936.

Costituzioni della Pia Società dei Missionari di S. Carlo per gli italiani emigrati (Scalabriniani), Rome 1948.

Dom Joâo Baptista Scalabrini, Caxias do Sul 1955.

Gruppi etnici e comunità nazionali. Il pensiero di Mons Krol, Arcivescovo di Philadelphia, in: *Problemi di storia, sociologia e pastorale dell'emigrazione*, Rome 1965, pp. 140-144.

Il Monitore Diocesano di Piacenza. Numero dedicato alla memoria del compianto nostro Vescovo, I, n. 14, 6-30-1905.

Il Monumento ricordo a Mons. Scalabrini (Special issue), Como 9-11-1913.

Il Servo di Dio Mons. G. B. Scalabrini Vescovo di Piacenza e Fondatore dei Missionari per gli Italiani all'Estero (Fiori di cielo, N. 146), Turin 1941.

Il Servo di Dio Mons. Giovanni B. Scalabrini nella luce delle celebrazioni del 50° della sua morte (1905-1 June-1955), Rome 1957 (abbreviated as: *Celebrazioni del 50°*).

In memoria di Mons. Giovanni Battista Scalabrini. Biographical and commemorative notes, Piacenza 1905.

In memoriam. La solenne traslazione della salma di Mons. Gio. Battista Scalabrini Vescovo di Piacenza dal cimitero alla cattedrale. (18-19 Apr. 1909), Piacenza 1909.

La lettera dell'Em.mo Cardinale Pitra: i commenti, la parola del Papa, Milan-Basilea, n.d., 1885.

La Madre Francesca Saverio Cabrini, Turin 1928.

La Società San Raffaele per la protezione degli immigranti italiani in Boston, New York 1906.

L'Opera Bonomelli, in: *Problemi di storia, sociologia e pastorale dell'emigrazione*, Rome 1965, pp. 73-80.

L'Opera di Assistenza agli Operai Italiani emigrati in Europa. In homage to Bishop Geremia Bonomelli, on his 80th birthday, Milan 1911.

Missioni Scalabriniane in America. Monograph (edited by G. Sofia), Rome 1939.

Mons. Giovanni Battista Scalabrini Vescovo di Piacenza. Trent'anni di Apostolato. Memorie e documenti (edited by Prof. Angelo Scalabrini, brother of the Servant of God), Rome 1909 (cited in its abbreviated form: *Trent'anni di Apostolato*).

Mons. Scalabrini apostolo degli emigranti, Milan 1951.

Per l'assistenza dei nostri operai emigranti in Europa e nel Levante, n.d. 1900.

Primo Centenario dell'apertura di Sant'Abbondio, Como 1936.

Problemi di storia, sociologia e pastorale dell'emigrazione. (Grant Series, 1, Centro Studi Emigrazione), Rome 1965.

Raccolta di lettere della venerata Madre Clelia Merloni, Rome 1948.

Rapporto della Società di San Raffaele Arcangelo per la protezione degli italiani immigranti, Boston Mass. 1902-1904, Boston, Mass. 1905.

Regola della Congregazione dei Missionari di S Carlo per gli italiani emigrati (1895), Piacenza 1895.

Regolamento della Congregazione dei Missionari per gli emigranti (1888), in: M. Caliaro, *La Pia Società dei Missionari di S. Carlo (Scalabriniani)*, Rome 1956, appendix IV, pp. 167-180.

Regolamento dell'Istituto dei Missionari di S. Carlo per gli italiani emigrati (1908), Piacenza 1909.

Regolamento generale per la Casa Madre della Congregazione dei Missionari di S. Carlo per gli emigrati italiani, Piacenza 1904.

Regole principali pei Missionari degli italiani all'estero, Piacenza 1890.

Relazione della Società Italiana di San Raffaele in New York nel primo anno della sua fondazione (1 luglio 1891-30 giugno 1892), II ed., Piacenza, 1892.

Statuti della Pia Società dei Missionari di S. Carlo per gli italiani emigrati, Rome 1925.

Statuto della Società Italiana di Patronato per l'Emigrazione, Piacenza 1892.

30 gennaio 1896. Ventesimo anniversario della consacrazione episcopale dell'eccellentissimo nostro Vescovo Monsignor Scalabrini, Piacenza 1896.

Una vita e un'opera. On the centenary of the birth of Mother Clelia Merloni, Rome 1961.

XXV anni di Episcopato. Mons. Scalabrini Vesc. di Piacenza (1876-1901), Milan 1901.

Venticinque anni di missione fra gli italiani immigrati di Boston, Mass., Milan 1913 (see Gregori V.).

Viaggi della Madre Francesca Saverio Cabrini, Rome.

Vita di Madre Clelia Merloni Fondatrice delle Suore Missionarie Zelatrici del Sacro Cuore, scritta da una Religiosa dell'Istituto, Rome 1954.

Vita e virtù del Servo di Dio Mons. Giovanni Battista Scalabrini, Bassano del Grappa 1936 (see Prevedello F.).

Periodical publications:

L'Emigrato Italiano. Under this title we designate the periodical by the Congregazione Scalabriniana which began publication in 1903 with the title: *"Congregazione dei Missionari di S. Carlo per gli italiani emigrati nelle Americhe."* Interrupted for several months after the death of Bishop Scalabrini it resumed publication in Feb. 1906 with the title: *"L'Emigrato Italiano in America."* The publication was once again interrupted in the period 1925-1930. From 1939 to 1953 it came out under the title: *"Le Missioni Scalabriniane"*; from January 1954 it took up once again the title *"L'Emigrato Italiano."* It is published monthly.

Il Catechista Cattolico. Founded in 1876 by Bishop Scalabrini; the first issue came out on July 5, 1876. Its first director was Can. Carlo Uttini. Monthly. Series I (1876-1889): "a religious monthly periodical for the Christian Doctrine schools in the diocese of Piacenza" (in this first period the activities of Bishop Scalabrini are often reported, especially in the catechetical field). Series II (1890-1908) "organ of the permanent committee of the first Catechetical Congress." Series III (1909-1940): "it services the Diocesan Catechetical Bureaus and the dependent schools." The legacy of the first Catechetical periodical was taken up in 1952 by the *Revista del Catechismo.*

Studi Emigrazione. A quarterly journal of pastoral sociology and history of emigration, edited by the Centro Studi Emigrazione (Via della Scrofa 70), Rome. The first number appeared in October 1964.

Selezione CSER. Bimonthly bulletin of the Centro Studi Emigrazione, Rome.

We have consulted the following collections of journals and periodicals published in Piacenza contemporary with Scalabrini:

L'amico del Popolo, La Voce catolica, La Voce del Paese, Il Giubileo episcopale di Mons. Scalabrini, Il Progresso, Il Piccolo, La Libertà, Il Lavoro, Il Monitore Diocesano di Piacenza;

and numerous other publications:

Rassegna Nazionale, L'Osservatore Cattolico, L'Osservatore Romano, L'Unità Cattolica, La Difesa, Il Veridico, Il Cittadino (di Genova), Il Cittadino (di Brescia), La Civiltà Cattolica, La Scuola Cattolica, La Lega Lombarda, La Perseveranza, Il Leonardo da Vinci, L'Ateneo Religioso, Cultura sociale, La Voce della Verità, etc.

CHAPTER NOTES

HISTORICAL BACKGROUND

1. J.B. Scalabrini, *Discorso per il giubileo episcopale di Mons. Bonomelli*, Cremona 1896, pp. 14-18.
2. Idem, *Il Concilio Vaticano*, Como 1873, pp. xiv-xv and xii.
3. Idem, *Il Socialismo e l'azione del Clero*, 2nd ed., Turin, 1899, p. 37.
4. A. Ferrari Toniolo in *Aspetti della cultura cattolica nell'età di Leone XIII*, Rome, 1961, p. 394.
5. E. Passerin D'Entrèves, *L'eredita della tradizione cattolica risorgimentale*, in *Aspetti della cultura cattolica*, etc. quoted on pp. 277-278.
6. G. Martina, *Il liberalismo cattolico italiano*, Appendix IV to Volume XXI of the *Storia della Chiesa*, by Fliche-Martin: *Il Pontificato di Pio IX (1846-1878)* by R. Aubert, Turin, 1964, p. 793.
7. Letter of the S.C. of the Index to the Editors of the *Osservatore Cattolico* of Milan, published in its issue of July 1, 1876.
8. E. Soderini, *Il Pontificato di Leone XIII*, Vol. I, Milan, 1932, p. 283.
9. The Collegio Alberoni was established by Card. Giulio Alberoni for the support and training of sixty seminarians from Piacenza to the conclusion of their studies. It was completed in 1751 and entrusted to the Vincention Order for direction and teaching.
10. A. Fermi: *Mons. Antonio Ranza, filosofo, teologo, vescovo di Piacenza*, Volume I, Part I, *Gli inizi dell'episcopato*, Piacenza, 1956. Volume I, Part II appeared in 1966, with the collaboration of Father Molinari. Volume II, dealing with Ranza's philosophical and theological thought, is under preparation.

11. Ibid., Vol. I., Part I, p. VII. I cannot agree with the author's verdict that "the principal reason why Ranza's was treated with neglect and even hostility" was "the sudden change in ecclesiastical policy. We know that policy has philosophical and doctrinal bases, which are its logical frame of reference and which do in fact determine it many times" (Ibid., p. VIII, n. 3). This casts doubt on Scalabrini's Thomism (i.e. the "Rocca case" is described as "in a certain sense the culmination" of the abrupt change). Fermi's theory continues the confusion between politics and philosophy which Scalabrini himself strove to dissipate, thus continuing, even in this sense, the work of his predecessor, at the end of whose episcopate "the just conviction was gaining ground that philosophical disputes, and much less political difference, should not crack the solid edifice of Christian charity" (Ibid., Vol. I, Part II, p. 402).

12. J. B. Scalabrini, Discourse for the dedication of the monument to Msgr. Ranza, April 13, 1883.

Chapter I — EARLY LIFE

1. G. Gattaneo, witness, *Processus, cop. publ.*, f. 914; Luisa Scalabrini (sister of the Servant of God), witness, ibid., f. 919 v.; R. Cantaluppi, ibid., f. 925 r.

2. G. Cattaneo, "Discourse in San Bartolomeo (Como) for the unveiling of the monument Bishop Scalabrini" in *L'Emigrato Italiano*, Sept. 15, 1914, suppl., p. 4.

3. G. Cardinali, witness, *Processus*, iuxta 6, p. 90.

4. F. Gregori, *La vita e l'opera di un grande Vescovo. Giov. Batt. Scalabrini*, Turin, 1934, p. 6. The archives of the Generalate of the Scalabrini Fathers in Rome contain several letters from the pastor of Fino Mornasco, which acknowledge receipt of Bishop Scalabrini's offerings for anniversary Masses for his parents.

5. Ibid.

6. A. Bianchi, witness, *Processus* iuxta 6, pp. 220-221.

7. Ibid.

8. S. Piccinelli, witness, *Processus, cop. publ.* f. 909 v.

9. F. Torta, witness, ibid., p. 114.

10. On the evening before his wedding, Angelo Scalabrini wrote to his brother, the Bishop: "These are the last moments of my youth and I dedicate them to you, to you because you hold a place in my heart second to none, not even to the young woman I adore who will be my bride within a few hours, and because among the ghosts of the past, some of them sad, some of them happy, all of them dear, your beloved fatherly image shines clear, pure and beautiful. Let me make a little confession. You see, throughout my life I have always had a guiding principle, to avoid any action that could displease or compromise (harm) you. And therefore I have always kept away from the meetings and congresses. I could have earned a splendid position for myself from a financial as well as a prestige viewpoint, and I certainly lacked neither the will nor the courage, and perhaps not even the ability, but I have never pushed myself forward because of consideration for you. I am telling you these things now as a kind of introduction to the answer I owe your last dear letter, which I have read and reread and which moved me most deeply. But I am sorry I cannot satisfy you, for morally and intellectually it is impossible for me at this time to perform an external act which would be a solemn hypocrisy, a profanation. This certainly is not what you want from me. As I read your letter, though, I earnestly promise myself to return to the study of religion and I assure you that if I find in your faith the pure and beautiful truth that satisfies and quiets the intellect I shall make it mine with all the strength of my soul and I shall declare it openly with all the courage I possess." (AGS).

11. L. Mondini, witness, *Processus*, iuxta 40 p. 56.

12. *Mons. Giovanni Battista Scalabrini, Trent'anni di Apostolato. Memorie e documenti*, Rome, 1909 (cited hereafter as *Trent'anni di Apostolato*).

13. G. Cattaneo, op. cit., p. 4.

14. *Il Servo di Dio, Mons. G. B. Scalabrini*, Turin, 1941, p. 3. The statement is based on the deposition of Don Alfonso Bianchi, who also provides the recollections of his mother, Scalabrini's sister (*Processus*, iuxta 7, p. 221).

15. Gregori, op. cit., p. 17.
16. *Il Servo Di Dio Mons. G. B. Scalabrini*, Turin, 1941. p. 3.
17. Invited to Como in 1880 to lecture on the Holy Crucifix, he began his address as follows: "I have no words to express how moved I am, the joy I feel at addressing you on this most happy occasion and in this place. And how could I feel otherwise, speaking to people to whom I belonged and among whom I lived the best years of my life...For the sons of St. Abbondio, the veneration of Christ Crucified was truly a need of the soul. As toddlers, at our mother's knee we learned to love Him and this love is woven through the dearest memories of our life. Who of us has not wept with emotion...at the sight of the entire town pouring into that shrine to venerate the blessed image of the Crucified? Who of us has not been profoundly moved when it was carried every year through these streets in triumph?... Even far from here it is not possible to forget our miraculous Crucifix. Oh! How often our weary thoughts fly to rest at its foot! There are days of inexplicable bitterness when our whole soul lies prostrate before it to seek comfort and relief. It seems almost as if a mysterious bond unites the children of this diocese to the Crucifix wherever Providence may transport them, and for them the time of their return always seem long delayed." J.B. Scalabrini, *Discorso per il SS. Crocifisso*, Como, 1880.
18. G. Cattaneo, op. cit., pp. 4-5.
19. C. Monti to Bishop Scalabrini, Sept. 9, 1882 (AGS).
20. His biographer, Gregori, summed up the poem in these words: "In his concept. St. Louis is an angel come down from heaven; life in all its forms smiles upon him, and nature is so prodigal with her gifts to him that the world hastens to surround him with its blandishments...But he does not forget that he has a mission to fulfill on this earth: namely, to demonstrate the miracle of purity."
21. G. Cattaneo, Disc. cit., p. 4.
22. See C. Mangot, witness, *Processus*, iuxta 10, p. 5; A. Bianchi, ibid. pp. 221-222.
23. A. Bianchi and G. Cattaneo, witnesses, *Processus*, iuxta 10, pp. 221-222; and *Processus, cop. publ.* ff. 914v.-915r.
24. Ibid. See L. Sterlocchi, *Cenni biografici di Mons. G.B. Scalabrini*, Como, 1912, p. 7: "He is always among the most distinguished in his class."
25. G. Cattaneo, op. cit., p. 5.
26. Ibid.
27. P. Salvetti to Bishop Scalabrini, Feb. 17, 1876 (AGS).
28. Gregori, op. cit., pp. 23-24.
29. G. Cattaneo, op. cit., p. 6.
30. Gregori, op. cit., pp. 26-27. In the archives of the Chancery Office of Piacenza there is the following rough draft of Scalabrini's reply to Msgr. Marinoni: "I would consider myself very fortunate if many of my clergy dedicated themselves to the sublime work of the missions. Although even here we are beginning to feel the shortage of priests, nevertheless far from opposing them I would have nothing but praise and encouragement for them, convinced as I am that the most effective means to preserve the faith among us is to bring it to those who do not yet possess it."
31. G. Marinoni to Bishop Scalabrini, Jan. 1, 1884 (AGS).
32. From the magazine, *Le Missioni Cattoliche*, June 13, 1884. The homily is also in the appendix of the book by U. Colli, *Opilio Negri missionario ad Hyderabad Deccan, India. Reminiscenze*, Milan, 1939, pp. 173-178.
33. Gregori, op. cit., p. 24.
34. *Primo Centenario dell'apertura di S. Abbondio*, Como, 1936, p. 7.
35. L. Sterlocchi, op. cit., pp. 8-9.
36. J. B. Scalabrini to Bishop Bonomelli, Sept. 1, 1883 (Abba).
37. G. Colombo to Bishop Scalabrini, Milan, Nov. 13, 1897: "I still remember the poem in Hebrew which Gazola wrote to Your Excellency when you were named Bishop of Piacenza. I still remember some note or other which you made on that eulogy, which the author himself immediately noted" (AGS).
38. Gregori, op. cit., p. 479.
39. J. B. Scalabrini to Msgr. Mangot, Boston, Sept. 7, 1901 (AGS).

40. Idem, St. Paul, Sept. 26, 1901 (AGS).
41. Gregori, op. cit., p. 487 (AGS).
42. J. B. Scalabrini to Msgr. Mangot, Sao Paulo, July 25, 1904 (AGS).
43. Idem, Sao Paulo, July 26, 1904 (AGS).
44. Idem, Encantado, Sept. 15, 1904 (AGS).
45. Idem to Father Attilio Bianchi, Encantado, Sept. 21, 1904 (AGS). Bishop Bonomelli confirms this, although he confused Spanish and Portuguese: "He not only understood Latin and Greek but could write in them correctly and with elegance. He spoke French and Spanish, and could understand English and German." (G. Bonomelli, "1 Giugno," in L'Emigrato Italiano, June, 1906, p. 75).
46. A. Bianchi, witness, Processus, iuxta 12, p. 222.
47. L. Mondini, witness, ibid., p. 40.
48. G. Cattaneo, witness, Processus, cop. publ., iuxta 12, f. 915 r.
49. D. Bolzani to J. B. Scalabrini, Lenno, Aug. 26, 1867 (AGS).
50. G. Cattaneo, op. cit., pp. 7-8.
51. A. Bianchi, witness, Processus, iuxta 13, pp. 222-223.
52. L. Sterlocchi, op. cit., p. 9.
53. It would take too long here to go into the relationship between Scalabrini and Bonomelli. For the latter, see C. Bellò, Geremia Bonomelli, Brescia, 1961.
54. G. Bonomelli, "1 Giugno," in L'Emigrato Italiano, June, 1906, pp. 74-75.
55. Ibid., Bonomelli's first letter to Scalabrini is dated Dec. 12, 1868 (See Gregori, op. cit., p. 45).
56. The latter was especially fond of the young rector. He had known him as a student and foretold a bright future for him, "Now seated at the same table, in happy moments and intimate conversation, he kept telling him that he was born to govern." (G. Cattaneo, op. cit., p. 7).
57. G. Bonomelli, op. cit., p. 75.
58. Il Concilio Vaticano, Conferences held in the Cathedrals of Como by Rev. J. B. Scalabrini, Como, 1873. On p. 111, n. 1, after quoting from Chrysostom's homily "Quod Christus sit Deus," Scalabrini adds: "If years ago some scholar had had the happy thought of translating this treatise into Italian, keeping as much of the eloquence and strength of the Greek text as possible and had added several of the letters of St. Athanasius in reply to the Aryans, he would have provided a triumphant response to Renan's notorious romance, Vie de Jesus. Some one did indeed have the idea, but he did not feel equal to the task and did not finish it. I hope that some one more competent will finish it." The some one who did have the idea was evidently Scalabrini himself.
59. G. Cattaneo, op. cit., p. 9.
60. J. B. Scalabrini to Msgr. Piccinelli, Oct. 16, 1896 (AGS).
61. According to Rev. Alfonso Bianchi, witness, (Processus, iuxta 55, p. 229) the kindergarten and the youth center for boys established by Scalabrini were the first in Como.
62. A. Miotti, Report to the National Catechetial Congress at Piacenza, 1889, in: Atti e documenti del Primo Congresso Catechistico, Piacenza, 1890, p. 124.
63. E. Dominioni, witness, Processus.
64. Il Monumeno ricordo a Mons. Scalabrini, Special Issue, Como, Sept. 11, 1913.
65. See A. Bianchi and S. Piccinelli, Processus, iuxta 38.
66. J. B. Scalabrini, Il Socialismo e l'azione del Clero, 2nd ed., 1899, pp. 10-13.
67. S. Piccinelli to Msgr. Gregori, s.d. (AGS).
68. J. B. Scalabrini. Written on the occasion of the beginning of the work in San Bartolomeo (manuscript in AGS). Please note that all the manuscripts of Bishop Scalabrini are found in AGS.
69. F. Poggia to Bishop Scalabrini, Biella, Feb. 24, 1876 (AGS).
70. See Bollettino parrocchiale di Salsomaggiore, Sept. 13, 1931.
71. See Litterae Apostolicae Pii PP. IX, Jan. 1, 1876 (AVP).
72. L. Sterlocchi, op. cit., pp. 14-15.
73. J. B. Scalabrini to Msgr. Piccinelli, Oct. 16, 1896 (AGS).
74. Gregori, op. cit., pp. 40-41.

75. J. B. Scalabrini to Msgr. Piccinelli, Mar. 26, 1899 (AGS).
76. Gregori, op. cit., p. 42.

Chapter II — BISHOP OF PIACENZA

1. *La Stampa*, Jan. 22, 1904.
2. J. B. Scalabrini, First Pastoral Letter, *Al Clero e al Popolo*, Jan. 30, 1876, pp. 3-4.
3. J. B. Scalabrini to a Bishop, Feb. 22, 1904 (AGS).
4. J. B. Scalabrini, *Discorso per il giubileo episcopale di Mons. Bonomelli*, Cremona, 1896, pp. 10, 11, 14.
5. Ibid., pp. 8-9.
6. Ibid., pp. 7-8.
7. Ibid., pp. 15-16.
8. Idem, Pastoral Letter, *Unione colla Chiesa, obbedienza ai legittimi pastori*, Feb. 8, 1896, pp. 19-20.
9. Idem to Bishop Bonomelli, June 10, 1892 (Abba).
10. Idem, s.d. (Abba).
11. Idem to Father Faustino Consoni, April 12, 1897 (AGS).
12. Idem, *Ai Missionari per gl'Italiani nelle Americhe*, Piacenza, 1882, pp. 7-8.
13. Idem, Discourse on the 20th Anniversary of the Episcopal Consecration.
14. A. Ferini — F. Molinari, op. cit., Vol. I, part II, p. 83.
15. P. M. Schiaffino, Discourse of Feb. 16, 1876 for the B. Gregorio X *VI Centenario del B. Gregorio PP. X*, Piacneza, 1876, p. 62.
16. J. B. Scalabrini, First Pastoral Letter, *Al Clero e al Popolo*, Jan. 30, 1876, pp. 4, 6, 7.

Chapter III — THE FATHER OF HIS FLOCK

1. See *Il Veridico* (Reggio Emilia), May 2, 1876.
2. J. B. Scalabrini, Discourse for his episcopal jubilee, 1901.
3. See witnesses I, II, XIII, XIV, XV, etc., *Processus*, iuxta 37, 26.
4. L. Mondini, witness, ibid., iuxta 37, p. 53.
5. C. Mangot, witness, ibid., iuxta 26, p. 11.
6. L. Cornaggia Medici, ibid., iuxta 55, p. 257.
7. Idem, *Le caratteristiche di Mons. G. B. Scalabrini*, Reggio Emilia, 1935, pp. 21-22.
8. L. Sterlocchi, *Cenni biografici di Mons. G. B. Scalabrini*, Como, 1912, p. 24. See witnesses I, V, IX, XI, XVII, XVIII, XXII, XXIX, XXXI, etc., *Processus*, iuxta 36.
9. *Il Progresso*, Dec. 11, 1879.
10. *Atti della Camera*, session of Dec. 21, 1879, Rome, 1879, p. 8.
11. A. Grili, Vice-President of the Committee for Soup Kitchens of Piacenza, to Bishop Scalabrini, Mar. 3, 1893 (AGS).
12. S. F. Motta to Bishop Scalabrini, Oct. 13, 1900 (AGS).
13. G. Vaciago to Angelo Scalabrini, June 2, 1905 (AGS). The kitchens had already operated successfully in 1874, during Bishop Ranza's tenure, but they had had to close in 1875. See A. Fermi — F. Molinari, *Mons. Antonio Ranza*, Piacenza, 1966, Vol. I, Part II, pp. 166-167.
14. Muriuri, manager of the pawnshop, to Bishop Scalabrini, June 11, 1901 (AGS).
15. A. Onesti Zangrandi to Bishop Scalabrini, June 24, 1901 (AGS).
16. See the numerous letters of thanks from the bishops cited (AGS).
17. See *La Voce del Paese*, Piacenza, Aug. 10, 1883.
18. J. B. Scalabrini to the editor of the *Voce del Paese*, May 6, 1883 (AGS).
19. The Archbishop of Pontremoli to Bishop Scalabrini, Aug. 6, 1884 (AGS).
20. J. B. Scalabrini, Circular to the Clergy and to the People, Aug. 16, 1884, p. 7.
21. Idem, Pastoral Letter, Sept. 15, 1884, p. 6.
22. See the letters of G. Boccali, Sept. 30, 1884, and of the bishops of Sarzana, Oct. 10, 1884, Bergamo, Nov. 15, 1884, Parma, Nov. 16, 1884 and Cuneo, Nov. 15, 1884, to Bishop Scalabrini and to Father G. Pinazzi, the chancellor of the diocese (AGS).
23. J. B. Scalabrini to the Marchese F. Landi, Mar. 10, 1887 (AGS); Circular, Oct. 8, 1889

24. See *L'Amico del Popolo*, Feb. and Mar. 11, 1887.
25. J. B. Scalabrini, Circular on the landslide of the Villanova of Bettola, May 20, 1904; See Announcement of the Landslide of Tollara, Mar. 23, 1895.
26. Idem, Discourse on the death of Casamicciola, Aug. 4, 1883.
27. G. Bonomelli, "1 Giugno" in *L'Emigrato Italiano*, June, 1906, p. 75.
28. Gregori, op. cit., p. 582. G. Cazinari, witness, *Processus*, iuxta 18, p. 210. A lira of the time was equivalent to about 500 lire of 1967.
29. G. Cardinali, witness, *Processus*, iuxta 15, p. 91.
30. G. Cattaneo, witness, *Processus, cop. publ.*, iuxta 36, f. 916 v.
31. L. Scalabrini, witness, ibid., f. 919 r.
32. Gregori, op. cit., p. 583.
33. C. Mangot, witness, *Processus*, iuxta 26, p. 11; L. Mondini, witness, ibid., iuxta 36, p. 51; C. Spallazzi, witness, ibid., p. 33.
34. *Il Monitore Diocesano di Piacenza*, June 30, p. 160.
35. J. B. Scalabrini to a recipient, note s.d. (AGS).
36. Gregori, op. cit., p. 583.
37. Card. L. Parocchi to Bishop Scalabrini, Nov. 11, 1877 (AGS).
38. The Bishop of Osimo to Bishop Scalabrini, Feb. 21, 1904 (AGS).
39. The Bishop of Como to Bishop Scalabrini, Oct. 30, 1878 (AGS).
40. A. Ratti to Bishop Scalabrini, June 26, 1902 (AGS).
41. See Chap. V. A. Mizzi to Bishop Scalabrini, May 14, 1891 (AGS).
42. See Chap. XXI, pp. 374-375.
43. V. Vignali to Bishop Scalabrini, Mar. 16, 1880 (AGS).
44. C. Spallazzi, witness, *Processus*, iuxta 36, p. 32.
45. For obvious reasons of delicacy the names of those who wrote the many letters of thanks are omitted.
46. See Chapter I, pp. 33-35.
47. L. Scalabrini to her brother, the bishop, June 18, 1889 (AGS).
48. A. Scalabrini to Bishop Mangot, Dec. 14, 1905 (AGS).
49. These letters are in AGS.
50. See Appendix II.
51. L. Gorlin, witness, *Processus*, iuxta 26, p. 307.
52. A. Bianchi, "Mons. Scalabrini e don Orione," in *L'Emigrato Italiano*, Oct. 1955, p. 118.
53. G. Dodici, witness, *Processus, cop. publ.*, f. 171 v.; C. Mangot, witness, p. 15; L. Mondini, witness, pp. 52-53.
54. F. Gregori, witness, ibid., p. 187.
55. E. Caccialanza, witness, ibid., f. 225 rv.
56. G. Squeri, witness, ibid., f. 531 r.
57. *L'Italiano in America*, New York, Aug. 31, 1901.
58. *Trent'anni di Apostolato*, cit. p. 103.
59. E. Morisi, witness, *Processus*, iuxta 37, pp. 140-141.
60. Douglas Scotti, witness, *Processus, cop. publ.*, iuxta 37, p. 327 v.
61. See the correspondence between Duke Roberto di Borbone and Bishop Scalabrini, and the letters of the marquis in question, in AGS.
62. F. Cattivelli, witness, *Processus, cop. publ.* iuxta 37, p. 389 v.
63. G. Squeri, witness, ibid., iuxta 37, p. 165.
64. F. Torta, witness, ibid., iuxta 4, p. 113.
65. F. Morisi, witness, ibid., iuxta 18, p. 134.
66. F. Torta, witness, ibid., iuxta 37, p. 122.
67. G. Cardinali, witness, ibid., p. 104.
68. L. Mondini, witness, ibid., p. 53. Adele Bracchi, who was a teacher, the mother of Venerable Lazzaro Chiappa, recounts that during his pastoral visit to Scopolo, Bishop Scalabrini had said to her: "When your son finishes elementary school, remind me about him." When time came for him to apply for admission to the seminary, she overcame her timidity and went to see the Bishop. "How scared I was when I found myself in front of the door to the Bishop's study. I couldn't even turn the doorknob, and the Bishop himself came to help

me. He appeared with a broad smile and asked, 'Well, teacher, what do you want of me?' Encouraged by his warm welcome, I took heart and reminded him of his pastoral visit to Scopolo and what he had said to me at the time about little Lazzaro. 'I remember, I remember,' he answered kindly. Then he said, 'But do you have the money for his studies?' I told him frankly what I had...'Don't you know,' he added gently, 'how much studying for the priesthood will cost?' And so, he kept me in suspense with a number of questions, although his smile told me he intended to help. 'Fine,' he said, 'the Rector has showed me your son's records; let him enter the Seminary, tell him to behave himself and to study; if in three months, he proves his record in his examination, he will be given full scholarship.' I could not find words to thank him. 'Pray, pray.for me,' he said, and dismissed me with these words." (*Monsignor Lazzaro Chiappa Arciprete di Caorso*, Piacenza, 1952, p. 15.)

69. See Scalabrini's letters to Bishop Bonomelli, passim (Abba); the letters of the Bishop of Vicenza, Jan. 19, 1894, and of the Bishop of Pavia, Oct. 26, 1878, to Bishop Scalabrini (AGS).

70. A. De Martini, witness, *Processus,*, iuxta 26, p. 83.

71. F. Torta, witness, ibid., iuxta 14, p. 114.

72. E. Preti, witness, ibid., iuxta 38, p. 75.

73. G. Cardinali, witness, ibid., iuxta 25, p. 98.

74. Idem, iuxta 43, pp. 105-106.

75. G. Squeri, witness, ibid., iuxta 44, p. 166.

76. G. Cardinali, witness, ibid., iuxta 44, p. 106.

77. Idem, iuxta 25, p. 98.

78. See Chap. V, pp. 103-107.

79. L. Mondini, witness, *Processus*, iuxta 20, p. 43.

80. X to Bishop Scalabrini, Dec. 22, 1904 (AGS).

81. X to Bishop Scalabrini, Dec. 24, 1904 (AGS).

82. X to Bishop Scalabrini, Jan. 15, 1903 (AGS).

83. X to Bishop Scalabrini, Aug. 23, 1881 (AGS).

84. Omodei Zorini to Bishop Scalabrini, Dec. 2, 1887 (AGS).

85. J. B. Scalabrini, Lenten Pastoral Letter, 1889, p. 17.

Chapter IV — SCALABRINI AS TEACHER

1. E. Sanguinetti in *Il Servo di Dio Mons. G. B. Scalabrini nella luce delle celebrazioni del 50° della sua morte*, Rome, 1957, p. 232 (referred to hereafter as *Celebrazioni del 50°*).

2. J. B. Scalabrini, *Discorso per il giubileo episcopale di Mons. Bonomelli*, Cremona, 1896, p. 9.

3. L. Biginelli in *Ateneo Religioso* XXL, 1899, pp. 581 ff.

4. *Atti e documenti del primo Congresso Catechistico*, Piacenza, 1890, p. 120.

5. U. Malchiodi, Preface to *Considerazioni catechistiche del Servo di Dio Mons. G. B. Scalabrini*, ed. by Father Luigi Rebecchi, Piacenza, 1956, p. 7.

6. Ibid., Introduction, pp. 9-10.

7. See E. Mangenot, *Catéchisme* in *Dict. de Théol Cath.*, II, 2, coll 1895-1968; C. Testore, *Catechesi, La catechesi nei secc. XIX e XX* in *Enciclopedia Cattolica*, III, coll. 1111-1112; *Catechismo dal Concilio di Trento ai nostri giorni*, ibid, 1123-1124 and the respective bibliographies. Among the numerous recent publications we might note U. Gianetto — G. Gianolo, *Il movimento catechistico in Italia dal 1870* in *Linee per un direttorio di pastorale catechistica*, Turin, 1967.

8. J. B. Scalabrini, *Prezioso dono ai bambini o Piccolo Catechismo proposto agli asili d'infanzia*, Milan, 1875, p. 84. In the preface he praises the catechism as "the book which takes the place of all books," and maintains that public instruction in the catechism "is, by divine institution, an imprescriptible right, a sacred duty of the Bishops" (now sanctioned by Can. 1336 of the Code of Canon Law). "And this inalienable right of the Bishops cannot be taken from them or limited, not even by parental authority," once a father has presented his child for baptism. The Kingdom of Italy, by virtue of Art. 1 of the Constitution "cannot permit teaching of the Catechism unless this is done by the Church." Therefore,

only the Bishop can approve the catechism to be used in his diocese. He observes that unfortunately diocesan catechisms were not suitable for children. "We have tried to remedy this with the present little catechism for use in kindergarten; it was written after consulting the best of the known catechisms and especially the catechism organized for the regular study of religion by Father C.U.M.L. of whose observations and study I availed myself." (The reference is to the Vincentian missionary Ciriaco Uttini, whose work Bishop Scalabrini later used in Piacenza along with that of his brother Canon Carlo Uttini.)

9.   S. Riva, Introduction to *Considerazioni catechistiche del Servo di Dio Mons. G. B. Scalabrini*, ed. by Father L. Rebecchi, Piacenza, 1956, pp. 6 and 13.

10.   Idem, *Mons. Giovanni Battista Scalabrini pioniere della catechesi moderna*, I, in *Rivista del Catechismo*, 1955, n. 3, pp. 223-229.

11.   *Programma per la pubblicazione di un foglietto religioso mensile intitolato Il Cathechista Cattolico Piacentino*, Piacenza, 1876.

12.   J. B. Scalabrini, Pastoral Letter, *Sull'Insegnamento del Catechismo*, Apr. 23, 1876, p. 35.

13.   S. Riva, art. cit., ibid., III, 1955, n. 6, pp. 468-469; IV, 1956, n. 1, p. 67.

14.   J. B. Scalabrini, Pastoral Letter, *Ai Maestri e alle Maestre delle Scuole Catechistiche della città e della diocesi*, Nov. 4, 1877, p. 36.

15.   Idem, Pastoral Letter, *Premessa alla ristampa del Catechismo Diocesano*, Jan. 1, 1881, p. 18. This prescribed the text, as revised by Scalabrini, of Bishop Terin Bonesio of Bobbio. In the 1893 Synod he prescribed a new revised and corrected edition (*Synodus Placentina Secunda*, 1893, p. 25). In 1899, along with the other bishops of the Emilian Region, his revision of the *Compendio della Dottrina Cristiana* by Bishop Michele Casati, which was already in use in Lombardy, Piedmont and Liguria.

16.   Idem, *Il Catechismo Cattolico, Considerazioni*, Piacenza, 1877, p. 180. "An excellent manual of formation, both pedagogical and didactic..., it has even today a wonderful relevancy and validity; we may only wonder why...it has not occurred to anyone to give this book again to Italian catechists" (S. Riva, in *Revista del Catechismo*, 1956, n. 1, p. 69).

17.   See *L'Unità Cattolica, Il Congresso Catechistico di Piacenza*, Sept. 28, 1889; *La Difesa* (Venice), Sept. 28, 1889.

18.   F. Salvestrini, *L'anno giubilare di due fondamentali documenti pontifici* in *Catechesi*, ed. Scuole Medie, n. 1, Jan., 1965, p. 7.

19.   *Atti e documenti del Primo Congresso Catechistico, tenutosi a Piacenza nei giorni 24, 25, 26 Settembre 1889*, Piacenza, 1890, p. 396.

20.   *Il Catechista Cattolico*, May, 1901, pp. 277-278.

21.   Ibid., June, 1902, p. 382.

22.   The *Catechista Cattolico*, Mar., 1905, pp. 129-130, reproduces Pius X's Brief and, immediately following it, the plan for the second catechetical congress approved by Bishop Scalabrini. This merely set forth the ideological bases, contained in the 1901 plan, quoted above, and is limited to a general outline (ibid., pp. 133-136). The second congress was finally held in Milan in 1910.

23.   L. Orione, witness, *Processus*, iuxta 16, p. 289.

24.   *Atti e documenti del Primo Congresso Catechistico*, quoted on pp. 98-120.

25.   J. B. Scalabrini to D. G. Allesi, note s.d., in answer to Allesi's letter of Sept. 9, 1891 (AGS).

26.   *Atti e documenti del Primo Congresso Catechistico*, quoted on pp. 63-74.

27.   Ibid., p. 160.

28.   Ibid., pp. 281-284.

29.   Card. A. Capecelatro to Bishop Scalabrini, Dec. 12, 1889 (AGS).

30.   Idem, Mar. 23, 1891 (AGS).

31.   Gregori, op. cit., pp. 240-242.

32.   L. Orione, witness, *Processus*, iuxta 16, p. 289.

33.   G. Varischi in *L'Avvenire d'Italia*, Jan. 30, 1931.

34.   G. Tessarolo in *L'Emigrato Italiano*, May, 1956, p. 86.

35.   L. Rebecchi, op. cit., p. 83.

36.   J. B. Scalabrini, *Il Catechismo Cattolico*, p. 127. See L. Rebecchi, op. cit., pp. 74-75.

37.   Rev. Leone di Maria, *Mons. G. B. Scalabrini Apostolo del Catechismo*, in *Celebrazioni del 50°*, p.. 254. See *Il Catechista Cattolico*, May 2, 1877, p. 86.

38. *Il Cittadino* (Genoa), Dec. 9, 1890.
39. *Trent'anni di Apostolato*, p. 439.
40. L. Rebecchi, op. cit., p. 73. In 1950 Bishop Ranza had devoted a pastoral letter to the subject of the catechism and he had encouraged the work of the Congregation of Christian Doctrine. "In later years...he could not take part in catechetical activity, and left this duty to his young and competent successor" (A. Fermi-F. Molinari, op. cit., Vol. I, Part II, p. 35).
41. *La Voce del Paese*, letter from Rome dated Sept. 30, 1883.
42. S. Riva, Mons. *Scalabrini "catechista,"* in the Introduction to L. Rebecchi, op. cit., p. 9.
43. J. B. Scalabrini, *Premessa alla ristampa de Catechismo Diocesano*, Jan. 1, 1881, pp. 4, 8.
44. Idem, *Il Catechismo cattolico*, quoted on pp. 54, 57, 59, 62, etc.
45. Idem, Pastoral Letter, *Ai Maestri e alle Maestre delle Scuole della città e della diocesi*, Nov. 4, 1877, pp. 18-19.
46. Idem, First Conference on Emigration, pp. 12, 7.
47. Idem, *Il Catechismo Cattolico*, quoted on p. 7.
48. See *Synodus Placentina Tertia, Part I, cap. V, De praedicatione Eucharistica*, Piacenza, 1900, pp. 29-31: Part IV, Chap. I, *De prima Communione*, nn. 1, 6, 7, pp. 64-67. See also Chapter XV, pp. 275-276.
49. S. Riva, Mons. *Scalabrini "catechista,"* in the Introduction to L. Rebecchi, op. cit., p. 10.
50. E. Sanguinetti in *Celebrazioni del 50°*, p. 235.
51. O. Alusi, letter quoted in *Trent'anni di Apostolato*, p. 492.
52. J. B. Scalabrini to Msgr. Mangot, Aug. 25, 1901 (AGS).
53. V. Sorrentino to Bishop Scalabrini, Aug. 26, 1901 (AGS).
54. G. Gelfi, witness, *Processus*, iuxta 4, p. 310.
55. *In memoria di Mons. G. B. Scalabrini*, Piacenza, 1905, p. 6. His predecessor had a weak voice and often no voice at all; therefore he could rarely preach (A. Fermi-F. Molinari, op. cit., Vol. I, Part II, pp. 35-36).
56. J. B. Scalabrini to Bishop Bonomelli, July 8, 1884 (Abba).
57. L. Mondini, witness, *Processus*, iuxta 25, p. 45.
58. *L'Eco d'Italia*, quoted in *Trent'anni di Apostolato*, p. 391.
59. *La Gazzetta Piemontese*, Mar., 1891, quoted in *Trent'anni di Apostolato*, p. 405.
60. E. Morisi, witness, *Processus*, iuxta 30, p. 138.
61. *La Nazione* (Florence), Mar. 9, 1891.
62. *Il Fanfulla* (Rome), Feb. 9, 1891.
63. F. Crispolti in *L'Amico del Popolo*, Feb. 9, 1901.
64. *L'Amico del Popolo*, Nov. 17-18, 1894.
65. *La Voce Cattolica*, July 17, 1901.
66. Antonio Fogazzaro, *Una visita a Mons. Scalabrini*, in *Rassegna Nazionale*, July 1, p. 9. See *Il Secolo XIX* (Genoa), Dec. 12, 1904: "L'arrivo di Mons. Scalabrini," an interview.
67. *La Trebbia* (Bobbio), May 15, 1905.
68. J. B. Scalabrini, Pastoral Letter, *Il prete Cattolico*, 1892, p. 15.
69. Idem, *Communicazione dell'Enciclica Etsi Nos*, Mar. 19, 1882, p. 16.
70. *Synodus Placentina Tertia, Monitiones*, n. 11, Piacenza, 1900, pp. 213-214.
71. L. Cornaggia Medici, witness, *Processus*, iuxta 25, p. 252.
72. Gregori, op. cit., pp. 594-595.
73. *Synodus Placentina Secunda, Part I, cap. II*, nn. 18-19, Piacenza, 1893, p. 31.
74. J. B. Scalabrini, *La stabilità della Chiesa*, Lenten Pastoral Letter, 1877, p. 15.
75. Ibid., p. 20.
76. Idem, *La Religione Cattolica*, Lenten Pastoral Letter, 1880, p. 20.
77. Idem, *L'indifferenza religiosa*, Lenten Pastoral Letter, 1882, pp. 3-4.
78. Idem, *La Famiglia cristiana*, Pastoral Letter, 1894, p. 7.
79. See *Trent'anni di Apostolato*, passim. In 1887 Giacomo Zanella sent Bishop Scalabrini some autographed poems and asked for a copy or copies of the pastoral (G. Zanella to Msgr. Mangot, Feb. 2, 1887). Several offers came to publish a volume of his writings. The first was from Father Circenzio Bertucci (letter to Bishop Scalabrini, Broni, Jan. 1, 1903, AGS). A year later still another request came from M. Zecca (letter to Bishop Scalabrini,

Aug. 6, 1903, AGS). The Bishop did not accept any of the offers, and the volume of his collected writings was never published.

There are numerous evidences of the esteem in which he was held by intellectual circles. Adolph Tanquerey asked his judgment on his works on dogmatic and moral theology (See his letter to Scalabrini, Baltimore, Dec. 12, 1901, AGS).

Francesco Saverio Nitti, who had just published a work on Catholic socialism wrote Scalabrini for permission to publish his pastorals and discourses. Later, when he became editor of the review, *La Riforma sociale*, he again wrote to Bishop Scalabrini, this time for an article on the Italian Catholics and the social question. "Italian Catholics are dull and indolent," he wrote. "You can do a great deal of good and set in motion a whole new movement." (See his letters to Scalabrini, of Mar. 17, 1899 and Feb. 25, 1894, AGS).

He was a member of the Philosophical-Medical Academy of St. Thomas in Rome, and of the literary-scientific Christopher Columbus Association of Genoa. There are extant numerous invitations from other Academies. The Bishop of Parma invited him to accept honorary membership in the scientific "St. Thomas Academy" in that city. He was made honorary chairman of the Italian organizing committee of the fourth International Catholic Scientific Congress (1897).

80. L. Bertola, witness, *Processus*, cop. publ., iuxta 15, f. 718 r.
81. A. Fermi-F. Molinari, op. cit., Vol. I, Part II, p. 26, n. 2.
82. J. B. Scalabrini, Pastoral Letter, *Sull'Opera di S. Opilio*, May 1, 1892, pp. 7-8.
83. A. Fermi-F. Molinari, op. cit., Vol. I, Part II, pp. 87-110. Bishop Ranza's relations with the Collegio Alberoni were difficult at first, but gradually became more cordial (ibid., pp. 85-87; Part I, pp. 299-403).

   On day students in the 19th century, see G. Martina in Appendix I of R. Aubert's *Il Pontificato di Pio IX*, Turin, 1964, pp. 754-756; P. Stella, *Don Bosco nella storia della religiosità cattolica*, Vol. I, Zurich, 1968, pp. 54-55.
84. J. B. Scalabrini, Pastoral Letter, *Sull'Opera di S. Opilio*, May, 1892, pp. 13, 19.
85. Gregori, op. cit., p. 67.
86. Scalabrini to the Rector of the Seminary of Bedonia, Oct. 16, 1890, (in the Archives of the Seminary of Bedonia).
87. Idem, Sept. 15, 1876. (Ibid.)
88. Idem to Cardinal Giuseppe Pecci, note s.d. (AGS).
89. A. Stoppani to Bishop Scalabrini, Jan. 1, 1889 (AGS).
90. Idem, Apr. 27, 1889 (AGS).
91. N. Zaccarino to Bishop Scalabrini, Oct. 27, 1889 (AGS).
92. A. Mascarini to Bishop Scalabrini, Ascoli Piceno, Feb. 15, 1890 (AGS). The noted geologist, Torquato Taramelli, was also among Scalabrini's admirers.
93. J. B. Scalabrini, Decree of Oct. 18, 1876 (AVP). The same Decree established the office of Spiritual Director, modeled after the well-known rules of St. Charles.
94. See A. Fermi, *Vincenzo Buzzetti e la filosofia in Piacenza*, Piacenza, 1923, pp. 21-22.
95. *Synodus Placentina Secunda*, Pars. IV, cap. VII, n. 27, Piacenza, 1893, p. 115.
96. See G. F. Rossi, *La filosofia nel Collegio Alberoni e il neotomismo*, Piacenza, 1959, p. 224.
97. J. B. Scalabrini, *Allocutio in Prolusione ad Synodum, Synodus Placentina*, 1879, Piacenza 1880, p. XXI.
98. Ibid., *De Seminario Clericorum*, nn. 5-6, p. 190.
99. E. Soderini, *Il pontificato di Leone XIII*, Milan, 1932, Vol. I, pp. 283-286.
100. L. Cornaggia Medici, witness, *Processus*, Iuxta 16, pp. 250-251.
101. G. Cardinali, ibid., p. 92. When this witness speaks of Giobertian and Rosminian currents in the Collegio Alberoni, he is repeating a commonly understood belief, which has been disproved by G. F. Rossi (op. cit.) and earlier by Bishop Scalabrini.
102. F. Lotteri, witness, *Processus*,, iuxta 16, p. 238.
103. G. B. Nasalli Rocca, witness, ibid., p. 258.
104. G. Semeria, *Mons. G. B. Scalabrini*, Piacenza, 1905, p. 18.
105. J. B. Scalabrini, *Allocutio...in dimissione Synodi, Synodus Placentina 1879*, Piacenza, 1880, p. 227.
106. *Synodus Placentina Tertia, Monitiones*, n. 5, Piacenza, 1900, p. 208.

107. J. B. Scalabrini, *Oratio III, Synodus Placentina Secunda*, Piacenza, 1893, pp. 185-197, passim.
108. Idem, Discourse to the Academy on the 40th Anniversary of the Cardinalate of Leone XIII, Oct. 14, 1893.
109. Idem, Discourse on St. Philip Neri.
110. Idem, *Oratio II, Synodus Placentina Secunda*, Piacenza, 1893, pp. 177-184, passim.
111. Idem, Pastoral Letter, *Il prete cattolico*, 1892, p. 9.
112. Ibid., p. 11.
113. *Synodus Placentina Tertia, Monitiones*, Piacenza, 1900, n. 2, pp. 205-206.
114. J. B. Scalabrini, *Allocutio...in dimissione Synodi, Synodus Placentina*, 1879, Piacenza, 1880, pp. 228-229.
115. Idem, *Oratio II, Synodus Placentina Secunda*, Piacenza, 1893, p. 182.
116. *Synodus Placentinus Tertia, Monitiones*, nn. 2-3, pp. 205-206.
117. J. B. Scalabrini, *Oratio III, Synodus Placentina Secunda*, pp. 192-196.
118. *Synodus Placentina, Tertia Monitiones*, Piacenza, 1900, n. 4, pp. 206-208.
119. J. B. Scalabrini to Bishop Bonomelli, Aug. 9, 1877 (Abba).
120. Card. E. Borromeo to Bishop Scalabrini, Aug. 4, 1877 (AGS).
121. Idem, Oct. 9, 1878 (AGS).
122. *XXV Anniversario dei Missionari di Mons. Scalabrini*, Rome, 1912, p. 9.
123. J. B. Scalabrini to Bishop Fontant, Sept. 27, 1887 (note in AGS).
124. Card. Lambini to Bishop Scalabrini, Dec. 12, 1887 (AGS).
125. Undated note (AGS).
126. J. B. Scalabrini, Pastoral Letter, *Pel suo ritorno da Roma*, Oct. 18, 1882, p. 18.
127. J. B. Scalabrini to Bishop Bonomelli, Mar. 28, 1882 (Abba). From all the above it is easy to understand the basis for the suspicions we find echoed in the correspondence between Patriarch Paolo Ballerini of Alexandria and Card. Ludovico Jacobini, the Secretary of State. This is recorded in an article by P. Bondioli, *Bonomelli e Albertario in documenti inediti della Segreteria di Stato di Leone XIII (1881-1884)* in *Memorie storiche della diocesi di Milano*, Vol. V, Milan, 1958, pp. 39-110. Among other things mention is made of a pastor in Como who noted Scalabrini's "partiality" for the Vincentians, including a certain Buroni. In his reply, dated Nov. 6, 1881, Card. Jacobini noted that these observations on the diocese of Piacenza had caught the attention of the Holy Father. Bishop Bonomelli called Scalabrini's attention to the pamphlet by Buroni which was causing some concern (letter to Scalabrini, Mar. 23, 1882, AGS). Scalabrini replied Mar. 3, 1882 (Abba) in the letter quoted below. G. Buroni, a native of Piacenza, had taught philosophy in the seminary there. At the time he wrote the pamphlet in question he was professor of philosophy in the Seminary of Turin.
128. J. B. Scalabrini to Bishop Bonomelli, Mar. 28, 1883 (Abba).
129. Ibid., "Every day I pray, and impose special duties on myself, in imploring God to raise up another Francis de Sales, who will be able to put an end to this ill-omened philosophical question, as that saint ended the controversy *de auxiliis*."
130. *Il Pedrotti della Sapienza e la Civiltà Cattolica* in *La Civiltà Cattolica*, Feb. 23, 1884, p. 587.
131. J. B. Scalabrini to Bishop Bonomelli, Aug. 10, 1883, and Sept. 1, 1883 (Abba).
132. A. Stoppani, *Gli Intransigenti alla stregua dei fatti vecchi, nuovi e nuovissimi*, dated 1886 but published in Oct. 1885. (See A. Stoppani to Bishop Bonomelli, Oct. 28, 1885, in G. Astori, *Corrispondenza di Mons. G. Bonomelli e Don. A. Stoppani*, Brescia, 1959, pp. 118-119.)
133. J. B. Scalabrini to Bishop Bonomelli, Rome, Nov. 13, 1885; Piacenza, Nov. 28, 1885 (Abba).
134. G. Bonomelli to Bishop Scalabrini, Oct. 29, 1886 (AGS); J. B. Scalabrini to Bishop Bonomelli, Oct. 31, 1886 (Abba).
135. Card. P. M. Schiaffino to Bishop Scalabrini, Nov. 6, 1886 (AGS).
136. J. B. Scalabrini to Bishop Bonomelli, Nov. 12, 1886 (Abba).
137. Idem, Nov. 29, 1886 (Abba).
138. J. B. Scalabrini to Card. Schiaffino, undated note, written probably around the middle of Nov., 1886 (AGS).

139. The letter in which Stoppani complained that the Bishop was forcing him to "extinguish *scintillam meam*" was not, however, addressed to Scalabrini (as G. Baraldi says in *I Vescovi Scalabrini e Bonomelli e la questione rosminiana, Segni dei Tempi*, Apr. 2, 1934, p. 57) but to Bonomelli.

140. He is referring to *Il nuovo Rosmini*.

141. J. B. Scalabrini to P. Cornoldi, Jan. 4, 1891 (AGS). Father Stoppani had died on Jan. 1, 1891.

142. J. B. Scalabrini to Leo XIII, Mar. 17, 1888 (note, AGS).

143. A. Stoppani to Bishop Bonomelli, Mar. 27, 1888 (G. Astori, op. cit., p. 131).

144. Bishop Angeli to Bishop Scalabrini, Mar. 20, 1888 (AGS).

145. J. B. Scalabrini, *Universo nostro Clero*, etc., Mar. 21, 1888, pp. IV-7.

146. Eight months later, Bishop Scalabrini recalled Moglia, since he had sent a contribution for a monument to Rosmini in Milano, the decision to erect it having been made in 1880. Moglia answered pointing out the date of the decision and the fact that his pledge to contribute had been made two years earlier. It was not his intention therefore to protest the decree *Post obitum* in fact, he took the occasion to reconfirm the freedom, sincerity and immutability of his submission to the decree, concluding: "I am ready to declare in the newspaper my unalterable obedience to the Holy Church of Rome, for which I would break not only the monument of my teacher Rosmini, but even that of my parents if that were necessary to dispel any misunderstanding." (A. Moglia to Bishop Scalabrini, Nov. 26, 1888, AGS). It is no wonder then that Scalabrini trusted him; Moglia was proposed as examiner because he was an examplary, zealous, cultivated priest, sincerely devoted to the Holy See and universally esteemed. If he then defended Rosmini, it was because he was free to do so, as Leo XIII himself assured him of this through me, until Rome had made some statement on the subject. And in fact as soon as he heard that the 40 propositions had been condemned, he made an act of complete submission, thereby arousing the anger of his friends, and he confined himself to his parish duties" (J. B. Scalabrini to the Cardinal Prect of the Sacred Congregation of the Council, July 5, 1895; note in AVP).

147. G. Cornoldi to Bishop Scalabrini, Apr. 4, 1888 (AGS). The witness Msgr. F. Torta (*Processus*, iuxta 16, p. 115) recalls that on that occasion, the Bishop gave Prof. Rossignoli the task of refuting the condemned propositions in the Seminary's school of philosophy. His lectures lasted six months. The witnesses at the process of inquiry are unanimous in noting the obedience of the Servant of God in this situation, but they prefer to bring out the prudence and charity with which he brought his priests to obedience and healed the dissension among the various currents. In 1892, he took action immediately against an anonymous pamphlet, printed in Piacenza, which attacked the decree *Post obitum*, ordered it sequestered, threatened the author with ecclesiastical censure, and reported him to the Holy Office.

148. J. B. Scalabrini, *Discorso per il giubileo episcopale di Mons. Bonomelli*, Cremona, 1896, pp. 10-11.

149. Idem, Pastoral Letter, *Per il riconoscimento delle reliquie dei SS. Antonino e Vittore*, 1880, p. 29.

150. Idem, First Pastoral Letter, *Al Clero e al popolo*, Jan. 30, 1876, p. 5.

151. Idem, Pastoral Letter, *Per la visita pastorale*, Nov. 11, 1876, p. 11.

152. G. Bonomelli, quoted in *Trent'anni di Apostolato*, p. 687.

153. Quoted by L. Cornaggia Medici, *Un Profilo di Mons. G. B. Scalabrini*, Rome, 1930, p. 4.

154. Antonio Fogazzaro, *Una visita a Mons. Scalabrini*, in *Rassegna Nazionale*, July 1, 1905, p. 11.

155. A. Labò, *In memoria di Mons. G. B. Scalabrini*, Piacneza, 1906, pp. 8-9.

156. *Commemorazione*, in the Basilica of San Antonino, in *Trent'anni Apostolato*, p. 657.

157. J. B. Scalabrini to Bishop Bonomelli, Sept. 17, 1883 (Abba).

Chapter V — THE FIVE PASTORAL VISITS

1. J. B. Scalabrini, Pastoral Letter, *Per la visita pastorale*, Nov. 4, 1876, pp. 4-5, 8, 10, 11.

2. Ibid., pp. 11-17.

3. *30 gennaio 1896. Ventesimo anniversario della Consacrazione episcopale di Mons. Scalabrini*, Piacenza, 1896, p. 7. Scalabrini's immediate predecessor had followed the custom, established for some time, of reducing the pastoral visit "to a bureaucratic contact with the juridical and external framework of the Mystical Body" (A. Fermi-F. Molinari, op. cit., Vol. I, Part II, p. 42).
4. Gregori, op. cit., p. 77.
5. J. B. Scalabrini, Pastoral Letter, *Per la visita pastorale*, Nov. 4, 1876, pp. 19, 17, 8.
6. P. Piacenza in *Il Giubileo Episcopale*, June 16, 1900, n. 6.
7. Gregori, op. cit., p. 81.
8. J. B. Scalabrini to Bishop Bonomelli, June 17, 1884 (Abba).
9. A. Bracchi, witness, *Processus*, iuxta 4, p. 146.
10. P. Agazzi, witness, *Processus*, iuxta 14, p. 148.
11. *Commemorazione*, Basilica of San Antonino, in *Trent'anni di Apostolato*, p. 651.
12. See *Trent'anni di Apostolato*, pp. 15-83.
13. Gregori, op. cit., p. 81.
14. J. B. Scalabrini, Pastoral Letter, *In occasione del compimento della Prima Visita Pastorale*, Sept. 26, 1880, p. 4.
15. Idem, *Disposizioni e Norme per la Terza Visita Pastorale*, May 10, 1888, pp. 3 ff.
16. G. Bonomelli to Bishop Scalabrini, Nigoline, Oct. 13, 1889; Cremona, Nov. 12, 1889 (AGS).
17. J. B. Scalabrini to Bishop Bonomelli, Nov. 4, 1889 (Abba).
18. Idem, May 21, 1890 (Abba).
19. Idem, Rabbi, Aug. 4, 1890 (Abba).
20. See Chapter V, p. 100.
21. *L'Amico del Popolo*, Oct. 29, 1890.
22. Ibid.
23. J. B. Scalabrini to Bishop Bonomelli, Jan. 27, 1896 (Abba).
24. Idem, Pomaro, Nov. 9, 1896 (Abba).
25. Idem, July 15, 1903 (Abba).
26. Idem, Caverzago Val Trebbia, Aug. 8, 1902 (Abba).
27. Idem, Piacenza, Aug. 11, 1903 (Abba).
28. Idem, Trevozzo, Oct. 4, 1903 (Abba).
29. Idem, *Circolare per la Sesta Visita Pastorale*, May 5, 1905.
30. A. Cavagna, *Un Vescovo tra due epoche*, Milan, 1963, p. 164.
31. J. B. Scalabrini, First Pastoral Letter, *Al Clero e al popolo*, Jan. 30, 1876, p. 5.
32. A. Bracchi, witness, *Processus, cop. publ.*, iuxta 14, f. 468 r.
33. J. B. Scalabrini, Pentecostal Discourse, 1895.
34. Idem, Pastoral Letter, *Communicazione dell'Enciclica, Supremi Apostolatus*, Sept. 16, 1883, pp. 3-4.
35. Idem, to Bishop Bonomelli, Aug. 16, 1887 (Abba).
36. *L'Amico del Popolo*, June 13, 1894.
37. A. Bracchi, witness, *Processus*, iuxta 4, p. 16.
38. *Synodus Placentina Secunda, Pars IV, cap. 4*, nn. 10-12, Piacenza, 1893, pp. 98-99.
39. J. B. Scalabrini to a Bishop, Feb. 22, 1904 (note in AGS).
40. Idem, Pastoral Letter, *Il prete cattolico*, 1892, pp. 38-39.
41. *Synodus Placentina Tertia, Monitiones*, Piacenza, 1900, n. 11, p. 213.
42. F. Torta, witness, *Processus*, iuxta 55, p. 128.
43. C. Mangot, witness, *Processus*, ibid., iuxta 19, p. 7.
44. F. Calzinari, witness, ibid., iuxta 35, p. 213.
45. G. Cardinali, witness, *Processus*, iuxta 28, p. 99.
46. L. Mondini, witness, ibid., iuxta 40, p. 56; iuxta 35, p. 50.
47. F. Gregori, witness, ibid., iuxta 53, p. 194.
48. G. B. Nasalli Rocca, witness, ibid., iuxta 43, p. 265.
49. See Chapter V, pp. 103-107.
50. L. Bertola, witness, *Processus, cop. publ.*, f. 719 v.
51. A. Ghizzoni, witness, ibid., iuxta 38, p. 276.

52. L. Mondini, witness, ibid., iuxta 25, pp. 50-51.
53. Idem, iuxta 38, pp. 53-54.
54. H. De Thierry to Bishop Scalabrini, Feb. 17, 1901 (AGS).
55. C. Squeri, witness, *Processus*, iuxta 3, pp. 285-286.
56. J. B. Scalabrini to Bishop Mangot, Bento Gonçalves, Oct. 12, 1904, (AGS).
57. G. Cardinali, witness, *Processus* iuxta 38, p. 104.
58. L. Tammi, witness, ibid., p. 299.
59. G. Cardinale, witness, ibid., iuxta 19 and 40, pp. 94 and 105.
60. F. Calzinari, witness, ibid., iuxta 35, p. 213.
61. J. B. Scalabrini to the Prefect of Piacenza (undated note, AGS).
62. J. B. Scalabrini, *Lettera di communicazione dell' Enciclica Etsi Nos.*, 1882, p. 15.
63. *Synodus Placentina Secunda*, Pars III, cap. I, nn. 17-19, Piacenza, 1893, pp. 57-58.
64. J. B. Scalabrini, Christmas Discourse, 1885. The Italian Protestant churches, especially the Evangelicals, at that time were noted for the virulence of their anti-papal and anti-Catholic propaganda, in which they were supported by the Liberal governments.
65. J. B. Scalabrini, New Years Day Discourse, 1886.
66. See Lenten Pastoral Letter, 1888: "It is certain that the ways of God are not our ways, Beloved Brethren, and that among the dissident churches, the Catholic Church has, Children, if not in fact, at least in desire, generous souls, worthy to have been born within the fold of unity and who perhaps already belong to it through invisible, hidden bonds known only to God" (p. 45). Similarly for the Orthodox: "Separated from the body of the Church, they belong to its soul...; when the great law of evangelical charity is better understood and practiced by all..., the universal Shepherd will see with glad surprise a great number of sheep who belonged to him there where perhaps the eye of man saw only wolves. Then East and West will embrace as brothers in the same sanctuary and St. Sophia in Constantinople will echo with the *Te Deum*" (idem, Pastoral Letter, *La Chiesa Cattolica*, Jan. 25, 1888, 2nd ed., pp. 45-46).
67. Idem, Epiphany Discourse, 1895.
68. Idem, Pastoral Letter, *Communicazione dell' Enciclica Humanum Genus*, June 1, 1884, pp. 14-15.
69. Idem, Epiphany Discourse, 1895.
70. F. Gregori, witness, *Processus* iuxta 20, p. 178.
71. L. Mondini, witness, ibid., p. 43; E. Preti, witness, ibid., p. 71; F. Torta, witness, ibid., p. 117. The latter confirmed that the Bishop was disposed to help Miraglia financially if there was need. He had hoped, perhaps not without foundation, to convince the schismatic with kindness, so that he disapproved, as contrary to his plan, the public intervention of the thirteen priests, who had acted independently of the diocesan authority and contrary to the prescriptions of the Synod: "It is certain that if Canon Rossi had not spoiled the plan of prudent reserve with his ill-advised and ill-fated letter to the civil authorities, the whole thing would have ended quietly and Miraglia would have left. Miraglia himself has said this to several persons" (J. B. Scalabrini to Card. Rampolla, Dec. 19, 1895; to Canon G. B. Rossi, Aug. 29, 1895, note in AVP).
72. Deposition given by J. B. Scalabrini, at home, for the Miraglia trial, 1896, pp. 1-6 (note in AGS).
73. Decree of the Inquisition (June 13, 1900) excommunicating Miraglia (AVP).
74. See G. Randini Tedeschi, witness, *Processus, cop. publ.*, iuxta 20, f. 368 r.; G. Squeri, witness, ibid., p. 162.
75. See Chapter VIII, pp. 162-164.
76. See the witnesses quoted above and the journalist E. Galimberti, *Processus*, iuxta 20, p. 199.
77. J. B. Scalabrini to Bishop Bonomelli, Pomaro, Nov. 9, 1895 (Abba).
78. Idem, Piacenza, Feb. 21, 1896 (Abba).
79. Idem, Holy Thursday, 1896 (Abba).
80. L. Cella, witness, *Processus*, iuxta 20, p. 202.
81. F. Torta, witness, ibid., p. 117.
82. L. Mondini, witness, ibid., p. 44.

83. F. Torta, witness, ibid., iuxta 30, p. 120.
84. E. Ottolenghi, witness, *Processus, cop. publ.,* f. 689 r.
85. L. Mondini, witness, ibid., p. 44.
86. G. Cardinali, witness, ibid., p. 95.
87. *Documenta vitae spiritualis,* Aug. 28, 1896 and Aug. 1900 *Processus,* pp. 328 and 330.
88. G. Cardinali, witness, *Processus,* iuxta 46, p. 106.
89. *Synodus Placentina Secunda, Pars III, caput I,* n. 12, Piacenza, 1893, p. 55. See E. Caccialanza, witness, *Processus,* iuxta 46, p. 71, typescript.
90. See Witnesses III, X, XIV, XV, XVII, XXXV, XLIV, LI, etc., *Processus,* iuxta 46.
91. J. B. Scalabrini, Sermon for the inauguration of an organ (notes).
92. See n. 98, below.
93. *Synodus Placentina Secunda, Pars III, Caput II,* Piacenza, 1893, pp. 62-65.
94. Ibid., *Pars IV, caput VII,* n. 15, p. 113.
95. See Witnesses III, IV, XLV, XXII, XXXII, etc., *Processus,* iuxta 46.
96. L. Mondini, witness, ibid., p. 59; E. Morisi, witness, ibid., p. 143.
97. J. B. Scalabrini, Lenten Pastoral Letter, 1904, *Come santificare le feste,* Avvisi, p. 39.
98. J. B. Scalabrini to the Benedictines, Apr. 10, 1904 (note in AGS). He favored the then young Father Lorenzo Perosi who, on the occasion of the Bishop's episcopal jubilee, performed the oratorio *Il Natale* three times in the Municipal Theatre of Piacenza. From Rome the composer wrote to Scalabrini expressing his happiness at having participated in the jubilee celebration and his happy memory of "the fatherly and affectionate kindness" with which he had surrounded him during his stay in Piacenza (L. Perosi to Bishop Scalabrini, June 21, 1901, AGS).

His rules for church music were "translated into French and published in the review of sacred music in Liege" (*Courrier de St. Grègoire,* November, 1895) *(30 gennaio 1896. Ventesimo anniversario della Consacrazione epsicopale di Mons. Scalabrini,* Piacenza, 1893, p. 77).
99. *Synodus Placentina Secunda, Pars III, caput V,* n. 7, Piacenza, 1893, p. 77.
100. Ibid., n. 14, p. 78.
101. Gregori, op. cit., p. 595.
102. See *Appendix ad Breviarium Romanum seu Officia propria Ecclesiae Placentinae,* approved by Leo XIII and by the Sacred Congregation of Rites, Sept. 9, 1883 and Feb. 4, 1884 (AVP).
103. V. Pancotti, *Mons. G. B. Scalabrini nella luce della storia,* Piacenza, 1930, p. 11.
104. L. Bertola, witness, *Processus, cop. publ.,* iuxta 18, f. 719 r.
105. See F. Torta's defense of Scalabrini (*Processus,* iuxta 43,, pp. 125-126). The pamphlet quoted above, *30 gennaio 1896*...says: "In fact, the motivation and organization of the project was considered so wise that the reigning Pontiff, (Leo XIII) asked for another copy for the Archbishop of Perugia, so that a similar reorganization might be carried out there" (p. 14).
106. J. B. Scalabrini, Pastoral Letter, *Pel nostro Duomo,* Feb. 9, 1894, p. 4. Some restorations had already been started, due especially to Canon G. B. Rossi, at considerable expense, but without an organized plan (See L. Tagliaferri, *La Cattedrale di Piacenca,* Piacenza, 1964).
107. Ibid., pp. 6-7.
108. L. Beltrami in *Il Corriere della Sera* quoted in *Trent'anni di Apostolato,* pp. 125-127.
109. C. Nava, quoted in *Trent'anni di Apostolato,* p. 123.
110. J. B. Scalabrini, *Circolare per la conservazione dei monumenti e altre opere d'arte,* Mar. 22, 1879. Scalabrini generously helped various artists. The most conspicuous example is his interest in the young Alessandro Moretti, whose story was carried in the *Provincia di Como.* The article recounted Moretti's poor childhood and the fact that when he got to Piacenza, Bishop Scalabrini noted "his extraordinary talent for sculpture...and helped him in every way, persuading him to study and to create." Moretti won success as a sculptor of portrait busts, and he kept up his correspondence with Scalabrini, often mentioning his gratitude for the kindness he had received at his hands (See Correspondence between A. Moretti and Bishop Scalabrini, AGS).
111. E. Sanguinetti, *Celebrazione del 50°,* pp. 236-237.

112. J. B. Scalabrini, Lenten Pastoral Letter, *Santificare le feste*, 1903, pp. 25,   26, 30.
113. Idem, Lenten Pastoral Letter, *Come santificare le feste*, 1904, pp. 6, 23.
114. *Synodus Placentina Tertia*, Piacenza, 1900, pp. 143 ff.
115. F. Torta, *Processus*, iuxta 38, p. 122.
116. J. B. Scalabrini to Msgr. Mangot, Alfredo Chaves, Oct. 4, 1904 (AGS).
117. L. Mondini, witness, *Processus*, iuxta 38, p. 54.
118. A. Carini, witness, *Processus*, cop. publ., f. 433 r.
119. E. Caccialanza, witness, ibid., F. 225 v.
120. J. B. Scalabrini to Msgr. Mangot, Bardi, May 28, 1891 (AGS).
121. Idem, Borgotaro, June 27, 1904 (AGS).
122. *Il Catechista Cattolico*, June 5, 1878.
123. F. Lotteri, witness, *Processus*, iuxta 25, p. 242.
124. L. Tammi, witness, ibid., iuxta, 30, p. 298.
125. See Scalabrini's discourses for All Saints Day, 1891, 1897, 1903.
126. Gregori, op. cit., p. 115.
127. *Synodus Placentina Secunda*, Piacenza, 1893, pp. 405 ff. The list forms an appendix to the
     Second Synod, and includes historical information associated with the reform of the
     Proper of the Saints of the church of Piacenza. Msgr. Piacenza, whose work Pius X
     later used for the reform of the Roman Breviary, was the principal collaborator.
128. G. Polledri, witness, *Processus*, cop. publ., iuxta 30, f. 590 v.
129. Gregori, op. cit., p. 119.
130. J. B. Scalabrini, Discourse for All Saints Day, 1903.
131. E. Caccialanza, witness, *Processus*, cop. publ., iuxta 30, f. 221 v.
132. C. Mangot, witness, ibid., pp. 13-14.
133. L. Mondini, witness, ibid., iuxta 25, p. 45.
134. Witnesses IX, XII, XVII, XXI, XXXIII, etc., ibid. iuxta 14.
135. Quoted by L. Cornaggia Medici in *Un profilo di Mons. Scalabrini*, Rome, 1930, p. 5.
136. L. Orione, witness, *Processus*, iuxta 25, p. 290.
137. S. Piccinelli, witness, *Processus*, cop. publ., f. 911 r.
138. *La Lega di Messina*, Oct. 5, 1889.
139. Quoted by *La Perseveranza*, Apr. 17, 1891.

Chapter VI — SCALABRINI AS ADMINISTRATOR

1. G. Semeria, *Mons. G. B. Scalabrini*, Piacenza, 1905, pp. 9-11.
2. *In memoriam, La solenne traslazione della salma di Mons. G. B. Scalabrini*, Piacenza, 1909,
   p. 18.
3. E. Sanguinetti, in *Celebrazioni del 50°*, pp. 239-240.
4. E. Martini, witness, *Processus*, cop. publ., iuxta 43, f. 205 r. See statements of Witnesses
   VII, XXXIII, XXXIV, etc., iuxta 43.
5. A. Carini, witness, ibid., f. 434 r.
6. E. Morisi, witness, ibid., p. 42.
7. F. Torta, witness, ibid., p. 124.
8. J. B. Scalabrini to Bishop Bonomelli, Nov. 11, 1881 (Abba).
9. C. Mangot, witness, *Processus*, iuxta 26, p. 11.
10. See statements of Witnesses VII, IX, XII, etc., ibid.
11. Tondini to Bishop Scalabrini, Turin, June 8, 1888 (AGS).
12. L. Mondini, witness, *Processus*, iuxta 41, p. 57; see Witnesses XI, XXII, XXXII, ibid.
13. G. B. Nasalli Rocca, witness, ibid., iuxta 42, p. 264.
14. *Vita e virtù del S. d. D. Mons. G. B. Scalabrini*, Bassano del Grappa, 1936, pp. 82-83.
15. L. Mondini, witness, *Processus*, iuxta 43, p. 57. During his thirty years as bishop he main-
    tained cordial relations with about forty cardinals and a hundred bishops. In addition to
    those already mentioned, those closest to him among the cardinals were Capecelatro, Di
    Canossa, Moretti, Galeati, Czacki, Schiaffino, Buasa, Galimberti, Svampa, Richelmy,
    Borromeo, as well as Cardinal Sarto and the future Pope Benedict XV. There were also the

cardinals he had met during his journeys in France and the Americas, especially Card. Gibbons and Archbishops Ireland, Quigley and Corrigan. His friendships among the bishops included Porrati of Bobbio, Foschi of Perugia, Fiorini of Pontremoli, Sarti of Guastalla, Morganti of Ravenna. He also numbered many friends among the ecclesiastical scholars of the time: Mercier, then rector of the University of Louvain, Stoppani, Arosio, Fathers Cornoldi, Lepidi and Torregrossa and many others. Friends in public life included Toniolo, Cantù, Fogazzaro, De Gubernatis, Crispolti, Soderini, Rezzara, Conti, Schiaparelli, Lampertico, Villari, and others.

16. F. Gregori, witness, *Processus*, iuxta 45, p. 192; D. F. Lotteri, p. 245; Witnesses IV, IX, XI, XXXIII, XXXIV, iuxta 45.
17. G. Bonomelli, "1 Giugno," *L'Emigrato Italiano*, June, 1906, p. 75. Scalabrini's characteristic sincerity and candor compelled him to speak frankly: "What are you doing? What are you thinking about? You are intelligent, but you don't understand...One would say you act first and think afterwards." That's how it occurred on the occasion of the 20th of September. When the Servant of God went to Cremona, he was surprised to see the tricolor waving from the bishop's residence. As soon as he saw Bonomelli he expressed his surprise and disapproval, pointing out that in addition to the seriousness of the matter he was also prejudicing his dignity as a bishop. (L. Mondini, witness, *Processus*, iuxta 45, p. 58.) Leo XIII was also convinced that Scalabrini's influence on his friend was all to the good, and "out of esteem for the Servant of God he charged him many times, sending him a special envoy (Bishop Giacomo della Chiesa), to moderate the too lively and explicit behavior of the Bishop of Cremona." (F. Lotteri, witness, ibid., p. 245.)
18. A. Ghizzoni, witness, ibid., iuxta 44, p. 278.
19. A. Buzzetti, witness, *Processus*, cop. publ., iuxta 44, f. 786 r.
20. G. Squeri, witness, ibid., p. 166.
21. C. Mangot, witness, ibid., p. 16; G. Cardinali, witness, p. 106; A. Carini, witness, *Processus, cop. publ.*, f. 434 r. See Chapter III, pp. 50-51.
22. J. B. Scalabrini to Father Francesco Zaboglio, Mar. 29, 1891 (ASMC).
23. J. B. Scalabrini, Pentecost Discourse, 1881.
24. Idem, Epiphany Discourse, 1880.
25. L. Tammi, witness, *Processus*, iuxta 26, p. 296.
26. E. Morisi, witness, ibid., iuxta 53, p. 144.
27. *Il Piccolo*, quoted by L. Corneggia Medici, in *Un Profilo di Mons. Scalabrini*, Rome, 1930, p. 9.
28. L. Orione, witness, *Processus*, iuxta 26, p. 292.
29. Gregori, op. cit., p. 152.
30. J. B. Scalabrini to Bishop Bonomelli, Dec. 30, 1882 (Abba).
31. Idem to Card. Di Pietro, Feb. 11, 1897. See also Scalabrini's letter to Msgr. G. De Lai. Oct. 11, 1897 (Note in AVP and AGS).
      With respect to Scalabrini's views on modernism, several writers recently have quoted Fogazzaro's "Una Visita a Mons. Scalabrini," in *Rassegna Nazionale*, July 1, 1905, p. 10: "He did not absolve Loisy from the charge that he lacked prudence, but he knew him personally and praised his talent, his learning, and his priestly integrity. Certainly he did not adopt the most recent theories of the author of *L'Evangile et l'Eglise* but he foresaw that some of those theories, which seem reckless and offensive today, would seem otherwise in a not too distant future and would be accepted by most. He foresaw a rapid diffusion of the new ideas among the young clergy. He spoke to them with a kindly tolerance, as one who does not wish to say that he accepts them but at the same time is disinclined to say he fears them."
      It is interesting to compare this passage with Fogazzaro's first account of the visit in a letter to his daughter: "Loisy is talked about...'He has been imprudent, yes. After all, what seems bold today everyone will be thinking in twenty years. — Under Leo, I had something to do with preventing his condemnation.' — Evolution is mentioned: 'I once went to Como during a congress of Catholic scientists...The other began to speak of evolution and a storm broke. When he had finished I took the liberty of saying a word or two myself, as some one who knew nothing about it, and I spoke of good Christians who

are and remain Christian and support that theory...' — I then ventured to say to the bishop that perhaps on the subject of evolution it was understandable that a churchman had to be more prudent than a layman and be somewhat reserved. — 'But why?' — the Bishop exclaimed. 'Must we always bring up the rear?' " (A. Fogazzaro to his daughter Gina, Feb. 19, 1905; the letter is quoted in O. Morra, *Fogazzaro nel suo piccolo mondo*, Bologna, 1960, pp. 556-557). P. Scoppola (*Crisi modernista e rinnovamento cattolico in Italia*, Bologna, 1961, p. 168) has this comment: "Sympathy and detachment, then, which is a sign of prudence matured through difficult years and painful conflicts and perhaps also an indication of a certain lack of understanding of the deeper motives of the crisis." There might also be reasons for certain reservations regarding Fogazzaro's acount since other parts of the same article in the *Rassegna* are literary additions (see the account of Scalabrini's visit to the Indians in Brazil, p. 268). Scalabrini died before the first pangs of the modernist crisis were felt, and he was fearful above all of the "plague of insubordination on the part of the clergy," the cause of which he believed was in poor training. "The period we are passing through is worse than it seems," he wrote. "Something malignant is working among the Clergy, not yet very well defined, and for the moment only the boldest are revealing themselves...Perhaps we Bishops have been too restrictive of individual liberty and detailed discipline administered like pills has lost the quality of austere grandeur it once had...Then, philosophy and Catholic social action, which are of such great value, have served as a cloak for some, a defense for others and a source of excitement for several, etc. etc....God help us. It is truly a time to pray hard and to be prepared for everything." (Bishop Bonomelli, Jan. 24, 1897 Abba). His views on the progress being made in various studies was quite different: "I do not entirely share your fears with respect to the biblical controversies. It is Jesus Christ who governs the Church, which always profits from the intellectual labor of her sons" (Idem, Feb. 16, 1904, Abba).

32. His firmness was criticized for being excessive with respect to theatrical productions during Lent. (See F. Lotteri, witness, *Processus*, iuxta 24, pp. 241-242). His actions should be viewed in the context of his struggles with the civil authorities who were promoting such productions in Lent for a purpose. These episodes are reminiscent of St. Charles Borromeo's problems with the Spanish authorities, who organized theatricals during Lent as a weapon against him.

33. C. Riva, in *Aspetti della cultura cattolica nell'età di Leone XIII*, Rome, 1961, p. 238.

34. Msgr. G. B. Vinati (1847-1917), cofounder of *Divus Thomas*, was appointed Vicar General in 1896, and Capitular Vicar at the death of Bishop Scalabrini. In 1906 he was named Bishop of Bosa in Sardinia where he became known as the "holy Bishop." He resigned from his diocese in 1916 for reasons of health and died in Rome in 1917.

35. *L'Osservatore Cattolico*, Sept. 3-4, 1881.

36. Ibid., Oct. 1-2, 1881.

37. J. B. Scalabrini to the Card. Prefect of the Sacred Congregation of the Council, July 5, 1895 (note in AVP).

38. G. Cardinali, witness, *Processus*, iuxta 22, p. 97.

39. L. Tammi, witness, ibid., pp. 295-296.

40. F. Torta, witness, ibid., p. 118.

41. G. Dodici, witness, *Processus*, *cop. publ.*, iuxta 22, f. 161 r.

42. G. Squeri, witness, ibid., p. 163.

43. G. B. Nasalli Rocca, witness, ibid., p. 260.

44. J. B. Scalabrini to the Card. Prefect of the Sacred Congregation of the Council, July 7, 1895 (note in AVP).

45. Idem to Bishop Bonomelli, Sept. 11, 1881 (Abba).

46. Idem, Sept. 22, 1881 (Abba).

47. *L'Osservatore Cattolico*, Oct. 1-2, 1881.

48. *La Verità* (Piacenza), Oct. 4, 1881. The protest is dated Oct. 3, 1881.

49. J. B. Scalabrini to Leo XIII, Sept. 26, 1881 (note in AGS).

50. J. B. Scalabrini to Card. Jacobini, Oct. 8, 1881 (note in AGS).

51. Card. Jacobini to Bishop Bonomelli, Nov. 8, 1881 and Nov. 12, 1881 (AGS).

52. *L'Osservatore Cattolico*, Nov. 10-11, 1881.

53. Note in AGS. It is undated but it is to be placed between the Nov. 12, 1881,, the date of Card. Jacobini's letter, and Nov. 22, according to a letter from Scalabrini to Bonomelli of the latter date (Abba).
54. J. B. Scalabrini to Bishop Bonomelli, Piacenza, Nov. 30, 1881, (Abba).
55. Idem to Msgr. Boccali, Secret Chamberlain of Leo XIII, Nov. 29, 1881 (note in AGS).
56. We are speaking here only of Bishop Scalabrini, but Bishop Bonomelli was involved in the same question. See G. Astori, *Mons. Bonomelli, Mons. Scalabrini e Don Davide Albertario*, Brescia, 1939; G. Pecora, *Don Davide Albertario*, Turin, 1934; L. Cornaggia Medici, *Antesignani della Conciliazione*, Fidenza, 1936; C. Bellò, *Geremia Bonomelli*, Brescia, 1961, pp. 60-76; Gregori, op. cit., pp. 125-145; G. Grabinski, *Storia documentata del giornale L'Osservatore Cattolico di Milano*, Milan, 1887; P. Bondioli, *Bonomelli e Albertario in documenti inediti della Segreteria di Stato di Leone XIII (1881-1884)*, in *Memorie storiche della diocesi di Milano*, vol. V, Milan, 1958, pp. 39-110.
57. Brief of Leo XIII to Bishop Scalabrini, Oct. 10, 1882, carried in *Il Catechista Cattolico*, Nov., 1882, pp. 65-67.
58. J. B. Scalabrini to Bishop Bonomelli, Mar. 2, 1883 (Abba).
59. Idem to Card. Jacobini, Mar. 15, 1883 (note in AGS).
60. Idem, Apr. 8, 1883 (note in AGS).
61. *L'Osservatore Cattolico*, Apr. 5-6, 1883.
62. J. B. Scalabrini to Card. L. Jacobini, Apr. 8, 1883 (note in AGS).
63. Card. L. Jacobini to Bishop Scalabrini, June 19, 1883 (AGS).
64. See G. Pecora, *Don Davide Albertario*, Turin, 1934, pp. 181-182.
65. *La Voce del Paese* (Piacenza), June 28, 1883.
66. **See Chapter XXIV, pp. 406-407.**
67. J. B. Scalabrini, *Discorso per il giubileo episcopale di Mons. Bonomelli*, Cremona, 1896, p. 10.
68. J. B. Scalabrini to Bishop Bonomelli, July 1, 1883 (Abba).
    In the Seminario Urbano, along with the dismissal of the Rector, Bishop Scalabrini was constrained to take other serious measures to heal the discord and confusion there. He had the consolation of seeing his actions bear good fruit. (See Idem, Dec. 30, 1882 Abba).
69. Idem, Sept. 17, 1883 (Abba).
70. Idem, to the Card. Prefect of the Sacred Congregation of the Council, July 5, 1895 (note in AVP).
71. R. Orfel, "La morte di Vittorio Emanuele II e i cattolici," in *Vita e Pensiero*, June, 1961, pp. 391-392.
72. F. Cattivelli, witness, *Processus, cop. publ.*, iuxta 53, f. 393 vr.
73. L. Mondini, witness, ibid, iuxta 38, p. 54.
74. Gregori, op. cit., p. 86. To discourage other outbursts of "nationalist clergy," which had often occurred during the tenure of his predecessor, he threatened to place the cathedral under interdict.
75. F. Torta, witness, *Processus*, iuxta 38, p. 122.
76. Gregori, op. cit., pp. 86-87. The chalice was sent on Feb. 4 not Feb. 6.
77. J. B. Scalabrini to the Minister of Grace and Justice (undated note in AGS).
78. Idem to the Prefect of Piacenza, Jan. 26, 1897 (note in AGS).
79. G. Squeri, witness, *Processus*, iuxta 53, p. 169.
80. A. Carini, witness, *Processus, cop. publ.*, iuxta 53, f. 437 v.
81. L. Mondini, witness, ibid., p. 62.
82. Gregori, op. cit., p. 227; he is quoting the opinion of the *Osservatore Cattolico*, June 14-15, 1888.
83. L. Cela, witness, *Processus*, iuxta 53, p. 207.
84. L. Tammi, witness, ibid., iuxta 15, p. 53.
85. A. Scarani, witness, *Processus, cop. publ.*, iuxta 53, f. 415 v.
86. G. Borelli, "Il clero cattolico e le condizioni politico-sociali d'Italia. Un colloquio con Mons. Scalabrini," in *L'Alba* (Milan), July 15, 1900.
87. F. Giarelli in *Il Caffaro* (Genoa) quoted by Gregori, op. cit., p. 323.
88. Gregori, op. cit., p. 323-324. See Witnesses II, III, IV, V, XVI, XVIII, etc., *Processus*,

iuxta 53.

89. J. B. Scalabrini to Bishop Bonomelli, July 7, 1895 (Abba).
90. Gregori, op. cit., p. 260.
91. See Chapter XIV, p. 247 ff.
92. *Synodus Placentina 1879, De Sacramento Ordinis*, n. 1, Piacenza, 1880, p. 104.
93. J. B. Scalabrini to the rector of the Seminary of Bedonia, Jan. 26, 1888 (Seminary Archives).
94. Idem, Feb. 16, 1885 (ibid.).
95. A. De Martini, witness, *Processus*, iuxta 25, p. 82.
96. E. Preti, witness, ibid., iuxta 25, pp. 71-72; iuxta 20, p. 70.
97. G. Cardinali, witness, ibid., iuxta 25, p. 98.
98. J. B. Scalabrini, address to his priests, 1896.
99. L. Tammi, witness, *Processus*, iuxta 15, p. 294. Unfortunately a kind of master diary, in which Scalabrini noted down anything that might be useful for the administration of the diocese, has been destroyed, perhaps because of its confidential nature. (See the testimony of Cardinal Nasalli Rocca, p. 397.

Gregori recorded a few notes that escaped destruction. For example: "Father...is suffering from scruples. He spends a great part of the day and night reciting his breviary. I bade him...One must keep this in mind in order to cheer him up when the need arises, and in order to have some one write to him from time to time. He deserves it, and if he recovers from this malady he can do a great deal of good." — "I esteem and am very fond of the Archpriest of...but he seems to me a man who is not very content with himself. I did not find in him that simple joy that shines forth from holy pastors on similar occasions. It may be his personality but it could also be that something is bothering or worrying him. However, he deserves to be comforted; he can do a great deal of good, and is doing so." — "I hope I'm mistaken but it seems to me that the pastor of..., who is not a bad man, is just doing the job for a living, and everything there suffers from the character of its leader. When the post is vacant, an active priest must be provided for it, one who is filled with the spirit of Jesus Christ." — "I found everything in such disorder, and instruction so poor, that I did not hesitate to say in public that if things continued as they were, pastor and parishioners would all end up in the house of the devil. Before leaving, I spoke privately with the pastor and he promised he would carry out my directives." — "There is in this parish a priest from the...diocese who is getting himself talked about. I suspended him, urging him to mend his ways. I hope he will...." "May the Most Holy Virgin bless and fulfill the desires of this Shepherd." (Gregori, op. cit., pp. 590-591).
100. A. Carini, witness, *Processus, cop. publ.*, iuxta 41, f. 433 v.; G. B. Nasalli Rocca, iuxta 43, p. 265.
101. J. B. Scalabrini to Bishop Mascaretti (undated note in AGS).
102. N. Bruni to the editor of *Giubileo Episcopale di Mons. Scalabrini*, Dec. 8, 1900 (published in the same journal).
103. *La Voce Cattolica*, June 20, 1901.
104. *L'Amico del Popolo*, April 9, 1896.
105. Ibid., Feb. 1, 1896.
106. J. B. Scalabrini, *Per il suo Guibileo Episcopale*, Dec. 8, 1900.
107. Ibid., p. 4.
108. G. B. Nasalli Rocca, witness, *Processus*, Iuxta 59, p. 268.
109. Note, unaddressed (AGS), probably to Card. Agliardi.
110. J. B. Scalabrini to Bishop Bonomelli, Mar. 3, 1901 (Abba).
111. Idem, Jan. 17, 1904 (Abba).
112. *La Stampa*, Jan. 22, 1904.
113. *Documenta vitae spiritualis, Processus*, pp. 328, 330.
114. J. B. Scalabrini to Bishop Bonomelli, Feb. 16, 1904 (Abba).
115. Gregori, op. cit., p. 535.
116. A. Samorè in *Celebrazioni del 50°*, p. 48.

Chapter VII — SOCIAL WORKS

1. J. B. Scalabrini, *Il prete cattolico*, 1892, pp. 21-22.

2. Idem, Pastoral Letter, *Intorno all'istruzione dei Sordo-muti*, Sept. 8, 1880, passim. See *Synodus Placentina* 1879, *De Scholis Doctrinae Christianae*, n. 15, Piacenza, 1880, p. 32.
3. Idem, Discourse on the Trial of the Deafmutes, Oct. 6, 1888.
4. G. Ceruti, *I Sordo-muti e Mons. Scalabrini*, *L'Emigrato Italiano*, June 1913, pp. 4-6.
5. *Enciclopedia Cattolica*, v. *Balestra Don Serafino* (vol. II, col. 747).
6. J. B. Scalabrini, Pastoral Letter, *Intorno all'istruzione dei Sordo-muti*, p. 16.
7. Idem, Discourse on the Trial of the Deafmutes, Oct. 9, 1886.
8. Idem, Discourse on the Trial of the Deafmutes, Oct. 6, 1888.
9. The Servant of God, Mother Rosa Gattorno, foundress of the Daughters of St. Anne, had already started working on the education of deaf and dumb girls and had a number with her in Piacenza (See A. Fiocchi, *La serva di Dio Rosa Gattorno*, Rome, 1937-41, pp. 170-171).
10. See the tributes in the anticlerical paper of Piacenza, *Il Progresso*, quoted in *Trent'anni di Apostolato*, pp. 85-89.
11. J. B. Scalabrini, Pastoral Letter, *Intorno all'istruzione dei Sordo-muti*, p. 17.
12. *L'Amico del Popolo*, Feb. 6,, 1886.
13. J. B. Scalabrini, Discourse on the Trial of the Deafmutes Oct. 6, 1888; *Regolamento delle Sordomute Terziarie;* Letters from the Third Order of Deafmutes to Bishop Scalabrini, Dec. 19, 1895, and Apr. 13, 1900 (AGS).
14. Gregori, op. cit., p. 111.
15. G. Ceruti, "I Sordo-muti e Mons. Scalabrini," in *L'Emigrato Italiano*, June, 1913, p. 5.
16. J. B. Scalabrini to Msgr. Mangot, Sao Paulo, July 14, 1904 (AGS).
17. *L'Emigrato Italiano*, Nov., 1906, p.. 164.
18. G. Ceruti, art, cit., pp. 5-6.
19. J. B. Scalabrini, Pastoral Letter, *Intorno all'istruzione dei Sordo-muti*, p. 18.
20. Idem, Discourse on the Trial of the Deafmutes, Oct. 9, 1886.
21. The Prefect of Piacenza (V. Tacconi) to Bishop Scalabrini, Oct. 12, 1880 (AGS).
22. G. Pinazzi to Bishop Scalabrini, Aug. 19, 1885 (AGS).
23. F. Molinari, *Mons. Francesco Torta apostolo della carità*, Turin, 1963.
24. F. Torta, *Cenni storici intorno all'Istituto dei Sordomuti alla Madonna della Bomba, con appendice sul nuovo Istituto dei Ciechi*, Piacenza, 1915, p. 7.
25. Ibid., p. 34.
26. Ibid., p. 55.
27. F. Molinari, op. cit., pp. 113-128.
28. E. Morisi, *Brevi cenni storici dell'Istituto Scrofolosi*, Piacenza, 1919; C. Spallazzi, witness, *Processus*, iuxta 36, p. 33.
29. *La Libertà* (Piacenza), July 6, 1903; *L'Osservatore Cattolico*, Aug. 28, 1903.
30. J. B. Scalabrini, *Circolare ai Vicari Foranei, etc., per una statistica dei Mondariso*, Aug. 22, 1903.
31. *Il Lavoro* (Piacenza), Dec. 21, 1903.
32. *Memoriale del Comitato dell'Opera dei Mondariso all'On. Consiglio del Lavoro*, Piacenza, Jan. 31, 1904.
33. Gregori, op. cit., p. 540.
34. F. Vistalli, *Giuseppe Toniolo*, Rome, 1954, p. 556.

Chapter VIII — THE LABOR PROBLEM

1. G. Bonomelli in *Il Monumento ricordo a Mons. Scalabrini, Le voci del cuore*, Como, Sept. 11, 1913.
2. Ibid.
3. See Chapter I, pp. 30-31.
4. J. B. Scalabrini, *Il Socialismo e l'azione del Clero*, 2nd ed. Turin, 1899, pp. 21-22.
5. Ibid., p. 89.
6. Ibid., pp. 37-38.
7. Ibid., p. 40.
8. Ibid., p. 81.

9. Idem, Circular Letter, *Associazione Cattoliche*, Mar. 2, 1885, p. 5.
10. Ibid., p. 4.
11. Idem, Pastoral Letter, *Unione, azione, preghiera*, May 11, 1890, pp. 5-6.
12. Idem, Pastoral Letter, *Azione Cattolica*, Oct. 16, 1896, pp. 6-7.
13. Idem, *Il Socialismo e l'azione del Clero*, p. 39.
14. Idem, Circular Letter, *Associazioni Cattoliche*, Mar. 3, 1885, p. 4.
15. See A. Cistellini, "I motivi dell'opposizione cattolica allo stato liberale," in *Vita e Pensiero*, Dec., 1959, p. 944.
16. J. B. Scalabrini, *Il Socialismo e l'azione del Clero*, 1899, p. 4.
17. Ibid., pp. 5-6.
18. Ibid., pp. 39-49.
19. See Ibid., p. 68, where he recommends socioeconomic legislation to remedy or at least lessen economic hardship, a renewal of spiritual strength through education, especially of the leaders, a strengthening of the sense of religious and civic duty, "and we shall have taken every basis for action from socialism."
20. Ibid., pp. 12-13.
21. Ibid., pp. 78-80.
22. Ibid., pp. 66-67, 75.
23. Ibid., p. 75.
24. Ibid., p. 78.
25. Ibid., p. 80. He was, however, very cautious about strikes. "Is it not one of those double-edged weapons which often wounds its user more than the one against whom it is used?" This is in the context of the government's bloody repression of strikes at that time.
26. Ibid., p. 62.
27. Ibid., pp. 81-83.
28. Ibid., pp. 85-86.
29. Ibid., pp. 76-77.
30. Ibid., pp. 81-84.
31. Ibid., pp. 85-86. Scalabrini recalled with pleasure the example of one of his young priests, who had a background of economics and social studies, and whom he sent to a country parish with the injunction to "take over all the uncultivated land of the benefice, with the free cooperation of the parishioners and transform it into a direct source of local activity and well-being." The young priest accomplished a miracle in a short time. The parishioners offered their work even on Sunday afternoons. The economic situation in the area was astonishingly changed and one day the priest returned to the bishop and said, "Bishop, I I have no more socialists in my parish. We are all well off and I am too rich." The bishop answered, "Bring me what you don't need for the use of poor seminarians, who will model themselves after you." The young priest was later decorated by the government, but according to Scalabrini "he will enjoy the greatest reward now in heaven, where God has prematurely called him. His successor continues along the lines he laid down and is giving my clergy a worthy example." (G. Borelli, "Il clero cattolico e le condizioni politico-sociali d'Italia. Un colloquio con Mons. Scalabrini," in *L'Alba* (Milan), July 15, 1900.
32. Idem, Pastoral Letter, *Per il Centenario di S. Luigi*, pp. 11-12.
33. Idem, Pastoral Letter, *Azione Cattolica*, p. 14.
34. Idem, Pastoral Letter, *Per il Cenetenario di S. Luigi*, pp. 11-12.
35. Idem, *Il Socialismo e l'azione del Clero*, p. 37.
36. Idem, Pastoral Letter, *Unione, azione, preghiera*, pp. 7-8.
37. Ibid., p. 8.
38. Idem, *Il Socialism e l'azione del Clero*, pp. 66-67. See Idem, *La premiere Croisade*, Clermont, 1895, pp. 8-9.
39. Idem, Pastoral Letter, *Unione, azione, preghiera*, pp. 8-9.
40. Ibid., pp. 9-10.
41. Idem, Pastoral Letter, *Azione Cattolica*, pp. 16-17.
42. Idem, Discourse to the Catholic Associations in San Antonio, July 4, 1883.
43. Idem, Lenten Pastoral Letter, 1893, p. 23.
44. Idem, Discourses on the First and Second Meeting of the Catholic Committees.

45. Idem, Discourse on the First Regional Meeting of the Catholic Committees, June 11, 1897.
46. Ibid. (A reference to the loss of political and territorial independence with the loss of the Papal States, and the need for "real freedom and independence" for the exercise of the Papal ministry. — Ed.)
47. Idem, Discourse on the Second Meeting of the Catholic Committees, Apr. 24, 1889.
48. Idem, Pastoral Letter, *Unione, azione, preghiera,* p. 10.
49. Idem, Discourse on the Second Meeting of the Catholic Committees, Apr. 24, 1889.
50. Idem, Circular Letter, *Associazioni Cattoliche,* Mar. 2, 1885.
51. Idem, Pastoral Letter, *Comunicazione dell'Enciclica Humanum genus,* June 1, 1884, pp. 5 and 12; *Synodus Placentina Secunda,* Pars. I, cap. III, n. 6, Piacenza, 1893, p. 34; *Avisi alla Congregazione dei Vicari Foranei,* May 13, 1903, p. 4.
52. Herein, perhaps, lies one of the reasons for certain differences with the *Opera dei Congressi,* which had the tendency, especially under Paganuzzi, to centralize and monopolize all forms of lay activity.
53. J. B. Scalabrini, *Il Socialismo e l'azione del Clero,* pp. 81-83.
54. L. Cerutti to Bishop Scalabrini, Venice, May 9, 1893 (AGS).
55. *Il Catechista Cattolico,* May, 1895: "The Bishop became their apostle." In 1897 at the second regional Catholic congress in Emilia, held in Piacenza, the principal topic was the development of rural banks. The speaker was the very active champion of this initiative, Father Giuseppe Manzini of Legnago (See *L'Amico del Popolo,* June 16, 1897).
56. J. B. Scalabrini, Lenten Pastoral Letter, 1899, p. 27.
57. G. Radini Tedeschi, witness, *Processus, cop. publ.,* iuxta 18, f. 367 r.; E. Martini, witness, iuxta 15, f. 185 r.
58. C. Spassazzi, witness, ibid., iuxta 18, pp. 23-24.
59. E. Martini, witness, ibid., *cop. publ.,* f. 185 v. See Scalabrini's Circular Letter of Dec. 25, 1890, pp. 6-7.
60. G. Cardinale, witness, ibid., p. 93.
61. E. Morisi, witness, ibid., p. 134. In the Dec. 25 Circular he recommended that the whole diocese take on the support of the *Oratorio di San Giovanni* and expressed the hope that similar institutions would be established at least in the larger towns.
62. G. Polledri, witness, ibid., *cop. publ.,* f. 585 r.
63. E. Martini, witness, ibid., iuxta 15, ff. 185 v. — 186 r. See D. Mazzadi, iuxta 18, p. 154; P. Agazzi, ibid., p. 148; A. Buzzetti, *cop. publ.,* f. 511 rv. Bishop Scalabrini, however, did not favor involvement of the clergy in strictly commercial or economic enterprises, "because, in the long view, he felt that the clergy in practice would not have a very good image... (G. Squeri, *Processus,* iuxta 18, p. 162).
64. Circular on the Episcopal Curia of Piacenza, May 15, 1902, pp. 3-4.
65. *Circolo Scalabrini di Studi Sociali,* Piacenza, June 4, 1901 (pamphlet containing the constitution of the *Circolo*). See *La Voce Cattolica* of Piacenza, June 8, 1901.
66. A. Gambasin, *Il movimento sociale nell'Opera dei Congressi,* Rome, pp. 704-705.
67. Gregori, op. cit., p. 306.
68. J. B. Scalabrini, Letter dated May 4, 1898 (note in AGS).
69. G. Ferrerio, "Mons. G. B. Scalabrini, Commemorazione," in *L'Emigrato Italiano,* July, 1906, p. 96.
70. G. Borelli, "Il clero cattolico e le condizioni politico-sociali d'Italia. Un colloquio con Mons. Scalabrini," in *L'Alba* (Milan), July 15, 1900.
71. Ibid.
72. Ibid. On Scalabrini's "conservatism" see note 115 of Chapter XVII.
73. For the earlier history of Catholic Action in the diocese of Piacenza, see op. cit., A. Fermi — F. Molinari, Vol I, Part II, pp. 167-205. The Marchese Alfonso Landi of Piacenza appears among the pioneers of the movement at the constituent meeting of the "Italian Catholic Association for the Freedom of the Church in Italy," founded by G. B. Casoni in Bologna, Dec. 3, 1865. The same Landi participated in the inauguration of the Italian Catholic Youth movement (*Gioventù Cattolica Italiana*) on June 19, 1867. The "Società Primaria Romana per gli interessi cattolici" (Principal Roman Society for Catholic Interests) had an affiliate

in Piacenza in 1871. In 1872 Bishop Ranza established the *Pio Sodalizio* (Pious Sodality) for holy days, which was suppressed soon afterwards. In 1871 the Carmelite Father Vittorio di San Giovanni Battista founded the *Circolo della Gioventù Cattolica* (Catholic Youth Circle) as an affiliate of the one in Bologna. A little earlier another Carmelite priest, Father Adeodato of Santa Croce, had started a Sunday youth center for workers' children, which was given the status of "congregation" by Bishop Ranza in 1873. The center ceased operating in 1878 when Father Adeodato resigned; it was reopened in 1890 through the efforts of Bishop Scalabrini and Msgr. Torta. In 1873 the above mentioned Father Vittorio had also founded the *Circolo della Gioventù Operaia* (Circle of Working Youth). Among the various initiatives of Bishop Ranza's episcopate the following had remained especially active: the *Obolo di San Pietro* (Peter's Pence); participation in religious manifestations whose promoter became Father Gherardo Casella, founder also of the center which from 1876 throughout Scalabrini's episcopate was the meeting place of the Catholic youth of Piacenza (ibid., p. 196).

74.   *La Verità* (Piacenza), Apr. 23, 1881. See also the issues of Apr. 24, 26 and 27.
75.   Bishop Giacomo M. Radini Tedeschi, was born in Piacenza July 22, 1857. Scalabrini sent him to study at the *Collegio Lombardo* in Rome, later ordained him and appointed him professor of canon law at the seminary of Bedonia, and soon afterwards at the *Seminario Urbano*. In 1890 Leo XIII gave him the same assignment at the Pontifical Academy of Ecclesiastics for the Nobility. With his father he supported the *Opera dei Congressi* in Piacenza, served as a member of the diocesan committee, became president of the regional Roman committee and from 1895 served as vice-president of the Permanent Committee. On Jan. 29, 1905, he was consecrated a bishop by Pope Pius X, assisted by Bishop Scalabrini and Bishop Arcangeli of Asti. Noted for his holiness, he governed the diocese of Bergamo until his death, May 22, 1914. (See A. Roncalli, *Mons. Giacomo Maria Radini Tedeschi*, 3rd. ed. Rome, 1963; F. Vistalli, *Monsignore Conte Giacomo Maria Radini Tedeschi*, Milan, 1935).
76.   See A. Gambasin, *Il movimento sociale nell'Opera dei Congressi*, Rome, 1958, pp. 130-131; D. Secco Suardo, *I Cattolici Intransigenti*, Brescia, 1962, p. 66.
77.   *L'Amico del Popolo*, Apr. 4, 1886.
78.   *Il Diritto Cattolico* (Modena), Apr. 25, 1889.
79.   Ibid.
80.   *Il Vessillo* (Cremona), Apr. 25, 1889; See *L'Amico del Popolo*, Apr. 27, 1889. At the 1892 meeting there emerged what seemed, from the beginning, the weak point in the organization and expansion of the parish committees in the diocese of Piacenza. Count Francesco Nasalli Rocca, secretary of the Diocesan Committee, thought the reasons for the poor results obtained thus far lay in the "five wounds" described by Filippo Meda: lack of harmony, scant financial resources, few members, an "indifferent or hostile clergy," legitimism. Bishop Scalabrini, who had worked so hard for the establishment of parish committees, reacted vigorously. "The word *wound*, which you have used, my dear Count, is not your own, but appears to be imposed by others. In any case it implies corruption. And that is enough to determine that it cannot in any way be attributed to my Clergy." The principal aim of the ecclesiastical mission, he continued, is the salvation of souls, and in this his clergy was second to none; in the second place the clergy also had in hand the other works desired by the Pope and called for by contemporary circumstances. "The institution and extension of the work of the Parish Committees is slow because of serious difficulties: but hope that with time all the committees will be established, and then the future will yield better and more fruitful results."
      Paganuzzi appears to have understood quite well the Bishop's thinking when he reminded some impatient member of the Committee that "the initiative for action in the diocese belongs primarily to the Bishop: and after him to the pastors of the various parishes... They alone are and must be our guide, leaders, teachers; we shall always be their disciples." (*L'Amico del Popolo*, Apr. 27-28, 1892).
81.   Gregori, op. cit., p. 537.
82.   Ibid., pp. 537-538. See ibid., p. 178.
83.   Leo XIII, Encyclical *Sapientiae Christianae*, 1890 (quoted in P. Dabin, *Insegnamenti Pon-*

tifici sull'Azione Cattolica in *Enciclopedia del Papato*, vol. II, Paoline ed., Catania, 1961, p. 1001).

84. Leo XIII, the Encyclical *Longinqua Oceani*, 1895 (ibid.).
85. J. B. Scalabrini, Pastoral Letter, *Azione Cattolica*, Oct. 16, 1896.
86. *L'Amico del Popolo*, July 25-26, 1896.
87. F. Lotteri, witness, *Processus*, iuxta 18, p. 239. "We must want what the Pope wants, and we must want it sincerely, constantly, at all costs...He desires that all the parishes in Italy have their committee, and this must be established in every parish of the diocese of Piacenza; it must not only be established, it must remain active. My words this time are not an exhortation but a *command.*" (J. B. Scalabrini, Pastoral Letter, *Azione Cattolica*, Oct. 16, 1896).
88. A. Gambasin, op. cit., p. 337.
89. See ibid., the statistical tables, pp. 611-741.
90. J. B. Scalabrini to Father Giovanni (?), Mar. 13, 1897 (AGS).
91. Idem, Pastoral Letter, *Comunicazione dell'Enciclica Etsi Nos*, Mar. 19, 1882, p. 20.
92. *Trent'anni di Apostolato*, p. 69.
93. J. B. Scalabrini, *Lettera Pastorale sull'Enciclica Immortale Dei*, Jan. 17, 1886. The quotation is from the Encyclical.
94. E. Sanguineti, *Celebrazione del 50°*, pp. 235-236.
95. J. B. Scalabrini, *Lettera Pastorale Comunicazione dell'Enciclica Etsi Nos*, Mar. 19, 1882, pp. 26-28.
96. Ibid., pp. 24-25.
97. L. G. Pelloux to Bishop Scalabrini, Feb. 9, 1899 (AGS).
98. Gregori, op. cit., p. 309.
99. Ibid., p. 310.
100. Thus the testimony of F. Torta, witness, *Processus*, iuxta 18, p. 116.
101. J. B. Scalabrini to Bishop Bonomelli, Apr. 24, 1900 (Abba).
102. F. Fonzi, "Dall'intransigentismo alla democrazia cristiana," in *Aspetti della cultura cattolica nell'età di Leone XIII*, Rome, 1961, pp. 334-335.
103. G. Borelli, art. cit.
104. F. Fonzi, op. cit., p. 339.
105. E. Manacorda, *Movimento cattolico, errori democratici e relativi doveri dei sacerdoti*, Fossano, 1897. For the Manacorda episode, see G. De Rosa, *Storia del movimento cattolico in Italia*, Vol. I, Bari, 1966, pp. 338-341.
106. J. B. Scalabrini to the President of the Board of *L'Amico del Popolo*, Centenaro, June 9, 1897 (note in AGS).
107. G. Borelli, art. cit.
108. See G. De Rosa, op. cit., p. 485.
109. A. Fogazzaro, "Una visita a Mons. Scalabrini," in *Rassegna Nazionale*, July 1, 1905, p. 10.
110. E. Martini, witness, *Processus, cop. publ.*, iuxta 15, f. 185 rv.
111. J. B. Scalabrini, *Alle cattoliche Istituzioni e Associazioni della diocesi*, Mar. 12, 1905.
112. Gregori, op. cit., p. 539.
113. F. Vistalli, *Giuseppe Toniolo*, Rome 1954, pp. 555-557.
114. D. Secco Suardo, *I cattolici intransigenti*, Brescia, 1962, p. 66.
115. See A. Gambasin, op. cit., p. 458. (*L'Opera dei Congressi* while officially professing to be non-political was working de facto and with unofficial Vatican inspiration against the government, which the Vatican considered guilty of usurping the Papal State. Scalabrini felt the demise of the Papal State was overdue and that Catholics should have participated in Italian politics through the vote and by running for office. In his view this was the way to end the hostility between government and Vatican. Hence while he was considered "transigent" regarding the government question, he was considered "conservative" vis-a-vis the *Opera dei Congressi* — Ed.)
116. R. Maerker, "Uno studio sulla vita e sulle opere di Mons. Scalabrini," in *Charitas* (Friburg i. Br.) and reproduced in the *Catechista Cattolico*, Oct., 1906, pp. 299-301.

Chapter IX — THE EMIGRANTS

1. G. Toniolo, Letter dated Nov. 1, 1911, quoted in *L'Emigrato Italiano*, 1918, n. 4., p. 17.
2. M. Caliaro, *La Pia Società dei Missionari di S. Carlo (Scalabriniani), Studio storico-giuridico dalla fondazione al Capitolo Generale dell'anno 1951*, pro mns., Rome, 1956, p. 10.
3. J. B. Scalabrini, Letter to the Cardinal Prefect of *Propaganda Fide*, Arch. S.C.P.F., Collegi d'Italia, Piacenza, ff. 1492 ss.
4. Benedict XV, Autograph, June 30, 1915, to the Institute of the Missionaries of St. Charles. See *L'Emigrato Italiano*, Sept. 15, 1915, p. 2.
5. J. B. Scalabrini, *L'emigrazione italiana in America*, Piacenza, 1887, pp. 3-6.
6. Space does not permit a full treatment of or bibliography on the work of Scalabrinians. Among the vast literature on the emigration phenomenon, we mention only two books, which have been of greatest use to us: F. Manzotti's, *La polemica sull'emigrazione nell' Italia unita (fino alla prima guerra mondiale)*, Milan, 1962; and G. Dore's *La democrazia italiana e l'emigrazione in America*, Brescia, 1964.
7. A. Perotti, "Documentazione sul pensiero sociale di G. B. Scalabrini sui fenomeni migratori," in *Problemi di storia, sociologia e pastorale dell'emigrazione*, Rome, 1965, p. 22.
8. J. B. Scalabrini, *L'emigrazione italiana in America*, Piacenza, 1887, p. 7.
9. Idem, First conference on emigration, p. 5 (this was held in Rome in the church of Sant' Andrea della Valle, Feb. 8, 1891).
10. Idem, *Il disegno di legge sulla emigrazione italiana: Osservazioni e proposte*, Piacenza, 1888, p. 33.
11. Idem, *L'Italia all'estero*, (conference held in the hall of the Exposition of Sacred Art in Turin) in *Il Conferenziere*, Jan., 1900, p. 15.
12. Ibid., p. 9.
13. Ibid., p. 10.
14. Ibid., "For our country the hope for any extensive political colonization was swept away and postponed indefinitely by the African disasters, the memory of which saddens every Italian heart." But in 1887 he had written: "Italy does not have colonies, even if one doesn't wish to consider those two margins of land occupied on the banks of the Red Sea, and it cannot get any for itself without obvious violations of international law and without bloody conflicts." (*L'emigrazione italiana in America*, Piacenza, 1887, p. 16).
15. *L'emigrazione italiana in America*, Piacenza, 1887, p. 13.
16. Ibid., p. 16.
17. Ibid., p. 28. The idea of agricultural colonies of Italians overseas has been taken up again in recent years by private enterprises and also through international treaties, e.g. the Italo-Brazilian Treaty of Oct. 8, 1949. See G. Pesci, *Lineamenti moderni dell'emigrazione italiana*, Rome, 1956, pp. 36-41.
18. Ibid., p. 26.
19. Ibid., p. 27.
20. Idem, *Il disegno di legge sull'emigrazione italiana*, Piacenza, 1888, p. 33.
21. Idem, *L'Italia all'estero*, p. 15.
22. A. Perotti, "Contributo di G. B. Scalabrini e dei suoi missionari alle prime leggi organiche sull'emigrazione," in *L'Emigrato Italiano*, June, 1962, p. 11.
23. J. B. Scalabrini, *Il disegno di legge sull'emigrazione italiana*, p. 32. "The law...in giving agents the right to recruit may be liberal but it is imprudent; it may be, as is said, the logical consequence of the right to emigrate. But a law is not a syllogism...Let us not impute this new sin, therefore, to liberalism, and much less to logic; they already have too many to account for!" (ibid.).
24. A. Perotti, art. cit., ibid.
25. J. B. Scalabrini, *Il disegno di legge sull'emigrazione italiana*, Piacenza, 1888, pp. 51-54.
26. Idem, *L'Italia all'estero*, p. 16. See A. Perotti, "Scalabrini e Governo," in *L'Emigrato Italiano*, 1962, n. 10-11, pp. 13-15.
27. J. B. Scalabrini, *L'emigrazione italiana in America*, Piacenza, 1887, p. 25.
28. Ibid., p. 30.

29. Ibid., p. 39.
30. Idem, *L'Italia all'estero*, p. 12.
31. Ibid., p. 23.
32. Idem, *L'emigrazione italiana in America*, p. 45.
33. Ibid.
34. Ibid., p. 46.
35. Ibid.
36. Ibid., pp. 47-48.
37. Idem, Letter of Feb. 16, 1887 to the Prefect of *Propaganda Fide*, Arch. S.C.P.F., Collegi d'Italia, Piacenza, ff. 1491 and ss.
38. Idem, *L'Italia all'estero*, pp. 22-23.
39. Idem, *L'emigrazione italiana in America*, pp. 41-42.
40. M. Caliaro, op. cit., pp. 17-18. Bishop Scalabrini's letter is preserved in the Archives of the S.C.P.F., Collegi d'Italia, f. 1490 r.
41. Ibid., pp. 21-23. Scalabrini continued to suggest a papal letter to the American bishops, until Leo XIII issued the *Quam Aerumnosa*, Dec. 10, 1888 (*Acta Leonis* XIII, vol. VIII, pp. 380-384).

Chapter X — MISSIONARIES FOR THE EMIGRANTS

1. M. Caliaro, op. cit., p. 24.
2. Ibid., pp. 27-28.
3. Ibid., pp. 29-30. In the beginning the members of the new Institute did not take perpetual vows but made a solemn promise to live in community and to obey the Pope, the Founder, and their Superior. In addition, before setting out for the missions, they promised not to keep anything as their own property but to assign any income to the Superior. They were obliged to remain in the Institute for five years, but had the option to prolong their service for another period or even for life (See ibid., pp. 40-43).
4. Ibid., pp. 44-45.
5. J. B. Scalabrini to the editor of the *Voce del Paese*, Piacenza, May 6, 1883.
6. M. Caliaro, op. cit., p. 45.
7. *L'Amico del Popolo*, July 14, 1888.
8. M. Caliaro, op. cit., p. 45. Bishop Scalabrini wrote to the Cardinal Prefect of Propaganda Fide about a request he had received from a high ranking Italian army officer to provide priests for the (Italian) possessions in Africa, saying he was disposed to comply with the request in the hope of doing a great deal of good. He asked, however, that the Italian district be taken out of the jurisdiction of the French Apostolic Vicar and that his missionaries be made responsible directly either to the Bishop of Piacenza or the Propaganda, through the establishment of a kind of Apostolic Prefecture. The Propaganda Fide replied in the negative and Bishop Scalabrini accepted the refusal "not only with deference but cheerfully" and discreetly passed on the information to the Government emissary (Scalabrini's notes to the Cardinal Prefect of Propaganda Fide, Oct. 4, 1890, and Aug. 20, 1891, AGS).
   The Servant of God received requests for help from many places. In 1888 there came an appeal from peasants that had emigrated to Rumania, presented by a certain Innocenzo Serrazanetti and transmitted to Scalabrini by Count Acquaderni (I. Serrazanetti to Bishop Scalabrini, Bologna, Nov. 14, 1888). Later the Archbishop of Bucharest appealed to him on behalf of the Italian colony in the Rumanian capital. Scalabrini found a priest for him but in the meantime the Archbishop decided to take two other religious (Xavier de Honstein to Bishop Scalabrini, Bucharest, Nov. 25, 1902 and Mar. 27, 1903, AGS).
   In 1903 the Patriarch of Jerusalem invited Scalabrini to take a trip to the Middle East to see the unhappy circumstances in which the Italian emigrants were living (the Patriarch of Jerusalem to Bishop Scalabrini, Mar. 4, 1903, AGS), but Bonomelli's order was already considering the Middle East. An earlier request had come, in 1893, from a nun concerned about the Italians working on the Lebanese railroad (G. Bogliassino, Daughter of Charity, to Bishop Scalabrini, Damascus, July 16, 1893, AGS). "Deeply grieved to be unable to

help" her as he wished, Scalabrini was obliged to reply in the negative as he already had done to another Daughter of Charity who had made a similar appeal on behalf of 300 families living in Paris (A. Giannini, Daughter of Charity, to Bishop Scalabrini, Paris, Sept. 26, 1888, AGS).

It would appear from a letter of the Card. Secretary of State, L. Nina, that Scalabrini had taken an interest in the Italians in Paris in 1879. Nina wrote: "As for Your Excellency's wise observations on the need in Paris for a Church to minister to the Italians living there, and especially the working class, I assure you that I shall without fail call this to the attention of the Nuncio and interest him in taking the matter up with the Eminent Archbishop there" (May 27, 1879, AGS).

Lack of personnel prevented him from carrying out his intentions to send missionaries to Costa Rica (See Letter of J. B. Scalabrini to the Superior General, probably of the Franciscans, s.d., and the Letter of J. B. Scalabrini to Senator Pasquale Vilari, s.d. in reply to Villari's letter, May 28, 1901, AGS).

9. *Regolamento della Congregazione dei Missionari per gli Emigranti* approved by the Sacred Congregation of Propaganda Fide in 1888, Chapter I, nn. 2-3. See M. Caliaro, op. cit., pp. 167-168.

10. *Regolamento* quoted 1888, Chap. VIII, n. 2.

11. M. Caliaro, op, cit., pp. 50-51.

12. J. B. Scalabrini to Rev. Domenico Vicentini, Mar. 5, 1892 (AGS).

13. *Regolamento*, quoted 1888, Chap. V., n. 5.

14. *Ai Missionari per gl'Italiani nelle Americhe il Vescovo di Piacenza*, Mar. 15, 1892, pp. 3-4.

15. Ibid., p. 8.

16. Ibid., p. 11.

17. Ibid., pp. 12-13.

18. Ibid., p. 13.

19. J. B. Scalabrini, *Il disegno di legge sull'emigrazione Italiana*, Piacenza, 1888, pp. 47-48. Scalabrini's intention to concern himself with all the dimensions of emigration as well as with the "whole" emigrant is confirmed in a letter addressed to a "most illustrious sir," which is undated but which certainly belongs to the beginning of 1889. In it he says that the purpose of the Congregation is "to ensure religious ministry and also the civil well-being of the Italian emigrants, especially in America." The purpose of the St. Raphael Society is "to give the migrant flows from our country rational and reliable direction." He adds: "I have it in mind to do something about the colonization of those lands for the benefit of our people and, in fact, I am attending to this; I should also like to have a pertinent newsletter published about it etc., etc., but there we are. I would need a powerful purse to come to my aid..." (AGS).

20. Idem, First Conference on Emigration, p. 12.

21. J. B. Scalabrini to Rev. Domenico Vicentini, Sept. 1894 (AGS).

22. Ibid. See the letter of Card. Bausa, the first Patron of the Institute, to Scalabrini, Florence, Dec. 27, 1894: "You have reason to be pleased about the vows, not solemn but nevertheless perpetual, made by a select group of young men. That permanence places the Institute among the great creations of the Church" (AGS).

23. Card. Satolli, Archives of the S.C.P.F., Rub. 8, pos. 41447/900: "The Reverend Commission, after a careful examination, was of the opinion that it was not expedient to approve the present Rules...The permanence of the vows is not only contrary to the very nature of the Institute, which...as soon as emigration ceased would also come to an end or would have to change, but also to the kind of life the Missionaries must lead, being for the most part isolated and far from their Superior..."

24. J. B. Scalabrini to the Cardinal Prefect of Propaganda Fide, Jan. 21, 1901 (AGS).

25. Idem, *L'emigrazione italiana in America*, pp. 7-9.

26. Pius XII, *Exsul Familia*, in *Acta Apostolicae Sedis*, XLIV (1952), p. 682.

27. M. Caliaro, op. cit., p. 152: "What Pius XII said about secular Institutes has therefore proved true also in our case, namely, that the specific goal creates the general purpose. In fact, it was precisely the necessity of making the apostolate to the emigrants both productive and lasting and his desire to strengthen the bonds among the members of the Institute

that soon led Bishop Scalabrini to introduce the five-year promises and later the perpetual vows, and that still later persuaded the Holy See of the opportuneness of granting the request to restore perpetual vows to the Society."

28. J. B. Scalabrini, Discourse to Departing Missionaries, Jan. 24, 1889.
29. Idem, *Note di viaggio* (letter to Msgr. Mangot) June 21, 1904 (AGS).
30. See "L'arrivo di Mons. Scalabrini. Il ricevimento all'Associazione C. Colombo," in *Il Caffaro* (Genoa), Dec. 6-7, 1904: Dec. 5, 1904, on his arrival from Brazil, Scalabrini recounted "several anecdotes about his visit in Brazil. An interesting one was that about his visit — in neutral territory — to the chief of the Indians, who showed him two very old goblets that had belonged to the first Catholic missionaries to visit those places. The conversation he had with that personage was marked by the greatest cordiality." See also "Gli Emigrati italiani e Mons. Scalabrini," in *La Vera Roma*, Jan. 21, 1905: "All these labors," Bishop Scalabrini declared to R. Mazzi, his interviewer, "are not ended, because a new road has been opened to the zeal of the missionaries. We made contact with the Indians, the ancient masters of Brazil, people still almost savage, who for three hundred years have been without any religious comfort whatever."

Rev. Marco Simoni has a different version of the episode according to which the meeting was with an ordinary Indian in the house of a Brazilian priest in Florianopolis (Letter of Rev. Marco Simoni to Rev. Carlo Pedrazzani, Mar. 5, 1938, (AGS).

31. A. Fogazzaro, "Una visita a Mons. Scalabrini" in *La Rassegna Nazionale*, July 1, 1905, pp. 7-8:

"Once while he was preaching in the church of one of those parishes that stretched over 70,000 square kilometers, he noticed the feathered headdress of a savage among the congregation. When the function was ended he sent for him and this laconic little dialogue took place:
— Is your tribe near here or far away?
— Near.
— How near?
— Only twenty hours on horseback.
— Go to your Chief and tell him that the Italian bishop would be happy to see him and is waiting for him here.
"The Indian leaped on his horse and went off. Two days later he returned from the forest.
— Well? Is your Chief not coming?
— The Chief says that he would be very happy to see the Italian bishop and is waiting for him in the forest.
— Fine, said the Bishop, we shall go to the forest.
"Everyone crowds around him begging him not to trust (him), not to go...
"The Bishop laughs at those who would make him afraid and bravely mounts, setting out with a small group in which there was a Venetian missionary. They arrive in the forest twenty hours later. They receive their first welcome from a pack of monkeys who gave them a 'devil of a stoning.' The travelers are thinking, 'Now we've had it,' and the Bishop puts on his episcopal robes. 'I was all in purple,' he told me. They proceed on their way and out from the thick of the wood comes a magnificent spectacle, three or four hundred savage horsemen led by their Chief, who is also in ceremonial dress. Feathers, necklaces, furs, 'nothing missing.' They all dismount and the Chief approaches the Bishop in a manner at once dignified and respectful and delivers a little speech in *guarani*. He recalls the missions of two centuries ago, reproves the Church for having abandoned them, and thanks the visitor. And the visitor, to the great astonishment of the Chief and his men answers in *guarani*. He conveys the greetings of the Great Priest in Rome, apologizes for the Church, ('why not — they are right, those poor souls') and its involuntary neglect, promises that when he returns to Italy he will speak of them to the Great Priest. The Indians take a great liking to the Venetian missionary, crowd around him and want him to stay with them. The missionary is moved and is about to say yes, but the Bishop intervenes: 'What do you expect to do here my dear boy, when you don't know a word of *guarani*?' To the Indians he says, 'I will have him study *guarani* and then I will send him back to you.' This is agreed and everyone is happy, the Indians and the missionary. 'Be careful though

not to eat him or me,' Scalabrini says to the Chief, and the Chief laughs. 'Oh, I told this to the Holy Father!' the good Bishop exclaimed, interrupting his story."

32. C. Spallazzi, witness, *Processus*, iuxta 29, pp. 27-28.

33. M. Simoni to Bishop Scalabrini, S. Felicidade, Feb. 26, 1905 (AGS). See the account of Father Simoni's companion, Rev. A. Buonaiuti in *L'Emigrato Italiano*, Feb., 1906, pp. 15-17.

34. J. B. Scalabrini, *Dell'assistenza alla emigrazione nazionale*, Piacenza, 1891, pp. 7-9.

35. This was not only domestic service. "The laymen who have a teacher's certificate or sufficient education will teach reading and writing, arithmetic, Italian history and especially Catechism" (*Regolamento* quoted 1888, Chap. IV, n. 6).

36. J. B. Scalabrini, First Conference on Emigration, p. 14.

37. Ibid., p. 15.

38. Idem, *Dell'assistenza alla emigrazione nazionale*, p. 7.

39. Idem, First Conference on Emigration, p. 15.

40. See Appendix I.

41. D. Vicentini, Letter dated July 6, 1906 (AGS).

42. See pp. 238-239.

43. Pius XII, *Exsul Familia* in *Acta Apostolicae Sedis*, XLIV (1952), p. 673.

44. M. Caliaro, op. cit., pp. 124-125.

45. Letters from A. Cicognani to Card. De Lai, Sept. 7, 1924 and Oct. 9, 1924 (Archives of the S.C.P.F., n. 773/24).

46. Rev. Francesco Tirondola (1886-1962) had run away from home at the age of fourteen to join the Combonian Missionaries. He was considered too old to start his studies but remained with them as a lay brother in the hope of becoming a missionary. When he saw his dream was not coming true he applied to Scalabrini's Congregation and was accepted by Father Vicentini. But then during World War I he had to spend four years at the front in the medical corps, where he earned seven decorations. When he returned in 1919 at age of 33 it was suggested that he study for the priesthood. He was ordained in 1924 and was immediately named pro-rector of the Motherhouse. He later became, successively, Superior of the House in Italy, Visitor to the Missions in America, and Vicar General of the Congregation. He was largely responsible for the numerical and geographical growth of the Congregation from 1924 to 1951. His dream of becoming a missionary came true only when he was 73 years old, when he was granted leave to go to the mission in Geneva, where he died April 21, 1962.

47. F. Prevedello, in *Cinquantesimo*, special issue of *L'Emigrato Italiano*, n. 5-6, 1955, pp. 8-11. "The first to take vows in the Society after it again became a religious order were the Priests, Professors and graduates of the seminaries in Italy. On Sunday, Apr. 8th, Albis 1934, His Eminence Card. Rossi went to Piacenza and in a solemn ceremony in the Chapel of the Motherhouse received the profession of perpetual vows from the Rector, eight Priests and twenty-four theology students, and then received the vows *ad annum* of thirty-six first year theology students and first and second year philosophy students. On the 10th the Cardinal, accompanied by those who were Professed, went to pray at the tomb of the Servant of God, Bishop Scalabrini, in the Cathedral, and there recited aloud the formula of the vows, bidding those who were with him to repeat the words after him, in the name also of those who were absent. It was an inspired gesture as well as a very delicate thought to confirm before the revered remains of the Founder, the profession of the life once more assumed by the Congregation he had founded, the kind of life that was his because he was the one who wished it so" (M. Caliaro, op. cit., p. 140).

48. See the Declarations of Card. Piazza at the Chapter meeting on July 6, 1951 (*Ricordi e richiami del Capitolo Generale Scalabriniano*, Rome, July 5-14, 1951, p. 11).

49. G. Ferretto, *Sua Santità Pio XII, provvido padre degli esuli, sapiente coordinatore dell' assistenza spirituale agli emigranti*, Rome, 1954.

50. The Scalabrini Fathers gathered in most of what was left of the Opera Bonomelli for the emigrants in Europe. Did a dream of the Founder thus come true? Unfortunately, we have no way of knowing this for sure. There are only Bonomelli's words to Scalabrini's secretary two months after the Bishop's death: "As for me, if we could achieve this ideal

union, I should be happy. But I see serious difficulties" (G. Bonomelli to Msgr. Mangot, Aug. 1, 1905,) (AGS). The Scalabrini missionaries remain sincere admirers of the pioneering work carried out by the Bonomelli Fathers, especially in Europe, where there are now two hundred mission centers for Italians.

Chapter XI — THE TWO "PASTORAL VISITS" TO THE EMIGRANTS

1. See Vatican Council II, Decree *Christus Dominus*, n. 23: "In similar circumstances, provision is to be made for the faithful of different languages either through priests or parishes; or through an Episcopal Vicar who knows their language well, and even, if necessary, one who is a bishop; or through other opportune means."
2. Card. Rampolla's letter is quoted and commented on by G. B. Volpe-Landi in the article, "Assistenza religiosa degli europei cattolici emigrati agli Stati Uniti," in *L'Amico del Popolo* of Aug. 12, 1891. Scalabrini asked to go to America in 1898, but the reply was that it did not seem "expedient"; "it might excite the sensitivities of the American Ordinaries" (Card. Ledóchowski to Bishop Scalabrini, Jan. 15, 1898, AGS).
3. *Venticinque anni di Missione fra gli Italiani immigrati di Boston, Mass.*, Milan, 1913, pp. 239-240.
4. *La Voce Cattolica* (Piacenza), July 20, 1901.
5. From *Note di viaggio*, J. B. Scalabrini, published in *La Voce Cattolica*, Aug. 21, 1901.
6. Ibid.
7. *Il Progresso italo-americano* (New York), Aug. 4, 1901.
8. J. B. Scalabrini, letter dated Aug. 9, 1901 (AGS).
9. *La Voce Cattolica*, Aug. 28, 1901, from its New York correspondent.
10. Scalabrini's interview with the editor of *L'Italia Cattolica* (Genoa), quoted in *Trent'anni di Apostolato*, p. 511.
11. J. B. Scalabrini to Msgr. Mangot, Aug. 9, 1901 (AGS).
12. *La Voce Cattolica*, Aug. 28, 1901, from its New York correspondent.
13. Ibid.
14. *The Italian Herald* (New York), Nov. 11, 1901.
15. J. B. Scalabrini to Msgr. Mangot, Aug. 12, 1901 (AGS).
16. Idem, Aug. 15, 1901 and Sept. 23, 1901 (AGS).
17. See Chapter VI, p. 65.
18. J. B. Scalabrini to Msgr. Mangot, Aug. 25, 1901 (AGS).
19. Idem, Sept. 2, 1901 (AGS).
20. *The New Haven Union*, Sept. 2, 1901.
21. Ibid.
22. *Post-Dispatch* (St. Louis), Oct. 3, 1901.
23. *The Italian Herald*, Oct. 21, 1901.
24. *Venticinque anni di missione fra gli Italiani immigrati di Boston, Mass.*, Milan 1913, pp. 19-20.
25. *The Italian Herald*, Oct. 30, 1901.
26. *La Libertà* (Piacenza), Dec. 7, 1901.
27. J. B. Scalabrini to Msgr. Mangot, Mar, 7, 1901 (AGS).
28. Idem, Sept. 10, 1901 (AGS).
29. Idem, Sept. 12, 1901 (AGS).
30. Idem, Sept. 17, 1901 (AGS).
31. Ibid. It is now recognized that certain bishops were mistaken in attempting to eradicate national characteristics. Italian immigrants would have made an extremely important religious contribution if Scalabrini's ideas had been followed from the beginning. The character of most of the ecclesiastical institutions in the United States was Irish, and in many places they tried in one way or another to shape everyone to the same mold. It was a far cry from the concept of preserving the values in every culture and of avoiding any method of evangelization based on the structure of a particular culture different from that of the people to be evangelized.
32. J. B. Scalabrini to Msgr. Mangot, Sept. 26, 1901 (AGS).

33. Idem, Oct. 1, 1901 (AGS).
34. Idem, Oct. 6, 1901 (AGS).
35. Ibid.
36. Gregori, op.cit., p. 478.
37. See pp. 204-205.
38. Scalabrini, in his letter of Sept. 12, 1901 to Msgr. Mangot (AGS), mentions that the arch-bishop of Boston had told him that as a young man he knew by name all the Catholics in Boston, who could meet in one room. In 1901 they already numbered 600,000. This helps to explain what seems to us a rather optimistic forecast.
39. *Venticinque anni di missione*, quoted pp. 19-20.
40. Ibid., p. 246.
41. J. B. Scalabrini to Msgr. Mangot, Nov. 6, 1901 (AGS).
42. "Il primo Vescovo italiano nell'America del Nord, Intervista con Mons. Scalabrini," in *La Lega Lombarda*, Dec. 7, 1901.
43. O. Alussi, letter dated Nov. 12, 1901 and carried in *Trent'anni di Apostolato*, p. 492.
44. Ibid., p. 489.
45. A. Bianchi to Msgr. Mangot, Rome, Nov. 21, 1901 (AGS).
46. *Trent'anni di Apostolato*, pp. 495-496.
47. Interview Scalabrini granted the editor of *L'Italia Coloniale* (Genoa), carried in *Trent'anni di Apostolato*, p. 511.
48. Ibid., p. 512.
49. J. B. Scalabrini to Bishop Bonomelli, Dec. 8, 1901 (Abba).
50. Idem, Trevozzo, Oct. 4, 1903 (Abba).
51. A. Scalabrini to Bishop Scalabrini, Rome, Mar. 30, 1904 (AGS).
52. J. B. Scalabrini, *Note di viaggio*, June 30, 1904 (See following note).
53. The *Note di viaggio*, or notes on his journey which Scalabrini sent his secretary were published in *Lavoro* (Piacenza) and *Il Citadino* (Genoa).
54. Diary of Rev. Alfredo Buonaiuti (limited to the first eight days of the voyage) in *L'Emigrato Italiano*, July, 1904, pp. 54-56.
55. See Chap. XVI, "Bishop Scalabrini and Pope Pius X."
56. "Dall'Italia al Brasile e viceversa," in *La Libertà* (Piacenza), Dec. 8, 1904.
57. J. B. Scalabrini to Msgr. Mangot, July 11, 1904 (AGS).
58. Interview in *Fanfulla*, carried in *Trent'anni di Apostolato*, pp. 527-532.
59. Ibid. Despite Bishop Scalabrini's clarifications on this point, the newspaper *O Estado de S. Paulo* persisted in seeing in the Italian missionaries and even in their Founder so many emissaries of the Italian government sent to prevent the assimilation of the immigrants and to prepare the way for colonial conquest (issue of July 16, 1904). This brought sharp rebuttals from the *Tribuna*, *Fanfulla*, and especially the *Estandarte Catholico*. The latter, in its July 30th (1904) issue wrote: "Only God knows how much material and spiritual good these missionaries do among the farmers and other Italian immigrants. And only God will reward them and their Founder. The world never recognizes true merit; and then, the fact that this apostolic prelate has adversaries can only be explained from a super-natural viewpoint. *Omnes qui pie volunt vivere in Christo Jesu persecutionem patientur*, he said recently in a certain situation. These words are quite applicable to himself. He sacrifices everything, comfort, what funds he has (and he is poor as a Franciscan), and even his health to do good to the poor and the disadvantaged — and notwithstanding this, there are those in Sao Paulo who slander him, attributing to him political motives for the works he is setting up! The Bishop is preparing the way for Italy to conquer Brazil, the United States, Germany, Argentina, etc., etc.! This writer thanks God that He granted him the grace to live for a few days in the company of this holy bishop, a true rival of the great Charles Borromeo."
60. L. Gorlin, witness, *Processus*, iuxta 5, p. 306.
61. J. B. Scalabrini to Msgr. Mangot, S. Paulo, July 11, 1904 (AGS).
62. Idem. To the Rector of the Motherhouse, S. Felicidade, Aug. 26, 1904 (AGS).
63. Idem. To Msgr. Mangot, Ypiranga, July 14, 1904 (AGS).
64. His servant, C. Spalazzi wrote, "We visited very many, in town after town, along the

splendid railway" "Dall'Italia al Brasile e viceversa" in *La Libertà*, Dec. 8, 1904). But they did not always travel by train. Bishop Pietro Massa of Rio Negro (Amazonia) recounted in 1958 that "in the month of August, if I remember rightly, in 1904, while I was visiting the Italian colonies in the State of Sao Paulo, I met on the road, or rather on a path in one of the coffee "plantations"...about two in the afternoon three priests who were traveling the same way on horseback. They were visiting the families of the plantation workers. We stopped and dismounted and I realized that one of them was a Bishop, our apostolic Bishop John Baptist Scalabrini, Bishop of Piacenza, who during those months was visiting his Missionaries and the immigrants in various states of Brazil. We had a long conversation, full of precious memories of Italy, while I, a young priest, was filled with admiration for the great apostle who, full of zeal and holy enthusiasm, spoke to me in his own language, gently and at the same time seriously, about the ideals and programs of his then new Congregation. Seated on the grass, in the shade of a jaquitibà, we spoke of many things while we sipped some fragrant coffee...I remember this episode among others...This is what he told me: 'When I went to pay my farewell respects to the Holy Father, he kept blessing me and giving me his advice. We have been friends since our youth, and he treated me with wonderful informality; at a certain point, as I kept asking for various special faculties for the benefit of our Italians...he said these very words with his amused smile: "Listen Scalabrini, let's take care of it this way: put my white cassock in your suitcase." This was the gracious way the great and holy Pope granted me all the faculties I might need for the good of our beloved Italians.' — Fifty-four years have passed since that happy encounter, and even now, almost eighty years old that I am, I remember the beloved figure of our unforgettable Bishop, in the sweet recollection of that far-off time, on the lonely sunfilled road in the Guadiroba plantation, in 1904" (*L'Emigrato Italiano*, Oct., 1958, pp. 14-15).

65.   J. B. Scalabrini to Msgr. Mangot, Sept. 3, 1904 (AGS).
66.   Idem, Sept. 9-10, 1904 (AGS).
67.   L. Gorlin, witness, *Processus*, iuxta 26, p. 307.
68.   D. Vicentini, *L'Apostolo degli italiani emigrati nelle Americhe*, Piacenza, 1909, p. 55.
69.   Sabinus (P. M. Rinaldi), "Cronaca," Encantado, Sept. 14, 1904, in *L'Emigrato Italiano*, Oct., 1904, pp. 75-78.
70.   Thus, in July 1941, the Scalabrinian Father Massimo Rinaldi, then the Bishop of Rieti, recalled the days he had spent with Scalabrini in Encantado (*L'Emigrato Italiano*, July, 1941, p. 91).
71.   J. B. Scalabrini to Msgr. Mangot, S. Lourenco, Sept. 25, 1904 (AGS).
72.   Scalabrini's servant, C. Spallazzi recalled the "terrible (journey) through the hilly land we encountered·after Encantado...The only food we carried with us was a bottle or two of milk and some bread and cheese...The Bishop rode in low, heavy carts covered with matting and drawn by six mules. The farmers guided this bizarre caravan. The Bishop's cart, creaking and bumping, seemed about to turn over at any moment. The rain, driven by the wind, dripped through the matting so that we always arrived wet to the bone, despite our raincoats, after an interminable odyssey. One evening we reached a settlement, having had almost no food, and there was nothing in the inn but bread and cheese. We spent the night there...Oh, there were many days that the Bishop ate in some rough peasant kitchen, where there was no tablecloth or napkins" ("Dall'Italia al Brasile a viceversa," in *La Libertà* Dec. 8, 1904).
73.   D. Vincentini, op. cit., p. 57.
74.   From correspondent, Alfredo Chaves, Oct. 9, 1904 in *Trent'anni di Apostolato*, p. 540.
75.   D. Vicentini, op. cit., p. 57.
76.   J. B. Scalabrini to Msgr. Mangot, Rio Grande, Oct. 29, 1904 (AGS).
77.   Quoted in *Trent'anni di Apostolato*, pp. 563-564.
78.   D. Vicentini, op. cit., p. 58.

Chapter XII — THE ST. RAPHAEL SOCIETY — EMIGRATION LAWS

1.   J. B. Scalabrini, *L'emigrazione italiana in America*, pp. 41-44.

2. Idem, *Dell'assistenza alla emigrazione nazionale*, p. 13.

3. Idem, Letter of Feb. 16, 1887, to the Cardinal Prefect of Propaganda Fide (Arch. S.C.P.F., Lettere e decreti, 1887, vol. 383, ff. 1491 ff.).

4. Arch. S.C.P.F., Collegi d'Italia, Piacenza, f. 1382 v. On the other hand, at the audience granted Nov. 11, 1887, to Bishop Jacobini, Secretary of Propaganda Fide, Leo XIII stated the following: "We believe the establishment of Committees in Italy and America should be postponed for the present." (Arch. S.C.P.F., Collegi d'Italia, Piacenza, f. 1388 rv.) Nevertheless in 1888 the Rule of the Congregation of Missionaries for the Emigrants was approved, and this stated in Chap. I, n. 3, among the means by which the Congregation was to pursue its aims, "the organization of Committees at the ports of embarkation and debarkation, to assist, direct, and counsel the emigrants." Apparently, Bishop Scalabrini had presented in person to Rome the necessary clarifications and had convinced the Holy See of the benefits and opportuneness of these committees.

5. *Rassegna Nazionale* (July 1, 1887), in its announcement of the election of Bishop Scalabrini as President of the Committee in Piacenza, wrote: "He yielded to the great pressures put upon him and in the interests of the work which he had proposed he accepted the high office and has already gathered about him, on the basis of Christian charity, several prominent men of various political persuasions, as well as members of the clergy and the laity."

6. "The two founders had tried in 1886 to obtain formal approval from the Congregation of Propaganda Fide. With Leo XIII's assent, this was not granted in order to avoid competition with the Propagation of the Faith in Lyons and also because there were quite a few Liberals among its promoters. The latter, however, had persisted, claiming that the articles in the constitution which determined its Catholic nature had been declared essential and immutable. The Association remained in unofficial contact with Propaganda Fide and benefitted missions and missionaries, and the latter accepted prior instructions from the ecclesiastical authorities." (A. Martini, "Leone XIII e l'emigrazione temporanea italiana," in *La Civiltà Cattolica*, a. 105, vol. III, Sept. 4, 1954, p. 474, n. 9.)

7. *L'Amico del Popolo*, July 14, 1888.

8. Ibid., Nov. 3, 1888.

9. Ibid., Dec. 19, 1888. In reporting the imminent departure of Prof. Angelo Scalabrini for America, *L'Amico del Popolo* wrote: "His journey has to do with the aim of the Society for the Protection of Italian Emigrants, founded by our Bishop, namely, to provide a rational direction for the emigrant flow, to get it out of the greedy exploitation of the agents and to direct it to fertile and healthy places of resettlement, and also to establish schools and committees according to the needs."

10. The Opera Bonomelli did not escape these difficulties precisely because it relied on the National Association for Aid to Italian Missionaries (See C. Bellà, *Geremia Bonomelli*, Brescia, 1961, pp. 156-169; the art. cit. by A. Martini in *La Civiltà Cattolica*, Sept. 4, 1954, and the note "Dalle Missioni Bonomelliane alle attuali missioni fra gli emigrati italiani in Europa" in *Selezione Centro Studi Emigrazione*, Rome, n. VII-VIII, Sept. 15, 1964).

     According to a letter of Schiaparelli's secretary of the National Association, it would appear that Propaganda Fide had advised Bishop Scalabrini to keep the Society he was about to establish in Piacenza completely independent, with only indirect and financial support from the National Association (E. Schiaparelli to Bishop Scalabrini, ? 14, 1887 AGS).

11. *L'Amico del Popolo*, May 1, 1889.

12. Ibid., May 4, 1889.

13. D. Secco Suardo, *I cattolici intransigenti*, Brescia, 1962, p. 66.

14. A. Gambasin, op. cit., p. 177.

15. Bishop Scalabrini addressed an appeal to the diocese on Dec. 25, 1890, urging everyone to contribute "to this work of redemption, to this religious, moral and civic undertaking."

16. S. Medolago Albani to G. B. Casoni, Dec. 20, 1888, cited by A. Gambasin, op. cit., p. 247. In January of the same year a periodical of the Opera dei Congressi had published a review of the first migratory work of Scalabrini by Cesare Sardi who maintained cordial relations with the Bishop of Piacenza marked by reciprocal esteem.

17. S. Medolago Albani to G. B. Volpe-Landi, June 15, 1889 (AGS). Toniolo wrote directly to

Scalabrini, Nov. 1, 1890, and Mar. 30, 1892, urging him to attend the First Congress of Social Sciences in Genoa since emigration was one of the principal items on the agenda. It seems that Scalabrini did not participate directly because of the "lengthy and notorious prejudices," against the Scalabrinian institutions on the part of Opera dei Congressi, as Toniolo described them in a letter to Scalabrini dated Sept. 18, 1894. See also Toniolo's letters to Bishop Callegari of Padua, president of the Union for Social Studies (G. Toniolo, *Opera omnia*, Series VI, *Epistolario*, vol. I, Rome, 1952, pp. 189-190, 263-264, 345-347, 243-245, 287-289).

18. "Archbishop of Genoa. Respectful greetings Your Excellency, colleagues and illustrious assemblage. I applaud this noble initiative and am happy to declare with you social problems cannot be solved except through faith and knowledge working together. Every true Italian is with you. The emigration question is the most important of all for our country. I recommend it especially to your study. If you bring some relief to the innumerable and serious ills that afflict it, if you give new impetus to the institution for protection happily inaugurated under the...auspices of the Holy Father Leo XIII, you will accomplish a particularly religious, patriotic civic work and God will bless your efforts." The text of the telegram was carried by *L'Amico del Popolo*, Oct. 15-16, 1892. A brief report from G. B. Volpe-Landi was presented at the Congress: "Emigrazione sue cause, suoi provvedimenti," published in *Atti del I Congresso Cattolico Italiano degli Studiosi di Scienze sociali, tenuto in Genova nei giorni 8, 9, 10, 11, ottobre 1892*, vol. I, Padua, 1893, pp. 236-238.

19. A. Gambasin, op. cit., p. 439. In 1897 Volpe-Landi published an article, "Il problema dell' emigrazione" in *Revisita Internazionale di scienze sociali e discipline ausiliarie*, vol. XIII, pp. 500-520. See also *Atti e Documenti del Secondo Congresso Cattolico Italiano degli Studiosi di Scienze sociali, tenutosi in Padova nei giorni, 26, 27 and 28 agosto 1896*, Padua, 1896, pp. 36, 169, 304-306.

20. G. B. Paganuzzi to Bishop Scalabrini, Apr. 1, 1899 (AGS). "Your Most Reverend Excellency will choose the subject that seems best but do not fail to give us your message. It will be all the more beneficial and salutary the more Italian Catholics need comfort, direction and encouragement in this time of trial."

21. A. Perotti, "Azione Sociale cattolica alla fine dell'800. Scalabrini e Governo," in *L'Emigrato Italiano*, 1962, n. 1-11, pp. 15-17.

22. Outline note of G. B. Volpe-Landi, undated but probably belonging in May-June, 1900 (AGS).

23. S. Medolago Albani to Bishop Scalabrini, June 28, 1900 (AGS).

24. A. Gambasin, op. cit., p. 535.

25. *St. Raphaels-Verein zum Schutze Katholiacher Auswanderer.* The German St. Raphael Society was founded by Peter Paul Cahensly (1838-1923), "father" of the German emigrants, in Mainz 1871. It was a completely lay organization, supported financially by its members, with an admirable organization. The first affiliate in the United States was established in 1883 (See Cost. Apost. *Exsul Familia*, in *Acta Apostolicae Sedis*, XLIV, 1952, p. 659).

At the invitation of Bishop Scalabrini, Toniolo, together with Prof. Luigi Olivi, was present at the 1894 general assembly. Toniolo reported to Bishop Callegari the decisions taken, stressing the one to place the St. Raphael Society under the collective patronage of the Italian bishops. The proposal that the chairmanship of the diocesan committees be subject to the approval of the Ordinary was rejected by a tie vote. "Nevertheless, Bishop Scalabrini, to whom we reported the result this morning, while he made no secret of what more was desirable, was most kind, stating that he was in full agreement given the need for a strictly Catholic orientation even in the membership of the committees, and the Marchese Volpe-Landi said the same thing, confessing that the attempt to attract...to the work the support of other elements of different political or ecclesiastical persuasion had failed" (G. Toniolo to Bishop Callegari, July 26, 1894, in *Epistolario*, vol. I, pp. 336-337).

26. *L'Amico del Popolo*, Dec. 5-6, 1894.

27. Ibid., Apr. 3, and Apr. 20, 1889.

28. A. Perotti, "Contributo dei Missionari Scalabriniani alla formazione delle prime leggi

sulla emigrazione in Italia," in *L'Emigrato Italiano*, Sept., 1962, pp. 5-22. The officials mentioned by Maldotti were to perform functions which we now ascribe to "social workers."

29.   Gregori, op. cit., p. 387.

30.   Fr. Villeneuve to Bishop Scalabrini, Oct. 11, 1891 (AGS).

31.   A wealthy gentleman of New York together with Prince Ruspoli, the mayor of Rome, proposed the foundation of a model (or pilot) colony in Arkansas and Bishop Scalabrini, at the request of Ruspoli, assigned Fr. Bandini to the work. He was happy to accept and soon built a church and school there. The rosy expectations of the beginning, however, were soon cut off by the death of the colony's founder. His heirs leased it to speculators, malaria took its toll of victims, and the settlers scattered. A certain number of families united around the missionary, however, urging him to do something about the future. He moved them to a healthier locale, had them clear the land, and built modest houses of wood and adobe. But a sudden frost and then a cyclone destroyed the crops. Their neighbors, who looked with disfavor on the settlers because they were Italian and Catholic, took to harrassing them even setting fire to their school. Fr. Bandini managed to put out the fire and the next morning, when their neighbors came to gloat over the destruction, they were met by the priest, who firmly declared that he would arm the settlers and that they woulld defend themselves at gunpoint. And that is what he did. The Italians were armed and kept close guard over their houses and fields, and they succeeded in having the county court adopt drastic measures to protect them. All their sacrifices finally bore fruit. The land was paid for, houses, shops, stores, schools, a post and telegraph office and a fine church were built. Fr. Bandini baptized the new town Tontitown, in memory of Enrico Tonti, an Italian explorer of the 17th Century. Fr. Bandini was the soul of the new town: its pastor, notary, school inspector, postmaster, agricultural director, and teacher of Italian. He himself remained so poor that he died in a home for old people (See Gregori, op. cit., pp. 429-431; P. C. Sassi, *Parrocchia della Madonna di Pompei in New York*, Marino, 1946, pp. 19-29; *L'Emigrato Italiano*, Apr., 1934, pp. 19-20; A. L. Fletcher, Bishop of Little Rock, Arkansas, "P. Bandini a Tontitown" in *L'Emigrato Italiano*, Oct., 1967, p. 18).

32.   P. C. Sassi, op. cti., pp. 21-22.

33.   Ibi., p. 51.

34.   J. B. Scalabrini, *Il disegno di legge sull'emigrazione italiana*, p. 6.

35.   "Il Papa e l'emigrazione," in *Riforma*, Dec. 14, 1888.

36.   Report of the Luzzatti Commission on the Visconti Venosta proposal (1900) quoted by Gregori, op. cit., p. 346.

37.   Rev. P. Colbachini, "Le condizioni degli emigrati nello Stato del Paranà in Brasile." Annex to Part III of *L'Europa all conquista dell'America Latina*, Venice, 1894, pp. 423-437.

38.   Idem, "Relazione presentata a S. E. il Ministro degli Esteri intorno alle condizioni presenti dell'emigrazione negli Stati Uniti del Brasile, ed ai provvedimenti opportuni per migliorare," in *Rassegna Nazionale*, Mar. 1, 1895.

39.   Colbachini's plans, concrete proposals and just observations merited every attention. That his Memorandum was seriously valued by scientists and men with unimpeachable technical credentials in emigration matters, is attested by the following letter from the Director General of the Statistical Office to Bishop Scalabrini, dated Jan. 14, 1895: "I have spoken with Father Colbachini, who gave me his report on Brazil to read. It is an excellent piece of work. What he proposes should be done. But who will do it? I do not think that the government, with the ideas prevailing at present, will commit itself to guarantee the interest on the capital of the societies to be established. Nor would any Minister today have the courage to propose such a measure to the Chamber of Deputies, although I believe that no money could be better spent, no expense better justified than whatever was devoted to effective aid in ennabling our emigrants to acquire land in the Americas. The guarantees would have to be found outside of Government. Devotedly yours, L. Bodio."

"Francesco Saverio Nitti, though very far from Scalabrini's ideology and pastoral cares, noted the indefatigable activity of the Bishop of Piacenza and his missionaries and acknowledged, in a well-known article in 1896, "the need to have the clergy with us to carry out an effective action for the protection of the emigrants." (A. Perotti, Contribution of "Missionari Scalabriniani alla formazione delle prime leggi sulla emigrazione in Italia" in *L'Emigrato Italiano*, July, 1962,, pp. 3-20).

40. Ibid., Spet., 1962, p. 6.
41. Gregori, op. cit., p. 347.
42. *Relazione a S. E. il Ministro degli Esteri*, Società di Patronato per gli emigranti, Piacenza, 1896, p. 37.
43. A. Perotti, art. cit., Sept. 1, 1962, pp. 5-22.
44. J. B. Scalabrini, *L'Italia all'Estero*, p. 13.
45. Ibid., p. 16.
46. L. Einaudi, "Il problema dell'emigrazione in Italia," in *Cronache politiche ed economiche di un trentennio*, vol. I, Turin, 1959, p. 115. "Last September I happened to act as secretary at a conference where a Bishop, several senators and deputies, many missionaries, several diplomatic and consular representatives of Italy abroad, representatives of powerful shipping enterprises and business houses had met, at the initiative of the national association for aid to Italian Catholic missionaries abroad and the organizing committee for the Italian exposition abroad, in order to study and discuss the serious problem of Italian emigration."
47. Einaudi defended the thesis, previously championed by Scalabrini, that emigration was necessary, while internal colonization was too slow a remedy and was costly and inadequate. And he added: "The creation of hostels for emigrants in Genoa, Naples and Palermo; prohibition of the unworthy traffic in persons carried on by unscrupulous agents and sub-agents; making the shipping companies responsible; strict regulations regarding the speed of the ships, the cubic measurements of the cabins, the food served and the medicines available during the voyage; hostels for emigrants at the arrival ports and various stations in the interior; aid at the embarkation points by sufficient personnel assisted by ecclesiastical and lay missionaries; these in general were the recommendations of the conference in Turin" (ibid., pp. 118-119). See by the same author, "Un missionario Apostolo degli emigrati (Father Maldotti)," ibid., p. 92.
48. The two plans were in agreement on the establishment of a central Commissariat, a consultative Council for emigration services, the services of traveling commissioners and doctors, the setting up of local district committees for aid and consultation. The point of difference turned on the emigration agents. The compromise regarding travel expenses under State control was then adopted. "In this law the Catholic saw official recognition by the Liberals of the work they had done on behalf of the emigrants. In the district or town committees the pastor sat with the local leaders. The requests Scalabrini had put forward for many years were partly met with regard to lightening the term of military duty for missionary seminarians and the missionaries going abroad to places and accordind to terms set by the Foreign Ministry. The aid institutions could be granted faculties which the law gave to the functionaries of the Commissariat and could be assigned (as they were in fact) subsidies for the emigration fund. To facilitate the work of the missionaries of the institutions for the protection of emigrants it was provided that they could enjoy free round trip passage on the ships. The Catholics thus succeeded in making a breach in the legislation of the Liberal State and in establishing their presence in this very important sector" (F. Manzotti, op. cit., pp. 140-141).
49. Rev. Maldotti to Bishop Scalabrini, Dec. 21, 1899 (AGS).
50. Idem, Dec. 30, 1899 (AGS).
51. Idem, Jan. 2, 1901 (AGS).
52. "I Missionari italiani all'estero. Intervista col Vescovo Mons. G. B. Scalabrini," in *Il Corriere della Sera*, June 1, 1901.
53. From the interview accorded the editor of *Italia Coloniale* (Genoa) in *Trent'anni di Apostolato*, p. 511.
54. A. Perotti, "Scalabrini e Governo" in *L'Emigrato Italiano*, 1962, p.. 26. The series of articles by an unknown author in the issues of Feb. 10-11, p. 26, July, Oct.-Nov., 1962 of the same

periodical deal in full with the contribution of Scalabrini and his missionaries to the legislation on emigration.

Chapter XIII — FOR THE EMIGRANTS OF ALL NATIONS

1. G. B. Sofia, "Mons. G. B. Scalabrini e l'attuale organizzazione dell'assistenza religiosa agli emigrati," in *Celebrazione del 50°*, pp. 223-226; see Gregori, op. cit., pp. 503-508. For the beginnings of the Opera Bonomelli, see C. Bellò, op. cit., pp. 156-169 (and bibliography on p. 159, n. 16). As for the encouragement Bonomelli received from Scalabrini, see the statement of Msgr. Emilio Lombardi, former secretary of the Bishop of Cremona: "I do not hesitate to say that if the Bishop of the Italian emigrants in Europe succeeded in his great religious and patriotic mission, despite conflicts, difficulties and trials of every kind, this is due to the advice and comfort he received from the great Bishop of Piacenza, who was in his turn father to the Italian emigrants overseas." (In *M.r Giovanni Battista Scalabrini nel 40° di sua elevazione episcopale*, Piacenza, Aug. 16, 1916, p. 6).

2. F. Milini, "Attualità del pensiero di Mons. G. B. Scalabrini sull'assistenza agli emigrati," in *L'Emigrato Italiano*, June, 1952; *Comitati e Segretariati*, ibid., July-Aug., 1960, pp. 3-4.

3. Pius X, *Motu Proprio — Degli Italiani emigranti all'estero, Iam pridem*, Mar. 19, 1914, in *A.A.S.* VI (1914), pp. 174-175.

4. Pius XII, Cost. Apost. *Exsul Familia*, Cap. V, nn. 43, 45, 46, 47, in *A.A.S.*, XLIV (1952), pp. 701-702.

5. See *Direttorio di pastorale per le migrazioni*, ed. by UCEI, Rome, 1965, pp. 37-48.

6. Sacred Consistorial Congregation, Letter to the Bishops of the Dioceses of Italy on the spiritual care of the emigrants, *Il dolore e le preoccupazioni*, Dec. 6, 1914, in *A.A.S.* VI (1914), pp. 699-701.

7. Pius XII, *Exsul Familia*, Cap. V, nn. 48-49, in *A.A.S.*, XLIV (1952), p. 702.

8. Sacred Consistorial Congregation, Notification of the creation of a Prelature for Italian emigration, *Esistono in Italia*, Oct. 23, 1920, in *A.A.S.* XII (1920), pp. 534 ff.

9. *L'Emigrato Italiano*, July, Aug., Sept., 1920, pp. 18-19.

10. *L'Amico del Popolo*, Oct. 6-7, 10-11, 20-21, 1894.

11. See Appendix I.

12. Pius XII, *Exsul Familia*, in *A.A.S.* XLIV (1952), p. 662.

13. *L'Emigrato Italiano*, Jan., Feb., Mar., 1920, pp. 25-26.

14. Pius XII, *Exsul Familia*, in *A.A.S.* XLIV (1952), pp. 673, 697-699.

15. G. Ferretto, *S.S.*, *Pio XII provido padre degli esuli e sapiente ordinatore dell'assistenza spirituale agli emigranti*, Rome, 1954, p. 19.

16. J. B. Scalabrini, *Il disegno di legge sull'emigrazione italiana*, p. 43.

17. Idem, First Conference on Emigration, p. 15.

18. Ibid., p. 13.

19. Idem, *Il Socialismo e l'azione del Clero*, p. 84.

20. Idem, *L'Italia all'estero*, p. 17.

21. Idem, *L'emigrazione italiana in America*, p. 46.

22. Idem, Letter dated Feb. 16, 1887, to the Cardinal Prefect of Propaganda Fide (Arch. S.C.P.F., *Lettere e decreti*, 1887, vol. 383, ff. 1491 ff.).

23. See the passages quoted on pp. 174-175 and 214-215.

24. J. B. Scalabrini, *Il disegno di legge sull'emigrazione italiana*, p. 48.

25. M. Ciufoletti, "Le Scuole Parrocchiali negli Stati Uniti ed in particolare le italiane," in *L'Emigrato Italiano*, Oct., Nov., Dec., 1917, p. 26.

26. Ibid., p. 25.

27. Idem, "Importanza sociale delle parrocchie italiane in America," Oct., Nov., Dec., 1924, pp. 1-6.

28. Mention has already been made of Fr. Chimielinski and Fr. Duda, true missionaries, whom Scalabrini sent to minister to the Polish immigrants in the United States. He also took an interest in the German immigrants (see his letter to Bishop Bonomelli, Piacenza, Dec. 21, 1904 Abba: "If the two Germans are really good and want to go to the missions I will accept them on your say-so. They will be very helpful, for there are often mixed settle-

ments"). He provided an Italian-Greek priest for the Albanian colony in New York (see letter to Bishop Corrigan, 1901, AGS). He was asked to take charge of an Institute that was to be established in Belgium for all the European immigrants in America, but he declined because the initiative had been undertaken without the approval of the Holy See (J. B. Scalabrini to D. Hengens, May 15, 1888; and to Card. Simeoni, July 10, 1888, AGS).

29. See Chapter XIII, pp. 237-239.
30. See Chapter XI, p. 206 ff.
31. M. Ciufoletti, "Importanza sociale delle parrocchie italiane in America," in *L'Emigrato Italiano*, Oct., Nov., Dec., 1924, pp. 3-6.
32. See Chapter XI, pp. 206-207 and 210.
33. "Gruppi etnici e comunità nazionale. Il pensiero di Mons. Krol, Arcivescovo di Philadelphia," in *Problemi di storia, sociologia, e pastorale dell'emigrazione*, Rome, 1965, pp. 140-144.
34. Pius XII, Allocution, *La elevatezza e la nobiltà dei sentimenti*, Feb. 20, 1946, in *A.A.S.* XXXVIII (1946), pp. 141 ff.
35. John XXIII, address to the World Pilgrimage of Emigrants and Refugees, Aug. 5, 1962 in *A.A.S.* LIV (1962), p. 578.
36. See L. Salvucci, "L'influsso degli immigrati nello sviluppo religioso e sociale delle collettività italiane del Rio Grande," in *L'Emigrato Italiano*, Aug., 1962, pp. 16-24.
37. A. Perotti, "Scalabriniani in Brasile," in *L'Emigrato Italiano*, Apr., 1966, pp. 4-10.
38. "Una visita in forma di Missione nelle due parrocchie Cupim e Prudentopolis," in *Periodico mensile della Congregazione dei Missionari di San Carlo (L'Emigrato Italiano)*, a. 2, n. 5, May, 1904, pp. 36-38.
39. F. Milini, "Una diocesi in cambio di una parrocchia," in *L'Emigrato Italiano*, Dec., 1954, pp. 173-174.
40. J. B. Scalabrini, *L'emigrazione italiana in America*, Piacenza,   1887, pp. 53-54.

Chapter XIV — THE HEART OF THE CHURCH

1. J. B. Scalabrini, Pastoral Letter, *Il prete cattolico*, 1892, p. 7.
2. Ibid., p. 12.
3. Idem, *Oratio III, Synodus Diocesana Placentina Tertia Eucharistics* (1889), Piacenza, 1900, p. 259. Future references will be abbreviated to *Syn. Plac. Tertia.*
4. Idem, *Allocutio pro commemoratione Summi Pontificis Pii VI*, ibid., p. 260.
5. Idem, *Oratio II*, ibid., p. 239.
6. Idem, *Oratio I*, ibid., p. 230.
7. Idem, *Oratio I*, ibid., pp. 219-224.
8. Idem, *Indictio Tertiae Synodi*, June 6, 1899, ibid., pp. 9-12.
9. Idem, *Oratio I*, ibid., pp. 219-233.
10. Idem, *Oratio II*, ibid, p. 240. Since Vatican Council II we can understand the full impact of these statements, which in Bishop Scalabrini's time must have seemed quite bold. Soon afterwards, he asserted that preaching the Gospel and the *fractio panis* are almost one and the same thing. Communion is the natural consequence of the preaching. The frequent, even daily Communion habitual in Rome and in Spain up to the time of St. Jerome, he explained, was due to the frequency with which the Gospel was preached.
11. All of Scalabrini's most important discourses end on a note of Christian optimism, the fruit of faith, hope and love. It is an optimism that he consciously set against a view of reality that tended to deepen the somewhat pessimistic bias of his own temperament. Here again, it is his will which, with the help of grace, conquers nature through the persistent effort to overcome human weakness that is characteristic of his asceticism (Idem, *Oratio II*, ibid., pp. 234-235).
12. Idem, *Oratio III*, ibid., p. 246-259.
13. Idem, Lenten Pastoral Letter, 1902, *La devozione al SS.mo Sacramento*, p. 34.
14. For this purpose he brought to Piacenza the Daughters of St. Joseph, founded by Father Clemente Marchisio, who were "specialists" in making the hosts and the wine for Mass and the sacred vestments. (See A. Costa to Bishop Scalabrini, Piacenza, Feb. 27, 1905, AGS).

15. J. B. Scalabrini, Lenten Pastoral Letter, 1902, pp. 33-34.
16. *Syn. Plac. Tertia*, Pars IV, cap. IV, n. 3, p. 84.
17. Ibid., no. 10, pp. 86-87.
18. Ibid., n. 11, p. 87.
19. Ibi., nn. 12-14, pp. 87-90.
20. In the Synod on the Eucharist there are frequent exhortations to joy, to gaiety, which should characterize all manifestations of Eucharistic devotion. For this reason, it was forbidden to carry symbols of the Passion in the processions in honor of *Corpus Domini* and those on the third Sunday of the month.
21. J. B. Scalabrini, Lenten Pastoral Letter, 1902, pp. 22-24.
22. *Syn. Plac. Tertia*, Pars IV, cap. I, n. 5, p. 66.
23. Ibid., cap. II, n. 15, p. 73.
24. Ibid., n. 17, p. 74.
25. Ibid., n. 18, p. 74.
26. Ibid., n. 20, p. 75.
27. Ibid., Pars III, cap. III, pp. 61-62.
28. J. B. Scalabrini, Discourses (notes).
29. J. B. Scalabrini to the Rector of the Seminary, Jan. 5, 1899 (Archives of the Seminary of Bedonia).
30. Idem, Lenten Pastoral Letter, 1902, p. 13.
31. *Syn. Plac. Tertia*, Pars II, cap. I, pp. 32-33.
32. Ibid., n. 5, p. 34.
33. Ibid., n. 9, p. 34.
34. Ibid., cap. VI, nn. 5-6, p. 53.
35. Ibid., cap. III, n. 7, p. 40.
36. Ibid., Pars VII, cap. VII, n. 1, p. 143.
37. Ibid., n. 5, p. 145.
38. Ibid., n. 7, p. 146.
39. Ibid., n. 12, pp. 147-148.
40. In 1891 he had already associated the diocese to the *Associazione Reparatrice delle Nazioni Cattoliche* (Society of Reparation of the Catholic Nations) which obliged the members to a half hour of adoration every Tuesday, the day assigned to Italy.
41. See V. Pancotti, *Il XX anniversario dell'Opera dei Tabernacoli*, Piacenza, 1924.
42. See Chapter VII, p. 143.
43. C. Molinari to Bishop Scalabrini, Rome, Mar. 29, 1905 (AGS).
44. L. Mondini, witness, *Processus*, iuxta 30, p. 47.
45. *Documenta vitae spiritualis, Processus*, p. 324.
46. Ibid., p. 330.
47. G. Cardinale, witness, *Processus*, iuxta 30, p. 101.
48. L. Cornaggia Medici, *Le caratteristiche di Mons. G. B. Scalabrini*, Reggio Emilia, 1935, p. 20.
49. E. Caccialanza, witness, *Processus, cop. publ.*, f. 221 v.
50. C. Tomedi, witness, ibid., iuxta 26, pp. 303-304.
51. E. Caccialanza, witness, *Processus, cop. publ.*, iuxta 30, f. 221 v.
52. P. Scarani, witness, biid., f. 485 r.
53. L. Cornaggia Medici, *Un profilo di Mons. Scalabrini*, Rome, 1930, p. 4.
54. Idem, *Processus*, iuxta 44, p. 255.
55. L. Mondini, witness, ibid., iuxta 41, p. 57.
56. L. Cornaggia Medici, witness, ibid., iuxta 4, pp. 249-250.
57. J. B. Scalabrini to a priest, Apr. 12, 1902 (note in AGS).
58. Idem to Fr. Natale Bruni, Sept. 12, 1894 (Archives of the Seminary of Bedonia).
59. Idem, note of letter to a priest (AGS).
60. Idem to Fr. Giovanni (?), Mar. 13, 1897 (AGS).
61. See *Trent'anni di Apostolato*, pp. 437-440.
62. Ibid., pp. 521-524.
63. F. Torta, witness, *Processus*, iuxta 30, p. 120.

64. "I asked him what time he got up. At five o'clock, he answered — And do you say Mass right away? — No, I say it much later. It is necessary to pray also for those who do not pray." (Antonio Fogazzaro, "Una visita a Mons. Scalabrini," in *Rassegna Nazionale*, July 1, 1905, p. 11.)

65. F. Gregori, witness, *Processus*, iuxta 30, p. 184. See L. Mondini, witness, ibid., p. 37. "He looks like an angel," the people used to say. "I often went to see him during the years I was in the seminary and later at the Alberoni College. And it was in this long period that I came to recognize the validity of their phrase, because especially when he preached and conducted the services, he seemed to be transformed, as it were, and to reveal a soul filled with ardor, eager and full of love for Jesus in the Eucharist," (F. Pallaroni, witness, *Processus de non-culto* f. 14 v.). "When we thought he had already gone to bed (during the Pastoral Visit) I often found him in Church before the Blessed Sacrament" (A. Gona, witness, ibid., f. 28 v.). "I cannot forget his enraptured look when he was in adoration before the Blessed Sacrament" (M. Risi, witness, ibid., f. 36 r.).

66. C. Spallazzi, witness, *Processus*, iuxta 30, p. 28. But even when he had his private chapel, "he very often went to make a long act of adoration before the Blessed Sacrament when the Church (cathedral) was empty." (E. Rossi, witness, *Processus de non-culto* f. 38 v.).

67. J. B. Scalabrini, *Lettera Pastorale*, Oct. 15, 1891, p. 14.

68. L. Mondini, witness, *Processus*, iuxta 30, p. 47. "During his lifetime he often observed that he would like to have in his coffin everything necessary to say Mass: the chalice, the cruets, wine and a host. And so, in fact, I placed them in there."

69. See Chapter XXIII, pp. 391-393.

70. J. B. Scalabrini, Lenten Pastoral Letter, 1902, p. 37.

71. Idem, Lenten Pastoral Letter, 1881, *La Religione e l'individuo*, p. 26.

Chapter XV — THE MOTHER OF THE CHURCH

1. J. B. Scalabrini, Pentecostal Discourse, 1900.

2. Idem, Assumption Discourse, 1882.

3. Idem, Pastoral Letter, *A ricordo del primo faustissimo Giubileo della definizione dommatica dell'Immacolato Concepimento*, Dec. 8, 1879; Idem, *Il Concilio Vaticano*, pp. 216-217. See Idem, Mary Immaculate Discourse, 1904.

4. Idem, Pastoral Letter quoted on p. 27.

5. Ibid., p. 7.

6. Idem, Mary Immaculate Discourse, 1904.

7. G. Cardinali, witness, *Processus*, iuxta 30, p. 101. See F. Lotteri, witness, ibid., p. 243: "he spoke of her with so much affection he seemed a seraph"; F. Calzinari, witness, ibid., p. 212: "he often spoke with emotion and in moving terms of the most holy Virgin"; L. Tammi, witness, ibid., p. 298: "he spoke as if he were inspired."
   With regard to Dec. 8, 1904, we read in a note by Scalabrini: "On that happy day in the city alone there were 30,000 persons who received communion. *Laus Deo!*" (AGS).

8. Devotion to the Immaculate Conception had flourished previously in the diocese, during the episcopates of Sanvitale and of Ranza. It was the latter who had had the column with the statue of the Immaculate Conception erected in the Piazza del Duomo (See A. Fermi-F. Molinari, op. cit., vol. I, part II, pp. 55-59.

9. J. B. Scalabrini, Pastoral Letter, *Per la visita pastorale*, Nov. 4, 1876, pp. 19-20.

10. Idem, to Msgr. Mangot, Curityba, Aug. 14, 1904 (AGS).

11. See *Fiori di cielo, Mons. G. B. Scalabrini*, p. 28.

12. J. B. Scalabrini, Pastoral Letter of Sept. 15, 1884, pp. 3-4.

13. Idem, *Associazione di preghiere per ottenere mediante l'intercessione di Maria SS. la buona educazione dei bambini*, Aug. 30, 1899 — As noted above, catechists gathered in the church of Santa Maria in Cortina for their monthly instruction or lecture by the Bishop or one of the priests.

14. See Chapter XIX, p. 352.

15. G. B. Nasalli Rocca, witness, *Processus*, iuxta 30, p. 262.

16. *L'Amico del Popolo*, Jan. 10, 14-15, 1893.

17. It is the public walk on the walls of Piacenza (a distortion of London's *Vauxhall Gardens*). According to tradition — but not historically certain — during the war between the Germans and the Franco-Spaniards in 1746, the city was bombarded for fifteen days, and one of the shells struck the Virgin's picture but remained stuck in the wall without damaging the house or its inhabitants.

18. F. Molinari, *Mons. Francesco Torta, apostolo della carità*, Turin, 1963, pp. 95-105. See Msgr. Torta's *Diario*, p. 8 (ibi cit.).

19. J. B. Scalabrini to the Rector of the Seminary of Bedonia, May 29, 1898 (Archives of the Seminary).

20. Idem, Nov. 27, 1893, ibid.

21. Idem, Sept. 13, 1892, ibid.

22. Idem, Sept. 27, 1892, ibid.

23. Idem, Feb. 3, 1889, ibid.

24. Idem, Feb. 3, 1904, ibid.

25. Idem, May 29, 1898, ibid.

26. Idem, Oct., 1, 1891, ibid.

27. *Vita e virtù del S.d.D. Mons. G. B. Scalabrini*, Bassano del Grappa, 1936, p. 57.

28. J. B. Scalabrini to the Rector of the Seminary of Bedonia, Nov. 27, 1888 (Seminary Archives).

29. Idem, Feb. 3, 1889, ibid.

30. Gregori, op. cit., p. 579.

31. G. Squeri, witness, *Processus*, iuxta 30, p. 164. See A. Bracchi, witness, ibid., *cop. publ.*, f. 472 r.: "And while the Servant of God was preaching, and even more as he crowned the miraculous statue, he wept and everyone wept."

32. D. Mazzadi, witness, *Processus*, iuxta 30, p. 156.

33. *L'Amico del Popolo*, July 25-26, 1896.

34. Ibid., Oct. 15, 1896.

35. Ibid., June 30, 1897.

36. See pp. 274-275.

37. G. Cardinali, witness, *Processus*, iuxta 30, p. 101.

38. J. B. Scalabrini, *Lettera ai MM. RR. Parroci*, May 5, 1895.

39. Idem, Assumption Discourse, 1895.

40. J. B. Scalabrini to Bishop Bonomelli, Mar. 21, 1883 (Abba).

41. Idem, June 5, 1882 (Abba).

42. J. B. Scalabrini, Discourse on the Virgin of Graces, Sept. 6, 1896.

43. G. Montini to Bishop Scalabrini, Sept. 10, 1896 (AGS). See A. Cistellini, *Giuseppe Tovini*, Brescia, 1964, p. 215.

44. Vicar General of Ravenna to Bishop Scalabrini, Dec. 17, 1899 (AGS).

45. G. B. Scalabrini, Discourse on the Coronation of the Madonna of San Savino, June 5, 1900.

46. Idem, *Communicazione dell'Enciclica, Supremi apostolatus*, Sept. 16, 1883, pp. 5-7.

47. Ibid., p. 9.

48. Idem, *Communicazione dell'Enciclica, De Rosario mariali*, Sept. 17, 1893, p. 2.

49. Idem, Discourse on the Rosary, 1894.

50. *Synodus Placentina 1879, De vita et honestate clericorum*, n. 4, pp. 140-141; *Synodus Placentina Secunda*, 1893, Oratio III, p. 193; *Synodus Placentina Tertia, Monitiones*, n. 2, p. 206.

51. A. Scarani, witness, *Processus, cop. publ.*, iuxta 30, p. 408 r. The reference is probably to the Encyclical *Supremi Apostolatus* of 1883.

52. See *Documenta vitae spiritualis, Processus*, pp. 294 ff. of the typescript.

53. E. Preti, witness, ibid., iuxta 30, p. 74.

54. Ibid., iuxta 30.

55. *Documenta vitae spiritualis, Processus*, Aug. 24, 1893, p.. 324.

56. Ibid., Aug., 1900, p. 330.

57. Ibid., Feb. 23, 1901, p. 331.

58. F. Gregori, witness, *Processus*, iuxta 30, p. 184.

59. Ibid.
60. J. B. Scalabrini, Discourse on the Virgin of Graces, Sept. 6, 1896.
61. Idem, Discourse on the Madonna of the People, Castelsangiovanni, Aug. 5, 1880.
62. F. Calzinari, witness, *Processus*, iuxta 30, p. 212.
63. *Vita e virtù del S.d.D. Mons. G. B. Scalabrini*, Bassano del Grappa, 1936, p. 50.
64. A. Labo, *In memoria di Mons. G. B. Scalabrini*, Piacenza, 1906, pp. 19-20.
65. See, among others, E. Martini, witness, *Processus, cop. publ.*, iuxta 30, f. 198 r.
66. Since 1927 the shrine of the Blessed Virgin of the Castello has been entrusted to Bishop Scalabrini's Missionaries of St. Charles. For the history of the shrine of Rivergaro, see G. Malchiodi, *Il Santuario della B. Vergine del Castello di Rivergaro*, Piacenza, 1905.

Chapter XVI — DEVOTION TO THE CHURCH AND TO THE POPE

1. *Il Concilio Vaticano.* Conference held in the Cathedral of Como by J. B. Scalabrini, Como, 1873.
2. Ibid., pp. XXIV-XXV. The Guardian of the Capuchin monastery in Lugano, Fr. Cherubino da Ligornetto, wrote to the author: "I could not name a better apologist, nor a better apostle of the truth...and of such truths...preached with such courage...and in these truly exceptional times...and from *that pulpit"* (the emphasis is Fr. Cherubino's) (AGS).
3. Ibid., p. XXVI.
4. Ibid., p. 161.
5. Ibid., pp. 203-204. Part II, conf. III, *Della forza e natura del Primato del Romano Pontefice*, pp. 191-207.
6. Ibid., pp. 204-205.
7. Ibid., p. 236.
8. Ibid.
9. Ibid., pp. 209-210. Part II, conf. IV, *Del Magistero infallibile del Romano Pontefice*, pp. 209-241.
10. Among the seven Italian bishops who abstained on the vote, one was too hastily compared to Bishop Scalabrini, Bishop Luigi Nazari di Calabiana, the archbishop of Milan since 1867. It is also well known that the Italian government had tried indirectly to prevent the proclamation of the dogma, fearing that the definition of infallibility would lead to a dogmatic definition of the necessity of temporal power for the papacy.
11. Idem, *Conferenze sul Concilio Vaticano*, 1873, p. 5.
12. Ibid., p. 6.
13. Ibid., p. 7.
14. Ibid., pp. 11-12.
15. Ibid., p. 13.
16. Ibid., pp. 22-23.
17. Idem, Lenten Pastoral Letter, 1888, pp. 16-17.
18. Ibid.
19. Ibid., pp. 18-22.
20. Ibid., p. 23.
21. Ibid., p. 41.
22. Ibid., pp. 41-43.
23. Idem, *Intransigenti e transigenti, Osservazioni di un Vescovo italiano*, Bologna, 1885, p. 5.
24. Ibid., p. 9.
25. Ibid., p. 17.
26. Ibid.
27. Ibid., p. 29.
28. Ibid., p. 31.
29. Idem, Pastoral Letter, *Unione colla Chiesa, obbedienza ai legittimi pastori*, Feb. 8, 1896, pp. 24-25.
30. Idem, Easter Discourse, 1879.
31. Ibid.

32. Idem, Lenten Pastoral Letter, 1888, *La Chiesa Cattolica*, 2nd ed. p. 37. He does not say, as we would expect, that we should be united to Christ, but to the Church. To be united to Christ it is indispensable to be united to the Church.

33. Ibid., pp. 38-39.

34. Idem, Pastoral Letter, *Unione colla Chiesa, obbedienza ai legittimi pastori*, Feb. 8, 1896, p. 4.

35. Ibid., p. 6.

36. Ibid.

37. Ibid., pp. 7-9.

38. Ibid., pp. 9-10.

39. Ibid., pp. 11-17.

40. Ibid., p. 18.

41. Ibid., pp. 22-23.

42. Idem, *L'Enciclica Sapientiae Christianae*, Letter of Jan. 1, 1890, p. 5.

43. G. B. Lemoyne, *Memorie biografiche del Venerabile Servo di Dio Don Giovanni Bosco*, vol. IX, Turin, 1917, p. 803.

44. C. Nocella to J. B. Scalabrini, Rome, May 7, 1873 (AGS).

45. *Venerabili Fratri Joanni Baptistae Episcopo Placentino Pius PP IX, Romae*, Feb. 2, 1876 (AVP).

46. L. Cornaggia Medici, *Un profilo di Mons. Scalabrini*, Rome, 1930, pp. 7-10.

47. J. B. Scalabrini, *Lettera Pastorale al Clero e al Popolo*, Jan. 30, 1876, pp. 7-10.

48. *Ad ejusmodi vero opus suscipiendum alacri animo jam propensis Nobis ac penitus inclinatis Sedis Apostolicae desiderium atque iterata insinuatio, quam nos veluti praeceptum venerati sumus, ardentiores stimulos addidere* (Allocution in *Prolusione Synodi, Synodus Dioecesana 1879*, Piacenza, 1880, pp. XIV-XV).

49. Ibid., p. XIX.

50. Ibid., *De fide Catholica*, pp. 2-3.

51. Ibid., pp. 239-270.

52. Ibid., *De Summo Pontifice*, p. 129.

53. Ibid., pp. 130-134.

54. Ibid., pp. 372-374.

55. *Leonis XIII ad litteras synodales responsum*, Oct. 18, 1879, ibid., pp. 375-376.

56. *Synodus Placentina Secunda*, Pars VI, cap. VI, n. 2, Piacenza, 1893, p. 157.

57. Ibid., n. 3.

58. Ibid., *Notificazioni*, n. 19, pp. 289-290.

59. *Monitiones*, which Bishop Scalabrini addressed to the Synod and which were to be reread every year at the meeting held on moral and liturgical subjects. *Synodus Placentina Tertia*, Piacenza, 1900, pp. 208-209, n. 6.

60. Pius IX's Brief to Bishop Scalabrini, Sept. 25, 1876 (AVP).

61. Gregori, op. cit., pp. 82-83.

62. Ibid., p. 87.

63. "The June festivities," he wrote in his Pastoral Letter of Mar. 3, 1877, on the occasion of Pius IX's jubilee as a bishop, pp. 6-7, "have various very important aims. First of all to thank the Most High for having with special assistance preserved for us until now Pius IX, the best of Fathers, to pray Our Lord that he will keep him for us a long time to come; to praise our glorious Pontiff; to console him in his difficulties, to help him in his needs; to make up for the ingratitude of others; to show him that we are always with him and desire to be always with him...but more than anything else the purpose of the June festivities is to proclaim the Divine Authority and *Infallible* Magisterium of the Pope. Therefore, by taking part in them, we shall make a solemn profession that we believe with full submission and embrace with the utmost respect what was recently defined by the Ecumenical Vatican Council with regard to the Roman Pontiff."

64. "Pius IX, the most authoritative of fathers for me and for you, who deigned to receive me with expressions of the greatest affection, who honored me with the precious gift which is the honor of a Bishop and his flock; who heard with great joy that you...love him sincerely, that you have an unalterable attachment to the Chair of Peter and reverent affection for

the unworthy pastor he sent you and who forms and will continue to form the object of your most fervent and frequent prayers. — I heartily congratulate you, dear Bishop of Piacenza, the glorious Pontiff deigned to reply, and I bless you with all my heart; on your return take to your good people and clergy of Piacenza my thanks and the Apostolic Benediction with a plenary indulgence." (J. B. Scalabrini, Discourse on the Feast of St. Peter, 1877.)

65. J. B. Scalabrini, *Lettera circolare per la morte di Pio IX*, Feb. 9, 1878, p. 1.

66. The Mastai family came originally from Crema, which was once part of the diocese of Piacenza. They received the title of Count from Duke Francesco Farnese, in a decree dated from Piacenza on Sept. 21, 1705 (Gregori, op. cit., p. 118, n. 1).

67. *La Verità*, (Piacenza), May 30, 1880. "Pius IX, when he gave the Piacentinians Bishop Scalabrini, said of him publicly: 'We have given a gift to Piacenza.'" (G. B. Nasalli Rocca, *Commemorazione di Mons. G. B. Scalabrini*, Piacenza, 1909, p. 12, n. 1). When the cathedral was restored, the statue of Pius IX was moved from the left nave to the outside.

68. J. B. Scalabrini, Pastoral Letter, Aug. 15, 1881, p. 5.

69. *Il Catechista Cattolico*, June 5, 1878, p. 146.

70. L. Nina to Bishop Scalabrini, Dec. 1, 1879 (AGS). See J. B. Scalabrini, Pastoral Letter, *Intorno all'istruzione dei Sordo-muti*, Sept. 8, 1880, p. 17.

71. Leo XIII to Bishop Scalabrini, July 26, 1880 (AVP).

72. J. B. Scalabrini, *Lettera Pastorale per la pubblicazione dell'Enciclica sul Matrimonio Cristiano*, Mar. 3, 1880, pp. 3, 7-8, 13, 14.

73. Idem, Pastoral Letter, Sept. 26, 1880, pp. 16-17.

74. Gregori, op. cit., p. 122.

75. See the letter of Canon Celli to the *Voce della Verita*, Oct. 19, 1881.

76. J. B. Scalabrini to Msgr. Boccali, Nov. 29, 1881 (note in AGS).

77. Idem, Pastoral Letter, Aug. 15, 1881.

78. The passage about the Catholic press was translated into Spanish and thousands of copies were distributed by the Catholic Youth Organization of Buenos Aires.

79. J. B. Scalabrini, *Comunicazione dell'Enciclica etsi nos e proibizione del giornale Il Penitente*, Mar. 19, 1882.

80. Idem, *Comunicazione dell'Enciclica Supremi Apostolatus*, Sept. 16, 1883.

81. Idem, *Comunicazione dell'Enciclica Humanum Genus*, June 1, 1884.

82. Idem, *Associazioni Cattoliche: Discorso del S. Padre*, Mar. 2, 1885. See the Lenten Pastoral, Jan. 30, 1885.

83. Idem, *Sull'Enciclica Immortale Dei*, Jan. 17, 1886.

84. Idem, Lenten Pastoral, Feb. 9, 1886.

85. Idem, to Count G. Acquaderni, Mar. 27, 1885 (note in AGS).

86. Idem, *Pel Guibileo sacerdotale del Sommo Pontefice Leone XIII*, Sept. 26, 1886, pp. 6-8. Some criticized the Pastoral for being "conciliatory," but it earned the sovereign pleasure" of the Pope. See *L'Amico del Popolo*, Oct. 16, 1886.

87. The purpose of the Zanardelli Law, especially articles 182-183 against the "abuses of the clergy," was to subject the clergy to more rigid state controls. It defined new crimes, such as public criticism of the laws of the State and the actions of the authorities; incitement to contempt of liberal institutions or infringement of the duties toward the fatherland. When it was adopted by the Parliament, Scalabrini was in Rome and he commented: "I was in the Vatican the day the Penal Code was adopted; no one said a word to me about it, almost as if it were the most unimportant thing in the world." (J. B. Scalabrini to Bishop Bonomelli, June 23, 1888.) (Abba.)

88. J. B. Scalabrini, Circular, Aug. 10, 1888.

89. See Chapter IV, pp. 86-87.

90. J. B. Scalabrini, Pastoral Letter, *L'educazione cristiana*, Feb. 7, 1889 (AGS).

91. M. Rampolla to Bishop Scalabrini, July 1;2, 1889 (AGS).

92. J. B. Scalabrini, Letter of Aug. 27, 1889, pp. 2-3. On the eve of the "cowardly outrage" he had sent a personal telegram to the Pope in which he said he shared his holy indignation "at this authorized offense to Catholic consciences, civil liberties and Italian honor" (June 8, 1889); this was quoted in *Osservatore Romano* and the *Voce della Verità*.

93. Idem, *L'enciclica Sapientiae Christianae*, Jan. 27, 1890. *Presentazione dell'Enciclica Dall' Alto*, Oct. 24, 1890.

94. Idem, Pastoral Letter, *Unione, azione e preghiera*, May 11, 1890; *Sulla Redenzione degli schiavi in Africa. Devozione alla S. Famiglia. Scuola di Religione ed oratorii*, Dec. 12, 1890. To the leader of the anti-slavery movement in Italy, Filippo Tolli, Bishop Scalabrini wrote: "The anti-slavery society of Italy fills a gap in our nation, which has always been the mother and author of glorious initiatives. This work strikes at the heart of slavery and needs support and money. If I were not committed with my missionaries to the emigrants, I would embrace your cause with enthusiasm, in fact I would become its standard-bearer" (Letter reported by F. Vistalli, *Giuseppe Toniolo*, Rome, 1954, p. 562).

95. J. B. Scalabrini to Bishop Bonomelli, Mar. 22, 1891 (Abba).

96. There are extant receipts for sizeable sums Scalabrini contributed to the building of the Church of St. Joachim in Rome. See letters from the institute *Adoratrice reparatrice*, etc. to Scalabrini, Dec. 4, 1889 and Oct. 26, 1897 (AGS). See J. B. Scalabrini, *Per il giubileo episcopale di Leone XIII*, Oct. 15, 1891.

97. J. B. Scalabrini, Pastoral Letter, May 1, 1892.

98. Idem, Lenten Pastoral Letter, *Il Papa*, Jan. 18, 1893.

99. Brief from Leo XIII to Bishop Scalabrini, May 11, 1895 (AVP).

100. Brief from Leo XIII to Bishop Scalabrini, Sept. 19, 1895 (AVP). The Bishop had organized a communication in tribute to the Pope on the occasion of the 25th anniversary of his Pontificate.

101. J. B. Scalabrini, Circular, Sept. 16, 1895, pp. 2-3.

102. *I diritti cristiani e i diritti dell'uomo*, Pastoral Letter of Jan. 25, 1898 of the Bishops of the Region of Emilia, Bologna, 1898; *L'Obolo di S. Pietro*, Joint Pastoral of the Bishops of the Emilian Region, Jan. 6, 1900, Bologna, 1900.

103. J. B. Scalabrini to Leo XIII, Jan. 22, 1901 (note in AGS).

104. Leo XIII to Bishop Scalabrini, Jan. 30, 1901 (AVP).

105. J. B. Scalabrini, Circular, Dec. 15, 1902.

106. Idem, Circular, Jan. 18, 1903.

107. Idem, Notification, July 21, 1903.

108. Idem, Notification, Aug. 4, 1903. See Card. Agliardi's letter to Bishop Scalabrini, Dec. 15, 1904 (AGS).

109. J. B. Scalabrini to a pastor, undated note (AGS).

110. Idem to Bishop Bonomelli, Piacenza, Aug. 11, 1903 (Abba).

111. Idem, Trevozzo, Oct. 4, 1903 (Abba).

112. Idem, Rome, undated, probably of Nov. 23, 1903 (Abba).

113. Idem, Pastoral Letter, *La prima lettera enciclica di S.S. Pio X*, Oct. 7, 1903, pp. 6-7.

114. Idem, *Note di viaggio* to Msgr. Mangot, June 18, 20, 29, 1904 (AGS).

115. *El Mensajero* (Buenos Aires), Nov. 18, 1904.

116. G. Bressan to Msgr. Mangot, June 9, 1905 (AGS).

117. Pius X to the Archbishops and Bishops of the Emilian Region, June 13, 1905 (AVP).

Chapter XVII — OBEDIENCE TO THE POPE AND THE CHURCH

1. J. B. Scalabrini, *Ai nostri amatissimi diocesani*, Jan. 23, 1878, pp. 2-3, 5.

2. Idem, Pastoral Letter, May 26, 1878, p. 5.

3. Idem, *Lettera a Leone XIII nell'anniversario dell'esaltazione al Sommo Pontificato*, Feb. 15, 1879.

4. Idem, Lenten Pastoral Letter, 1879, *La Religione Cattolica e la Società*, p. 5.

5. *Atti e documenti del Primo Congresso Catechistico*, Piacenza, 1890, p. 238.

6. J. B. Scalabrini, *Notificazione dell'elezione di Pio X*, Aug. 4, 1903, p. 6.

7. Idem, Discourse of the Feast of St. Peter, 1899.

8. Idem, *Lettera Pastorale di Monsignor Vescovo di Piacenza sull'opuscolo, "La Lettera dell'E.mo Card. Pitra. I commenti — La parola del Papa,"* Oct. 5, 1885.

9. See Chapter II, pp. 37-38.

10.   L. Mondini, witness, *Processus*, iuxta 53, p. 62.
11.   See Chapter IV, p. 119 ff.
12.   See E. Soderini, op. cit., vol. II, pp. 75-80; G. Martina, "L'Enciclica Libertas nei commenti della stampa contemporanea," in *Aspetti della cultura cattolica nell'età di Leone XIII,* Rome, 1961, pp. 597-630. On Card. Pitra, See F. Cabrol, *Histoire du Cardinal Pitra,* Paris, 1891; A. Battandier, *Le Cardinal Pitra,* Paris, 1886.
13.   *Acta Leonis XIII,* vol. V., pp. 68 ff: "Dilecto...Cardinal Guibert, Archiepiscopo Parisiensi," June 17, 1885.
14.   J. B. Scalabrini to Leo XIII, Aug. 16, 1885 (letter reproduced on p. 144 of the volume, *Leonis XIII Epistola ad Archiepiscopum Parisiensem,* Rome, 1885).
15.   *Lettera dell'E.mo Card. Pitra. I commenti. La parola del Papa,* Basilea — Milano, 1885.
16.   J. B. Scalabrini to Card. Jacobini, Sept. 16, 1885 (note in AGS).
17.   Card. L. Jacobini to Bishop Scalabrini, Sept. 23, 1885 (AGS).
18.   Card. L. Jacobini to Bishop Scalabrini, Oct. 8, 1885 (AGS). The notes Card. Jacobini sent — "Alcune idee per una Pastorale sull'Opuscolo *La Lettera del Card. Pitra,* etc." — are reproduced in their entirety in C. Bello, *Geremia Bonomelli,* Brescia, 1961, pp. 273-276.
19.   *Lettera Pastorale di Monsignor Vescovo di Piacenza sull'opuscolo: "La Lettera dell'E.mo Card. Pitra. I commenti. La Parola del Papa,"* Oct. 5, 1885, p. 15. The reference to Stoppani is clear, who used to say: "As long as I can believe that my poor pen can accomplish something, *Deo juvante,* for the good of the Church and the glory of God, I shall use it with holy freedom and with courage. As soon as I suspect the contrary, I shall break it!" (A. Stoppani to Bishop Bonomelli, Aug. 3, 1884. See G. Astori, *Corrispondenza di Mons. G. Bonomelli e Don A. Stoppani,* Brescia, 1959, p. 93.)
20.   Card. L. Jacobini to Bishop Scalabrini, Oct. 17, 1885 (AGS). *L'Osservatore Romano* carried it in full, calling it "an important writing of the illustrious Prelate" (Oct. 23, 1885). Several editions were published, including one in French put out in Paris by the Archbishop of Rouen. All the more significant, therefore, is the silence of the *Osservatore Cattolico,* to which the Secretariat of State had addressed an explicit invitation to speak of it: "I am sending the Pastoral of the Bishop of Piacenza. This pastoral has been praised by Italian Catholic journalists for the Catholic doctrine and devotion to the Holy See which it expresses. It is desired that the *Osservatore Cattolico* also speak of it with praise." (M. Mocenni to D. G. Rossi, Oct. 25, 1885, quoted by F. Vistalli, *Mon. Guindani,* Bergamo, 1943, p. 349).
21.   J. B. Scalabrini to Bishop Bonomelli, Oct. 24, 1885 (Abba).
22.   Idem, Nov. 28, 1885 (Abba).
23.   *Intransigenti e Transigenti,* quoted on pp. 3-4.
24.   Ibid., pp. 4-5.
25.   Ibid., pp. 6-7.
26.   Ibid., p. 22.
27.   Ibid., p. 28. The ideas expressed by Scalabrini coincide with those in the encyclical *Immortale Dei* issued the previous month: "In general total abstention from public life would be no less blameworthy than the refusal to participate in any way in the public good; especially since Catholics, by reason of their principles, are more than ever obliged to bring integrity and zeal to the management of affairs. On the other hand, as they keep themselves apart, men will easily come to power whose opinions leave little hope for the good of the State. And this would likewise turn to the detriment of religion, since those who hate the Church would be able to do very much, and those who love it very little." (*Acta Leonis XIII,* vol. V., p. 146.)
28.   Ibid., pp. 31-33.
29.   Ibid., p. 35. The pamphlet *Intransigenti e Transigenti* has a fundamental importance for the interpretation of the life of the Bishop of Piacenza, for it explains to what type of "transigents" he belonged, namely the current so precisely defined by Cistellini: "It was, therefore, sound political realism and especially a clear perception of the facts, from a Christian religious viewpoint, that prevented them from turning back to a past that could not be repeated and prompted them to stretch out, without compromising their principles, toward possibilities for action and to define the new problems that were besetting the

conscience of Catholics. From that time to the present the classification "liberal-Catholics" or "liberal-clergy" has been facile and frequent, a charge the intransigents tossed about without the least respect for episcopal dignity and which has been unfortunately taken up again by modern historians with astonishing lack of seriousness and even of scientific integrity. In addition to this type of categorizing, accepted unquestioningly, tends to make numerous pages of the religious history of Italian Catholics at that time quite incomprehensible. In any case, if one goes back to the sources it is not difficult to find proud and dignified protests against such charges, which kept being made repeatedly and were just as repeatedly denied. Not liberal-Catholics but integral-Catholics, and to attach to them the adjective transigent or conciliationist seems to diminish the purity of their faith and the sincerity of their obedience." (A. Cistellini, "I motivi dell'opposizione cattolica allo Stato liberale," in *Vita e Pensiero*, Dec., 1959, pp. 953-954.)

30. G. Borelli, "Il clero cattolico e le condizioni politico-sociali d'Italia. Un colloquio con Mons. Scalabrini," in *L'Alba* (Milan), July 15, 1900. There is great confusion even today. See A. Ferrari-Toniolo in *Aspetti della cultura cattolica nell'eta di Leone XIII*. Rome, 1961, p. 393. Who would not characterize Bishop Scalabrini as "intransigent according to the definition given by Gambasin? "...In speaking of the intransigents, the reference is not to those Catholics who through excessive zeal were trying to be more intransigent than the Pope, nor to those who in their desire to hurry things along, openly moved away from the discipline of the Catholic Movement; (the term refers rather) to those Catholics who discussed political programs, weighed the advantages and the disadvantages of the *non expedit*, prompted or dampened Catholic public opinion regarding the abrogation of the prohibition to take part in elections, or took one or another position regarding the two equally serious questions, i.e. the Roman question and the social question, did not foment nor pursue any doctrinal deviations nor did they rebel against the discipline imposed by the papacy." (A. Gamabsin, "L'Azione Cattolica e l'ingresso dei cattolici nella politica," in *Vita e Pensiero*, Dec., 1959, pp. 977, n. 1.)

31. See *L'Osservatore Cattolico*, Dec. 19-20; 21-22; 22-23; 23-24, 1885. This paper, which had carried no words of criticism against the booklet *La Lettera del Card. Pitra*, etc., bitterly attacked Scalabrini's pamphlet, accusing it of lying, calling it outrageous, an insolent outburst of personal resentments and antipathies, prompted by mean self-interest and malicious passions, an insult to the Pontiff, a distillate of liberal Jansenistic hypocrisy. The author (who practically speaking had been the pope himself) was accused of being arrogant toward Catholics, disrespectful to the Pope, ridiculous, among the most fanatic and injust sectarians, ignorant, cynical, dishonest, flea-brained, erratic and frenetic, conniving with the Free Masons, etc., etc. Even in the context of the polemical journalism of the period, this episode clearly demonstrates the difference in stature, and also in obedience and devotion to the Pope, between Bishop Scalabrini and the author of this hostile article.

32. G. Bonomelli to Bishop Scalabrini, Dec. 30, 1885 (AGS).

33. J. B. Scalabrini to Bishop Bonomelli, Dec. 31, 1885 (Abba).

34. G. Bonomelli to Bishop Scalabrini, Jan. 22, 1886 (AGS).

35. J. B. Scalabrini to Bishop Bonomelli, undated but written at the beginning of Jan., 1886 (Abba).

36. Draft in AGS.

37. Idem, in the same letter there is this proposal: "To complete this truly holy and salutary work, it would be well to consider another pamphlet which would treat the philosophical question with a view to dispelling the numerous ambiguities, even those contrived deliberately (liberal Rosminians, etc.). I shall gladly work at this, Holy Father, prepared to undertake whatever Your Holiness is disposed to support, etc."

38. N. Marzolini to Bishop Scalabrini, Jan. 7, 1886 (AGS).

39. Leo XIII to Bishop Scalabrini, Jan. 5, 1886. The Brief was published in *Amico del Popolo* only on Feb. 3, 1886.

40. The Pastoral is the Letter directed against the libel, *Il Card. Pitra*, etc.; the pamphlet is *Intransigenti e Transigenti*. Both were written, as we have seen at the behest of the Holy See.

41. J. B. Scalabrini to Leo XIII, undated draft, 1886 (AGS).

42. Idem to Card. Schiaffino, Jan. 21, 1887 (draft in AGS).
43. Idem to Card. Jacobini, July 11, 1886 (draft in AGS).
44. See *La Verità*, May 29, 1880 and May 30, 1880.
45. J. B. Scalabrini to Bishop Boccali, Nov. 29, 1881 (draft in AGS).
46. The six questions are quoted in their entirety in C. Bello, *Geremia Bonomelli*, pp. 82-83.
47. Undated draft, placed in May, 1886 or a little later (AGS).
48. J. B. Scalabrini to Bishop Bonomelli, Oct. 8, 1882 (Abba).
49. Ibid. The Marxist historian, G. Carocci, basing himself on the works of G. Manfroni and G. Candeloro, relates that Scalabrini took part in negotiations between the government and the Vatican with a view to permitting Catholics to participate in the elections of 1882 and especially those of 1886 when "Depretis used Minghetti as mediator, who, in turn, through Codronchi, was in contact with Scalabrini, and through the latter with the Pope. In fact, the negotiations would have succeeded if Tajani's anticlerical resistance during the trial of the reporter De Dorides, had not upset the clandestine idyll between the government and the Vatican. In Piacenza, the Intransigents supported the antigovernment list of candidates, made up of pentarchists, radicals, socialists, and supported also by the anarchists; the Transigents, on the other hand, followed Scalabrini's advice and supported the ministerial candidates" (G. Carocci, *Agostino Depretis e la politica interna italiana dal 1876*, Turin, 1956, pp. 322-325). The author here unquestioningly accepts the point of view of the Prefect of Piacenza with respect to his relations with the Minister of the Interior...More interesting is this letter of the deputy from Bologna, G. Codronchi to Minghetti, dated Apr. 10, 1886: "He (Scalabrini) says that he had come to an understanding with the Pope regarding participation in the elections, which would have been dangerous, but in the sense of supporting honest men, would support order...I saw from the correspondence that all was settled when Tajani's reply (...) disgusted the Pope so much that he did not want to hear any more about the matter" (Ibid., p. 323).
50. G. Boccali to Bishop Scalabrini, May 1, 1886 (AGS).
51. Idem, May 8, 1886 (AGS).
52. *L'Amico del Popolo*, May 8, 1886.
53. It should be noted that the declaration of the Holy Office had not yet been issued which restricted the previous interpretations and it was no longer a question of whether the matter was opportune but whether it was licit: *non expedit* is the same as *non licet*. On Jan. 5, 1883, the Sacred Apostolic Penitentiary had replied as follows to the Bishops who had asked whether it was a serious sin to take part in the elections: "One is to be regulated in each case according to the dictates of one's conscience and prudence, taking into account all the circumstances."
54. *L'Amico del Popolo*, May 12, 1886.
55. J. B. Scalabrini to Msgr. Mangot, May 11, 1886 (See *L'Amico del Popolo*, May 12, 1886).
56. Unfortunately the statement in *Amico del Popolo* of June 19, 1886, was true, which deplored the fact that "there are Catholics who call themselves *pure* and *intransigent*, and support the *Piccolo*, a *radical-democratic* paper, with anything but tender inclinations toward our religion, in order to get support for their party and to compromise the Bishop!.. What transigents!"
57. The note is carried by *Amico del Popolo*, which states *Piccolo* had published Marchese Landi's letter (June 19, 1886).
58. See *L'Amico del Popolo*, June 12, and 19, 1886.
59. See ibid., June 2 and 9, 1886.
60. Count Galeazzo Calciati was one of the four deputies in Piacenza elected at the polls on May 23, 1886, along with the lawyers Vittorio Cipello and Ernesto Pasquali and Prince Emmanuele Ruspoli of Rome.
61. J. B. Scalabrini to Mons. Mangot, Bedonia, May 22, 1886 (AGS).
62. Card. Monaco La Valletta to Bishop Scalabrini, June 6, 1886 (AGS).
63. Card. L. Jacobini to Bishop Scalabrini, July 11, 1886 (AGS). See Gregori, op. cit., p. 178.
64. Undated draft in AGS. To understand certain passages in the letter it is necessary to recall the fact that in June, 1886, right after the elections, Count Radini Tedeschi, president of The Diocesan Committee of Piacenza for the *Opera dei Congressi*, had received an

honor from the Holy See in recognition of the work he had done for Catholic Action. Scalabrini was displeased because, contrary to the usual practice, the honor was bestowed without the Bishop's knowledge, and he certainly had no reason to second this recognition bestowed on a man who, with all his merits, had not conducted himself very well with respect to the diocesan authorities, but he was especially displeased that the honor was given him at that particular moment. In fact it was bruited about as an open rebuke from the Holy See to Bishop Scalabrini, a point made especially by *Osservatore Cattolico*, which published two letters from Card. Jacobini to Commendatore Venturoli, president of the Permanent Committee of the *Opera dei Congressi*, through whom the Holy See had communicated the honor to the Count (See *L'Osservatore Cattolico*, July 5-6, and 7-8, 1886, which infers, contrary to Scalabrini, that the Pope can communicate his will without going through the bishop...). Radini, however, hastened to write to Scalabrini, stating his deep regret that the honor had been thus misused in disrespectful polemics against the person of the Bishop and authorizing him to publish the contents of the letter.

65. J. B. Scalabrini to Bishop Bonomelli, undated. Bonomelli's reply carries the date of Jan. 10, 1887 (Abba).
66. L. Galimberti to Bishop Scalabrini, Nov. 24, 1886 (AGS).
67. See E. Soderini, *Il Pontificato di Leone XIII*, Vol. II, pp. 152-154.
68. C. Mangot, witness, *Processus*, iuxta 26, p. 12.
69. L. Mondini, witness, ibid., iuxta 19, p. 42.
70. Idem, iuxta 42, p. 57.
71. F. Torta, witness, ibid., iuxta 17, pp. 115-116.
72. G. Radini Tedeschi, witness, ibid., *cop. publ.*, f. 366 v.
73. F. Gregori, witness, ibid., iuxta 19, pp. 177-178.
74. L. Cornaggia Medici, witness, ibid., p 252.
75. Card. G. B. Nasalli Rocca, witness, ibid., p. 260.
76. See Chapter XII, p. 233.
77. See G. Astori, "San Pio X e il Vescovo Geremia Bonomelli," in *Revista di Storia della Chiesa in Italia*. a. X n. 2 (May-Aug.), 1956.
78. A. Bianchi, witness, *Processus*, iuxta 19, p. 224.
79. G. Borelli, "Il clero cattolico e le condizioni politico-sociali d'Italia. Un colloquio con Mons. Scalabrini, Vescovo di Piacenza," in *L'Alba* (Milan), June 15, 1900. "Dogma no... I am quite free to discuss the opportuneness and efficacy of the measure. I rest on the word of the Pope, who is more enlightened than I, a humble pastor, and I accept the recommendation because I understand, as I have understood throughout my life as a bishop, the absolute necessity of observing the discipline, the foundation of the unbreakable unitary organism of the Church." Obedience and unity therefore, De Rosa has demonstrated that these were the constants on which Leo XIII and Pius X laid principal stress (See *Storia del movimento cattolico in Italia*, vol. I, Bari, 1966, pp. 265-268, where he underlines Leo's idea of "the realization of a social movement in Italy and the rest of the world, wherever there were Catholics, which would again put the Church at the head of the expectations of the working classes," pp. 372, 376, 428-431, etc.). Certainly Scalabrini judged the *non expedit* differently from Leo XIII, and he was always personally in favor of the idea set forth in the *Osservatore Romano* of June 14, 1904: "The means, precisely *qua* means, are never to be confused with the end. When the end may be gained equally well or better with another means, one may, and sometimes it is a moral obligation, give up the first and adopt the second" (quoted ibid., pp. 436-437). But for a moral evaluation of Scalabrini's attitude the greatest importance is to be given the essential points: obedience, harmony, "reChristianization" of society, always and only with a view to the "salvation of souls."
80. The summary is from Gregori, op. cit., pp. 207-209.
81. This section was not quoted literally by Gregori.
82. J. B. Scalabrini to Bishop Bonomelli, Aug. 16, 1887 (Abba).
83. Idem, Nov. 6, 1887 (Abba).
84. G. Bonomelli to Bishop Scalabrini, Mar. 13, 1887 (Gregori, op. cit., pp. 209-210).
85. J. B. Scalabrini to Bishop Bonomelli, Apr. 30, 1887 (Abba).

86. G. Bonomelli to Bishop Scalabrini, Dec. 14, 1887 (Gregori, op. cit., p. 215).
87. J. B. Scalabrini to Bishop Bonomelli, Dec. 12, 1887 (Abba).
88. Idem, Nov. 13, 1887 (Abba).
89. Idem, Feb. 26, 1889 (Abba).
90. Idem, Apr. 4, 1889 (G. Astori, "L'opuscolo di Mons. Bonomelli Roma e l'Italia e la realtà delle cose!" Excerpt from *Revista di Storia della Chiesa in Italia*, XV, n. 3, Sept.-Oct., 1961. Rome, 1961, p. 14). See *Acta Leonis XIII*, vol. IX, pp. 79-81: *Epistola Grtam scito*.
91. G. Bonomelli to Bishop Scalabrini, Apr. 5, 1889 (Abba). Bonomelli's act of confession and submission to the Pope and the letter quoted are reproduced in G. Astori, op. cit., pp. 14-15.
92. J. B. Scalabrini to Bishop Bonomelli, Apr. 5, 1889 (Abba).
93. See A. Fappani, *Un Vescovo "intransigente,"* Brescia, 1964, pp.. 24-25.
94. G. Bonomelli to Bishop Scalabrini, Apr. 13, 1889 (Gregori, op. cit., p. 217).
95. See *L'Amico del Popolo*, Apr. 13, 1889.
96. See *Il Messaggero* (Cremona), Apr. 22, 1889: "The author, as soon as he learned of the letter of the Holy Father, hastened to carry out what he had promised many times in his book and he immediately sent a trusted priest to Piacenza so that through the good offices of the Venerable Bishop there his submission and his acknowledgement that he was the author of the work could be forwarded. For serious reasons it was thought best not to go through with this edifying action and instead an anonymous submission was sent to *Rassegna Nazionale* to be passed on to *Osservatore Romano*...He was assured by a person charged to do so that the Holy Father was pleased by that submission and nothing further was required."
97. J. B. Scalabrini to Bishop Bonomelli, Apr. 12, 1889 (Abba).
98. G. Bonomelli to Bishop Scalabrini, Apr. 20, 1889 (AGS).
99. J. B. Scalabrini to Bishop Bonomelli, Apr. 20, 1889 (Abba).
100. The principal reasons for the public retraction are given in the text of the retraction itself. See G. Astori, op. cit., p. 17; C. Bello, op. cit., pp. 113-114.
101. G. Bonomelli to Bishop Scalabrini, Apr. 21, 1889 (Gregori, op. cit., p. 219).
102. J. B. Scalabrini to Bishop Boccali, Apr. 21, 1889 (ibid., p. 220).
103. Idem to Bishop Bonomelli, Apr. 22, 1889 (G. Astori, op. cit., pp. 17-18).
104. Reference to Scalabrini's telegram to the Holy Father. On the other hand, Scalabrini's letter to Agliardi contained the exploratory inquiry we mentioned.
105. A. Agliardi to Bishop Scalabrini, Apr. 22, 1889 (G. Astori, op. cit., p. 18).
106. On Apr. 29 Leo XIII sent through Scalabrini an Epistle in which he accepted with pleasure Scalabrini's. suggestion to compare Bonomelli with Fenelon (*Acta Leonis XIII*, vol. IXX, pp. 89-90: *Libenter intelleximus, Epistola ad Ep.um Cremonensem*).
107. J. B. Scalabrini to Card. Schiaffino, May 10, 1889 (Gregori, op. cit., pp. 222-223).
108. Idem to Bishop Bonomelli, May 11, 1889 (Abba).
109. G. Bonomelli to Bishop Scalabrini, May 29, 1889 (AGS).
110. An allusion to the "mad party" Bonomelli had written him about.
111. J. B. Scalabrini to Bishop Bonomelli, June 6, 1889 (Abba).
112. J. B. Scalabrini, *Il disegno di legge sulla emigrazione italiana*, Piacenza, 1888, p. 46.
113. See G. Dalla Torre, "La natura e i caratteri del movimento cattolico nell'Italia unita," in *Vita e Pensiero*, Dec., 1959, pp. 99 ff.
114. J. B. Scalabrini, *Il Socialism e l'azione del Clero*, Turin, 1899, p. 75.
115. For Scalabrini "conservation" is preferable to socialism: "in relation to the socialist party all the others become conservative" (ibid., p. 37). "Young priests must come out of the temple and the sacristy and confront the enemy who is setting his snares. But it is active practical efforts that are needed, and a powerful organization. Civil society must be convinced that where an organization of Catholic forces develops the most wholesome and profound principle of political and social conservation takes on vigor and triumphs. I say conservation, not reaction, and the civil authorities are mistaken if they continue to think that the clergy is dreaming of reversionary movements and does not sense the inescapable and fated movement of society...toward more noble forms of civil society...The liberal conservationists are filled with prejudices and fears and do not realize that by placing ob-

stacles in the way of Catholic organization...they not only flagrantly belie their own liberal program, but they offend the most powerful and legitimate guarantees of order...The Government of Italy should appeal directly to the Holy Father's wisdom and love of country. I am deeply convinced that the Pope would accept the invitation...Let the Government, therefore, have the courage to face the formidable problem and we shall all be happy. But if the house burns down meanwhile? — It certainly will not be the Catholics who will set the fires nor help the arsonists...Italian society is sick, there is no doubt and its collective functions do not always correspond to the principles of what is good and just. Nevertheless, I again state that the clergy cannot be the instrument of subversion. This is a sectarian calumny." (G. Borelli, art. cit.). Scalabrini's conservationism can be summed up in the following words: "The Church, along with revealed faith, preserves the principles on which rest the state, the family and property" (J. B. Scalabrini, Pastoral Letter, *Unione, azione, preghiera*, May 11, 1890, p. 10).

116. See Chapter XVII, pp. 325-326.
117. J. B. Scalabrini's *L'emigrazione italiana in America*, Piacenza, 1887, p. 54.
118. Idem, "L'Italia all'estero," in *Il Conferenziere*, Jan., 1900, p. 25.
119. J. B. Scalabrini to Bishop Bonomelli, Mar. 22, 1891 (Abba). The previous year, Fr. Agostino da Montefeltro had obtained the Pope's permission to invoke a blessing on Italy in his Lenten sermon and shortly afterwards he was obliged to make a public retraction (See A. Cistellini, "Il Vescovo Geremia Bonomelli, la Chiesa e i tempi moderni," in *Commentari dell'Ateneo di Brescia per il 1963*, p. 54, n. 52).
120. Idem, Jan. 19, 1892 (Abba).
121. L. Mondini, witness, *Processus*, iuxta 40, p. 55. The reference is to the Attorney General, Honorable Costa, to whom Bishop Scalabrini had occasion to write: "Certainly, if some way could be found to come to an accord, this would be the beginning, the foundation of an era of prosperity and greatness, an entirely new period for our Country. Oh, if the Government would ask the Pope to solve the problem! In his noble mind, this most prudent Leo XIII would find a way, there is no doubt, to reconcile the exigencies of the Church and of Italy, the two strongest and highest loves of every good Italian, love of Religion and love of Country. This is what he has wanted for so long and he has made it known many times" (Oct. 31, 1896, draft in AGS). There is no doubt that Scalabrini always affirmed it was up to the Italian State to take the first step and leave the decision to the Pope, as we have seen in several of the passages quoted.
122. G. Dodici, witness, *Processus, cop. publ.*, f. 172 v.
123. A. De Martini, witness, ibid., p. 89.
124. L. Tammi, witness, *ex officio*, ibid., pp. 299-300.
125. See various witnesses, iuxta 40. The following excerpts from the *Storia di Piacenza* by E. Ottolenghi is interesting (vol. IV, Piacenza s.d., p. 182): "Bishop Scalabrini...blessed the Commander and the whole troop leaving for Africa, commending them all to God's protection and wishing them a happy journey and a glorious return, and evoked demonstrations of sympathy and praise in the press throughout Italy."
126. G. B. Nasalli Rocca, witness, ibid., p. 264.
127. In this connection, we read in an undated draft of a letter, probably addressed to the Card. Secretary of State: "Most Eminent Prince, this is the second time that the civil authorities of this city have invited me to go and pay my respects to the King...My answer has always been the same: I cannot come, the conditions of the Church and of the Holy See do not allow it, etc. I was never able to give them a reply that satisfied them, however, when they put before me the examples of Bishops and Archbishops and even Cardinals who go to visit the King when he comes into the cities where they reside. It is useless to tell you the great differences of opinion among certain Bishops have given rise to the idea that the Holy Father's prescriptions of 1878 in this regard have been explicitly withdrawn, and for this reason several, and among them the principal Bishops of Italy, have decided to do what they do." (See also C. Spallazzi, witness, *Processus*, iuxta 13, p. 22: "In this connection with the Centennial celebration of Volta, I must attest that the King was present at the festivities. Although the Servant of God was urgently invited, even in writing, to attend the performance of an Oratorio by Perosi, at which the King and royal

family were present, he did not accept."

128. Scalabrini himself reminded the Pope: "I have refused honors, very great ones with the right of a generous pension in order to protest the violation of the rights of the Church (J. B. Scalabrini, to Leo XIII, Sept. 26, 1881, draft in AGS; See the letter of Card. Rampolla to Bishop Scalabrini, Dec. 17, 1892). The Bishop is referring to the *Collare dell'Annunziata*, which it was proposed to bestow on him for the aid he had given the people of Piacenza during the winter of 1879-1880. He did not permit his missionaries to accept honors from the government either: Fr. Maldotti, Scalabrinian Missionary, nominated to receive the Knighthood of the Crown asked permission of the Servant of God, who instructed me to inform him that since the *Ordine Cavalleresco della Corona d'Italia* (Order of the Knights of the Crown) had been instituted on the occasion of the capture of Rome, no priest in particular could accept it" (L. Mondini, witness, *Processus*, iuxta 40, p. 56).

He was also most prudent about asking the government's assistance for his work for emigrants. When he was accused by *Osservatore Cattolico* of having engaged in dealings with the "excommunicated" government for this purpose, he declared to the Cardinal Prefect of *Propaganda Fide:* "I am very well aware of my delicate position, especially where the government is concerned. The Government is ruthlessly working against me, although secretly for the present, especially since I told the Missionaries in New York, when the consul suggested they ask for a subsidy from the Ministry, to be careful not to do so: "You must neither be servile," I answered them, "nor uselessly hostile. Keep on the best terms with the local authorities, but never ask for anything from the Government." And he added the following highly significant words: "It is a very ugly thing, Your Eminence, to live in the midst of all these fires! Please assure the Holy Father that I pay no attention to anyone but Him, and my sole ambition is to please Him, knowing that in this way I shall please God" (J. B. Scalabrini to Card. Simeoni, Jan. 14, 1889. Arch. S.C.P.F., Collegi di Italia, Piacenza).

129. In the letter to Card. Simeoni quoted above, the following note, which he had put in the first draft, with respect to Prof. Angelo Scalabrini, does not appear: "Some years ago he was nominated as a deputy to Parliament and I let him know that just by permitting himself to be nominated, I could no longer receive him in my house, and he immediately refused the nomination and never spoke to me about it again." To this same brother Scalabrini wrote: "I have read your book on Rio della Plata. To tell you that I like it is saying little. However, there are certain phrases that won't do...Why needle the good Jesuit Fathers here and there about the colossal work they have achieved in Paraguay?... Without those blemishes your book would have been golden, a book to read, to give as a present, to recommend to everyone; with those defects and at this time of passionate emotionalism, this cannot be done" (Aug. 12, 1894, AGS).

130. A. Stoppani to Bishop Bonomelli, June 10, 1887 (G. Astori, *Corrispondenza di Mons. Geremia Bonomelli e Don Antonio Stoppani*, Brescia, pp. 128-130).

131. J. B. Scalabrini to A. Stoppani (Gregori, op. cit., p. 184).

132. Card. Rampolla to Bishop Scalabrini (AGS).

133. J. B. Scalabrini to Card. Rampolla, June 24, 1887 (draft in AGS).

134. Idem, to Bishop Bonomelli, June 29, 1887 (Abba).

Chapter XVIII — INTEGRITY, LOVE, OBEDIENCE

1. J. B. Scalabrini, Pastoral Letter, *Cattolici di nome e cattolici di fatto*, Feb. 1, 1887, pp. 16-17. It should be noted that the strong expressions in the Pastoral are inspired by and often copied from Leo XIII's letter to Card. Guibert (June 17, 1885), beginning with the first: "There are those among Catholics...who, not content with the role of subject believe they are able to play a part in its government."

2. Ibid., pp. 21-22.

3. Idem, *Lettera dell'Em.no Card. Pitra. I commenti — La parola del Papa*, Oct. 5, 1885, pp. 18-20.

4. Letters from Card. Jacobini to Bishop Scalabrini, Sept. 23, Oct. 8, Oct. 17, 1885 (AGS). See Chapter XVII, p. 313.

5.   J. B. Scalabrini, *Cattolici di nome e cattolici di fatto*, quoted on p. 24.
6.   Idem, *Conferenze sul Concilio Vaticano*, 4th ed., Piacenza, 1877, p. 161.
7.   Ibid., p. 159.
8.   Idem, *Cattolici di nome e cattolici di fatto*, quoted on p. 22.
9.   J. B. Scalabrini to Bishop Bonomelli, Nov. 22, 1881 (Abba).
10. Idem, undated (Abba).
11. Idem, undated (Abba).
12. Some object that taking part in the elections meant a *de facto* recognition of the usurping State and that therefore it was a question of principle and an act of collusion with Liberalism. This may be answered by the fact that Pius X did permit Catholics to vote. If a question of principle was necessarily implicit in this how could his permission be justified? What *de facto* legitimization had intervened that was not the same as that which could be invoked in Scalabrini's time?
13. F. Fonzi, *I cattolici e la società italiana dopo l'unità*, Rome, 1960, p. 62.
14. Ibid., p. 57. See P. Scoppola, *Chiesa e Stato nella storia d'Italian*, Bari, 1967, p. 263.
15. See St. Ignatius of Antioch, *Trall.*, 3, 1; *Symrn.*, 8, 1; *Magn.* 7, 1. Scalabrini maintained that a Bishop, precisely because he was "called to share the pastoral solicitude for all the churches" (*Cattolici di nome e cattolici de fatto*, Feb. 2, 1887, p. 21), cannot be content with purely passive obediences: "*In omnibus,*" wrote one Father of the Church, I think St. Ambrose, *cupio sequi Ecclesiam Romanam: sed tamen et nos homines sensum habemus:* I think he meant, just because I am a Bishop must I allow myself to be imposed upon like a beast of burden?" (J. B. Scalabrini to Bishop Bonomelli, Apr. 28, 1890, Abba.) The passage from St. Ambrose is to be found in *De Sacramentis*, lib. III (Migne, PL, XVI, 452, 5).
16. J. B. Scalabrini to Bishop Bonomelli, undated, 1885 (Abba).
17. Idem, *Cattolici di nome e cattolici di fatto*, Feb. 1, 1887, pp. 16-20.
18. J. B. Scalabrini, *Intransigenti e transigenti*, Bologna, 1885, pp. 22-23.
19. Vatican Council II, *Gaudium et Spes* (Constitution on the Church in the Modern World), n. 4.
20. G. Borelli, "Il clero e le condizioni politico-sociali di Italia. Un colloquio con Mons. Scalabrini, Vescovo di Piacenza," in *L'Alba* (Milan), July 15, 1900.

Chapter XIX — A LIFE OF FAITH

1.   J. B. Scalabrini, Oratio II, *Synodus Placentina Secunda*, Piacenza, 1893, pp. 177-184.
2.   Idem, All Saints Day Discourse, 1893.
3.   Idem, All Saints Day Discourse, 1882.
4.   Idem, Oratio II, *Synodus Placentina Secunda*, pp, 181-183.
5.   *Documenta vitae spiritualis, Processus*, pp. 322-333, passim.
6.   Ibid., Aug. 24, 1894 (ibid., p. 326).
7.   Ibid., Oct. 31, 1893 (ibid., p. 324).
8.   Ibid., Jan. 30, 1894 (ibid., p. 325).
9.   Idem, Lenten Pastoral Letter, 1883, p. 10. We find similar expressions in his Lenten Pastoral of 1878, pp. 33-34: "Our manner of speaking must be that of Jesus..., the glance of the eyes that of Jesus, the gentleness of our manners that of Jesus. Jesus for mirror, Jesus for model, Jesus for seal. It is He who must make the judgments, plan the way, make the choices; it is He who must govern, direct, control our life. Finally, He is our love, our joy, our crown, our all pervading thought, the beat of our heart, the wings of our aspiration, the sound that soothes our ears, the balm that softens our pain, the staff that supports us on our pilgrimage, the hymn and canticle which rises from our lips and accompanies us from time to eternity."
10. Ibid., Lenten Pastoral Letter, 1883, p. 12.
11. Idem, Lenten Pastoral Letter, 1878, p. 6.
12. Ibid., p. 29.
13. Idem, Lenten Pastoral Letter, 1883, p. 16.
14. Idem, Oratio II, *Synodus Placentina Secunda*, pp. 180-181.

15. Idem, *Documenta vitae spiritualis*, Aug. 24, 1893, *Processus*, p. 324.
16. Ibid., Jan. 30, 1894, p. 325; See Jan. 29, 1901, p. 330.
17. Ibid., Aug. 28, 1896, p. 328.
18. L. Scalabrini, witness, *Processus*, *cop. publ.*, iuxta 52, f. 919 v.
19. See Witnesses, I, II, III, XXII, XXVIII, *Processus*, iuxta 51.
20. L. Mondini, witness, ibid., p. 61.
21. F. Gregori, witness, ibid., p. 193.
22. A. Bianchi, witness, iuxta 51, pp. 227-228.
23. See Witnesses VIII, X, XXII, XXXII, etc., iuxta 51.
24. L. Gorlin, witness, iuxta 26, p. 308.
25. G. Radini Tedeschi, witness, *cop. publ.*, iuxta 51,, f. 377 r.
26. See Witnesses I, VII, XXI, XXXII, etc. iuxta 51.
27. E. Preti, witness, ibid., p. 76.
28. Idem, iuxta 52, p. 76.
29. J. B. Scalabrini to D. L. Cornaggia Medici, Dec. 22, 1896 (AGS).
30. Idem to a canon, s.d. (AGS).
31. Idem to a cardinal, s.d. (AGS).
32. G. M. Pellizzari, *In memoria di Mons. Scalabrini*, June 1, 1906, p. 20.
33. J. B. Scalabrini to Bishop Bonomelli, Nov. 13, 1884 (Abba).
34. Idem, Sept. 10, 1884 (Abba).
35. Idem, Nov. 13, 1884 (Abba).
36. Idem to the Rector of the Seminary of Bedonia, Nov. 28, 1884 (Archives of the Seminary of Bedonia).
37. A. Bianchi, witness, *Processus*, iuxta 14,, p. 223.
38. J. B. Scalabrini to Msgr. Mangot, s.d. (AGS).
39. Idem to D. L. Cornaggia Medici, May 12, 1896 (AGS).
40. C. Spallazzi, witness, *Processus*, iuxta 17, p. 23.
41. I. Puppo, witness, iuxta 26, p. 315.
42. J. B. Scalabrini to Card. Agliardi, Mar. 20, 1899 (AGS).
43. Idem to Duchess Clelia Fogliani ved. Pallavicino, Jan. 24, 1903 (AGS).
44. Idem to Bishop Bonomelli, s.d. (probably 1881) (Abba).
45. *Documenta vitae spiritualis*, Aug. 24, 1893, *Processus*, p. 323.
46. Ibid.
47. Ibid., Aug. 24, 1894, p. 327.
48. Ibid., Aug.. 28, 1896, p. 328.
49. Ibid., Aug., 1900, pp. 329-330.
50. Ibid., Jan. 29, 1901, p. 330.
51. Witnesses XVII and X, iuxta 26; III and X *ex officio*, iuxta 56, XI and XIII *ex officio*, iuxta 26.
52. Witnesses, XV; IV *ex officio*, iuxta 56.
53. Witnesses III, XIV, XV, XXXII; IV *ex officio*, iuxta 56.
54. F. Gregori, witness, iuxta 26, p. 182.
55. L. Mondini, witness, iuxta 56, p. 3.
56. F. Calzinari, witness, iuxta 26, p. 211. It was precisely this virtue, practiced to a heroic degree that indirectly caused his premature death. While he was on his pastoral visit to Bardi, his horse reared and in his effort to avoid a fall he hurt himself badly, but his scrupulous modesty kept him from saying anything about this to his companions (Witness III and X *ex officio*, iuxta 26 and 56). If he had mentioned the hurt in time, he could easily have been cured (Witnesses I, iuxta 26; I *ex officio*, 56). The bruise grew worse, became hydrocele and for many years he suffered annoying pain. When finally his strength failed, he was forced to take to his bed and to allow himself to be examined by a doctor. "Scalabrini is a love," his personal physician, Dr. Luigi Marchesi said, "of extraordinary purity; he is an angel." And he added: "If he is not in paradise, no one will get there." (L. Cella, witness, iuxta 26, p. 203.)
57. J. B. Scalabrini to Bishop Bonomelli, Sept. 19, 1882, see Mar., 3, 1901; Aug. 11, 1903 (Abba).

58. *Documenta vitae spiritualis, Processus*, passim.
59. See the *Discorsi di Capodanno*.
60. J. B. Scalabrini, Oratio II, *Synodus Placentina Secunda*, Piacenza, 1893, p. 184.
61. J. B. Scalabrini to Bishop Bonomelli, Jan. 24, 1897 (Abba).
62. G. B. Nasalli Rocca, witness, *Processus*, iuxta 27, p. 261. See Witnesses II, VI, VII, VIII, XI, XVI, XX, XXII, XXV, XXX, I *ex officio*, etc., iuxta 27.
63. A. Carini, witness, *Processus, cop. publ.*, iuxta 27, f. 429.
64. Douglas Scotti, witness, ibid., iuxta 25, f. 321 v.
65. A. Labo, *In memoria di Mons. G. B. Scalabrini*, Piacenza, 1906, p. 17.
66. L. Cornaggia Medici, *Le caratteristiche di Mons. G. B. Scalabrini*, Reggio Emilia, 1935, p. 19.
67. Idem, *Processus*, iuxta 26, p. 253.
68. G. B. Nasalli Rocca, *Commemorazione di Mons. G. B. Scalabrini*, Piacenza, 1909, p. 7.
69. G. Dodici, *Processus, cop. publ.*, iuxta 26, f. 163 v.
70. Idem, juxta 28, f. 167 r.
71. L. Mondini, witness, ibid., iuxta 30, p. 47.
72. J. B. Scalabrini, Pastoral Letter, *La Pregliera*, Feb. 12, 1905, p. 20.
73. Ibid., pp. 23-24.
74. Ibid., p. 26.
75. A. Fogazzaro, "Una visita a Mons. Scalabrini," in *Rassegna Nazionale*, July 1, 1905.
76. J. B. Scalabrini, Discourse for the Inauguration of the Temple of Carmine, Piacenza, Oct. 16, 1896.
77. Idem, Discourse for the Centenary of the First Crusade, Rome, 1895.
78. J. B. Scalabrini to the Rector of the Seminary of Bedonia, May 7, 1878 (Archives of the Seminary of Bedonia).
79. Idem to Bishop Bonomelli, Aug. 10, 1883 (Abba).
80. Idem, Feb. 5, 1884 (Abba).
81. Idem to Sr. Clelia Merloni, FEb. 22, 1899 (AGS).
82. Idem to D. L. Cornaggia Medici, s.d. (AGS).
83. Idem, s.d. (AGS).
84. Gregori, op cit., p. 575.
85. J. B. Scalabrini to a bishop. Feb. 22, 1904 (note in AGS).
86. Idem to Bishop Bonomelli, Sept. 22, 1881 (Abba).
87. Idem, May 20, 1884 (Abba).
88. Idem, Aug. 11, 1903 (Abba).
89. Idem to Fr. Giuseppe Alessi, note s.d. 1891 (AGS).
90. Idem to Msgr. Mangot, June 30, 1904 (AGS).
91. Idem to Fr. Attilio Bianchi, Encantado, Sept. 21, 1904 (AGS).
92. Idem to Msgr. Mangot, Bento Gonzalves, Oct. 12, 1904 (AGS).
93. Idem, Porto Alegre, Oct. 23, 1904 (AGS).
94. G. Cardinali, witness, *Processus*, iuxta 28, p. 99.
95. E. Morisi, witness, ibid., iuxta 30, p. 138.
96. G. Dodici, witness, ibid., iuxta 29, *cop. publ.*, f. 167 v.
97. G. Squeri, witness, ibid., p. 164.
98. G. B. Nasalli Rocca, witness, ibid., p. 262.
99. A. Ranza, witness, ibid., *cop. publ.*, f. 647 v.
100. J. B. Scalabrini, All Saints Day Discourse, 1876.
101. Idem, Lenten Pastoral Letter, 1884, p. 27.
102. Idem, New Year's Day Discourse, 1899.
103. Idem, Lenten Pastoral Letter, 1899, p. 15.
104. Idem, Epiphany Discourse, 1904.

Chapter XX — HOPE

1. J. B. Scalabrini, Epiphany Discourse, 1904.
2. Idem, *Documenta vitae spiritualis*, Nov. 30, 1894, *Processus*, p. 325.

3. J. B. Scalabrini to P. F. Zaboglio, Nov. 29, 1895 (ASMC).
4. Idem, Feb. 4, 1895 (ASMC).
5. Idem to P. O. Alussi, Feb. 12, 1899 (note in AGS).
6. Idem to Bishop Bonomelli, May 28, 1889 (Abba).
7. Idem to the Fr. Provincial in the United States, Nov. 22, 1893 (note in AGS).
8. Idem to P. F. Zaboglio, Nov. 20, 1888 (ASMC).
9. Idem, July 28, 1895 (ASMC).
10. Idem to D. Luigi, May 4, 1895 (AGS).
11. A. Carini, witness, *Processus, cop. publ.*, iuxta 31, f. 430 r.
12. F. Torta, witness, ibid., p. 120.
13. E. Morisi, witness, ibid., p. 139.
14. F. Gregori, witness, ibid., p. 185.
15. See Chapter V, pp. 103-107.
16. G. B. Nasalli Rocca, witness, *Processus*, iuxta 31, p. 262.
17. J. B. Scalabrini to P. F. Zaboglio, Dec. 11, 1896 (ASMC).
18. Idem to P. Beccherini, 1895 (note in AGS).
19. See Chapter XXIV, pp. 406-407.
20. J. B. Scalabrini to Bishop Bonomelli, Jan. 24, 1897 (Abba).
21. C. Mangot, witness, *Processus*, iuxta 31, p. 14.
22. G. Dodici, witness, ibid., *cop. publ.*, f. 168, rv.
23. F. Torta, witness, ibid., iuxta ;33, p. 121.
24. J. B. Scalabrini to an Archpriest, Aug. 1, 1880 (AGS)
25. E. Caccialanza, witness, *Processus, cop. publ.*, iuxta 31, f. 223 v.
26. G. Dodici, witness, ibid., iuxta 33 ff., 168 v.-169 r.
27. L. Mondini, witness, ibid., pp. 47-48.
28. F. Gregori, witness, ibid., iuxta 33, p. 185.
29. D. Mazzadi, witness, ibid., p. 157.
30. L. Mondini, witness, ibid., p. 49.
31. E. Morisi, witness, ibid., p. 139.
32. P. Agazzi, witness, ibid., p. 149.
33. L. Cornaggia Medici, witness, ibid., iuxta 31, p. 254.
34. J. B. Scalabrini to P. O. Alussi, June 10, 1891 (AGS).
35. F. Cattivelli, witness, *Processus, cop. publ.*, iuxta 33, f. 388 rv.
36. L. Mondini, witness, ibid., iuxta 18, 32, pp. 41,48.
37. Idem, iuxta 32, p. 48.
38. L. Cella, witness, ibid., iuxta 33, p. 204.
39. E. Caccialanza, witness, ibid., iuxta 18, *cop. publ.*, f. 218 r.
40. G. Cardinali, witness, ibid., iuxta 33, pp. 102-103.
41. F. Torta, witness, ibid., iuxta 32, pp. 120-121.
42. E. Morisi, witness, ibid., p. 139.
43. See C. Mangot, witness, ibid., p. 14.
44. C. Spallazzi, witness, ibid., p. 29.
45. J. B. Scalabrini to the Vicar General of Crema, s.d. (note in AGS).
46. J. B. Scalabrini to a benefactor, note s.d. (AGS).
47. "I Missionarii italiani all'estero. Un'intervista col Vescovo Mons. Scalabrini," in *Il Corriere della Sera*, June 1, 1901. It is probably the same incident as that narrated in D. E. Morisi's testimony (above).
48. E. Martini, witness, *Processus, cop. publ.*, iuxta 31, f. 200 r.
49. G. Polledri, witness, ibid., p. 199 of the typescript.
50. J. B. Scalabrini, Ascension Discourse.
51. E. Preti, witness, *Processus*, iuxta 29, p. 73.
52. L. Scalabrini, witness, ibid., iuxta 34, *cop. publ.*, f. 919 r.

Chapter XXI — THE PRINCIPAL VIRTUE

1. Autographed Brief of Benedict XV, June 30, 1915. See *L'Emigrato Italiano*, Sept., 1915, p. 1.

2.   C. Mangot, witness, *Processus*, iuxta 35, p. 15.

3.   L. Mondini,w itness, ibid., p. 50. His valet C. Spallazzi testified "that he goes to confession often. Certainly every eight days to his usual confessor and often to his secretary before the eight days are up" (ibid., p. 32).

4.   E. Caccialanza, witness, ibid., *cop. publ.*, f. 224 v.

5.   E. Preti, witness, ibid., p. 74.

6.   G. Cardinali, witness, ibid., p. 103.

7.   See Witnesses VI, XIII, XVI, XXII, XXIII, ibid., iuxta 35.

8.   See Witnesses IV, XVIII, XXI, XXIII: III and V *ex officio*, ibid.

9.   F. Lotteri, witness, ibid., p. 244.

10.   F. Torta, witness, ibid., p. 121. The Bishop had asked the secretary to pull on his cassock when he was on the verge of losing his patience with priests.

11.   A. De Martini, witness, ibid., p. 85. We have previously quoted the judgments of many famous and holy persons, contemporaries of Scalabrini or who came after him.

12.   C. Mangot, witness, ibid., iuxta 59, 5, pp. 20, 4.

13.   C. Spallazzi, witness, ibid., iuxta 26, pp. 25-26.

14.   L. Mondini, witness, ibid., p. 46.

15.   Idem, iuxta 57, p. 64.

16.   F. Gregori, witness, ibid., p. 196. See G. B. Nasalli Rocca: "He was considered a man of saintly life, but his manner was natural and normal in every way; he avoided any display of external austerity which makes such an impression on the masses, and he did not create an image of altar holiness as the people commonly think of it. As we read of many other saints who were able to hide their interior holiness" (ibid., p.. 268).

17.   F. Lotteri, witness, ibid., iuxta 27, p. 242.

18.   L. Tammi, witness, ibid., p. 297.

19.   L. Orione, witness, ibid., iuxta 5, p. 289.

20.   J. B. Scalabrini, Lenten Pastoral Letter, 1878, p. 9.

21.   G. Ferrerio, "Mons. G. B. Scalabrini, Commemorazione," in *L'Emigrato Italiano*, July, 1906, pp. 92-94.

22.   See *ex officio* witnesses A. Ghizzoni and L. Tammi, *Processus*, iuxta 26, p. 274, 296. "He allowed himself to be controlled by his generous heart."

23.   G. B. Nasalli Rocca, *Commemorazione di Mons. G. B. Scalabrini*, Piacenza, 1909, pp. 21-22.

24.   J. B. Scalabrini, Pastoral Letter, *Unione colla Chiesa, obbedienza ai legittimi pastori*, Feb. 8, 1896, p. 38.

25.   Ibid., p. 42.

26.   Idem, *Notificazione al Clero e al popolo piacentino*, May 1, 1896.

27.   See Chap. V., p.

28.   See Letters of Giovanni Asaro to Bishop Scalabrini, 1901-1902; and a letter of the former's father, Luigi Asaro to the Bishop (AGS).

29.   F. Lotteri, witness, *Processus*, iuxta 38, p. 245.

30.   Ibid., See Letters of Bishop Giacomo M. Radini Tedeschi to Bishop Scalabrini, Apr. 20, 1898, Apr. 23, 1898, July 4, 1898 (AGS).

31.   A. Mizzi to Bishop Scalabrini, Apr. 23, 1898 (AGS).

32.   F. Gregori, witness, *Processus*, iuxta 39, p. 188.

33.   C. Mangot, witness, ibid., iuxta 23, p. 8.

34.   G. B. Nasalli Rocca, witness, ibid., pp. 260-261. In a letter from Bishop Gaetano De Lai, then in the Council and later a Cardinal, we read: "I admire your long patience, which, I might say we thought to be a little too long by the Sacred Congregation" (To Bishop Scalabrini, Aug. 7, 1895, AGS).

35.   F. Calzinari, witness, ibid., iuxta 24, p. 211.

36.   L. Mondini, witness, ibid., p. 45.

37.   G. B. Rossi to Bishop Scalabrini, May 19, 1901 (AGS).

38.   See L. Mondini, witness, *Processus*, iuxta 39, p. 55.

39.   G. B. Nasalli Rocca, witness, ibid., p. 263.

40.   From the *Commemorazione* delivered in St. Antoninus and published in *Trent'anni di*

Apostolato, p. 659.

41. J. B. Scalabrini to the Albertario Anniversary Committee, Oct. 30, 1894 (AGS — Comitato promotore dei festeggiamenti di D. Albertario).

42. From the *Commemorazione* quoted in *Trent'anni di Apostolato*, p. 657.

43. Gregori, op. cit., p. 272. See G. Pecora, *Don Davide Albertario*, Turin, 1934, p. 290.

44. J. B. Scalabrini to the President of the Committee, Oct. 5, 1894 (see G. Pecora, op. cit., ibid.).

45. J. B. Scalabrini to Bishop Bonomelli, Dec. 6, 1894. G. Bonomelli to Bishop Scalabrini, Dec. 6, 1894 (Abba).

46. J. B. Scalabrini to Bishop Bonomelli, Jan. 7, 1895 (Abba).

47. D. Albertario to Bishop Scalabrini, Dec. 24, 1894 (AGS).

48. From the *Commemorazione* quoted in *Trent'anni di Apostolato*, p. 657-658. See L. Mondini, witness, *Processus*, iuxta 19, p. 41. "On that occasion he was the quest of the Servant of God, who treated him as a person with whom he had always been on the best of terms."

49. Gen. Genova di Revel to Bishop Scalabrini, June 11, 1898 (AGS).

50. J. B. Scalabrini to N. Rezzara, Oct. 5, 1898 (note in AGS).

51. Idem to Minister Pelloux, Sept. 2, 1898 (note in AGS).

52. Bonomelli wrote to the King on the same day, Sept. 2, 1898.

53. L. G. Pelloux to Bishop Scalabrini, Sept. 7, 1898 (AGS). The ministerial provision for Fr. Albertario arrived at Finalborgo on the same day.

54. J. B. Scalabrini to Paganuzzi Oct. 21, 1898 (note in AGS).

55. D. Albertario to Bishop Scalabrini, Finalborgo, May 14, 1899 (AGS).

56. E. Morisi, witness, *Processus*, iuxta 19, p. 135.

57. G. Dodici, witness, ibid., *cop. publ.*, f. 159 v.

58. G. B. Nasalli Rocca, witness, ibid., iuxta 38, p. 263.

59. G. Squeri, witness, ibid., p. 166.

60. See Chapter VI, pp. 131-132.

61. J. B. Scalabrini, Circular, Jan. 23, 1878, pp. 6-7.

62. L. Mondini, witness, *Processus,,* iuxta 38, p. 55.

63. G. Dodici, witness, ibid., *cop. publ.*, f. 172 r.

64. D. Mazzadi, witness, ibid., iuxta 29, p. 156.

65. C. Spallazzi, witness, ibid., iuxta 17, p. 23.

66. J. B. Scalabrini to Msgr. Mangot, Oct. 12, 1904 (AGS).

Chapter XXII — HUMBLE AND POOR

1. See Witnesses XXII, XXV, XXVI, XVI, etc., *Processus*, iuxta 26.

2. L. Mondini, witness, ibid., iuxta 55, p. 63.

3. See Witnesses III, VI, XVII, XXI: X *ex officio*, etc., ibid.

4. L. Cornaggia Medici, witness, ibid., p. 257.

5. A. Sarani, witness, ibid., *cop. publ.*, f. 416 r.

6. See J. B. Scalabrini to the Rector of the Seminary of Bedonia, Jan. 31, 1903 (Archives of the Seminary of Bedonia).

7. See *Documenta vitae spiritualis*, *Processus,,* pp. 322-333, passim.

8. G. Polledri, witness, *Processus, cop. publ.*, iuxta 55, ff. 598 v., 599 r.

9. See Witnesses, XXV, XXVI, XXXII; III *ex officio*, etc., *Processus*, iuxta 55.

10. C. Mangot, witness, ibid., iuxta 26, p. 12. See *Documenta vitae spiritualis*, ibid., passim.

11. F. Torta, witness, ibid., iuxta 55, p. 128.

12. G. B. Nasalli Rocca, witness, ibid., p. 267.

13. A. Carini, witness, ibid., *cop. publ.*, ff. 437 v.-438 r. See G. Squeri, witness, ibid., p. 169.

14. F. Gregori, witness, ibid., iuxta 55, p. 195.

15. G. Squeri, witness, ibid., iuxta 4, p. 159.

16. *Il Monitore Diocesano di Piacenza*, June 30, 1905, p. 160.

17. E. Galimberti, witness, *Processus*, iuxta 24, pp 200-201.

18. F. Calzinari, witness, ibid., iuxta 55, p. 217.

19. J. B. Scalabrini to the Rector of the Seminary of Bedonia, Jan. 15, 1884 (Archives of the Seminary of Bedonia).
20. Idem to Bishop Bonomelli, Feb. 16, 1904 (Abba).
21. G. Bonomelli, "1 Giugno," in *L'Emigrato Italiano*, June, 1906, p. 75.
22. J. B. Scalabrini to Bishop Bonomelli, Feb. 2, 1886 (Abba).
23. E. Soderini, *Il Pontificato di Leone XIII*, vol. II, p. 172, n. 1.
24. L. Mondini, witness, *Processus*, iuxta 55, p. 62.
25. See Chapter VI, p. 139.
26. G. B. Bonomelli to Bishop Scalabrini, Mar.. 2, 1901; J. B. Scalabrini to Bishop Bonomelli, Mar. 3, 1901 (Abba).
27. G. Chiodin to Msgr. Mangot, Venice, Feb. 11, 1904 (AGS).
28. J. B. Scalabrini to Bishop Bonomelli, Jan. 17, 1904 (Abba).
29. P. Piacenza to Bishop Scalabrini, Rome, Jan. 23, 1904: "Your Excellency twice replied that you were not disposed to accept." See the letters to Bishop Scalabrini from the Bishop of Guastalla, Jan. 12, 1904 and of Antonietta Giacomelli, Terviso, Jan. 9, 1904 (AGS).
30. Card. Agliardi to Bishop Scalabrini, Feb. 15, 1904 (AGS).
31. G. Bonomelli to Bishop Scalabrini, Feb. 13, 1904 (Gregori, op. cit., p. 534).
32. J. B. Scalabrini to Bishop Bonomelli, Feb. 16, 1904 (Abba). When writing to another colleague that "the storm was passed," he wrote beside the draft: *Noli laetari nisi cum benefeceris. Brevis gloria, quae ab hominibus datur et accipitur.* (AGS).
33. J. B. Scalabrini to P. V. Astorri, Aug. 6, 1894 (AGS).
34. A. Bianchi, witness, *Processus*, iuxta 55, p. 229.
35. G. Cardinali, witness, ibid., p. 109. See L. Cella, witness, ibid., p. 207.
36.. J. B. Scalabrini, Christmas Discourse, 1879.
37. See Witnesses, *Processus*, iuxta 26.
38. L. Mondini, witness, *Processus*, iuxta 36, pp. 51-52. "One day in Rome he met a poor shamefaced man...who in a low voice asked the Servant of God for help, holding out his hand. He gave him five lire. The beggar, surprised at what was at the time a generous sum, was greatly moved and murmured: 'Look, I am a Jew.' At this the Servant of God asked him, 'Are you truly in need?' When the man answered yes, he doubled his gift. At this generosity, I said, 'It would be well if Your Excellency gave me the money, because if you go on distributing it like this we shall have to be sent home by mail.' At this the Servant of God replied smiling, 'Well, take it then, since you are afraid of losing the ground under your feet...' "
39. G. Gregori, witness, ibid., p. 182; L. Tammi, witness, iuxta 26, p. 296.
40. Msgr. Mangot attests that the incident of the torn will is true (*Processus*, iuxta 48, p. 17). Other witnesses (iuxta 48) said the story about this was frequently told; others, on the other hand, (e.g. L. Cornaggia Medici, ibid., p. 256) say that Bishop Scalabrini refused to accept the will. With respect to the will of the Marchesa Fanny Visconti Anguissola (see C. Spallazzi and F. Torta, ibid., pp. 34-35 and 127) there is a note from Scalabrini himself to the nephew of the deceased, in which we read: "With this I renounce whatever claim I may have. I prefer to receive some help from you as a favor for my charitable works rather than to come into the possession of a colossal sum that is not due me at all." (AGS).
41. Witnesses XII and XVII, iuxta 26.
42. L. Mondini, witness, iuxta 32, p. 48.
43. See Witnesses, I, II, III, VI, XXII, iuxta 52.
44. See Witnesses I, II, III, VI, XII, XXI, XXII, XXVI, XXVII; I and III, *ex officio*, ibid.
45. *Synodus Placentina Secunda*, Pars VI, *De cleri et populi disciplina*, caput I, *De vita et honestate clericorum*, nn. 9-10, Piacenza, 1893, pp. 144-145.
46. L. Cella, witness, *Processus*, iuxta 26, p. 203.
47. L. Cornaggia "Ricordi di un grande Vescovo Patriota," in *La Tribuna*, Sept. 16, 1930.
48. Scalabrini was accused of wastefulness and poor administration of diocesan property. But a true evaluation of these insinuations was given by those who knew him best. "As for wastefulness," one witness stated, "I have never seen anything to prove it; it was only in giving charity that he did not recognize any limits" (L. Mondini, witness, *Processus*, iuxta 50, p. 67). Even Galimberti, who at times, even in published articles, had raised cer-

tain doubts about the administration of the contributions and inheritances received by the Bishop, had to admit that he "had spent everything for the Church, especially for the great restorations in the Cathedral, for the poor, for the Institute for Deafmutes, and for his Missionaries, for the emigrants, and he had kept nothing for himself." (E. Galimberti, witness, ibid., p. 198). In any case, it would not be surprising to find some inaccuracy or other amid the great and rapid developments of the Bishop's numerous projects. In this field he was not one to be frightened off by any difficulties, confident as he was that Providence would come to the rescue. "With credits one does nothing, but with debts one accomplishes something" (E. Caccialanza, witness, ibid., iuxta 18, cop. publ., f. 218 r.). According to his philosophy, "the works are carried out and the means to pay for them sooner or later will not be lacking" (A. Ghizzoni, witness, ibid., p. 272). He was proved right because he left no debts (Witnesses II, IV, XXII; III ex officio, ibid.). In fact, one witness stated: "I refuted with documentation in my possession those who spoke this calumny" (C. Spallazzi, witness, ibid., p. 24).

49.   At the first Synod he had decreed that there should not be more than two or three courses. At the second Synod, he renewed the prescription under pain of a three-day suspension and other penalties (Synodus Placentina Secunda, Pars III, cap I, nn. 14-15; cap. III, n. 27, Piacenza 1893, pp. 56 and 71). The strictness of these provisions should not be surprising when one recalls that at the time, in certain places, there were excesses in terms of more than fifteen courses at a dinner (A. Scarani, witness, Processus, cop. publ., iuxta 51, f. 414 v.).

50.   See Witnesses, XIV, XV, XXV, XXX, iuxta 51.
51.   A. Carini, witness, ibid., cop. publ., f. 436 v.
52.   L. Cella, witness, ibid., p. 206.
53.   L. Tammi, witness, iuxta 52, p. 301.
54.   P. Scarani, witness, ibid., cop. publ., f. 492 r.
55.   A. Bracchi, witness, ibid., ff. 474 v.-475 r.
56.   F. Calzinari, witness, ibid., p. 217.
57.   See Witnesses XI, XVII, XIX, iuxta 52.
58.   G. Polledri, witness, ibid., cop. publ., f. 597 v.
59.   See Witnesses, I, II, III, XIII, XX, XXIII, iuxta 51.
60.   C. Spallazzi, witness, ibid., p. 35.
61.   L. Mondini, witness, ibid., p. 61.
62.   G. Polledri, witness, ibid., cop. publ., f. 597 rev. A certain Mme. Zangrandi wrote to the Bishop on July 8, 1881, as follows: "Last evening at St. Antonino's you were literally exhausted. I beg you as a favor and for the love of the good Jesus, whose sheep you care for, to take care of yourself constantly and conscientiously. Your body is not your own, Bishop; it is a servant whom God has given you to serve Him and He does not want to place a greater burden on it than its strength can bear...And don't you even let it sleep? And, sick as it is, you make the 'poor thing' say Mass at four in the morning; but to say it at four, you must get up at three, etc." (AGS).

Chapter XXIII — HIS MEMORY IS BLESSED

1.   F. Torta, witness, Processus, iuxta 48, p. 129.
2.   C. Spallazzi, witness, ibid., iuxta 58, pp. 36-37.
3.   L. Cella, witness, ibid., p. 208.
4.   J. B. Scalabrini, New Year's Discourse, 1905.
5.   L. Tammi, witness, Processus, iuxta 29, p. 297.
6.   Cronache riguardanti la Parrocchia di Borghetti, from 1900-1905.
7.   L. Mondini, witness, Processus, iuxta 56, p. 64.
8.   C. Spallazzi, witness, ibid., iuxta 34, p. 30.
9.   Idem, p. 31.
10.   Il Monitore Diocesano di Piacenza, June 30, 1905, pp. 129-130.
11.   C. Spallazzi, witness, Processus, iuxta 34, pp.. 29-30.
12.   Il Monitore Diocesano di Piacenza, June 30, 1905, p.. 130.

13. C. Spallazzi, witness, *Processus*, iuxta 34, pp. 29-30.
14. "He bade me clothe him in robes of little value, with a metal ring and cross, not gold, so that the latter might be used for the poor." (C. Spallazzi, witness, ibid., p. 32.)
15. The next day Bishop Bonomelli's golden anniversary Mass was being celebrated. They gave him the news of the death of his closest friend only that evening.. See G. Bonomelli's letter to Bishop Scalabrini's brother and sister, June 1, 1905 (AGS).
16. *Il Monitore Diocesano di Piacenza*, June 30, 1905, p. 130.
17. C. Spallazzi, witness, *Processus*, iuxta 34, p. 32.
18. *Il Monitore Diocesano di Piacenza*, June 30, 1905, p.. 130.
19. See Witnesses, *Processus*, iuxta 57 and 59.
20. E. Morisi, witness, ibid., iuxta 59, p. 146.
21. F. Pallaroni, witness, *Processus de non-culto*, f. 15 r.
22. *La Libertà*, June 5, 1905.
23. *Il Piccolo*, June 7, 1905.
24. *Il Monitore Diocesano di Piacenza*, June 30, 1905, p. 156.
25. Thus one of the inscriptions dictated by Msgr. Dallepiane, later Bishop of Iglesias.
26. *Il Monitore Diocesano di Piacenza*, June 30, 1905, pp. 156-157.
27. Gregori, op. cit., p. 563.
28. F. Pallaroni, witness, *Processus de non-culto*, f. 10 r. See the other witnesses, *Processus*, iuxta 59.
29. Published in the single number: *Il Monumento ricordo a Mons. Scalabrini*, Como, Sept. 11, 1913.
30. *L'Emigrato Italiano*, Nov.-Dec., 1912, p. 26.
31. Pius X to the bishops of the Emilian Region, June 13, 1905 (AVP).
32. The Brief is dated Oct. 18, 1913. See the Brief of Pius X to Fr. Domenico Vicentini for the 25th anniversary of the Missionaries of St. Charles, dated Sept. 4, 1912 (*L'Emigrato Italiano*, Nov.-Dec., 1912, pp. 5-6).
33. *L'Emigrato Italiano*, Sept., 1915, pp. 2-4. The Brief is dated June 30, 1915.
34. A. Ratti to Bishop Scalabrini, Jan. 8, 1904 (AGS).
35. Idem to Msgr. Attilio Bianchi, May 22, 1913 (AGS). The letter was confirmed, so to speak, by the Holy Father who, 25 years later, added his signature as *Pius PP. XI*, Mar. 13, 1938.
36. *L'Emigrato Italiano*, Apr., 1934, pp. 4-5.
37. Ibid., Apr., 1936, pp. 2-3.
38. Pius XII, Apostolic Constitution, *Exsul Familia* in *Acta Apost. Sedis*, XLIV (1952), p. 659. The Holy Father is referring to the Letter of Decree, *Spiritus Domini*, of July 7, 1946 (*Acta Apost. Sedis*, XXXVIII, 1946, p. 44).
39. Card. Angelo Roncalli, *Lettera Postulatoria a S.S. Pio XII, S.C. dei Riti*, July 9, 1955. Card. Roncalli had seen and heard Scalabrini in Bergamo in 1898 on the occasion of the celebrations of St. Alexander, but his knowledge and opinion of him were based on the impressions and recollections of the intransigent Bishop Giacomo Radini Tedeschi. To the above quotation he added: "Now that several decades have elapsed since the delicate and difficult situations which may have raised a little dust here and there, it is up to the absolute competence of the Supreme Authority to say the last word, if, that is, the Lord has blown that dust off the tomb of the bishop of Piacenza, raising heavenly signs of greatness. This is my prayer." (AGS).
40. *Il Monitore Diocesano di Piacenza*, June 30, 1905, p. 149.
41. Card. Capecelatro, Nov. 4, 1912 (AGS).
42. Card. Agliardi to Att. Calda, Feb. 27, 1909 (AGS).
43. Card. Schiaffino to Msgr. Mangot, 1901 (AGS).
44. Card. Moretti to Msgr. Mangot, June 20, 1880 (AGS).
45. Card. Ferrari, June 23, 1916 (in *Il Nuovo Giornale*, Aug. 16, 1916). The Servant of God, Card. Ferrari, whom Scalabrini held in great esteem for his goodness and extraordinary activity, understood very well the position of the Bishop of Piacenza, for he too found himself in similar situations. It is enough to note for example the exemption from the *non expedit* obtained in 1897 for Deputy Emanuele Greppi and, by way of contrast, the great effort it took in the same year to get permission from the Secretariat of State to speak with

the King in order to request a permit for a procession (see G. Rossi, *Il Cardinal Ferrari, Assisi*, 1956, pp. 125 and 53-54), although Card. Sarto had visited the Sovereign only a few months before. Card. Ferrari's situation parallelled that of Scalabrini when he was accused of modernism: "There was one universal tactic: act bold on the strength of the alleged approval of the distant Pope, rebel against the bishop close at hand, thus falling into doctrinal error and intolerable lack of discipline which Card. Ferrari stamped in blood with a condemnation that has become history: *new-minted modernism*" (G. B. Penco-B. Galbiati, *Vita del Cardinale Andrea Carlo Ferrari, Arcivescovo di Milano*, Milan-Rome, s.d. p. 179). The phrase (of the Pastoral Letter N. 134, Feb. 23, 1908) evidently derives from the well known expression of Scalabrini: *liberalism of new coinage*.

46. Card. A. Richelmy, Oct. 28, 1912 (*L'Emigrato Italiano*, Nov.-Dec., 1912, p. 8).
47. Card. G. B. Nasalli Rocca, Oct. 16, 1913 (*Il Monumento ricordo a Mons. Scalabrini*, single issue, Como, Sept. 11, 1913).
48. *L'Emigrato Italiano*, Sept., 1939, p. 130.
49. *Celebrazioni del 50°*, p. 34.
50. Card. A. G. Piazza, *Discorso nella Cattedrle di Piacenza*, June 5, 1955, Ibid., pp. 139-149.
51. Idem, Preface to the life of Bishop Scalabrini by I. Felici: *Il Padre degli Emigrati*, Monza, pp. 7-8.
52. From a stenographic summary of the lecture given by Fr. Giulio Bevilacqua, later Cardinal, in Piacenza on June 2, 1955, on the subject, "Mons. Scalabrini difensore dei diritti della Chiesa e delle anime" (AGS).
53. G. Bonomelli, "1 Giugno" in *L'Emigrato Italiano*, June, 1906, p. 76.
54. *Il Monumento ricordo a Mons. Scalabrini*, single issue, Como, Sept. 11, 1913.
55. *La solenne traslazione della salma di Mons. G. B. Scalabrini*, Piacenza, 1909, p. 11.
56. G. M. Pellizzari, *Elogio funebre. In memoria di Mons. G. B. Scalabrini*, Piacenza, 1906, pp. 10, 20, 21.
57. L.Lacroix to Bishop Scalabrini, Mar. 25, 1904 (AGS).
58. *Il Monitore Diocesano di Piacenza*, June 30, 1904, passim.
59. *Celebrazione del 50°*, passim.
60. See Appendix II.
61. Decree of Beatification of Blessed Luigi Guanella, Oct. 24, 1964.
62. "L'uomo provvidenziale," in *L'Emigrato Italiano*, Dec., 1915, pp. 22-26.
63. L. Sterlocchi, *Cenni biografici di Mons. G. B. Scalabrini*, Como, 1912, p. 5.
64. See Appendix I.
65. See Chapter VII, pp. 144-145.
66. M. Rinaldi, witness, *Processus*, iuxta 59, p. 235.
67. F. Torta, witness, ibid., iuxta 10, p. 114.
68. See Chapter XXI, pp. 371-372.
69. L. Orione, witness, *Processus*, iuxta 5, p. 291.
70. G. Calabria to P. F. Milini, May 15, 1954 (in *Celebrazioni del 50°*, p. 38).
71. See Chap. IX, pp. 171-172. Similar opinions are expressed by other well known figures in the Catholic Movement. Grosoli called him "apostle of faith and civilization." Crispolti said he was the "glory of the Church and of Italy...,Father to all who approached him" (see *Il Monitore Diocesano di Piacenza*, June 30, 1905, p. 149; and F. Crispolti to Bishop Scalabrini, Dec. 4, 1890, AGS). For Msgr. Alessi, Bishop Scalabrini's judgment was equivalent to that of the whole Italian hierarchy, because he was "the man for our time" (G. Alessi to Msgr. Mangot, Sept. 12, 1889 AGS). Prof. Olivi wrote: "A soul aglow with youthful enthusiasm for all good causes, rich in new initiatives for those who weep, who suffer... We have suffered an immense loss...A new Paul in works of faith, in sowing the seeds of charity...His memory will be always alive because it is linked with what we have in Italy that is most precious and most holy" (L. Olivi to Msgr. Mangot, June 3, 1905, AGS).
    It might be useful to cite some of the opinions of the civil authorities of the period, whose anticlericalism was official. First, from the Royal Decree of the Ministry of the Interior, permitting the transferral of Bishop Scalabrini's body to the Cathedral in Piacenza, signed by Minister Facta on Nov. 21, 1908:
    "The figure of the lamented Bishop, illustrious in life for his singular patriotic and

civic merits, earned throughout his active and virtuous life through works of eminent charity, and through the Catholic apostolate he carried out always with great zeal and exemplary equanimity, assumes a special importance because of his innumerable merits, the memory of which lives on...These merits and excellence, to make brief mention of them, reside in the thirty years of his episcopate which was so productive in fostering every most noble ideal, in his simple, upright life, in his exquisite artistic sense..., in his tireless diligence in the exercise of his episcopal ministry..., in his spirit of sacrifice and of philanthropy which found expression in infinite works of charity to relieve the misfortunes and the misery of those in humble circumstances, his unwearying activity, carried on with the faith of an apostle, with a sense of charity and of country for noble civic intentions on behalf of our emigrants" (*Trent'anni di Apostolato*, pp. 697-699).

Some of the provincial authorities were even more deeply moved. Royal Commissioner Bellini asserted that all Italy envied Piacenza her bishop, "for the admirable nobility of his mind open to all ideas of human progress, alight with the brillance of his projects, and for the goodness of his soul, which radiated so much light around his person" (*Il Monitore Diocesano di Piacenza*, June 30, 1905, p. 145).

Prefect Trinchier, recalling the religious and civic merits of the Bishop added: "I am perhaps better able to testify to the precious cooperation which, without ever losing sight of his sacred mission and with all due respect for my civic and political mandate, he gave me on many occasions and thus made easier for me the administration of the province" (ibid., p. 146).

This testimony constitutes one of the clearest proofs of the sense of balance, illumined by singular charity in matters of policy, which Scalabrini had showed in a period of the greatest confusion in the relations between the ecclesiastical and civic authorities.

72.   A. Malpeli, witness, *Processus*, p. 284. See witnesses C. Squeri, p. 286 and F. Sbarbori, p. 287. Bishop Scalabrini, on the other hand, simply wrote, "The fire, which could have had the most disastrous consequences, was brought under control and extinguished in a few hours" (to Msgr. Mangot, July 15, 1902, AGS).

73.   C. Polledri, witness, *Processus*, pp. 281-282. See E. Morisi, witness, iuxta 59, p. 146.

74.   F. Gregori, witness, ibid., p. 197.

75.   L. Gorlin, witness, ibid., p. 309; C. Tomedi, witness, p. 305.

76.   See *L'Emigrato Italiano*, of 1936, passim.

77.   See pp. 395-396.

78.   Witnesses, I, II, III, IV, V, VI, VII, VIII, IX, X, XI, XII, XVI, XVII, XVIII, XIX, XX, XXI, XXII, XXV, XXVI, XXVIII, XXIX, XXX, XXXI, XXXII; and *ex officio* witnesses, I, II, III, IV, V, IX, X, XI, XII, XIII, XIV; witnesses I and II in the rogatory process first in Como; I of the second and I of the rogatory process in Camerino.

79.   Card. A. G. Piazza, Discourse on the Cathedral of Piacenza, June 5, 1955 (*Celebrazioni del 50°*, pp. 146-147).

Chapter XXIV — THE HUMAN AND CHRISTIAN FEATURES OF BISHOP SCALA-BRINI'S PERSONALITY

1.   In fact, the austerity of his life, his pastoral preoccupations, and the multiple duties of administration in no way affected his simplicity of manner. His human side was reflected in his use of his native dialect, his predilection for simple things, the affability that inspired a respectful confidence in others (see *L'Amico del Popolo*, June 13, 1894). His contemporaries are unanimous in describing him as a strong and balanced personality. "The death of Bishop Scalabrini," one Bishop declared, "is a grave loss to the Italian hierarchy: a personality has disappeared" (the Bishop of Novara to Msgr. Mangot, quoted in *L'Emigrato Italiano*, July, 1905, p. 25). The journalist Galimberti, who often wrote in opposition to Scalabrini in liberal papers, nevertheless said of him, "he was always well-balanced, one of those who give to God what is God's and to Caesar what is Caesar's" (E. Galimberti, *Processus*, iuxta 57, p. 200).

2.   G. Ferrerio, "Commemorazione di Mons. G. B. Scalabrini," in *L'Emigrato Italiano*, July, 1906, p. 94.

3. G. Borelli, "Il clero cattolico e le condizioni politico-sociali d'Italia. Un colloquio con Mons. Scalabrini," in *L'Alba* (Milan) July 15, 1900.

4. J. B. Scalabrini to Bishop Bonomelli, Nov. 1, 1886 (Abba).

5. Idem, Aug. 16, 1887 (Abba).

6. Idem, Oct. 4, 1887 (Abba).

7. Idem, beginning of 1887 (Abba).

8. For example, we read in his correspondence with Bonomelli: "I have read that men of talent are ordinarily very naive. I must have had some talent myself, because I was always very trusting. But now I must have lost it completely because I have become almost cynical, *salva fide* of course, for the faith through the grace of God increasingly cheers my spirit and gives me a lively joy even though I am often disturbed at the sight of so much evil." (J. B. Scalabrini to Bishop Bonomelli, Nov. 25, 1882, Abba.) "Experience with the world, dear brother, has made me rethink many, many things, and I regret the loss of those days when my soul, all zeal, saw the Church as perfect and everything pertaining to it through rose colored glasses. But there have been changes, and these too have their reason. They detach me more and more from the things of this poor world and incline me toward the type of program I proposed to you one day: to prepare for death and meanwhile do as much good as possible for the souls of the diocese" (Idem, May 23, 1883, Abba).

9. J. B. Scalabrini, Discourses: Obedience, Unity, Discipline.

10. Idem, *Avvertenze alla Congregazione dei Vicari Foranei*, 1903 (AVP).

11. "Sometimes he was a little quick to react, but he immediately controlled himself, and generously rendered the greatest satisfaction" (F. Torta, witness, *Processus*, iuxta 26, p. 119). "If at times he gave vent to a sudden outburst, I was greatly edified by the way he immediately controlled himself" (L. Mondini, witness, *Processus*, iuxta 18, p. 67). Sometimes, however, "deliberately and out of a sense of duty he acted indignant toward some one he wished to correct" (E. Preti, witness, *Processus*, iuxta 26, pp. 112-113).

12. Interview in *Fanfulla* (Sao Paulo), July, 1904 (quoted in *Trenti'anni di Apostolato*, p. 528).

13. J. B. Scalabrini, *Ai Missionari per gl'Italiani nelle Americhe*, Piacenza, 1892, p. 5.

14. Idem, *L'emigrazione italiana in America*, Piacenza, 1887, p. 6.

15. Idem to Bishop Bonomelli, Oct. 4, 1903 (Abba).

16. A. Scalabrini, *Trent'anni di Apostolato*, p. 5.

17. E. Preti, witness, *Processus*, iuxta 29, p. 73.

18. See L. Cornaggia Medici, *Un profilo di Mons. Scalabrini*, Rome, 1903, p. 5.

19. J. B. Scalabrini, to P. F. Zaboglio, Nov. 20, 1888 (ASMC).

20. P. Gazzola, in *L'Emigrato Italiano*, Nov.-Dec., 1912, pp. 30-31.

21. Ibid.

22. Especially Card. Capecelatro, Card. Bevilacqua, Fr. Orione, and Fr. Semeria.

23. J. B. Scalabrini, *Ai Missionari per gl'Italiani nelle Americhe*, Piacenza, 1905, p. 12.

24. G. Semeria, *Mons. G. B. Scalabrini*, Piacenza, 1905, p. 11.

25. L. Cornaggia Medici, *Le caratteristiche di Mons. G. B. Scalabrini*, Reggio Emilia, 1935, p. 11.

26. Card. A. Agliardi to Bishop A. Bianchi, Oct. 10, 1912 (AGS). Scalabrini was sometimes accused of being weak with his secretary and of placing too much confidence in him; other times he was accused of favoritism. The witnesses at the Process were unanimous in testifying to his impartiality in assigning posts and duties (See Witnesses, I, II, III, IV, V, VII, VIII, IX, XI, XIV, XV, XX, XXI, XXII, XXIII, XXV, XXVI, XXIX, XXX, XXXI, XXXII, and III *ex officio*, *Processus*, iuxta 50). "In the matter of appointments, he used to say: I do not regard the color but the competence" (C. Mangot, witness, ibid., p. 17). It is not surprising that he had a real affection for his secretary Mangot, who was "his confidant, his adviser, invariably ready to undergo any sacrifice to save the Bishop trouble or annoyance, taking on himself in all things the distasteful part" (G. Cardinali, witness, ibid., p. 108). Nevertheless the Bishop "was not a man to let anyone impose on him, including Msgr. Mangot, when the affairs of the Diocese were concerned" (E. Torta, witness, ibid., p. 127). If at times, the secretary exceeded his powers, "Scalabrini cancelled any acts that did not correspond to what was true and just" (E. Morisi, witness, ibid., p. 143).

27. J. B. Scalabrini, *Ai Missionari per gl'Italiani nelle Americhe*, Piacenza, 1892, p. 13.

28. G. Cardinali, witness, *Processus*, pp. 94, 99, 105.
29. J. B. Scalabrini, *Discorso per il giubileo episcopale di Mons. Bonomelli*, Cremona, 1896, p. 10.
30. See the judgment of Card. Bevilacqua, Chapter XXIII, pp. 398-399.
31. J. B. Scalabrini, Discourse on St. Colombano, 1894.
32. J. B. Scalabrini to Bishop Bonomelli, July 10, 1893 (Abba).
33. See Chapter XXIII, p. 395.
34. See Chapter XXI, pp. 375-376.
35. J. B. Scalabrini, *Discorso al Catholic Club di New York*, 1901; see Chapter XI, pp. 209-210.
36. Idem, *Il disegno di legge sulla emigrazione italiana*, Piacenza, 1888, p. 46.
37. G. Semeria, *Commemorazione di Mons. G. B. Scalabrini*, Piacenza, pp. 18, 3. As an example of Scalabrini's foresightedness we may cite his perception that the United States would guide a kind of peaceful revolution destined to unite all nations in a spirit of liberty: "Note that this great far-seeing man perceived this when no one would have dared think that America not only would not abandon her isolationism but would take on the function of leadership. He sensed this was possible not because of the technical progress of modern civilization but by virtue of the spirit of Christianity, lived under the leadership of the Vicar of Christ on earth." This idea expressed at a time when Catholics formed only a seventh of the population of the United States and for the most part were among the poorest people "has an undeniable accent of prophecy" (From a talk by Msgr. F. Firoentino, New York, 1955 in *Celebrazione del 50°*, pp. 110-111. See Felici-Della Chiesa, *Father to the Immigrants*, New York, 1955, pp. 202-203).
38. See Card. G. B. Nasalli Rocca in: *A Mons. Giovanni Battista Scalabrini nel 40° di sua elezione episcopale*, Piacenza, Aug. 16, 1916, p. 4.
   "Whoever has had the good fortune to be near that admirable man, even for a short time, has been immediately won by the power which the goodness of his heart, the clarity of his mind and the sincerity of his spirit, exercised over all who approached him without distinction" (*L'Emigrato Italiano*, 1912, n. VI, p. 81). "He was so good! So good to everyone! He had such kind words for everyone. He could sympathize with every weakness!...Oh! When I think that I can no longer go and tell him all my sufferings and difficulties, that I can never again hear his gentle and discerning words, which always calmed me and did me so much good, I seem not to have the strength to go on living!" (Alfonso Bianchi to Msgr. Mangot, June 1, 1905, AGS).
39. *Il Monitore Diocesano di Piacenza*, June 30, 1905, pp. 159-160.
40. J. B. Scalabrini, Lenten Pastoral Letter, 1878, p. 16.
41. Idem, *Documenta vitae spiritualis*, *Processus*, p. 325.

APPENDIX NOTES

Appendix I — THE FIRST SCALABRINIAN MISSIONARIES

1. J. B. Scalabrini, "L'Italia all'estero" in *Il Conferenziere*, Jan., 1900, pp. 24-25.
2. Ibid., p. 24.
3. In August, 1967, Card. Amleto G. Cicognani, Secretary of State and Legate of His Holiness Pope Paul VI brought the Gold Rose to the national Shrine of Brazil, N. Senhora Aparecida. In his address to the Governor of the State of Sao Paulo, recalled that during a previous visit to Brazil he had been told that a "young Italian priest had founded there (in Ipiranga), in 1895, an institute for abandoned children. It was Fr. Giuseppe Marchetti, of the Pious Society of the Missionaries of St. Charles, who died, after a heroic life at the age of 27. Making up for his lack of means with zealous love for Christ, and with the help of his good mother and dear sister, this apostle to the emigrants, who at that time were settling in great numbers in the state and city of Sao Paulo, was able to lay the foundations of a providential work which found faithful supporters as the years went by and today carries on its flourishing and beneficent work"(See *L'Osservatore Romano*, Aug. 17-18, 1967: "Gli alti motivi del dono pontificio espositi dal Cardinale Legato al Governatore dello Stato di S. Paolo").
4. J. B. Scalabrini to P. F. Consoni, Jan. 15, 1897 (AGS).
5. The program the Founder gave his missionaries — to become an emigrant with the emigrants — remained by no means a dead letter. We believe that the success of their efforts is explained by the fact that they identified themselves with their brother exiles: "That certain spontaneous and irresistible sympathy with the Missionary which the emi-

grant feels," one of the first Scalabrinians wrote, "comes from the intimate harmony the emigrant senses between his own situation and that of the missionary who is his fellow countryman. He knows quite well what labors and discomforts his Father undergoes to bring a word of comfort to his brother compatriots scattered across interminable distances, in places...with only the most rudimentary roads...The settlers want to see in their Missionary the faithful friend who remains at their side even through misfortune, the benefactor who knows all their deficiencies. They know very well that he had had to leave a loving mother and an affectionate father to follow them to these far-off lands, so how could they not feel, more than a simple sympathy for him, a real love?... (See "Religione e Patria nel cuore dell'emigrato," in *L'Emigrato Italiano*, Apr., 1911, pp. 56-57).

6.   Fr. Colbachini to Bishop Scalabrini, Jan. 26, 1901 (AGS).
7.   See E. Negrin, *P. Pietro Colbacchini Missionario*, Bassano del Grappa, 1951. The servant who assisted Fr. Colbachini later became a Scalabrinian nun, Sister Lucia Gorlin, and gave testimony at the diocesan process of Bishop Scalbrini.
8.   See *L'Emigrato Italiano*, 1920, n. 1, pp. 33-34.
9.   See C. Porrini, "P. Giuseppe Pandolfi," in *L'Emigrato Italiano*, Jan., 1951, pp. 16-17.
10. See *Venticinque anni di missione fra gli italiani immigrati di Boston, Mass.*, Milan, 1913, pp. 120-122; C. Sassi, *Parrocchia della Madonna di Pompei in New York*, Marino, 1942, pp. 49-51; *L'Emigrato Italiano*, Oct., 1934, pp. 18-20.
11. J. B. Scalabrini to the Prefect of *Propaganda Fide*, Feb. 2, 1887 (Arch. S.C.P.F., Collegi d'Italia, Piacenza, ff. 1492, ff.).
12. Idem to Fr. Francesco Zaboglio, Sept. 7, 1893 (ASMC). See M. Caliaro, op. cit., p. 22, n. 21.
13. Gregori, op. cit., pp. 434-435.
14. From a letter of Fr. Teodoro Paroli, Mar. 28, 1913, quoted in *Venticinque anni di missione fra gli Italiani immigrati di Boston*, Milan, 1913, p. 143.
15. See *L'Emigrato Italiano*, June, 1913, pp. 6-16.
16. The biography of the Bishop of Rieti was written by the Scalabrinian G. B. Sofia: *Massimo Rinaldi, Missionario e Vescovo*, Rome, 1960, p. 208.
17. M. Rinaldi, *Processus*, iuxta 4, pp. 230-231.
18. *Il Fanfulla* (Sao Paulo), June 4, 1941.

Appendix II — RELIGIOUS ORDERS OF SISTERS FOR THE EMIGRANTS

1.   J. B. Scalabrini, Report to the Sacred Congregation of Propaganda Fide, Aug. 10, 1900 (noted in AGS).
2.   Card. R. C. Rossi, "La Beata Cabrini e il Servo Di Dio Mons. Scalabrini," in *L'Osservatore Romano*, Nov. 11, 1938. The authors consulted the following biographies of St. Frances Cabrini: *La Madre Francesca Saverio Cabrini* (by one of her Daughters), Turin, 1928; T. Maynard, *Il mondo e troppo piccolo*, Milan, 1948; N. Vian, *Madre Cabrini*, IV ed., Brescis, 1956; S. C. Lorit, *La Cabrini*, Rome, 1965; *Viaggi della Madre Francesca Saverio Cabrini*, Rome.
3.   *La Madre Francesca Saverio Cabrini*, Turin, 1928, pp. 80-81.
4.   Ibid., pp. 84-85.
5.   Ibid., p. 85.
6.   Ibid., pp. 90-91.
7.   Ibid., p. 97.
8.   Three months before, on January 3 to be precise, Bishop Scalabrini had received the following telegram (preserved in AGS): "Convent for Sisters ready, Mme. di Cesnola." In a letter dated May 8, 1889, Archbishop Corrigan explained his position this way: "With respect to the Salesian Sisters, I was opposed to the plan for an Italian orphanage since I considered it premature and had a well-founded fear that they would not be able to maintain it. But, without awaiting for an answer from me, the Mother Superior came to America. I personally explained to her all the difficulties of the undertaking; but since $5000 had been collected for this purpose, I gave permission for the plan to be tried for as long as the above mentioned money lasted" (AGS).

The Scalabrinian Missionaries, who had arrived eight months earlier, could not provide much help; they were still using as a church a warehouse they had rented (Archbishop Corrigan to Bishop Scalabrini, Aug. 10, 1888, AGS). The Archbishop then explained where they would live: "(Fr. Felice Morelli) promised to give up to them the house where he was living, at least for two or three months, until a few rooms could be build for them (the Cabrini Sisters). Mother Cabrini, noting that Father's ideas are not very practical, is afraid that these rooms will not be suitable for her Religious either. These "holes" as she called them are so low that Father Felice could not enter them without taking off his hat" (Archbishop Corrigan to Bishop Scalabrini, May 8, 1889, AGS).

9. F. S. Cabrini to Bishop Scalabrini, New York, June 10, 1899 and Dec. 10, 1888 (AGS).
10. N. Vian, *Madre Cabrini*, IV ed., Brescia, 1956, pp. 114 ff.
11. J. B. Scalabrini to F. Morelli, letter of 1891, perhaps written in May (note in AGS).
12. *La Madre Francesca Saverio Cabrini*, Turin, 1928, p. 150. Bishop Scalabrini recognized this difficulty and admired Mother Cabrini's holiness: "Notwithstanding the humiliation she suffered in having the direction of the hospital taken from her, she seems disposed to take responsibility, and is even thinking of soliciting funds. I have personally experienced that she is a very virtuous woman of great heart" (J. B. Scalabrini to F. Morelli, May 18, 1891, AGS).
13. *La Madre Francesca Saverio Cabrini*, Turin, 1928, pp. 150-151.
14. Ibid.
15. F. S. Cabrini to Bishop Scalabrini, New York, June 14, 1892.
16. Bishop Scalabrini to P. F. Morelli, Oct. 10, 1892 (AGS).
17. F. S. Cabrini to Bishop Scalabrini, Rome, Dec. 12, 1890 (AGS).
18. Idem, Codogno, June 23, 1897 (AGS).
19. Idem, New York, Dec. 10, 1898 (AGS).
20. Idem, Codogno, Nov. 27, 1900 (AGS).
21. Idem, Buenos Aires, Jan. 24, 1901 (AGS).
22. Idem, Codogno, Dec. 22, 1899 (AGS).
23. Idem, New York, Dec. 11, 1894 (AGS).
24. Idem, New York, June 16, 1899 (AGS).
25. J. B. Scalabrini, Letter of Recommendation, Dec. 8, 1897, preserved in the Motherhouse of the Missionary Sisters of the Sacred Heart in Codogno.
26. Card. R. C. Rossi, art. cit.
27. J. B. Scalabrini, Report to the Sacred Congregation of Propaganda Fide, Aug. 10, 1900, cit. It is not easy to determine from the documents it has been possible to consult the nature of the approval and of the rule of the very first Missionary Sisters of St. Charles. Father Faustino Consoni, wrote to Bishop Scalabrini in 1897 saying that he had gone to see the Bishop of Sao Paulo who had asked him, "What are those women doing up there in the orphanage?" — "I answered that I would write immediately to Your Excellency to approve the rules the late Father Joseph had given them, basing them on those of St. Francis de Sales and the Visitation Sisters, and that then I would reorganize everything and he was satisfied with this. Another important matter is that of regularizing the Sisters once Your Excellency has approved the rules, which I can have printed here in our shop in paragraphs and articles and I could receive the vows of the others...It is necessary to accept them soon for the need is urgent. I spoke with the Bishop today and he assured me that as soon as Your Excellency transmits the faculty to confer the veil and accept their profession, he himself will do so, or, if he cannot, he will delegate either myself or a person of confidence to do so. Please write and I will present it all. The Bishop wants to know what title to give them and if this one will do, but I should like to see Your Excellency named in it, e.g. Founded by His Excellency Bishop Scalabrini of Piacenza for the Italian orphans and abandoned children overseas" (Fr. Faustino Consoni to Bishop Scalabrini, Sao Paulo, Mar. 9, 1897. Copy preserved in the Provincial House of the Missionary Sisters of St. Charles in Piacenza).

Bishop Scalabrini, then, was considered the Founder and Superior of the Sisters both by Fr. Consoni and by the Bishop of Sao Paulo. He replied as follows: "As for the Sisters there was a Regulation approved *ad experimentum;* if you do not find it, write to me right away. It was desired to begin with temporary vows; let us see what God's will will be. Meanwhile accept the young women you wrote me about, but be careful that they are all that they should be" (Bishop Scalabrini to Fr. Consoni, Apr. 12, 1897, AGS).

In 1908, after the Sisters were separated from those of Mother Merloni, Fr. Consoni wrote to Fr. Domenico Vicentini, Superior General of the Missionaries of St. Charles: "Confer with Bishop Duarte (of Sao Paulo) who had separated the two communities of Sisters and goodnaturedly promised that he would give them his support and the necessary means to continue the work founded by Bishop Scalabrini and ratified by three Bishops, among them Antonio Alverenga, who wanted them to be called, like us, Sisters of St. Charles (Sao Paulo, Dec. 12, 1908, AGS).

28.   From: *Brevi cenni*, written by the first Superior General of the Missionary Sisters of St. Charles, Mother Assunta M. Marchetti (Generalate Archives of the Missionary Sisters of St. Charles, Rome, pos. 514/2).

29.   The Scalabrinian Fathers were also popularly called "Colombians" because of the name of the motherhouse, Istituto Cristoforo Colombo.

30.   *Vita di Madre Clelia Merloni fondatrice delle Suore Missionarie Zelatrici del Sacro Cuore, scritta da una Religiosa dell'Istituto*, Rome, 1954, pp. 80-81. Bishop Scalabrini's intention to join the two Orders into one is confirmed in the testimony of some of the Sisters of both Congregations, who were eyewitnesses at the time at the Diocesan Process. See C. Tomedi, witness, *Processus*, iuxta 4, p. 303; I. Puppo, witness, ibid., p. 314; G. Gelfi, witness, ibid., p. 310.

31.   Mother Clelia Merloni's letter to Bishop Scalabrini, quoted in *Vita di Madre Clelia Merloni*, cit., p. 117. St. Frances Xavier Cabrini also pressed Bishop Scalabrini, with his authority as "common Father," to remove the inconvenience of having two Congregations with a similar title (See Mother Cabrini's letters to Bishop Scalabrini, from Codogno, Nov. 27, 1900, and from Chicago, June 10, 1903). During the first novitiate in the temporary convent in Castelnuovo Fogliani, letters of some of Mother Merloni's Sisters were signed "Missionary Sisters of St. Charles" (See letters to Mother Merloni dated Dec. 12, 1899, and Dec. 19, 1899, and to Bishop Scalabrini, dated Dec. 22, 1899). Mother Merloni herself wrote to Bishop Scalabrini that she had received the Rules of the Missionary Sisters of St. Charles (Mother Merloni to Bishop Scalabrini, Apr. 1, 1900). All the letters cited are preserved in AGS.

32.   J. B. Scalabrini, Report to the Sacred Congregation of Propaganda Fide, Aug. 10, 1900 (note in AGS).

33.   See Chapter X, p. 198.

34.   A little later, in fact, Bishop Scalabrini wrote to the Foundress: "There is little I can add to what I have told you. Given the truly providential circumstances it seems to me and to the Fathers resident here that God wills this thing. It will certainly succeed if we deserve it and make ourselves worthy through fervent prayer and with the sincere desire to consecrate ourselves completely to the glory of God. I have written to the Superiors of the houses in America and I await their answers. I hope they will accord with our wishes. Now I am working on the house and the Rule, since as I told you, we must begin from the beginning and establish a regular novitiate, which all the Sisters, without exception, must complete, being formed thus in the true spirit of Jesus Christ. Awaiting the hour of God, live with the Sisters, all in Him, with Him, and for Him, and He in His mercy will help us in the great work we wish to undertake. (Bishop Scalabrini to Mother Merloni, Feb. 22, 1899, AGS.)

35.   I. Puppo, witness, *Processus*, iuxta 4, pp. 313-314.

36.   See p. 432.

37.   *Vita di Madre Clelia Merloni*, cit., p. 97.

38.   *Una vita e un'opera. Nel Centenario della nascita di Madre Clelia Merloni*, Rome, 1961, p. 48.

39.   *Vita di Madre Clelia Merloni*, cit., pp. 124-125.

Name Index

Subject Index

Divine Providence, 364-367. The trust of S. rewarded, 365-367. Hope and prudence, 364-365.

HUMANITY: The human dimensions of S.: friendship, 28, 117-118, 370-371; realism, 405-406; pessimism, 406-107; sensitivity, 407; transigence and intransigence, 407; actions and activities, 408-410; justice, 409-410; emotionalism, 413-414. See: TRUTH.

HUMILITY: The — of S., 38, 106-107, 138-140, 144, 304-305, 369-370, 381-385.

TRANSIGENTS: Historical sketch, 3, 5-13. Positive, negative and controversial aspects of the —, 7-8. The — and the Rosminians, 12-14. The — at Piacenza, 16-17, 119-130, 160-161, 320-326, 336. Confusion between — and Thomists, 12-14, 120-122. Relations between S. and Fr. Albertario, 120-130, 376-379. Relations between S. and Carlo Radini Tedeschi, 324. — and the Letter of Card. Pitra, 311-313. The pamphlet *Intransigenti e Transigenti*, 313-318. See: RECONCILIATION, NON-EXPEDIT, WORKS OF THE CONGRESSES, ROSMINIANS, TRANSIGENTS, UNITY.

LIBERALS: Historical facts regarding Italian —, 2-12. The — in Piacenza, 16-17, 105-106, 132-133. S. accused of liberalism, 99-102, 130-131, 324-326. S. makes a rapprochement with the — for apostolic reasons, 99-102, 370-371. S. takes a stand against economic liberalism, 150-154. S. and liberal legislation regarding emigration, 177-179, 230-233. The "conservatism" of S., 333-334. See: CATHOLIC LIBERALS, ROSMINIANS, TRANSIGENTS.

LITURGY: Love of S. for the —, 107-114. See: EUCHARIST

LOVE: — of S. for God, 347, 355-356, 357-360, 369-372, 413-414. Hatred of sin, 353-354, 369-372. Forgiveness, 48, 128-129, 372-380, 392-393. — of S. for the poor, 21, 43-49, 50-51, 158-159; for those stricken with cholera, 27, 44; for the sick, 30-32, 44, 146; for the deaf and dumb, 143-146; for the blind, 146; for prisoners, 49-50; for poor seminarians, 51, 303-304; for priests, 51-52; for Miraglia, 52-53, 158-162, 372-373; vis à vis the polemics of the day, 88-89, 128-129, 150-156, 162-164, 345, 374-375, 411-412.

MADONNA: The devotion to the — in the 19th century, 14. The devotion to the — of S.: the boy, 20-21; the pastor, 32; the bishop, 281-284. The rosary, 79, 281-282. The — and the Church, 272-273, 285-286. The Immaculate Conception, 272-275. The devotion to the — and the catechism, 275. The patroness of Piacenza, 275-276. The — of S. Marco, 276-279. The Blessed Virgin of the Castle, 282-284. Popular celebrations promoted by S., 276-282.

MISSIONARIES OF ST. CHARLES: See: SCALABRINIAN ORDER

MISSIONARIES OF ST. CHARLES: See: SISTERS TO THE EMIGRANTS.

NON EXPEDIT: Historical sketch, 4-6, 7-8, 10, 318-319, 322-323. Opinion of S. regarding —, 315, 319, 323, 324-326, 334. Obedience of S. to, 20-21, 318-326. See: RECONCILIATION, INTRANSIGENTS, TRANSIGENTS.

OBEDIENCE: The — of S. to the Church and the Pope, see The POPE. The — requested by S. of the clergy, 119-124; of his missionaries, 188-189.

PATIENCE: The — of S., 103-105, 125-126, 129-130, 131-132, 215-216, 349-353, 358-359, 362, 370, 379, 430.

PATRIOTIC OR NATIONALIST CLERGY: — in Lombardy, 1-2; — in Piacenza, 15-17. See: CATHOLIC LIBERALS, TRANSIGENTS.

THE PHILOSOPHICAL QUESTION: See: POPE, ROSMINIANS, THOMISM.

PIETY: — in the 19th century, 14-15. The — of S.: the boy, 20-21; the youth, 21-22; the pastor, 32. Education in priestly —, 77-79. Prayer, 354-356. The practices of —, 77-79, 256-258, 265, 282, 369-370.

THE POPE: The opinion of S. regarding the primacy and infallibility of the —, 285-291, 341. Love of S.: for Pius IX, 295-299; for Leo XIII, 299-305; for Pius X, 215, 218, 305-308. S. instructs the people in love and obedience to the —, 295-297, 300-303, 305-306. Peter's Pence, 296, 297-298, 300, 302, 304-305. Opinion of S. regarding obedience to the —, 293-295, 305-307, 309-310. Obedience to the — in political and philosophical matters, 82-90, 290-291, 310, 314-315, 324-326, 333-337, 342-343. Obedience of S. to the — in the matter

have her go to America, 426-428. Invites her to take charge of the Italian Hospital of New York, 428-430. S.-Cabrini correspondence, 429-431. S. founds the Congregation of the Missionary Sisters of St. Charles Borromeo, 416-417, 431-434. The development of the above congregation, 433. S. the savior and cofounder of the Sister Apostles of the Sacred Heart of Jesus, 432-433, 434-435.

TEACHING: S. the teacher, 55-89. The pastoral letters, 67-68. The Synods, 75-76, 134, 254-258. See: CATECHISM, CLERGY, PREACHING.

THOMISM: Historical facts regarding — and Rosminianism, 12-14. — at Piacenza, 17. The Thomist reform enacted by S. in Piacenza, 69-74. — at the Urbano Seminary and the Rocca case, 119-122. The — of S., 28-29, 69-70, 82-83.

TRUTH: Love of —, a characteristic of S., 87-89, 128-129, 303, 318-319, 323-342, 395-396, 411-412. See: POPE.

UNITY: — within the hierarchy defended and urged by S., 39-41, 122-124, 273, 292-294, 340-341; — in the clergy, 135-136, 412-413; — among all Catholics, 162-163, 292-294, 301-302, 340-341, 393-394, 407, 412-413; between the faithful and the bishops, 40-41, 122-124, 159-163, 293-294, 340-341. See: EPISCOPACY, POPE.

WORKERS: S. the pastor and the —, 30-32. Zeal of S. for —, 99-100, 150-152. The concern of S. for the problems of the —, 149-154. Works of social action promoted by S., 151-152. See: SOCIAL ACTION, EMIGRATION, RICE FIELD WORKERS, WORKS OF THE CONGRESSES, SOCIALISM.

WORKS OF THE CONGRESSES: Historical sketch, 6-7, 9-12. Relation of S. to the —, 159-161, 166-169, 221-224, 328, 343-344. The — at Piacenza, 160-165, 298-299, 301. The *Opera pro Mondariso* and the —, 145-147. The — and emigration, 168-169, 221-224. The contribution of S. to the restoration of the — after 1898, 163-164. See: CATHOLIC ACTION, SOCIAL ACTION, CHRISTIAN DEMOCRACY, INTRANSIGENTS.

ZEAL: — of S. for the salvation of souls, 97-102, 113-114, 194-195, 262, 361-362, 410-411; for his brothers, 20-21; for those "far away," 99-102; for the sick, 27, 32, 101-102; for children, 29-31, 98-99; for workers, 99, 150-152; for emigrants, 181-185; for administering of the sacraments, 92-94, 111-113, 210, 216-217; in pastoral visits, 91-97; for the liturgy, 32-35, 107-113; for vocations, 69; in preaching, 65-67. — as the single reason for S.'s reconciliation doctrine, 333-337, 358-359; and for his tireless activity, 407-409.